Major Problems in
American History
Volume II

MAJOR PROBLEMS IN AMERICAN HISTORY SERIES

GENERAL EDITOR

THOMAS G. PATERSON

Major Problems in
American History

Volume II
Since 1865

DOCUMENTS AND ESSAYS

SECOND EDITION

EDITED BY

ELIZABETH COBBS HOFFMAN

SAN DIEGO STATE UNIVERSITY

JON GJERDE

UNIVERSITY OF CALIFORNIA, BERKELEY

Australia • Brazil • Japan • Korea • Mexico • Singapore • Spain • United Kingdom • United States

WADSWORTH
CENGAGE Learning

Major Problems in American History: Volume II, Since 1865: Documents and Essays, Second Edition
Edited by Elizabeth Cobbs Hoffman, Jon Gjerde

Publisher: Patricia Coryell

Sponsoring Editor:
Sally Constable

Senior Development Editor:
Lisa Kalner Williams

Project Editor: Aimee Chevrette

Editorial Assistant:
Katherine Leahey

Senior Art and Design
Coordinator: Jill Haber Atkins

Photo Editor: Michael Farmer

Cover Design Manager:
Anne S. Katzeff

Composition Buyer:
Chuck Dutton

Associate Manufacturing Buyer:
Susan Brooks

Senior Marketing Manager:
Katherine Bates

Marketing Assistant:
Lauren Bussard

Cover Image: © Smithsonian
American Art Museum,
Washington, DC / Art
Resource, NY

For product information and technology assista nce, contact us at
Cengage Learning Customer & Sales Support, 1-800-354-9706

For permission to use material from this text or product,
submit all requests online **www.cengage.com/permissions**
Further permissions questions can be emailed to
permissionrequest@cengage.com

Library of Congress Control Number: 2006928408

ISBN-13: 978-0-618-67833-4

ISBN-10: 0-618-67833-6

Wadsworth
10 Davis Drive
Belmont, CA 94002
USA

Cengage Learning is a leading provider of customized learning solutions with office locations around the globe, including Singapore, the United Kingdom, Australia, Mexico, Brazil, and Japan. Locate your local office at **www.cengage.com/global**

Cengage Learning products are represented in Canada by Nelson Education, Ltd.

To learn more about Wadsworth, visit
www.cengage.com/wadsworth

Purchase any of our products at your local college store or at our preferred online store **www.ichapters.com**

Printed in the United States of America
5 6 7 11 10 09

Contents

CHAPTER 4
Imperialism and World Power
Page 87

CHAPTER 5
The Progressive Movement
Page 110

C H A P T E R   6
America in World War I
Page 135

C H A P T E R   7
Crossing a Cultural Divide: The Twenties
Page 162

C H A P T E R   8
The Depression, the New Deal, and Franklin D. Roosevelt
Page 192

C H A P T E R   9
The Ordeal of World War II
Page 222

C H A P T E R   1 0
The Cold War and the Nuclear Age
Page 253

CHAPTER 11
The 1950s "Boom": Affluence and Anxiety
Page 282

CHAPTER 12
Making the Great Society: Civil Rights
Page 313

C H A P T E R   1 3
The Sixties: Left, Right, and the Culture Wars
Page 344

C H A P T E R   1 4
Vietnam and the Downfall of Presidents
Page 375

C H A P T E R   1 5
End of the Cold War and New International Challenges: Globalization and Terrorism
Page 403

For
Victoria and Gregory Shelby
and
Christine and Kari Gjerde

Preface

History is a matter of interpretation. Individual scholars rescue particular stories from the welter of human experience, organize them into a pattern, and offer arguments to suggest how these phenomena reflected or reshaped human society at a given moment. This means that yet other historians might select different stories, organize them into a pattern, and arrive at a contrasting interpretation of the same period of time or even the same event. All scholars use evidence, but the choice and interpretation of evidence is to some extent inevitably an expression of personal judgment. History is not separate from historians.

The goal of *Major Problems in American History* is to place meat on this bare bones description of how the study of the past "works." Like most instructors, we want students to learn and remember the "important" facts, yet at the same time we want to make clear that historians often disagree on what is important. And, even when historians do agree on what is worthy of commentary, they often disagree on what a certain piece of evidence signifies. For example, scholars agree fifty-six men signed the Declaration of Independence in 1776, but they may well debate why these colonists felt compelled to take this dramatic step.

The two volumes that comprise this book bring together primary documents and secondary sources on the major debates in American history. The primary sources give students evidence to work with. They represent a mix of the familiar and unfamiliar. Certain documents are a "must" in any compilation for a survey course because they had a powerful, widely noted impact on American history, such as Tom Paine's *Common Sense* (1776) or *Brown v. the Board of Education* (1954). We have also selected pieces that evoke the personal experiences of individuals who reflected their times but may not have changed them. Included are statements from letters, sermons, speeches, and government reports by European explorers, colonial preachers, pioneer women on the frontier, immigrant workers, soldiers, eyewitnesses to the terrors of World War I, and children in rebellion against their parents during the 1960s. These documents often show conflicting points of view, from the "bottom up," as well as the "top down."

The secondary sources in these volumes fulfill a different goal, which is to expose students to the elemental historical debates for each broad period. We have chosen, therefore, to focus on classic debates, often combining very recent essays with more seasoned pieces by eminent historians who set the terms of discussion for an entire generation or more. Our purpose is to make the interpretive contrasts as clear as possible for students who are just learning to distinguish interpretation from fact, and to discern argument within description. In addition, the essays often make direct reference to one of the primary documents, demonstrating to students how historians integrate evidence in an interpretation. Sometimes historians refer explicitly to one another, pointing to the process of revisionism.

Volume II, prepared by Elizabeth Cobbs Hoffman in collaboration with Jon Gjerde, begins with Reconstruction and ends at the start of the twenty-first century. This volume focuses on some of the enduring themes of United States history, including the impact of changing technologies on the lives of workers and families, and the periodic waves of reform that have defined the nation since its inception. The transformation of gender expectations and race relations are also highlighted throughout the volume.

The second edition of *Major Problems in American History* continues the primary pedagogical objectives of the first edition. We've also retained many of the documents and essays that reviewers told us work well in their survey courses. However, each chapter in the second edition has been updated to reflect the latest in historical scholarship. Chapter 15 brings the American story through the cataclysmic events of September 11, 2001, and their aftermath, including the war in Iraq. This edition incorporates even more voices of everyday folk, including those of a union member, a Japanese-American internee, and a Chinese immigrant, to name a few. Documents and essays in this volume highlight the connections between events in America and world trends, consistent with recent initiatives in our profession to internationalize the study of U.S. history.

New essays provide new contrasts in Volume II. The pair of essays by Steven Hahn and David Blight in Chapter 1 present different approaches to the Reconstruction era. Chapter 5 has essays by Daniel Rodgers and Eric Rauchway that unveil diverse interpretations of American progressivism. In Chapter 15, essays by Bernard Lewis and Thomas Friedman speak of discrete global issues that have emerged since the dawn of the twenty-first century.

This book follows the same general format as other volumes in the Major Problems in American History series. Each chapter begins with a short introduction that orients the student to the topic. Following this, we include a section called "Questions to Think About" to help students focus their reading of the subsequent material. Next come seven to ten primary documents, followed by two essays that highlight contrasting interpretations. Headnotes at the start of the document and essay sections help readers identify key themes and debates. These headnotes also show how the documents relate to each other, and how the essays differ in perspective. Each chapter concludes with a brief "Further Reading" section to tempt readers into further research. In addition, at the start of the volume, we give suggestions on how to read sources and critically analyze their content, point of view, and inferences. This introduction encourages students to draw their own conclusions and use evidence to back up their reasoning.

Many friends and colleagues have contributed to these volumes. For the first edition, we especially wish to thank Robin Einhorn, David Henkin, and Mary Ryan from the University of California at Berkeley; William Cheek, Sarah Elkind, John Putman, Harry McDean, William Weeks, and Andrew Wiese from San Diego State University; Brian Balogh of the University of Virginia; Drew Cayton at Miami University of Ohio; Eric Hinderaker at University of Utah; David Kennedy of Stanford University; Phil Morgan at Johns Hopkins; Bruce Schulman from Boston University;

James Stewart at Macalaster College; and Louis Warren from the University of California at Davis.

For this edition, we received detailed and extremely helpful reviews from Donna Alvah, St. Lawrence University; Charles E. Brooks, Texas A&M University; C. Dallett Hemphill, Ursinus College; Stacey Ingrum Randall, Northern Illinois University; and Robert B. Kane, Troy State University–Montgomery. Thomas G. Paterson, the editor of the Major Problems series, provided sound advice. We are obliged to our editors at Cengage Learning, Sally Constable and Lisa Kalner Williams, for their kind encouragement and insightful recommendations.

The life of the mind is exceptionally fulfilling, but it is happiest when set within the life of the family. We wish to express our deep gratitude to our spouses, Ruth Gjerde and Daniel Hoffman. We dedicate the book to our four children and the young people of their generation, for whom it is written. To paraphrase the poet Emily Dickinson, this is our letter to their world.

E. C. H.
J. G.

Introduction: How to Read
Primary and Secondary Sources

College study encompasses a number of subjects. Some disciplines, such as mathematics, are aimed at problems and proofs. Students learn methods to discover the path to a correct answer. History is different. Unlike math, it is focused much more on interpretation and imagination. Historians study and analyze sources to construct arguments about the past. They generally understand that there is no "right" answer, even if there are some arguments that are more convincing than others. They search less for a proof than an interpretation, less for absolute truth than for understanding. A historical imagination is useful in creating these interpretations. People in the past thought and acted differently than we do today. Their views of science, of religion, of the place of women and men—to cite only a few examples—were not the same as our views. When we as historians create an argument about the past, we must imagine a world unlike the one we now inhabit.

The "problems" in U.S. history on which this text focuses, then, are different from math "problems." They are a series of issues in the American past that might be addressed, discussed, and debated, but not necessarily solved. The text provides readers with two types of tools to grapple with these problems. The first is the *primary source,* which is a piece of evidence that has survived from the period we are analyzing. Primary sources come in a variety of forms, including pictures, artifacts, and written texts. And they may have survived in a number of ways. Archaeologists might uncover pieces of evidence when they undertake digs of lost civilizations; ethnologists might transcribe stories told by people; economists might take bits of evidence to create numerical measures of past behavior; and historians might scrutinize surviving written sources. This volume by and large presents written texts, varying from political tracts to private letters. Some of the texts, however, are transcriptions, that is, texts written by someone who noted what another person said.

As historians, we must be critical of primary sources for a number of reasons. First of all, we must consider whether a source is really from the historical period we are studying. You might have occasionally read stories in the newspaper about paintings that had been attributed to famous artists but were discovered to be frauds painted by an unknown copyist. When the fraud is discovered, the painting's value plummets. The same can be said for a primary source. If it is not valid, it is not as valuable. A letter alleged to have been written by George Washington clearly is not of much use for revealing his innermost thoughts if we discover the document was written in 1910. But we should also be aware of the opposite: not all pieces of evidence have survived to the present. We might ask if there is a bias in the likelihood of one point of view surviving and another being lost. Or we might ask if some points of view were not given as much voice in the era we are studying. The experiences of slaveholders, for example, might have been more commonly written and published than those of slaves. Because they were rarely given the opportunity to publish their thoughts, slaves—in addition to others such as Native Americans and women—have bequeathed us some sources that have survived as transcriptions. As essential as these sources are in reconstructing the past, as historians we must be critical of them as well. Did the people writing down the spoken words accurately set them to paper or did they inject their own thoughts?

Once we consider the validity of sources and understand that some sources were more likely to survive than others, another reason to critique the sources is that they are not "objective" portrayals of the past. By nature, they are points of view. Like anyone in a society, the writer of each primary source provides us with his or her viewpoint and thus gives us a window through which to view his or her world, complete with its biases. When we read about the American Revolution, for example, we will see many different perspectives on the events leading up to the Declaration of Independence by the American colonies. Those who opposed independence saw the events in a very different light from those who led the independence movement. We have often read about the advocates of independence who saw the British as threats to American freedom. Theirs is a story of realizing that the American colonies would be better off as an independent nation and bringing this vision to fruition. Americans for generations have viewed this as a truly heroic episode in U.S. history. But many contemporaries were not as sure that independence was the correct course of action. Many British American colonists opposed independence because they felt they were more secure if they remained in the British Empire. Countless members of Indian nations were suspicious of the intentions of the American "patriots" and remained loyal to the king. African American slaves were often leery of the aims of their patriot owners. The fact that people had different viewpoints allows us to grapple with the multiple perspectives of the past. In the end, there is no single story that encompasses the American past, but rather a series of competing narratives.

When you are reading the documents in this volume, then, you are urged to criticize each document. We are certain that these are valid sources, and so you should be especially critical of the point of view contained in each document. Consider both the document and its author. Who wrote or spoke the words in the document? What was his or her reason for expressing the thoughts? Given the background and motivations of the authors, what are their perspectives and potential biases? How do they see the world differently from the way others do? And why do you think these different perspectives exist? Whose viewpoint do you agree with most? Why? It is not too much to say that the student of history is similar to a detective who seeks out sources and clues that illuminate the lives and events of the past.

In addition to primary sources, each chapter in this volume contains two essays that represent what we call a *secondary source.* Secondary sources are the written work of historians who have conducted painstaking research in primary sources. Historians work with an array of primary sources that they uncover and use as evidence to construct an argument that addresses one of the major problems in American history. A secondary source is so named because it is one step removed from the primary source. As you will notice, the writers of the essays in each chapter do not necessarily reach similar conclusions. On the contrary, they illustrate differing opinions about why events occurred and what they mean for us today.

Hence secondary sources, like primary sources, do not provide us with the "truth," even to the extent that they are based on verifiable facts. Rather, historians' conclusions vary just as your ideas about the documents might differ from those of someone else in your class. And they differ for a number of reasons. First, interpretations are influenced by the sources on which they depend. Occasionally, a historian might uncover a cache of primary sources heretofore unknown to other scholars, and these new sources might shed new light on a topic. Here again historians are like detectives.

Second and more important, however, historians carry their own perspectives to the research. As they read secondary sources, analyze primary texts, and imagine the past, historians usually develop arguments that differ in emphasis from those developed by others. As they combine their analyses with their own perspectives, they create an argument to explain the past. Historians' individual points of view and even society's dominant point of view influence their thinking. If analyzing sources resembles working as a detective, writing history is similar to being a judge who attempts to construct the most consistent argument from the sources and information at hand. And historians can be sure that those who oppose their viewpoints will analyze their use of sources and the logic of their argument. Those who might disagree with them—and that might include you—will criticize them if they make errors of fact or logic.

The essays were selected for this text in part because they reflect differing conclusions with which you may or may not agree. For example, what caused the Civil War? For decades, historians have given us a number of answers. Some have said the war could have been prevented if politicians had been more careful to avoid sectional divisions or if the U.S. political system had been suitable for compromise. Others have observed that the divisions that developed between North and South over time became so acute that they could not be compromised away. A civil war in their view was well nigh inevitable. Or what are we to make of the "Age of Jackson"? Some historians have celebrated this period as a flowering of American democracy. The increased voting rights for men fostered raucous political parades that celebrated the American freedoms. Others have noted that these rights were given only to white men and that the "freedoms" were in name only. Or how do we make sense of the Vietnam War nearly forty years after the first American troops landed? Was it a terrible mistake that undermined confidence in the United States both at home and abroad, or was it, in President Reagan's words, a "noble cause"?

An important question left unanswered in all of these chapters is what do *you* think is the correct interpretation? In the end, maybe you don't agree completely with any of the essayists. In fact, you might wish to create your own argument that uses primary sources found here and elsewhere and that accepts parts of one essay and parts of another. When you do this, you have become a historian, a person who attempts to analyze texts critically, someone who is actively engaged in the topic. If that occurs, this volume is a success.

When we discuss the discipline of history with people, we typically get one of two responses. One group of people says something like "I hated history in school." The other group says something like "history was my favorite subject when I went to school." Invariably the people who hated history cite all the boring facts that they had to memorize. In contrast, those who loved history remember a teacher or professor who brought the subject alive by invoking the worlds of people in the past. As we have tried to indicate in this short overview, history is not about memorizing boring facts but rather an active enterprise of thought and interpretation. Historians are not rote learners; studying history does not entail simply memorization. Instead, historians are detectives and judges, people who interpret and imagine what happened in history and why, individuals who study the past in order to understand the world in which they live in the present. Facts are important, but they are only building blocks in a larger enterprise of interpretation. In sum, our intent with this text is to show how primary and secondary sources can be utilized to aid you in understanding and interpreting major problems in the American past. It is also aimed at keeping that group of people who hates studying history as small as possible and enlarging that second group who considers history their passion. Frankly, it's more fun to talk to the latter.

Major Problems in
American History
Volume II

Reconstruction, 1865–1877

*Even before the Civil War was over, President Lincoln and congressional leaders
began to puzzle over how best to reintegrate the people of the South into the Union.
Before he was assassinated, President Lincoln proposed the "10 percent plan,"
which would have allowed a state government to reestablish itself once one-tenth of
those who had voted in 1860 took an oath of loyalty to the United States. Radicals
in Congress were appalled by the seemingly lenient plan and pushed through
their own bill, which increased the proportion to one-half of the voters who were
required to swear that they had never supported secession. Lincoln's assassination
cut short this increasingly scathing debate, but it did not end the controversy of
Reconstruction, a controversy that would engross the nation for nearly fifteen years.
Political disagreements over Reconstruction policy were vast, and the strategies
advocated were so varied that Reconstruction took a crooked road. As approaches
to rebuilding the South shifted, the hopes among some to transform southern society
grew and then were dashed. Ultimately, despite important legal precedents that
were made in the era, many of the social, political, and economic conventions
that had characterized antebellum society endured after Reconstruction ended.*

*Although people differed on what was the best policy for Reconstruction, every-
one agreed that the Confederate states were in dire straits. The war had devastated
the South: entire cities lay in ruins; two-thirds of the southern railroads had been
destroyed; and at least one-third of its livestock had disappeared. Likewise, the
abolition of slavery unalterably transformed southern society at the same time that
it gave hope to people freed from their bondage (known as freedmen). Following
Lincoln's death, many believed that Andrew Johnson, who succeeded Lincoln as
president, would advocate a severe Reconstruction of the South. Instead Johnson
engineered a plan that seemed to many Northerners as much too charitable. Ironically, Johnson's course of action, combined with the intransigence of unrepentant
Southern leaders, was a major force in bringing about the era of Radical Reconstruction beginning in 1866. Because he was so impolitic, Johnson strengthened
the resolve of Congress to enact a more radical policy. After the Republican Party
won a resounding victory in the elections of 1866, Congress reconvened in 1867
and set a much harsher and more radical plan of Reconstruction.*

*If Reconstruction was engineered in Washington, new social conventions were
forged in the South that would be extremely important in the future. The lives
of former slaves were dramatically changed and freedmen expressed their understanding of freedom in a variety of ways. Significantly, many African Americans*

played important roles in the new Republican Party of the South, and by 1868 black men were seated for the first time in southern state legislatures. These political gains, however, were short-lived. In spite of the electoral successes of African Americans, the Democratic Party enjoyed increasing political success in the South as former Confederates eventually had their political rights restored. Changes in the electorate in conjunction with intimidation shifted the trajectory of Reconstruction once again as radical transformation was replaced with a movement toward "redemption," the white South's term for reclaiming the world they had known before the Civil War.

The end of Reconstruction was hastened by events in the North as well as the South. Ulysses S. Grant, elected president in 1868, was a better general than politician and his administration was already mired in scandal shortly after he took office. By 1873, the nation was rocked by a financial panic that led Americans into a depression lasting six years. Scandal and depression weakened the Republican Party. Meanwhile Congress and the Supreme Court were weakening in their resolve to continue a strict policy of Reconstruction. The death knell of Reconstruction was the national election of 1876, when it became clear that the North was no longer willing to pursue its earlier goals. The election of the Democratic candidate for president was avoided only by a compromise in 1877 wherein Rutherford B. Hayes would be declared president if he promised to withdraw federal troops from those states in the South where they still remained. The deal was made. Reconstruction was over.

QUESTIONS TO THINK ABOUT

What were the failures of Reconstruction and what were its successes? Why did it collapse, to the extent that it did? Did Reconstruction come to an end primarily because the North abandoned it or because it was opposed by the South?

DOCUMENTS

The South was in a state of astonishing flux after the collapse of the Confederacy. Document 1 consists of reminiscences of former slaves about the coming of freedom and the challenges they faced in the early years of Reconstruction. These hazards were heightened by the "black codes" enacted in many southern states, one of which is given in Document 2. This example from Louisiana in 1865 illustrates the many ways in which the rights of "freedom" were abridged. The next two documents illustrate the many viewpoints on how the federal government should reconstruct the South in the years immediately after the war. In Document 3, President Andrew Johnson argues against black suffrage. In contrast, Thaddeus Stevens, a Radical representative in Congress, argues for passage of the Reconstruction Act of 1867 in Document 4 because he believes that only an unfaltering federal presence will prevent "traitors" from ruling the South. The bitterness that ensued resulted in the impeachment of President Andrew Johnson. Document 5, the opening argument in the impeachment trial, enumerates the accusations against President Johnson. The radical implications of the debate on Reconstruction had an impact in other arenas of political debate, as Document 6 shows. Elizabeth Cady Stanton argues that the very radicals who are pushing for increased rights for freed slaves are deferring the issue of women's suffrage. Document 7 is the text of the Fourteenth and Fifteenth Amendments, which among other things provided the due process of law and suffrage for freed male slaves. As radical as these measures were, their successful implication was made difficult by conditions in the United States. Document 8 is a recollection by a freedman in 1871 of a visit in the night by the Ku Klux Klan. Consider how difficult it would be to retain one's political leanings in the face of such threats. Document 9 illustrates the enduring notion of a "lost cause" that was maintained by many white southerners well after war and reconstruction.

1. African Americans Talk About Their Personal Experiences of Newfound Freedom, c. 1865

FELIX HAYWOOD From San Antonio, Texas. Born in Raleigh, North Carolina. Age at Interview: 88

The end of the war, it come just like that—like you snap your fingers. . . . How did we know it! Hallelujah broke out—

> Abe Lincoln freed the nigger
>   With the gun and the trigger;
> And I ain't going to get whipped any more.
>   I got my ticket,
> Leaving the thicket,
>   And I'm a-heading for the Golden Shore!

Soldiers, all of a sudden, was everywhere—coming in bunches, crossing and walking and riding. Everyone was a-singing. We was all walking on golden clouds. Hallelujah!

> Union forever,
>   Hurrah, boys, hurrah!
> Although I may be poor,
>   I'll never be a slave—
> Shouting the battle cry of freedom.

Everybody went wild. We felt like heroes, and nobody had made us that way but ourselves. We was free. Just like that, we was free. It didn't seem to make the whites mad, either. They went right on giving us food just the same. Nobody took our homes away, but right off colored folks started on the move. They seemed to want to get closer to freedom, so they'd know what it was—like it was a place or a city. Me and my father stuck, stuck close as a lean tick to a sick kitten. The Gudlows started us out on a ranch. My father, he'd round up cattle—unbranded cattle—for the whites. They was cattle that they belonged to, all right; they had gone to find water 'long the San Antonio River and the Guadalupe. Then the whites gave me and my father some cattle for our own. My father had his own brand—7 B)—and we had a herd to start out with of seventy.

B. A. Botkin, ed., *Lay My Burden Down: A Folk History of Slavery* (Chicago: University of Chicago Press, 1945), pp. 65–70, 223–224, 241–242, 246–247. Copyright 1945 by B. A. Botkin. Reprinted by permission of Curtis Brown, Ltd.

We knowed freedom was on us, but we didn't know what was to come with it. We thought we was going to get rich like the white folks. We thought we was going to be richer than the white folks, 'cause we was stronger and knowed how to work, and the whites didn't, and they didn't have us to work for them any more. But it didn't turn out that way. We soon found out that freedom could make folks proud, but it didn't make 'em rich.

Did you ever stop to think that thinking don't do any good when you do it too late? Well, that's how it was with us. If every mother's son of a black had thrown 'way his hoe and took up a gun to fight for his own freedom along with the Yankees, the war'd been over before it began. But we didn't do it. We couldn't help stick to our masters. We couldn't no more shoot 'em than we could fly. My father and me used to talk 'bout it. We decided we was too soft and freedom wasn't going to be much to our good even if we had a education.

WARREN MCKINNEY, From Hazen, Arkansas. Born in South Carolina. Age at Interview: 85

I was born in Edgefield County, South Carolina. I am eighty-five years old. I was born a slave of George Strauter. I remembers hearing them say, "Thank God, I's free as a jay bird." My ma was a slave in the field. I was eleven years old when freedom was declared. When I was little, Mr. Strauter whipped my ma. It hurt me bad as it did her. I hated him. She was crying. I chunked him with rocks. He run after me, but he didn't catch me. There was twenty-five or thirty hands that worked in the field. They raised wheat, corn, oats, barley, and cotton. All the children that couldn't work stayed at one house. Aunt Mat kept the babies and small children that couldn't go to the field. He had a gin and a shop. The shop was at the fork of the roads. When the war come on, my papa went to build forts. He quit Ma and took another woman. When the war close, Ma took her four children, bundled 'em up and went to Augusta. The government give out rations there. My ma washed and ironed. People died in piles. I don't know till yet what was the matter. They said it was the change of living. I seen five or six wooden, painted coffins piled up on wagons pass by our house. Loads passed every day like you see cotton pass here. Some said it was cholera and some took consumption. Lots of the colored people nearly starved. Not much to get to do and not much houseroom. Several families had to live in one house. Lots of the colored folks went up North and froze to death. They couldn't stand the cold. They wrote back about them dying. No, they never sent them back. I heard some sent for money to come back. I heard plenty 'bout the Ku Klux. They scared the folks to death. People left Augusta in droves. About a thousand would all meet and walk going to hunt work and new homes. Some of them died. I had a sister and brother lost that way. I had another sister come to Louisiana that way. She wrote back.

I don't think the colored folks looked for a share of land. They never got nothing 'cause the white folks didn't have nothing but barren hills left. About all the mules was wore out hauling provisions in the army. Some folks say they ought to done more for the colored folks when they left, but they say they was broke. Freeing all the slaves left 'em broke.

That reconstruction was a mighty hard pull. Me and Ma couldn't live. A man paid our ways to Carlisle, Arkansas, and we come. We started working for Mr. Emenson.

He had a big store, teams, and land. We liked it fine, and I been here fifty-six years now. There was so much wild game, living was not so hard. If a fellow could get a little bread and a place to stay, he was all right. After I come to this state, I voted some. I have farmed and worked at odd jobs. I farmed mostly. Ma went back to her old master. He persuaded her to come back home. Me and her went back and run a farm four or five years before she died. Then I come back here.

2. Louisiana Black Codes Reinstate Provisions of the Slave Era, 1865

SECTION 1. *Be it therefore ordained by the board of police of the town of Opelousas,* That no negro or freedman shall be allowed to come within the limits of the town of Opelousas without special permission from his employers, specifying the object of his visit and the time necessary for the accomplishment of the same. . . .

SECTION 2. *Be it further ordained,* That every negro freedman who shall be found on the streets of Opelousas after 10 o'clock at night without a written pass or permit from his employer shall be imprisoned and compelled to work five days on the public streets, or pay a fine of five dollars.

SECTION 3. No negro or freedman shall be permitted to rent or keep a house within the limits of the town under any circumstances, and any one thus offending shall be ejected and compelled to find an employer or leave the town within twenty-four hours. . . .

SECTION 4. No negro or freedman shall reside within the limits of the town of Opelousas who is not in the regular service of some white person or former owner, who shall be held responsible for the conduct of said freedman. . . .

SECTION 5. No public meetings or congregations of negroes or freedmen shall be allowed within the limits of the town of Opelousas under any circumstances or for any purpose without the permission of the mayor or president of the board. . . .

SECTION 6. No negro or freedman shall be permitted to preach, exhort, or otherwise declaim to congregations of colored people without a special permission from the mayor or president of the board of police. . . .

SECTION 7. No freedman who is not in the military service shall be allowed to carry firearms, or any kind of weapons, within the limits of the town of Opelousas without the special permission of his employer, in writing, and approved by the mayor or president of the board of police. . . .

SECTION 8. No freedman shall sell, barter, or exchange any articles of merchandise or traffic within the limits of Opelousas without permission in writing from his employer or the mayor or president of the board. . . .

SECTION 9. Any freedman found drunk within the limits of the town shall be imprisoned and made to labor five days on the public streets, or pay five dollars in lieu of said labor.

Condition of the South, Senate Executive Document No. 2, 39 Cong., 1 Sess., pp. 92–93.

SECTION **10.** Any freedman not residing in Opelousas who shall be found within the corporate limits after the hour of 3 p.m. on Sunday without a special permission from his employer or the mayor shall be arrested and imprisoned and made to work. . . .

SECTION **11.** All the foregoing provisions apply to freedmen and freed-women. . . .

E. D. ESTILLETTE,
President of the Board of Police.
JOS. D. RICHARDS, *Clerk.*

Official copy:

J. LOVELL,
Captain and Assistant Adjutant General.

3. President Andrew Johnson Denounces Changes in His Program of Reconstruction, 1867

It is manifestly and avowedly the object of these laws to confer upon negroes the privilege of voting and to disfranchise such a number of white citizens as will give the former a clear majority at all elections in the Southern States. This, to the minds of some persons, is so important that a violation of the Constitution is justified as a means of bringing it about. The morality is always false which excuses a wrong because it proposes to accomplish a desirable end. We are not permitted to do evil that good may come. But in this case the end itself is evil, as well as the means. The subjugation of the States to negro domination would be worse than the military despotism under which they are now suffering. It was believed beforehand that the people would endure any amount of military oppression for any length of time rather than degrade themselves by subjection to the negro race. Therefore they have been left without a choice. Negro suffrage was established by act of Congress, and the military officers were commanded to superintend the process of clothing the negro race with the political privileges torn from white men.

The blacks in the South are entitled to be well and humanely governed, and to have the protection of just laws for all their rights of person and property. If it were practicable at this time to give them a Government exclusively their own, under which they might manage their own affairs in their own way, it would become a grave question whether we ought to do so, or whether common humanity would not require us to save them from themselves. But under the circumstances this is only a speculative point. It is not proposed merely that they shall govern themselves, but that they shall rule the white race, make and administer State laws, elect Presidents and members of Congress, and shape to a greater or less extent the future destiny of the whole country. Would such a trust and power be safe in such hands?

The peculiar qualities which should characterize any people who are fit to decide upon the management of public affairs for a great state have seldom been

Andrew Johnson, "Third Annual Message" (December 3, 1867), in *A Compilation of Messages and Papers of the Presidents, 1789–1897,* VI, ed. James D. Richardson (Washington, D.C.: Bureau of National Literature and Art, 1899), 564–565.

combined. It is the glory of white men to know that they have had these qualities in sufficient measure to build upon this continent a great political fabric and to preserve its stability for more than ninety years, while in every other part of the world all similar experiments have failed. But if anything can be proved by known facts, if all reasoning upon evidence is not abandoned, it must be acknowledged that in the progress of nations negroes have shown less capacity for government than any other race of people. No independent government of any form has ever been successful in their hands. On the contrary, wherever they have been left to their own devices they have shown a constant tendency to relapse into barbarism. In the Southern States, however, Congress has undertaken to confer upon them the privilege of the ballot. Just released from slavery, it may be doubted whether as a class they know more than their ancestors how to organize and regulate civil society.

4. Congressman Thaddeus Stevens Demands a Radical Reconstruction, 1867

. . . It is to be regretted that inconsiderate and incautious Republicans should ever have supposed that the slight amendments [embodied in the pending Fourteenth Amendment] already proposed to the Constitution, even when incorporated into that instrument, would satisfy the reforms necessary for the security of the Government. Unless the rebel States, before admission, should be made republican in spirit, and placed under the guardianship of loyal men, all our blood and treasure will have been spent in vain. I waive now the question of punishment which, if we are wise, will still be inflicted by moderate confiscations, both as a reproof and example. Having these States, as we all agree, entirely within the power of Congress, it is our duty to take care that no injustice shall remain in their organic laws. Holding them "like clay in the hands of the potter," we must see that no vessel is made for destruction. Having now no governments, they must have enabling acts. The law of last session with regard to Territories settled the principles of such acts. Impartial suffrage, both in electing the delegates and ratifying their proceedings, is now the fixed rule. There is more reason why colored voters should be admitted in the rebel States than in the Territories. In the States they form the great mass of the loyal men. Possibly with their aid loyal governments may be established in most of those States. Without it all are sure to be ruled by traitors; and loyal men, black and white, will be oppressed, exiled, or murdered. There are several good reasons for the passage of this bill. In the first place, it is just. I am now confining my argument to negro suffrage in the rebel States. Have not loyal blacks quite as good a right to choose rulers and make laws as rebel whites? In the second place, it is a necessity in order to protect the loyal white men in the seceded States. The white Union men are in a great minority in each of those States. With them the blacks would act in a body; and it is believed that in each of said States, except one, the two united would form a majority, control the States, and protect themselves. Now they are the victims of daily murder. They must suffer constant persecution or be exiled. The

Thaddeus Stevens, speech in the House (January 3, 1867), *Congressional Globe,* 39 Cong., 2 Sess., Vol. 37, pt. 1, pp. 251–253. This document can also be found in *Radical Republicans and Reconstruction,* ed. Harold M. Hyman (Indianapolis, Ind., and New York: Bobbs-Merrill, 1967), 373–375.

convention of southern loyalists, lately held in Philadelphia, almost unanimously agreed to such a bill as an absolute necessity.

Another good reason is, it would insure the ascendancy of the Union party. Do you avow the party purpose? exclaims some horror-stricken demagogue. I do. For I believe, on my conscience, that on the continued ascendancy of that party depends the safety of this great nation. If impartial suffrage is excluded in rebel States then every one of them is sure to send a solid rebel representative delegation to Congress, and cast a solid rebel electoral vote. They, with their kindred Copperheads of the North, would always elect the President and control Congress. While slavery sat upon her defiant throne, and insulted and intimidated the trembling North, the South frequently divided on questions of policy between Whigs and Democrats, and gave victory alternately to the sections. Now, you must divide them between loyalists, without regard to color, and disloyalists, or you will be the perpetual vassals of the free-trade, irritated, revengeful South. For these, among other reasons, I am for negro suffrage in every rebel State. If it be just, it should not be denied; if it be necessary, it should be adopted; if it be a punishment to traitors, they deserve it.

But it will be said, as it has been said, "This is negro equality!" What is negro equality, about which so much is said by knaves, and some of which is believed by men who are not fools? It means, as understood by honest Republicans, just this much, and no more: every man, no matter what his race or color; every earthly being who has an immortal soul, has an equal right to justice, honesty, and fair play with every other man; and the law should secure him those rights. The same law which condemns or acquits an African should condemn or acquit a white man. The same law which gives a verdict in a white man's favor should give a verdict in a black man's favor on the same state of facts. Such is the law of God and such ought to be the law of man. This doctrine does not mean that a negro shall sit on the same seat or eat at the same table with a white man. That is a matter of taste which every man must decide for himself. The law has nothing to do with it.

5. Representative Benjamin Butler Argues That President Andrew Johnson Be Impeached, 1868

This, then, is the plain and inevitable issue before the Senate and the American people:

Has the President, under the Constitution, the more than kingly prerogative at will to remove from office and suspend from office indefinitely, all executive officers of the United States, either civil, military, or naval, at any and all times, and fill the vacancies with creatures of his own appointment, for his own purposes, without any restraint whatever, or possibility of restraint by the Senate or by Congress through laws duly enacted?

The House of Representatives, in behalf of the people, join this issue by affirming that the exercise of such powers is a high misdemeanor in office. . . .

Trial of Andrew Johnson, President of the United States, on Impeachment by the House of Representatives for High Crimes and Misdemeanors (Washington, D.C.: Government Printing Office, 1868), 96, 121–123.

Who does not know that Andrew Johnson initiated, of his own will, a course of reconstruction of the rebel States, which at the time be claimed was provisional only, and until the meeting of Congress and its action thereon? Who does not know that when Congress met and undertook to legislate upon the very subject of reconstruction, of which he had advised them in his message, which they alone had the constitutional power to do, Andrew Johnson last aforesaid again changed his course, and declared that Congress had no power to legislate upon that subject; that the two houses had only the power *separately* to judge of the qualifications of the members who might be sent to each by rebellious constituencies, acting under State organizations which Andrew Johnson had called into existence by his late *fiat,* the electors of which were voting by his permission and under his limitations? Who does not know that when Congress, assuming its rightful power to propose amendments to the Constitution, had passed such an amendment, and had submitted it to the States as a measure of pacification, Andrew Johnson advised and counselled the legislatures of the States lately in rebellion, as well as others, to reject the amendment, so that it might not operate as a law, and thus establish equality of suffrage in all the States, and equality of right in the members of the electoral college, and in the number of the representatives to the Congress of the United States? . . .

Who does not know that from the hour he began these, his usurpations of power, he everywhere denounced Congress, the legality and constitutionality of its action, and defied its legitimate powers, and, for that purpose, announced his intentions and carried out his purpose, as far as he was able, of removing every true man from office who sustained the Congress of the United States? And it is to carry out this plan of action that he claims the unlimited power of removal, for the illegal exercise of which he stands before you this day. Who does not know that, in pursuance of the same plan, he used his veto power indiscriminately to prevent the passage of wholesome laws, enacted for the pacification of the country and, when laws were passed by the constitutional majority over his vetoes, he made the most determined opposition, both open and covert, to them, and, for the purpose of making that opposition effectual, he endeavored to array and did array all the people lately in rebellion to set themselves against Congress and against the true and loyal men, their neighbors, so that murders, assassinations, and massacres were rife all over the southern States, which he encouraged by his refusal to consent that a single murderer be punished, though thousands of good men have been slain; and further, that he attempted by military orders to prevent the execution of acts of Congress by the military commanders who were charged therewith. These and his concurrent acts show conclusively that his attempt to get the control of the military force of the government, by the seizing of the Department of War, was done in pursuance of his general design, if it were possible, to overthrow the Congress of the United States; and he now claims by his answer the right to control at his own will, for the execution of this very design, every officer of the army, navy, civil, and diplomatic service of the United States. He asks you here, Senators, by your solemn adjudication to confirm him in that right, to invest him with that power, to be used with the intents and for the purposes which he has already shown.

The responsibility is with you; that safeguards of the Constitution against usurpation are in your hands; the interests and hopes of free institutions wait upon your verdict. The House of Representatives has done its duty. We have presented the facts in the constitutional manner; we have brought the criminal to your bar, and demand judgment at your hands for his so great crimes.

Never again, if Andrew Johnson go quit and free this day, can the people of this or any other country by constitutional checks or guards stay the usurpations of executive power.

I speak, therefore, not the language of exaggeration, but the words of truth and soberness, that the future political welfare and liberties of all men hang trembling on the decision of the hour.

6. Elizabeth Cady Stanton Questions Abolitionist Support for Female Enfranchisement, 1868

To what a depth of degradation must the women of this nation have fallen to be willing to stand aside, silent and indifferent spectators in the reconstruction of the nation, while all the lower stratas of manhood are to legislate in their interests, political, religious, educational, social and sanitary, moulding to their untutored will the institutions of a mighty continent. . . .

While leading Democrats have been thus favorably disposed, what have our best friends said when, for the first time since the agitation of the question [the enfranchisement of women], they have had an opportunity to frame their ideas into statutes to amend the constitutions of two States in the Union.

Charles Sumner, Horace Greeley, Gerrit Smith and Wendell Phillips, with one consent, bid the women of the nation stand aside and behold the salvation of the negro. Wendell Phillips says, "one idea for a generation," to come up in the order of their importance. First negro suffrage, then temperance, then the eight hour movement, then woman's suffrage. In 1958, three generations hence, thirty years to a generation, Phillips and Providence permitting, woman's suffrage will be in order. What an insult to the women who have labored thirty years for the emancipation of the slave, now when he is their political equal, to propose to lift him above their heads. Gerrit Smith, forgetting that our great American idea is "individual rights," in which abolitionists have ever based their strongest arguments for emancipation, says, this is the time to settle the rights of races; unless we do justice to the negro we shall bring down on ourselves another bloody revolution, another four years' war, but we have nothing to fear from woman, she will not revenge herself! . . .

Horace Greeley has advocated this cause for the last twenty years, but to-day it is too new, revolutionary for practical consideration. The enfranchisement of woman, revolutionizing, as it will, our political, religious and social condition, is not a measure too radical and all-pervading to meet the moral necessities of this day and generation.

Why fear new things; all old things were once new. . . . We live to do new things! When Abraham Lincoln issued the proclamation of emancipation, it was a new thing. When the Republican party gave the ballot to the negro, it was a new thing, startling too, to the people of the South, very revolutionary to their institutions, but Mr. Greeley did not object to all this because it was new. . . .

Elizabeth Cady Stanton, "Who Are Our Friends?" *The Revolution,* 15 (January 1868).

And now, while men like these have used all their influence for the last four years, to paralyze every effort we have put forth to rouse the women of the nation, to demand their true position in the reconstruction, they triumphantly turn to us, and say the greatest barrier in the way of your demand is that "the women themselves do not wish to vote." What a libel on the intelligence of the women of the nineteenth century. What means the 12,000 petitions presented by John Stuart Mill in the British Parliament from the first women in England, demanding household suffrage? What means the late action in Kansas, 10,000 women petitioned there for the right of suffrage, and 9,000 votes at the last election was the answer. What means the agitation in every State in the Union? In the very hour when Horace Greeley brought in his adverse report in the Constitutional Convention of New York, at least twenty members rose in their places and presented petitions from every part of the State, demanding woman's suffrage. What means that eloquent speech of George W. Curtis in the Convention, but to show that the ablest minds in the State are ready for this onward step?

7. The Fourteenth and Fifteenth Amendments Grant Citizenship and Due Process of Law to African Americans and Suffrage to African American Men, 1868, 1870

Amendment 14

Section 1. All persons born or naturalized in the United States, and subject to the jurisdiction thereof, are citizens of the United States and of the State wherein they reside. No State shall make or enforce any law which shall abridge the privileges or immunities of citizens of the United States; nor shall any State deprive any person of life, liberty, or property, without due process of law; nor deny to any person within its jurisdiction the equal protection of the laws.

Section 2. Representatives shall be apportioned among the several States according to their respective numbers, counting the whole number of persons in each State, excluding Indians not taxed. But when the right to vote at any election for the choice of electors for President and Vice-President of the United States, Representatives in Congress, the executive and judicial officers of a State, or the members of the legislature thereof, is denied to any of the male inhabitants of such State, being twenty-one years of age, and citizens of the United States, or in any way abridged, except for participation in rebellion, or other crime, the basis of representation therein shall be reduced in the proportion which the number of such male citizens shall bear to the whole number of male citizens twenty-one years of age in such State.

Section 3. No person shall be a Senator or Representative in Congress, or elector of President and Vice-President, or hold any office, civil or military, under the United States or under any State, who, having previously taken an oath as a member of Congress, or as an officer of the United States, or as a member of any State legislature, or as an executive or judicial officer of any State, to support the Constitution

U.S. Constitution, Amendments 14 and 15.

of the United States, shall have engaged in insurrection or rebellion against the same, or given aid or comfort to the enemies thereof. But Congress may, by a vote of two-thirds of each house, remove such disability.

Amendment XV

Section 1. The right of citizens of the United States to vote shall not be denied or abridged by the United States or by any state on account of race, color, or previous condition of servitude.

Section 2. The Congress shall have power to enforce this article by appropriate legislation.

8. Elias Hill, an African American Man, Recounts a Nighttime Visit from the Ku Klux Klan, 1871

On the night of the 5th of last May, after I had heard a great deal of what they had done in that neighborhood, they came. It was between 12 and 1 o'clock at night when I was awakened and heard the dogs barking, and something walking, very much like horses. As I had often laid awake listening for such persons, for they had been all through the neighborhood, and disturbed all men and many women, I supposed that it was them. . . . Some one then hit my door. It flew open. One ran in the house, and stopping about the middle of the house, which is a small cabin, he turned around, as it seemed to me as I lay there awake, and said, "Who's here?" Then I knew they would take me, and I answered, "I am here." He shouted for joy, as it seemed, "Here he is! Here he is! We have found him!" and he threw the bedclothes off of me and caught me by one arm, while another man took me by the other and they carried me into the yard between the houses, my brother's and mine, and put me on the ground beside a boy. The first thing they asked me was, "Who did that burning? Who burned our houses?"—gin-houses, dwelling-houses and such. Some had been burned in the neighborhood. I told them it was not me; I could not burn houses; it was unreasonable to ask me. Then they hit me with their fists, and said I did it, I ordered it. They went on asking me didn't I tell the black men to ravish all the white women. No, I answered them. They struck me again with their fists on my breast, and then they went on, "When did you hold a night-meeting of the Union League, and who were the officers? Who was the president?" I told them I had been the president, but that there had been no Union League meeting held at that place where they were formerly held since away in the fall. This was the 5th of May. They said that Jim Raney, that was hung, had been at my house since the time I had said the League was last held, and that he had made a speech. I told them he had not, because I did not know the man. I said, "Upon honor." They said I had no honor, and hit me again. . . . Generally, one asked me all the questions, but the rest were squatting over me—some six men I counted as I lay there. Said one, "Didn't you preach against the Ku-Klux," and wasn't that what Mr. Wallace was writing to me about. "Not at all," I said. "Let me see the

Report to the Joint Select Committee to Inquire into the Condition of Affairs in the Late Insurrectionary States, 42 Cong., 2 Sess., December 4, 1871–June 10, 1872, Vol. I, Serial 1483, pp. 44–46.

letter," said he; "what was it about?" I said it was on the times. They wanted the letter. I told them if they would take me back into the house, and lay me in the bed, which was close adjoining my books and papers, I would try and get it. They said I would never go back to that bed, for they were going to kill me—"Never expect to go back; tell us where the letters are." I told them they were on the shelf somewhere, and I hoped they would not kill me. Two of them went into the house. . . . They staid in there a good while hunting about and then came out and asked me for a lamp. I told them there was a lamp somewhere. They said "Where?" I was so confused I said I could not tell exactly. They caught my leg—you see what it is—and pulled me over the yard, and then left me there, knowing I could not walk nor crawl, and all six went into the house. I was chilled with the cold lying in the yard at that time of night, for it was near 1 o'clock, and they had talked and beat me and so on until half an hour had passed since they first approached. After they had staid in the house for a considerable time, they came back to where I lay and asked if I wasn't afraid at all. They pointed pistols at me all around my head once or twice, as if they were going to shoot me, telling me they were going to kill me; wasn't I ready to die, and willing to die? Didn't I preach? That they came to kill me—all the time pointing pistols at me. This second time they came out of the house, after plundering the house, searching for letters, they came at me with these pistols, and asked if I was ready to die. I told them that I was not exactly ready; that I would rather live; that I hoped they would not kill me that time. They said they would; I had better prepare. One caught me by the leg and hurt me, for my leg for forty years has been drawn each year, more and more year by year, and I made moan when it hurt so. One said "G-d d——n it, hush!" He had a horsewhip, and he told me to pull up my shirt, and he hit me. He told me at every lick, "Hold up your shirt." I made a moan every time he cut with the horsewhip. I reckon he struck me eight cuts right on the hip bone; it was almost the only place he could hit my body, my legs are so short—all my limbs drawn up and withered away with pain. I saw one of them standing over me or by me motion to them to quit. They all had disguises on. I then thought they would not kill me. One of them then took a strap, and buckled it around my neck and said, "Let's take him to the river and drown him." "What course is the river?" they asked me. I told them east. Then one of them went feeling about, as if he was looking for something, and said, "I don't see no east! Where is the d——d thing?" as if he did not understand what I meant. After pulling the strap around my neck, he took it off and gave me a lick on my hip where he had struck me with the horsewhip. One of them said, "Now, you see, I've burned up the d——d letter of Wallace's and all," and he brought out a little book and says, "What's this for?" I told him I did not know; to let me see with a light and I could read it. They brought a lamp and I read it. It was a book in which I had keep an account of the school. I had been licensed to keep a school. I read them some of the names. He said that would do, and asked if I had been paid for those scholars I had put down. I said no. He said I would now have to die. I was somewhat afraid, but one said not to kill me. They said "Look here! Will you put a card in the paper next week like June Moore and Sol Hill?" They had been prevailed on to put a card in the paper to renounce all republicanism and never vote. I said, "If I had the money to pay the expense, I could." They said I could borrow, and gave me another lick. They asked me, "Will you quit preaching?" I told them I did not know. I said that to save my life. They said I must stop that republican paper that was coming to Clay Hill. It has been only a few weeks since it stopped. The republican weekly paper was then coming to me from Charleston. It came to my name. They said I must stop it, quit preaching, and put a card in the newspaper renouncing republican-ism, and they would not kill me; but if I did not they would come back the next week and kill me. . . .

[Satisfied that he could no longer live in that community, he had written to make inquiry about the means of going himself to Liberia.]

9. Confederate General Jubal Early Memorializes the "Lost Cause," 1894

When the question of practical secession from the United States arose, as a citizen of the State of Virginia, and a member of the Convention called by the authority of the Legislature of that State, I opposed secession with all the ability I possessed, with the hope that the horrors of civil war might be averted and that a returning sense of justice on the part of the masses of the Northern States would induce them to respect the rights of the people of the South.

While some Northern politicians and editors were openly and sedulously justi-fying and encouraging secession, I was laboring honestly and earnestly to preserve the Union.

As a member of the Virginia Convention, I voted against the ordinance of seces-sion on its passage by that body, with the hope that even then, the collision of arms might be avoided and some satisfactory adjustment arrived at. The adoption of that ordinance wrung from me bitter tears of grief; but I at once recognized my duty to abide the decision of my native State, and to defend her soil against invasion. Any scruples which I may have entertained as to the right of secession were soon dis-pelled by the unconstitutional measures of the authorities at Washington and the frenzied clamor of the people of the North for war upon their former brethren of the South. I recognized the right of resistance and revolution as exercised by our fathers in 1776 and without cavil as to the name by which it was called, I entered the military service of my State, willingly, cheerfully, and zealously. . . .

During the war, slavery was used as a catch-word to arouse the passions of a fanatical mob, and to some extent the prejudices of the civilized world were excited against us; but the war was not made on our part for slavery. High dignitaries in both church and state in Old England, and puritans in New England, had partici-pated in the profits of a trade by which the ignorant and barbarous natives of Africa were brought from that country and sold into slavery in the American Colonies. The generation in the Southern States which defended their country in the late war, found amongst them, in a civilized and Christianized condition, 4,000,000 of the descendants of those degraded Africans. The Creator of the Universe had stamped them, indelibly, with a different color and an inferior physical and mental organi-zation. He had not done this from mere caprice or whim, but for wise purposes. An

Lieutenant General Jubal Anderson Early, C.S.A, *Autobiographical Sketch and Narrative of the War Between the States* (Philadelphia: J. B. Lippincott, 1912), vii.

amalgamation of the races was in contravention of His designs or He would not have made them so different. This immense number of people could not have been trans-ported back to the wilds from which their ancestors were taken, or if they could have been, it would have resulted in their relapse into barbarism. Reason, common sense, true humanity to the black, as well as the safety of the white race, required that the inferior race should be kept in a state of subordination. The conditions of domestic slavery, as it existed in the South, had not only resulted in a great improvement in the moral and physical condition of the negro race, but had furnished a class of laborers as happy and contented as any in the world if not more so. Their labor had not only developed the immense resources of the immediate country in which they were located, but was the main source of the great prosperity of the United States, and furnished the means for the employment of millions of the working classes in other countries. Nevertheless, the struggle made by the people of the South was not for the institution of slavery but for the inestimable right of self-government, against the domination of a fanatical faction at the North; and slavery was the mere occasion of the development of the antagonism between the two sections. That right of self-government has been lost, and slavery violently abolished. . . .

Each generation of men owes the debt to posterity to hand down to it a correct history of the more important events that have transpired in its day. The history of every people is the common inheritance of mankind, because of the lessons it teaches.

For the purposes of history, the people of the late Confederate States were a separate people from the people of the North during the four years of conflict which they maintained against them.

No people loving the truth of history can have any object or motive in suppress-ing or mutilating any fact which may be material to its proper elucidation.

E S S A Y S

The collapse of Reconstruction had enormous costs for the African American population of the South. Arguably, its failure also postponed the economic and social recovery of the entire region until well into the twentieth century. Historians have long debated the meaning of Reconstruction and particularly the reasons for its abandonment. In the first essay, Steven Hahn of the University of Pennsylvania shows that former slaves and Confederates were both prepared to mount an armed defense of their goals, reflecting a long tradition of Southern violence that had previously undergirded slavery. He argues that Reconstruction came to an end when freedmen lost the military support of the North, which had tired of the sixteen-year conflict (1861–1877). Essentially, the freedmen were outgunned. David Blight of Yale University takes a somewhat different tack. He depicts Reconstruction as a process in which two important but incompatible goals vied for attention: reconcilia-tion and emancipation. The nation needed to heal the sectional divide in order to function as one country, yet it had also fought the war, at least in part, to bring justice to the former slaves. As it turned out, Southern resistance narrowed the terms on which reconciliation was possible. The emancipationist promise of the war was stunted as a result, and eventually forgotten in the attempt to minimize the differences between "the Blue and the Grey." Reconstruction became a contest over the memory and meaning of the war. Black southerners lost.

Continuing the War: White and Black
Violence During Reconstruction

STEVEN HAHN

In March 1867, nearly two years after the Confederate armies had begun to surrender and more than a year after Congress had refused to seat representatives from the former Confederate states, the mark of Radicalism was indelibly inscribed into the cornerstone of the reconstructed American republic. It did not herald the draconian policies—imprisonments and executions, massive disfranchisement, or confiscation of landed estates—that some Republicans had advocated and many Rebels had initially feared. And it required a combination of white southern arrogance and vindictiveness, presidential intransigence, and mounting African American agitation before it could be set. But with the Military Reconstruction Acts, Congress gave the federal government unprecedented power to reorganize the ex-Confederate South politically, imposed political disabilities on leaders of the rebellion, and, most stunning of all, extended the elective franchise to southern black males, the great majority of whom had been slaves. Never before in history, and nowhere during the Age of Revolution, had so large a group of legally dependent people been enfranchised. . . .

By the summer of 1867, complaints of "armed organizations among the freedmen," of late-hour drilling, and of threatening "assemblages" had grown both in volume and geographical scope. The entire plantation South appeared to pulse with militant and quasi-military activity. But now, in the months after the passage of the Reconstruction Acts, investigation revealed a more formal process of politicization, and one tied directly to the extension of the elective franchise and the organizational initiatives of the Republican party. From Virginia to Georgia, from the Carolinas to the Mississippi Valley and Texas, the freed people showed "a remarkable interest in all political information," were "fast becoming thoroughly informed upon their civil and political rights," and, most consequentially, were avidly "organizing clubs and leagues throughout the counties." Of these, none was more important to the former slaves or more emblematic of the developing character of local politics in the postemancipation South than the often vilified and widely misunderstood body known as the Union League.

Emerging out of a network of organizations formed in the northern states in 1862 and 1863 to rally public support for the Lincoln administration and the war effort, the Union League embraced early the practices of both popular and patrician politics. Bound by secrecy, requiring oaths and rituals much in the manner of the Masons, and winning a mass base through local councils across the Midwest and Northeast, the league also took hold among loyalist elites meeting in stately clubs and townhomes in Philadelphia, New York, and Boston. In May 1863, a national convention defined goals, drew up a constitution, and elected officers, and councils were soon being established in Union-occupied areas of the Confederate South to

Reprinted by permission of the publisher from *A Nation Under Our Feet: Black Political Struggles in the Rural South* by Steven Hahn, pp. 165, 177, 178–181, 183, 184, 186, 189, 190, 219, 224–226, 265–269, 280, 281, 286, 288–292, 307, 308, 310–312, Cambridge, Mass.: The Belknap Press of Harvard University Press, Copyright © 2003 by the President and Fellows of Harvard College.

advance the cause. Once the war ended, the league continued its educational and agitational projects and spread most rapidly among white Unionists in southern hill and mountain districts, where membership could climb into the thousands. But committed as the league was "to protect, strengthen, and defend all loyal men without regard to sect, condition, or race," it began as well to sponsor political events and open a few councils for the still unfranchised African Americans—chiefly in larger cities like Richmond, Norfolk, Petersburg, Wilmington, Raleigh, Savannah, Tallahassee, Macon, and Nashville.

With the provision for a black franchise and voter registration encoded in the Reconstruction Acts, league organizers quickly fanned out from these urban areas into the smaller towns and surrounding countryside, and particularly into the plantation belt. . . .

It was arduous and extremely dangerous work, for as organizers trekked out to where the mass of freedpeople resided, they fell vulnerable to swift and deadly retaliation at the hands of white landowners and vigilantes. Having organized the Mount Olive Union League Council in Nottoway County, Virginia, in July of 1867, the Reverend John Givens reported that a "colored speaker was killed three weeks ago" in neighboring Lunenberg County. But Givens determined to "go there and speak where they have cowed the black man," hoping "by the help of God" to "give them a dose of my radical Republican pills and neutralize the corrosive acidity of their negro hate." . . .

The formation of a Union League council officially required the presence of at least nine loyal men, each twenty-one years of age or older, who were, upon initiation, to elect a president and other officers from among those regarded as "prudent, vigilant, energetic, and loyal," and as "possess[ing] the confidence of their fellow citizens." They were expected to hold meetings weekly, to follow the ceremony, and to "enlist all loyal talent in their neighborhood." . . .

The experience and operations of local councils depended to some extent on the training and ability of the organizer, but perhaps even more on the social and political conditions in the specific counties and precincts. In hilly Rutherford County, North Carolina, where only one in five inhabitants was black and where the Whig party had been dominant before the Civil War, the Union League seemed to function—at least initially—in an unusually open and relaxed manner. One Saturday a month at noon, the courthouse bell in the village of Rutherfordton would be rung to announce a meeting and summon "every citizen who wished to come." Membership in the league was not concealed and some men who had served in the Confederate army belonged. . . .

Yet where blacks made up between one-third and two-thirds of the population—and where, not incidentally, the great majority of Union League councils was to be found—the situation was rather different. Here, most league members were black and they encountered a substantial and largely antagonistic population of whites. Whether they met weekly, biweekly, or monthly (and there was considerable variation), they relied on word of mouth rather than bells, horns, or posters; they usually assembled at night; and they generally favored sites that would attract as little adverse attention as possible, often posting armed sentinels outside. Some league councils either organized their own drilling companies or linked with companies that already existed. One observer in the South Carolina piedmont district of Abbeville fretfully reported that local leagues with "their Captains, and other Officers," were meeting

"with their Guns . . . in secret places, but do not meet twice in the same place."
Recognizing the dangers, the freedman Caleb, who worked for a particularly hostile landowner in Maury County, Tennessee, where blacks formed just under half
of the population, chose another course: he went to his employer in April 1867 "and
whol[l]y den[i]ed having any thing to do with the Un[i]on League," insisting that
he "has not joined it nor never will." . . .

The Union League sprang to life through the plantation districts because its goal
of mobilizing black support for the national government and the Republican party
fed on and nourished the sensibilities and customs that organizers found in many
African American communities. League councils served as crucial political schools,
educating newly enfranchised blacks in the ways of the official political culture. New
members not only were instructed in the league's history, in the "duties of American
citizenship," and in the role of th[e] Republican party in advancing their freedom, but
also learned about "parliamentary law and debating," about courts, juries, and militia
service, about the conduct of elections and of various political offices, and about
important events near and far. With meetings often devoted, in part, to the reading
aloud of newspapers, pamphlets, and government decrees, freedmen gained a growing political literacy even if most could neither read nor write. . . .

Indeed, league councils quickly constituted themselves as vehicles not only of
Republican electoral mobilization, but also of community development, defense, and
self-determination. In Harnett County, North Carolina, they formed a procession
"with fife and drum and flag and banner" and demanded the return of "any colored
children in the county bound to white men." In Oktibbeha County, Mississippi, they
organized a cooperative store, accepting "corn and other products . . . in lieu of
money," and, when a local black man suffered arrest, "the whole League" armed and
marched to the county seat. In Randolph County, Alabama, and San Jacinto County,
Texas, they worked to establish local schools so that, as one activist put it, "every
colored man [now] beleaves in the Leage." . . .

Among the diverse activities that Union League councils across the former Confederate South pursued in 1867, few commanded more immediate attention than
those required to implement the provisions and goals of the Reconstruction Acts.
Within months, the Republican party had to be organized in the states and counties,
delegates had to be nominated and elected to serve in state constitutional conventions, new state constitutions enfranchising black men and investing state governments with new structures and responsibilities had to be written and ratified, and the
general congressional expectations for readmission to the Union had to be fulfilled.
First and foremost, the outlines of a new body politic had to be drawn and legitimated
through a process of voter registration. . . .

During Reconstruction, black men held political office in every state of the former
Confederacy. More than one hundred won election or appointment to posts having
jurisdiction over entire states, ranging from superintendent of education, assistant
commissioner of agriculture, superintendent of the deaf and dumb asylum, and member of the state land commission to treasurer, secretary of state, state supreme court
justice, and lieutenant governor. One African American even sat briefly as the governor of Louisiana. A great many more—almost eight hundred—served in the state

legislatures. But by far the largest number of black officeholders were to be found at the local level: in counties, cities, smaller municipalities, and militia districts. Although a precise figure is almost impossible to obtain, blacks clearly filled over 1,100 elective or appointive local offices, and they may well have filled as many as 1,400 or 1,500, about 80 percent of which were in rural and small-town settings. . . .

Union League and Republican party activists therefore had to prepare carefully for election day lest their other efforts be nullified. They had to petition military commanders and Republican governors to appoint favorable (and dismiss hostile) election officials and to designate suitable polling sites, particularly if Democrats still controlled county governing boards. They had to get their voters to the polls, at times over a distance of many miles, and make sure that those voters received the correct tickets. They had to minimize the opportunities for bribery, manipulation, and intimidation. And they had to oversee the counting of ballots. Voting required, in essence, a military operation. Activists often called a meeting of fellow leaguers or club members the night before an election to provide instructions and materials. The chairman of the Tunica County, Mississippi, Republican executive committee had men come to the town of Hernando from all over the county on the day before the election and distribute tickets to those political clubs meeting that night. At times groups of black voters might spend the night before an election on a safe plantation or in the woods, perhaps sending a small party ahead to check for possible traps or ambushes, and then move out at first light to arrive at the polls well before their opponents or "rebel spies" could gather. Henry Frazer, who organized for the Republican party in Barbour County, Alabama, claimed that he went out with as many as "450 men and camped at the side of the road" before going into the town of Eufaula at eight in the morning where they would "stand in a body until they got a chance to vote." . . .

Protecting black Republican voters from white intimidation was only the most obvious goal of such martial organization and display, however. There was also the need to prod the timid and punish the apathetic or disloyal within their own communities. Activists learned early that elections could only be carried by securing overwhelming allegiance to the Republican party and then by ensuring that the eligible voters overcame fear or inertia to cast ballots. Political parades and torchlight processions during election campaigns and on the eve of polling—often with black men dressed in their club uniforms, beating drums, "hallooing, hooping," and, on occasion, riding full gallop through the streets—thereby served several purposes: to inspire enthusiasm, advertise numbers and resolve, and coax the participation of those who might otherwise abstain. Where coaxing proved insufficient, more coercive tactics could be deployed. Union League members in a North Carolina county, upon learning of three or four black men who "didn't mean to vote," threatened to "whip them" and "made them go." In another county, "some few colored men who declined voting" were, in the words of a white conservative, "bitterly persecut[ed]." One suffered insults, the destruction of his fences and crops, and "other outrages."

Especially harsh reprisals could be brought against blacks who aligned with conservatives and Democrats, for they were generally regarded not merely as opponents but as "traitors." As black Mississippian Robert Gleed put it, "[W]e don't believe they have a right to acquiesce with a party who refuse to recognize their right to participate in public affairs." In the rural hinterlands of Portsmouth, Virginia, black

Republicans attacked "colored conservatives" at a prayer meeting and beat two of them badly. In southside Virginia's Campbell County, a black man who betrayed the Union League was tied up by his heels and suspended from a tree for several hours until he agreed to take an oath of loyalty. . . .

When the U.S. Congress conducted an investigation of the Ku Klux Klan in the early 1870s, more than a few of the reputed leaders testified that the organization was a necessary response to the alarming activities and tactics of the Union League. They complained of secret oaths, clandestine meetings, accumulations of arms, nocturnal drilling, threatening mobilizations, and a general flaunting of civilities among former slaves across the plantation South. In so doing, they helped construct a discourse, later embraced by apologists for slavery and white supremacy, that not only justified vigilantism but also demonized Radical Reconstruction for its political illegitimacies. The enfranchisement of ignorant and dependent freedmen by vengeful outsiders, the Klansmen insisted, marked a basic corruption of the body politic and a challenge to order as it was widely understood. . . .

Ku Klux Klan leaders and sympathizers who blamed the Union League for their resort to vigilantism were at least right about the chronology. Union League mobilizations generally preceded the appearance of the Klan. But the character and activities of the league itself reflected a well-established climate of paramilitarism that assumed both official and unofficial forms. Already during the summer and fall of 1865, despite the presence of a Union army of occupation, bands of white "regulators," "scouts," and cavalrymen rode the countryside disciplining and disarming freedpeople who looked to harvest their crops, make new labor and family arrangements, and perhaps await a federally sponsored land redistribution. . . .

From the first, the Klan proved particularly attractive to young, white men who had served in the Confederate army. All of the founders in Pulaski, Tennessee, were youthful Confederate veterans, and most everywhere former Confederate officers, cavalrymen, and privates sparked organization and composed the bulk of membership. Klan dens and other vigilante outfits often became magnets for returning soldiers and, at times, they virtually mirrored the remainders of specific Confederate companies. Powell Clayton, the Republican governor of Arkansas who effectively combated the Klan, complained in retrospect about the Confederates being paroled or allowed to desert without surrendering their arms, ammunition, and horses. To this extent, the Klan not only came to embody the anger and displacement of a defeated soldiery and to capitalize on the intensely shared experiences of battlefields and prison camps; it also may be regarded as a guerilla movement bent on continuing the struggle or avenging the consequences of the official surrender.

But the very associations between the Klan and the Confederate army suggest a deeper historical and political context, for Confederate mobilization itself was enabled by longstanding and locally based paramilitary institutions. Militias were perhaps most important because state governments required the enrollment of all able-bodied white men while leaving much of the organizational initiative to counties and neighborhoods, where volunteer companies could elect their own officers, make their own by-laws, and then secure recognition by the legislature. The militias, in turn, were closely connected with slave patrols—for a time through formal control, and more generally by way of personnel and jurisdiction—which policed the

African American population, instructed all white men in their responsibilities as citizens in a slave society, and could be enlisted as something of a posse by the state in the event of emergency. A martial spirit and military presence thus suffused the community life of the antebellum South. . . .

The geography of Klan activity was, in essence, a map of political struggle in the Reconstruction South. Klan-style vigilantism surfaced at some point almost anywhere that a substantial Republican constituency—and especially a black Republican constituency—was to be found: from Virginia to Florida, South Carolina to Texas, Arkansas to Kentucky. Reports of "outrages" and "depredations" emanated from areas that were heavily black (eastern North Carolina, west-central Alabama), heavily white (east Tennessee, northwest Georgia), and racially mixed (eastern Mississippi, northwest South Carolina, east-central Texas). But whether the eruptions were brief or prolonged and whether they achieved their objectives depended on the nature and effectiveness of black resistance and, by extension, the readiness of the state Republican governments to respond with necessary force. . . .

Union Leagues and Republican party clubs had, in some places, already begun to mount a response to Klan violence, at times bringing pressure against suspected Klan leaders. Black members of a Pickens County, Alabama, Union League boycotted a white landowner thought to be "head of the Ku Klux." They were so effective that, in his words, he "could not hire a darkey at any price." In a number of locales scattered across the plantation districts, they appear to have taken even more direct and destructive action by torching the mills, barns, and houses of former slaveholders. But the leagues and clubs more likely moved to put themselves on a paramilitary footing, if they had not embraced rituals of armed self-defense from the outset. Black Union Leaguers in Darlington County, South Carolina, fearing Klan violence, gathered weapons, took control of a town, and threatened to burn it down in the event of attack. Near Macon, Mississippi, the combination of local outrages and the very bloody Meridian riot led blacks to organize "secretly" and ready themselves to "meet the mob." "There will be no more 'Meridians' in Mississippi," a white ally of theirs declared. "Next time an effort of this kind is made there will be killing on both sides." The tenor of conflict and mobilization in Granville County, North Carolina, in the fall of 1868 was such that a prominent Democrat offered Union League members a bargain: "If we would stop the leagues he would stop the Ku Klux." . . .

Like Tennessee, neighboring Arkansas had a white population majority, a solid base of Unionist sentiment in the mountains of the northwest, and a Republican party that looked to punish former Confederates. But Arkansas had been remanded to military rule by the Reconstruction Acts of 1867, and in the spring of 1868 eligible voters put Republicans in command of the general assembly and the carpetbagger Powell Clayton in the governor's chair. A native of Pennsylvania and a civil engineer by training, Clayton had been out in Kansas during the 1850s and commanded a Union cavalry regiment in Arkansas during the war, where he saw a good deal of action against Confederate guerillas. After the surrender, he settled in Arkansas and bought a plantation, but run-ins with ex-Confederate neighbors led him into politics; he first helped to organize the state Republican party and then accepted the party's nomination for governor. By the time of Clayton's inauguration in July, Klan activity was sufficiently pronounced in the southern and eastern sections of the state that he wasted no time in responding: with the approval of the legislature, he began mobilizing a state militia and, as intimidation of Republican voters and local officials intensified and a Republican congressman fell victim to a Klan ambush, he declared marital law in ten counties. Armed skirmishes between militiamen and Klansmen, together with arrests, trials, and a few executions, followed. By early 1869, the Klan had pretty well "ceased to exist" in Arkansas. . . .

The accession of Republican Ulysses S. Grant to the presidency in March of 1869 offered some welcome possibilities to those governors who stood ready to deploy state militia units. Previously, the Johnson administration had refused requests for arms, and governors were left scrambling to equip their troops. Arkansas's Powell Clayton first tried to borrow guns from various northern states and then, when this failed, sent an emissary to New York to purchase rifles and ammunition. Unfortunately, a contingent of well-prepared Klansmen intercepted the shipment between Memphis and Little Rock. Florida's carpetbag governor Harrison Reed chose to go personally to New York to procure arms soon after the legislature passed a militia law in August 1868, but the result was even more embarrassing. Under the nose of a federal detachment, Klansmen boarded the train carrying the armaments to Tallahassee and destroyed them. Grant, on the other hand, proved more receptive than Johnson and made substantial supplies of weapons available to Governors Holden and Scott in the Carolinas. . . .

The Klan's effectiveness depended on a wider political climate that gave latitude to local vigilantes and allowed for explosions of very public violence. Louisiana and Georgia, which alone among the reconstructed states supported Democrat Horatio Seymour for the presidency in 1868, had at least seven bloody riots together with Klan raiding that summer and fall. The term "riot," which came into wide use at this time, quite accurately captures the course and ferocity of these eruptions, claiming as they did numerous lives, often over several days, in an expanding perimeter of activity. But "riot" suggests, as well, a disturbance that falls outside the ordinary course of political conduct, and so by invoking or embracing it we may miss what such disturbances can reveal about the changing dynamics and choreography of what was indeed ordinary politics in the postemancipation South. . . .

Consider the Camilla riot in southwest Georgia, which captured the greatest attention but shared many features of the others. In late August 1868, Republicans in the state's Second Congressional District, most of whom were black, met in the town of Albany and nominated William P. Pierce, a former Union army officer, failed planter, and Freedmen's Bureau agent, for Congress. It would not be an easy campaign. . . . A "speaking" in the town of Americus on September 15 brought menacing harassment from local whites and Pierce barely escaped violence. But he did not interrupt plans for a similar event in Camilla on Saturday, September 19.

News of the rally—which would feature Pierce, several other white Republicans, and Philip Joiner, a former slave, local Loyal League president, and recently expelled state legislator—circulated through the neighboring counties. So, too, did rumors of a possible attack by armed whites who, it was said, proclaimed that "this is our country and we intend to protect it or die." Freedpeople did have ample cause for alarm. Camilla, the seat of relatively poor, white-majority Mitchell County in an otherwise black majority section of the state, crackled with tension.

Gunfire had broken out there during the April 1868 elections, and many of the blacks had resolved that they would "not dare . . . go to town entirely unarmed as they did at that time." The white Republican leaders tried to quell these fears when the Dougherty County contingent gathered on their plantations on Friday night the 18th; and as the group moved out on Saturday morning for the twenty-odd mile trek to Camilla, most heeded the advice to leave their weapons behind and avoid a provocation. . . .

But to the whites of Camilla, such a procession could only constitute a "mob," with no civil or political standing, and mean "war, revolution, insurrection, or riot of some sort." Once spotted on Saturday morning, it thereby sparked another round of rumors, these warning of an "armed body of negroes" heading toward the town. Although evidence suggests that local Democrats had been busy for at least two days accumulating weapons and preparing to respond with force, the rumors clearly sped the mobilization of the town's "citizens," who appointed a committee to ride out with the sheriff and "meet the approaching crowd." A tense exchange followed, with the Republican leaders explaining that they only wished "to go peaceably into Camilla and hold a political meeting," and the sheriff warning them not to enter the town with arms. . . .

Suddenly, a local drunkard, waving a double-barreled shotgun, ran out to the wagon and, significantly, demanded that the drumming (associated both with a citizens' militia and slave communication) cease. A moment later he fired, and the "squads" of white townsmen immediately joined in. Freedmen who had guns briefly returned the volleys and then, with the others, commenced a desperate flight for safety. The sheriff and his "deputies" followed them into the woods and swamps with deadly purpose, some looking for "that d——d Phil Joiner." Joiner escaped, but eleven days later he reported that "the mobbing crowd is still going through Baker County and every Colored man that is farming to his self or supporting the nominee of Grant and Colfax he either have to leave his home or be killed."

Prospects for black retaliation briefly ran very high. As word of the shooting spread through Dougherty County that Saturday evening, agitated freedmen in Albany sought out the local Freedmen's Bureau agent. Some talked of going immediately to Camilla to rescue and protect those who remained at risk. A few hours later, African Methodist minister Robert Crumley heatedly reminded his congregants that he had advised those bound for Camilla the night before not to go with fewer than 150 well-armed men, and then suggested traveling there en masse the next day to "burn the earthy about the place." The Freedmen's Bureau agent managed to discourage such a course by promising a full investigation and urging his superiors in Atlanta to send federal troops. The investigation showed Camilla to be a massacre that had left at least nine African Americans dead and many more wounded. But all that came out of Atlanta was a proclamation by Republican governor Rufus Bullock urging civil authorities to keep the peace and safeguard the rights of the people. Election day proved to be remarkably quiet in southwest Georgia because the contest was over well before. Only two Republicans bothered to cast ballots in Camilla, and the turnout was so low elsewhere in the district that the Democrats, despite being greatly outnumbered among eligible voters, registered an official victory. There would be resurgences of local black power in the future, but this was the beginning of the end for Republican rule in Georgia. . . .

And yet we must not underestimate the extent and tenacity of black resistance. White toughs did, to their misfortune, in the village of Cainhoy, a short distance from Charleston. Attempting to intimidate a Republican speaker at a "joint discussion" in mid-October, they found themselves outgunned as well as outnumbered by a black crowd that included several militia companies. When the smoke cleared, five whites lay dead and as many as fifty had been wounded. Most in evidence among the coast, such militance was nonetheless to be found at various points in the interior. As rifle club activity intensified in Barnwell County, a "company of negroes," acting on their own authority, appropriated arms issued during Governor Scott's administration and threaten[ed] to destroy the town" of Blackville. In Darlington County, a "negro militia company consisting," according to a local Democrat, "of the worst elements in this section," continued to drill and cause "a great deal of trouble," coming in one instance to the aid of a favored trial justice. Sporadically, there were acts of arson and sabotage, ambushes and assaults. . . .

The paramilitary politics of the Reconstruction South had previously produced dual state governments in Louisiana (1872), Texas (1873), and Arkansas (1874), but in 1876–1877 they also provoked a national crisis of governance. Not only were the state returns contested in both South Carolina and Louisiana, but there, as well as in Florida, the electoral college returns were contested too, leaving the outcome of the Presidential race—and control of the executive branch—in doubt. As Republicans and Democrats struggled to reach an accord before Grant's term expired in early March, tensions and threats that harked back to the winter of 1860–1861 seemed to abound. Yet through all of this, what appeared to be taking shape was less a "compromise" than a shared political sensibility in northern ruling circles that questioned the legitimacies of popular democracy. That sensibility had always been in evidence among conservatives and had spread during the 1850s, only to be pressed to the margins by the revolutionary mobilizations of the 1860s. It now expressed itself as weariness with the issues of Reconstruction, as skepticism about the capabilities of freedpeople, as concerns about the expansion of federal powers, as revulsion over political corruption, and, especially, as exasperation with the "annual autumnal outbreaks" in the Deep South and the consequent use of federal troops to maintain Republican regimes there.

It required elaborate fictions and willful ignorance for critics to argue, as some did, that the military had no business rejecting the popular will in the South. For if detachments of federal troops at the statehouses in Columbia, South Carolina, and New Orleans, Louisiana, alone enabled Republicans to hang onto the last threads of power, their Democratic rivals made no effort to conceal their own dependence on superior force of arms. In Louisiana, Democratic gubernatorial claimant and former Confederate brigadier general Francis T. Nicholls quickly demonstrated his understanding of political necessities. He designated local White League units as the legal state militia, commandeered the state arsenal, and took control of the New Orleans police. In South Carolina, Wade Hampton's allies succeeded in garrisoning the state capitol with as many as six thousand Red Shirts, while rifle clubs drove out Republican officeholders in upcountry counties. . . .

The withdrawal of federal troops from the statehouses of South Carolina and Louisiana in April of 1877 did not therefore mark the end of their role in protecting the rights and property of American citizens; it only marked the end of their role, at least for nearly another century, in protecting the rights and property of African Americans and other working people. . . .

Ending the War: The Push for National Reconciliation

DAVID W. BLIGHT

Americans faced an overwhelming task after the Civil War and emancipation: how to understand the tangled relationship between two profound ideas—*healing* and *justice*. On some level, both had to occur; but given the potency of racial assumptions and power in nineteenth-century America, these two aims never developed in historical balance. One might conclude that this imbalance between outcomes of sectional healing and racial justice was simply America's inevitable historical condition, and celebrate the remarkable swiftness of the reunion, as Paul Buck did in his influential book, *The Road to Reunion* (1937). But theories of inevitability—of irrepressible conflicts or irrepressible reconciliations—are rarely satisfying. Human reconciliations—when tragically divided people unify again around aspirations, ideas, and the positive bonds of nationalism—are to be cherished. But sometimes reconciliations have terrible costs, both intentional and unseen. The sectional reunion after so horrible a civil war was a political triumph by the late nineteenth century, but it could not have been achieved without the resubjugation of many of those people whom the war had freed from centuries of bondage. This is the tragedy lingering on the margins and infesting the heart of American history from Appomattox to World War I. . . .

Reconstruction was one long referendum on the meaning and memory of the verdict at Appomattox. The great challenge of Reconstruction was to determine how a national blood feud could be reconciled at the same time a new nation emerged out of war and social revolution. The survivors on both sides, winners and losers in the fullest sense, would still inhabit the same land and eventually the same government. The task was harrowing: how to make the logic of sectional reconciliation compatible with the logic of emancipation, how to square black freedom and the stirrings of racial equality with a cause (the South's) that had lost almost everything except its unbroken belief in white supremacy. Such an effort required both remembering and forgetting. During Reconstruction, many Americans increasingly realized that remembering the war, even the hatreds and deaths on a hundred battlefields—facing all those graves on Memorial Day—became, with time, easier than struggling over the enduring ideas for which those battles had been fought. . . .

In the immediate aftermath of the war, defeated and prostrate, it appeared to many that white Southerners would accept virtually any conditions or terms laid upon them. This was the initial conclusion of the northern journalist Whitelaw Reid, who believed that even black suffrage would be "promptly accepted"—that is, until

Reprinted by permission of the publisher from *Race and Reunion: The Civil War in American Memory* by David W. Blight, pp. 3, 31, 44–47, 51, 64, 65, 69–71, 77–81, 83, 86, 87, 89, 91, 92, 97, Cambridge, Mass.: The Belknap Press of Harvard University Press, Copyright © 2001 by the President and Fellows of Harvard College.

he observed white Southern defiance revived by President Johnson's conciliatory Reconstruction measures. After his Southern tour, Reid left a mixed warning to policymakers about the disposition of white Southerners in 1866. "The simple truth is," Reid concluded, "they stand ready to claim everything, if permitted, and to accept anything, if required." Other Northern journalists observing the South reached similar conclusions. The initial war-bludgeoned compliance on the part of white Southerners gave way within a year to what Trowbridge called a "loyalty . . . of a negative sort: it is simply disloyalty subdued." A correspondent for the *New York Tribune* reported from Raleigh, North Carolina, that "the spirit of the Rebellion is not broken though its power is demolished." And a Northerner who had just returned from six months in South Carolina and Georgia informed Thaddeus Stevens in February 1866 that "the spirit which actuated the traitors . . . during the late rebellion is only subdued and *allows* itself to be *nourished* by *leniency.*"

Against this backdrop, Andrew Johnson offered to the South his rapid Reconstruction policy. In late May 1865, Johnson announced his plan for the readmission of Southern states. It included a broad provision for amnesty and pardon for those participants in the rebellion who would take a loyalty oath to the Union. High-ranking ex-Confederate government officials were excluded from pardons for the time being, as were all Southerners who owned $20,000 or more worth of property. The latter group had to apply personally to the President for a pardon. Johnson's plan further required each former Confederate state to call a convention to revise its antebellum constitution, renounce secession, and accept the Thirteenth Amendment abolishing slavery; they would then be promptly restored to the Union.

Johnson's plan put enormous authority back in the hands of white Southerners, but without any provisions for black civil or political rights. Indeed, Johnson himself was a thoroughgoing white supremacist and a doctrinaire state rightist. He openly encouraged the South to draft its notorious Black Codes, laws enacted across the South by the fall of 1865 that denied the freedmen political liberty and restricted their economic options and physical mobility. Designed as labor controls and a means for plantation discipline, such laws were part of the new constitutions produced by these "Johnson governments," and they expressed clearly white Southerners' refusal to face the deeper meanings of emancipation. Presidential Reconstruction, as it evolved in 1865, allowed Southerners to recreate governments of and for white men. Moreover, Johnson was openly hostile to the Freedmen's Bureau, the agency created by Congress in the last months of the war to provide food, medical care, schools, and labor contract adjudication for the freedpeople. The President overruled military and Freedmen's Bureau efforts to redistribute some land from masters to ex-slaves. By the fall of 1865, pardoned ex-Confederates were reclaiming their lands, and with such presidential encouragement, reclaiming political power. . . .

Profoundly different memories and expectations collided in 1865–67, as presidential Reconstruction collapsed and the Republicans in Congress wrested control of the process away from Johnson. "These people [white Southerners] are not loyal; they are only conquered," wrote Union Brigadier General James S. Brisbin to Thaddeus Stevens in December 1865. "I tell you there is not as much loyalty in the South today as there was the day Lee surrendered to Grant. The moment they lost their cause in the field they set about to gain by politics what they had failed to obtain by force of arms." Brisbin thought the Black Codes would "reduce the blacks to a slavery worse than that from which they just escaped." Johnson's leniency seemed only to restore an old order and risk losing the very triumph that the Union forces had just won with so much sacrifice. . . .

The radical Republicans had a genuine plan for Reconstruction. Their ideology was grounded in the notion of an activist federal government, a redefinition of American citizenship that guaranteed equal political rights for black men, and faith in free labor in a competitive capitalist system. The radicals greatly expanded federal authority, fixing their vision, as Sumner put it, on "the general principles" of "a national security and a national faith." Their cardinal principle was *equality before the law,* which in 1866 they enshrined in the Fourteen Amendment, expanding citizenship to all those born in the United States without regard to race. The same year Congress renewed the Freedmen's Bureau over Johnson's veto and passed the first civil rights act in American history.

Such legislation became reality because most Northerners were not ready to forget the results, and especially the sacrifices, of the war. The Southern states' rejection of the Fourteenth Amendment and Johnson's repeated vetoes of Reconstruction measures (as well as his repudiation at the polls in the Congressional elections of 1866) gave the radicals increased control over federal policy. In 1867 Congress divided the ex-Confederate states into five military districts and made black suffrage a condition of readmission to the Union. By 1870 all ex-Confederate states had rejoined the Union, and in most, the Republican Party—built as a coalition of "carpetbaggers" (Northerners who moved South), "scalawags" (native Southerners who gave allegiance to the new order), and thousands of black voters—held the reins of state government. Indeed black voters were the core constituency of Southern Republicanism and the means of power in 1867–68. . . .

As Congress engaged in the fateful debates over national policy in 1866–67, the floors of the House and Senate became arenas of warring memories. Many Republicans were clearly driven by a combination of retribution against the South, a desire to remake the Constitution based on black equality, and a quest for long-term political hegemony. Stevens left no doubt of his personal attitude toward ex-slaveholders and ex-Confederates. "The murderers must answer to the suffering race," he said on May 8, 1866. "A load of misery must sit heavily upon their souls." The public debate in Congress was often sanguinary; it challenged everyone's ability to convert primal memory into public policy. "I know that there is a morbid sensibility, sometimes called mercy," declared Stevens, "which affects a few of all classes, from the priest to the clown, which has more sympathy for the murderer on the gallows than for his victim." Yankee retribution never had a more vehement voice than Stevens, and no one ever waved the "bloody shirt" with greater zeal. "I am willing they shall come in when they are ready," Stevens pronounced. "Do not, I pray you, admit those who have slaughtered half a million of our countrymen until their clothes are dried, and until they are reclad. I do not wish to sit side by side with men whose garments smell of the blood of my kindred."

"Bloody shirt" rhetoric lasted a long time in American politics; it was more than a slogan, and in these early years, it had many uses and diverse practitioners. As both raw personal memory and partisan raw material, the "bloody shirt" was a means to establish war guilt and a method through which to express war-induced hatreds. . . .

Death and mourning were everywhere in America in 1865; hardly a family had escaped its pall. In the North, 6 percent of white males aged 13–43 had died in the war; in the South, 18 percent were dead. Of the 180,000 African Americans who served in the Union army and navy, 20 percent perished. Diseases such as typhoid, dysentery, and pneumonia claimed more than twice as many soldiers as did battle. The most immediate legacy of the war was its slaughter and how to remember it.

Death on such a scale demanded meaning. During the war, soldiers in countless remote arbors, or on awful battlefield landscapes, had gathered to mourn and bury their comrades, even while thousands remained unburied, their skeletons lying about on the killing fields of Virginia, Tennessee, or Georgia. Women had begun rituals of burial and remembrance in informal ways well before the war ended, both in towns on the homefront and sometimes at the battlefront. Americans carried flowers to graves or to makeshift monuments representing their dead, and so was born the ritual of "Decoration Day," known eventually also as Memorial Day.

In most places, the ritual was initially a spiritual practice. But very soon, remembering the dead and what they died for developed partisan fault lines. The evolution of Memorial Day during its first twenty years or so became a contest between three divergent, and sometimes overlapping, groups: blacks and their white former abolitionist allies, white Northerners, and white Southerners. With time, in the North, the war's two great results—black freedom and the preservation of the Union—were rarely accorded equal space. In the South, a uniquely Confederate version of the war's meaning, rooted in resistance to Reconstruction, coalesced around Memorial Day practice. Decoration Day, and the ways in which it was observed, shaped Civil War memory as much as any other cultural ritual. The story of the origins of this important American day of remembrance is central to understanding how reconciliationist practices overtook the emancipationist legacies of the Civil War. . . .

The "First Decoration Day," as this event came to be recognized in some circles in the North, involved an estimated ten thousand people, most of them black former slaves. During April, twenty-eight black men from one of the local churches built a suitable enclosure for the burial ground at the Race Course. In some ten days, they constructed a fence ten feet high, enclosing the burial ground, and landscaped the graves into neat rows. The wooden fence was whitewashed and an archway was built over the gate to the enclosure. On the arch, painted in black letters, the workmen inscribed "Martyrs of the Race Course." At nine o'clock in the morning on May 1, the procession to this special cemetery began as three thousand black schoolchildren (newly enrolled in freedmen's schools) marched around the Race Course, each with an armload of roses and singing "John Brown's Body." The children were followed by three hundred black women representing the Patriotic Association, a group organized to distribute clothing and other goods among the freedpeople. The women carried baskets of flowers, wreaths, and crosses to the burial ground. The Mutual Aid Society, a benevolent association of black men, next marched in cadence around the track and into the cemetery, followed by large crowds of white and black citizens. . . .

According to a reminiscence written long after the fact, "several slight disturbances" occurred during the ceremonies on the first Decoration Day, as well as "much harsh talk about the event locally afterward." But a measure of how white Charlestonians suppressed from memory this founding in favor of their own creation of the practice a year later came fifty-one years afterward, when the president of the Ladies Memorial Association of Charleston received an inquiry for information about the May 1, 1865, parade. A United Daughters of the Confederacy official wanted to know if it was true that blacks and their white abolitionist friends had engaged in such a burial rite. Mrs. S. C. Beckwith responded tersely: "I regret that I was unable to gather any official information in answer to this." In Southern and national memory, the first Decoration Day was nearly lost in a grand evasion.

As a Northern ritual of commemoration, Memorial Day officially took hold in May 1868 and 1869, when General John A. Logan, commander-in-chief of the Grand Army of the Republic (GAR), called on all Union veterans to conduct ceremonies and decorate the graves of their dead comrades. In general orders issued each of the two springs, Logan called for a national commemoration unlike anything in American experience save possibly the Fourth of July. In "almost every city, village, and hamlet church-yard in the land," charged Logan's circular, those who died to "suppress the late rebellion" were to be honored annually "while a survivor of the war remains." On May 30, 1868, when flowers were plentiful, funeral ceremonies were attended by thousands of people in 183 cemeteries in twenty-seven states. The following year, some 336 cities and towns in thirty-one states (including the South) arranged Decoration Day parades and orations. The observance grew manifold with time. In 1873, the New York legislature designated May 30 a legal holiday, and by 1890 every other Northern state had followed its lead. . . .

For white Southerners, Memorial Day was born amidst the despair of defeat and the need for collective expressions of grief. By 1866, local memorial associations had formed in many Southern communities, organized largely by women. Some new cemeteries were founded near battlefields, while existing ones in towns and cities were expanded enormously to accommodate the dead. In both sections, but especially in the South, the first monuments erected tended to be placed in cemeteries— the obvious sites of bereavement. By the 1890s, hardly a city square, town green, or even some one-horse crossroads lacked a Civil War memorial of some kind. But through most of the Reconstruction years, the cemetery remained the public site of memorialization; obelisks and stone pyramids appeared as markers of the recent past that so haunted every community. Often directed by social elites who could fund monuments, the Southern "memorial movement . . . helped the South assimilate the fact of defeat," as Gaines Foster writes, "without repudiating the defeated." . . .

By the early 1870s, a group of ex-Confederate officers in Virginia had forged a coalition of memorial groups that quickly took over the creation of the Lost Cause tradition. They did so through print as much as through ritual commemorations. In 1866, former Confederate general Daniel H. Hill founded the magazine *The Land We Love,* a periodical devoted to demonstrating the skill and prowess of Confederate armies against all odds. By 1869, Hill's journal had become *Southern Magazine,* and most importantly, the Southern Historical Society (SHS) was founded as the vehicle for presenting the Confederate version of the war to the world. By 1876, the SHS began publishing its regular *Southern Historical Society Papers,* a series that ran for fourteen years under the editorship of a former Confederate chaplain, John William Jones. The driving ideological and emotional force behind the SHS was the former Confederate general Jubal Early. Early had fled to Mexico at the end of the war and vowed never to return to his native Virginia under the federal flag. Despite such bluster, and because of threatening poverty, Early returned to his hometown of Lynchburg in 1869. He made himself, as Gaines Foster observes, into the "prototypical unreconstructed Rebel." His principle aim was not only to vindicate

Southern secession and glorify the Confederate soldier, but also to launch a propaganda assault on popular history and memory. . . .

In the South, monument unveiling days took on a significance equal to, if not greater than, Memorial Day. In Richmond, Virginia, on October 26, 1875, Confederate veterans by the thousands staged their first major coming-out as a collective force. At the unveiling of the first significant monument to a Confederate hero, a standing statue of Stonewall Jackson sculpted by the British artist T. H. Foley, nearly fifty thousand people gathered for an unprecedented parade and a ceremony. . . .

At major intersections on the parade route, veterans, ladies memorial associations, and "the indefatigable K.K.K." (Ku Klux Klan) had assembled artisans to construct arches and towers with elaborate decorations honoring Jackson. The largest arch, at Grace and Eighth Streets, included huge letters that read: "Warrior, Christian, Patriot." Above the inscription was a painting representing a stone wall, "upon which was resting a bare sabre, a Bible, and a Confederate cap." . . .

One dispute among the planners of the Jackson statue unveiling nearly derailed the event. Governor Kemper was the grand marshal of the ceremonies and had carefully planned the parade to the Capitol Square in Richmond. Kemper was nervous that "nothing shall appear on the 26th to hurt the party" (Democrats). He feared that the "least excess" in the Confederate celebration would give yet another "bloody shirt" to Northern Republicans, and he asked the leaders of the Confederate veterans to restrain their displays of battle flags. Only days before the big event, Jubal Early wrote to Kemper complaining of rumors that black militia companies and civilians were to be "allowed in the procession." "I am inexpressibly shocked at the idea," said Early. He considered the involvement of blacks "an indignity to the memory of Jackson and an insult to the Confederates." Black Richmonders, the total of which Early judged to be between twenty thousand and thirty thousand, would swarm into the square, he believed, and whites would be forced to "struggle for place with buck negroes . . . anxious to show their consequence." Believing that blacks would wave "pictures of Lincoln and Fifteenth Amendment banners," Early threatened not to attend, and to take other veterans with him, if Kemper executed the plan.

In ferocious responses, Kemper told Early to mind his own business and begged him to "stay at home." Black militia officers and ministers in Richmond had petitioned Kemper to take part in the procession. For racial "peace" in the city, the governor accepted the petitioners' request. The small contingent of blacks were placed at the extreme rear of a parade several miles long, numbering many thousands of white marchers. . . . The position of blacks in this bitter argument between the ultimate irreconcilable [Jubal Early] and a redeemer-reconciliationist governor remained utterly subordinate. One would eliminate them altogether from Confederate memory; the other would declare them loyal and dispatch them to the rear of parades. In the long history of Lost Cause tradition, both got their wish.

As the immense crowd assembled at the state capital grounds where the Jackson monument was to be unveiled, Kemper welcomed them as the Democrat-redeemer governor of Virginia. He announced that Jackson was a national hero, not merely a Southern saint, whose memory was to be a "common heritage of glory" for both sections. The massive ceremony served as the South's reminder to the North of its insistence on "respect." The unveiling declared, in effect, that Reconstruction, as Northern Republicans had imagined it, was over. . . .

In 1874–75, Union and Confederate veterans began to participate in Memorial Day exercises together in both North and South. In the wake of Memorial Day, 1875, in North Carolina, a black citizen in Raleigh, Osborne Hunter, anxiously observed in a letter to a newspaper "a noticeable spirit of reconciliation pervading the political atmosphere of both the Republican and Democratic parties of this state." In August 1874, the Democrats had regained power in North Carolina, and the highly racialized election had hinged, in part, on Southern resistance to federal enforcement of black civil rights. Until May 1875, blacks in Raleigh had always played a major role in Decoration Day ceremonies in that city. That year they were discouraged from participating, as the occasion was declared to be only a "soldier's turn-out." At the mark of a "decade in the history of freedom," concluded Hunter, Decoration Day seemed to be only an occasion for "ignoring the colored citizen and the colored voter." . . .

The disputed election of 1876 and the electoral crisis that culminated in the Compromise of 1877 brought the Republican Rutherford B. Hayes to the presidency, as well as the final three remaining Southern states not under Democratic control into that party's fold. Reconciliation seemed to sweep over the country's political spirit, as the Union survived another potential severing by sectional and partisan strife. Although it was hardly the first time that commentators in both sections had declared the final conclusion to the issues of the war, the political settlement of 1877 easily took its place as the traditional "end" of Reconstruction (a label it has carried ever since).

On Memorial Day, May 30, 1877, New York City experienced an array of parades and ceremonies unprecedented since the formal inception of the holiday nine years earlier. Virtually every orator and editorial writer declared the day one of forgetting, forgiveness, and equality of the Blue and the Gray veterans. . . .

Decoration Day, 1877 in New York culminated with a special indoor event at the Brooklyn Academy of Music. The planning committee, dominated by Democrats, had invited the prominent ex-Confederate general, lawyer, and then Brooklyn resident Roger A. Pryor to be orator of the evening. A committee member, Joseph Neilson, opened the proceedings with an explicit appeal for reconciliation. Neilson declared all the "causes" of the "late domestic contention" forgotten. As the voice of "healing," Pryor took the podium before an audience of nearly one thousand to deliver his extraordinary address, "The Soldier, the Friend of Peace and Union." . . .

Unlike many Memorial Day orators, Pryor did not hide the issue of race behind a rhetoric of reunion. The war had nothing directly to do with slavery, he proclaimed, in what became an article of faith to Southern vindicationists and their Northern allies. Southerners were comfortably reconciled to the destruction of slavery because it had only been the "occasion not the cause of secession." Slavery was an impersonal force in history, a natural phenomenon subject only to divine control and beyond all human responsibility. It was good while it lasted, good once it was gone; no Southerner fought in its defense, and no Northerner died to end it. It just went away, like a change in the weather. . . .

Following Pryor, former Union general Isaac S. Catlin delivered the final address of the evening. In full sympathy with the former Confederate's speech, Catlin spoke of military pathos and glory, of the victimhood and heroism of all soldiers on both sides. "I love the memory of a soldier," said Catlin. "I love the very dust that covers his mouldering body." Catlin called on all to be "exultant" that slavery was dead. "Is this not enough?" he asked. "Is it not enough that we are all American citizens, that our country is saved, that our country is one?" In this doctrine of "enough," the emancipationist legacy of the war had become bad taste among gentlemen soldiers. The "divine doctrine of forgiveness and conciliation" was the order of the day.

Dissent from this Blue-Gray reconciliationist version of the war's memory, while now on the margins, was by no means silenced in the larger culture or in New York. One year later, as though they had decided to invite a direct response to Pryor and his ilk, the integrated Abraham Lincoln Post of the GAR asked Frederick Douglass to address them in Madison Square on Decoration Day. As he did on so many occasions during the last quarter of his life, Douglass rose to the challenge with fire and indignation, offering an alternative, emancipationist memory of the war. "There was a right side and a wrong side in the late war," insisted Douglass "that no sentiment ought to cause us to forget." . . . The reconciliationists were using memory to send the nation down the wrong road to reunion, he believed. Douglass had no patience for endless tales of Southern woes. "The South has suffered to be sure," he said, "but she has been the author of her own suffering." . . .

The story of Civil War memory and the ritual of Decoration Days continued well beyond 1885 with the emancipationist legacy fighting endless rearguard actions against a Blue-Gray reconciliation that was to sweep through American culture. Those who remembered the war as the rebirth of the republic in the name of racial equality would continue to do battle with the growing number who would remember it as the nation's test of manhood and the South's struggle to sustain white supremacy.

FURTHER READING

Eric Anderson and Alfred Moss, eds., *The Facts of Reconstruction* (1991).
Michael Les Benedict, *A Compromise of Principle: Congressional Republicans and Reconstruction* (1974).
Laura Edwards, *Gendered Strife and Confusion: The Political Culture of Reconstruction* (1997).
Eric Foner, *A Short History of Reconstruction, 1863–1877* (1990).
Tera Hunter, *To 'Joy My Freedom: Southern Black Women's Lives and Labors After the Civil War* (1997).
Leon Litwack, *Been in the Storm So Long: The Aftermath of Slavery* (1979).
Nell Irvin Painter, *Exodusters: Black Migration to Kansas After Reconstruction* (1977).
Michael Perman, *The Road to Redemption* (1984).
Howard Rabinowitz, *Southern Black Leaders of the Reconstruction Era* (1982).
Heather Cox Richardson, *The Death of Reconstruction: Race, Labor, and Politics in the Post-Civil War North* (2001).
Jonathan Wiener, *Social Origins of the New South* (1978).
Gavin Wright, *The Political Economy of the Cotton South* (1978).

Western Settlement
and the Frontier

*The nineteenth-century historian Frederick Jackson Turner described the frontier
as "an area of free land" that was continually receding as American settlers moved
westward. The frontier closed, he said, when settlers reached the outer limit of the
western wilds, which had "constituted the richest free gift that was ever spread out
before civilized man." In Turner's portrayal, the West was an empty landscape
that was gradually peopled. It was also the place where a uniquely American
identity was forged: individualistic but cooperative, and deeply egalitarian. Today,
historians view the frontier very differently. To them, a frontier is not a line mark-
ing the start of an empty place but a zone of interaction where two or more societies
vie for the use of land. A frontier "opens" when one hsuman group intrudes upon
another, and "closes" when one of them establishes dominance. The process is often
a brutal one.*

*The Civil War spurred the opening of the Far West by removing southern
resistance to settlement of the territories by "free labor." In 1862, in the midst of the
war, the Republican-dominated Congress passed the Homestead Act. This legislation
offered 160 acres of western public land free of charge to any citizen who was over
the age of twenty-one or who headed a family, so long as he or she stayed on the
land for five continuous years. Congress also funded the first transcontinental railroad in 1862, the Union Pacific. These two events placed Indians, soldiers, freed
slaves, migrants from the East, and immigrants from Europe and Asia in conflict
for the following four decades.*

*The clash between these competing peoples led to murder and massacre during
the last quarter of the nineteenth century. Military spending on the Indian
wars amounted to 60 percent of the federal budget in 1880. The U.S.-Indian wars
reached their climax and ended with the defeat of the Sioux under Sitting Bull
in 1881 and the Apaches under Geronimo in 1886, at a cost of twenty-five
white soldiers for every Indian warrior killed. But the frontier still remained
open. "Whites" battled the Chinese, non-Mormons attacked Mormons, and
Indians struggled to hold onto their diminishing lands and rights well into*

the twentieth century. Native Americans, as well as Norwegians, Germans, Czechs, Mexicans, Chinese, and African Americans struggled to sustain their cultures and establish safe homesteads. All vied for the land "pacified" by the U.S. cavalry.

❧ Q U E S T I O N S   T O   T H I N K   A B O U T

"Westerns" (both movies and novels) told generations of Americans "how the West was won." Is frontier settlement best understood as a saga of English-speaking pioneers, or as the story of competing ethnic and racial groups? Was the West truly the place where Americans were most free and most "American," or was it a place riddled with inequalities?

❧ D O C U M E N T S

The following documents reveal a variety of perspectives on the western migration. Document 1 is Governor Lilburn Boggs's order to the Missouri state militia to drive out Mormons and exterminate them, if necessary, as a plague on the frontier. Document 2 is the Homestead Act of 1862, passed by the Civil War Congress. This act effected a massive public land transfer to migrants (like the Mormons, among others), fulfilling the promise of "free soil, free labor." Mary Barnard Aguirre, the author of Document 3, was one of the individuals whom the "cruel war" encouraged to move west. The document recounts her favorable impressions of the vibrant Hispanic southwest, soon to be opened to Anglo homesteaders. Some Indian tribes, in their ongoing resistance to the United States, elected to join the Confederacy. Document 4 shows how the United States used their "disloyalty" to consolidate control over the Indian nations after the war. Documents 5 and 6 give Indian perspectives on the United States's wars of conquest. In Document 5, Katie Bighead, a Cheyenne eyewitness to the massacre of U.S. troops under General George Armstrong Custer, notes the superiority of arrows over guns in an ambush. Chief Joseph of the Nez Percé, the tribe that had come to the aid of the Lewis and Clark expedition seventy years earlier and that had welcomed teachers and missionaries, evokes the tragedy of American expansionism in his famous surrender speech of 1877, Document 6. Document 7 shows that the struggle for land was not just between Indians and whites. African Americans also sought a piece of earth they could call their own, where they could live separately and without fear. In May 1879, a convention of 189 representatives from 19 states met in Nashville, Tennessee, to organize the "colored" western migration movement. Document 8 shows that the frontier attracted people from several continents, who frequently clashed. Miners in Wyoming responded violently to the perceived threat of Chinese laborers, struggling to make new lives on the frontier. Finally, historian Frederick Jackson Turner helped to create for the American public the image of the romantic West, where (white) men were strong, women virtuous, and democracy triumphant. In his 1893 statement (Document 9), Turner described the effects of the frontier both on democracy and on the American personality. He also pronounced the frontier "closed."

1. The Governor of Missouri Orders the Militia to Exterminate Mormons, 1838

The Exterminating Order.

On the following day the famous "Exterminating Order" was issued, which is as follows:

Headquarters Militia, City of Jefferson,
October 27, 1838.

Sir:

Since the order of the morning to you, directing you to cause four hundred mounted men to be raised within your division, I have received by Amos Reese, Esq., and Wiley E. Williams, Esq., one of my aids, information of the most appalling character, which changes the whole face of things, and places the Mormons in the attitude of open and avowed defiance of the laws and of having made open war upon the people of this State. Your orders are therefore, to hasten your operations and endeavor to reach Richmond, in Ray County, with all possible speed. The Mormons must be treated as enemies, and *must be exterminated,* or driven from the State, if necessary, for the public good. Their outrages are beyond all description. If you can increase your force you are authorized to do so, to any extent you may think necessary. I have just issued orders to Major General Wallock, of Monroe County, to raise five hundred men and to march them to the northern part of Daviess and there to unite with General Doniphan, of Clay, who has been ordered with five hundred men to proceed to the same point, for the purpose of intercepting the retreat of the Mormons to the north. They have been directed to communicate with you by express. You can also communicate with them if you find it necessary. Instead, therefore, of proceeding, as at first directed, to reinstate the citizens of Daviess in their homes, you will proceed immediately to Richmond, and there operate against the Mormons. Brigadier General Parks, of Ray, has been ordered to have four hundred men of his brigade in readiness to join you at Richmond. The whole force will be placed under your command.

L. W. Boggs,
Governor and Commander in Chief.

2. The Homestead Act Provides Free Land to Settlers, 1862

May 20, 1862.

Be it enacted by the Senate and House of Representatives of the United States of America in Congress assembled, That any person who is the head of a family, or who has arrived at the age of twenty-one years, and is a citizen of the United States,

---

From: Missouri Extermination Order, found in *Missouri Historical Review,* V. 13, n. 3 (April 1919) pp. 295–296. (Imprint: Columbia, Mo. State Historical Society).

The Statutes at Large, Treaties, and Proclamations of the United States 1859–1863, vol. 12 (Boston: Little, Brown, 1865), 392.

or who shall have filed his declaration of intention to become such, as required by the naturalization laws of the United States, and who has never borne arms against the United States Government or given aid and comfort to its enemies, shall, from and after the first January, eighteen hundred and sixty-three, be entitled to enter one quarter section or a less quantity of unappropriated public lands . . . which shall not, with the land so already owned and occupied, exceed in the aggregate one hundred and sixty acres.

SEC. 2. *And be it further enacted,* That the person applying for the benefit of this act shall, upon application to the register of the land office in which he or she is about to make such entry, make affidavit . . . that said entry is made for the purpose of actual settlement and cultivation, and not either directly or indirectly for the use of benefit of any other person or persons whomsoever; and upon filing the said affidavit with the register or receiver, and on payment of ten dollars, he or she shall thereupon be permitted to enter the quantity of land specified.

3. Pioneer Mary Barnard Aguirre Marries into the Spanish West, 1863

In September '63 we made preparations for another trip—this time it was to be to unknown lands "across the plains" & by the 19th all was ready & we started from Westport in ambulances—quite a party of us. There was my father & oldest sister, my husband, myself, Pedro (then not quite three months old) & a nursegirl 13 years old, named Angeline. . . . I was like a child with no more knowledge of the responsibilities of life or the care of a baby & only glad to leave that cruel war & the horrors behind me. . . .

. . . That first winter was delightful to us all. The weather was so warm & the constant sunshine so lovely that we States-people enjoyed it to the fullest extent—staying out of doors the most of the time. . . . On New Years day (1864) my husband & myself were invited to be "Padrinos"—(godparents) for the New Years high Mass, which we attended sitting in chairs in front of the altar with highly decorated wax candles in our hands. These were lit & my whole attention was devoted to keeping that candle straight—for I was so interested with the newness of every thing that I'd forget the candle for a moment & it would bob over to the imminent danger of my hat. This was a special attention we were shown because my husband was much beloved in the town.

Next came Pedro's christening which was a grand affair. He being the first grandson in the family an especial celebration was made. For three days before there was a baker & two assistants in the house. They baked no end of cakes & confectionary, roasted fowls & pigs & were highly entertaining to me, on account of the way they made & baked things. Everything was baked in one of those bee hive shaped adobe ovens, that opened into the kitchen. It was heated red hot & then all the coals scraped out & things put in on flat pieces of tin & shallow pans. The number of eggs that were used was a marvel & in fact it was all a wonder to me. There were

Mary Barnard Aguirre, " Autobiography," Aguirre Collection, Arizona State Historical Society Library, pp. 7–17 of typed copy.

two hundred guests. People from far & near were invited, some coming from El Paso—60 miles away. . . .

There was something new to see all the time. The annual feasts came on in due time. Each town has its patron saint whose day was celebrated by high mass & then a week of games & bull fights & dancing in the open air by the populace. There were three towns near together—Dona Ana, Las Cruces & La Mesilla & their feasts came in Jan, Feb & March & we attended all of them. At the Mesilla feast which was in March there were much more elaborate preparations made. I was again invited to be the "Madrina" . . . & was dressed in a way that would be astonishing now adays, for part of my attire was an elaborate satin cloak, made in the City of Mexico & embroidered a half a yard wide on three capes, reaching to my feet. I had to go also to the vespers & the evening was cool. It was brown satin & the embroidery white. So you can fancy my astonishing appearance as we sailed up that church, climbing over the kneeling crowds—for there were no seats & all sat on the floor—till we reached the chairs set for us before the altar. Some one remarked that I must be the Virgin Mary.

The next afternoon we all attended a bull fight. The ring was in the church plaza, built of logs tied together with raw hide. Above one side were the private boxes "Palcos" they were called—which were made of boards loosely put together & covered with canvas. These were reached by ladders of the rudest description & the widest apart rungs one could imagine. It was terrible climbing for short folks like me. When we ladies started up that ladder (me in that wonderful cloak) two men held blankets over us as we went up. When we arrived at the top the boards of the floor were so wide apart that we came near stepping thro'. But we all enjoyed the bull fight immensely tho' there were no bulls killed & no blood shed. . . . I lived in Las Cruces seven months & then went to Las Vegas to be with my husband who had what was then called the Interior freight contract from the government to supply all the military posts of the territory with provisions & freight. The shipping point was Ft Union—& Las Vegas was the nearest point. There I lived very happily.

4. The Federal Government Punishes Confederate Indians, 1865

. . . The council assembled at Fort Smith, September 8, and delegates were present in the course of the sittings (though not all in attendance at first) representing the Creeks, Choctaws, Chickasaws, Cherokees, Seminoles, Osages, Senecas, Shawnees, Quapaws, Wyandotts, Wichitas, and Comanches. Immediately upon the opening of the proceedings, the tribes were informed generally of the object for which the commission had come to them; that they for the most part, as tribes, had, by violating their treaties—by making treaties with the so-called Confederate States, forfeited all *rights* under them, and must be considered as at the mercy of the government; but that there was every disposition to treat them leniently, and above all a determination to recognize in a signal manner the loyalty of those who had fought upon the side of the government, and endured great sufferings on its behalf. On the next day

Annual Report of the Commissioner of Indian Affairs, 1865.

the delegates were informed that the commissioners were empowered to enter into treaties with the several tribes, upon the basis of the following propositions:

1st. That each tribe must enter into a treaty for permanent peace and amity among themselves, each other as tribes, and with the United States.

2d. The tribes settled in the "Indian country" to bind themselves, at the call of the United States authorities, to assist in compelling the wild tribes of the plains to keep the peace.

3d. Slavery to be abolished, and measures to be taken to incorporate the slaves into the tribes, with their rights guaranteed.

4th. A general stipulation as to final abolition of slavery.

5th. A part of the Indian country to be set apart, to be purchased for the use of such Indians, from Kansas or elsewhere, as the government may desire to colonize therein.

6th. That the policy of the government to unite all the Indian tribes of this region into one consolidated government should be accepted.

7th. That no white persons, except government employees, or officers of employees of internal improvement companies authorized by government, will be permitted to reside in the country, unless incorporated with the several nations.

Printed copies of the address of the commissioners involving the above propositions were placed in the hands of the agents, and of members of the tribes, many of whom were educated men.

On the third day the delegates from the loyal Chickasaws, Choctaws, Senecas, Osages, and Cherokees, principally occupied the time with replies to the address and propositions of the commissioners, the object being partly to express a willingness to accept those propositions, with some modifications, if they had been clothed with sufficient power by their people, but chiefly in explanation of the manner in which their nations became involved with the late confederacy. The address of the Cherokees was especially noteworthy, inasmuch as they attempted to charge the causes of their secession upon the United States, as having violated its treaty obligations, in failing to give the tribe protection, so that it was *compelled* to enter into relations with the confederacy. The next day the loyal Seminoles expressed their willingness to accede to the policy of the government, and to make peace with those of their people who had aided the rebellion. The president of the commission then read a reply to the address of the loyal Cherokees above referred to, showing, from original and official documents, that, *as a tribe,* by the action of their constituted authorities, John Ross being then, as at the time of the council, their head, they had, at the very opening of the rebellion, entered into alliance with it, and raised troops for it, and urged the other tribes to go with them, and that they could not now, under the facts proven, deny their original participation in the rebellion. . . .

The loyal Creeks on this day presented their address of explanation, setting forth the manner in which their nation, by the unauthorized action of its chief, entered into treaty relations with the confederacy, and the terrible sufferings which the loyal Creeks endured in battle and on the march to Kansas seeking protection from the United States, and asking "to be considered not guilty."

5. Katie Bighead (Cheyenne) Remembers Custer and the Battle of Little Big Horn, 1876

I was with the Southern Cheyennes during most of my childhood and young woman-hood. I was in the camp beside the Washita river, in the country the white people call Oklahoma, when Custer and his soldiers came there and fought the Indians (November, 1868). Our Chief Black Kettle and other Cheyennes, many of them women and children, were killed that day. It was early in the morning when the soldiers began the shooting. There had been a big storm, and there was snow on the ground. All of us jumped from our beds, and all of us started running to get away. I was barefooted, as were almost all of the others. Our tepees and all of our property we had to leave behind were burned by the white men.

The next spring Custer and his soldiers found us again (March, 1869). We then were far westward, on a branch of what the white people call Red river, I think. That time there was no fighting. Custer smoked the peace pipe with our chiefs. He promised never again to fight the Cheyennes, so all of us followed him to a soldier fort (Fort Sill). Our people gave him the name Hi-es-tzie, meaning Long Hair.

I saw Long Hair many times during those days. One time I was close to where he was mounting his horse to go somewhere, and I took a good look at him. He had a large nose, deep-set eyes, and light-red hair that was long and wavy. He was wearing a buckskin suit and a big white hat. I was then a young woman, 22 years old, and I admired him. All of the Indian women talked of him as being a fine-looking man.

My cousin, a young woman named Me-o-tzi, went often with him to help in finding the trails of Indians. She said he told her his soldier horses were given plenty of corn and oats to eat, so they could outrun and catch the Indians riding ponies that had only grass to eat. All of the Cheyennes liked her, and all were glad she had so important a place in life. After Long Hair went away, different ones of the Cheyenne young men wanted to marry her. But she would not have any of them. She said that Long Hair was her husband, that he had promised to come back to her, and that she would wait for him. She waited seven years. Then he was killed. . . .

I had seen other battles, in past times. I always liked to watch the men fight-ing. Not many women did that, and I often was teased on account of it. But this time [at the battle of Little Big Horn] I had a good excuse, for White Bull's son, my nephew, named Noisy Walking, had gone. I was but twenty-nine years old, so I had not any son to serve as a warrior, but I would sing strongheart songs for the nephew. He was eighteen years old. Some women told me he had expected me to be there, and he had wrapped a red scarf about his neck in order that I might know him from a distance. . . .

The Indians were using bows and arrows more than they were using guns. Many of them had no guns, and not many who did have them had also plenty of bullets. But even if they had been well supplied with both guns and bullets, in that

---

As told to Thomas B. Marquis, reprinted in Thomas B. Marquis, *Custer on the Little Bighorn* (Algonac, Mich.: Reference Publications, 1986), 35–43.

fight the bow was better. As the soldier ridge sloped on all sides, and as there were no trees on it nor around it, the smoke from each gun fired showed right where the shooter was hidden. The arrows made no smoke, so it could not be seen where they came from. Also, since a bullet has to go straight out from the end of a gun, any Indian who fired his gun had to put his head up so his eyes could see where to aim it. By doing this his head might be seen by a soldier and hit by a soldier bullet. The Indian could keep himself at all times out of sight when sending arrows. Each arrow was shot far upward and forward, not at any soldier in particular, but to curve down and fall where they were. Bullets would not do any harm if shot in that way. But a rain of arrows from thousands of Indian bows, and kept up for a long time, would hit many soldiers and their horses by falling and sticking into their heads or their backs. . . .

I may have seen Custer at the time of the battle or after he was killed. I do not know, as I did [not] then know of his being there. . . .

But I learned something more about him from our people in Oklahoma. Two of those Southern Cheyenne women who had been in our camp at the Little Bighorn told of having been on the battlefield soon after the fighting ended. They saw Custer lying dead there. They had known him in the South. While they were looking at him some Sioux men came and were about to cut up his body. The Cheyenne women, thinking of Me-o-tzi, made signs, "He is a relative of ours," but telling nothing more about him. So the Sioux men cut off only one joint of a finger. The women then pushed the point of a sewing awl into each of his ears, into his head. This was done to improve his hearing, as it seemed he had not heard what our chiefs in the South said when he smoked the pipe with them. They told him then that if ever afterward he should break that peace promise and should fight the Cheyennes the Everywhere Spirit surely would cause him to be killed.

Through almost sixty years, many a time I have thought of Hi-es-tzie as the handsome man I saw in the South. And I often have wondered if, when I was riding among the dead where he was lying, my pony may have kicked dirt upon his body.

6. Chief Joseph (Nez Percé) Surrenders, 1877

Tell General Howard I know what is in his heart. What he told me before, I have in my heart. I am tired of fighting. Our chiefs are killed. Looking Glass is dead. Tulhul-hutsut is dead. The old men are all dead. It is the young men who say yes or no. He who led the young men is dead. It is cold and we have no blankets. The little children are freezing to death. My people, some of them, have run away to the hills and have no blankets, no food; no one knows where they are—perhaps freezing to death. I want to have time to look for my children and see how many of them I can find. Maybe I shall find them among the dead. Hear me, my chiefs. I am tired; my heart is sick and sad. From where the sun now stands I will fight no more, forever.

As quoted in Allen P. Slickpoo, *Noon-Nee-Me-Poo: We, the Nez Perce* (Lapwi, Idaho: Nez Perce Tribe, 1973), 193–194.

7. Southern Freedmen Resolve to Move West, 1879

Fifteen years have elapsed since our emancipation, and though we have made material advancement as citizens, yet we are forced to admit that obstacles have been constantly thrown in our way to obstruct and retard our progress. Our toil is still unrequited, hardly less under freedom than slavery, whereby we are sadly oppressed by poverty and ignorance, and consequently prevented from enjoying the blessings of liberty, while we are left to the shame and contempt of all mankind. This unfortunate state of affairs is because of the intolerant spirit exhibited on the part of the men who control the state governments of the South today. Free speech in many localities is not tolerated. The lawful exercise of the rights of citizenship is denied when majorities must be overcome. Proscription meets us on every hand; in the school-room, in the church that sings praises to that God who made of one blood all the nations of the earth; in places of public amusement, in the jury box, and in the local affairs of government we are practically denied the rights and privileges of freemen.

We can not expect to rise to the dignity of true manhood under the system of labor and pay as practically carried out in some portions of the South today. . . .

Resolved, That it is the sense of this conference that the great current of migration which has for the past few months taken so many of our people from their homes in the South, and which is still carrying hundreds to the free and fertile West, should be encouraged and kept in motion until those who remain are accorded every right and privilege guaranteed by the constitution and laws.

Resolved, That we recommend great care on the part of those who migrate. They should leave home well prepared with certain knowledge of localities to which they intend to move; money enough to pay their passage and enable them to begin life in their new homes with prospect of ultimate success.

8. Wyoming Gunfight: An Attack on Chinatown, 1885

ROCK SPRINGS, WYO., *September 18, 1885.*

HON. HUANG SIH CHUEN,
Chinese Consul:

YOUR HONOR: We, the undersigned, have been in Rock Springs, Wyoming Territory, for periods ranging from one to fifteen years, for the purpose of working on the railroads and in the coal mines.

Up to the time of the recent troubles we had worked along with the white men, and had not had the least ill-feeling against them. The officers of the companies employing us treated us and the white men kindly, placing both races on the same footing and paying the same wages.

W. E. B. DuBois, "Economic Cooperation Among Negro Americans," *Twelfth Annual Atlanta Conference* (Atlanta: Atlanta University Publications, 1907), 52–53.

House, *Providing Indemnity to Certain Chinese Subjects,* 49th Cong., 1st Sess., 1886, 26–29.

Several times we had been approached by the white men and requested to join them in asking the companies for an increase in the wages of all, both Chinese and white men. We inquired of them what we should do if the companies refused to grant an increase. They answered that if the companies would not increase our wages we should all strike, then the companies would be obliged to increase our wages. To this we dissented, wherefore we excited their animosity against us.

During the past two years there has been in existence in "Whitemen's Town," Rock Springs, an organization composed of white miners, whose object was to bring about the expulsion of all Chinese from the Territory. To them or to their object we have paid no attention. About the month of August of this year notices were posted up, all the way from Evanston to Rock Springs, demanding the expulsion of the Chinese, &c. On the evening of September 1, 1885, the bell of the building in which said organization meets rang for a meeting. It was rumored on that night that threats had been made against the Chinese. . . .

About 2 o'clock in the afternoon [of September 2] a mob, divided into two gangs, came toward "Chinatown," one gang coming by way of the plank bridge, and the other by way of the railroad bridge. The gang coming by way of the railroad bridge was the larger, and was subdivided into many squads, some of which did not cross the bridge, but remained standing on the side opposite to "Chinatown;" others that had already crossed the bridge stood on the right and left at the end of it. Several squads marched up the hill behind Coal-pit No. 3. One squad remained at Coal-shed No. 3, and another at the pump-house. The squad that remained at the pump-house fired the first shot, and the squad that stood at Coal-shed No. 3 immediately followed their example and fired. The Chinese by name of Lor Sun Kit was the first person shot, and fell to the ground. At that time the Chinese began to realize that the mob were bent on killing. . . .

Whenever the mob met a Chinese they stopped him, and pointing a weapon at him, asked him if he had a revolver, and then approaching him they searched his person, robbing him of his watch or any gold or silver that he might have about him, before letting him go. Some of the rioters would let a Chinese go after depriving him of all his gold and silver, while another Chinese would be beaten with the butt ends of the weapons before being let go. Some of the rioters, when they could not stop a Chinese, would shoot him dead on the spot, and then search and rob him. Some would overtake a Chinese, throw him down and search and rob him before they would let him go. Some of the rioters would not fire their weapons, but would only use the butt ends to beat the Chinese with. Some would not beat a Chinese, but rob him of whatever he had and let him go, yelling to him to go quickly. Some, who took no part either in beating or robbing the Chinese, stood by, shouting loudly and laughing and clapping their hands.

There was a gang of women that stood at the "Chinatown" end of the plank bridge and cheered; among the women, two of them each fired successive shots at the Chinese. This was done about a little past 3 o'clock p.m. . . .

Some of the Chinese were killed at the bank of Bitter Creek, some near the railroad bridge, and some in "Chinatown." After having been killed, the dead bodies of some were carried to the burning buildings and thrown into the flames. Some of the Chinese who had hid themselves in the houses were killed and their bodies burned; some, who on account of sickness could not run, were burned alive in the houses. One Chinese was killed in "Whitemen's Town" in a laundry house, and his house demolished. The whole number of Chinese killed was twenty-eight and those wounded fifteen.

9. Historian Frederick Jackson Turner Articulates the "Frontier Thesis," 1893

The American frontier is sharply distinguished from the European frontier—a fortified boundary line running through dense populations. The most significant thing about the American frontier is, that it lies at the hither edge of free land. In the census reports it is treated as the margin of that settlement which has a density of two or more to the square mile. . . .

In the settlement of America we have to observe how European life entered the continent, and how America modified and developed that life and reacted on Europe. Our early history is the study of European germs developing in an American environment. Too exclusive attention has been paid by institutional students to the Germanic origins, too little to the American factors. The frontier is the line of most rapid and effective Americanization. The wilderness masters the colonist. It finds him a European in dress, industries, tools, modes of travel, and thought. It takes him from the railroad car and puts him in the birch canoe. It strips off the garments of civilization and arrays him in the hunting shirt and the moccasin. It puts him in the log cabin of the Cherokee and Iroquois and runs an Indian palisade around him. Before long he has gone to planting Indian corn and plowing with a sharp stick; he shouts the war cry and takes the scalp in orthodox Indian fashion. In short, at the frontier the environment is at first too strong for the man. He must accept the conditions which it furnishes, or perish, and so he fits himself into the Indian clearings and follows the Indian trails. Little by little he transforms the wilderness, but the outcome is not the old Europe. . . . The fact is, that here is a new product that is American. At first, the frontier was the Atlantic coast. It was the frontier of Europe in a very real sense. Moving westward, the frontier became more and more American. . . .

But the most important effect of the frontier has been in the promotion of democracy here and in Europe. As has been indicated, the frontier is productive of individualism. Complex society is precipitated by the wilderness into a kind of primitive organization based on the family. The tendency is anti-social. It produces antipathy to control, and particularly to any direct control. . . . The frontier individualism has from the beginning promoted democracy. . . .

From the conditions of frontier life came intellectual traits of profound importance. The works of travelers along each frontier from colonial days onward describe certain common traits, and these traits have, while softening down, still persisted as survivals in the place of their origin, even when a higher social organization succeeded. The result is that to the frontier the American intellect owes its striking characteristics. That coarseness and strength combined with acuteness and inquisitiveness; that practical, inventive turn of mind, quick to find expedients; that

---

Reprinted in Ray Allen Billington, ed. *The Frontier Thesis: Valid Interpretation of American History?* (New York: Robert Krieger, 1977), 10–20.

masterful grasp of material things, lacking in the artistic but powerful to effect great ends; that restless, nervous energy; that dominant individualism, working for good and for evil, and withal that buoyancy and exuberance which comes with freedom— these are traits of the frontier, or traits called out elsewhere because of the existence of the frontier. . . . But never again will such gifts of free land offer themselves. For a moment, at the frontier, the bonds of custom are broken and unrestraint is triumphant. There is not *tabula rasa*. The stubborn American environment is there with its imperious summons to accept its conditions; the inherited ways of doing things are also there; and yet, in spite of environment, and in spite of custom, each frontier did indeed furnish a new field of opportunity, a gate of escape from the bondage of the past; and freshness, and confidence, and scorn of older society, impatience of its restraints and its ideas, and indifference to its lessons, have accompanied the frontier. What the Mediterranean Sea was to the Greeks, breaking the bond of custom, offering new experiences, calling out new institutions and activities, that, and more, the ever retreating frontier has been to the United States directly, and to the nations of Europe more remotely. And now, four centuries from the discovery of America, at the end of a hundred years of life under the Constitution, the frontier has gone, and with its going has closed the first period of American history.

E S S A Y S

The western frontier looms large in the history of the United States. Historians Frederick Jackson Turner and Theodore Roosevelt helped to enshrine the frontier experience by portraying the West as the rough-and-tumble setting in which Americans forged their commitment to political democracy and social equality. Whether one agrees with this may depend on whether one sees the drama as featuring a multiethnic cast, or as being primarily a tale of Anglo-American migration westward. Today, historians debate whether the West was really the cradle of American equality and individualism. Ray Allen Billington, an intellectual heir of Frederick Jackson Turner, shows how the western environment fostered an easy-going social equality among Yankee pioneers. Patricia Nelson Limerick of the University of Colorado at Boulder speaks for a generation of "new western historians" when she argues that western settlement was continuously multiethnic and fundamentally antidemocratic.

The Frontier as a Cradle of Liberty

RAY ALLEN BILLINGTON

To understand the uniqueness of *American* democracy we must consider not only the form of government and the extent of popular participation, but the way in which the people of the United States view government and society as a whole. Do they regard the state as the master or servant of its citizens? Do they consider their fellow men as equals, or as inferiors and superiors? . . . If the image of the social

Ray Allen Billington, *America's Frontier Heritage* (New York: Holt, Rinehart and Winston, 1967), 139–157. Reprinted with permission of Wadsworth, an imprint of the Wadsworth Group, a division of Thomson Learning.

order common among Americans differs from that usual among Europeans, and if the differences can be explained by the pioneering experience, we can conclude that the frontier has altered the national character as well as institutions.

In this quest, two concepts are especially important: that of "individualism" and that of "equality." Visitors from abroad feel that the people of the United States have endowed these words with distinctive meanings. In no other nation is the equality of all men so loudly proclaimed; in no other country is the right of individual self-assertion (within certain areas) so stoutly defended. . . .

. . . Was frontier individualism a myth, and if not, how did it differ from traditional individualism? One conclusion is obvious: in the social realm the pioneer was a complete traditionalist, leaning on the community no less than his city cousins. Cooperation with his neighbors was commonplace for defense, the accomplishments of essential pioneering tasks, law enforcement, and a host of other necessities. In the economic realm the frontiersman's attitudes were less sharply defined. Consistency was not one of his sins; he favored regulation that seemed beneficial to his interests, and opposed regulation that threatened immediate or potential profits. His views were, in other words, comparable to those of Eastern business leaders who demanded from the government protective tariffs, railroad land grants, and federal subsidies, while mouthing the virtues of "rugged individualism."

Yet in one sense, the frontiersman moved somewhat beyond his counterparts in the East. He was, to a unique degree, living in a land where everyone was a real or potential capitalist. Nowhere could a stake in society be more easily obtained, and nowhere was the belief that this was possible more strongly entrenched. . . .

. . . The widespread property holdings in the West, and the belief that every man would achieve affluence, inclined the Westerner to insist on his right to profits somewhat more stridently than others. His voice spoke for individualism louder than that of his fellows, even though he was equally willing to find haven in cooperation when danger threatened or need decreed. . . .

Basically, frontier individualism stemmed from the belief that all men were equal (excluding Negroes, Indians, Orientals, and other minority groups), and that all should have a chance to prove their personal capabilities without restraint from society. This seemed fair in a land of plenty, where superabundant opportunity allowed each to rise or fall to his proper level as long as governments did not meddle. Faith in the equality of men was the great common creed of the West. Only an understanding of the depth of this belief can reveal the true nature of social democracy on successive frontiers.

To European visitors, this was the most unique feature of Western life and thought: the attitude that set that region apart from Europe or the East. "There is nothing in America," wrote one, "that strikes a foreigner so much as the real republican equality existing in the Western States, which border on the wilderness." The whole attitude of the people was different; calmly confident of their own future, they looked on all men as their peers and acted accordingly. One Westerner who defined the frontier as a region where a poor man could enter a rich man's house without feeling uneasy or unequal was not far astray. Menial subservience was just as unpopular there as haughty superiority. Dame Shirley, writing from the California gold fields, felt the "I'm as good as you are" spirit all about her, and believed that only an American frontiersman could

> Enter a palace with his old felt hat on—
> To address the King with the title of Mister,
> And ask the price of the throne he sat on.

Everywhere men of all ranks exuded that easy air of confidence that went with complete self-assurance, meeting travelers on terms of equality that charmed those democratically inclined and shocked those of opposite prejudice. "The wealthy man assumes nothing to himself on account of his wealth," marveled one, "and the poor man feels no debasement on account of his poverty, and every man stands on his own individual merits." The spirit of Western democracy was captured by a cowboy addressing a disagreeable scion of British nobility: "You may be a son of a lord back in England, but that ain't what you are out here."

In the give and take of daily life, Western egalitarianism was expressed in the general refusal to recognize the class lines that were forming in every community. Some of the self-proclaimed "better sort" might hold themselves aloof and put on aristocratic airs, but they were atypical of the great mass of the people. The majority, in evaluating those about them, applied value judgments that differed from those in communities where tradition played a stronger role. Men were weighed on their present and future contributions to society, with total disregard for their background. Each played a role in the developing social order, and as long as he played it well he was respected. "To be useful is here the ruling principle," wrote a Swedish visitor to the West; "it is immaterial what one does so long as he is respected and does his work efficiently." Drones and aristocratic idlers were not bearing their fair share and were outcasts; men of menial rank were contributing to the community welfare and were respected. "There is in the West," noted an unusually acute observer during the 1830s, "a real equality, not merely an equality to talk about, an equality on paper; everybody that has on a decent coat is a gentleman."

Contemporaries speculated often on the reasons for frontier social democracy. Most agreed that the burgeoning Western economy was basically responsible, offering as it did a chance for the lowliest to acquire prestige through accumulated wealth. All had an equal chance to improve themselves, and so all should be treated as equals; conversely, the servant who believed that he would someday be a millionaire saw no reason to be servile to his temporary betters. This was common sense, since every new community boasted dozens of living examples of rags-to-riches success: the tenant farmer who was now a county judge, the mechanic newly elected to the legislature, the farmer grown rich by the sale of lands. As a British traveler saw, "the means of subsistence being so easy in the country, and their dependence on each other consequently so trifling, that spirit of servility to those about them so prevalent in European manners, is wholly unknown to them." Why be servile when the man above today might be the man below tomorrow? Why cling to traditional views of rank when the heir apparent to a British earldom could be seen mowing hay, assisted by two sons of a viscount, while nearby the brother of an earl was feeding grain into a threshing machine? Clearly standards on the frontier were different, and equality more nearly a fact of life.

The common level of wealth encouraged this spirit, for while differences did exist, the gulf between rich and poor was relatively less in frontier regions than in older societies. Poverty was rare in pioneer communities that had graduated from the backwoods stage; one governor complained that the number of dependent paupers in his state was "scarcely sufficient to give exercise to the virtue of charity in individuals." Wealth might and did exist on rural frontiers, but its presence was less obvious than in the East, for money would buy little but land and land was available to all. Ostentatious spending existed but was uncommon, partly because luxuries and leisure were largely unavailable, partly because it would breed hostility in neighbors who resented display. "Their wealth," it was observed, "does very little in the way of purchasing even the outward signs of respect; and as to *adulation,* it is not to be purchased with love or money." This leveling process underlined the sense of equality that was so typical of the frontier.

It was further emphasized by the fact that on the newer frontiers rich and poor lived, dressed, and acted much more alike than in the East. Most owned their own houses, though some might be of logs and some of bricks. Most dressed in homespun clothes and shunned the powdered wigs and knee breeches that were the badge of the gentry in the early nineteenth century; travelers frequently complained that it was impossible to distinguish the well-born from the lowly by the garments they wore. Most bore themselves proudly, scorning the humble mien that marked the lower classes in Europe. "The clumsy gait and bent body of our peasant is hardly ever seen here," wrote an Englishman from Kentucky in 1819; "every one walks erect and easy." When people looked and acted alike, as they did along the frontiers, treating them alike came naturally.

No less important in fanning the spirit of egalitarianism was the newness of the West, and the lack of traditional aristocratic standards there. No entrenched gentry governed social intercourse, setting the practices of those below them and closing their ranks against newcomers. Those who rose in station did not have to surmount the barrier of learning new customs as do those achieving higher status today, for conventions, deferences, and distinctions were rare among the "tree-destroying sovereigns" of the West. A man's ancestry and prior history were less important than the contribution that he could make to a new society badly in need of manpower. One Westerner who remarked: "It's what's above ground, not what's under, that we think on," and another who added: "Not, 'What has he done in the East?' but 'What does he intend to do in Kansas and for Kansas?' " summed up the reasons for much of the social democracy that thrived along the frontiers.

This combination of causal forces—economic equality, commonly shared living standards, and the absence of traditional aristocratic values—enshrined belief in equality as the common faith of Western society. Class distinctions did exist, of course; innate differences in talent, ambition, and skill divided the various strata at an early stage in the evolution of every Western community. But relatively, these distinctions played a lesser role in the West than in the East. Instead belief in equality compelled frontiersmen to uplift the lowly and degrade the superior as they sought a common democratic level.

Elevation of the lowly was most commonly expressed by refusal to use terms designating class distinctions. Every man on the frontier, whatever his status in life, was a "gentleman," and every woman a "lady." Travelers from older societies were frequently amused to find the ragged wagoner or the ill-kempt seller of old bones addressed in this fashion; one who asked a tavern keeper in an infant settlement in New York to find his coachman was delighted when that worthy called out: "Where is the gentleman that brought this man here?" "Ladies" were as carelessly designated; one traveling in the West might hear, as did Mrs. Trollope, references to "the lady over the way that takes in washing," or "that there lady, out by the Gulley, what is making dip-candles." If titles could serve as social escalators, no one on the frontiers need stay long in menial ranks.

The leveling spirit of Western democracy sought not only to elevate the lowly but also to dethrone the elite. Any attempt at "putting on airs," was certain to be met with rude reminders of the equality of all men. New settlers were warned by guidebooks to mingle freely and familiarly with neighbors, and above all to pretend no superiority, if they wished to be accepted. They were told that nothing ruined a man's chances on the frontier so fatally as a suspicion of pride, which, once established, would ruin his reputation. . . . One English newcomer who asked to be addressed as "Esquire" found that within a few days not only his host but the hired hands were calling him "Charlie"; another had the brass buttons unceremoniously ripped from his coat by a frontiersman who objected to such display. Texas rangers gambled or gave away the fancy uniforms issued to them, and stole the gold-braided suits of officers so that these aristocratic evidences of rank would not be seen. "Superiority," observed an English visitor, "is yielded to men of acknowledged talent alone."

Outward signs of social snobbery might arouse resentment in the West, but so did any conduct that seemed to suggest superiority. Families with sizable incomes found themselves better accepted if they lived and dressed as simply as their poorest neighbors; politicians soon realized that for success they must insist on being addressed as "Mister" or "Governor," and not as "Excellency." Even such a born-to-the-purple native aristocrat as Theodore Roosevelt took pains to understate his wealth and ancestry when on his Dakota ranch. When Colonel Thomas Dabney appeared at a frontier cabin raising in the Southwest with twenty slaves to do his work he was ostracized by the community; when a traveler had the good sense to dispose of expensive luggage, he was at last accepted on friendly terms. Natives and visitors alike learned that in the West refusal to drink with a stranger was interpreted as a sign of social superiority; unless they could convince their would-be hosts that they had "sworn off," even redeye whisky was preferable to the trouble that followed if word spread that they were "too good" for the community.

So strong was the spirit of equality along the frontiers that any deviation was met with resentment that was sometimes carried to ludicrous ends. Frontier housewives found themselves in disfavor if they kept their homes neater or cleaner than those of their neighbors; one who had waited three years for her first caller was told: "I woulda come before but I heard you had Brussels carpet on the floor." Another who offered to lend teaspoons for a party was rudely informed that no such luxuries were wanted, for the guests would not be used to them. Even those with a few choice possessions apologized; carpets were excused a "*one* way to hide the dirt," a mahogany table as "dreadful plaguy to scour," and kitchen conveniences as "lumberin' up the house for nothin'." When an Englishman remonstrated about the lack of ceremony in Western life he was told: "Yes, that may be quite necessary in England, in order to overawe a parcel of ignorant creatures, who have no share in making the laws; but with us a man's a man, whether he have a silk gown on him or not." The spirit of Western social democracy could have found no more eloquent expression than that.

In practice this spirit found its most outspoken expression in the attitude of hired workers. A "servant" in the traditional sense was impossible to find in the West because any form of servility was demeaning and hence intolerable; some of the most wealthy hosts and hostesses interrupted their dinner parties to wait on table or busy themselves in the kitchen. When servants could be drafted from the ranks of newly arrived immigrants or the families of less well-to-do pioneers they refused to accept that designation, but insisted on being called "helps," or "hired hands," or "ladies." The term "waiter" was equally unpopular, and was likely to call forth a spirited rejoinder from the person so addressed. Still more insulting was the word *master.* A misguided traveler asking "Is your master at home?" would probably be told "I have no master"; one in the Wyoming cattle country was heatedly informed that "the son of Baliel ain't been born yet." So deep was the resentment against any implication of servility that young men and women preferred to labor at poor pay under bad conditions rather than accept a post as servant.

Those who did so guarded their respectability by abolishing all traditional symbols of servitude. Livery was never used; bells to summon servants in Western inns were unknown because the "helpers" refused to respond. All insisted on being treated as equals, dining with the family, meeting guests, and joining in all social functions under threat of immediate departure. One who had been told she must eat in the kitchen turned up her lip, announced "I guess that's cause you don't think I'm good enough to eat with you," and flounced from the house. Nor was this rebellious spirit peculiar to household help. The oft-heard remark: "If a man is good enough to work for me, he is good enough to eat with me" was literally applied. A family who had hired several carpenters to build a barn made the mistake of an early breakfast without them one day; the next day they left. A honeymooning couple were abandoned by their hired driver when they tried to eat alone just once. In public houses or conveyances the story was the same; travel accounts abound with tales of stewards who joined the card game after serving drinks, of waitresses who leaned over chairs to join in the conversation or borrow a guest's fan, or messengers who seated themselves and demanded a drink while serving their messages, of waiters in inns who joined their patrons when their tasks were done. In the West men felt equal, and acted the part.

Menial tasks were as resented by servants as were menial titles. Travelers were often forced to clean their own boots in frontier inns, or to rub down their own horses while "helpers" looked on disdainfully. One who asked to be awakened in the morning was answered "call yourself and be damned." On another occasion a titled Englishman in the Wyoming wilds was told to take a swim instead of a bath when he asked his hired helper to fill a tub; when he refused the angry helper shot the tub full of holes, shouting: "You ain't quite the top-shelfer you think you is, you ain't even got a shower-bath for cooling your swelled head, but I'll make you a present of one, boss!" Nor did servants alone resent the suggestion of servility. A pioneer Michigan housewife who tired of seeing a guest attack the roast with his own knife and offered to carve was rudely informed: "I'll help myself, I thankye. I never want no waitin' on."

Travelers who were shocked by these evidences of social democracy in the West were equally appalled by the democratic spirit which prevailed in frontier inns. There no "First Class" or "Second Class" accommodations separated patrons; tradesmen, slave dealers, farmers, congressmen, generals, fur trappers, and roustabouts ate side by side at the long tables, and all were treated the same. Sleeping accommodations were allotted on a first-come-first-serve basis, with governors and herdsmen, senators and farmers, rich and poor, clean and unclean, all crowded three or four to a bed. "It has been my lot," recorded an experienced traveler, "to sleep with a diversity of personages; I do believe from the driver of the stage coach, to men of considerable name." Complaints against these arrangements were summarily rejected by pioneer landlords; one visitor from overseas who objected to using a dirt-encrusted wash-bowl with a dozen other guests was told that "one rain bathes the just and the unjust, why not one wash-bowl"; another's protest that the sheets were dirty was answered with: "since *Gentlemen* are all alike, people do not see why they should not sleep in the same sheets." The frontier inn was, as one traveler put it "a most almighty beautiful democratic amalgam."

The social democracy and frontier-type individualism that characterized America's growing period have not persisted unchanged into the twentieth century. . . .

. . . The United States is no longer a country free of class distinctions and so wedded to egalitarianism that manifestations of wealth arouse public resentment. But its social democracy does differ from that of older nations, marked by its relative lack of class awareness, and by the brash assurance of the humble that they are as worthy of respect as the elite. The house painter who addresses a client by his first name, the elevator operator who enters into casual conversation with his passengers, the garage mechanic who condescendingly compares his expensive car with your aging model, could exist only in the United States. Their counterparts are unknown in England or on the Continent partly because America's frontiering experience bred into the people attitudes toward democracy that have persisted down to the present.

The Frontier as a Place of Conquest and Conflict

PATRICIA NELSON LIMERICK

In 1871 an informal army of Arizona civilians descended on a peaceful camp and massacred over one hundred Apaches, mostly women and children. Who were the attackers at Camp Grant? The usual images of Western history would suggest one answer: white men. In fact, the attackers were a consortium of Hispanics, Anglo-Americans, and Papago Indians. However different the three groups might have been, they could agree on the matter of Apaches and join in interracial cooperation. Hostility between Apaches and Papagoes, and between Apaches and Hispanics, had in fact begun long before conflict between Apaches and Anglo-Americans.

In the popular imagination, the frontier froze as a biracial confrontation between "whites" and "Indians." More complex questions of race relations seemed to be the terrain of other regions' histories. The history of relations between blacks and whites centered in the South, while "ethnic conflict" suggested the crowded cities of the Northeast, coping with floods of immigrants in the late nineteenth and early twentieth centuries. As blacks moved north and European immigrants crossed the Atlantic, new populations put the adaptability of American society to the test. Could native Americans of northern European stock tolerate these "others"? Was it better to deal with them through assimilation or through exclusion? How could old-stock Americans defend their valued "purity" against these foreign threats?

These are familiar themes in the history of the Southern and Northeastern United States, but ethnic conflict was not exclusive to the East. Western America shared in the transplanted diversity of Europe. Expansion involved peoples of every background: English, Irish, Cornish, Scottish, French, German, Portuguese, Scandinavian, Greek, and Russian. To that diversity, the West added a persistent population of Indians, with a multitude of languages and cultures; an established Hispanic population, as well as one of later Mexican immigrants; Asians, to whom the American West was the East; black people, moving west in increasing numbers in the twentieth century; and Mormons, Americans who lived for a time in isolation, evolving a distinctive culture from the requirements of their new faith. Put the diverse humanity of Western America into one picture, and the "melting pot" of the Eastern United States at the turn of the century begins to look more like a family reunion, a meeting of groups with an essential similarity—dominantly European, Judeo-Christian, accustomed to the existence of the modern state.

The diversity of the West put a strain on the simpler varieties of racism. In another setting, categories dividing humanity into superior white and inferior black were comparatively easy to steer by. The West, however, raised questions for which racists had no set answers. Were Indians better than blacks—more capable of civilization and assimilation—perhaps even suitable for miscegenation? Were Mexicans essentially Indians? Did their European heritage count for anything? Were "mongrel" races even worse than other "pure" races? Where did Asians fit in the racial ranking? Were they humble, menial workers—or representatives of a great center of civilization, art, and, best of all, trade? Were the Japanese different from, perhaps more tolerable than, the Chinese? What about southern and eastern Europeans? When Greek workers in the mines went on strike and violence followed, was this race war or class war? Western diversity forced racists to think—an unaccustomed activity.

Over the twentieth century, writers of Western history succumbed to the easy temptation, embracing a bipolar West composed of "whites" and "Indians." Relations between the two groups shrank, moreover, to a matter of whites meeting obstacles and conquering them. Fought and refought in books and film, those "colorful" Indian wars raged on. Meanwhile, the sophisticated questions, the true study of American race relations, quietly slipped into the province of historians who studied other parts of the country.

In 1854, in the case of *People v. Hall,* California Supreme Court Chief Justice J. Murray demonstrated the classic dilemma of an American racist wrestling with the questions raised by Western diversity. Ruling on the right of Chinese people to testify in court against white people, Murray took up the white man's burden of forcing an intractable reality back into a unified racist theory.

No statute explicitly addressed the question of Chinese testimony, but Murray found another route to certainty. State law, he argued, already prevented blacks, mulattoes, and Indians from testifying as witnesses "in any action or proceeding in which a white person is a party." Although state law did not refer explicitly to Asians, this was, Murray argued, an insignificant omission. Columbus, he said, had given the name "Indians" to North American natives while under the impression that he was in Asia and the people before him were Asians. "Ethnology," having recently reached a "high point of perfection," disclosed a hidden truth in Columbus's error. It now seemed likely that "this country was first peopled by Asiatics." From Columbus's time, then, "American Indians and the Mongolian, or Asiatic, were regarded as the same type of the human species." Therefore, it could be assumed, the exclusion of "Indians" from testifying applied to Asians as well.

Judge Murray found an even more compelling argument in the essential "degraded" similarity of nonwhite races. The laws excluding "Negroes, mulattoes, and Indians" from giving testimony had obviously been intended to "protect the white person from the influence of all testimony" from another caste. "The use of these terms ["Negro," "mulatto," and "Indian"] must, by every sound rule of construction, exclude everyone who is not of white blood."

Concluding that Asians could not testify, Murray spelled out the "actual and present danger" he had defused. "The same rule which would admit them to testify, would admit them to all the equal rights of citizenship, and we might soon see them at the polls, in the jury box, upon the bench, and in our legislative halls." With a smoke screen of scientific racism, using anthropology, Murray thus declared the essential unity of darker mankind. He did his best to keep power, opportunity, and justice in California in the hands of God's chosen, lighter-skinned people. And he did a good job of it. . . .

To white workingmen, post–gold rush California did not live up to its promise. Facing limited job opportunities and uncertain futures, white laborers looked both for solutions and for scapegoats. Men in California came with high hopes; jobs proved scarce and unrewarding; someone must be to blame. In California, capital had at its command a source of controllable, underpaid labor. White workers, the historian Alexander Saxton has said, "viewed the Chinese as tools of monopoly." The workers therefore "considered themselves under attack on two fronts, or more aptly from above and below." Resenting big business and resenting competition from Chinese labor, frustrated workers naturally chose to attack the more vulnerable target. The slogan "The Chinese must go" could make it through Congress and into federal law; "Big business must go" was not going to earn congressional approval.

The issue of the Chinese scapegoat became a pillar of California politics, a guaranteed vote getter. In 1879, a state referendum on the Chinese question brought out "a margin of 150,000 to 900 favoring total exclusion." Opposition to the Chinese offered unity to an otherwise diverse state; divisions between Protestants and Catholics temporarily healed; Irish immigrants could cross the barrier separating a stigmatized ethnic group from the stigmatizing majority. Popular democratic participation in the rewriting of the California constitution showed this majority at work. "[N]o native of China, no idiot, insane person, or person convicted of any infamous crime," the constitution asserted, ". . . shall ever exercise the privileges of an elector of this State." Moreover, in the notorious Article XIX, the framers went on to prohibit the employment "of any Chinese or Mongolian" in any public works projects below the federal level or by any corporation operating under state laws. These provisions, the historian Mary Roberts Coolidge wrote early in the twentieth century, "were not only unconstitutional but inhuman and silly." They were also directly expressive of the popular will.

"To an American death is preferable to a life on a par with a Chinaman," the manifesto of the California Workingmen's Party declared in 1876. ". . . Treason is better than to labor beside a Chinese slave." Extreme threat justified extreme actions; extralegal, violent harassment followed closely on violent declarations. In harassing the Chinese, white Californians did not seek to violate American ideals and values; they sought to defend them. "They call us a mob," a female organizer said, single-handedly demolishing the image of women as the "gentle tamers" of the West. "It was a mob that fought the battle of Lexington, and a mob that threw the tea over-board in Boston harbor, but they backed their principles. . . . I want to see every Chinaman—white or yellow—thrown out of this state."

California may have "catalyzed and spearheaded the movement for exclusion," but, as Stuart Miller has shown, this was not a matter of a narrow sectional interest pushing the rest of the nation off its preferred course. Negative images gleaned from traders, missionaries, and diplomats in China predisposed the whole country to Sinophobia; the use of Chinese workers as strikebreakers in Eastern industries clinched the question. The 1882 Chinese Exclusion Act, a product of national consensus, met little opposition. . . .

In their anti-Oriental crusading, white Westerners often referred to the South and its "problem." In a search for case studies of discrimination and conflict in black / white relations, they did not need to go so far afield. During the nineteenth century, black people were sparsely represented in the West. Their numerical insignificance, however, did not stop white people from being preoccupied with the issues of black migration. Despite visions of Western fresh starts and new beginnings, the South's "problem" had long ago moved West.

The extension of slavery into the Western territories had, of course, been a prime source of sectional tension before the Civil War. The struggles over the admission of new states, free or slave, had alarmed those concerned with the survival of the Union; "a firebell in the night," Thomas Jefferson called the conflicts preceding the 1820 Missouri Compromise. Fantasies of Western innocence aside, the Western territories were deeply implicated in the national struggle over slavery.

In 1850, California was admitted as a free state; in 1857, Oregon was admitted with a similar status. That fact alone can give the impressions that the Westerners were, in some principled way, opposed to slavery. That impression needs closer examination.

Most white settlers in Oregon opposed the intrusion of slavery into their territory. However, they also opposed the intrusion of free blacks. Following on earlier territorial laws, the 1857 Oregon state constitution included a provision excluding free blacks and received heavy voter support. "The object," one early Oregon leader explained, "is to *keep* clear of this most troublesome class of population. We are in a new world, under most favorable circumstances, and we wish to avoid most of these great evils that have so much afflicted the United States and other countries." To the white Oregonians, this was a principled position. The project was to create and preserve a better social order and to steer clear of the problems and mistakes that plagued other, less pure regions. Oregon's exclusion of blacks thus appeared to be "a clear victory for settlers who came to the Far West to escape the racial troubles of the East."

The particular conditions of Oregon added another reason for black exclusion. The question of the admission of free blacks, Oregon's delegate to Congress explained in 1850,

> is a question of life and death to us in Oregon. . . . The negroes associate with the Indians and intermarry, and, if their free ingress is encouraged or allowed, there would a relationship spring up between them and the different tribes, and a mixed race would ensure inimical to the whites; and the Indians being led on by the negro who is better acquainted with the customs, language, and manners of the whites, than the Indian, these savages would become much formidable than they otherwise would, and long and bloody wars would be the fruits of the comingling of the races. It is the principle of self preservation that justifies the actions of the Oregon legislature.

Beyond actual armed conspiracy, white Westerners saw in black rights the first link in a chain reaction. Permit blacks a place in American political and social life, and Indians, Asians, and Hispanics would be next. Western diversity thus gave an edge of urgency to each form of prejudice; the line had to be held against each group; if the barrier was breached once, it would collapse before all the various "others." White Southerners could specialize, holding off one group; white Westerners fought in a multifront campaign.

Post–Civil War Reconstruction thus posed a challenge to the institutions of the West as well as to those of the South. Western members of Congress could often join in imposing black rights on the South; the South had rebelled, after all, and deserved punishment. One punishment was black suffrage. But imposing black suffrage on Western states that had not rebelled—that was another matter, and the occasion for another round in the westward-moving battle of states' rights.

Confronted with the Fifteenth Amendment, giving blacks the vote, both California and Oregon balked. "If we make the African a citizen," an Oregon newspaper argued in 1865, "we cannot deny the same right to the Indian or the Mongolian. Then how long would we have peace and prosperity when four races separate, distinct and antagonistic should be at the polls and contend for the control of government?" In California, opposition to the Fifteenth Amendment hinged on the prospect that suffrage without regard to "race, color or previous condition of servitude" might include the Chinese. The Fifteenth Amendment became law without ratification by California or Oregon. The Oregon legislature "in a gesture of perverse defiance rejected the amendment in October, 1870, fully six months after its incorporation into the federal Constitution." The amendment, the state senate declared, was "in violation of Oregon's sovereignty, an illegal interference by Congress in Oregon's right to establish voting qualifications, and a change in law forced on the nation by the bayonet." White Southerners might have been reduced to a state of temporary impotence, but they could take comfort in the fact that others had adopted their favored arguments.

In their ongoing preoccupation with purity, various Western state legislatures also moved to hold the line against racial mixing. California, Oregon, and—most extraordinary, in light of its current flexibility in matrimonial matters—Nevada all passed laws against miscegenation. Below the level of law, white Westerners practiced their own, more casual versions of discrimination. Labor unions excluded black workers; owners of restaurants, inns, and hotels limited their clientele; housing segregation was common. Scattered through historical records are incidents in which individual communities abruptly resolved to expel their black residents. "In 1893," Elizabeth McLagan has reported, "the citizens of Liberty, Oregon, requested that all black people leave town." In 1904, facing high unemployment, the town of Reno, Nevada, set out to reduce its problems by "arresting all unemployed blacks and forcing them to leave the city." "There are too many worthless negroes in the city," the Reno police chief explained.

In the twentieth century, as black migration from the South to the West accelerated, Western states' discriminatory laws stayed on the books. Although never consistently enforced, Oregon's prohibition on free blacks was not formally repealed until 1926. California's ban on miscegenation lasted until 1948; Nevada's remained until 1959. Oregon and California finally consented to a symbolic ratification of the Fifteenth Amendment—in 1959 and 1962, respectively. . . .

Race, one begins to conclude, was the key factor in dividing the people of Western America. Its meanings and distinctions fluctuated, but racial feeling evidently guided white Americans in their choice of groups to persecute and exclude. Differences in culture, in language, in religion, meant something; but a physically distinctive appearance seems to have been the prerequisite for full status as a scapegoat. If this conclusion begins to sound persuasive, then the Haun's Mill Massacre restores one to a realistic confusion.

On an October day, the Missouri militia attacked a poorly defended settlement of the enemy, killed seventeen, and wounded fifteen more. One militiaman discovered a nine-year-old boy in hiding and prepared to shoot him. Another intervened. "Nits will make lice," the first man said, and killed the boy.

Is this the classic moment in an Indian massacre? The murdered boy, like the other victims at the 1838 Haun's Mill Massacre, was white—and Mormon.

In the 1830s, Missourians hated Mormons for a variety of reasons. They had unsettling religious, economic, and political practices; they were nonetheless prosperous, did not hold slaves, and could control elections by voting in a bloc. They were a peculiar people, seriously flawed to the Gentile point of view. Mormons were white, but the Missourians still played on most of the usual themes of race hatred. When the governor of Missouri suggested a war of extermination against the Mormons, he made one point clear: the absence of a racial difference could not keep white people from thoroughly hating each other.

Mormonism, moreover, was an American product. In the 1820s, in upstate New York the young Joseph Smith had brooded about American religious diversity. With so many sects making competing claims to certainty, how was the seeker to make the right choice? "I found," Smith said, "that there was a great clash in religious sentiment; if I went to one society they referred me to one plan, and another to another. . . ." It was obvious that "all could not be right" and "that God could not be the author of so much confusion." Wrestling with this chaos, Smith began to experience revelations, he said, leading him to the acquisition of buried golden plates. Translated, the golden plates became the Book of Mormon, and the basis of a new American religion, offering the certainty of direct revelation in modern times. To its believers, Mormonism was not so much a new religion as an old one restored. Over the centuries, true Christianity had become corrupted and factionalized, broken into the competing sects that had once perplexed Smith. The Church of Latter-day Saints of Jesus Christ restored the lost unity.

Against that backdrop of sects and denominations, Mormonism offered its converts certainty and community. In Mormon doctrine, earthly labors carried a direct connection to spiritual progress; one's exertions in the material world directly reflected one's spiritual standing. With nearly every daily action "mormonized," as a later observer put it, Saints clearly had to cluster, constructing communities in which they could keep each other on track. In converting to Mormonism, one converted to a full way of life within a community of believers. In their first decade, Mormons were already on their way to becoming a new ethnic group, something new under the American sun.

As Mormon numbers grew, and the majority of the converts clustered in the Midwest, they came into increasing conflict with their Gentile neighbors. Their novel religion, their occasional experiments in communitarianism, their ability to vote in a bloc, their very separatism, made them targets for suspicion and hostility. When Joseph Smith summarized his people's experience, he could not be accused of much exaggeration: "the injustice, the wrongs, the murders, the bloodshed, the theft, misery and woe that has been caused by the barbarous, inhuman and lawless proceedings" of their enemies, especially in the state of Missouri. . . .

When the "Indian problem" grew heated in the early nineteenth century, the remote and isolated West had presented itself as a geographical solution: place the Indians in locations white people would not want anyway, and end the friction by a strategy of segregation. Geography appeared to offer the same solution to "the Mormon problem." Relocated in the remote and arid Great Basin, the Mormons could escape persecution by a kind of spatial quarantine; the dimensions of the continent itself would guard them. Even when the gold rush broke the quarantine and when Gentiles—and even Missourians—were suddenly provoked into crossing the continent, the Mormons had had the chance to reverse the proportions and become an entrenched majority in the territory of Utah. . . .

The aridity of Utah meant that prosperity depended on a cooperation that the Mormons, uniquely, could provide. Land might be privately held, but water and timber were held in common and allocated by church authorities. The church leadership ordained the founding of towns and farms; communally organized labor could then build the dams and ditches that made irrigation possible. In their prosperity and good order, the settlements of the Mormons impressed even those who could find nothing else to admire in this peculiar people's way of life.

That peculiarity had become suddenly more dramatic. Established in their own territory, far from disapproving neighbors, leaders had felt empowered to bring the church's peculiar domestic practice into the open. In 1852, the Mormons stood revealed as practitioners of polygamy.

For the rest of the nineteenth century, the idea of one man in possession of more than one woman would strike most non-Mormon Americans as deviant, licentious, and *very* interesting—a shocking matter of sexual excess. In fact, Mormon polygamy was a staid and solemn affair. If the patriarchal family was a good thing, if bringing children into the world to be responsibly raised in the right religion was a major goal of life, then it was a logical—and very American—conclusion that more of a good thing could only be better. The Mormon family, properly conducted through this world, would reassemble in the afterlife. Adding more personnel to this sanctified unit gave Mormon patriarchs even greater opportunity to perform their ordained function. . . .

. . . For thirty years, Congress tried to make the Mormons behave. Antipolygamy laws added up to a sustained campaign to change personal behavior, a campaign without parallel except in Indian affairs. . . .

Antipolygamy laws finally drove the Mormon leaders into hiding, concealed— in defiance of federal law—by their loyal followers. The church had been placed in receivership; cohabitation prosecutions went on apace; zealous federal agents pursued the concealed leaders. Then, on September 24, 1890, President Wilford Woodruff of the LDS issued an official manifesto, advising the Latter-day Saints "to refrain from contracting any marriage forbidden by the law of the land." The year was 1890, and one kind of frontier opportunity had indeed closed. . . .

Whatever else it tells us, the Mormon example shows that race was not the only provocation for strong antipathies and prejudices. White people could also become aliens, targets for voyeuristic exploitation, for coercive legislation, even for the use of the U.S. Army. But, the Mormon example also shows that in the long run it paid to be white.

At the Utah statehood convention in 1895, Charles S. Varian gave a speech of reconciliation. Varian had earlier been U.S. district attorney for Utah Territory "and relentless in his prosecution of polygamy." He had, however, found the convention to be an occasion of harmony. Every member, he thought, had "been taught by his fellowmen that, after all, we are very much alike, and that the same passions, and the same motives, actuate us all."

"After all, we are very much alike"—it was a statement no one at the time made to the Chinese or the Japanese. Once polygamy had been formally settled, the "differentness" of Mormons could be subordinated and their essentially American qualities celebrated. . . .

When it came to pitting Western people against each other, politics and economics could work as well as race or religion. When White people appeared to threaten order and prosperity, the lesson was once again clear: race was no protector from vicious conflict. Consider three examples:

•   In May 1912, the middle-class citizens of San Diego, California, forcibly expelled the anarchist speakers Emma Goldman and Ben Reitman. San Diego was, in that year, "an established city of more than 40,000 people," "progressive Republican" in politics. In their radicalism and also in their association with the Wobblies, the Industrial Workers of the World, Goldman and Reitman represented a threat that the city's boosters would not tolerate. Goldman "escaped violence only by the narrowest margin," a San Diego newspaper reported. But "treatment that the vigilantes would not give the woman was accorded to the man. Reitman was mysteriously spirited away from the hotel some time near midnight . . . and, it is reported, tarred and feathered and branded on the back with the letters 'I.W.W.' He is furthermore said to have been forced to kneel and kiss the American flag. The branding was done with a lighted cigar, which was traced through the tar. . . ." The concerned citizens and policemen of San Diego were not always so gentle. In other confrontations, "at least two radicals were killed."

•   On April 20, 1914, the Colorado militia attacked a tent colony of strikers and their families. Both sides had guns and used them, but bullets were not the major source of injury. In the middle of the battle, the tents burst into flames. Two women and eleven children burned to death. The Ludlow massacre "climaxed a labor struggle in Colorado which erupted into a civil war all over the state."

•   On November 5, 1916, two steamboats carrying Wobblies left Seattle for the town of Everett, to support a strike under way against the timber industry. Armed vigilantes and policemen tried to prevent them from landing; in the exchange of bullets, five workers and two vigilantes died, while over fifty were wounded and seven were reported missing. "The water turned crimson," one historian has written, "and corpses were washing ashore for days afterward."

The conventional approach of blaming Western violence on the "frontier environment" does not explain these incidents. Although most of the strikers at Ludlow were of southern or eastern European origin, racial or ethnic explanations of conflict are also of limited help. Judging by the written record alone, a historian blind to actual physical characteristics might think that there were at least eight oppressed races in the West: Indians, Hispanics, Chinese, Japanese, blacks, Mormons, strikers, and radicals.

Exploring the ways in which "Mexicans, Chinese and Indians were shamefully abused by the Yankee majority," Ray Allen Billington in 1956 placed the responsibility on the "corrosive effect of the environment" and "the absence of social pressures." The abuse, he said, represented "a completely undemocratic nativism."

This explanation has an innocent certainty now beyond our grasp. Nativism was only in an ideal sense "undemocratic." The California votes on Chinese exclusion and the Oregon votes on black exclusion made the voice of democracy in these matters clear. Second, blaming "the corrosive effect of the environment" for nativism involved doubtful logic; white Americans brought the raw material for these attitudes with them, with little help from the "environment." And finally, on close examination, over the duration of Western history, the very concept of "the Yankee majority" was a coherent entity only if one retreated to a great distance, from which the divisions simply could not be seen. . . .

When the weight of Southern civilization fell too heavily on Huckleberry Finn, Mark Twain offered the preferred American alternative: "I reckon I got to light out for the Territory ahead of the rest, because Aunt Sally she's going to adopt me and sivilize me, and I can't stand it. I been there before." The West, the theory had gone, was the place where one escaped the trials and burdens of American civilization, especially in its Southern version. Those "trials and burdens" often came in human form. Repeatedly, Americans had used the West as a mechanism for evading these "problems." Much of what went under the rubric "Western optimism" was in fact this faith in postponement, in the deferring of problems to the distant future. Whether in Indian removal or Mormon migration, the theory was the same: the West is remote and vast; its isolation and distance will release us from conflict; this is where we can get away from each other. But the workings of history carried an opposite lesson. The West was not where we escaped each other, but where we all met.

 F U R T H E R   R E A D I N G

William Cronon, George Miles, Jay Gitlin, eds., *Under an Open Sky: Rethinking America's Western Past* (1992).
Kenneth M. Hamilton, *Black Towns and Profit: Promotion and Development in the Trans-Appalachian West, 1877–1915* (1991).
Andrew Isenberg, *The Destruction of the Bison: An Environmental History* (2000).
Peter Iverson, *When Indians Became Cowboys: Native Peoples and Cattle Ranching in the American West* (1994).
Joy Kasson, *Buffalo Bill's Wild West: Celebrity, Memory, and Popular History* (2000).
Glenda Riley and Richard Etulain, eds., *By Grit and Grace: Eleven Women Who Shaped the American West* (1997).
Richard Slotkin, *Gunfighter Nation: The Myth of the Frontier in Twentieth Century America* (1992).
Frederick Jackson Turner, *The Frontier in American History* (1920).
Robert M. Utley, *The Indian Frontier of the American West, 1869–1886* (1982).
Louis Warren, *Buffalo Bill's America: William Cody and the Wild West Show* (2005).
Elliott West, *The Contested Plains: Indians, Goldseekers, and the Rush to Colorado* (1998).
Richard White, *It's Your Misfortune and None of My Own: A New History of the American West* (1991).

CHAPTER
3

Industrialization, Workers, and the New Immigration

The Industrial Revolution and the migration of Europeans to the Americas were well under way before the American Civil War, but in the years after the war these phenomena restructured the American landscape in ways that would have made it unrecognizable to previous generations. Improvements in steel production allowed architects to design buildings that shot into the sky out of the flat prairie. Railroads built by laborers from China and Ireland linked the East Coast to the West Coast. Huge processing centers took the products of farms and ranches and converted them into consumer goods with a rapidity that made country and city folk alike rub their eyes in disbelief. Industrialists amassed fortunes in a way never before seen in human history, while knowledgeable artisans found their training and judgment less and less called for in an age of mass production. Skilled and unskilled alike competed for jobs that often paid hardly enough to keep a family from starving.

In the midst of this industrial transformation, a second giant wave of immigration hit the United States. Sometimes called the "new immigration" to distinguish it from the influx of Germans and Irish earlier in the nineteenth century, this wave brought Poles, Italians, Scandinavians, and eastern European Jews. Crowded together in tenements and jostled into factories and sweatshops, these immigrants struggled to adapt their old skills to new working conditions. They also sought to maintain their sense of themselves in the midst of change. At work, they organized labor unions to create decent working conditions. During their leisure, they gathered in churches, saloons, and public parks, where they could escape the watchful eye of employers and reformers and enjoyed the camaraderie of their "own kind." Sometimes they decided that America was not for them, and they returned home.

Across the economic spectrum, Americans struggled to define the meaning of industrial concentration for democracy and social justice. Unions like the American Federation of Labor focused on specific reforms for particular classes of skilled workers. Congressmen and journalists investigated social conditions for the poorest of immigrants. Industrialists may have occasionally worried about justice, but they obsessed about profits. Competition to achieve ever more profitable advantages of scale led to a rush of corporate mergers between 1897 and 1900. Integrating vertically and horizontally, the largest companies formed "trusts" into which smaller companies disappeared. By 1900, seventy-three such trusts had swallowed up more than 3,000 companies, creating combinations like Standard Oil, U.S. Steel, and the American Tobacco Company. Industrialists defended their actions as the inevitable outcome of "progress" and industrial development. Although they violently resisted the demands of workers for a more equitable sharing of profits, a few also sought to express traditional American concerns for equality and "uplift" through the creation of a new set of institutions—philanthropic foundations and free libraries. Increased immigration, industrialization, and urbanization all contributed to making this a particularly turbulent transition in U.S. history.

QUESTIONS TO THINK ABOUT

How did immigrants cope with conditions as they found them in America's brimming cities? Did industry crush immigrants or provide them with new opportunities? In what ways did workers resist the forces of industrialization and shape the terms of their own lives?

DOCUMENTS

The documents in this chapter present different reactions to immigration and industrialization. In Document 1 a laborer from China reflects upon his conflicts with immigrants from other parts of the world, and their prejudice towards the Chinese. Document 2 is a poem by Emma Lazarus, the daughter of a prosperous Jewish family in New York. She wrote it to help raise funds for a pedestal for the Statue of Liberty. The verse appears at the base of the statue, which was often the first thing that immigrants saw when they sailed into New York Harbor. Document 3 is an immigrant account drawn from congressional testimony on the replacement of skilled adult labor with unskilled child labor in factories. It shows the devastating poverty encountered by immigrant and working families. Document 4 expresses the Social Darwinism of Andrew Carnegie, a Scottish immigrant and self-made millionaire who during his lifetime gave 90 percent of his wealth to establish free public libraries and a variety of nonprofit foundations. Carnegie's statement helps to explain how some industrialists rationalized to themselves the often-painful consequences of industrialization. Document 5 reveals the practical emphasis of the American Federation of Labor, which focused its efforts on bettering conditions for skilled labor and giving workers "eight hours for what we will." Document 6 is by the Pulitzer Prize–winning novelist and socialist Upton Sinclair. His masterpiece of muckraking, *The Jungle,* helped Progressives pass the Pure Food and Drug Act, but Sinclair also created one of the most disturbing descriptions of immigrant life ever written. In this selection, the defeated Polish immigrant Jurgis discovers the saloon. Document 7 is a European boy's perspective on the stories of the "Golden Country" told by returned immigrants. It gives insight into the forces beguiling immigrants to the New World, and it suggests that at least some returned to the old country as heroes. In the last selection, Document 8, the famous efficiency expert Frederick Winslow Taylor details how he persuaded men to work faster by selecting an "ideal worker" and training him to follow instructions slavishly—leaving no room for "unscientific" personal initiative. If immigrants were to find avenues for self-expression, they would have to look for them in places other than their work.

1. Chinese Immigrant Lee Chew Denounces Prejudice in America, 1882

I worked on my father's farm till I was about sixteen years of age, when a man of our tribe came back from America and took ground as large as four city blocks and made a paradise of it. He put a large stone wall around and led some streams through and built a palace and summer house and about twenty other structures, with beautiful bridges over the streams and walks and roads. Trees and flowers, singing birds, waterfowl and curious animals were within the walls.

The man had gone away from our village a poor boy. Now he returned with unlimited wealth, which he had obtained in the country of the American wizards. After many amazing adventures he had become a merchant in a city called Mott Street, so it was said. . . .

The wealth of this man filled my mind with the idea that I, too, would like to go to the country of the wizards and gain some of their wealth, and after a long time my father consented, and gave me his blessing, and my mother took leave of me with tears, while my grandfather laid his hand upon my head and told me to remember and live up to the admonitions of the Sages, to avoid gambling, bad women and men of evil minds, and so to govern my conduct that when I died my ancestors might rejoice to welcome me as a guest on high.

My father gave me $100, and I went to Hong Kong with five other boys from our place and we got steerage passage on a steamer, paying $50 each. Everything was new to me. All my life I had been used to sleeping on a board bed with a wooden pillow, and I found the steamer's bunk very uncomfortable, because it was so soft. The food was different from that which I had been used to, and I did not like it at all. I was afraid of the stews, for the thought of what they might be made of by wicked wizards of the ship made me ill. Of the great power of these people I saw many signs. The engines that moved the ship were wonderful monsters, strong enough to lift mountains. When I got to San Francisco, which was before the passage of the Exclusion act, I was half starved, because I was afraid to eat the provisions of the barbarians, but a few days' living in the Chinese quarter made me happy again. A man got me work as a house servant in an American family, and my start was the same as that of almost all the Chinese in this country.

The Chinese laundryman does not learn his trade in China; there are no laundries in China. The women there do the washing in tubs and have no washboards or flat irons. All the Chinese laundrymen here were taught in the first place by American women just as I was taught.

When I went to work for that American family I could not speak a word of English, and I did not know anything about housework. The family consisted of husband, wife, and two children. They were very good to me and paid me $3.50 a week, of which I could save $3. . . .

. . . Men of other nationalities who are jealous of the Chinese, because he is a more faithful worker than one of their people, have raised such a great outcry about Chinese

As found in David M. Katzman and William M. Tuttle, Jr. (eds.), *Plain Folk: The Life Stories of Undistinguished Americans* (Chicago: University of Illinois Press, 1982). Reprinted in Jon Gjerde, ed. *Major Problems in American Immigration and Ethnic History* (Boston: Houghton Mifflin, 1998), 172–174.

cheap labor that they have shut him out of working on farms or in factories or building railroads or making streets or digging sewers. He cannot practice any trade, and his opportunities to do business are limited to his own countrymen. So he opens a laundry when he quits domestic service.

The treatment of the Chinese in this country is all wrong and mean. It is persisted in merely because China is not a fighting nation. The Americans would not dare to treat Germans, English, Italians or even Japanese as they treat the Chinese, because if they did there would be a war.

There is no reason for the prejudice against the Chinese. The cheap labor cry was always a falsehood. Their labor was never cheap, and is not cheap now. It has always commanded the highest market price. But the trouble is that the Chinese are such excellent and faithful workers that bosses will have no others when they can get them. If you look at men working on the street you will find an overseer for every four or five of them. That watching is not necessary for Chinese. They work as well when left to themselves as they do when someone is looking at them.

It was the jealousy of laboring men of other nationalities—especially the Irish—that raised all the outcry against the Chinese. No one would hire an Irishman, German, Englishman or Italian when he could get a Chinese, because our countrymen are so much more honest, industrious, steady, sober and painstaking. Chinese were persecuted, not for their vices, but for their virtues. There never was any honesty in the pretended fear of leprosy or in the cheap labor scare, and the persecution continues still, because Americans make a mere practice of loving justice. They are all for money making, and they want to be on the strongest side always. They treat you as a friend while you are prosperous, but if you have a misfortune they don't know you. There is nothing substantial in their friendship. . . .

Irish fill the almshouses and prisons and orphan asylums, Italians are among the most dangerous of men, Jews are unclean and ignorant. Yet they are all let in, while Chinese, who are sober, or duly law abiding, clean, educated and industrious, are shut out. There are few Chinamen in jails and none in the poor houses. There are no Chinese tramps or drunkards. Many Chinese here have become sincere Christians, in spite of the persecution which they have to endure from their heathen countrymen. More than half the Chinese in this country would become citizens if allowed to do so, and would be patriotic Americans. But how can they make this country their home as matters now are! They are not allowed to bring wives here from China, and if they marry American women there is a great outcry.

2. Poet Emma Lazarus Praises the New Colossus, 1883

> Not like the brazen giant of Greek fame,
> With conquering limbs astride from land to land;
> Here at our sea-washed, sunset gates shall stand
> A mighty woman with a torch, whose flame
> Is the imprisoned lightning, and her name

Mother of Exiles. From her beacon-hand
Glows world-wide welcome; her mild eyes command
The air-bridged harbor that twin cities frame.
"Keep, ancient lands, your storied pomp!" cries she
With silent lips. "Give me your tired, your poor,
Your huddled masses yearning to breathe free,
The wretched refuse of your teeming shore.
Send these, the homeless, tempest-tost to me,
I lift my lamp beside the golden door!"

3. Immigrant Thomas O'Donnell Laments the Worker's Plight, 1883

BOSTON, MASS., *October 18, 1883*

THOMAS O'DONNELL examined.

By the CHAIRMAN:

Question. Where do you live? *Answer.* At Fall River.
Q. How long have you lived in this country? *A.* Eleven years.
Q. Where were you born? *A.* In Ramsbotham, England.
Q. Have you been naturalized here? *A.* No, sir.

Life of a Mule-Spinner

Q. What is your business? *A.* I am a mule-spinner by trade. I have worked at it since I have been in this country—eleven years.

Q. Are you a married man? *A.* Yes, sir; I am a married man; have a wife and two children. I am not very well educated. I went to work when I was young, and have been working ever since in the cotton business; went to work when I was about eight or nine years old. I was going to state how I live. My children get along very well in summer time, on account of not having to buy fuel or shoes or one thing and another. I earn $1.50 a day and can't afford to pay a very big house rent. I pay $1.50 a week for rent, which comes to about $6 a month. . . .

Q. Do you have work right along? *A.* No, sir; since that strike we had down in Fall River about three years ago I have not worked much more than half the time, and that has brought my circumstances down very much.

Q. Why have you not worked more than half the time since then?—*A.* Well, at Fall River if a man has not got a boy to act as "back-boy" it is very hard for him to get along. In a great many cases they discharge men in that work and put in men who have boys.

Q. Men who have boys of their own? *A.* Men who have boys of their own capable enough to work in a mill, to earn 30 or 40 cents a day.

Testimony of Thomas O'Donnell, Fall River mule-spinner, *Report of Senate Committee upon the Relations Between Labor and Capital*, III (1883), 451–457.

Child Labor Necessary to the Employment of Parents

Q. Is the object of that to enable the boy to earn something for himself?

A. Well, no; the object is this: They are doing away with a great deal of mule-spinning there and putting in ring-spinning, and for that reason it takes a good deal of small help to run this ring work, and it throws the men out of work because they are doing away with the mules and putting these ring-frames in to take their places. For that reason they get all the small help they can to run these ring-frames. There are so many men in the city to work, and whoever has a boy can have work, and whoever has no boy stands no chance. Probably he may have a few months of work in the summer time, but will be discharged in the fall. That is what leaves me in poor circumstances. Our children, of course, are very often sickly from one cause or another, on account of not having sufficient clothes, or shoes, or food, or something. And also my woman; she never did work in a mill; she was a housekeeper, and for that reason she can't help me to anything at present, as many women do help their husbands down there, by working, like themselves. My wife never did work in a mill, and that leaves me to provide for the whole family. I have two children. . . .

Supporting a Family on $133 a Year

. . .

Q. Taking a full year back can you tell how much you have had?—*A.* That would be about fifteen weeks' work. Last winter, as I told you, I got in, and I worked up to about somewhere around Fast Day, or maybe New Year's day; anyway, Mr. Howard has it down on his record, if you wish to have an exact answer to that question; he can answer it better than I can, because we have a sort of union there to keep ourselves together.

Q. Do you think you have had $150 within a year? *A.* No, sir.

Q. Have you had $125? *A.* Well, I could figure it up if I had time. The thirteen weeks is all I have had. . . .

Q. That would be somewhere about $133, if you had not lost any time? *A.* Yes, sir.

Q. That is all you have had? *A.* Yes, sir.

Q. To support yourself and wife and two children? *A.* Yes, sir.

Q. Have you had any help from outside? *A.* No, sir.

Q. Do you mean that yourself and wife and two children have had nothing but that for all this time? *A.* That is all. I got a couple dollars' worth of coal last winter, and the wood I picked up myself. I goes around with a shovel and picks up clams and wood. . . .

Too Poor to Go West

Q. Well, I want to know why you do not go out West on a $2,000 farm, or take up a homestead and break it and work it up, and then have it for yourself and family? *A.* I can't see how I could get out West. I have got nothing to go with.

Q. It would not cost you over $1,500. *A.* Well, I never saw over a $20 bill, and that is when I have been getting a month's pay at once. If some one would give me $1,500 I will go. . . .

Q. Has there been any day in the year that you have had to go without anything to eat? *A*. Yes, sir, several days.

Q. More than one day at a time? *A*. No.

Q. How about the children and your wife—did they go without anything to eat too?

The Children Crying for Food

A. My wife went out this morning and went to a neighbor's and got a loaf of bread and fetched it home, and when she got home the children were crying for something to eat.

Q. Have the children had anything to eat to-day except that, do you think? *A*. They had that loaf of bread—I don't know what they have had since then, if they have had anything.

Q. Did you leave any money at home? *A*. No, sir. . . .

4. Steel Magnate Andrew Carnegie Preaches a Gospel of Wealth, 1889

The problem of our age is the proper administration of wealth, that the ties of brotherhood may still bind together the rich and poor in harmonious relationship. The conditions of human life have not only been changed, but revolutionized, within the past few hundred years. In former days there was little difference between the dwelling, dress, food, and environment of the chief and those of his retainers. The Indians are to-day where civilized man then was. When visiting the Sioux, I was led to the wigwam of the chief. It was like the others in external appearance, and even within the difference was trifling between it and those of the poorest of his braves. The contrast between the palace of the millionaire and the cottage of the laborer with us to-day measures the change which has come with civilization. This change, how-ever, is not to be deplored, but welcomed as highly beneficial. It is well, nay, essen-tial, for the progress of the race that the houses of some should be homes for all that is highest and best in literature and the arts, and for all the refinements of civilization, rather than that none should be so. Much better this great irregularity than universal squalor. Without wealth there can be no Mæcenas. The "good old times" were not good old times. Neither master nor servant was as well situated then as to-day. A relapse to old conditions would be disastrous to both—not the least so to him who serves—and would sweep away civilization with it. But whether the change be for good or ill, it is upon us, beyond our power to alter, and, therefore, to be accepted and made the best of. It is a waste of time to criticize the inevitable. . . .

The price we pay for this salutary change is, no doubt, great. We assemble thousands of operatives in the factory, and in the mine, of whom the employer can know little or nothing, and to whom he is little better than a myth. All intercourse between them is at an end. Rigid castes are formed, and, as usual, mutual ignorance breeds mutual distrust. Each caste is without sympathy with the other, and ready

Andrew Carnegie, *Gospel of Wealth* (North American Review, 1889), 1–4, 7, 10–11, 13, 17.

to credit anything disparaging in regard to it. Under the law of competition, the employer of thousands is forced into the strictest economies, among which the rates paid to labor figure prominently, and often there is friction between the employer and the employed, between capital and labor, between rich and poor. Human society loses homogeneity.

The price which society pays for the law of competition, like the price it pays for cheap comforts and luxuries, is also great; but the advantages of this law are also greater still than its cost—for it is to this law that we owe our wonderful material development, which brings improved conditions in its train. But, whether the law be benign or not, we must say of it, as we say of the change in the conditions of men to which we have referred: It is here; we cannot evade it; no substitutes for it have been found; and while the law may be sometimes hard for the individual, it is best for the race, because it insures the survival of the fittest in every department. . . .

We start, then, with a condition of affairs under which the best interests of the race are promoted, but which inevitably gives wealth to the few. Thus far, accepting conditions as they exist, the situation can be surveyed and pronounced good. The question then arises,—and if the foregoing be correct, it is the only question with which we have to deal,—What is the proper mode of administering wealth after the laws upon which civilization is founded have thrown it into the hands of the few? And it is of this great question that I believe I offer the true solution. . . .

. . . The budget presented in the British Parliament the other day proposes to increase the death duties; and, most significant of all, the new tax is to be a graduated one. Of all forms of taxation this seems the wisest. Men who continue hoarding great sums all their lives, the proper use of which for public ends would work good to the community from which it chiefly came, should be made to feel that the community, in the form of the State, cannot thus be deprived of its proper share. By taxing estates heavily at death the State marks its condemnation of the selfish millionaire's unworthy life.

It is desirable that nations should go much further in this direction. . . . This policy would work powerfully to induce the rich man to attend to the administration of wealth during his life, which is the end that society should always have in view, as being by far the most fruitful for the people. Nor need it be feared that this policy would sap the root of enterprise and render men less anxious to accumulate, for, to the class whose ambition it is to leave great fortunes and be talked about after their death, it will attract even more attention, and, indeed, be a somewhat nobler ambition, to have enormous sums paid over to the State from their fortunes. . . .

Poor and restricted are our opportunities in this life, narrow our horizon, our best work most imperfect; but rich men should be thankful for one inestimable boon. They have it in their power during their lives to busy themselves in organizing benefactions from which the masses of their fellows will derive lasting advantage, and thus dignify their own lives. . . .

This, then, is held to be the duty of the man of wealth: To set an example of modest, unostentatious living, shunning display or extravagance; to provide moderately for the legitimate wants of those dependent upon him; and, after doing so, to consider all surplus revenues which come to him simply as trust funds, which he is called upon to administer, and strictly bound as a matter of duty to administer in the manner which, in his judgment, is best calculated to produce the most beneficial results for the community—the man of wealth thus becoming the mere trustee and agent for his poorer brethren, bringing to their service his superior wisdom, experience, and ability to administer, doing for them better than they would or could do for themselves. . . .

. . . The day is not far distant when the man who dies leaving behind him millions of available wealth, which was free for him to administer during life, will pass away "unwept, unhonored, and unsung," no matter to what uses he leaves the dross which he cannot take with him. Of such as these the public verdict will then be: "The man who dies thus rich dies disgraced."

Such, in my opinion, is the true gospel concerning wealth, obedience to which is destined someday to solve the problem of the rich and the poor, and to bring "Peace on earth, among men good will."

5. Unionist Samuel Gompers Asks "What Does the Working Man Want?" 1890

. . . My friends, we have met here today to celebrate the idea that has prompted thousands of working-people of Louisville and New Albany to parade the streets of y[our city]; that prompts the toilers of Chicago to turn out by their fifty or hundred thousand of men; that prompts the vast army of wage-workers in New York to demonstrate their enthusiasm and appreciation of the importance of this idea; that prompts the toilers of England, Ireland, Germany, France, Italy, Spain, and Austria to defy the manifestos of the autocrats of the world and say that on May the first, 1890, the wage-workers of the world will lay down their tools in sympathy with the wage-workers of America, to establish a principle of limitations of hours of labor to eight hours for sleep [applause], eight hours for work, and eight hours for what we will. [Applause.]

It has been charged time and again that were we to have more hours of leisure we would merely devote it to debauchery, to the cultivation of vicious habits—in other words, that we would get drunk. I desire to say this in answer to that charge: As a rule, there are two classes in society who get drunk. One is the class who has no work to do in consequence of too much money; the other class, who also has no work to do, because it can't get any, and gets drunk on its face. [Laughter.] I maintain that that class in our social life that exhibits the greatest degree of sobriety is that class who are able, by a fair number of hours of day's work to earn fair wages—not overworked. The man who works twelve, fourteen, and sixteen hours a day requires some artificial stimulant to restore the life ground out of him in the drudgery of the day. [Applause.] . . .

We ought to be able to discuss this question on a higher ground, and I am pleased to say that the movement in which we are engaged will stimulate us to it. They tell us that the eight-hour movement cannot be enforced, for the reason that it must check industrial and commercial progress. I say that the history of this country,

"A News Account of an Address in Louisville," in *The Samuel Gompers Papers: The Early Years of the American Federation of Labor, 1887–90,* ed. Stuart Kaufman (Chicago: University of Illinois Press, 1987), 307–314.

in its industrial and commercial relations, shows the reverse. I say that is the plane on which this question ought to be discussed—that is the social question. As long as they make this question an economic one, I am willing to discuss it with them. I would retrace every step I have taken to advance this movement did it mean industrial and commercial stagnation. But it does not mean that. It means greater prosperity; it means a greater degree of progress for the whole people; it means more advancement and intelligence, and a nobler race of people. . . .

They say they can't afford it. Is that true? Let us see for one moment. If a reduction in the hours of labor causes industrial and commercial ruination, it would naturally follow increased hours of labor would increase the prosperity, commercial and industrial. If that were true, England and America ought to be at the tail end, and China at the head of civilization. [Applause.]

Is it not a fact that we find laborers in England and the United States, where the hours are eight, nine and ten hours a day—do we not find that the employers and laborers are more successful? Don't we find them selling articles cheaper? We do not need to trust the modern moralist to tell us those things. In all industries where the hours of labor are long, there you will find the least development of the power of invention. Where the hours of labor are long, men are cheap, and where men are cheap there is no necessity for invention. How can you expect a man to work ten or twelve or fourteen hours at his calling and then devote any time to the invention of a machine or discovery of a new principle or force? If he be so fortunate as to be able to read a paper he will fall asleep before he has read through the second or third line. [Laughter.] . . .

The man who works the long hours has no necessities except the barest to keep body and soul together, so he can work. He goes to sleep and dreams of work; he rises in the morning to go to work; he takes his frugal lunch to work; he comes home again to throw himself down on a miserable apology for a bed so that he can get that little rest that he may be able to go to work again. He is nothing but a veritable machine. He lives to work instead of working to live. [Loud applause.]

My friends, the only thing the working people need besides the necessities of life, is time. Time. Time with which our lives begin; time with which our lives close; time to cultivate the better nature within us; time to brighten our homes. Time, which brings us from the lowest condition up to the highest civilization; time, so that we can raise men to a higher plane. . . .

We want eight hours and nothing less. We have been accused of being selfish, and it has been said that we will want more; that last year we got an advance of ten cents and now we want more. We do want more. You will find that a man generally wants more. Go and ask a tramp what he wants, and if he doesn't want a drink he will want a good, square meal. You ask a workingman, who is getting two dollars a day, and he will say that he wants ten cents more. Ask a man who gets five dollars a day and he will want fifty cents more. The man who receives five thousand dollars a year wants six thousand dollars a year, and the man who owns eight or nine hundred thousand dollars will want a hundred thousand dollars more to make it a million, while the man who has his millions will want everything he can lay his hands on and then raise his voice against the poor devil who wants ten cents more a day. We live in the latter part of the Nineteenth century. In the age of electricity and steam that has produced wealth a hundred fold, we insist that it has been brought about by the intelligence and energy of the workingmen, and while we find that it is now easier to produce it is harder to live. We do want more, and when it becomes more, we shall still want more. [Applause.] And we shall never cease to demand more until we have received the results of our labor.

6. Jurgis Rudkus Discovers Drink in *The Jungle,* 1905

With one member trimming beef in a cannery, and another working in a sausage factory, the family had a first-hand knowledge of the great majority of Packing-town swindles. For it was the custom, as they found, whenever meat was so spoiled that it could not be used for anything else, either to can it or else to chop it up into sausage. . . .

It was only when the whole ham was spoiled that it came into the department of Elzbieta. Cut up by the two-thousand-revolutions-a-minute flyers, and mixed with half a ton of other meat, no odor that ever was in a ham could make any difference. There was never the least attention paid to what was cut up for sausage; there would come all the way back from Europe old sausage that had been rejected, and that was mouldy and white—it would be dosed with borax and glycerine, and dumped into the hoppers and made over again for home consumption. . . .

Such were the new surroundings in which Elzbieta was placed, and such was the work she was compelled to do. It was stupefying, brutalizing work; it left her no time to think, no strength for anything. She was part of the machine she tended, and every faculty that was not needed for the machine was doomed to be crushed out of existence. There was only one mercy about the cruel grind—that it gave her the gift of insensibility. Little by little she sank into a torpor—she fell silent. She would meet Jurgis and Ona in the evening, and the three would walk home together, often without saying a word. Ona, too, was falling into a habit of silence—Ona, who had once gone about singing like a bird. . . .

Yet the soul of Ona was not dead—the souls of none of them were dead, but only sleeping; and now and then they would waken, and these were cruel times. The gates of memory would roll open—old joys would stretch out their arms to them, old hopes and dreams would call to them, and they would stir beneath the burden that lay upon them, and feel its forever immeasurable weight. They could not even cry out beneath it; but anguish would seize them, more dreadful than the agony of death. It was a thing scarcely to be spoken—a thing never spoken by all the world, that will not know its own defeat.

They were beaten; they had lost the game, they were swept aside. It was not less tragic because it was so sordid, because that it had to do with wages and grocery bills and rents. They had dreamed of freedom; a chance to look about them and learn something; to be decent and clean, to see their child grow up to be strong. And now it was all gone—it would never be! They had played the game and they had lost. Six years more of toil they had to face before they could expect the least respite,

Upton Sinclair, *The Jungle* (1905), 135–139.

the cessation of the payments upon the house; and how cruelly certain it was that they could never stand six years of such a life as they were living! . . .

Jurgis, being a man, had troubles of his own. There was another specter following him. He had never spoken of it, nor would he allow anyone else to speak of it—he had never acknowledged its existence to himself. Yet the battle with it took all the manhood that he had—and once or twice, alas, a little more. Jurgis had discovered drink.

He was working in the steaming pit of hell; day after day, week after week— until now there was not an organ of his body that did its work without pain, until the sound of ocean breakers echoes in his head day and night, and the buildings swayed and danced before him as he went down the street. And from all the unending horror of this there was a respite, a deliverance—he could drink! He could forget the pain, he could slip off the burden; he would see clearly again, he would be master of his brain, of his thoughts, of his will. His dead self would stir in him, and he would find himself laughing and cracking jokes with his companions—he would be a man again, and master of his life.

It was not an easy thing for Jurgis to take more than two or three drinks. With the first drink he could eat a meal, and he could persuade himself that that was economy; with the second he could eat another meal—but there would come a time when he could eat no more, and then to pay for a drink was an unthinkable extravagance, a defiance of the age-long instincts of his hunger-haunted class. One day, however, he took the plunge, and drank up all that he had in his pockets, and went home half "piped," as the men phrase it. He was happier than he had been in a year.

7. A Slovenian Boy Remembers Tales of the Golden Country, 1909

As a boy of nine, and even younger, in my native village . . . I experienced a thrill every time one of the men of the little community returned from America.

Five or six years before, as I heard people tell, the man had quietly left the village for the United States, a poor peasant clad in homespun, with a mustache under his nose and a bundle on his back; now, a clean-shaven *Amerikanec,* he sported a blue-serge suit, buttoned shoes very large in the toes and with india-rubber heels, a black derby, a shiny celluloid collar, and a loud necktie made even louder by a dazzling horseshoe pin, which, rumor had it, was made of gold, while his two suitcases of imitation leather, tied with straps, bulged with gifts from America for his relatives and friends in the village. In nine cases out of ten, he had left in economic desperation, on money borrowed from some relative in the United States; now there was talk in the village that he was worth anywhere from one to three thousand American dollars. And to my eyes he truly bore all the earmarks of affluence. Indeed, to say that he thrilled my boyish fancy is putting it mildly. With other boys in the village, I followed him around as he went visiting his relatives and friends and distributing presents, and hung onto his every word and gesture.

Then, on the first Sunday after his homecoming, if at all possible, I got within earshot of the nabob as he sat in the winehouse or under the linden in front of the winehouse in Blato, surrounded by village folk, ordering wine and *klobase*—Carniolan sausages—for all comers, paying for accordion-players, indulging in tall talk about America, its wealth and vastness, and his own experiences as a worker in the West Virginia or Kansas coal-mines or Pennsylvania rolling-mills, and comparing notes upon conditions in the United States with other local *Amerikanci* who had returned before him. . . .

I remember that, listening to them, I played with the idea of going to America when I was but eight or nine.

My notion of the United States then, and for a few years after, was that it was a grand, amazing, somewhat fantastic place—the Golden Country—a sort of Paradise—the Land of Promise in more ways than one—huge beyond conception, thousands of miles across the ocean, untellably exciting, explosive, quite incomparable to the tiny, quiet, lovely Carniola; a place full of movement and turmoil, wherein things that were unimaginable and impossible in Blato happened daily as a matter of course.

In America one could make pots of money in a short time, acquire immense holdings, wear a white collar, and have polish on one's boots like a *gospod*—one of the gentry—and eat white bread, soup, and meat on weekdays as well as on Sundays, even if one were but an ordinary workman to begin with. In Blato no one ate white bread or soup and meat, except on Sundays and holidays, and very few then. . . .

In America everything was possible. There even the common people were "citizens," not "subjects," as they were in Austria and in most other European countries. A citizen, or even a non-citizen foreigner, could walk up to the President of the United States and pump his hand. Indeed, that seemed to be a custom in America. There was a man in Blato, a former steel-worker in Pittsburgh, who claimed that upon an occasion he had shaken hands and exchanged words with Theodore Roosevelt, to whom he familiarly referred as "Tedi"—which struck my mother very funny. To her it seemed as if someone had called the Pope of Rome or the Emperor of Austria by a nickname. But the man assured her, in my hearing, that in America everybody called the President merely "Tedi."

Mother laughed about this, off and on, for several days. And I laughed with her. She and I often laughed together.

8. Engineer Frederick Winslow Taylor Manufactures the Ideal Worker, 1910

Our first step was the scientific selection of the workman. In dealing with workmen under this type of management, it is an inflexible rule to talk to and deal with only one man at a time, since each workman has his own special abilities and limitations, and since we are not dealing with men in masses, but are trying to develop each individual man to his highest state of efficiency and prosperity. Our first step was to find the proper workman to begin with. We therefore carefully watched and studied these 75 men for three or four days, at the end of which time we had picked out four men who appeared to be physically able to handle pig iron at the rate of 47 tons [as

F. W. Taylor, *Scientific Management* (New York: Harper & Brothers, 1910), 5–8.

opposed to the customary 12½ tons] per day. A careful study was then made of each of these men. We looked up their history as far back as practicable and thorough inquiries were made as to the character, habits, and the ambition of each of them. Finally we selected one from among the four as the most likely man to start with. He was a little Pennsylvania Dutchman who had been observed to trot back home for a mile or so after his work in the evening about as fresh as he was when he came trotting down to work in the morning. We found that upon wages of $1.15 a day he had succeeded in buying a small plot of ground, and that he was engaged in putting up the walls of a little house for himself in the morning before starting to work and at night after leaving. He also had the reputation of being exceedingly "close," that is, of placing a very high value on a dollar. As one man whom we talked to about him said, "A penny looks about the size of a cart-wheel to him." This man we will call Schmidt.

The task before us, then, narrowed itself down to getting Schmidt to handle 47 tons of pig iron per day and making him glad to do it. This was done as follows. Schmidt was called out from among the gang of pig-iron handlers and talked to somewhat in this way:

"Schmidt, are you a high-priced man?"

"Vell, I don't know vat you mean."

"Oh yes, you do. What I want to know is whether you are a high-priced man or not."

"Vell, I don't know vat you mean."

"Oh, come now, you answer my questions. What I want to find out is whether you are a high-priced man or one of these cheap fellows here. What I want to find out is whether you want to earn $1.85 a day or whether you are satisfied with $1.15, just the same as all those cheap fellows are getting."

"Did I vant $1.85 a day? Vas dot a high-priced man? Vell, yes, I vas a high-priced man.". . .

"Well, if you are a high-priced man, you will load that pig iron on that car to-morrow for $1.85. Now do wake up and answer my question. Tell me whether you are a high-priced man or not."

"Vell—did I got $1.85 for loading dot pig iron on dot car to-morrow?"

"Yes, of course you do, and you get $1.85 for loading a pile like that every day right through the year. That is what a high-priced man does, and you know it just as well as I do."

"Vell, dot's all right. I could load dot pig iron on the car to-morrow for $1.85, and I get it every day, don't I?"

"Certainly you do—certainly you do."

"Vell, den, I vas a high-priced man."

"Now, hold on, hold on. You know just as well as I do that a high-priced man has to do exactly as he's told from morning till night. You have seen this man here before, haven't you?"

"No, I never saw him."

"Well, if you are a high-priced man, you will do exactly as this man tells you to-morrow, from morning till night. When he tells you to pick up a pig and walk, you pick it up and you walk, and when he tells you to sit down and rest, you sit down. You do that right straight through the day. And what's more, no back talk. Now a high-priced man does just what he's told to do, and no back talk. Do you understand that? When this man tells you to walk, you walk; when he tells you to sit down, you sit down, and you don't talk back at him. Now you come on to work here to-morrow morning and I'll know before night whether you are really a high-priced man or not."

This seems to be rather rough talk. And indeed it would be if applied to an educated mechanic, or even an intelligent laborer. With a man of the mentally sluggish type of Schmidt it is appropriate and not unkind, since it is effective in fixing his attention on the high wages which he wants and away from what, if it were called to his attention, he probably would consider impossibly hard work. . . .

Schmidt started to work, and all day long, and at regular intervals, was told by the man who stood over him with a watch, "Now pick up a pig and walk. Now sit down and rest. Now walk—now rest," etc. He worked when he was told to work, and rested when he was told to rest, and at half-past five in the afternoon had his 47½ tons loaded on the car. And he practically never failed to work at this pace and do the task that was set him during the three years that the writer was at Bethlehem. And throughout this time he averaged a little more than $1.85 per day, whereas before he had never received over $1.15 per day, which was the ruling rate of wages at that time in Bethlehem. That is, he received 60 percent higher wages than were paid to other men who were not working on task work. One man after another was picked out and trained to handle pig iron at the rate of 47½ tons per day until all of the pig iron was handled at this rate, and the men were receiving 60 percent more wages than other workmen around them.

The writer has given above a brief description of three of the four elements which constitute the essence of scientific management: first, the careful selection of the workman, and, second and third, the method of first inducing and then training and helping the workman to work according to the scientific method.

E S S A Y S

Immigration history is deeply intertwined with industrialization because workers from Europe provided much of the muscle for the new factories. The great immigration historian Oscar Handlin, retired from Harvard University, articulates convincingly what some have dubbed the "melting pot" theory: that factory work and polyglot cities sheared immigrants of their cultural roots, reduced them to a common human mass, and remolded them in the forms desired by capitalists. In the first essay, an excerpt from Handlin's classic book, *The Uprooted,* he shows how factories simplified their mechanical processes so that they could utilize unskilled peasants and how peasants came to adapt themselves to the new life. He also argues that industrial labor left the immigrant just as vulnerable to poverty as conditions in the Old World, but with considerably less psychic compensation. A generation and more of younger historians have emphasized the ways in which immigrants and other workers resisted the new industrial work discipline by creating vibrant ethnic enclaves. Mark Wyman of Illinois State University takes this discussion one step further. He argues that immigrants never gave up the fight for personal autonomy, and in fact quite a few returned to their home countries, sometimes sadder and wiser, but sometimes much richer. Wyman's essay leads readers to question if immigrants were genuinely uprooted, or if they simply transplanted themselves according to their own calculations of risks and benefits. Wyman acknowledges the difficult conditions under which immigrants struggled, but he emphasizes the choices they made, rather than the ones made for them by industrialization.

Uprooted and Trapped:
The One-Way Route to Modernity

OSCAR HANDLIN

Let the peasant, now in America, confront his first problem; time enough if ever this is solved to turn to other matters.

How shall a man feed himself, find bread for his family? The condition of man is to till the soil; there is no other wholeness to his existence. True, in retrospect, life on the soil in the old home had not yielded a livelihood. But that was because there was not there soil enough. In consequence, the husbandmen, in their hundreds of thousands, have left their meager plots. They have now come to a New World where open land reaches away in acre after acre of inexhaustible plenty. Arrived, they are ready to work.

Yet only a few, a fortunate few, of these eager hands were destined ever to break the surface of the waiting earth. Among the multitudes that survived the crossing, there were now and then some who survived it intact enough in body and resources to get beyond the port of landing and through the interior cities of transit. Those who were finally able to establish themselves as the independent proprietors of farms of their own made up an even smaller number.

All the others were unable to escape from the cities. Decade after decade, as the Federal government made its count, the census revealed a substantial majority of the immigrants in the urban places; and the margin of that majority grew steadily larger. Always the percentage of the foreign-born who lived in the cities was much higher than that of the total population.

Yet the people who were to live the rest of their days amidst a world of steel and stone and brick were peasants. If they failed to reach the soil which had once been so much a part of their being, it was only because the town had somehow trapped them. . . .

What could the peasant do here? He could not trade or do much to help the traders. There was some room for petty shopkeepers; he lacked the training and the capital. Some handicraftsmen supplied clothes and furniture and a variety of other products to the townsfolk; he lacked the skill and tools. Back on the docks at which he had landed were a number of casual jobs with the stevedores. Here and there in the warehouses and stores were calls for the services of porters. But there was a limit to the amount of lifting and carrying to be done. Wandering about in the first days of their arrival, these immigrants learned that beyond these few opportunities there was, at first, no demand for their capacities.

As time went by, they became restless seekers after employment. Yet many remained unsuccessful in the quest or, drifting about, picked up odd jobs that tided them over from week to week. They joined a growing army of the anxious for work, for they could certainly not remain long without income. Perpetually on the verge of destitution, and therefore of starvation, eager to be hired at any rate, these redundant hands accumulated in a fund of available but unused labor. . . .

In the 1820's and 1830's, factory employment was the province of groups relatively high in social status. North of Boston, the bulk of the labor force was made up of respectable young girls, many the daughters of neighborhood farmers, girls willing to work for a few years in anticipation of the marriageable young man. In southern New England the general practice was to employ whole families of artisans. Everywhere, paternalistic organization and the closely knit communal life of the boarding-houses did not allow the easy entrance of newcomers. The only immigrants who then found a place in industry were the few skilled operatives who had already mastered the craft in the Old Country and were hired for the sake of their skills.

The reservoir of unskilled peasant labor that mounted steadily higher in the cities did not long remain untapped, however. In the 1840's and 1850's came a succession of new inventions that enterprising men of capital used to transform the productive system of the United States. The older industries had disdained the immigrants; but the new ones, high in the risks of innovation and heavy initial investments, drew eagerly on this fund of workers ready to be exploited at attractively low wages. The manufacture of clothing, of machines, and of furniture flourished in the great commercial cities precisely where they could utilize freely the efforts of the newcomers, hire as many as they needed when necessary, lay off any surplus at will. A completely fluid labor supply set the ideal conditions for expansion.

Thereafter, whatever branch of the economy entered upon a period of rapid expansion did so with the aid of the same immigrant labor supply. At midcentury the immigrants went to dig in the mines that pockmarked the great coal and iron fields of Pennsylvania, first experienced Welshmen and Cornishmen, later raw Irishmen and Germans, and still later Slavs—a vague term that popularly took in Bohemians, Slovaks, Hungarians, and also Italians. These people spread with the spread of the fields, southward into West Virginia and westward to Illinois, in a burst of development from which impressive consequences followed.

The wealth of new power extracted from the earth, after 1870, set off a second revolution in American industry. Steam replaced water power. Iron replaced wood in the construction of machines. Factories became larger and more mechanized and the place of unskilled labor more prominent. On the payrolls of new enterprises, immigrant names were almost alone; and the newcomers now penetrated even into the older textile and shoe industries. The former peasants, first taken on for menial duties as janitors and sweepers, found themselves more often placed at machines as the processes of production were divided into ever simpler tasks open to the abilities of the unskilled. . . .

This process, so rich in rewards for the country as a whole, paid mostly dividends of pain for the immigrants involved in it. It cost the peasants this to make the adjustment, that the stifling, brazen factories and the dark, stony pits supplanted the warm, living earth as the source of their daily bread. Year after year they paid the price in innumerable hardships of mind and body.

When he reviewed his grievances the man who went to work said that the conditions of his labor were oppressively harsh. His day was long, he pointed out; not until the 1880's was the ten-hour limit an objective seriously to be struggled for, and for many years more that span remained a pleasing ideal rather than a reality. His week was full, he added; seven days, when they could be had, were not unusual. And, he complained, along with the Sunday there vanished that whole long calendar of holidays that had formerly marked the peasant year. Here the demands of industry and the availability of employment alone determined when a man should work and when he should rest.

These were such wrongs as the ache in his muscles recalled. Others were summoned up by an ache of the spirit. For this matter of time reflected an unhuman lack of concern with human needs that was characteristic of the entire system. In these great concerns, no one seemed troubled with the welfare of the tiny men so cheap to come by who moved uneasily about in the service of the immense expensive machines. A high rate of industrial accidents and a stubborn unwillingness to make the most elementary provisions for the comfort of the employees, to the immigrant were evidence of the same penetrating callousness.

In the terms of his own experience, the laborer could come to understand his total insecurity by recollecting the steady decline in the span of the labor contract. In the Old Country, and in the old America, a man was hired for the year or for the season. But that period was altogether out of place under these conditions. Now it was not even by the month or by the week that the worker was taken on, but by the day or by the hour. Such an arrangement released the employer from the compulsion of paying hands when he had no need of them. But it left the hands uncertain, from moment to moment, as to how much work and how much income they would have.

The ultimate refinement was the shift to piecework in which the laborer, rewarded in accord with his output, received payment only for the instants he was actually at his task. The peasant sometimes conceived of this as an attractive alternative, for he hated the idea of selling his time, of taking directions like a servant, of cringing under the frowns of a foreman who judged all performances inadequate. Piecework brought the consolation of independence—one's time was one's own—and the illusion that additional effort would bring additional returns. But, though the immigrants often clung to the illusion as a token of hope, the reality was inescapably different. There was no independence and rewards would not rise. For the employer who set the rates manipulated them to his own interest while the employee had no choice but to accept. The net effect was to shift from the employer to the employee the whole burden of labor insecurity.

These elements of insecurity, the immigrant learned, were not confined to the conditions of the working day; they pervaded the total relationship of the worker to the economy. The fluid labor supply that gave the employer complete liberty to hire as many workers as he wished, when he wished, also gave him the ability, at will, to dismiss those whose toil he no longer needed. Under such circumstances there were always some men without jobs. Each industry came to have its seasons, peaks and troughs in the level of employment dictated either by the weather as in construction, or, more generally, by the convenience of the managers. It was a rare individual who did not go on the bricks for some part of the year, for periodic unemployment was an expected aspect of the laborer's career.

Then there were the years when unemployment deepened and spread out. The intervals of idleness grew longer and were less frequently interrupted until unemployment was no longer intermittent but continuous. More men appeared on the streets during the day; children were seen, pail in hand, on the way to the police station for the doled-out soup. First in the mill and mining towns where there was only one employer or one industry and where a closing had an immediate cataclysmic effect, then in the cities where the impact was delayed by diversity of occupations, but in time everywhere, the laborer knew a depression was upon him.

At such times, the burdens of his economic role became intolerable. The hunger left behind in Europe was again an intimate of the household, and the cold and raggedness. Endurance stretched to the bursting point, and the misery of regret was overwhelming. It was a golden land here in America as long as there was work, but without work it was worth nothing. In the miry slough of inactivity into which he now sank, the peasant had leisure to meditate upon the meaning of his lot in the New World. . . .

Only by calling upon the earnings of more than one of its members could the immigrant household make ends meet. Not unless it utilized the efforts of wife and child, as well as those of the husband, could the family be certain that there would always be someone working and that the income of the whole would be large enough, secure enough, to withstand the recurrent shocks of American economic life.

It was not the mere fact that wife and child must exert themselves that was hurtful. These were no strangers to toil in the Old World, or in the New. The degradation lay in the *kind* of work. The boys drifted into street occupations, blacked boots or hawked newspapers, missed thus the opportunity to acquire a trade and fell into all sorts of outlandish ways. Or they, and girls too for that matter, entered the shops, where they did men's work at child's wages. For the women, there was "domestic service"—maid's work in strangers' homes or back-breaking laundering in their own; or, more often as time went on, service to industry in the factory or by homework. If it was characteristic of these families that they somehow found the room for a boarder, that was only another method of adding to their ranks another breadwinner.

But in America bread never came without complications. The peasant, new to the means of earning his livelihood, was also new to the means of spending it. To his misfortune he discovered that he himself added to the difficulties in making ends meet through inability to use efficiently whatever money came to his hands. In his old life, he had thought of objects in their individuality and uniqueness; the chair, the hat, the cow. Here he had to learn to think of them as commodities, subject to a common quantitative standard of price. Without a clear conception of the relationship of money to things, every transaction involved a set of totally new conditions. . . .

Often, they would try to understand. They would think about it in the pauses of their work, speculate sometimes as their minds wandered, tired, at the close of a long day.

What had cut short the continuous past, severed it from the unrelated present? Immigration had transformed the entire economic world within which the peasants had formerly lived. From surface forms to inmost functionings, the change was complete. A new setting, new activities, and new meanings forced the newcomers into radically new roles as producers and consumers of goods. In the process, they became, in their own eyes, less worthy as men. They felt a sense of degradation that raised a most insistent question: Why had this happened? . . .

Every element of the immigrants' experience since the day they had left home added to this awareness of their utter helplessness. All the incidents of the journey were bound up with chance. What was the road to follow, what the ship to board, what port to make? These were serious questions. But who knew which were the right answers? Whether they survived the hazards of the voyage, and in what condition, these too were decisions beyond the control of the men who participated in it. The capricious world of the crossing pointed its own conclusion as to the role of chance in the larger universe into which the immigrants plunged.

It was the same with their lives after landing. To find a job or not, to hold it or to be fired, in these matters laborers' wills were of slight importance. Inscrutable, distant persons determined matters on the basis of remote, unknown conditions. The most fortunate of immigrants, the farmers, knew well what little power they had to influence the state of the climate, the yield of the earth, or the fluctuations of the market, all the elements that determined their lot. Success or failure, incomprehensible in terms of peasant values, seemed altogether fortuitous. Time and again, the analogy occurred to them: man was helpless like the driven cog in a great machine.

Loneliness, separation from the community of the village, and despair at the insignificance of their own human abilities, these were the elements that, in America, colored the peasants' view of their world. From the depths of a dark pessimism, they looked up at a frustrating universe ruled by haphazard, capricious forces. Without the capacity to control or influence these forces men could but rarely gratify their hopes or wills. Their most passionate desires were doomed to failure; their lives were those of the feeble little birds which hawks attack, which lose strength from want of food, and which, at last surrendering to the savage blasts of the careless elements, flutter unnoticed to the waiting earth.

Sadness was the tone of life, and death and disaster no strangers. Outsiders would not understand the familiarity with death who had not daily met it in the close quarters of the steerage; nor would they comprehend the riotous Paddy funerals who had no insight of the release death brought. The end of life was an end to hopeless striving, to ceaseless pain, and to the endless succession of disappointments. There was a leaden grief for the ones who went; yet the tomb was only the final parting in a long series of separations that had started back at the village crossroads.

Coming and Going: Round Trip to America

MARK WYMAN

The Polish priest was surprised as he went over the parish census for 1894. He had known for some time that people were emigrating from the village of Miejsce, and so there was nothing startling in the total of 121 persons going to America in the ten years since the first traveler set out across the Atlantic.

Mark Wyman, *Round-Trip to America: The Immigrants Return to Europe, 1880–1930* (Ithaca: Cornell University Press, 1993), pp. 3–6, 17–19, 32, 39–40, 53, 60–62, 67–68, 76–77, 79, 83–87, 127, 129, 201–202. Used by permission of the publisher, Cornell University Press.

What surprised him was the return flow: fifty-eight persons had come home to stay, just under half the overseas migration. . . .

What surprised the Polish priest in 1894 continues to offer unexpected findings to those who look beneath the surface of American immigration. For the incoming tidal wave of peoples has always had an outflow, a reverse movement of immigrants turning their backs on the United States. Ignored by Fourth of July orators, overlooked by historians who concentrate on the newcomers' assimilation, return migration looms so large in world history, with critical implications for the homelands and the United States, that it cries out for attention. . . .

The perils of ocean travel in these early periods, during the age of sail, helped keep return totals low. But by the middle of the nineteenth century a different picture emerged as railroads crisscrossed the continents and steamships began to ply the Atlantic. Not only were the European masses on the move for America, Canada, and elsewhere, but for large numbers it had become a round-trip. During this era of mass immigration, from approximately 1880 until 1930 when restriction laws and the Great Depression choked it off, from one-quarter to one-third of all European immigrants to the United States permanently returned home. The total may have reached four million persons.

European peasant villages that once seemed impenetrable in their backwardness, their isolation, now boasted residents who could describe the wonders of the New World—skyscrapers, elevated trains, deep tunnels. (Had not they themselves worked on these wonders?) Men and women who formerly quailed at the thought of a visit from the landlord now proudly described how they had seen the president of the United States in person, and one returned Slovenian even claimed to have shaken the hand of "Tedi." European politicians suddenly had to contend with subjects who knew different governmental systems, and clergymen confronted parishioners who had come into contact with other religious ideas. Life was not the same in Miejsce, nor in the Mezzogiorno, nor in thousands of peasant communities across the Continent. . . .

The new migration was all built on the centuries-old European tradition of seasonal migration for work in nearby areas. This practice was so old, so extensive, that recent scholars have referred to it as "a way of life" among Russian and Galician Poles; as "the thing to do . . . an accepted and socially supported form of behavior" in many areas of east-central Europe; as "a way of life for hundreds of thousands of Slovaks" and "as almost an ordinary routine of village life" in the Italian Apennines. It was known everywhere in Europe. . . .

This movement within Europe was not new to the late nineteenth century, despite claims to the contrary by some writers. The modern world has struggled hard to maintain the comforting, nostalgic thought of a static peasant culture rooted to the soil, unchanging. Oscar Handlin wrote of "the enormous stability in peasant society. . . . From the westernmost reaches of Europe, in Ireland, to Russia in the east, the peasant masses had maintained an imperturbable sameness." He described a world where the village's self-sufficiency only rarely yielded to products or influences from outside, while cities were "regions of total strangeness into which the peasant never ventured, where not the people alone, but the very aspect of the earth, was unfamiliar."

But recent examinations into the past of European communities contradict the view of peasant life as stable and unchanging; this picture is inaccurate not only for the nineteenth century but for many centuries before. The Nordic countries' population "has been very mobile for centuries," one scholar found, and another showed that conditions in central Sweden's Dalarna province were driving people to seek work elsewhere perhaps as far back as the Middle Ages. . . . It was the same in Italy, where two scholars who examined the exodus from a northern community for 1865–1921 noted that this emigration really demonstrated "continuity in an apparently long-standing pattern of intense but short-distance migration." The inhabitants traditionally traveled for work away from home, but not overseas. Balkan men similarly trekked across much of southern Europe looking for jobs. An Irishman was therefore speaking for generations and an entire continent, not just for his 1881 peers, when he told the royal commissioners investigating the vast farm labor migration into England, "We are like wild geese, your honor." . . .

Frequently it was specific information from America that drew the emigrant. As an Italian politician put it, "the strongest emigration agent is the postage-stamp." Branko M. Colakovic's interviews with 500 Yugoslavs who had crossed the ocean before 1925 led him to conclude that the pull from America was more important than the push from even the harshest Yugoslav conditions. Higher wages were crucial, and pamphlets from American railroads and state immigration bureaus bombarded the would-be immigrant with statistics to support the agents' claims. "It was almost heaven," a Finn said in recalling tales of the wealth that allegedly awaited workers in the United States. "You could almost just grab the money!" And Swedish children in Småland called the distant land where their relatives were heading not America but *mer rika*—"more rich." . . .

As this emigration to America mushroomed, its makeup began to shift. It remained a heavily rural, peasant movement, but no longer did family groups dominate. Single women arrived, but their numbers were overwhelmed by those of men, especially young men. "They came in droves of males," a U.S. congressman remarked, and the change was dramatic enough to draw attention: the U.S. Census report for 1910 observed that with the increased immigration from southern and eastern Europe the foreign-born showed "a very marked excess of males"—154.6 males to 100 females from Austria, 160.8 to 100 from Hungary, 190.6 to 100 from Italy, 137.3 to 100 from Russia. . . .

The transformation in the makeup of this emigration was apparently not driven by racial or regional factors but by economic ones. In the decade ending in 1910, in fact, almost 70 percent of *all* immigrants into the United States were males, mainly young males. Women continued to arrive, but many found work not in the factories but as servants, or they remained within family groups. And for both men and women it was a migration of youth. Some of the Austro-Hungarian groups had more than 80 percent in the 14–44 age category after 1900; for U.S. immigration as a whole, persons in that age group accounted for 83.4 percent of the total in the exploding influx of 1906–10. This changing flow had a large impact on the emigration districts of Europe, too: the exodus of men from Slovak regions of Hungary was so heavy that by 1910 there were only 532 men in Slovakia for every 1,000 women.

Part of the change in the exodus was that immigrants increasingly planned only a short stay in America—nothing to put down roots for, just enough to pile up some savings that could be used for better living or a specific project at home. . . .

No one expected such work to be easy. "Everyone works like hell," a Finn wrote home from Michigan, and the experiences gave rise to a Polish saying: "America for the oxen, Europe for the peasant." A YMCA leader examining the immigrants' situation in Pittsburgh found that as a rule they earned the lowest wages and worked the "full stint" of hours, including twelve hours daily on a seven-day week at the blast furnaces. Long hours were common for immigrant workers; so was energy-sapping labor. . . .

They agreed: you worked hard in America. One had to "sweat more during a day than during a whole week in Poland," a peasant immigrant wrote home. Returnees to Ireland said that they had worked like slaves, and some argued that "if people worked hard at home they would make as much money at home as anyone in America." Interviewers with Norwegian immigrants found general agreement that they had to work harder in America than in Norway. Similar comments appeared across the Continent as remigrants recounted their experiences. . . .

Stories of the enormous sacrifices immigrants made to build up savings circulated in the industrial centers and even in the halls of Congress. Common laborers in Pittsburgh were reported to be putting away up to $15 a month; this is consistent with Ewa Morawska's conclusion that the savings by east-central European men in Johnstown averaged $100–200 annually. Italian laborers had the highest savings rate among European laborers, according to a 1907 Bureau of Labor report, putting away $25–27 monthly from railroad work. Floating immigrant workers in the western Midwest and Plains states were reported to have "clear saving" of $1 per day from wages of only $1.25–1.65. An American working in a steel mill found many employees who did not save, but he said that "practically all the 'Hunkies' of twenty-eight or thirty and over saved very successfully"—and these were expecting to return to Europe. One told him: "A good job, save money, work all time, go home, sleep, no spend." . . .

Closely related to the immigrants' desire to save and their willingness to put up with dismal job conditions was their acceptance of housing that was primitive and congested in the extreme. Some of this acquiescence stemmed from peasant backgrounds, but much arose also from "the desire of employees from the south and east of Europe to decrease expenses," as a government investigator put it. If they crowded together in sleeping rooms, their rent could be sharply reduced; if all went together in a communal cooking and eating plan, or hired a wife or "boss" to handle cooking—the Italian *bordo,* the Bulgarian *boort,* the "boarding boss" system—then costs could be cut even further. . . .

In coal mining areas the immigrants sometimes lived in deserted pigpens and cowsheds: "You might call them outhouses," one critic said. A manufacturer told of seeing the homes of Italian and Hungarian miners at Honey Brook, Pennsylvania, where the huts were seven feet high, "built of slabs and rotten planks and poles, and I supposed when I saw them that they were places where these people, the miners around there, kept their pigs or something. I didn't really suppose, to look at them, that they were the habitations of human beings." Similarly, a Knights of Labor official encountered a settlement of Hungarian brick workers near Detroit: it had 127 persons living in a building ten feet by fifty feet, including five families cooped into a single room, "eating from one common kettle of food and sleeping in one common bed." . . .

Lacking a long-term commitment, these immigrants often rebuffed those seeking to enlist them in broader campaigns. They suffered their own maltreatment in silence rather than fight for justice. "These creatures are willing to take anything offered them, because they do not intend to remain, and will sacrifice anything to acquire a little fortune," the Brass-Workers national leader asserted contemptuously. Finns working in a Colorado mine drew a similar complaint from a coworker, who said that they were "ignorant of the language and ways of working in this country, and will take from the bosses any insult they may offer, and are willing to accept any usage in the company's boardinghouse." The central European peasant in America, it was said, "kissed the hand of the boss who sent him to work." Ultimately, then, the lower levels of America's booming industries were filling up with persons who willingly endured lower wages, coarse treatment, and poor conditions. They avoided friction with the boss so the paychecks would not stop coming. Because of this, they were widely regarded as a retarding influence in the drive for better conditions in the nation's workplaces. . . .

It did not take long for reaction to build against such workers. A reporter covering Pennsylvania's mining strikes testified in 1888 that he saw Hungarians, Poles, and Italians "marched up to the shanties" from the train at the Highland mines in the Lehigh region; they were blamed with "breaking down the strike" there.

Recruitment of immigrants to break strikes was sometimes blatant, but often the onrushing tide made recruitment unnecessary: they arrived regardless. The *Chicagoer Arbeiter-Zeitung* was both pro-union and pro-immigrant and was therefore in a quandary as the influx began to affect the city's labor market: "We are not enemies of immigration and hence cannot choose to fight it; but we must still raise the question: What should be done to lessen, or eliminate, the decrease in wages resulting from the huge labor supply?" Given Chicago's scarcity of jobs, the newspaper asked, "What, then, can the new immigrants do save offer their labor below the established pay scale?" It feared the result: Chicago's established workers would be forced to give way to the cheaper immigrant labor. . . .

Without a doubt, many immigrants returned because they had succeeded in America. The Finn who predicted that he would go home as soon as "the pockets [were] full of money" spoke for legions. And though a variety of explanations, including failure, appeared among those returning to Szamosszeg, Hungary, an investigator found that "more considered that they had fulfilled their purpose for going"—that is, they reached their savings target. Three to five years was the most frequent length to stay in America to reach the immigrant's goal, although many stayed longer and some, less. Slovaks reportedly set $1,000 as the "fortune" to be amassed before they would return, and among the workers in a 1919 steel mill pit was "a quiet-eyed Pole, who was saving up two hundred dollars to go to the old country." But interviews with other Poles who returned after World War I turned up many who were much more successful, including one who left the United States with $6,000 in his money belt—and on the ship discovered more: a vest with double lining sewed up with banknotes. Immediately he encountered a Croat running wildly and yelling, "Has anyone seen my vest?" It was returned to him. Such funds carried in belts, bags, clothing, and pockets formed an important portion of the transfer of American wealth across the ocean.

Interviews with returned Finns and questionnaire data disclosed the fact that, although these immigrants had performed some of the hardest drudgery in American capitalist enterprises during the 1880–1930 years—in such jobs as logging, mining, and steel mill work—they were still overwhelmingly positive about their achievements. A 1934 study found that 40.3 percent (255 persons) reported good results in America, 17.3 percent (109) had "quite good" results, and 16.4 percent (104) had a "fair result." Only 18.5 percent reported a bad result. Later studies uncovered similar findings. . . .

If the journey to America was based heavily on the expectation of finding employment in American industry, it was therefore vulnerable to the vicissitudes of that industry. The label "migrant industrials" was fastened on these immigrants by an American scholar, but it was contemporary Italians who called the United States "the workshop." Italians flocked to this land of labor mainly in March, April, and May, and their heaviest returns were in October, November, and December, when layoffs were often most numerous. And the workshop could close, as it did at times, abruptly, sending throngs eastward across the Atlantic. One remigrant in late 1894 was a Pole who encountered many of his compatriots "running away from America. The stagnation existing there has now driven them out of their 'new homeland,'" he said. Remigration data revealed that a large proportion of those returning had been in factory work, mills, or mining, occupations especially vulnerable to the boom-and-bust nature of the American economy. . . .

Many immigrants viewed the increasing returns not as a reason to celebrate the American economy but as grounds to condemn it. Some European observers charged that there would be even more returns if not for the shame that prevented some immigrants from going home; better to hang on and hope for improvement than return in disgrace. And many who went back were seemingly "worse than when they came, for many had failed and were broken in spirit," Edward Steiner observed after his steerage interviews.

Embitterment against America often followed, as with the Irishman who had arrived in Cleveland just in time for an economic depression. His brother was already there but had lost his savings when a bank failed, and only because a sister was married to a still-employed policeman was the Irishman able to remain alive—barely—until he could make his way back to Ireland. "He hates to talk about it, and he even hates the Yanks that come home," a friend later recalled; "he said America ruined his life." Another told of returning Irishmen who were so destitute when they landed that they had to walk all the way home to Kilkenny from the Dublin docks, some seventy miles. They were not proud of their time in America. . . .

Other travelers on returning ships were repeatedly struck by the large numbers of injured, broken, or ill immigrants on board and the multiplicity of widows. One American was surprised that more than a fifth of those coming back on the steamship *Canopic* were sick. Steiner looked at returning Polish women who seemed crushed (their cheeks pale and pinched, their skin severely wrinkled) and asked himself how it could be otherwise: "They had lived for years by the coke ovens of Pennsylvania, breathing sulphur with every breath; their eyes had rarely seen the full daylight and their cheeks had not often felt the warm sunlight." . . .

Looming behind these health problems, the missing limbs and diseased lungs, were the conditions of labor in America. A leading Hungarian-American newspaper, *Szabadság* of Pittsburgh, featured in its yearly almanac a chapter titled "Fatal Accidents and Mine Disasters." It had plenty of material to chronicle—cave-ins, explosions, haulage accidents—and one recent estimate is that 25 percent of the New Immigrant workers in Carnegie Steel's South Works in Pittsburgh were killed or injured in the 1907–10 years. Immigrants struggled against such conditions mainly by quitting but also by forming their own mutual aid societies, often a carryover from home. . . .

High on the list for condemnation, after unsafe working conditions, was the driving of workers in the American system—relentless, shoving, pushing, threatening. Peasants had been raised with different manners and a different pace of daily and yearly work. Gone now were the special holidays and festivals that dotted the work year in Europe; vanished as well were name days and wedding feasts when work was not allowed. And notably absent in the day-to-day handling of employment in large American concerns or labor gangs was consideration for individual problems: an illness, a need to visit a relative, a family problem that took someone away from work for a day.

Now there were supervisors who used fines or dismissal as weapons to enforce the speedup. Herbert Gutman stressed the personal costs of the peasant's transformation to wage laborer, and angry reactions by immigrants are not difficult to locate in the industrial records of the era. Many returned to Ireland to take up fishing again because, it was said, "they preferred that free life to bosses and clocks." One remigrant said that he was glad to be back where work was hard but free and easy, for "there is no clock or watch or boss to watch you here." . . .

New structures were going up all across Europe as the nineteenth century closed—houses with tile or slate roofs instead of thatch, a large window with a view to the road, walls of brick or plastered white, doorways sporting brass knobs and shiny varnish. Boards replaced logs, tile replaced thatch. . . . These "American" villages brought together many of the tangible, as well as intangible, results of return migration. The "American houses," which sprang up like mushrooms after a rain, were quickly noticed by visitors. When Carlo Levi was exiled to a tiny southern Italian town by Mussolini in the mid-1930s, his early walks through the poverty-stricken district brought him to some homes that were surprising, different. These had a second floor and balcony, even fancy varnish and doorknobs. They were exceptional among the drab huts of a peasant village. "Such houses belonged to the 'Americans,'" he noted.

The American houses were outward symbols of changes that affected not only the Continent's physical surfaces but also its inner life, customs, and traditions. For the remigrants were often different people when they returned, and their accomplishments soon reached beyond the Italian saying, "He who crosses the ocean can buy a house." Their determination, as well as the structures they built, could inspire their neighbors. It was said that "the people went wild from envy and desire" when a Pole returned and bought land on which he built two houses in his Galician community. He and his deeds were noted; his capacity for achievements and the source of his funds were obvious. All were explained by the fact of his round-trip journey abroad. Asked about the home he proudly showed, an Italian commented simply, "America bought this house." . . .

But, though negative experiences were abundant, travelers in Europe over the years encountered what seemed to be almost a single view among remigrants, a chorus that overwhelmed dissonant voices. This was a sentiment extolling the United States, an attitude that seemed surprising in view of the conditions they had known. It was surprising because most returners had seen firsthand the contradictions in American life; they could show missing fingers and arms and talk knowingly of the United States as "a challenging giant, both fair and unfair, ugly and beautiful." They accepted the view that life was cruel in America and that the nation's coarse citizenry did not appreciate beauty; as the Italian saying put it bluntly, "Had the peasant known all this, he wouldn't have gone to America." Critics at home feasted on such tales.

Still, despite their difficulties abroad, massive numbers of remigrants carried home attitudes toward America that were overwhelmingly positive. Some of this can be put down to the human tendency to remember happy times and submerge the difficult times. These contrasts did not survive in a simple relationship among remigrants, however: favorable memories involving the United States seem to have coexisted as an intricate part of some very bad experiences. Like a patent medicine that irritates the skin to produce a warm feeling, struggles in America's industrial cauldron were passed through the filter of memory and emerged as recollections of the proud role remigrants had played in creating the American industrial colossus. Their labors were essential. However small their part on the section gang or meatpacking line, they had helped build America.

FURTHER READING

Ron Chernow, *Titan: The Life of John D. Rockefeller, Sr.* (1998).

William Cronon, *Nature's Metropolis: Chicago and the Great West* (1991).

Wendy Gamber, *The Female Economy: The Millinery and Dressmaking Trades* (1997).

Elliot Gorn and Warren Goldstein, *A Brief History of American Sports* (1993).

Matthew Frye Jacobson, *Whiteness of a Different Color: European Immigrants and the Alchemy of Race* (1998).

Harold C. Livesay, *Andrew Carnegie and the Rise of Big Business* (2nd ed., 2000).

David Montgomery, *The Fall of the House of Labor* (1987).

Robert A. Orsi, *The Madonna of 115th Street: Faith and Community in Italian Harlem* (1985).

Kathy Peiss, *Cheap Amusements: Working Women and Leisure in Turn-of-the-Century New York* (1986).

Roy Rozenzweig, *Eight Hours for What We Will: Workers and Leisure in an Industrial City* (1983).

Philip Scranton, *Endless Novelty: Specialty Production and American Industrialization* (1997).

Stephen Thernstrom, *The Other Bostonians* (1973)

CHAPTER
4

Imperialism and
World Power

In 1898 the United States embarked on its first war on behalf of the rights of people other than its own. Revolutionaries in Cuba had fought for thirty years (1868–1898) to break Spain's grasp on its last colony in the New World. With U.S. help, they finally did. Eighty years earlier, John Quincy Adams had warned at a similar moment that entanglement in foreign revolutions should be avoided because it would involve the United States "beyond the power of extrication in all the wars of interest and intrigue." No matter how righteous the initial cause, he stated, "the fundamental maxims of her policy would insensibly change from liberty to force. . . . She might become dictatress of the world. She would no longer be the ruler of her own spirit." The war against Spain to secure Cuba's indepen-dence, in line with Adams's prediction, in fact did not end there. The United States Congress passed the Platt Amendment in 1903, requiring Cuba to agree to unilateral American intervention indefinitely. More shockingly, in the course of the war the United States took the Philippine Islands, Guam, and Puerto Rico from Spain. The United States had initially collaborated with Filipino independence fighter Emilio Aguinaldo, but then, against his wishes, it transformed the islands into an American colony. When Aguinaldo detected this U.S. treachery, he launched a new rebellion, which the American army brutally suppressed. The U.S.-Philippine war lasted three years. Over four thousand U.S. troops died, along with nearly 200,000 Filipino rebels and civilians.

These first conflicts of the twentieth century contained in full measure the contradictions and danger that were to shape relations between the United States and the rest of the globe for the coming century. Presidents William McKinley, Theodore Roosevelt, and Woodrow Wilson, under whose direction the United States took up a leading role on the world stage, agreed that the time had come to exercise America's tremendous potential for international influence. They disagreed on the reasons for doing so. Should the United States be an imperial power, or should it fight to eradicate colonialism? Should the United States promote stability and the status quo, or should it promote decolonization and democracy? Should the United States "speak softly and carry a big stick," as Roosevelt argued, or should it exercise a moral diplomacy?

Of course, even the existence of the debate reflected how far the United States had strayed from its traditional policy of "nonentanglement," dating back to George Washington. Any form of intervention involved the United States in disputes beyond its control and often beyond its understanding. Even the process of promoting democracy meant meddling in ways that undermined other peoples' self-determination. The United States did not have to exercise regional, and ultimately global, police power. But at the start of the twentieth century, it did so. Why?

QUESTIONS   TO   THINK   ABOUT

How could a nation with democratic values fight a colonial war? What rhetoric or reform aspirations made this undertaking palatable? Did democratic values stop at the water's edge?

DOCUMENTS

The documents in this chapter show the many sides to the debate over imperialism within the United States, and some of the ways in which people abroad perceived the American presence. In Document 1, President William McKinley asks Congress to declare war against Spain "in the cause of humanity." Document 2 is a speech by New York Governor and former "Rough Rider" Theodore Roosevelt, given a year after the Spanish-American War. Roosevelt scorned anti-imperialists as weak. Only "the overcivilized man, who has lost the great fighting, masterful virtues," distrusted his country's motives, according to Roosevelt. The pugnacious New Yorker was elected vice president in 1898, and became president following the assassination of William McKinley in 1901. In Document 3, the Filipino revolutionary Emilio Aguinaldo reveals what he thought of the United States in 1899: that it had sent an "army of occupation." The following documents also condemn the policy of the McKinley administration. In Document 4, the Anti-Imperialist League claims that the administration sought "to extinguish the spirit of 1776 in those islands." Mark Twain, author of *Tom Sawyer* and *Huckleberry Finn,* fiercely criticizes the racial and imperial assumptions of the United States in Document 5. In Document 6, a soldier writes that American troops made more enemies than friends in the Philippines by calling the natives "Niggers" and by burning the houses of rebels and peaceful civilians alike. Document 7 is the 1904 Roosevelt Corollary to the Monroe Doctrine. President Theodore Roosevelt's pronouncement expanded the meaning of the Monroe Doctrine of 1823, which had simply warned the great powers of Europe not to intervene in the affairs of, or attempt to recolonize, the independent nations of Latin America. In his annual speech to Congress on December 6, 1904, Roosevelt claimed a new role for the United States as "an international police power." In the last reading, Document 8, President Woodrow Wilson condemns placing economic interest ahead of moral principle and swears that the United States will "never again seek one additional foot of territory by conquest." Wilson soon thereafter sent U.S. troops into Mexico, Haiti, and the Dominican Republic, but all in the name of helping to teach Latin Americans to "elect good men."

1. President William McKinley Asks for War to Liberate Cuba, 1898

. . . Our people have beheld a once prosperous community reduced to comparative want, its lucrative commerce virtually paralyzed, its exceptional productiveness diminished, its fields laid waste, its mills in ruins, and its people perishing by tens of thousands from hunger and destitution. We have found ourselves constrained, in the observance of that strict neutrality which our laws enjoin and which the law of nations commands, to police our own waters and watch our own seaports in prevention of any unlawful act in aid of the Cubans. . . .

The war in Cuba is of such a nature that, short of subjugation or extermination, a final military victory for either side seems impracticable. The alternative lies in the physical exhaustion of the one or the other party, or perhaps of both—a condition which in effect ended the ten years' war by the truce of Zanjon. The prospect of such a protraction and conclusion of the present strife is a contingency hardly to be contemplated with equanimity by the civilized world, and least of all by the United States, affected and injured as we are, deeply and intimately, by its very existence. . . .

The grounds for . . . intervention may be briefly summarized as follows:

First. In the cause of humanity and to put an end to the barbarities, bloodshed, starvation, and horrible miseries now existing there, and which the parties to the conflict are either unable or unwilling to stop or mitigate. It is no answer to say this is all in another country, belonging to another nation, and is therefore none of our business. It is specially our duty, for it is right at our door.

Second. We owe it to our citizens in Cuba to afford them that protection and indemnity for life and property which no government there can or will afford, and to that end to terminate the conditions that deprive them of legal protection.

Third. The right to intervene may be justified by the very serious injury to the commerce, trade, and business of our people and by the wanton destruction of property and devastation of the island.

Fourth, and which is of the utmost importance. The present condition of affairs in Cuba is a constant menace to our peace and entails upon this Government an enormous expense. With such a conflict waged for years in an island so near us and with which our people have such trade and business relations; when the lives and liberty of our citizens are in constant danger and their property destroyed and themselves ruined; where our trading vessels are liable to seizure and are seized at our very door by war ships of a foreign nation; the expeditions of filibustering that we are powerless to prevent altogether, and the irritating questions and entanglements thus arising—all these and others that I need not mention, with the resulting strained relations, are a constant menace to our peace and compel us to keep on a semi war footing with a nation with which we are at peace. . . .

This document can be found in John Bassett Moore, *A Digest of International Law* (Washington, D.C.: Government Printing Office, 1906), VI, 211–223. Reprinted in Dennis Merrill and Thomas G. Paterson, eds., *Major Problems in American Foreign Relations,* Vol. I: to 1920, Sixth Ed. (Boston: Houghton Mifflin, 2005), 331–333.

In view of these facts and of these considerations I ask the Congress to authorize and empower the President to take measures to secure a full and final termination of hostilities between the Government of Spain and the people of Cuba, and to secure in the island the establishment of a stable government, capable of maintaining order and observing its international obligations, insuring peace and tranquillity and the security of its citizens as well as our own, and to use the military and naval forces of the United States as may be necessary for these purposes. . . .

2. Governor Theodore Roosevelt Praises the Manly Virtues of Imperialism, 1899

In speaking to you, men of the greatest city of the West, men of the state which gave to the country Lincoln and Grant, men who preeminently and distinctly embody all that is most American in the American character, I wish to preach not the doctrine of ignoble ease but the doctrine of the strenuous life; the life of toil and effort; of labor and strife; to preach that highest form of success which comes not to the man who desires mere easy peace but to the man who does not shrink from danger, from hardship, or from bitter toil, and who out of these wins the splendid ultimate triumph. . . .

We of this generation do not have to face a task such as that our fathers faced, but we have our tasks, and woe to us if we fail to perform them! We cannot, if we would, play the part of China, and be content to rot by inches in ignoble ease within our borders, taking no interest in what goes on beyond them; sunk in a scrambling commercialism; heedless of the higher life, the life of aspiration, of toil and risk; busying ourselves only with the wants of our bodies for the day; until suddenly we should find, beyond a shadow of question, what China has already found, that in this world the nation that has trained itself to a career of unwarlike and isolated ease is bound in the end to go down before other nations which have not lost the manly and adventurous qualities. If we are to be a really great people, we must strive in good faith to play a great part in the world. We cannot avoid meeting great issues. All that we can determine for ourselves is whether we shall meet them well or ill. Last year we could not help being brought face to face with the problem of war with Spain. All we could decide was whether we should shrink like cowards from the contest or enter into it as beseemed a brave and high-spirited people; and, once in, whether failure or success should crown our banners. So it is now. We cannot avoid the responsibilities that confront us in Hawaii, Cuba, Puerto Rico, and the Philippines. All we can decide is whether we shall meet them in a way that will redound to the national credit, or whether we shall make of our dealings with these new problems a dark and shameful page in our history. To refuse to deal with them at all merely amounts to dealing with them badly. We have a given problem to solve. If we undertake the solution there is, of course, always danger that we may not solve it aright, but to refuse to undertake the solution simply renders it certain that we cannot possibly solve it aright.

Theodore Roosevelt, *The Strenuous Life and Other Essays* (New York, The Century Company, 1900), 4–10.

The timid man, the lazy man, the man who distrusts his country, the over-civilized man, who has lost the great fighting, masterful virtues, the ignorant man and the man of dull mind, whose soul is incapable of feeling the mighty lift that thrills "stern men with empires in their brains"—all these, of course, shrink from seeing the nation undertake its new duties; shrink from seeing us build a navy and army adequate to our needs; shrink from seeing us do our share of the world's work by bringing order out of chaos in the great, fair tropic islands from which the valor of our soldiers and sailors has driven the Spanish flag. These are the men who fear the strenuous life, who fear the only national life which is really worth leading. . . .

. . . I have scant patience with those who fear to undertake the tasks of governing the Philippines, and who openly avow that they do fear to undertake it, or that they shrink from it because of the expense and trouble; but I have even scanter patience with those who make a pretense of humanitarianism to hide and cover their timidity, and who cant about "liberty" and the "consent of the governed," in order to excuse themselves for their unwillingness to play the part of men. Their doctrines, if carried out, would make it incumbent upon us to leave the Apaches of Arizona to work out their own salvation, and to decline to interfere in a single Indian reservation. Their doctrines condemn your forefathers and mine for ever having settled in these United States. . . .

I preach to you, then, my countrymen, that our country calls not for the life of ease, but for the life of strenuous endeavor. The twentieth century looms before us big with the fate of many nations. If we stand idly by, if we seek merely swollen, slothful ease, and ignoble peace, if we shrink from the hard contests where men must win at hazard of their lives and at the risk of all they hold dear, then the bolder and stronger peoples will pass us by and will win for themselves the domination of the world.

3. Filipino Leader Emilio Aguinaldo Rallies His People to Arms, 1899

By my proclamation of yesterday I have published the outbreak of hostilities between the Philippine forces and the American forces of occupation in Manila, unjustly and unexpectedly provoked by the latter.

In my manifest of January 8 [1899] last I published the grievances suffered by the Philippine forces at the hands of the army of occupation. The constant outrages and taunts, which have caused the misery of the people of Manila, and, finally the useless conferences and the contempt shown the Philippine government prove the premeditated transgression of justice and liberty.

I know that war has always produced great losses; I know that the Philippine people have not yet recovered from past losses and are not in the condition to endure others. But I also know by experience how bitter is slavery, and by experience I know that we should sacrifice all on the altar of our honor and of the national integrity so unjustly attacked.

Major-General E. S. Otis, *Report on Military Operations and Civil Affairs in the Philippine Islands, 1899* (Washington, D.C.: Government Printing Office, 1899), 95–96.

I have tried to avoid, as far as it has been possible for me to do so, armed conflict, in my endeavors to assure our independence by pacific means and to avoid more costly sacrifices. But all my efforts have been useless against the measureless pride of the American Government and of its representatives in these islands, who have treated me as a rebel because I defend the sacred interests of my country and do not make myself an instrument of their dastardly intentions. . . .

Be not discouraged. Our independence has been watered by the generous blood of our martyrs. Blood which may be shed in the future will strengthen it. Nature has never despised generous sacrifices.

4. The American Anti-Imperialist League Denounces U.S. Policy, 1899

We hold that the policy known as imperialism is hostile to liberty and tends toward militarism, an evil from which it has been our glory to be free. We regret that it has become necessary in the land of Washington and Lincoln to reaffirm that all men, of whatever race or color, are entitled to life, liberty and the pursuit of happiness. We maintain that governments derive their just powers from the consent of the governed. We insist that the subjugation of any people is "criminal aggression" and open disloyalty to the distinctive principles of our Government.

We earnestly condemn the policy of the present National Administration in the Philippines. It seeks to extinguish the spirit of 1776 in those islands. We deplore the sacrifice of our soldiers and sailors, whose bravery deserves admiration even in an unjust war. We denounce the slaughter of the Filipinos as a needless horror. We protest against the extension of American sovereignty by Spanish methods.

We demand the immediate cessation of the war against liberty, begun by Spain and continued by us. We urge that Congress be promptly convened to announce to the Filipinos our purpose to concede to them the independence for which they have so long fought and which of right is theirs.

The United States have always protested against the doctrine of international law which permits the subjugation of the weak by the strong. A self-governing state cannot accept sovereignty over an unwilling people. The United States cannot act upon the ancient heresy that might makes right.

Imperialists assume that with the destruction of self-government in the Philippines by American hands, all opposition here will cease. This is a grievous error. Much as we abhor the war of "criminal aggression" in the Philippines, greatly as we regret that the blood of the Filipinos is on American hands, we more deeply resent the betrayal of American institutions at home. The real firing line is not in the suburbs of Manila. The foe is of our own household. The attempt of 1861 was to divide the country. That of 1899 is to destroy its fundamental principles and noblest ideals. . . .

We hold, with Abraham Lincoln, that "no man is good enough to govern another man without the other's consent. When the white man governs himself, that is self-government, but when he governs himself and also governs another man, that is more than self-government—that is despotism. Our reliance is in the love of

Frederic Bancroft, ed., *Speeches, Correspondence, and Political Papers of Carl Schurz* (New York: G. P. Putnam's Sons, 1913), VI, 77–79.

liberty which God has planted in us. Our defense is in the spirit which prizes liberty as the heritage of all men in all lands. Those who deny freedom to others deserve it not for themselves, and under a just God cannot long retain it."

We cordially invite the cooperation of all men and women who remain loyal to the Declaration of Independence and the Constitution of the United States.

5. Mark Twain Satirizes "The Battle Hymn of the Republic," 1900

Mine eyes have seen the orgy of the launching of the Sword;
He is searching out the hoardings where the stranger's wealth is stored;
He hath loosed his fateful lightnings, and with woe and death has scored;
　His lust is marching on.

I have seen him in the watch-fires of a hundred circling camps,
They have builded him an altar in the Eastern dews and damps;
I have read his doomful mission by the dim and flaring lamps—
　His night is marching on.

I have read his bandit gospel writ in burnished rows of steel:
"As ye deal with my pretensions, so with you my wrath shall deal;
Let the faithless son of Freedom crush the patriot with his heel;
　Lo, Greed is marching on!"

We have legalized the strumpet and are guarding her retreat;
Greed is seeking out commercial souls before his judgment seat;
O, be swift, ye clods, to answer him! be jubilant my feet!
　Our god is marching on!

In a sordid slime harmonious, Greed was born in yonder ditch,
With a longing in his bosom—and for others' goods an itch—
As Christ died to make men holy, let men die to make us rich—
　Our god is marching on.

6. A Soldier Criticizes American Racism in the Philippines, 1902

Of late by reason of the conduct of the troops such as the extensive burning of the barrios in trying to lay waste the country so that the insurgents cannot occupy it, the torturing of natives by so-called water-cure and other methods to obtain information, the harsh treatment of natives generally, and the failure of inexperienced, lately-appointed lieutenants commanding posts to distinguish between those who are friendly and those unfriendly and to treat every native as if he were, whether or

Frederick Anderson, ed., *A Pen Warmed Up in Hell: Mark Twain in Protest* (New York: Harper & Row, 1972).

B. D. Flower, "Some Dead Sea Fruit of Our War Subjugation," *The Arena,* Vol. 27 (1902), 648–649.

no, an *insurrecto* at heart, . . . and a deep hatred toward us engendered. If these things need be done, they had best be done by native troops, so that the people of the United States will not be credited therewith.

Almost without exception, soldiers and also many officers refer to natives in their presence as "Niggers," and natives are beginning to understand what the word "Nigger" means. The course now being pursued in this province and in the provinces of Batangas, Laguna, and Samar is in my opinion sowing the seeds for a perpetual revolution against us hereafter whenever a good opportunity offers. Under present conditions the political situation in this province is slowly retrograding, the American sentiment is decreasing, and we are daily making permanent enemies. In the course above referred to, troops make no distinction often between the property of those natives who are insurgent or insurgent sympathizers, and the property of those who heretofore have risked their lives by being loyal to the United States and giving us information against their countrymen in arms. Often every house in a barrio is burned. In my opinion the small number of irreconcilable insurgents still in arms, although admittedly difficult to catch, does not justify the means employed, and especially when taking into consideration the suffering that must be undergone by the innocent and its effects upon the relations with these people hereafter.

7. The Roosevelt Corollary Makes the United States the Police of Latin America, 1904

It is not true that the United States feels any land hunger or entertains any projects as regards the other nations of the Western Hemisphere save such as are for their welfare. All that this country desires is to see the neighboring countries stable, orderly, and prosperous. Any country whose people conduct themselves well can count upon our hearty friendship. If a nation shows that it knows how to act with reasonable efficiency and decency in social and political matters, if it keeps order and pays its obligations, it need fear no interference from the United States. Chronic wrongdoing, or an impotence which results in a general loosening of the ties of civilized society, may in America, as elsewhere, ultimately require intervention by some civilized nation, and in the Western Hemisphere the adherence of the United States to the Monroe Doctrine may force the United States, however reluctantly, in flagrant cases of such wrongdoing or impotence, to the exercise of an international police power. If every country washed by the Caribbean Sea would show the progress in stable and just civilization which with the aid of the Platt amendment Cuba has shown since our troops left the island, and which so many of the republics in both Americas are constantly and brilliantly showing, all question of interference by this Nation with their affairs would be at an end. Our interests and those of our southern neighbors are in reality identical. They have great natural riches, and if within their borders the reign of law and justice obtains, prosperity is sure to come to them. While they thus obey the primary laws of civilized society they may rest assured that they will be treated by us in a spirit of cordial and helpful sympathy. We would interfere with them only in the last resort, and then only if it became evident that their inability or unwillingness

Congressional Record, XXXIX (December 6, 1904), Part I, 19.

to do justice at home and abroad had violated the rights of the United States or had invited foreign aggression to the detriment of the entire body of American nations. It is a mere truism to say that every nation, whether in America or anywhere else, which desires to maintain its freedom, its independence, must ultimately realize that the right of such independence cannot be separated from the responsibility of making good use of it.

8. President Woodrow Wilson Disavows Territorial Conquest, 1913

The future, ladies and gentlemen, is going to be very different for this hemisphere from the past. These States lying to the south of us, which have always been our neighbors, will now be drawn closer to us by innumerable ties, and I hope, chief of all, by the tie of a common understanding of each other. Interest does not tie nations together; it sometimes separates them. But sympathy and understanding does unite them, and I believe that by the new route that is just about to be opened, while we physically cut two continents asunder, we spiritually unite them. It is a spiritual union which we seek. . . .

There is one peculiarity about the history of the Latin American States which I am sure they are keenly aware of. You hear of "concessions" to foreign capitalists in Latin America. You do not hear of concessions to foreign capitalists in the United States. They are not granted concessions. They are invited to make investments. The work is ours, though they are welcome to invest in it. We do not ask them to supply the capital and do the work. It is an invitation, not a privilege; and States that are obliged, because their territory does not lie within the main field of modern enterprise and action, to grant concessions are in this condition—that foreign interests are apt to dominate their domestic affairs, a condition of affairs always dangerous and apt to become intolerable. What these States are going to see, therefore, is an emancipation from the subordination, which has been inevitable, to foreign enterprise. . . .

We must prove ourselves their friends and champions upon terms of equality and honor. You cannot be friends upon any other terms than upon the terms of equality. You cannot be friends at all except upon the terms of honor. We must show ourselves friends by comprehending their interest, whether it squares with our own interest or not. It is a very perilous thing to determine the foreign policy of a nation in the terms of material interest. It not only is unfair to those with whom you are dealing, but it is degrading as regards your own actions.

Comprehension must be the soil in which shall grow all the fruits of friendship, and there is a reason and a compulsion lying behind all this which is dearer than anything else to the thoughtful men of America. I mean the development of constitutional liberty in the world. Human rights, national integrity, and opportunity as against material interests—that, ladies and gentlemen, is the issue which we now have to face. I want to take this occasion to say that the United States will never again seek one additional foot of territory by conquest. She will devote herself to showing that

This document can be found in Thomas G. Paterson, *Major Problems in American Foreign Policy,* Vol. 1, 3d ed. (Boston: Houghton Mifflin, 1989), pp. 504–506.

she knows how to make honorable and fruitful use of the territory she has, and she must regard it as one of the duties of friendship to see that from no quarter are material interests made superior to human liberty and national opportunity. I say this, not with a single thought that anyone will gainsay it, but merely to fix in our consciousness what our real relationship with the rest of America is. It is the relationship of a family of mankind devoted to the development of true constitutional liberty.

☞ E S S A Y S

Historians have proposed many explanations for why the United States embarked on a war that spread far from its shores after having so long avoided what were called "foreign entanglements." Scholars have argued variously that it was for economic gain, that it grew out of concern for the Cuban people, that "yellow" journalists created a war hysteria to sell newspapers, and even that the war happened by accident. At base, most authors are troubled by a fundamental question: did the United States intend to exploit weaker nations by creating an empire, or did it intend to "spread the American dream"? These essays show two competing explanations: one that emphasizes an intentional will to dominance, and another that suggests a more complex blending of idealism and self-interest. Gail Bederman of Notre Dame University argues that Theodore Roosevelt, a leading proponent of the wars against Spain and the Philippines, was powerfully influenced by images of race and gender. These cultural concepts led him to see imperialism as the next stage in the healthy growth of the republic. As you read Bederman, think about how ideas of gender and race may influence the decisions of leaders. Anders Stephanson of Columbia University places the story in the context of global events. American leaders faced a world in which Japan and the European great powers were amassing new colonies at breakneck speed. They feared that the nation might soon be eclipsed. Influenced by this geopolitical reality, policy leaders broke with the tradition of nonentanglement to safeguard another tradition they considered even more important: "manifest destiny." America could no longer afford the luxury of isolation, they believed. It had a simple choice: act or be acted upon. To individuals like Theodore Roosevelt, advancing the United States meant advancing the democratic vision.

Gendering Imperialism: Theodore Roosevelt's Quest for Manhood and Empire

GAIL BEDERMAN

In 1882, a newly elected young state assemblyman arrived in Albany. Theodore Roosevelt, assuming his first elective office, was brimming with self-importance and ambition. He was only twenty-three—the youngest man in the legislature—and he looked forward to a promising career of wielding real political power. Yet Roosevelt was chagrined to discover that despite his intelligence, competence, and real legislative successes, no one took him seriously. The more strenuously he labored to play "a man's part" in politics, the more his opponents derided his manhood.

Gail Bederman, *Manliness and Civilization: A Cultural History of Gender and Race in the U.S., 1880–1917.* © 1995 University of Chicago Press. Reprinted by permission of the University of Chicago Press.

Daily newspapers lampooned Roosevelt as the quintessence of effeminacy. They nicknamed him "weakling," "Jane-Dandy," "Punkin-Lily," and "the exquisite Mr. Roosevelt." They ridiculed his high voice, tight pants, and fancy clothing. Several began referring to him by the name of the well-known homosexual Oscar Wilde, and one actually alleged (in a less-than-veiled phallic allusion) that Roosevelt was "given to sucking the knob of an ivory cane." While TR might consider himself a manly man, it was becoming humiliatingly clear that others considered him effeminate.

Above all other things, Roosevelt desired power. An intuitive master of public relations, he knew that his effeminate image could destroy any chances for his political future. Nearly forty years before women got the vote, electoral politics was part of a male-only subculture, fraught with symbols of manhood. Besides, Roosevelt, who considered himself a man's man, detested having his virility impugned. Although normally restrained, when he discovered a Tammany legislator plotting to toss him in a blanket, TR marched up to him and swore, "By God! if you try anything like that, I'll kick you, I'll bite you, I'll kick you in the balls, I'll do anything to you—you'd better leave me alone!" Clearly, the effeminate "dude" image would have to go.

And go it did. Roosevelt soon came to embody powerful American manhood. Within five years, he was running for mayor of New York as the "Cowboy of the Dakotas" [in reference to his taking up residence on a South Dakota ranch in 1884]. Instead of ridiculing him as "Oscar Wilde," newspapers were praising his virile zest for fighting and his "blizzard-seasoned constitution." In 1898, after a brief but highly publicized stint as leader of a regiment of volunteers in the Spanish American War, he became known as Colonel Roosevelt, the manly advocate of a virile imperialism. Never again would Roosevelt's name be linked to effeminacy. Even today, historians invoke Roosevelt as the quintessential symbol of turn-of-the-century masculinity.

Roosevelt's great success in masculinizing his image was due, in large part, to his masterful use of the discourse of civilization. As a mature politician, he would build his claim to political power on his claim to manhood. Skillfully, Roosevelt constructed a virile political person for himself as a strong but civilized white man.

Yet Roosevelt's use of the discourse of civilization went beyond mere public relations: Roosevelt drew on "civilization" to help formulate his larger politics as an advocate of both nationalism and imperialism. As he saw it, the United States was engaged in a millennial drama of manly racial advancement, in which American men enacted their superior manhood by asserting imperialistic control over races of inferior manhood. To prove their virility, as a race and a nation, American men needed to take up the "strenuous life" and strive to advance civilization— through imperialistic warfare and racial violence if necessary. . . .

. . . Beginning in 1894, unhappy with President Cleveland's reluctance to annex Hawaii, Roosevelt began to exhort the American race to embrace a manly, strenuous imperialism, in the cause of higher civilization. In Roosevelt's imperialistic pronouncements, as in *The Winning of the West* [a celebratory history of European American westward expansion published between 1889 and 1896], issues of racial dominance were inextricably conflated with issues of manhood. Indeed, when Roosevelt originally coined the term "the strenuous life," in an 1899 speech, he was explicitly discussing only foreign relations: calling on the United States to build up its army and to take imperialistic control of Cuba, Puerto Rico, and the Philippines. Ostensibly, the speech never mentions gender at all. Yet the phrase "the strenuous life" soon began to connote a virile, hard-driving manhood, which might or might not involve foreign relations, at all.

How did the title of an essay calling for American imperialism become a catch-phrase to describe vigorous masculinity? To answer this question, we need to understand the logic behind Roosevelt's philosophies about American nationalism and imperialism. For Roosevelt, the purpose of American expansionism and national greatness was always the millennial purpose behind human evolution—human racial advancement toward a higher civilization. And the race that could best achieve this perfected civilization was, by definition, the one with the most superior manhood.

It was not coincidental that Roosevelt's advocacy of manly imperialism in the 1890s was contemporaneous with a widespread cultural concern about effeminacy, overcivilization, and racial decadence. . . . [T]hroughout Europe and Anglo-America intellectuals were worried about the emasculating tendencies of excessive civilization. Roosevelt shared many of his contemporaries' fears about the future of American manly power; and this gave his imperialistic writings an air of especial urgency. . . .

. . . Roosevelt understood decadence in terms of the racial conflict through which he believed civilizations rose and fell. As he had shown in *The Winning of the West,* TR believed that manly racial competition determined which race was superior and deserved to control the earth's resources. A race which grew decadent, then, was a race which had lost the masculine strength necessary to prevail in this Darwinistic racial struggle. Civilized advancement required much more than mere masculine strength, of course; it also required advanced manliness. Intelligence, altruism, and morality were essential traits, possessed by all civilized races and men. Yet, as important as these refined traits were, they were not enough, by themselves, to safeguard civilization's advance and prevent racial decadence. Without the "virile fighting virtues" which allowed a race to continue to expand into new territories, its more civilized racial traits would be useless. If American men lost their primal fighting virtues, a more manful race would strip them of their authority, land, and resources. This effeminate loss of racial primacy and virility was what Roosevelt meant by overcivilized racial decadence. . . .

This concept of overcivilized decadence let Roosevelt construct American imperialism as a conservative way to retain the race's frontier-forged manhood, instead of what it really was—a belligerent grab for a radically new type of nationalistic power. As Roosevelt described it, asserting the white man's racial power abroad was necessary to avoid losing the masculine strength Americans had already established through race war on the frontier. Currently the American race was one of the world's most advanced civilized races. They controlled a rich and mighty continent because their superior manhood had allowed them to annihilate the Indians on the Western frontier. If they retained their manhood, they could continue to look forward to an ever higher civilization, as they worked ever harder for racial improvement and expansion. But if American men ever lost their virile zest for Darwinistic racial contests, their civilization would soon decay. If they ignored the ongoing racial imperative of constant expansion and instead grew effeminate and luxury-loving, a manlier race would inherit their mantle of the highest civilization.

From 1894 until he became president in 1901, Roosevelt wrote and lectured widely on the importance of taking up what Rudyard Kipling, in 1899, would dub "the White Man's burden." Kipling coined this term in a poem written to exhort American men to conquer and rule the Philippines. "The white man" . . . simultaneously meant the white race, civilization itself, and white males as a group. In "The White Man's Burden," Kipling used the term in all these senses to urge white males to take up the racial burden of civilization's advancement. "Take up the White Man's burden," he wrote, capitalizing the essential term, and speaking to the manly civilized on behalf of civilization. "Send forth the best ye breed"—quality breeding was essential, because evolutionary development (breeding) was what gave "the White Man" the right and duty to conquer uncivilized races.

> Go bind your sons to exile
>   To serve your captives' need;
> To wait in heavy harness,
>   on fluttered folk and wild—
> Your new-caught, sullen peoples,
>   Half-devil and half-child. . . .

Roosevelt called Kipling's poem "poor poetry but good sense from the expansionist standpoint." Although Roosevelt did not use the term "the white man's burden" in his writings on imperialism, he drew on the same sorts of race and gender linkages which Kipling deployed in his poem. TR's speeches of this period frequently conflate manhood and racial power, and draw extended analogies between the individual American man and the virile American race.

For example, "National Duties," one of TR's most famous speeches, represents both American men and the American race as civilized entities with strong virile characters—in popular parlance, both were "the white man." Roosevelt begins by outlining this racial manhood, which he calls "the essential manliness of the American character." Part of this manliness centered around individual and racial duties to the home. On the one hand, individual men must work to provide for the domestic needs of themselves and their families. On the other hand, the men of the race must work to provide for their collective racial home, their nation. Men who shirked these manly homemaking duties were despicably unsexed; or, as TR put it, "the willfully idle man" was as bad as "the willfully barren woman."

Yet laboring only for his own hearth and nation was not enough to satisfy a real man. Virile manhood also required the manly American nation to take up imperialistic labors outside its borders, just as manhood demanded individual men to labor outside the home: "Exactly as each man, while doing first his duty to his wife and the children within his home, must yet, if he hopes to amount to much, strive mightily in the world outside his home, so our nation, while first of all seeing to its own domestic well-being, must not shrink from playing its part among the great nations without." It would be as unmanly for the American race to refuse its imperialist destiny as it would be for a cowardly man to spend all his time loafing at home with his wife. Imperialist control over primitive races thus becomes a matter of manhood—part of a male-only public sphere, which TR sets in contradistinction to the home.

After setting up imperialism as a manly duty for both man and race, Roosevelt outlines the imperialist's appropriate masculine behavior—or, should we say, his appropriate masculine appendage? Roosevelt immediately brings up the "big stick." It may be a cheap shot to stress the phallic implications of TR's imagery, yet Roosevelt himself explained the meaning of the "big stick" in terms of manhood and the proper way to assert the power of a man: "A good many of you are probably acquainted with the old proverb: 'Speak softly and carry a big stick—you will go far.' If a man continually blusters, if he lacks civility, a big stick will not save him from trouble; and neither will speaking softly avail, if back of the softness there does not lie strength, power." Just as a manly man avoided bluster, relying instead on his self-evident masculine strength and power, so virile American men should build a powerful navy and army, so that when they took up the white man's burden in primitive lands, they would receive the respect due to a masterful, manly race. . . .

Roosevelt was not content merely to make speeches about the need for violent, imperialistic manhood. He always needed to embody his philosophy. The sickly boy had remade himself into an adventure-book hunter-naturalist; the dude politician had remade himself into a heroic Western rancher. The 1898 outbreak of the Spanish-American war—for which he had agitated long and hard—let Roosevelt remake himself into Colonel Roosevelt, the fearless Rough Rider.

Reinventing himself as a charismatic war hero allowed Roosevelt to model the manful imperialism about which he had been writing for four years. TR became a walking advertisement for the imperialistic manhood he desired for the American race. Indeed, from the moment of his enlistment until his mustering out four months later, Roosevelt self-consciously publicized himself as a model of strenuous, imperialistic manhood. In late April 1898, against all advice, Roosevelt resigned as assistant secretary of the navy and enlisted to fight in the just-declared war on Spain. Aged thirty-nine, with an important subcabinet post, a sick wife, and six young children, no one but Roosevelt himself imagined he ought to see active service. Roosevelt's decision to enlist was avidly followed by newspapers all over the country. . . .

The press, fascinated by the undertaking, christened [his] regiment "Roosevelt's Rough Riders." Roosevelt's heroic frontiersman identity thus came full circle, as he no doubt intended. As Richard Slotkin has pointed out, the term "Rough Riders" had long been used in adventure novels to describe Western horsemen. Thus, by nicknaming his regiment the "Rough Riders," the nation showed it understood the historical connections Roosevelt always drew between Indian wars in the American West and virile imperialism in Cuba and the Philippines. . . .

After his mustering out, TR the politician continued to play the role of virile Rough Rider for all he was worth. In November, he was elected governor of New York, campaigning as a war hero and employing ex–Rough Riders to warm up the election crowds. By January 1899, his thrilling memoir, *The Rough Riders,* was appearing serially in *Scribner's Magazine.* And in 1900 his virile popularity convinced Republican party leaders that Roosevelt could counter [Democrat William Jennings] Bryan's populism better than any other vice-presidential candidate. Roosevelt had constructed himself and the Rough Riders as the epitome of civilized, imperialistic manhood, a model for the American race to follow. His success in modeling that imperialistic manhood exceeded even his own expectations and ultimately paved the way for his presidency.

On April 10, 1899, Colonel Roosevelt stood before the men of Chicago's elite, all-male, Hamilton Club and preached the doctrine of "The Strenuous Life." As governor of New York and a fabulously popular ex–Rough Rider, he knew the national press would be in attendance; and though he spoke *at* the Hamilton Club, he spoke *to* men across America. With the cooperation of the press and at the risk of his life, TR had made himself into a national hero—the embodiment of manly virtue, masculine violence, and white American racial supremacy—and the antithesis of over-civilized decadence. Now he urged the men of the American race to live the sort of life he had modeled for them: to be virile, vigorous, and manly, and to reject over-civilized decadence by supporting a strenuously imperialistic foreign policy. When contemporaries ultimately adopted his phrase "the strenuous life" as a synonym for the vigorous, vehement manhood Roosevelt modeled, they showed they correctly understood that his strenuous manhood was inextricably linked to his nationalism, imperialism, and racism.

Ostensibly, "The Strenuous Life" preached the virtues of military prepared-ness and imperialism, but contemporaries understood it as a speech about man-hood. The practical import of the speech was to urge the nation to build up its army, to maintain its strong navy, and to take control of Puerto Rico, Cuba, and the Philippines. But underlying these immediate objectives lay the message that Amer-ican manhood—both the manly race and individual white men—must retain the strength of their Indian-fighter ancestors, or another race would prove itself more manly and overtake America in the Darwinian struggle to be the world's most dominant race.

Roosevelt began by demanding manliness in both the American nation and American men. Slothful men who lacked the "desire and power" to strive in the world were despicable and unmanly. "We do not admire the man of timid peace. We admire the man who embodies victorious effort." If America and its men were not man enough to fight, they would not only lose their place among "the great nations of the world," they would become a decadent and effeminate race. Roosevelt held up the Chinese, whom he despised as the most decadent and unmanly of races, as a cautionary lesson: If we "play the part of China, and be content to rot by inches in ignoble ease within our borders," we will "go down before other nations which have not lost the manly and adventurous qualities." If American men lacked the manly fortitude to go bravely and willingly to a foreign war, the race would decay, preached TR, the virile war hero.

In stirring tones, the Rough Rider of San Juan Hill ridiculed the overcivilized anti-imperialists who had lost the "great fighting, masterful virtues." Lacking the masculine impulse toward racial aggression and unmoved by virile visions of empire, these men had been sapped of all manhood.

> The timid man, the lazy man, the man who distrusts his country, the over-civilized man, who has lost the great fighting, masterful virtues, the ignorant man, and the man of dull mind, whose soul is incapable of feeling the mighty lift that thrills stern men with empires in their brains—all these, of course shrink from seeing the nation undertake its new duties; shrink from seeing us build a navy and an army adequate to our needs; shrink from seeing us do our share of the world's work. These are the men who fear the strenuous life. . . . They believe in that cloistered life which saps the hardy virtues in a nation, as it saps them in the individual.

Like "cloistered" monkish celibates, these "over-civilized" men "shrink, shrink, shrink" from carrying the "big stick." Dishonorably, they refused to do their manly duty by the childish Filipinos. Had the United States followed these anti-imperialists' counsel and refused to undertake "one of the great tasks set modern civilization," Americans would have shown themselves not only unmanly but also racially inferior. "Some stronger, manlier power would have to step in and do the work, and we would have shown ourselves weaklings, unable to carry to successful completion the labors that great and high-spirited nations are eager to undertake." As TR saw it, the man, the race, and the nation were one in their need to possess virile, imperialist manhood.

Then TR got down to brass tacks, dwelling at length on Congress' responsibility to build up the armed forces. After again raising the specter of Chinese decadence, which American men faced if they refused to strengthen their army and navy, Roosevelt stressed America's duty to take up the white man's burden in Cuba, Puerto Rico, and the Philippines. If the American race was "too weak, too selfish, or too foolish" to take on that task, it would be completed by "some stronger and more manful race." He ridiculed anti-imperialists as cowards who "make a pretense of humanitarianism to hide and cover their timidity" and to "excuse themselves for their unwillingness to play the part of men."

"The Strenuous Life" culminates with a Darwinian vision of strife between races for the "dominion of the world," which only the most manful race could win.

> I preach to you then, my countrymen, that our country calls not for the life of ease but for the life of strenuous endeavor. . . . If we stand idly by . . . then the bolder and stronger peoples will pass us by, and will win for themselves the domination of the world. Let us therefore boldly face the life of strife, resolute to do our duty well and manfully.

American men must embrace their manly mission to be the race which dominates the world. Struggle for racial supremacy was inevitable, but the most manful race—the American race—would triumph, if it made the attempt. Its masculine strength was proven by military victories over barbarous brown races. Its manly virtue was evident in its civilized superiority to the primitive childish races it uplifted. White American men must claim their place as the world's most perfect men, the fittest race for the evolutionary struggle toward a perfect civilization. This was the meaning of "The Strenuous Life."

We can now answer the question, "How did the title of an essay calling for American dominance over the brown races become a catchphrase to describe virile masculinity?" Roosevelt's desire for imperial dominance had been, from the first, intrinsically related to his views about male power. As he saw it, the manhood of the American race had been forged in the crucible of frontier race war; and to abandon the virile power of that violence would be to backslide toward effeminate racial mediocrity. Roosevelt wanted American men to be the ultimate in human evolution, the world's most powerful and civilized race. He believed that their victory over the Indians on the frontier proved that the American race possessed the racial superiority and masculine power to overcome any savage race; and he saw a glorious future for the race in the twentieth century, as it pressed on toward international dominance and the perfection of civilization. The only danger which Roosevelt saw menacing this millennial triumph of manly American civilization came from within. Only by surrendering to overcivilized decadence—by embracing unmanly racial sloth instead of virile imperialism—could American men fail. Thus, American men must work strenuously to uphold their civilization. They must refuse a life of ease, embrace their manly task, and take up the white man's burden. Only by living that "strenuous life" could American men prove themselves to be what Roosevelt had no doubt they were—the apex of civilization, evolution's most favored race, masterful men fit to command the barbarous races and the world's "waste spaces"—in short, the most virile and manly of men.

In later years, as Americans came to take international involvement for granted and as imperialism came to seem less controversial, the phrase "the strenuous life" underwent a subtle change of meaning. Always associated with Roosevelt, it came to connote the virile manhood which he modeled for the nation as imperialistic Western hero and Rough Rider—the peculiar combination of moral manliness and aggressive masculinity which he was able to synthesize so well. As Roosevelt's presidency wore on, Americans grew accustomed to taking up the white man's burden, not only in the Philippines, but also in Cuba, Panama, and the Dominican Republic. The "strenuous life" came to be associated with any virile, manly effort to accomplish great work, whether imperialistic or not. Yet on a basic level, "the strenuous life" retained TR's original associations with the evolutionary struggle of the American race on behalf of civilization. "The strenuous life," as it came to be used, meant the opposite of "overcivilized effeminacy." Or, as Roosevelt summed it up himself in his *Autobiography,* the man who lives the strenuous life regards his life "as a pawn to be promptly hazarded whenever the hazard is warranted by the larger interests of the great game in which we are all engaged." That great game, for Roosevelt, was always the millennial struggle for Americans to perfect civilization by becoming the most manly, civilized, and powerful race in the world.

Global Competition and Manifest Destiny on the Cusp of the Twentieth Century

ANDERS STEPHANSON

Between 1875 and 1914, one quarter of the world was claimed as colonies. Britain alone added 4 million square miles. European empires had of course existed for a long time, but only after 1870 was there a sustained attempt to turn the rapidly accumulating colonial possessions into a formal system. It was then, for example, that Queen Victoria officially added the title of Empress. In the imperialist "scramble for Africa," as the expression went, and in similar rivalries elsewhere, expectations of economic advantage played a significant role. Much less by way of profitable commerce and extraction of raw materials actually issued in the real world than expected; but once the race for territory had begun it took on strategic considerations. It became part of a globalized game among Great Powers. The United States, though an economic powerhouse, was in this respect still outside the range of serious players. The "civilized world," in sum, was developing into a configuration of national and potentially nationalist entities with colonial appendages and protectionist economies. Unlike, for example, the transnational aristocracy of earlier Europe, classes thus became increasingly rooted in the purely domestic sphere and its colonial extension.

Anders Stephanson, excerpts from "Blessings of Civilization, 1865–1914" from *Manifest Destiny: American Expansion and the Empire of the Right* (New York: Hill and Wang, 1995), pp. 72–78, 105–106. Copyright © 1995 by Anders Stephanson. Reprinted by permission of Hill and Wang, a division of Farrar, Straus and Giroux, LLC.

They confronted each other as nation-state against nation-state, empire against empire, alliance against alliance.

The effects were several. *Ideologically,* two convictions followed. First and most generally, "the West" was seen as obviously superior in every way because, equally obviously, it ruled the world; and it was justified in ruling the world because it was superior. New theories of evolution and race offered scientific confirmation of this circular idea. Second, war was understood by dominant circles to be rational policy. For war would either be short and decisive (witness Bismarck's successes in the 1860s and '70s); or, because massive armaments and civilized solidarity within the West made hostilities unthinkable there, it would be used *only against the barbaric outside,* by definition a zone of anarchy legitimately subject to forceful imposition of rational order as a step toward civilization. *Politically,* the uneven, gradual inclusion of wider segments of the populations into the established order reinforced the old privacy and secrecy that had always typified geopolitics in the European stale system. This seems odd at first, but the domestic nature of the popularization process actually served to keep foreign policy from public view, except in moments of crisis, Jingoism and superficial engagement, predicated on the advent of mass literacy and mass newspapers, could then easily be whipped up, to the point of overtaking events. War in the popular mind became what William James derogatorily but rightly called an "exciting kind of *sport.*"

Mass participation in politics had occurred in the United States long before this period; and, as noted, there was nothing much in postbellum times to keep from view in the first place. But James Polk and the Mexican War had shown how the Executive might use the conduct of foreign relations for its own purposes when the circumstances were right. The effects could be absurd. In 1889, for example, the United States almost ended up in war with Germany because of a conflict over tiny Samoa in the Pacific, a conflict that Secretary of State James Blaine was able to carry on largely at his leisure. In 1895, Grover Cleveland and his Secretary of State, Richard Olney, provided further evidence of manipulative power when they picked a quarrel with Great Britain over an essentially trivial question regarding the boundary between Venezuela and British Guiana. They informed London, much to popular acclaim, that the United States had the right to decide the issue because it was, to use Olney's formulation, "practically sovereign on this continent." That indelicate and erroneous formulation, a loose interpretation of the Monroe Doctrine, rubbed the British very much the wrong way. Cleveland and Olney themselves, meanwhile, were thoroughly unsettled by the instant success of their public excursion into power politics. A compromise saving face all around was worked out, ultimately possible because of the quiet but long-standing British policy of appeasement toward the United States: more important things were at stake outside the Americas. Three years later, indeed, the popular spirit was suddenly vociferously pro-British, as London had made a considerable effort of support during the Spanish-American War. To that crucial moment of expansionism we may now turn.

(3)

In 1893, the United States had been hit by the most severe economic depression it had ever experienced. Because of underlying deflationary tendencies going back to the 1870s, the widespread political discontent arising from the crisis came to center inordinately on currency questions, particularly on the monetarization of silver. Forces led by William Jennings Bryan committed the Democratic Party to this position, but in 1896, in the first crucial election since 1860, he lost to William McKinley, a less-than-spectacular machine politician from Ohio, or so it seemed. The election initiated a period of Republican hegemony in national politics that would last till the election of Franklin D. Roosevelt in 1932, the Wilsonian interlude having been made possible only through the Republican split in 1912.

Throughout but also beyond the depression, worries that the system would not be able to cope spread beyond the mugwumps into the mainstream. The dislocations were indeed massive: pressures of urbanization, immigration from new and unrecognizable places in southeastern Europe (20 million immigrants arrived between 1870 and 1910), labor and farmer unrest, populist and socialist agitation, giant corporations and trusts, and other swiftly emerging, unfamiliar phenomena. The cherished frontier had already been consigned to the past by the census of 1890. What remained, and powerfully so, was Frederick Jackson Turner's famous thesis, articulated in 1893, that the frontier had shaped the very essence of the (inheritable) American character. But Turner's argument merely underlined in the popular mind that the United States was no longer a society of sturdy pioneers. If American identity was indeed the process of pioneering the frontier and the latter had ceased to exist, what sort of new form might that identity then assume? Small wonder that the preeminent literary genre from the late 1880s to the turn of the century was utopian fiction, featuring a paradoxical desire to change the American present fundamentally in order to make it into something once again stable and unchanging, or at any rate into what was believed to have been something stable and unchanging.

In this general climate, expansionism returned to the political agenda, with a vengeance. It had made an early, pre-depression appearance in 1892–93 when American sugar interests in Hawaii had engineered independence, followed in time-honored fashion by calls for American annexation. But Grover Cleveland, the incoming Democratic President, had blocked it. In 1898, by contrast, the annexation of Hawaii sailed through Congress easily because of the war with Spain. It was through that war, then, that elements of similarity with the Western "model" came strongly to the fore: executive secrecy and manipulation against a backdrop of intense but momentary interest among a largely uninformed public; an imperial move to colonize overseas territories; a splashing entry, apparently, into the world of Great Powers. Thus, in 1898, the United States seized Cuba, Puerto Rico, Guam, Wake Island, and Manila in the Philippines; the following year, a bloody colonial war of subjugation began in the Philippines that would last until 1902. Washington also declared the "Open Door" policy with regard to China and followed it up by sending marines to Beijing to quell the so-called Boxer Rebellion. The coda of this extraordinary reorientation occurred in 1903 when Theodore Roosevelt assisted Panamanian separatists to break away from Colombia in exchange for American rights to extraterritoriality. The isthmian canal could finally be built.

The complexities of these events are beyond my scope; but an account of the Spanish-American War and its immediate aftermath is useful. The origins of this war lay in the revival in 1895 of the Cuban rebellion against the oppressive Spanish colonial authority. A coalition for national liberation, spanning the whole range of indigenous classes, was formed. The Spanish regime, on its part, decided to launch a last, all-out effort to preserve its rule over this remaining, profitable colony. The brutalities of the ferocious conflict turned it into an American issue in the highly charged political climate of that moment. Press lords William Randolph Hearst and Joseph Pulitzer, locked in a circulation war, made Cuba a feature story through continuous, graphic accounts of Spanish cruelty. Expressions of solidarity, moreover, from the oppositional silver forces resulted in demands for, at minimum, American recognition of rebel belligerency. Cleveland, a conservative gold Democrat, had no interest in pursuing the issue, maintaining instead a policy of neutrality that served in fact to support the Spanish. Business interests in general also opposed any potentially disturbing action.

Nothing was known about McKinley's views on the matter when he came into the White House. Insofar as he had any, he refused to divulge them. Unlike Cleveland, he proved selectively favorable to annexationism. Surprisingly little has been learned about his thinking since. He left few documentary traces and stuck to his own counsels. He was known (wrongly) by his opponents as a mere tool of Republican boss rule and (rightly) for his quasi-religious attachment to protectionism. Outwardly he continued Cleveland's line, but privately, during the summer of 1897, he peremptorily informed the Spanish government that the imbroglio was having a detrimental effect on the American recovery. In fact, he was open to purchasing or annexing the island. Spain, under a new, more liberal regime in the fall, responded to the crisis with various autonomy solutions. These met with no success. In early 1898, McKinley sent the battleship *Maine* to Havana to protect American interests, a mostly symbolic move that ended in the notorious, fatal explosion (most likely an accident). War eventually ensued after the President, cautious as always, had procrastinated and left it up to Congress to make the final decision. Conservative opinion on the eastern seaboard, accused of crass and heartless materialism, finally swung around to supporting war.

War, in fact, was probably unnecessary since the Spanish government had informed McKinley of its desire to settle preponderantly on his terms; but this he kept largely to himself. It was, in any case, an immensely popular war because it was experienced as a humanitarian effort, and it turned out to be short. Splendid it was not, on the other hand, at least not for the amateurish army, most of which never made it out of the country. Among those left behind were William Jennings Bryan and his Nebraska Guard. The excitable Teddy Roosevelt, however, was able to bully his way onto a ship with his Rough Riders. The navy did well. In accordance with existing contingency plans but to the great surprise of the public, the Pacific Squadron made the initial, decisive attack on the Spanish fleet in the Philippines.

When Spain capitulated in July 1898, however, the United States was physically in control only of the southeastern section of Cuba, a beachhead in Puerto Rico, and the environs of Manila. This crucial fact was ignored in the peace negotiations with Spain later in the fall. McKinley, having tested the waters thoroughly, had decided by then to opt for annexation. Hawaii had already been accepted as a territory of the Union during the summer. In the case of Cuba, McKinley's hands were tied by the Teller Amendment, attached by Congress to the war authorization in order to make clear that there was no "intention to exercise sovereignty, jurisdiction, or control, except for the pacification" of the island. Since then, it had been discovered that the

Cuban rebels were a lot blacker (meaning less "civilized") than anticipated and thus in need of extensive tutelage. "Pacification" nevertheless went relatively smoothly because, with Spain out of the way, the internal contradictions of the Cuban anti-colonials could be exploited. Thus, in 1901, the island became nominally independent under U.S. protection, conceding a naval base (Guantanamo) in perpetuity and American rights to intervene whenever order was deemed under threat. Five years later the marines were indeed back; and Cuba was well on its way to becoming an American sugar plantation. As for Puerto Rico, there was no Teller Amendment and no one made much noise when it was appropriated. Its population, generally pro-Spanish, had no means of resisting. It was transformed into a protectorate, legally modeled after the British crown colony of Hong Kong. A century later, a protectorate it largely remains.

Annexing and pacifying the Philippines was an altogether different kettle of fish: seven thousand miles away, a myriad of islands, peoples, and languages, and, most dauntingly, an indigenous nationalist movement under arms with no intention of letting the United States assume a sovereignty it did not physically possess. Domestic opposition in the United States, not surprisingly, was also at its strongest against imperial rule here. The peace treaty was ratified by the Senate in February 1899 with a margin of one vote. At the same time, there began a war of subjugation that would, directly or indirectly, cause the death of some 200,000 Filipinos and involve, throughout the three years it lasted, no less than 127,000 U.S. soldiers, led by officers with suitable experience of Indian warfare at home. The final, victorious campaign against the nationalists was headed by General Arthur MacArthur, who thus initiated what would be a long family presence in the islands. Lacking any class of colonial administrators, however, the United States had to rely on indigenous forces to run the place, thus creating not only a "nationalized" client class but also, ironically, the basis for the future Philippine nation as such. In the 1930s Congress decided that the islands would become independent fifteen years thereafter, chiefly because domestic economic interests were clamoring for protection against Philippine imports. . . .

In condensing the oppositional [anti-imperialist, anti-expansionist] view, I have made it more cohesive than it really was. Throughout one tended to come up against a basic contradiction, on which indeed the expansionists came down gleefully again and again: the United States had always been about subjugation and displacement, thus demonstrating, as Henry Cabot Lodge proudly declared, "a record of conquest, colonization, and territorial expansion unequalled by any people in the nineteenth century." If no more territory could be taken because it was contrary to essential American principles, one might as well give New Mexico back to the Apaches. Against this forceful point, the contiguity argument seemed quite lame.

(8)

The Apache example came from Theodore Roosevelt, and the moment has now come to return to this extraordinary figure, whom fortuitous (and tragic) circumstances put into the White House in 1901. His ascendancy had not appeared likely. When he became governor of New York after the highly visible heroics on San Juan Hill, Godkin said of him superciliously, if not inaccurately, that he would have made a good pal of Richard the Lion-hearted, for his outlook was "essentially a boy's view." Less accurately, Godkin went on to predict that if this view were ever turned into "national policy" the result "would make us the most turbulent people the world has ever seen." But, Godkin was happy to observe, only Roosevelt himself took his histrionics of war seriously.

There was indeed a good deal of Rooseveltian blustering about the need to become a great virile power. "We cannot, if we would, play the part of China, and be content to rot by inches in ignoble ease within our borders, taking no interest in what goes on beyond them, sunk in a scrambling commercialism; heedless of the higher life, the life of aspiration, of toil and risk," to quote a typical passage from 1899. Destiny he interpreted, very much in character, in voluntaristic terms. One had the choice of determining it with one's own hands, so to speak; it was up to each to show the will, desire, and decisiveness to act in accordance with one's historical duty. And that duty, in the American case, was not to be Great.

In office, Roosevelt actually performed on the whole with consummate skill and prudence in the foreign arena. He knew more about it and had greater intuitive feel for it than any U.S. President since John Quincy Adams. Unlike Woodrow Wilson, he was a superb tactician, with a nuanced grasp of threats, force, appearances, dissimulation, retreat, the whole technology of power politics. Yet Roosevelt's presidency was in fact marked by the growing domestic agenda of Progressivism and his moves to establish the Executive domestically as a relatively autonomous, policy-making institution. His geopolitical maneuvers, often out of sight of the public, were made with keen appreciation of how limited was the American willingness to enter into the high-stakes game of global politics, a game in which he himself took the greatest interest. Within a determinate range of geopolitics, he enjoyed complete privacy and freedom of action; but the range itself was not wide. The United States was now perceived by others as a Great Power, however, and Roosevelt consciously played his role when he could as though he were heading one. I bring him in here because of his articulate intelligence on the matter and the endlessly fascinating (and often-made) contrast with Woodrow Wilson, the exploration of which reveals something about the destiny of destinarian thinking after 1900.

Roosevelt's strategic approach has usefully been characterized as domination in the Caribbean, balance of power in the Far East, and nonentanglement in Europe, coupled with adjudication in Great Power conflicts when possible for the purpose of promoting civilized peace. The particulars of this are not my concern here; the interest lies in his long-term project of civilization and geopolitics, the place of the United States within it, and how it all changed. Let us begin with his historical understanding of time and space.

History appeared to Roosevelt as a linear movement from barbarism to civilization but through an intermediate or transitional stage of despotism. We recognize this view as essentially Spencer's, but Roosevelt used it spatially to divide the real world of 1900 in two: a sphere of civilization (Christian, Western civilization, the Anglophone version being the cutting edge) against a sphere of barbarism and despotism, civilization of course gradually expanding. Empire as civilized domination showed the historical necessity of establishing order by means of force in the unruly sphere and thus allowing "waste spaces" to be used in the interest of humanity. American history, in a way, was the story of just such a process. A certain amount of cruelty and brutality necessarily adhered to the endeavor, and it was useless, therefore, to moralize about that past. The result was in any case for the best. Putting down the Philippine "insurrection" was thus the equivalent of putting down the Seminoles in Jackson's days. One must, Roosevelt advised the Secretary of State in 1899, "harass and smash the insurgents in every way until they are literally beaten into peace."

FURTHER READING

César Ayala, *American Sugar Kingdom: The Plantation Economy of the Spanish Caribbean, 1898–1934* (1999).

H. W. Brands, *Bound to Empire: The United Sates and the Philippines* (1992).

Matthew Jacobson, *Barbarian Virtues: The United States Encounters Foreign Peoples at Home and Abroad, 1877–1900* (2000).

H. Paul Jeffers, *Colonel Roosevelt: Theodore Roosevelt Goes to War* (1996).

Stanley Karnow, *In Our Image: America's Empire in the Philippines* (1989).

Glenn May, *Social Engineering in the Philippines: The Aims, Execution, and Impact of American Colonial Policy* (1980).

Louis Perez, Jr., *On Becoming Cuban: Identity, Nationality, and Culture* (1999).

David Pletcher, *The Diplomacy of Trade and Investment: American Economic Expansion in the Hemisphere* (1998).

Robert Rydell, *All the World's a Fair: Visions of Empire at American International Expositions, 1876–1916* (1984).

Lars Schoultz, *Beneath the United States: A History of U.S. Policy Towards Latin America* (1999).

Edward Van Zile Scott, *The Unwept: Black American Soldiers and the Spanish-American War* (1996).

William Appleman Williams, *The Tragedy of American Diplomacy* (1959).

CHAPTER
5

The Progressive Movement

From the turn of the century up to the 1920s, Americans of all backgrounds wrestled with the notion of "progress." Giant cities peopled by impoverished immigrants, new technologies of mass production, political machines controlled by party bosses, and the spectacular concentration of wealth in the hands of the few left many people wondering, "Is this progress?" The nation had more money and technology, but it seemed to have more corruption, disease, and poverty as well.

A wide spectrum of middle- and upper-class activists throughout the nation called themselves Progressives. They sought to strengthen the moral fiber of American society and ameliorate the problems of modern life. They fought successfully for reforms such as woman suffrage, the prohibition of alcohol, antitrust legislation, laws curtailing child labor, the creation of a national income tax, conservation of natural resources, and the popular election of senators. But theirs was not the only definition of progress. Immigrants, politicians, businessmen, and experts in law, economics, engineering, and such newly invented fields as social work contended over what constituted progress, and on whose terms it would take place. African Americans, meanwhile, saw the progress contained in the Fourteenth and Fifteenth Amendments undermined by federal law and local practice. In the 1890s, white mobs on average lynched more than one hundred blacks every year. In 1896, in Plessy v. Ferguson, *the Supreme Court legalized segregation by race. Left to work out their own solutions, African American leaders also debated the meaning of progress and the methods of obtaining it.*

Progressive reformers particularly prized efficient planning to promote the "public good," but they often failed to see that what was good for one public might be bad for another. Cleaning up city politics made sense to political reformers, who hated to see party bosses buying votes. To immigrants, cleaning up city government meant losing those politicians who might look out for their specific interests. Regulating business helped consumers (as in the Pure Food and Drug Act), but it also gave big corporations an edge over less efficient small companies. Banning alcohol seemed an urgent moral reform to nondrinkers; banning cigarettes seemed an urgent moral reform to nonsmokers. Immigrants and the working class tended to favor both indulgences. Progressives in America looked abroad to other industrializing societies for ideas on how to solve the problems of modern life, but they also wrestled with some unique dilemmas, such as how to create a single nation out of the multi-lingual peoples suddenly inhabiting the land. They also struggled with how much power to give the state, considering America's particular tradition of hostility to centralized government.

Progressives attacked problems at the local level first. Both Woodrow Wilson and Theodore Roosevelt were reformist governors before they became president. Even before Congress passed Prohibition, nineteen states had banned alcohol. Sixteen states had outlawed cigarettes and passed the vote for women.

What followed was the greatest spate of Constitution-rewriting since the adoption of the Bill of Rights. Through women's suffrage and the direct election of senators, Progressives deepened America's commitment to democracy. By creating a federal income tax, they vastly amplified the power of the state. By prohibiting alcohol, they imposed their social values and medical advice on the nation. Reformers came from both political parties, and under former president Theodore Roosevelt some created a third party, the Progressive Party, in 1912. Politically, they may have been hard to categorize, but they were nothing if not bold.

QUESTIONS TO THINK ABOUT

What was Progressivism? Was it an inspirational movement to further the nation's democratic ideals, or was it an attempt at social control by self-important, moralistic busybodies? To what extent was Progressivism an expression of America's old utopian tendencies, and to what extent was it a reaction common to all industrializing nations?

DOCUMENTS

The documents in this chapter display different perspectives on the problems and solutions of the Progressive era. In Document 1, Frances Willard of the Women's Christian Temperance Union attacks the alcohol and tobacco interests. She makes an argument for women's suffrage by saying that women need more power in order to protect men and boys in their care, who are prey to such vices. Philosopher John Dewey inspired multiple generations of American educators to make teaching more interactive and democratic. In Document 2, he explains why popular education is particularly critical to an industrial society that otherwise reduces humans to mere cogs in a machine. Document 3 reflects the terrible predicament of African Americans in the Progressive era. W.E.B. DuBois was a founder of the National Association for the Advancement of Colored People (NAACP), along with Jane Addams. Like other Progressives, DuBois placed great emphasis on the power of education. In this document he denounces Booker T. Washington, the founder of Tuskegee Institute in Alabama, who promoted vocational training for blacks and tacitly accepted racial segregation as a necessary political compromise. In Document 4, "muckraking" journalist Lincoln Steffens blames the American people for their descent into political corruption. In *The Shame of the Cities,* Steffens urged citizens to vote according to their consciences, not for the machines. In Document 5, party boss George Washington Plunkitt offers a famous defense for machine politics. Politicians simply provided services, he said, for which they were compensated by getting privileged information that allowed them to become rich. In Document 6, social worker Jane Addams underscores the WCTU argument that women need a political voice in order to do a better job of "civic housekeeping." Republican President Theodore Roosevelt, like his successor Woodrow Wilson, advanced a new era of government regulation and oversight. In Document 7, he lectures state governors on the importance of conserving natural resources for future generations. In Document 8, Yale sociology professor William Graham Sumner vents the annoyance felt by some at Progressive zealotry. He criticizes the Progressives for their extravagant complaints, their attacks on business, and their overconfidence in the power of legislation to right all wrongs. Document 9 attests to the sweep of Progressive reform, despite pessimists like Sumner. The Progressive Era saw more additions to the U.S. Constitution than at any time since the Bill of Rights.

1. W. C. T. U. Blasts Drinking and Smoking, and Demands Power to Protect, 1893

The W. C. T. U. stands as the exponent, not alone of that return to physical sanity which will follow the downfall of the drink habit, but of the reign of a religion of the body which for the first time in history shall correlate with Christ's wholesome, practical, yet blessedly spiritual religion of the soul. "The kingdom of heaven is within you"—shall have a new meaning to the clear-eyed, steady-limbed Christians of the future, from whose brain and blood the taint of alcohol and nicotine has been eliminated by ages of pure habits and noble heredity. . . .

The saloon-keepers understand this new proverb,—"Through the eye to the heart." "King Gambrinus," in garb of green and red and purple, flourishing aloft his foaming mug of beer, and bestriding a huge cask of the same refining beverage, sits above the doors of all leading dram-shops. In Kansas, just after the [state] prohibition law went into force, I saw a picture displayed in the empty windows of the closed saloons, which was artfully contrived to arouse the dormant appetite of every drinking man who looked sorrowfully toward the scene of his former exploits. A generous glass of ale, brimming with beaded foam, was done in colors carefully laid on, and this tempting but now impossible draught was surrounded by separate hands, all the fingers of each one being represented in most ardent, expectant attitudes of grasping, clutching, and clawing all in vain, to reach the coveted but unattainable glass. The tobacconist, with similar wit and shrewdness, attracts attention to his demoralizing wares by placing before his door a statuesque Indian maiden, who offers a bunch of artificial cigars, while to get the real ones, of which she sets the foolish young man thinking, he must go inside. . . .

. . . [The] W. C. T. U., passing through the stages of petition work, local-option work, and constitutional-prohibition-amendment work, has come to the conviction that women must have the ballot as a "home protection" weapon. . . .

The men of the liquor traffic have themselves contributed not a little to our schooling. In their official organs, secret circulars to political aspirants, and by the mightier eloquence of votes paid for with very hard cash, they have united in the declaration (here given in their own words): "Woman's ballot will be the death knell of the liquor traffic!" . . .

Frances E. Willard, *Woman and Temperance* (Chicago: J. S. Goodman and Company, 1883), pp. 42, 283–284, 326, 459. Found on Microfilm, Research Publication, New Haven, CT.

[It] is women who have given the costliest hostages to fortune. Out into the battle of life they have sent their best beloved, with fearful odds against them, with snares that men have legalized and set for them on every hand. Beyond the arms that held them long, their boys have gone forever. Oh! by the danger they have dared; by the hours of patient watching over beds where helpless children lay; by the incense of ten thousand prayers wafted from their gentle lips to Heaven, I charge you give them power to protect, along life's treacherous highway, those whom they have so loved. Let it no longer be that they must sit back among the shadows, hopelessly mourning over their strong staff broken, and their beautiful rod; but when the sons they love shall go forth to life's battle, still let their mothers walk beside them, sweet and serious, and clad in the garments of power.

2. Philosopher John Dewey Advocates Democracy Through Education, 1899

Plato defined a slave as one who accepts from another the purposes which control his conduct. This condition obtains even where there is no slavery in the legal sense. It is found wherever men are engaged in activity which is socially serviceable, but whose service they do not understand and have no personal interest in. Much is said about scientific management of work. It is a narrow view which restricts the science which secures efficiency of operation to movements of the muscles. The chief opportunity for science is the discovery of the relations of a man to his work—including his relations to others who take part—which will enlist his intelligent interest in what he is doing. Efficiency in production often demands division of labor. But it is reduced to a mechanical routine unless workers see the technical, intellectual, and social relationships involved in what they do, and engage in their work because of the motivation furnished by such perceptions. . . . Intelligence is narrowed to the factors concerned with technical production and marketing of goods. No doubt, a very acute and intense intelligence in these narrow lines can be developed, but the failure to take into account the significant social factors means none the less an absence of mind, and a corresponding distortion of emotional life. . . .

 . . . The devotion of democracy to education is a familiar fact. The superficial explanation is that a government resting upon popular suffrage cannot be successful unless those who elect and who obey their governors are educated. Since a democratic society repudiates the principle of external authority, it must find a substitute in voluntary disposition and interest; these can be created only by education. But there is a deeper explanation. A democracy is more than a form of government; it is primarily a mode of associated living, of conjoint communicated experience. The extension in space of the number of individuals who participate in an interest so that each has to refer his own action to that of others, and to consider the action of others to give point and direction to his own, is equivalent to the breaking down of those barriers of class, race, and national territory which kept men from perceiving the full import of their activity. These more numerous and more varied points of contact

John Dewey, *Democracy and Education* (Illinois: Project Gutenberg). Accessed at http://www.netLibrary .com/nlreader/nlreader.dll?bookid=1085236&filename=Page_65. html through =Page_68.html.

denote a greater diversity of stimuli to which an individual has to respond; they consequently put a premium on variation in his action. They secure a liberation of powers which remain suppressed as long as the incitations to action are partial, as they must be in a group which in its exclusiveness shuts out many interests.

The widening of the area of shared concerns, and the liberation of a greater diversity of personal capacities which characterize a democracy, are not of course the product of deliberation and conscious effort. On the contrary, they were caused by the development of modes of manufacture and commerce, travel, migration, and intercommunication which flowed from the command of science over natural energy. But after greater individualization on one hand, and a broader community of interest on the other have come into existence, it is a matter of deliberate effort to sustain and extend them. Obviously a society to which stratification into separate classes would be fatal, must see to it that intellectual opportunities are accessible to all on equable and easy terms. A society marked off into classes need [be] specially attentive only to the education of its ruling elements. A society which is mobile, which is full of channels for the distribution of a change occurring anywhere, must see to it that its members are educated to personal initiative and adaptability.

3. NAACP Founder W. E. B. DuBois Denounces Compromise on Negro Education and Civil Rights, 1903

Mr. [Booker T.] Washington represents in Negro thought the old attitude of adjustment and submission; but adjustment at such a peculiar time as to make his programme unique. This is an age of unusual economic development, and Mr. Washington's programme naturally takes an economic cast, becoming a gospel of Work and Money to such an extent as apparently almost completely to overshadow the higher aims of life. Moreover, this is an age when the more advanced races are coming in closer contact with the less developed races, and the race-feeling is therefore intensified; and Mr. Washington's programme practically accepts the alleged inferiority of the Negro races. . . . In other periods of intensified prejudice all the Negro's tendency to self-assertion has been called forth; at this period a policy of submission is advocated. In the history of nearly all other races and peoples the doctrine preached at such crises has been that manly self-respect is worth more than lands and houses, and that a people who voluntarily surrender such respect, or cease striving for it, are not worth civilizing.

In answer to this, it has been claimed that the Negro can survive only through submission. Mr. Washington distinctly asks that black people give up, at least for the present, three things,—

First, political power,
Second, insistence on civil rights,
Third, higher education of Negro youth,—

W. E. B. DuBois, *The Souls of Black Folk* (New York: Signet, 1969), 87–89.

and concentrate all their energies on industrial education, and accumulation of wealth, and the conciliation of the South. This policy has been courageously and insistently advocated for over fifteen years, and has been triumphant for perhaps ten years. As a result of this tender of the palm-branch, what has been the return? In these years there have occurred:

1. The disfranchisement of the Negro.
2. The legal creation of a distinct status of civil inferiority for the Negro.
3. The steady withdrawal of aid from institutions for the higher training of the Negro.

These movements are not, to be sure, direct results of Mr. Washington's teachings; but his propaganda has, without a shadow of doubt, helped their speedier accomplishment. The question then comes: Is it possible, and probable, that nine millions of men can make effective progress in economic lines if they are deprived of political rights, made a servile caste, and allowed only the most meager chance for developing their exceptional men? If history and reason give any distinct answer to these questions, it is an emphatic *No.* And Mr. Washington thus faces the triple paradox of his career:

1. He is striving nobly to make Negro artisans business men and property-owners; but it is utterly impossible, under modern competitive methods, for workingmen and property-owners to defend their rights and exist without the right of suffrage.
2. He insists on thrift and self-respect, but at the same time counsels a silent submission to civic inferiority such as is bound to sap the manhood of any race in the long run.
3. He advocates common-school and industrial training, and depreciates institutions of higher learning; but neither the Negro common-schools, nor Tuskegee itself, could remain open a day were it not for teachers trained in Negro colleges, or trained by their graduates. . . .

. . . Such men feel in conscience bound to ask of this nation three things:

1. The right to vote.
2. Civic equality.
3. The education of youth according to ability.

4. Journalist Lincoln Steffens Exposes the Shame of Corruption, 1904

. . . The misgovernment of the American people is misgovernment by the American people.

When I set out on my travels, an honest New Yorker told me honestly that I would find that the Irish, the Catholic Irish, were at the bottom of it all everywhere.

Lincoln Steffens, *The Shame of the Cities* (New York: Hill and Wang, 1959), 2–7.

The first city I went to was St. Louis, a German city. The next was Minneapolis, a Scandinavian city, with a leadership of New Englanders. Then came Pittsburg, Scotch Presbyterian, and that was what my New York friend was. "Ah, but they are all foreign populations," I heard. The next city was Philadelphia, the purest American community of all, and the most hopeless. And after that came Chicago and New York, both mongrel-bred, but the one a triumph of reform, the other the best example of good government that I had seen. The "foreign element" excuse is one of the hypocritical lies that save us from the clear sight of ourselves.

Another such conceit of our egotism is that which deplores our politics and lauds our business. . . .

There is hardly an office from United States Senator down to Alderman in any part of the country to which the business man has not been elected; yet politics remains corrupt, government pretty bad, and the selfish citizen has to hold himself in readiness like the old volunteer firemen to rush forth at any hour, in any weather, to prevent the fire; and he goes out sometimes and he puts out the fire (after the damage is done) and he goes back to the shop sighing for the business man in politics. The business man has failed in politics as he has in citizenship. . . .

But there is hope, not alone despair, in the commercialism of our politics. If our political leaders are to be always a lot of political merchants, they will supply any demand we may create. All we have to do is to establish a steady demand for good government. The bosses have us split up into parties. To him parties are nothing but means to his corrupt ends. He "bolts" his party, but we must not; the bribe-giver changes his party, from one election to another, from one county to another, from one city to another, but the honest voter must not. Why? Because if the honest voter cared no more for his party than the politician and the grafter, then the honest vote would govern, and that would be bad—for graft. It is idiotic, this devotion to a machine that is used to take our sovereignty from us. If we would leave parties to the politicians, and would vote not for the party, not even for men, but for the city, and the State, and the nation, we should rule parties, and cities, and States, and nation. If we would vote in mass on the more promising ticket, or, if the two are equally bad, would throw out the party that is in, and wait till the next election and then throw out the other party that is in—then, I say, the commercial politician would feel a demand for good government and he would supply it. . . .

But do the people want good government? Tammany says they don't. Are the people honest? Are the people better than Tammany? Are they better than the merchant and the politician? Isn't our corrupt government, after all, representative? . . .

. . . [T]he corruption that shocks us in public affairs we practice ourselves in our private concerns. There is no essential difference between the pull that gets your wife into society or for your book a favorable review, and that which gets a heeler into office, a thief out of jail, and a rich man's son on the board of directors of a corporation; none between the corruption of a labor union, a bank, and a political machine; none between a dummy director of a trust and the caucus-bound member of a legislature; none between a labor boss like Sam Parks, a boss of banks like John D. Rockefeller, a boss of railroads like J. P. Morgan, and a political boss like Matthew S. Quay. The boss is not a political, he is an American institution, the product of a freed people that have not the spirit to be free.

5. Political Boss George Washington Plunkitt Defends "Honest" Graft, 1905

Everybody is talkin' these days about Tammany men growin' rich on graft, but nobody thinks of drawin' the distinction between honest graft and dishonest graft. . . .

There's an honest graft, and I'm an example of how it works. I might sum up the whole thing by sayin': "I seen my opportunities and I took 'em."

Just let me explain by examples. My party's in power in the city, and it's goin' to undertake a lot of public improvements. Well, I'm tipped off, say, that they're going to lay out a new park at a certain place.

I see my opportunity and I take it. I go to that place and I buy up all the land I can in the neighborhood. Then the board of this or that makes its plan public, and there is a rush to get my land, which nobody cared particular for before.

Ain't it perfectly honest to charge a good price and make a profit on my investment and foresight? Of course, it is. Well, that's honest graft.

Or supposin' it's a new bridge they're goin' to build. I get tipped off and I buy as much property as I can that has to be taken for approaches. I sell at my own price later on and drop some more money in the bank.

Wouldn't you? It's just like lookin' ahead in Wall Street or in the coffee or cotton market. It's honest graft, and I'm lookin' for it every day in the year. I will tell you frankly that I've got a good lot of it, too. . . .

For instance, the city is repavin' a street and has several hundred thousand old granite blocks to sell. I am on hand to buy, and I know just what they are worth.

How? Never mind that. I had a sort of monopoly of this business for a while, but once a newspaper tried to do me. It got some outside men to come over from Brooklyn and New Jersey to bid against me.

Was I done? Not much. I went to each of the men and said: "How many of these 250,000 stones do you want?" One said 20,000, and another wanted 15,000, and another wanted 10,000. I said: "All right, let me bid for the lot, and I'll give each of you all you want for nothin."

They agreed, of course. Then the auctioneer yelled: "How much am I bid for these 250,000 fine pavin' stones?"

"Two dollars and fifty cents," says I.

"Two dollars and fifty cents!" screamed the auctioneer. "Oh, that's a joke! Give me a real bid."

He found the bid was real enough. My rivals stood silent. I got the lot for $2.50 and gave them their share. That's how the attempt to do Plunkitt ended, and that's how all such attempts end.

I've told you how I got rich by honest graft. Now, let me tell you that most politicians who are accused of robbin' the city get rich the same way.

They didn't steal a dollar from the city treasury. They just seen their opportunities and took them. That is why, when a reform administration comes in and spends a half million dollars in tryin' to find the public robberies they talked about in the campaign, they don't find them.

William L. Riordan, *Plunkitt of Tammany Hall* (New York: McClure, Phillips, 1905), 3–10.

The books are always all right. The money in the city treasury is all right. Everything is all right. All they can show is that the Tammany heads of departments looked after their friends, within the law, and gave them what opportunities they could to make honest graft. Now, let me tell you that's never goin' to hurt Tammany with the people. Every good man looks after his friends, and any man who doesn't isn't likely to be popular. If I have a good thing to hand out in private life, I give it to a friend. Why shouldn't I do the same in public life?

Another kind of honest graft. Tammany has raised a good many salaries. There was an awful howl by the reformers, but don't you know that Tammany gains ten votes for every one it lost by salary raisin'?

The Wall Street banker thinks it shameful to raise a department clerk's salary from $1500 to $1800 a year, but every man who draws a salary himself says: "That's all right. I wish it was me." And he feels very much like votin' the Tammany ticket on election day, just out of sympathy.

6. Social Worker Jane Addams Advocates Civic Housekeeping, 1906

It has been well said that the modern city is a stronghold of industrialism quite as the feudal city was a stronghold of militarism, but the modern cities fear no enemies and rivals from without and their problems of government are solely internal. Affairs for the most part are going badly in these great new centres, in which the quickly-congregated population has not yet learned to arrange its affairs satisfactorily. Unsanitary housing, poisonous sewage, contaminated water, infant mortality, the spread of contagion, adulterated food, impure milk, smoke-laden air, ill-ventilated factories, dangerous occupations, juvenile crime, unwholesome crowding, prostitution and drunkenness are the enemies which the modern cities must face and overcome, would they survive. Logically their electorate should be made up of those who can bear a valiant part in this arduous contest, those who in the past have at least attempted to care for children, to clean houses, to prepare foods, to isolate the family from moral dangers; those who have traditionally taken care of that side of life which inevitably becomes the subject of municipal consideration and control as soon as the population is congested. To test the elector's fitness to deal with this situation by his ability to bear arms is absurd. These problems must be solved, if they are solved at all, not from the military point of view, not even from the industrial point of view, but from a third, which is rapidly developing in all the great cities of the world—the human-welfare point of view. . . .

City housekeeping has failed partly because women, the traditional housekeepers, have not been consulted as to its multiform activities. The men have been carelessly indifferent to much of this civic housekeeping, as they have always been indifferent to the details of the household. . . . The very multifariousness and complexity of a city government demand the help of minds accustomed to detail and variety of work, to a sense of obligation for the health and welfare of young children and to a responsibility for the cleanliness and comfort of other people. Because

Jane Addams, "The Modern City and the Municipal Franchise for Women" (speech at the NAWSA Convention, February 1906).

all these things have traditionally been in the hands of women, if they take no part in them now they are not only missing the education which the natural participation in civic life would bring to them but they are losing what they have always had.

7. President Theodore Roosevelt Preaches Conservation and Efficiency, 1908

This Conference on the conservation of natural resources is in effect a meeting of the representatives of all the people of the United States called to consider the weightiest problem now before the Nation; and the occasion for the meeting lies in the fact that the natural resources of our country are in danger of exhaustion if we permit the old wasteful methods of exploiting them longer to continue. . . .

. . . Nature has supplied to us in the United States, and still supplies to us, more kinds of resources in a more lavish degree than has ever been the case at any other time or with any other people. Our position in the world has been attained by the extent and thoroughness of the control we have achieved over nature; but we are more, and not less, dependent upon what she furnishes than at any previous time of history since the days of primitive man. . . .

Since the days when the Constitution was adopted, steam and electricity have revolutionized the industrial world. Nowhere has the revolution been so great as in our own country. The discovery and utilization of mineral fuels and alloys have given us the lead over all other nations in the production of steel. The discovery and utilization of coal and iron have given us our railways, and have led to such industrial development as has never before been seen. The vast wealth of lumber in our forests, the riches of our soils and mines, the discovery of gold and mineral oils, combined with the efficiency of our transportation, have made the conditions of our life unparalleled in comfort and convenience. . . .

The steadily increasing drain on these natural resources has promoted to an extraordinary degree the complexity of our industrial and social life. Moreover, this unexampled development has had a determining effect upon the character and opinions of our people. The demand for efficiency in the great task has given us vigor, effectiveness, decision, and power, and a capacity for achievement which in its own lines has never yet been matched. . . .

We have become great in a material sense because of the lavish use of our resources, and we have just reason to be proud of our growth. But the time has come to inquire seriously what will happen when our forests are gone, when the coal, the iron, and the gas are exhausted, when the soils shall have been still further impoverished and washed into the streams, polluting the rivers, denuding the fields, and obstructing navigation. These questions do not relate only to the next century or to the next generation. One distinguishing characteristic of really civilized men is foresight; we have to, as a nation, exercise foresight for this nation in the future; and if we do not exercise that foresight, dark will be the future! [Applause] We should exercise foresight now, as the ordinarily prudent man exercises foresight in conserving and wisely using the property which contains the assurance of well-being for himself and his children. . . .

Proceedings of a Conference of Governors in the White House (Washington, D.C.: U.S. Government Printing Office, 1909).

Just let me interject one word as to a particular type of folly of which it ought not to be necessary to speak. We stop wasteful cutting of timber; that of course makes a slight shortage at the moment. To avoid that slight shortage at the moment, there are certain people so foolish that they will incur absolute shortage in the future, and they are willing to stop all attempts to conserve the forests, because of course by wastefully using them at the moment we can for a year or two provide against any lack of wood. That is like providing for the farmer's family to live sumptuously on the flesh of the milch cow. [Laughter] Any farmer can live pretty well for a year if he is content not to live at all the year after. [Laughter and applause]

8. Sociologist William Graham Sumner Denounces Reformers' Fanaticism, 1913

As time runs on it becomes more and more obvious that this generation has raised up for itself social problems which it is not competent to solve, and that this inability may easily prove fatal to it. We have been boasting of the achievements of the nineteenth century, and viewing ourselves and our circumstances in an altogether rose-colored medium. We have not had a correct standard for comparing ourselves with our predecessors on earth, nor for judging soberly what we have done or what men can do. . . . We draw up pronunciamentos, every paragraph of which begins with: "we demand," without noticing the difference between the things which we can expect from the society in which we live, and those which we must get either from ourselves or from God and nature.

We believe that we can bring about a complete transformation in the economic organization of society, and not have any incidental social and political questions arise which will make us great difficulty, or that, if such questions arise, they can all be succinctly solved by saying: "Let the State attend to it"; "Make a bureau and appoint inspectors"; "Pass a law." But the plain fact is that the new time presents manifold and constantly varying facts and factors. It is complicated, heterogeneous, full of activity, so that its phases are constantly changing. Legislation and state action are stiff, rigid, inelastic, incapable of adaptation to cases; they are never adopted except under stress of the perception of some one phase which has, for some reason or other, arrested attention. Hence, the higher the organization of society, the more mischievous legislative regulation is sure to be. . . .

We think that security and justice are simple and easy things which go without the saying, and need only be recognized to be had and enjoyed; we do not know that security is a thing which men have never yet succeeded in establishing. History is full of instruction for us if we will go to it for instruction. . . .

We think that, if this world does not suit us, it ought to be corrected to our satisfaction, and that, if we see any social phenomenon which does not suit our notions, there should be a remedy found at once. A collection of these complaints and criticisms, however, assembled from the literature of the day, would show the most heterogeneous, contradictory, and fantastic notions.

William Graham Sumner, "Fantasies and Facts," in *Earth-Hunger and Other Essays* (New Brunswick, N.J.: Transaction, Inc., 1980), 207–210.

We think that this is a world in which we are limited by our wants, not by our powers; by our ideals, not by our antecedents.

We think that we are resisting oppression from other men, when we are railing against the hardships of life on this earth. . . .

We think that capital comes of itself, and would all be here just the same, no matter what regulations we might make about the custody, use, and enjoyment of it. . . .

We think that we can impair the rights of landlords, creditors, employers, and capitalists, and yet maintain all other rights intact.

We think that, although A has greatly improved his position in half a lifetime, that is nothing, because B, in the same time, has become a millionaire.

We throw all our attention on the utterly idle question whether A has done as well as B, when the only question is whether A has done as well as he could.

We think that competition produces great inequalities, but that stealing or almsgiving does not.

9. Rewriting the Constitution: Amendments on Income Tax, Election of Senators, Prohibition, and the Vote for Women, 1913–1920

Amendment XVI

The Congress shall have power to lay and collect taxes on incomes, from whatever source derived, without apportionment among the several States, and without regard to any census or enumeration.

Amendment XVII

The Senate of the United States shall be composed of two Senators from each State, elected by the people thereof, for six years; and each Senator shall have one vote. The electors in each State shall have the qualifications requisite for electors of the most numerous branch of the State legislatures.

When vacancies happen in the representation of any State in the Senate, the executive authority of such State shall issue writs of election to fill such vacancies: *Provided,* That the legislature of any State may empower the executive thereof to make temporary appointments until the people fill the vacancies by election as the legislature may direct.

This amendment shall not be so construed as to affect the election or term of any Senator chosen before it becomes valid as part of the Constitution.

Amendment XVIII

Section 1. After one year from the ratification of this article the manufacture, sale, or transportation of intoxicating liquors within, the importation thereof into, or the exportation thereof from the United States and all territory subject to the jurisdiction thereof for beverage purposes is hereby prohibited.

U.S. Constitution, amends. 16–19.

Section 2.   The Congress and the several States shall have concurrent power to enforce this article by appropriate legislation.

Section 3.   This article shall be inoperative unless it shall have been ratified as an amendment to the Constitution by the legislatures of the several States, as provided in the Constitution, within seven years from the date of the submission hereof to the States by the Congress.

Amendment XIX

The right of citizens of the United States to vote shall not be denied or abridged by the United States or by any State on account of sex.
Congress shall have power to enforce this article by appropriate legislation.

➤ E S S A Y S

Progressivism was so multidimensional that it has provoked a wide variety of historical arguments about everything from its effect on business profits to its consequences for marriage. The following two essays stake out new territory in the debates over the character of Progressivism. Daniel T. Rodgers of Princeton University argues that American Progressives learned their trade in Europe. They were part of a much larger transatlantic conversation over the best ways to provide for human welfare in the industrialized world. Fairly or not, Europeans tended to see the Americans as latecomers and borrowers in the process of reform. Eric Rauchway of the University of California at Davis doesn't deny the transatlantic connection, but he places more emphasis than Rodgers on the unique characteristics of American Progressivism. Reformers in the United States had to work around the nation's liberal, antistatist traditions. They also coped with high immigration and a polyglot population. Rauchway argues that these factors led American Progressives to place special emphasis on personal solutions to political problems. The goal of government should not be to supervise citizens for the rest of their lives and take care of their every need, Progressives thought, but to educate people properly so that they didn't require what Europeans themselves would later criticize as the "Nanny State."

American Progressivism in the Wider Atlantic World

DANIEL T. RODGERS

"Was there a world outside of America?" the muckraker Ray Stannard Baker tried to recollect his state of mind as an apprentice journalist in Chicago in the 1890s. "If there was, I knew next to nothing at all about it—as a reality . . . I knew something of European history—the old tyranny of kings, the absurdity of aristocracy, the futility of feudal wars—out of which America, the wonderful, had stepped proudly into the enlightenment of the Bill of Rights and the Declaration of Independence. I was a true geocentric American."

Daniel T. Rodgers, *Atlantic Crossings: Social Politics in a Progressive Age* (Cambridge: The Belknap Press of Harvard University Press, 1998), 12–13, 15–16, 52, 56, 58–59, 64, 69–72, 74, 142–144. Copyright © 1998 by the President and Fellows of Harvard College. Reprinted by permission of the publisher.

In the face of a provincialism this profound, it is hard to resist a knowing smile. Every serious reader of the past instinctively knows what Baker had yet to learn: that nations lie enmeshed in each others' history. Even the most isolated of nation-states is a semipermeable container, washed over by forces originating far beyond its shores. Even the most powerful act their part within world systems beyond their full control.

If complicity in world historical forces marks all nations, it especially marks outpost nations, like the United States, which begin as other nations' imperial projects. From the earliest European settlements in North America forward, the Atlantic functioned for its newcomers less as a barrier than as a connective lifeline—a seaway for the movement of people, goods, ideas, and aspirations. A key outpost for European trade and a magnet for European capital, the eighteenth- and nineteenth-century United States cannot be understood outside the North Atlantic economy of which it was a part. . . .

Social politics is a case in point. Of studies of progressive and New Deal politics there is no end. On the roots of the impulse to limit the social costs of aggressive, market capitalism, some of the very best American history writing has found its focus. As befits a large-order event, large-scale explanations have been employed to understand it. Thus the rise of the interventionist state in America has been traced to the shock of particularly rapid industrialization, the thin and distended nature of the mid-nineteenth-century American state and society, the status anxieties of a declining middle class, the scientistic ambitions of a new elite of experts and professionals, the social maternalism of middle-class women, the demands from below of farmers and wage workers, and the demands of industrial capitalists at the top for a more rationalized social order than capitalist competition, by itself, could create. But an unspoken "geocentrism," as Baker styled it, frames them all.

Familiar as these explanations are, they leave unstated what every contemporary who followed these issues knew: that the reconstruction of American social politics was of a part with movements of politics and ideas throughout the North Atlantic world that trade and capitalism had tied together. . . .

Every age, even the most calculating and material, needs a symbol, and Gustave Eiffel, who knew a promotional opportunity when it came his way, was eager to provide one. A "factory chimney," critics called his tower at its birth in 1889, "gigantic and hideous." An upended illustration of the principles of railroad bridge design, it defied the scale of the city below it. The tile roofs of old Paris's neighborhoods, the mansards and boulevards of the Second Empire, even the great towers of Notre Dame (as the sketches by Eiffel's engineers pointedly showed) all shrank to Lilliputian dimensions beside this display of engineering hubris. The Eiffel Tower was an advertisement for the tradition-shattering, revolutionary possibilities of industrial technology. Little wonder that Paris's artists immediately petitioned to have it torn down.

Eiffel's tower had a second purpose as well. Built for the Paris exposition of 1889, it was designed as a giant billboard for a great, temporary market of the wares of nineteenth-century industrial capitalism. The exposition's official purpose was to celebrate the centenary of the French Revolution and, in its reflected glory, the still fragile political fortunes of the Third Republic. In fact, trade—not politics—had dominated every world exposition since the iron and glass Crystal Palace Exposition in London in 1851, and the Paris exhibition was no exception. . . .

[I]n 1900, the French convened a still larger fair on the same site, this time to inventory the century itself. The Eiffel Tower was repainted a bright yellow for the occasion, its gas jets replaced by hundreds of new electric lights to keep it abreast of the onward rush of technological progress. On the fairground itself, a still larger stock of goods—the largest to be displayed in this fashion anywhere until the world's fairs of the 1930s—was crammed still more tightly into still more numerous galleries. The 1889 exposition, despite its planners' intentions, had been largely a French affair. This time both Germany, ostracized in 1889, and the United States were represented in force, elbowing Britain for exhibition space and prestige in their race for industrial primacy. . . .

For the 1900 exposition, the Musée Social's organizers determined to lay on a much more elaborate and centrally placed social economy display. In the meeting hall of the social economy pavilion they convened a summer of international conferences on phases of the *question sociale.* For the pavilion's display rooms, they solicited the best examples of practical social amelioration the nations of the Atlantic economy could muster. If there were in the industrialized countries social designs to compensate for the privations and pains of the market revolution, here one might hope to find their outlines.

At first glance, the sheer confusion of issues assembled under the social economy umbrella was all but overwhelming. The French tried to make order out of the whole by carving it into subsections: apprenticeship and the protection of child workers, wages and profit sharing, workers' and employers' associations, farm credit, regulation of the conditions of work, workers' housing, cooperative stores, institutions for the intellectual and moral development of workers, savings and insurance institutions, hygiene (by which they meant not only public sanitation but the public battle against intemperance, slums, and the moral contamination of poverty), poor relief, and a residual category for whatever public or private initiatives for the well-being of the citizens were left over. . . .

To move through the social economy exhibit hall, however, was to discover how far from unified the social economy experts were on solutions. From nation to nation, the shifts in theme were abrupt and arresting. The Russians brought a temperance exhibit. The Italians displayed the work of cooperative savings banks. The Belgians emphasized low-cost workers' housing. Great Britain, its government distracted by the escalating military hostilities in South Africa, barely mustered an exhibit at all. On one wall of the British alcove hung a chart illustrating the growth of the consumers' cooperative movement. On the other hung one of the maps created for Charles Booth's monumental survey of poverty in London—the class relations of the city outlined, street by street, in bright washes of wealth and dark masses of poverty.

In retrospect, Booth's poverty maps seem the most prescient exhibit of the display. It was the German exhibit, however, that stayed longest in visitors' minds. Even non-Germans in Paris were compelled to admit that Germany was the fair's overall victor in the contest of prestige. Germany's national pavilion boasted the exhibition's tallest tower, next to Eiffel's. The most impressive industrial exhibit was the Germans'. In deference to French sensibilities, the Germans had left their huge Krupp cannons and overt military displays at home, but their imperial ambitions were everywhere on exhibit.

In the social economy building, the Germans ignored the complex French categories. In the middle of their alcove they mounted instead a large, gilded obelisk representing the benefits the imperial social insurance funds had distributed to German workers since their inauguration sixteen years earlier. Compulsory, state-administered insurance against the risks of industrial accidents, sickness, and old age was Germany's great social-political invention of the 1880s. The second prong of Bismarck's campaign to crush the German socialists, state social insurance was Bismarck's device to win over the loyalty of the urban German masses through the preemptive, top-down "socialism" of the state. In a symbolic display of imperial largesse and power, surrounded by photos of the hospitals and sanitariums its agencies administered for the welfare of German workers, the state commanded the German exhibit, without a hint of competition.

The Germans spoke on the subject of the state with peculiar authority and zeal in 1900. From the imperial art collection in the German national pavilion to the gilded obelisk in the social economy palace, the German exhibits radiated the message of government's fostering and protective hand—over culture, art, labor, and the ravages of economic misfortune. What better alternative was there to the insecurities and predations of the market but the massive, countervailing, paternal power of the state? . . .

A visitor to the social economy building . . . would not have had an easy time locating the American exhibit. Despite its economic muscle in 1900, the United States was in many ways the exposition's stepchild. It had wrangled space in the front row of national pavilions only through vigorous effort. There, wedged between competitors, the American commissioners built a plaster building made up of the usual Greco-Roman architectural borrowings. The interior, however, they fitted out with American newspapers, typewriters, stenographers for hire, a telegraph, a money exchange, and a ticker tape—everything an American businessman on vacation might need. The Americans were the nouveau riche in Paris in 1900, scrambling hard for status, more eager than any others for the shoptalk of commerce. The German pavilion radiated learning, art, and empire. The French dwelt on politics and solidarity. The American pavilion, behind its classical false front, was about business.

In the social economy building, the same national themes recurred. There, too, the Americans scrambled for place. Squeezed into a tiny, twenty-seven-foot-square alcove, they crammed into their exhibition space a larger stock of material than in any display but France's itself. On hinged boards and ingenious folding cases, they hung out the nation's social wares. For the center of the room, the New York Tenement House Committee contributed a model of one of the city's most notorious slum blocks, together with a model of how much more fiercely crowded that block might become if built up to the density that the city's building code allowed. Nearby, as proof that a sense of the state was not wholly missing, was a handsome collection of the bound reports of the state and national bureaus of labor statistics. In one corner was tucked an exhibit on American Negro life, including examples of handwork made at the Tuskegee Institute and W. E. B. Du Bois's statistical display of African Americans' progress in Georgia since slavery.

Arrangements for the largest body of material in the American exhibit, however, fell to a fledgling social betterment clearinghouse, the League for Social Service. Organized two years earlier, it styled itself a general clearinghouse for information concerning "everything that tends to the social betterment of humanity." Its moving spirit, William Tolman, was in many ways typical of those now forgotten figures who shaped the early years of American social politics. From the position of general agent of the New York Association for Improving the Condition of the Poor, Tolman had been drawn into the Reverend Charles Parkhurst's antivice crusade in the 1890s, and from there into Mayor William Strong's reform administration in New York City, where he had made his particular concern the provision of public baths à la Berlin and London—no slight matter to a city population jammed together, more than two thousand persons to a city block, without benefit of bathrooms. . . .

For the social economy display, however, Tolman hung the walls with photos of the work of self-enlightened capitalism. The endeavors of the nation's model industrial employers were represented there: the Heinz company's spotless factory workrooms, the Cleveland Hardware company's employee restaurant, the employee housing constructed by the Westinghouse Airbrake firm, and the elaborate employee morale work of the National Cash Register Company in Dayton, Ohio. In the realm of *prévoyance* the welfare capitalist theme continued; the biggest, most eye-catching displays were those of the Prudential, Metropolitan, and Equitable life insurance companies. The normally acute reporter for *L'Exposition de Paris* never saw past the life insurance company advertisements; Charles Gide thought the American exhibit formless. But the message of the American display was clearer than Gide sensed: the most promising counterforce to the injuries of industrial capitalism was the enlightened conscience of capitalism itself. . . .

The new Atlantic economy of the late nineteenth century was to encourage a new Atlantic-wide politics. From its first stirrings in the 1890s, the new social politics was to emerge as a powerful political force by the 1910s, with representatives in every capital in the North Atlantic world. Even the Americans, so distant from the chief centers of policy and intellectual innovation, were to be drawn in.

Those who forged the new social politics in the generation before the First World War never shared a common name. Some of them never found a consistent referential language even for themselves. William Beveridge referred to himself variously as a "Tory democrat," a "Labour imperialist," "very nearly" a socialist, and a Liberal. Frederic C. Howe, the American municipal reformer, called himself a single-taxer, a "liberal," a "reformer," and a "radical." . . .

One comes close to a common denominator, however, with "progressive." As a political designation it was English before it was American, born in the heated municipal politics of 1890s London before crossing to the United States in the first decade of the new century. . . .

By the first decade of the twentieth century there was no party system within the North Atlantic economy that had not been profoundly shaken by the new social politics. In Britain, the Liberal government of 1906–1914 embarked on a flurry of legislation that, a quarter century later, still stuck in Franklin Roosevelt's mind for its daring. For the aged poor, it inaugurated an old-age pension system borrowed from New Zealand; for the crippling economic effects of sickness, a program of compulsory wage-earners' health insurance borrowed from Germany; for the most exploited of workers, a set of Australian-style wage boards empowered to establish legal minimum wages; for the sake of fiscal justice, progressive land and income taxes; for the unemployed, a German-style network of state-run employment offices;

and, for workers in trades of particularly uneven labor demand, an untried experiment in pooling the risks of unemployment through state-administered insurance. . . .

On both sides of the Atlantic, politicians rode the new issues to power and popularity: David Lloyd George and the young Winston Churchill in Britain, Georges Clemenceau in France, Theodore Roosevelt and Woodrow Wilson in the United States. Parties and pressure groups drew up sweeping social programs. For the rest of the twentieth century, although parties split and polarized over the new issues, no politics could be divorced from social politics. . . .

Within Europe itself, one of the most striking signs of the new transnational social politics was the phenomenon of legislation passed from one nation to another, sometimes despite acute distrust and rivalry. An early example was British-modeled factory legislation, which began to turn up in France, Germany, and elsewhere in the 1870s. A generation later, borrowings of this sort formed a crazy quilt of transnational influences and appropriations. Danish old-age pensions were imported (via New Zealand) to Britain, British industrial liability codes to France, and French subsidarism to Denmark, Holland, and Scandinavia, even as more radical French progressives turned to German-style compulsory state insurance. . . .

The settlement house movement was one of transatlantic social Protestantism's most striking productions. Here the innovators were English. From the opening of Toynbee Hall in Whitechapel at the edge of London's East End in 1884, Samuel Barnett's institution was a magnet for American visitors. Jane Addams made visits in 1887, 1888, and 1889. . . .

Inevitably, American and English settlement house developments diverged. Rooted in a women's college network unknown in England, the American movement was much more quickly and deeply feminized than its English model. Sharing neither the Oxford cultural pretensions of Toynbee Hall (with its fine arts exhibits and reading rooms wreathed in pipe smoke) nor its residents' easy, Oxbridge-greased access to government policy making, the American settlement houses were more alert to issues of family, immigrants, and neighborhoods. But the social investigations that from the outset kept the American settlements from becoming mere charity outposts were a direct offshoot of the London original. And the American settlement house residents worked extremely hard to sustain the English connection. . . .

Weave as it did the interests and experiences of American and European progressives together, bind them as it did in a common understanding of the forces at work on both sides of the Atlantic, this evolving web of connections could not erase two enduring peculiarities of the transatlantic progressive relationship. The first was the asymmetry of the exchange. The second was the mediating effects of travel.

That American progressives should have found themselves drawing so much more heavily on the experience and ideas of their European counterparts than Europeans did on theirs was no historical given. In the transatlantic radical world of the 1880s, the biggest splash of all had been made by the American radical economist Henry George. . . .

One of the painful signs of this imbalance was a marked contraction of European progressive interest in American politics. Where American attention to British progressive politics was "coherent and continuous," Kenneth Morgan writes of this period, the influences in the other direction were "intermittent and partial at best." The Marxian disillusionment with American politics is well known. . . .

Alfred Zimmern's seven-month pilgrimage in search of progressive America in 1911 and 1912 was more telling and more poignant. Fresh from studying civic republicanism in ancient Athens, Zimmern arrived in the United States fired with ideals of civic political culture, both ancient and modern. He worked hard to locate the centers of political vitality in the New World. In New York he looked in at the United Charities Building, hunted up the city's leading socialists, lunched with Theodore Roosevelt, and attended a mass meeting of protest and remembrance for the 146 garment workers who, locked in the Triangle Shirtwaist Company's loft, had been killed in a factory fire. . . .

"Lots of new ideas," Zimmern wrote his sister, "which may be applied at home." But from there on, progressive America unraveled for him. The more he talked with Americans, the thinner his confidence wore. The raw, unmitigated capitalism of Chicago unnerved him. The U.S. Steel Corporation's model city, Gary, Indiana, seemed to him a monstrous "fortress." Six months after he began, he wrote home: "I have long ago given up looking at America as the land of progress. The only question left in my mind is how many years it's behind England. I think it's somewhere in the eighties and not going our pace at that."

By the time Zimmern picked it up, the metaphor of American behind-handedness was already a hardened trope among European progressives. Sometimes it was used as a general rhetoric of dismissal, as when E. R. Pease of the Fabian Society concluded, on reading John Graham Brooks's latest account of labor relations in the United States, that "in the things that pertain to man as a social and intellectual being, America is decades, if not centuries, behind us." Sometimes it was employed more precisely. Thus in labor legislation the British Labourite J. R. Clynes put the United States twenty years behind Britain in 1909; in trade union development, fifteen years. . . .

The metaphor of laggards and leaders also helped to shield American progressives from the charges of political utopianism their antagonists were poised to hurl at them. It made their idealism hard-headed and practical. "Many persons think that the progressive movement proposes to usher in the millennium by legislation," Benjamin De Witt wrote in 1915. "Nothing could be farther from the minds of the men and women who call themselves progressive. What they propose to do is to bring the United States abreast of Germany and other European countries in the matter of remedial legislation." To catch up to the "civilized" nations of the world was a running progressive theme. Seconding Theodore Roosevelt's nomination at the Progressive Party convention of 1912, Jane Addams made the point official: "The new party has become the American exponent of a world-wide movement toward juster social conditions, a movement which the United States, lagging behind other great nations, has been unaccountably slow to embody in political action." . . .

What riveted the attention of most American admirers of European city life, however, were the absences: "No offensive bill boards; no heaps of offal and rubbish, no long stretches of untidy vacancy held for speculation in the midst of the city; no tumble-down tenements; no ragged, inebriate pedestrians," the National Municipal League's president William D. Foulke wrote of Frankfurt in 1911. No wretchedly paved streets and packed streetcars, no corrupt city bosses, no waste, no lawlessness, no anarchy. The "not"s multiplied as the European cities took shape in reverse of the American cities to which the reformers could not avoid contrasting them. Everything played into these judgments, from the width and paving of the streets and the comparative hideousness of the advertisements to the political convictions of the observers. The reflections and mirrors, the inner eye always focused on America while the outer eye saw Europe: all of this affected judgments.

But admirers of European civic life like Howe were not politically naive. Howe knew the difference between the Junkers and the forces expanding, as he put it, like molten lava below the crust—even if, for his purposes, he chose to elide party divisions as unimportant. He was under no illusion that the European cities moving rapidly into new realms of provision and collective enterprise were democratic in the American understanding of the term. The word portraits of handsome city baths and well-run municipal streetcars in which writers like Howe invested so much were more than travelogue prose. They were part of a struggle to socialize the language of democracy—to balance its rhetoric of rights and privileges with a new rhetoric of services, outcomes, and results. In their stress on cities that *did* things, they tried to forge a language of democratic, civil action rather than mere democratic forms. The German city, Howe admitted, in almost the same words Boston's Josiah Quincy had used sixteen years earlier, was not democratic in its administrative structure; but it was "democratic, even socialistic, in its services." . . .

Among advanced urban progressives in the early-twentieth-century United States, it is hard to exaggerate the ambitions bound up in these half-imported visions of cities free of their swarms of contractors, grafters, entrepreneurs, and franchisers, of cities conscious of their own administration and directing their own fate. Or to exaggerate their sense of affinity with events across the Atlantic. That the American issue might be thought to turn, even for a moment, on the experience of Glasgow streetcars—this was the primary event. "You know that one of the best governed cities in the world is the great Scotch city of Glasgow," Woodrow Wilson casually told a crowd in Fall River, Massachusetts, in the campaign of 1912. "They are 'way ahead of us," Lincoln Steffens wrote of the European municipalizers. "Liberals and radicals all of them, they are in harness and down to the details." The American municipal progressives' challenge was to see what could be done with their transatlantic enthusiasms where the political structures, whose importance they minimized, were so differently organized. . . .

A Distinctive American Progressivism: Women, Immigrants, and Education

ERIC RAUCHWAY

When historians of the United States talk about Progressivism, we refer to a politics of social responsibility that emerged in the United States at the turn of the twentieth century, analogous to but distinct from similar tendencies in other industrialized countries. Throughout Europe, North America, and the Antipodes—wherever railroads and telegraphs, steel rails and copper wire had begun to wring modernity from tradition—citizens struggled accordingly to reformulate their ideas about how society worked and what it was for. This struggle invariably began with a renunciation of old ways and the inauguration of a search for new morally and politically acceptable habits that made room for modern life. In many societies, the renunciation of the old meant moving away from conservative, organic ideas about social obligations and toward the recognition of individual liberties. Sometimes the renunciation of the old also meant relinquishing the revolutionary socialism of the earlier nineteenth century and embracing a democratic socialism that recognized the legitimacy of political processes. But in the United States, where neither true conservatism nor true radicalism had really flourished, the renunciation of old ways took on the form of an attack on traditional liberalism and a groping toward some conception of society that would permit a definition of social responsibility—of what citizens in a modern America might conceivably owe to each other as a matter of decency and duty—that might fit within the frame of liberal prejudices on which the thin canvas of American institutions was stretched. In a society where the dollar was almighty and the only really legal relationship was a contractual one, Americans struggled to explain what kinds of obligations might comprise a community life worth living.

For many years, Progressive-era Americans' "search for a public interest that would transcend particularity," or their "quest for union and meaning amid a decaying culture," has seemed to historians simply, in the words of one interpreter, a "search for order"—an order preferable only for its orderliness, without respect for liberty or regard for individual fulfillment. During this quest, states and state agencies (like courts and orphanages) acquired the power to look into even the most private of affairs so long as they evinced an interest in the welfare of children. The increasing power of the state to interfere with families has often seemed to buttress the orderly interpretation, seeming to expose Progressive reformers as coolly willing "to organize both sexual life and social life according to the principles of modern science." This interpretation seems to me to mix results with intentions, and to confuse the brackish trickle of the Progressives' legacy with its major tributaries. Progressives sought an organizing principle for society that would accommodate liberties, encourage individual self-fulfillment, and, most important, erode invidious social distinctions. They turned—and returned—to the family because it was a unique form of social order that fulfilled itself in its dissolution—in the release of grown children, now self-governing adults, into the society. For them the family was not a shelter from a harsh society, but a starting point in transforming such a society.

There were several structural features to the American case that encouraged Progressives to think about family rather than other species of social bonds. In the past, American political thinkers had expended their intellectual elbow grease on erasing arbitrary claims to citizens' duty. No king or sovereign parliament, let along local baron, could constrain the liberty of a citizen: only he himself (or, as women gained rights through the nineteenth century, she herself) could do that, by making a contract with another. Within the realm of contracts made, there were clear obligations people had incurred. But without contract—without money and property at stake—there were precious few ways to command an American's sense of duty. Christianity had tended to provide a certain dutiful leaven to Americans' daily bread. But by the turn of the twentieth century, even the traditional Protestant denominations, historically the conscience of American liberalism, had succumbed to such theological attenuation that they hardly dared compel believers to consider other members of the community of Christ as their brothers and sisters, without a wholesale rewriting of the gospel to make it social. The contagion of liberty had sapped the strength of all traditional institutions, even God's. New institutions would have to anticipate this assault, and to make room for liberty in their conception of duty.

Apart from the prevalence of liberal prejudices, the American case featured two further distinctive tendencies that determined its different political progress. First, the industrial problem that American Progressives confronted was not nearly so clearly a problem of labor as it was one of immigration. Between 1890 and 1914, the United States drew about fifteen million immigrants principally from countries in South and East Europe. Peasants and craftsmen left when shaken from their traditional places by industrialization, seeking higher wages and good (or good enough) work, which they expected to find in America. They left when pogroms or political upheaval stigmatized their people, expecting to endure less brutal stigmatization in America. The appearance of these immigrants, so different from the German, English, and other West European populations already well-represented in America, shook existing conceptions of who belonged, and how they belonged, to an American community. Did transients belong? Did believers in other gods? Did speakers of foreign tongues? And if so, how could they learn to belong responsibly—to act as citizens, self-governing and informed of their rights? American Progressives tended to address these questions first, whereas their European and Antipodean counterparts concerned themselves more with the emergence of a native-born industrial working class—a different, no more tractable, but largely internal phenomenon that raised different questions about the nature of society.

Progressivism in America also involved women much more thoroughly than the concurrent social politics of other countries did. The most important instance of women's role in Progressivism was the settlement-house movement, which saw middle-class, university-educated women living together in large houses in urban, immigrant neighborhoods for the purpose of educating and enlightening the newly arrived Americans. Although the settlement houses borrowed heavily and explicitly from English precedent, the English version of these houses relied much more extensively on reform-minded men with connections to Oxford University and other elite institutions than their American counterparts could, or would, do; in the United States, the houses comprised primarily unmarried and independent-minded women, such as Jane Addams, Lillian Wald, and Florence Kelley. The presence and political influence of the settlement-house women inspired a younger generation of American women to think beyond their duty to their families to their duty to society—and even their duty to themselves.

Both these latter two characteristics of Progressivism—the importance of immigrants and of women—made the issue of family into a matter of political discussion, and sometimes of controversy. Even though immigrants did not always arrive as the poorest of the poor, homeless and all but wholly ignorant of the world, reformers tended to see them that way: they believed the newcomers needed comfort and education, and an explanation of how the United States worked, so they might become independent, self-governing citizens. And nobody could better supply these needs than the well-educated, well-connected, and unmarried daughters of a professional class whose universities were open to them but whose professions were not. These women invented careers of their own, serving evident social needs. But mothering whole communities precluded (so one argument went) mothering one's own children. A settlement-house worker could have one or the other, but not both—certainly not easily. The women of the settlement houses tended to describe their careers as substitutes for family relations, and for many years historians have echoed this contemporary judgment, often referring explicitly to the writings of Jane Addams. Addams was one of the most eloquent of Progressive reformers and the best-known of the settlement-house workers, famous for her success in establishing and promoting Hull House in Chicago, where middle-class women lived and worked in the heart of one of the city's poorest immigrant districts. She justified the living and working arrangement of Hull House by identifying a conflict between social roles that tore at the consciences of educated middle-class women. These women's families believed they had a claim on them to serve as caretakers for older relatives and for children and also as marriageable links up the social ladder. But (Addams argued) educated women themselves recognized that the society in which they lived—and that had given them advantages so much greater than those it had given their fellow-citizens—required different behavior of them than it had of their mothers. Society, newly teeming with undereducated immigrants preyed upon by party bosses and ruthless employers, demanded that educated women give their time to the remedy of these public ills, rather than to the private matters of the household. Addams's counterposition of the family and the social claim suggested that even though it might be personally painful for them to do it, women had an obligation to forgo their traditional familial roles to serve a morally superior social role. She framed the choice in terms of sacrifice—"in the effort to sustain the moral energy necessary to work out a more satisfactory social relation, the individual often sacrifices the energy which should legitimately go into the fulfilment [*sic*] of personal and family claims, to what he considers the higher claim"—and she tended to use gender-neutral language, but the predicament she described and the solution she outlined specifically addressed the concerns of educated women. There appeared to be a basic conflict between women's familial role and their reform work, and indeed doing the latter sort of work often required that women forgo families and children of their own, even should they greatly want them. . . .

Addams identified her generation as belonging to a peculiar historical moment when secular social trends challenged the institution of the family. Because middle-class women had now attained university degrees they now possessed a measure of power and privilege. Further, because their society's promise of substantive equality was threatened by the pressures of immigration and industrialization as well as by the obviously inadequate responses to these developments, duty called: such educated women could not afford to consider themselves solely as creatures of their own homes. . . .

Addams would carry these convictions about the proper nature of social relations into party politics, delivering a speech nominating Theodore Roosevelt for the presidency at the Progressive Party convention in 1912. Addams, who mistrusted Roosevelt for his belligerency, sought influence by compromising her pacifist principles. They did, however, share more than political opportunism. When Roosevelt could be pried away from the lure of war, he shared Addams's vision of social relations.

If in time of war Roosevelt yielded too easily to a worse self, this tendency only highlights by contrast the open, liberal approach to social and family relations that mark him as a Progressive. For example, in a 1917 investigation of the relationship between middle-class society and the working-class or immigrant family, he reported himself fascinated by the adaptive philosophy of the Juvenile Workers' Bureau, which (he wrote) "never commits the dreadful fault of reducing all cases to the same test. It tries to keep the family together, so long as there is any possibility of good coming from the effort; but where necessary it unhesitatingly protects and separates the boy or girl from the drunken mother or brutal father." In dealing with illegitimate children, the juvenile courts had also played to Roosevelt's open-mindedness. "I was myself sufficiently under the rule of tradition to assume that the desirable thing was to secure the marriage of the parents; but the lady who was chief of the woman's division of the criminal department explained to me that in actual practice this had not been found desirable." Roosevelt approved of an open approach to families that responded to social needs. For him, family also expanded outward into society: "the meaning of free government" included his notion that what he called "the parent class" had to foster independence not only in their own children but in "the people as a whole." . . .

The favorite Progressive reform was a new school, a research bureau, a new publication, or an information clearinghouse. These measures are better characterized as educational than as interventionist. Even at their most activist, what Progressives most wanted was to teach, to make society "a school where democratic experiments could be worked out as they should be." Why? In part, of course, because it was financially and politically cheaper to teach than to do. Institutions of education were more politically acceptable and less accountable than programs that could compose what we might think of as a prototypical welfare state. But in their political cheapness, these measures for education reflected widespread and influential values. These institutions of reform acted toward their dependents as liberal parents did toward their children, teaching them to achieve their independence. Even when such reforms became arms of the state—like the federal Children's Bureau—they spent their time principally gathering and disbursing information. In the bureau's most active mode, it represented the state in the role of a library or an advice columnist, and its dependents—the mothers who relied on it—leaned on it of their own accord and did so only as long as they needed to. . . .

. . . The Progressives grew up in an explicitly imperialist world, where they believed their ambitions stood an excellent chance of global fulfillment. However paradoxical it may sound, when we descend to cases we see that these ambitions rested less on the increase of state power than on the spread of American institutions and customs—on the family and its relations to society, on small institutions more than on the central state. Progressives optimistically believed that beyond minimal cleanliness and shelter, all anyone really needed was to know better, to abandon ancient superstitions about social obligations (to the church, to Old World authority, to patriarchal families). They could hopefully launch their educational enterprises only because they believed that education was all any group really required to free themselves, that the proper education would create critically thinking, intelligently-self-governing citizens. Like the good liberals they were, they brought up their children in keeping with this precept, and they believed that if any social class needed bringing up or uplifting, the same principles should apply. They lived in an America where this sort of bourgeois condescension was acceptable, because without condescension there could be no perception of weakness on the part of other classes and thus no call for reform. They lived in an America where self-government meant self-discipline and individual independence, for the bonds between parents and children could only justify their existence if they ensured their ultimate dissolution. They lived in an America that did not yet tend toward statist solutions to social problems. . . .

FURTHER READING

Alan Dawley, *Struggles for Justice: Social Responsibility and the Liberal State* (1991).
Leon Fink, *Progressive Intellectuals and the Dilemmas of Democratic Government* (1997).
Gayle Gullett, *Becoming Citizens: The Emergence and Development of the California Women's Movement, 1880–1911* (2000).
Samuel Hays, *Conservation and the Gospel of Efficiency* (1969).
Gabriel Kolko, *The Triumph of Conservatism: A Re-interpretation of American History, 1900–1916* (1963).
Alan Kraut, *Silent Travelers: Germs, Genes, and the "Immigrant Menace"* (1995).
Christopher Lasch, *The True and Only Heaven: Progress and its Critics* (1991).
Leon Litwack, *Trouble in Mind: Black Southerners in the Age of Jim Crow* (1998).
Peter McCaffery, *When Bosses Ruled Philadelphia: The Emergence of the Republican Machine* (1993).
Kathryn Kish Sklar, *Florence Kelley and the Nation's Work* (1995).
Peter Stearns, *Schools and Students in Industrial Society: Japan and the West, 1870–1940* (1998).

CHAPTER
6

America in World War I

In 1918, President Woodrow Wilson broke the precedent of more than one hundred years and sent American soldiers "over there," across the Atlantic. George Washington had declared the "Great Rule" of staying out of Europe's troubles in 1796, and James Monroe had underscored the principle in his famous Monroe Doctrine of 1823. Essentially, the Monroe Doctrine asserted that Europeans should stay out of affairs in the Americas, and that Americans should stay out of political affairs in Europe. Following this venerable tradition, Wilson declared neutrality when the war first broke out on July 28, 1914. But the opportunity to sell food, arms, and other goods to the belligerents gradually led the United States deeper and deeper into the conflict. Britain declared a blockade of all German-occupied territory to prevent food and supplies from getting through to enemy soldiers and civilians on the continent. To enforce this blockade, Britain declared a war zone off the coast of Northern Europe and laced it with mines. Underwater bombs sent six U.S. merchant ships to the bottom along with their cargo and men. The British took no responsibility for these losses, claiming that all casualties resulted from mines that the Germans had sowed amongst theirs.

Germany retaliated against the blockade by declaring a war zone around the British Isles, enforced largely by the newly developed U-boats, which went after American ships heading for England, Ireland, and France. To Wilson, submarine warfare seemed particularly unfair and inhumane. When Kaiser Wilhelm of Germany resumed unrestricted submarine warfare in February 1917 in order to break Britain's starvation blockade, U-boats immediately sank two American merchant ships. By April 1, German submarines had sunk a total of ten American ships.

The difference in the number of ships sunk by anonymous mines (probably British) and by identifiably German U-boats is far too slight to explain why Wilson entered the so-named "Great War" on the side of the Allies, or even why he took the nation into a European conflict at all. Historians answer these questions in different ways. Some point to the German U-boat, which Wilson considered an especially heinous form of warfare, especially after one sunk the British passenger liner Lusitania in 1915. Other historians point to Wilson's personality: his religious faith and predilection for moralizing, or his Progressive commitment to political reform and his desire to "make the world safe for democracy." Scholars (and some Americans at the time) have also expressed the suspicion that the United States simply followed its economic interests in allying with the British and French. But while they disagree on why the U.S. went to war, historians concur that this decision set the nation on a course of intervention in world affairs. During the war Wilson called for a "peace without victory" and a League of Nations that would guarantee *the right of all peoples to self-determination. After the war, the U.S. Senate refused to ratify the President's peace treaty. Ever since, historians and politicians have called the notion of an American democratic mission abroad by the name "Wilsonianism."*

The consequences of America's new course were profound, both abroad and at home. The Wilson administration fostered hyperpatriotism through a Committee on Public Information, and repressed free speech through Espionage and Sedition Acts aimed at anyone who opposed the war. Americans rallied around the flag, and over 100,000 soldiers died under its colors. But afterwards, disillusionment set in quickly: disillusionment with profiteers who had helped drag the U.S. into the conflict, with idealists who had sought to remake the Old World, and with war itself as a patriotic or glorious undertaking. World War I ultimately provided few lessons about when or how the United States should intervene in conflicts beyond its borders. George Washington's Great Rule against foreign entanglements had been broken, but the Senate's vote against the League of Nations showed that it could be restored.

QUESTIONS TO THINK ABOUT

Progressives such as Presidents Woodrow Wilson and Theodore Roosevelt supported American entry into the war. But other Progressives, such as Senator Robert La Follette and Secretary of State William Jennings Bryan, bitterly opposed it. How did the war further the Progressive agenda, and how did the war undermine it?

What do you think of Woodrow Wilson's leadership? Was he a hopeless dreamer who bungled the attempt to restore peace, or was he the prescient architect of a new world order?

DOCUMENTS

The documents in this chapter illustrate a variety of attitudes about the decision to go to war and toward the war itself. In Document 1, President Wilson asks Congress to declare war and pledge "our lives and our fortunes" to make the world free. Progressive Senator Robert La Follette strenuously objected. In a speech to the U.S. Senate (Document 2), he argues that America stands to lose its own freedom through conscription and other measures that take away free speech and free choice. Document 3 is a sworn statement made out by union organizers who were whipped, tarred, and feathered for not buying Liberty Bonds. This selection testifies to the domestic intolerance that grew out of the war, fulfilling La Follette's prophecy. Document 4 is the Espionage Act of 1918, designed to punish pacifists and quell dissent. In a speech on January 8, 1918, Wilson outlined the war aims of the United States, which included self-determination for all peoples. His so-called Fourteen Points (Document 5) spoke to the historic ideals of the United States— ideals that would bedevil the nation's foreign policy for the ensuing century. The next two documents reveal contrasting perceptions of the war itself: as a patriotic opportunity to "make your mother proud of you," or as a gruesome, unpredictable bloodbath. Document 6 is "Over There," a rousing, patriotic song by George M. Cohan that helped stir millions to volunteer. Document 7 is an excerpt from the memoir of Harry Smith, an ambulance company surgeon. The events he describes helped fuel a genre of memoirs and novels after the war (including the works of former ambulance driver Ernest Hemingway) that deplored the slaughter. In Document 8, newspaperman George Creel recounts how the U.S. government used the newest propaganda techniques to "sell" the war and the international crusade for democracy. Document 9 shows cartoons that grappled with the essential choice faced by the United States once the guns went silent: to embrace "foreign entanglements" or to turn its back on the common cause of humanity.

1. President Woodrow Wilson Asks Congress to Declare War, 1917

On the third of February last I officially laid before you the extraordinary announcement of the Imperial German Government that on and after the first day of February it was its purpose to put aside all restraints of law of humanity and use its submarines to sink every vessel that sought to approach either the ports of Great Britain and Ireland or the western coasts of Europe or any of the ports controlled by the enemies of Germany within the Mediterranean. That had seemed to be the object of the German submarine warfare earlier in the war, but since April of last year the Imperial Government had somewhat restrained the commanders of its undersea craft in conformity with its promise then given to us that passenger boats should not be sunk and that due warning would be given to all other vessels which its submarines might seek to destroy, when no resistance was offered or escape attempted, and care taken that their crews were given at least a fair chance to save their lives in their open boats. The precautions taken were meagre and haphazard enough, as was proved in distressing instance after instance in the progress of the cruel and unmanly business, but a certain degree of restraint was observed. The new policy has swept every restriction aside. Vessels of every kind, whatever their flag, their character, their cargo, their destination, their errand, have been ruthlessly sent to the bottom without warning and without thought of help or mercy for those on board, the vessels of friendly neutrals along with those of belligerents. Even hospital ships and ships carrying relief to the sorely bereaved and stricken people of Belgium, though the latter were provided with safe conduct through the proscribed areas by the German Government itself and were distinguished by unmistakable marks of identity, have been sunk with the same reckless lack of compassion or of principle.

I was for a little while unable to believe that such things would in fact be done by any government that had hitherto subscribed to the humane practices of civilized nations. International law had its origin in the attempt to set up some law which would be respected and observed upon the seas, where no nation had right of dominion where lay the free highways of the world. By painful stage after stage has that law been built up, with meagre enough results, indeed, after all was accomplished that could be accomplished, but always with a clear view, at least of what the heart and conscience of mankind demanded. This minimum of right the German Government has swept aside under the plea of retaliation and necessity and because it had no weapons which it could use at sea except these which it is impossible to employ as it is employing them without throwing to the winds all scruples of humanity or of respect for the understandings that were supposed to underlie the intercourse of the world. I am not now thinking of the loss of property involved, immense and serious as that is, but only of the wanton and wholesale destruction of the lives of noncombatants, men, women, and children, engaged in pursuits which have always, even in the darkest periods of modern history, been deemed innocent and legitimate. Property can be paid for; the lives of peaceful and innocent people cannot be. The present German submarine warfare against commerce is a warfare against mankind.

It is a war against all nations. American ships have been sunk, American lives taken, in ways which it has stirred us very deeply to learn of, but the ships and people of other neutral and friendly nations have been sunk and overwhelmed in the waters in the same way. There has been no discrimination. The challenge is to all mankind. Each nation must decide for itself how it will meet it. The choice we make for ourselves must be made with a moderation of counsel and a temperateness of judgment befitting our character and our motives as a nation. We must put excited feeling away. Our motive will not be revenge or the victorious assertion of the physical might of the nation, but only the vindication of right, of human right, of which we are only a single champion. . . .

With a profound sense of the solemn and even tragical character of the step I am taking and of the grave responsibilities which it involves, but in unhesitating obedience to what I deem my constitutional duty, I advise that the Congress declare the recent course of the Imperial German Government to be in fact nothing less than war against the government and people of the United States; that it formally accept the status of belligerent which has thus been thrust upon it; and that it take immediate steps not only to put the country in a more thorough state of defense but also to exert all its power and employ all its resources to bring the Government of the German Empire to terms and end the war. . . .

It is a distressing and oppressive duty, Gentlemen of the Congress, which I have performed in thus addressing you. There are, it may be, many months of fiery trial and sacrifice ahead of us. It is a fearful thing to lead this great peaceful people into war, into the most terrible and disastrous of all wars, civilization itself seeming to be in the balance. But the right is more precious than peace, and we shall fight for the things which we have always carried nearest our hearts—for democracy, for the right of those who submit to authority to have a voice in their own governments, for the rights and liberties of small nations, for a universal dominion of right by such a concert of free peoples as shall bring peace and safety to all nations and make the world itself at last free. To such a task we can dedicate our lives and our fortunes, everything that we are and everything that we have, with the pride of those who know that the day has come when America is privileged to spend her blood and her might for the principles that gave her birth and happiness and the peace which she has treasured. God helping her, she can do no other.

2. Senator Robert M. La Follette
Passionately Dissents, 1917

The poor, sir, who are the ones called upon to rot in the trenches, have no organized power, have no press to voice their will upon this question of peace or war; but, oh, Mr. President, at some time they will be heard. I hope and I believe they will be heard in an orderly and a peaceful way. I think they may be heard from before long. I think, sir, if we take this step, when the people to-day who are staggering under the burden of supporting families at the present prices of the necessaries of the life find those prices multiplied, when they are raised a hundred percent, or 200 percent, as they will be quickly, aye, sir, when beyond that those who pay taxes come to have their taxes doubled and again doubled to pay the interest on the nontaxable bonds held by Morgan and his combinations, which have been issued to meet this war, there will come an awakening; they will have their day and they will be heard. It will be as certain and as inevitable as the return of the tides, and as resistless, too. . . .

Just a word of comment more upon one of the points in the President's address. He says that this is a war "for the things which we have always carried nearest to our hearts—for democracy, for the right of those who submit to authority to have a voice in their own government." In many places throughout the address is this exalted sentiment given expression. . . .

But the President proposes alliance with Great Britain, which, however liberty-loving its people, is a hereditary monarchy, with a hereditary ruler, with a hereditary House of Lords, with a hereditary landed system, with a limited and restricted suffrage for one class and a multiplied suffrage power for another, and with grinding industrial conditions for all the wageworkers. The President has not suggested that we make our support of Great Britain conditional to her granting home rule to Ireland, or Egypt, or India. We rejoice in the establishment of a democracy in Russia, but it will hardly be contended that if Russia was still an autocratic Government, we would not be asked to enter this alliance with her just the same. Italy and the lesser powers of Europe, Japan in the Orient; in fact all of the countries with whom we are to enter into alliance, except France and newly revolutionized Russia, are still of the old order—and it will be generally conceded that no one of them has done as much for its people in the solution of municipal problems and in securing social and industrial reforms as Germany. . . .

Who has registered the knowledge or approval of the American people of the course this Congress is called upon in declaring war upon Germany? Submit the question to the people, you who support it. You who support it dare not do it, for you know that by a vote of more than ten to one the American people as a body would register their declaration against it.

In the sense that this war is being forced upon our people without their knowing why and without their approval, and that wars are usually forced upon all peoples in the same way, there is some truth in the statement; but I venture to say that the response which the German people have made to the demands of this war shows that it has a degree of popular support which the war upon which we are entering has not and never will have among our people. The espionage bills, the conscription bills, and other forcible military measures which we understand are being ground out of the war machine in this country is the complete proof that those responsible for this war fear that it has no popular support and that armies sufficient to satisfy the demand of the entente allies can not be recruited by voluntary enlistments.

3. A Union Organizer Testifies to Vigilante Attack, 1917

"On the night of November 5, 1917, while sitting in the hall at No. 6 W. Brady Street, Tulsa, Okla. (the room leased and occupied by the Industrial Workers of the World, and used as a union meeting room), at about 8:45 P.M., five men entered the hall, to

Sworn testimony of the secretary of the Industrial Workers of the World local, Tulsa, Oklahoma, November 1917, from *Liberator,* April 1918.

whom I at first paid no attention, as I was busy putting a monthly stamp in a member's union card book. After I had finished with the member, I walked back to where these five men had congregated at the baggage-room at the back of the hall, and spoke to them, asking if there was anything I could do for them.

"One who appeared to be the leader, answered 'No, we're just looking the place over.' Two of them went into the baggage-room flashing an electric flashlight around the room. The other three walked toward the front end of the hall. I stayed at the baggage-room door, and one of the men came out and followed the other three up to the front end of the hall. The one who stayed in the baggage-room asked me if I was 'afraid he would steal something.' I told him we were paying rent for the hall, and I did not think anyone had a right to search this place without a warrant. He replied that he did not give a damn if we were paying rent for four places, they would search them whenever they felt like it. Presently he came out and walked toward the front end of the hall, and I followed a few steps behind him.

"In the meantime the other men, who proved to be officers, appeared to be asking some of our members questions. Shortly after, the patrol-wagon came and all the members in the hall—10 men were ordered into the wagon. I turned out the light in the back end of the hall, closed the desk, put the key in the door and told the 'officer' to turn out the one light. We stepped out, and I locked the door, and at the request of the 'leader of the officers,' handed him the keys. He told me to get in the wagon, I being the 11th man taken from the hall, and we were taken to the police station. . . .

"In about forty minutes, as near as we could judge about 11 P.M., the turnkey came and called 'Get ready to go out, you I.W.W. men.' We dressed as rapidly as possible, were taken out of the cells, and the officer gave us back our possessions, Ingersoll watches, pocketknives and money, with the exception of $3 in silver of mine which they kept, giving me back $27.87. I handed the receipt for the $100 bond I had put up to the desk sergeant and he told me he did not know anything about it, and handed the receipt back to me, which I put in my trousers' pocket with the 87 cents. Twenty-seven dollars in bills was in my coat pocket. We were immediately ordered into automobiles waiting in the alley. Then we proceeded one block north to 1st Street, west one-half block to Boulder Street, north across the Frisco tracks and stopped.

"Then the masked mob came up and ordered everybody to throw up their hands. Just here I wish to state I never thought any man could reach so high as those policemen did. We were then bound, some with hands in front, some with hands behind, and others bound with arms hanging down their sides, the rope being wrapped around the body. Then the police were ordered to 'beat it,' which they did, running, and we started for the place of execution.

"When we arrived there, a company of gowned and masked gunmen were there to meet us standing at 'present arms.' We were ordered out of the autos, told to get in line in front of these gunmen and another bunch of men with automatics and pistols, lined up between us. Our hands were still held up, and those who were bound, in front. Then a masked man walked down the line and slashed the ropes that bound us, and we were ordered to strip to the waist, which we did, threw our clothes in front of us, in individual piles—coats, vests, hats, shirts and undershirts. The boys not having had time to distribute their possessions that were given back to them at the police stations, everything was in the coats, everything we owned in the world.

"Then the whipping began, a double piece of new rope, ⅝ or ¾ hemp, being used. A man, 'the chief' of detectives, stopped the whipping of each man when he thought the victim had had enough. After each one was whipped another man applied the tar with a large brush, from the head to the seat. Then a brute smeared feathers over and rubbed them in.

"After they had satisfied themselves that our bodies were well abused, our clothing was thrown into a pile, gasoline poured on it and a match applied. By the light of our earthly possessions, we were ordered to leave Tulsa, and leave running and never come back."

4. The U.S. Government Punishes War Protesters: The Espionage Act, 1918

Be it enacted by the Senate and House of Representatives of the United States of America in Congress assembled, That section three of title one of the Act entitled, "An Act to punish acts of interference with the foreign relations, the neutrality, and the foreign commerce of the United States, to punish espionage, and better to enforce the criminal laws of the United States, and for other purposes," approved June fifteenth, nineteen hundred and seventeen, be, and the same is hereby, amended so as to read as follows:

"SEC. 3. Whoever, when the United States is at war, shall willfully make or convey false reports or false statements with intent to interfere with the operation or success of the military or naval forces of the United States, or to promote the success of its enemies, or shall willfully make or convey false reports or false statements, or say or do anything except by way of bona fide and not disloyal advice to an investor or investors, with intent to obstruct the sale by the United States of bonds or other securities of the United States or the making of loans by or to the United States, and whoever, when the United States is at war, shall willfully cause or attempt to cause, or incite or attempt to incite, insubordination, disloyalty, mutiny, or refusal of duty, in the military or naval forces of the United States, or shall willfully obstruct or attempt to obstruct the recruiting or enlistment service of the United States, and whoever, when the United States is at war, shall willfully utter, print, write, or publish any disloyal, profane, scurrilous, or abusive language about the form of government of the United States, or the Constitution of the United States, or the military or naval forces of the United States, or the flag of the United States, or the uniform of the Army or Navy of the United States, or any language intended to bring the form of government of the United States, or the Constitution of the United States, or the military or naval forces of the United States, or the flag of the United States, or the uniform of the Army or Navy of the United States into contempt, scorn, contumely, or disrepute, or shall willfully utter, print, write, or publish any language intended to incite, provoke, or encourage resistance to the United States, or to promote the cause of its enemies, or shall willfully display the flag of any foreign enemy, or shall willfully by utterance, writing, printing, publication, or language spoken, urge, incite, or advocate any curtailment

---

Espionage Act, U.S. Statutes at Large 40 (1918), 553ff.

of production in this country of any thing or things, product or products, necessary or essential to the prosecution of the war in which the United States may be engaged, with intent by such curtailment to cripple or hinder the United States in the prosecution of the war, and whoever shall willfully advocate, teach, defend, or suggest the doing of any of the acts or things in this section enumerated, and whoever shall by word or act support or favor the cause of any country with which the United States is at war or by word or act oppose the cause of the United States therein, shall be punished by a fine of not more than $10,000 or imprisonment for not more than twenty years, or both. . . ."

5. Wilson Proposes a New World Order in the "Fourteen Points," 1918

I. Open covenants of peace, openly arrived at, after which there shall be no private international understandings of any kind but diplomacy shall proceed always frankly and in the public view.

II. Absolute freedom of navigation upon the seas, outside territorial waters, alike in peace and in war, except as the seas may be closed in whole or in part by international action for the enforcement of international covenants.

III. The removal, so far as possible, of all economic barriers and the establishment of an equality of trade conditions among all the nations consenting to the peace and associating themselves for its maintenance.

IV. Adequate guarantees given and taken that national armaments will be reduced to the lowest point consistent with domestic safety.

V. A free, open-minded, and absolutely impartial adjustment of all colonial claims, based upon a strict observance of the principle that in determining all such questions of sovereignty the interests of the populations concerned must have equal weight with the equitable claims of the government whose title is to be determined.

VI. The evacuation of all Russian territory and such a settlement of all questions affecting Russia as will secure the best and freest cooperation of the other nations of the world in obtaining for her an unhampered and unembarrassed opportunity for the independent determination of her own political development and national policy and assure her of a sincere welcome into the society of free nations under institutions of her own choosing; and, more than a welcome, assistance also of every kind that she may need and may herself desire. The treatment accorded Russia by her sister nations in the months to come will be the acid test of their good will, of their comprehension of her needs as distinguished from their own interests, and of their intelligent and unselfish sympathy.

VII. Belgium, the whole world will agree, must be evacuated and restored, without any attempt to limit the sovereignty which she enjoys in common with all other free nations. No other single act will serve as this will serve to restore confidence among the nations in the laws which they have themselves set and determined for the government of their relations with one another. Without this healing act the whole structure and validity of international law is forever impaired.

Congressional Record, LVI (January 8, 1918), Part 1, 680–682.

VIII. All French territory should be freed and the invaded portions restored, and the wrong done to France by Prussia in 1871 in the matter of Alsace-Lorraine, which has unsettled the peace of the world for nearly fifty years, should be righted, in order that peace may once more be made secure in the interest of all.

IX. A readjustment of the frontiers of Italy should be effected along clearly recognizable lines of nationality.

X. The peoples of Austria-Hungary, whose place among the nations we wish to see safeguarded and assured, should be accorded the freest opportunity of autonomous development.

XI. Rumania, Serbia, and Montenegro should be evacuated; occupied territories restored; Serbia accorded free and secure access to the sea; and the relations of the several Balkan states to one another determined by friendly consul along historically established lines of allegiance and nationality; and international guarantees of the political and economic independence and territorial integrity of the several Balkan states should be entered into.

XII. The Turkish portions of the present Ottoman Empire should be assured a secure sovereignty, but the other nationalities which are now under Turkish rule should be assured an undoubted security of life and an absolutely unmolested opportunity of autonomous development, and the Dardanelles should be permanently opened as a free passage to the ships and commerce of all nations under international guarantees.

XIII. An independent Polish state should be erected which should include the territories inhabited by indisputably Polish populations, which should be assured a free and secure access to the sea, and whose political and economic independence and territorial integrity should be guaranteed by international covenant.

XIV. A general association of nations must be formed under specific covenants for the purpose of affording mutual guarantees of political independence and territorial integrity to great and small states alike.

6. Broadway Showman George M. Cohan Sings About Patriotism, 1918

Johnnie, get your gun,
Get your gun, get your gun,
Take it on the run,
On the run, on the run.
Hear them calling, you and me,
Every son of liberty.
Hurry right away,
No delay, no delay,
Make your daddy glad
To have had such a lad.

George M. Cohan, "Over There."

Tell your sweetheart not to pine,
To be proud her boy's in line.

Chorus

Over there, over there,
Send the word, send the word over there—
That the Yanks are coming,
The Yanks are coming,
The drums rum-tumming
Ev'rywhere.
So prepare, say a pray'r,
Send the word, send the word to beware.
We'll be over, we're coming over,
And we won't come back till it's over
Over there.

Johnnie, get your gun,
Get your gun, get your gun,
Johnnie show the Hun
Who's a son of a gun.
Hoist the flag and let her fly,
Yankee Doodle do or die.
Pack your little kit,
Show your grit, do your bit.
Yankee Doodle fill the ranks,
From the towns and the tanks.
Make your mother proud of you,
And the old Red, White and Blue.

(*repeat chorus twice*)

7. An Ambulance Surgeon Describes What It Was Like "Over There," 1918

We were in full view of the enemy and within easy reach of the shells the German gunners were sending toward the town with exceptional ferocity. Nothing happened to us on the first trip, On the second trip, however, as we approached the town at about dawn, we saw a strange sight in the valley below. A greenish-yellow cloud hovered thickly over the region in a dense, motionless pall. It was mustard gas, a violent irritant which would blister the skin at contact if the concentration were sufficient. Toward the end of the war this type of gas was used extensively in shells, being released when the projectiles exploded. Ville-Savoye had been bombarded mercilessly all the preceding night and the gas we saw had accumulated during the darkness.

Harry L. Smith, M.D., *Memoirs of An Ambulance Company Officer* (Rochester, Minn: Doomsday Press, 1940). Obtained from www.lib.byu.edu/~rdh/wwi/memoir/Ambco/officer3.html.

Dressing stations had been set up in two very deep stone cellars in Ville-Savoye. A man probably was as safe there as he would have been anywhere else in the village. The walls were thick, and the ceiling, which was formed by what was left of the first floor of the old building, was supported by great timbers that no doubt had been hewn by hand and fitted with infinite care, after the manner of most building in rural France. The doors of the two cellars had been hung with Army blankets drenched with water to keep out poison gas. I lived through what must have been one of the most deathly barrages of the war. The Germans sent tons of steel and iron crashing into the town for hours on end, and detonations were so monstrous that the earth and walls about us shuddered and trembled, even though we were far below the surface of the ground. Our ears rang with the mighty tumult, and the very air in the damp cellar vibrated until it was painful. At times we could not hear the spoken voice, so we sat with our backs to the wall, wondering speechless on the floor when the infernal din would cease, or whether we would live to know quiet when it returned again.

8. Publicist George Creel Recalls Selling the War, 1920

Back of the firing-line, back of armies and navies, back of the great supply-depots, another struggle waged with the same intensity and with almost equal significance attaching to its victories and defeats. It was the fight for the *minds* of men, for the "conquest of their convictions," and the battle-line ran through every home in every country. . . .

We strove for the maintenance of our own morale and the Allied morale by every process of stimulation; every possible expedient was employed to break through the barrage of lies that kept the people of the Central Powers in darkness and delusion; we sought the friendship and support of the neutral nations by continuous presentation of facts. We did not call it propaganda, for that word, in German hands, had come to be associated with deceit and corruption. Our effort was educational and informative throughout, for we had such confidence in our case as to feel that no other argument was needed than the simple, straightforward presentation of facts.

There was no part of the great war machinery that we did not touch, no medium of appeal that we did not employ. The printed word, the spoken word, the motion picture, the telegraph, the cable, the wireless, the poster, the sign-board— all these were used in our campaign to make our own people and all other peoples understand the causes that compelled America to take arms. All that was fine and ardent in the civilian population came at our call until more than one hundred and fifty thousand men and women were devoting highly specialized abilities to the work of the Committee, as faithful and devoted in their service as though they wore the khaki.

While America's summons was answered without question by the citizenship as a whole, it is to be remembered that during the three and a half years of our neutrality the land had been torn by a thousand divisive prejudices, stunned by the

George Creel, *How We Advertised America* (New York: Harper and Brothers, 1920), 3–8.

voices of anger and confusion, and muddled by the pull and haul of opposed interests. These were conditions that could not be permitted to endure. What we had to have was no mere surface unity, but a passionate belief in the justice of America's cause that should weld the people of the United States into one white-hot mass instinct with fraternity, devotion, courage, and deathless determination. The *war-will*, the will-to-win, of a democracy depends upon the degree to which each one of all the people of that democracy can concentrate and consecrate body and soul and spirit in the supreme effort of service and sacrifice. What had to be driven home was that all business was the nation's business, and every task a common task for a single purpose. . . .

. . . A speaking division toured great groups like the Blue Devils, Pershing's Veterans, and the Belgians, arranged mass-meetings in the communities, conducted forty-five war conferences from coast to coast, coordinated the entire speaking activities of the nation, and assured consideration to the crossroads hamlet as well as to the city.

The Four Minute Men, an organization that will live in history by reason of its originality and effectiveness, commanded the volunteer services of 75,000 speakers, operating in 5,200 communities, and making a total of 755,190 speeches, every one having the carry of shrapnel.

With the aid of a volunteer staff of several hundred translators, the Committee kept in direct touch with the foreign-language press, supplying selected articles designed to combat ignorance and disaffection. It organized and directed twenty-three societies and leagues designed to appeal to certain classes and particular foreign-language groups, each body carrying a specific message of unity and enthusiasm to its section of America's adopted peoples.

It planned war exhibits for the state fairs of the United States, also a great series of interallied war expositions that brought home to our millions the exact nature of the struggle that was being waged in France. In Chicago alone two million people attended in two weeks, and in nineteen cities the receipts aggregated $1,432,261.36.

The Committee mobilized the advertising forces of the country—press, periodical, car, and outdoor—for the patriotic campaign that gave millions of dollars' worth of free space to the national service.

It assembled the artists of America on a volunteer basis for the production of posters, window-cards, and similar material of pictorial publicity for the use of various government departments and patriotic societies. A total of 1,438 drawings was used.

It issued an official daily newspaper, serving every department of government, with a circulation of one hundred thousand copies a day. For official use only, its value was such that private citizens ignored the supposedly prohibitive subscription price, subscribing to the amount of $77,622.58. . . .

Through the medium of the motion picture, America's war progress, as well as the meanings and purposes of democracy, were carried to every community in the United States and to every corner of the world. "Pershing's Crusaders," "America's Answer," and "Under Four Flags" were types of feature films by which we drove home America's resources and determinations, while other pictures, showing our social and industrial life, made our free institutions vivid to foreign peoples.

9. Cartoons for and Against the League of Nations, 1920

INTERRUPTING THE CEREMONY

THE ACCUSER

▶ E S S A Y S

The stakes at the end of World War I turned out to be very high indeed, since in retrospect many historians have placed the blame for World War II on the failings of the Treaty of Versailles and the League of Nations. Walter McDougall of the University of Pennsylvania articulates the view that a messianic, egotistical Wilson ventured into matters far beyond his understanding. Wilson's idealistic but ill-considered crusade divided America and further unraveled the fabric of European stability. The president made terrible compromises in return for England and France's agreement to the Treaty of Versailles, while failing utterly to compromise with his rivals at home. Robert A. Pastor of American University in Washington, D.C., disputes the idea that Wilson was on a fool's errand, even though the president failed to get his treaty through Congress. The American model of a new world order did not come about in 1920, but it did become the basis for a more peaceable international system after 1945, Pastor points out. Wilson lamented at the end of his career: "I had to negotiate with my back to the wall. Men thought I had all the power. Would to God I had had such power." Considering the powers that Wilson did have, do you think he employed them well? Was he wise, or not, in breaking George Washington's "Great Rule?"

Woodrow Wilson: Egocentric Crusader

WALTER MCDOUGALL

"The only place in the world where nothing has to be explained to me is the South." An extraordinary admission by a man who would tell the whole world how to arrange its affairs, but that is what Wilson said. A Virginian descended from Presbyterian ministers on both sides of his family, he took the religion of his household for granted in the cerebral and sometimes smug way of the Calvinist elect. So certain was he of his spiritual correctness that a Catholic friend called him a "Presbyterian priest." And so deaf was Wilson to the aesthetics of other Christian liturgies that he pronounced the Episcopalian service "very stupid indeed . . . a ridiculous way of worshiping God, and one which must give very little pleasure to God." And yet this man who could parse a biblical text or dissect social ills with Presbyterian exactitude might also, of an evening, summon his family or friends to a naughty séance at the ouija board. He dabbled in numerology, too, his own lucky number being thirteen.

Wilson believed in predestination, not only in the hereafter but in time. He knew that God had chosen him to do great things, a faith that survived his indifferent schoolwork and utter failure while a student of law. As a Princeton undergraduate, "Tommy" Wilson drafted classmates into games and clubs so that he could play the leader and indulge his love of things British. In war games he fancied himself a British squadron commander, in political clubs a British minister swaying Parliament with his rhetoric. He kept a portrait of the crusading Christian prime minister William Ewart Gladstone on his desk, and he attributed the death of American oratory to the congressional system in which decisions were made through committee rather than debate on the floor. . . .

Not surprisingly, Wilson embraced Progressive Imperialism. It suited his belief in the white man's calling and his notion of presidential government. So he cheered annexation of the Philippines and Puerto Rico—"They are children and we are men in these deep matters of government and justice"—and the fact that foreign policy again dominated U.S. politics. Now there would be "greatly increased power and opportunity for constructive statesmanship given the President." A strong executive, he wrote, "must utter every initial judgment, take every first step of action, supply the information upon which [the country] is to act, suggest and in large measure control its conduct."

In time, Wilson was named president of Princeton University—or "prime minister," as he liked to say—where he acquired a Cromwellian reputation for being a bold reformer and thorough authoritarian. Looking to Oxford and Cambridge for models, he placed junior faculty and graduate students (preceptors) in charge of the undergraduates, and tried to break up Princeton's exclusive fraternal clubs in favor of residential quadrangles. His purpose was "to attract more high school students of slender means to Princeton and to make the sons of the wealthy as unlike their fathers as possible." The expensive and radical project angered alumni and faculty, but Wilson refused to budge: "As long as I am president of Princeton, I propose to dictate the architectural policy of the university."

If any trait bubbles up in all one reads about Wilson, it is this: he loved, craved, and in a sense glorified power. That may seem anomalous in a pious Progressive and contemporary of Lord Acton, who warned, "Power tends to corrupt; absolute power corrupts absolutely." But Acton was a Catholic who believed in original sin; he was making a statement about the nature of man, not about the abstraction called power. Wilson, by contrast, leaned on "God's all-powerful arm," and defined power as the "capacity to make effective decisions" so as to nudge people and institutions along their appointed road toward perfection. In *Congressional Government* Wilson confessed, "I cannot imagine power as a thing negative and not positive." And in a 1911 address, "The Bible and Progress," he said, "Let no man suppose that progress can be divorced from religion . . . the man whose faith is rooted in the Bible knows that reform cannot be stayed."

In the end, his one-crusader stance lost him the quad fight at Princeton but attracted the attention of New Jersey Democrats, who massaged Wilson's image into that of an incorruptible paladin of the common man. He was elected governor, then nominated for president in the year when Teddy Roosevelt's insurgency tore the Republican Party asunder. The campaign of 1912 thus became a three-way fight for the soul of industrial America. Taft represented stand-pat Republicanism in league with big business. Roosevelt praised corporations for their efficiency, but called for big government agencies to referee conflicts between capital and labor. Wilson blamed the ills of industrialism on simple greed, and promised a New Freedom based on competition and opportunity for all.

Everyone quotes Wilson's utterance that "it would be an irony of fate if my administration had to deal chiefly with foreign affairs." As it happened, he succeeded in introducing most of his domestic agenda, and won his fights for tariff reduction, the Federal Reserve Act, and the income tax. The real irony in his remark was that he had more latitude to exercise power and assert moral principles in foreign than in domestic policy—a fact that Wilson the political scientist had shrewdly observed. What is more, he did not shun foreign policy but jumped into it within days of his inauguration. . . .

. . . Thus did Wilson reaffirm the Roosevelt Corollary, but strip from it any intimation that U.S. strategic or economic self-interest was involved. On the contrary, Wilson renounced all territorial ambition and, in a speech at Mobile in October 1913, called it "a very perilous thing to determine the foreign policy of a nation in terms of material interest. It not only is unfair to those with whom you are dealing, but it is degrading as regards your own actions."

Let us pause for a moment to let that sink in. According to Wilson, it was dangerous, unfair, and disgraceful to pursue a foreign policy based on material self-interest. Now, we may applaud the fact that he refused to commit the nation to conflict just to pull some bankers' bonds out of the fire. But what would John Quincy Adams have said of a policy that not only renounced but denounced the governments' obligation to protect American property and suggested instead that a policy was just and prudent only if it served platonic abstractions like justice? . . .

The British gave Wilson a blank check to do what he liked in Mexico, but otherwise were dumbfounded. Ambassador Sir Cecil Spring Rice wrote that Wilson talked to newspapermen or members of Congress "at length in excellent language, but when they leave him they say to each other, 'What on earth did he say?'" . . . In 1914 British emissary Sir Edward Tyrrell told Wilson, "I shall be asked to explain your Mexican policy—can you tell me what it is?" Wilson replied, "I am going to teach the South American republics to elect good men."

A mystery indeed, because promising to make the Mexican revolution somehow turn out "right" only made Wilson a prisoner of events. . . .

American diplomacy during World War I is usually described in terms of Wilson's struggle to uphold neutral rights at sea, as if it were a reprise of the situation during the Napoleonic Wars. There were parallels, for again Britain and her continental rival—France then, now Germany—blockaded each other and interfered with neutral commerce in systematic and arrogant ways. U.S. trade with German-occupied Europe shrank almost to nothing within eighteen months of the outbreak of war. By contrast, the German submarine blockade did not prevent U.S. exports to Britain and France from almost quadrupling by 1916 to $2.75 billion. But submarines necessarily took lives as well as property, and were for that reason more heinous than the Royal Navy's surface blockade. What is more, most U.S. diplomatic activity from 1914 to 1917 did concern neutral rights at sea, and the timing of Wilson's ultimate decision to fight derived in part from the German decision to sink without warning all ships of any nationality bound for Britain ("unrestricted submarine warfare").

Notwithstanding all that, the damage done to U.S. commerce seems to have interested Wilson little. Nor did he cling to neutrality because it was American tradition, or because he was a pacifist (he was not), or because the American people were almost unanimously in favor of staying out of the war. He did it because he believed that remaining above the battle was the only way that he, Wilson, could exert the moral authority needed to end the war on terms that would make for a lasting peace. Within a few weeks of the outbreak of war on August 1, 1914, Wilson told his brother-in-law that the principles guiding the future must be: no more territorial gains achieved by conquest; equality of rights for small nations; government control of arms manufacture; and an "association of nations wherein all shall guarantee the territorial integrity of each." Compared with this lofty quest, the material losses of American shippers were small beer indeed. . . .

Buoyed by his [1916 electoral] victory, Wilson launched a final peace offensive. He had reason for optimism, since the German chancellor had quietly but urgently asked for a new U.S. initiative. (In truth, the German high command had given him a deadline to achieve a favorable peace or else it would resume unrestricted submarine warfare.) But the belligerents dared not trim their war aims sufficiently to interest their opponents, so Wilson aimed his Peace Without Victory speech of January 22, 1917, not at the governments but at "the peoples of the countries now at war." Any peace forced on the losers, he said, would be built on sand. Hence both alliances must renounce their ambitions and "with one accord adopt the doctrine of President Monroe as the doctrine of the whole world."

What sounded like reason and mercy to Wilson, however, was madness and cant in European ears. London and Paris took Wilson to mean that the United States had no intention of fighting Germany no matter what outrages the latter committed. Or, at best, the Americans might join the war but in opposition to Allied war aims as well as to Germany's. Bonar Law spoke for the British cabinet when he sighed, "What Mr. Wilson is longing for we are fighting for," and historian Sir George Trevelyan called Wilson "the quintessence of a prig. What a notion that the nations of Europe, after this terrible effort, will join him in putting down international encroachments by arms, at some future time, if he is afraid to denounce such encroachments even in words now!" Georges Clemenceau, soon to become French premier, said of Wilson's speech: "Never before has any political assembly heard so fine a sermon on what human beings might be capable of accomplishing if only they weren't human." But the bitterest critique of Peace Without Victory was Theodore Roosevelt's. Wilson's suggestion of a moral equivalence between the two sides was "wickedly false," talk of peacekeeping after the war "premature," and the reference to the Monroe Doctrine a contradiction in terms. "If his words mean anything, they would mean that hereafter we intended to embark on a policy of violent meddling in every European quarrel, and in return to invite Old World nations violently to meddle in everything American. Of course, as a matter of fact, the words mean nothing whatever." . . .

Historians have rarely asked *whether* the United States should have gone to war in 1917, but rather what Wilson's motives were for doing so. In the 1930s critics charged that U.S. policy had become a hostage of munitions makers and Wall Street bankers, and that Wilson's unneutral acts had given the United States a stake in an Allied victory. The former contention was unfounded: as we know, Wilson rejected materialist policies and was contemptuous of big business. The latter contention seems to have been obvious, since the United States had solid security reasons for preferring an Allied victory. As U.S. diplomat Lewis Einstein had written in 1913, "The European balance of power is a political necessity which can alone sanction in the Western Hemisphere the continuance of an economic development unhandicapped by the burden of extensive armaments." Any European war would damage American interests, thought Einstein, but a German victory would be a calamity. He boldly suggested that the United States "extend the Monroe Doctrine to England" and deter Germany from launching a war. But few Americans were aware of their dependence on a balance of power and Anglo-American command of the seas, and however much Wilson might have appreciated that truth, he anathematized balance-of-power politics. Instead of telling the American people that they had to fight to defend the Atlantic Ocean from Germany, Wilson "managed to convert a successful national effort into a lost crusade."

And as always, Wilson stood alone. He was careful to describe the United States as an "associated" not an "allied" power, by which he meant that he did not recognize the Allies' war aims as codified in their secret treaties. So even as the United States lent military assistance to the Allies, it was implicitly a political rival of them. As of November 1917, it was also a rival of the de facto government of Russia. That was when Lenin and the Bolsheviks seized power in Petrograd and Moscow and called on the workers and soldiers of all nations to stop fighting and overthrow their imperialist governments. Echoing Wilson, Lenin called for a peace of "No Annexations, No Indemnities!" Echoing Lenin, Wilson announced his own war aims in the Fourteen Points speech of January 1918, to which he later added twenty-four principles, ends, particulars, and declarations. So it was that four, not two, contestants fought to control the world's future in 1918: the German militarists, the democratic but imperialist Allies, Wilson with his program of Liberal Internationalism, and Communists preaching social revolution. . . .

Perhaps the greatest irony of the fight over the Treaty of Versailles, which contained the League Covenant, was that most Americans and members of the Senate were not especially hostile to its terms. Few Americans objected to the harsh conditions (disarmament, demilitarization and occupation of the Rhineland, loss of territories, seizure of Germany's fleet and overseas colonies) and open-ended reparations foisted on Germany (which Wilson himself called for in the Fourteen Points). Nor did most Americans care a fig for the fate of Fiume, which exercised the Italians, or the Chinese port of Kiao-Chow, which Japan had seized and would not give up. The Senate may even have been willing to ratify the guarantee against future German aggression that Wilson and Lloyd George promised to France even though it was an entangling alliance. The harshest critics of the peace terms, in fact, were disheartened Democrats.

What did disturb senators was that the League of Nations Covenant—especially the collective security obligation in Article Ten—seemed incompatible with the existing traditions of U.S. policy. . . .

Republican Herbert Hoover, for instance, did not like Article Ten because he thought the League's purpose should be "the pacific settlement of controversies among free nations," but he was willing to accept it with reservations. Roosevelt, too, wanted "to join the other civilized nations of the world in some scheme that in a time of great stress would offer a likelihood of obtaining settlements that will avert war." He insisted only that the League not be made a substitute for military preparedness and the national interest. Republicans Root and Hughes feared that Article Ten might prove to be "a trouble-breeder, and not a peace-maker." But they still viewed the League as a way to continue wartime cooperation, keep Germany down, and settle disputes so long as it complemented traditional deterrents. All were willing to follow Wilson's lead. They just wanted their doubts addressed before they were asked to endorse a new diplomatic tradition. . . .

Upon his return to Paris, Wilson did obtain amendments to the Covenant including a right of withdrawal, removal of immigration and tariffs from the League's purview, and recognition of the Monroe Doctrine. So he came home confident that the revised Covenant he deposed on the Senate on July 10, 1919, would win swift ratification. "The stage is set, the destiny disclosed. It has come about by no plan of our conceiving, but by the hand of God, who led us into the way." Reporters asked if he would entertain reservations to the treaty. "I shall consent to nothing," said Wilson. "The Senate must take its medicine."

The Republican leadership refused the spoon. Lodge bought time by reading the entire Treaty of Versailles on the floor of the Senate, then called sixty witnesses to testify before the Foreign Relations Committee. . . .

The Senate divided into four factions. Sixteen irreconcilables, led by Hiram Johnson (R., Calif.) and Borah, were opposed to the League in any form. As Borah said, "The proposition is force to destroy force, conflict to prevent conflict, militarism to destroy militarism, war to prevent war." It also meant the extinction of American nationality: "It is difficult to tell just how long the real Americans will sit still and permit the infamous propaganda to go on. I have just as much respect for the Bolshevist who would internationalize our whole system from below as I would for the broadcloth gentlemen who would internationalize it from above." The second and third factions were "hard" and "soft" reservationists, numbering twenty and twelve respectively. They were not "isolationists." As Root argued, "If it is necessary for the security of western Europe that we should agree to the support of France if attacked, then let us agree to do that particular thing plainly. . . . But let us not wrap up such a purpose in a vague universal obligation." All told, some fifty reservations and amendments were introduced, but Root and Lodge narrowed them down to fourteen and released them on November 19. . . .

Clearly these reservations were designed not to gut the peace that Wilson had fashioned, but to ensure that his new order did not gut the sovereignty and Constitution of the United States and the Monroe Doctrine. Had Wilson been willing to swallow them, or an even milder package promoted by some Senate Democrats, the Treaty of Versailles would have been ratified. But he was convinced that the reservations would castrate the League, and in any case he hated Lodge. "Never, never! I'll never consent to adopt any policy with which that impossible man is so prominently identified." So he drafted a letter urging loyal Democrats, the fourth Senate faction, to oppose all reservations, with the perverse result that most Republicans voted *for* the League (with reservations) and almost all Democrats *against* it. The treaty with reservations failed 39 to 55, and the treaty without reservations 38 to 53. . . .

Whether or not Wilsonianism was the message the world needed to hear after World War I, Woodrow Wilson was surely the wrong messenger—not because he was too religious, but because his religion was too personal, sanctimonious, gnostic. Senator Lawrence Y. Sherman (R., Ill.) put his finger on it when he called the League Covenant "a revolutionary document" inspired by the impossible dream of "a sinless world." Yet Wilson never doubted that he would be vindicated: "I would rather fail in a cause that will ultimately triumph than triumph in a cause that will ultimately fail."

Many historians would say that he was vindicated, since Wilson's Liberal Internationalist tenets informed the foreign policies of every administration after him. In

1920 the Republican platform endorsed an "agreement among the nations to preserve the peace of the world [but] without the compromise of national independence." . . .

As a blueprint for world order, Wilsonianism has always been a chimera, but as an ideological weapon against "every arbitrary power anywhere," it has proved mighty indeed. And that, in the end, is how Wilson did truly imitate Jesus. He brought not peace but a sword. . . .

Woodrow Wilson: Father of the Future

ROBERT A. PASTOR

The twentieth-century arrived two years early in American foreign policy. The Spanish-American War of 1898 constituted a watershed in America's relations with the world, separating an isolationist nineteenth century from a globally engaged twentieth century. Since its independence, America had viewed itself as special and different from Europe, but Americans were often divided as to how to translate this self-image into policy. Before 1898 the debates were largely resolved in favor of America standing aloof from the world as a "promised land." In the twentieth century, Americans gradually realized they had an important role to play in the world, but they still debated what that role should be—whether to be an example worthy of emulation or an activist shaping the world; whether or not to be imperialist; whether to define U.S. interests in a far-sighted or narrow way; and whether to act alone or with others.

The answers to those questions have not always been consistent, but a pattern became evident: U.S. policy was aimed not just to advance U.S. interests but to change the world. With deep roots in the country's unique heritage and favorable geography, an American idea of a new international system slowly began to crystallize. When it declared war against Spain, Washington shocked Europe by renouncing the war's main prize, Cuba. Theodore Roosevelt's goal of building a strong independent power that would open the world's doors to trade and pledge not to take its neighbors' territory added two more elements to the developing vision, but it was Woodrow Wilson who gave fullest expression to a truly revolutionary worldview.

Wilson's goal went beyond winning World War I: He wanted to prevent all future wars and at the same time make the world safe for democracy. His proposal was quintessentially American: The European balance of power system must be dismantled in favor of a "community of power"—a League of Nations—that would guarantee the self-determination of all nations and therefore eliminate the cause of wars. The countries defeated in World War I must be given a stake and a place in the new system; there must be "peace without victory"; there must be no indemnities and no colonies. These ideas were too radical to be accepted in 1918 but too compelling to be denied in 1945.

It was not just Europe that was unwilling to trade its sovereignty and self-defense for a new system based on collective security. The United States was never as

Robert A. Pastor, "The United States: Divided by a Revolutionary Vision" in Robert A. Pastor, ed., *A Century's Journey: How the Great Powers Shape the World* (New York: Basic Books, 1999), 191–193, 206–214, 233–235, 238. Reprinted by permission of Basic Books, a member of Perseus Books, L.L.C.

committed to Wilsonianism in practice as it was in its rhetoric. Always watching the rearview mirror to make sure it wouldn't be rear-ended by the old order, the United States never allowed an international institution to replace its hands on the steering wheel or its foot on the brake pedal. America's idealism defined the world's mission, but its realism safeguarded its own security. . . .

For a century following the Napoleonic Wars, the United States benefited from Europe's general peace and localized wars. When World War I began, the United States tried to avoid being drawn into it. Wilson declared U.S. neutrality and issued ten proclamations to define the rights of neutrals. Sensitive to their need for U.S. support but also wanting to prevent goods from reaching Germany, the British took care to respect U.S. rights. Germany's ability to compete against the British Navy depended on a new weapon, submarines, whose rules of engagement had not been defined. When German U-boats began to sink ocean liners, notably the *Lusitania,* whose passengers included 124 Americans, the United States protested vehemently. In an effort to keep the United States out of the war, Germany instructed its submarine commanders not to attack neutral merchant ships or any passenger ships. Nonetheless public opinion in the United States continued to turn against Germany, though Americans still did not want to fight.

Wilson had to walk a tightrope of neutrality. He was accused by Theodore Roosevelt of being too neutral in a war between democracy and autocracy, and by William Jennings Bryan, his secretary of state, of not being neutral enough. After Wilson sent a tough message to Germany condemning U-boat attacks, Bryan resigned on June 8, 1915. Wilson later healed the rift with Bryan, who endorsed him for a second term. Wilson won in a close election that included the slogan, "He kept us out of war."

Even before Wilson's second inaugural, the German government decided to try to bring the war to a quick end. On January 31, 1917, Germany informed the U.S. government that it would begin unrestricted submarine warfare in the war zone. The Germans believed that they could defeat England in five months and that even if the United States declared war, it could not mobilize quickly enough to affect the outcome. Wilson broke off relations with Germany. The British intercepted the "Zimmerman telegram" and three weeks later, turned over to Wilson this cable from the German foreign minister to his ambassador in Mexico City in which Germany proposed an alliance with Mexico against the United States. In the event of their victory, the Germans promised to help Mexico "reconquer the lost territory in Texas, New Mexico, and Arizona." The contents of the telegram were leaked to the press, and Americans were outraged.

The Zimmerman telegram and German attacks on three U.S. ships between March 12 and 18 were the events that finally convinced Wilson, his cabinet, and most Americans that they had to fight. On April 2, 1917, Wilson addressed Congress and asked for a declaration of war. He said that America must accept the "status of belligerent which thus has been thrust upon it" by German attacks on U.S. and other neutral ships. America must fight "for the rights of nations great and small and the privilege of men everywhere to choose their way of life. The world must be made safe for democracy."

Only five Senators spoke against the declaration. Senator George Norris said that he opposed entry into the war because the United States had not been completely neutral. Wall Street, in his judgment, was behind the war: "There is no doubt in my mind but the enormous amount of money loaned to the allies in this country has been instrumental in bringing about a public sentiment in favor of our country taking a course that would make every bond worth a hundred cents on the dollar." He urged his colleagues to recall George Washington's warning about entangling alliances: "Let Europe solve her problems as we have solved ours." Before the Germans sank U.S. ships, many Americans shared Norris's view. In April 1917, his was a lonely voice. The Senate voted for war 82 to 6, as did the House, 373 to 50.

By this time Wilson also wanted the United State to enter the war so that he could have a hand in constructing the peace. No other leader gave as much thought or solicited and synthesized more revolutionary ideas on how the world political system should be restructured to stop future wars. From the beginning of the war, Wilson's mind turned to the fundamental questions: How to mediate an end to the war? How to assure permanent peace? He sent his principal adviser, Colonel Edward House, to Europe several times in search of an answer to the first question, but the Europeans wanted to win, not settle. Wilson therefore spent most of his time on the longer-term issue. His first thought was to try to secure mutual guarantees of territorial integrity and political independence under republican forms of government, and he decided the power of this idea could be demonstrated in the Americas. He proposed to the ambassadors of Argentina, Brazil, and Chile a "Pan-American Pact" to "mutualize" the Monroe Doctrine and to be a model that Europe could follow to end the war. Argentina and Brazil approved the idea, but Chile had reservations. In the end, Wilson's interventions in Mexico and the Caribbean precluded hemispheric agreement, but the idea would be central in his subsequent peace proposals.

Beginning in May 1916 Wilson tried to awaken Americans to a new role as participants "in the life of the world" rather than as "disconnected lookers-on." In his "Peace Without Victory" address to a joint session of Congress on January 22, 1917, Wilson asked, "Is the present war a struggle for a just and secure peace, or only for a new balance of power?" He answered with a set of revolutionary principles that borrowed from James Monroe but reached all the way back to Immanuel Kant:

> There must be, not a balance of power, but a community of power; not organized rivalries, but an organized common peace . . . I am proposing, as it were, that the nations would with one accord adopt the doctrine of President Monroe as the doctrine of the world: that no nation should seek to extend its polity over any other nation or people, but that every people should be left free to determine its own polity.

If all sides would acknowledge the stalemate and accept "peace without victory," not only would the war end but there would be no defeated power seeking revenge in a second war. Acceptance of self-determination would eliminate the causes of war (colonies and reparations), and a concert of powers, greater than any nation, would be able to enforce the peace. Wilson was proposing nothing less than a complete change in the way states defined their interests and the way the international system should work.

A year later, after the U.S. had entered the war, Wilson and House sat down for two hours one morning and condensed their thoughts into a fourteen-point peace plan, which Wilson delivered to Congress on January 8, 1918. The first five points set out the basic elements of "progressive internationalism": no secret treaties ("open

covenants of peace, openly arrived at"); freedom of the seas; reduction of trade barriers and equality of trade conditions; reduction of national armaments to the lowest
possible level; and an impartial adjustment of colonial claims based on the principle
of self-determination. The next points called for the withdrawal of foreign armies
to their own lands, the welcoming of revolutionary Russia "into the society of free
nations," the adjustment of boundaries along clear lines of nationality, and the
creation of a Polish state with access to the sea. Wilson left the most important point,
his proposal for a League of Nations, for last: "A general association of nations must
be formed under specific covenants for the purpose of affording mutual guarantees
of political independence and territorial integrity to great and small states alike."

"These are American principles," Wilson proclaimed, and he added, "they are
the principles of mankind and must prevail." He also reached out to Germany: "We
have no jealousy of German greatness, and there is nothing in this program that
impairs it . . . We wish her only to accept a place of equality among the peoples of
the world."

The speech was praised widely, and it elicited some peace feelers. But the Germans then imposed a punishing peace treaty on Russia and moved its forces west.
The United States raised an army of 5 million men within one year, but they did not
arrive in large enough numbers to make a difference until the autumn of 1918,
when they helped blunt a German offensive. The Germans retreated to Belgium and
appealed to Wilson for talks based on the Fourteen Points, but the request came at a
politically awkward time. Congressional elections were approaching, and the Republicans, more attuned to American anger over 116,000 casualties, wanted Germany defeated, not accommodated. In order to win the congressional elections, the
Republican leadership united behind a strategy of attacking Wilson's peace plan.
Theodore Roosevelt demanded unconditional surrender and urged the Senate to reject
the Fourteen Points. Henry Cabot Lodge accused Wilson of accepting "peace at any
price" because his advisers were "socialists and Bolsheviks." Wilson stiffened his
demands to the Germans. He then tried to bring the Germans and the Allies to the
bargaining table and to win the congressional elections. He succeeded only in gaining German agreement to an armistice on November 11. Five days earlier, the Republicans had won control of both houses of Congress. Henry Cabot Lodge became
chairman of the Senate Foreign Relations Committee. The election campaign was so
poisonous that Wilson refused to appoint Lodge or any senior Republican to advise
him on the peace negotiations.

Europe's leaders dismissed Wilson's plan as naïve, but they could not ignore
the vast and enthusiastic crowds that met Wilson in England, France, and Italy or the
popular response to his speeches urging fundamental change in the international
system. Still, when Wilson sat down to negotiate, he found himself alone, asking his
European counterparts to discard the rules of a 400-year-old inter-state system in
exchange for a set of untried, idealistic principles. The first issue on the table was
the disposal of Germany's colonies, and every country except the United States made
claims based on the age-old principle "To the victor belongs the spoils." Wilson listened until his patience was exhausted. Then, like a professor who was frustrated
with his students because they could not grasp the point of his lecture, he reminded
the others of the purpose of their negotiations: "The world was against any further
annexations. [If they occurred] the League of Nations would be discredited from

the beginning." He explained his plan for ending colonialism and protecting the people "under the full view of the world, until they were able to take charge of their own affairs." The English were the most indignant, but all the Allied representatives responded as if they were from a different world, as indeed they were. All the major powers except the United States also opposed small power representation on the League's Executive Council. The Japanese requested a provision on racial equality, but the English blocked it, along with two American proposals, for freedom of religion and of the seas. Wilson nonetheless negotiated with great skill and perseverance and was able to preserve enough of his points that he could present a draft to the world on February 14, 1919, and return to the United States to consult and defend it.

Between February 23 and his return to France in early March, Wilson met with numerous groups and at least thirty-four senators for intensive discussions on the draft. There was great enthusiasm among the American public for the League of Nations Covenant, but on the day before Wilson's return to Paris to continue the peace talks, Lodge offered a stiff critique that mixed vitriol with some searing substantive points. After accusing the president of abandoning George Washington in favor of "Trotsky, the champion of internationalism," Lodge displayed a round-robin letter, signed by thirty-seven senators, indicating that the treaty would not be approved in its current form. He then recommended four changes: an affirmation of the Monroe Doctrine, a provision for withdrawal from the League of Nations, explicit exclusion of domestic issues (such as immigration) from the League of Nations Covenant, and clarification of how the League would use force.

Former President William Howard Taft and the Senate Democratic leader Gilbert Hitchkock assured Wilson that if he could amend the treaty along the lines recommended by Lodge, "the ground will be completely cut from under the opposition." The Allies were aware of the round-robin letter, and they were ready to amend the League Covenant in exchange for Wilson's accepting harsh provisions in the Treaty of Versailles. France wanted to annex the Saar but accepted a fifteen-year Allied occupation of the Rhineland, a separate Anglo-American defense treaty, and an exorbitant increase in reparations from Germany. The Italians demanded parts of Austria; the Japanese threatened to bolt the conference unless they received German concessions in Shandong. All insisted on a vengeful war-guilt clause against Germany. With a heavy heart, Wilson struck the compromises to accommodate Lodge. These changes diminished the enthusiasm of the progressive internationalists, the League's strongest supporters, which made selling the agreement that much harder. The Treaty of Versailles, which included the League Covenant, was signed on June 28, 1919, in the Hall of Mirrors, and Wilson turned to his next battle.

The Senate debate on the Treaty of Versailles has been described as having pitted internationalists against isolationists, but there were only twelve irreconcilably isolationist Republicans. The more interesting debate was not between them and the internationalists but between the "unilateral" and the "cooperative" internationalists. The unilateralists were thirty-seven Republican senators who supported Lodge; they wanted to constrain the League and ensure that the United States would retain the freedom to act unilaterally. The League's supporters, forty-seven Democratic senators, agreed with Wilson that international institutions should stop all wars.

Despite Wilson's success in amending the League Covenant and making it a part of the treaty, Lodge was still not reconciled to it because, in his words, it placed "the destiny of my country under the control of a politically selected tribunal of nine . . . sitting forever upon foreign soil . . . The spirit of this plan to subordinate this great Republic into this international socialistic combine is absolutely in the face and teeth and eyes of our Constitution." His second point also had the ring of tradition: "Before I go into the stabilizing business abroad, I believe in making the foundations of a republican-democratic form of government safe and stable in my own country."

President Wilson met with groups of Republican senators and realized they supported Lodge, who was stalling the debate. On September 2, despite poor health, the president decided to build support for the League around the country, and he began a national tour that would take him to twenty-nine cities to give thirty-seven speeches to rebut his opponents' arguments: "I want to call you to witness that the peace of the world cannot be established without America . . . [and] the peace and goodwill of the world are necessary to America."

He returned to Washington exhausted, and on October 2 he suffered a stroke that paralyzed one side of his body. Wilson became inflexible both physically and temperamentally at the very moment compromises were desperately needed, although it is by no means clear that a compromise was possible. Lodge had crafted fourteen reservations that struck at the League's heart. For example, as a substitute for the League's collective security provision, Lodge proposed a provision stating, "The U.S. assumes no obligation to preserve the territorial integrity or political independence of any country . . . unless . . . Congress . . . by act or joint resolution [shall] so provide." Other reservations were aimed at releasing the United States from commitments agreed in the League Covenant and the treaty unless Congress specifically approved. The treaty came to the Senate floor for a vote three times, the first time with Lodge's reservations, the second without, and the third with some support by Democrats for Lodge's reservations. Each time, it failed.

The tragedy was that in order to secure the League of Nations, Wilson had to compromise on so many of his Fourteen Points that the Treaty of Versailles reflected the old order more than the new. The harsh reparations and the war-guilt clause imposed on Germany sowed seeds that were to bear bitter fruit for Europe. The decision to transfer Germany's concession in China to Japan not only alienated the Chinese from the United States but set the stage for the next war in Asia. Worse, Wilson could not deliver his own country. It was not at all clear that the League of Nations would have been able to deter or confront aggressors if the United States had been a member, but it was reasonably clear that it could not do so without the United States. Moreover, the U.S. failure to approve the agreement to defend France against German attack left France naked, with neither a new institution nor a balance of power that could prevent the next war.

Perhaps a stronger, more flexible Wilson could have won a weakened League. But it is also possible that he was just too far in front of the American people at that time. Beneath the debate among internationalists was a powerful postwar undercurrent tugging Americans home, back to "normalcy," fearful of Europe's wars and the Russian Revolution. The United States succumbed to a Red Scare in 1920 when A. Mitchell Palmer, Wilson's attorney general, launched anticommunist raids in thirty-three cities in one night. By the end of the year, Warren G. Harding won a landslide victory that reflected the nation's yearning to turn inward. Lodge interpreted Harding's victory as his as well: "So far as the United States is concerned, the League is dead."

Besides the rejection of the League and the World Court, other signs that America wanted to close the door on the world included congressional approval of the country's first laws limiting worldwide immigration. The nation's leaders, predominantly Anglo-Saxon Protestants, reacted to the heavy influx of immigrants from southern and eastern Europe. Nearly 20 million people had immigrated in the two decades before the war. Congress accepted as "scientific fact" that the new immigrants were of lower quality than those who had preceded them and that a successful America required more of the original and fewer of the newer immigrants. The quotas set by the laws reflected the ethnic composition of America in 1890, before the new wave of immigration. The immigration debate coincided with an ugly mood of intolerance, reflected in the rise of the Ku Klux Klan and other nativist groups. . . .

The United States had the world's strongest economy at both the beginning and the end of the twentieth century, although over the course of the century it changed from a commodity producer and manufacturer to a nation that relied on information, technology, and services. Though it was still relatively autonomous economically as compared to most of the other powers, the United States was more than twice as dependent on trade in 1996 as it was in 1970, and that was roughly twice as dependent as in 1913. A century after emerging from its strategic cocoon, the United States stands alone, with a military capacity that dwarfs that of any plausible combination of rivals. The economic and military indicators, however, tell only a small part of the story of the U.S. impact on the international system in the twentieth century and its probable effect in the future. The real story is how unorthodox U.S. ideas changed the very character of the system.

In June 1914 Wilson posed the pivotal question for the United States:

> What are we going to do with the influence and power of this great nation? Are we going to play the old role of using that power for our aggrandizement and material benefit only? You know what that may mean. It may upon occasion mean that we shall use it to make the peoples of other nations suffer in the way in which we said that it was intolerable to suffer when we uttered the Declaration of Independence.

Wilson's answer was evident from the way he posed the question: The United States would not play the "old role." Wilson defined new goals not just for the United States but for the world, and new instruments—international institutions and norms—to secure these goals of world peace and freedom. Tapping deep roots of U.S. idealism, Wilson offered answers to the fundamental questions of why wars occur and how they could be stopped, questions that challenged the foundations of the Westphalian interstate system. Balance of power, Wilson concluded, was not the solution; rather, it was part of the problem. Wilson's proposal, despite its utopian dress, was eminently practical: to reduce the benefits and increase the costs of war by gaining universal agreement on a powerful idea, self-determination, and an institution to enforce it, the League of Nations. This norm denies war's gains, and it increases its costs by giving a voice and legitimacy to those struggling for independence.

Wilson's ideas slowly grew legs and began to walk, uncertainly at first but within a few years after World War II territorial acquisition had virtually disappeared as a goal of states. Since 1945 only one state has tried to annex forcefully another UN member. . . .

How can we explain the continuity and changes in U.S. foreign policy in the twentieth century? The continuity in U.S. foreign policy follows from both geography and political culture. Only a country sitting securely between two large oceans and weak or friendly neighbors could have afforded to devote so much time to its own affairs and so little time, relative to the other great powers, to the world. A country composed of middle-class citizens who distrust central authority and who fear that war would strengthen their government, reduce their democracy, and risk their children is a country that keeps its government out of war until a security threat compels it to act. Then it fights zealously to vanquish the foe and return home as quickly as possible. Only a country settled by refugees and blessed with distant threats and a puritan's heritage could imagine a world without war and would design institutions not just to defeat foes but to banish all war and injustice. And only a country whose reigning philosophy was pragmatism would preserve its own freedom of action even while proclaiming a new world order based on international institutions. . . .

The twenty-first century will be very different from the twentieth. Testimony to the distance that the world has traveled toward America's vision is the grudging acknowledgment by Henry Kissinger, the classic realist, in his book, *Diplomacy:* "It is above all to the drumbeat of Wilsonian idealism that American foreign policy has marched since his watershed presidency and continues to march to this day." The United States changed the rules and the game of international politics in the twentieth century. The world today is different because the United States is different.

FURTHER READING

Nancy Bristow, *Making Men Moral: Social Engineering During the Great War* (1996).

Thomas Britten, *American Indians in World War I: At Home and at War* (1997).

John Milton Cooper, Jr., *The Warrior and the Priest: Woodrow Wilson and Theodore Roosevelt* (1983).

Leslie Midkiff DeBauche, *Reel Patriotism: The Movies and World War I* (1997).

Gerard DeGroot, *The First World War* (2001).

Robert Ferrell, *Woodrow Wilson and World War I* (1985).

Milton and Susan Harries, *The Last Days of Innocence: America at War* (1997).

George F. Kennan, *American Diplomacy, 1900–1950* (1951).

David M. Kennedy, *Over Here: The First World War and American Society* (1980).

Thomas J. Knock, *To End All Wars: Woodrow Wilson and the Quest for a New World Order* (1992).

Ronald Schaffer, *America in the Great War: The Rise of the War Welfare State* (1991).

Susan Zeiger, *In Uncle Sam's Service: Women Workers with the American Expeditionary Force* (1999).

CHAPTER
7

Crossing a Cultural Divide:
The Twenties

The Nebraska-born novelist Willa Cather famously said of the 1920s that "the world broke in two in 1922 or thereabouts." In that decade, for the first time, more Americans lived in towns than on farms. Mass industrialization, higher wages, and the wide use of credit placed modern products like the car, the vacuum cleaner, and the washing machine at the disposal of millions. Science made new discoveries that appeared to challenge old truths. The vote for women became law in 1920, and though few women became politicians, millions became flappers. In six years, hemlines went from the ankle, where they had been for centuries, to the knee. Film, radio, and advertising came into the lives of everyday Americans, expressing and reshaping their desires and dreams, and reminding them constantly that they lived in a new era.

Cultural change provoked deep conflict over religion, sex, gender roles, and ethnicity. The decade that invented dating *also coined the term* fundamentalism. *The rural vision of America seemed deeply at odds with the urban one, and myriad organizations formed to defend "white Anglo-Saxon Protestant" (WASP) traditions. One such organization was the revitalized Ku Klux Klan, which won legislative and executive elections throughout the Midwest and had nearly 3 million members by 1923. The most famous trial of the decade, the Scopes "monkey trial," epitomized the clash over modernism and the battle to hold the line against "Godless science." Ironically, Progressive icon William Jennings Bryan, leading the prosecution, appeared to stand against progress. Meanwhile, on a day-to-day level, the police struggled and failed to implement the crowning reform of the preceding decade, the prohibition of alcohol. The twenties became known instead for the willful flouting of Progressive-era moralizing: men drank, women smoked, and, worst of all, they did these things in one another's company. Youth culture became distinct from adult culture in this decade, and many young people were discernibly amused by the puritanical streak of the older generation.*

The decade also witnessed the culmination of the buildup of xenophobic sentiment that had been going on since the turn of the century. Many Americans concluded that the best way to keep out foreign ideas was to keep out foreigners. In 1924, Congress passed a National Origins Act that was specifically designed to limit Catholic and Jewish immigration and abolish Asian immigration altogether. Proponents sought the triumph of "Nordic" (north European) whites and the

Protestant religion. But the gates swung closed on a population that was already enormously diverse in its religious beliefs and ethnic character, and whose face was turned to the future. The modern era was underway.

◤ Q U E S T I O N S   T O   T H I N K   A B O U T

Why was there a great debate in the 1920s about the future? Who won it, the modernists or the fundamentalists? Would you characterize this period primarily as the Age of Jazz or as the Age of Prohibition?

◤ D O C U M E N T S

The documents in this chapter illustrate many aspects of the cultural changes that took place in the 1920s. In Document 1, the Governor of California decries the economic competition of the Japanese and their shockingly high fertility. He articulates a commitment to ending Asian immigration that went from the citizenry to the highest levels of government. Document 2 is a fervent appeal by Reverend Amzi Dixon of Raleigh, North Carolina. The Reverend counters the theory of evolution, which he says denies the glory of God and enshrines the notion that "might makes right." The changing morality of modern youth is scrutinized in Document 3, taken from a survey of high school students sponsored by business executives in Michigan. Document 4 shows the famous clash between attorney Clarence Darrow and William Jennings Bryan in the Scopes "monkey trial." They spoke from opposite sides of the cultural divide noted by Willa Cather. Former Secretary of State Bryan defended a literal interpretation of the Bible, including the story of the Earth's origins as told in Genesis. Darrow, retained by the American Civil Liberties Union, spoke for modern science. Document 5 is by F. Scott Fitzgerald, the handsome young novelist who epitomized for many the glamour of the Jazz Age. *The Great Gatsby* reveals the flapper style at its height, the decline in female deference, and the appeal of racist ideology to men whose world was changing faster than they liked. Document 6 outlines the program of the Ku Klux Klan and reveals the extent to which religion, race, and patriotism were inseparably intertwined in the Klan definition of "American." Document 7 is from a famous sociological study of Muncie, Indiana (called Middletown), in the 1920s that showed how new mass products like the automobile reshaped people's values. The last selection (Document 8) shows the literary power that brought Langston Hughes to fame in the Harlem Renaissance and expresses the sentiments that propelled African Americans out of the South.

1. The Governor of California Tells of the "Japanese Problem," 1920

The Japanese in our midst have indicated a strong trend to land ownership and land control, and by their unquestioned industry and application, and by standards and methods that are widely separated from our occidental standards and methods, both in connection with hours of labor and standards of living, have gradually developed to a control of many of our important agricultural industries. Indeed, at the present

California State Board of Control, *California and the Oriental* (Sacramento: State Printing Office, June 1920), 8–13.

time they operate 458,056 acres of the very best lands in California. The increase in acreage control within the last decade, according to these official figures, has been 412.9 per cent. In productive values—that is to say, in the market value of crops produced by them—our figures show that as against $6,235,856 worth of produce marketed in 1909, the increase has been to $67,145,730 approximately tenfold.

More significant than these figures, however, is the demonstrated fact that within the last ten years Japanese agricultural labor has developed to such a degree that at the present time between 80 and 90 per cent of most of our vegetable and berry products are those of the Japanese farms. Approximately 80 per cent of the tomato crop of the state is produced by Japanese; from 80 to 100 per cent of the spinach crop; a greater part of our potato and asparagus crops, and so on. So that it is apparent without much more effective restrictions that in a very short time, historically speaking, the Japanese population within our midst will represent a considerable portion of our entire population, and the Japanese control over certain essential food products will be an absolute one. . . .

These Japanese, by very reason of their use of economic standards impossible to our white ideals—that is to say, the employment of their wives and their very children in the arduous toil of the soil—are proving crushing competitors to our white rural populations. The fecundity of the Japanese race far exceeds that of any other people that we have in our midst. They send their children for short periods of time to our white schools, and in many of the country schools of our state the spectacle is presented of having a few white children acquiring their education in classrooms crowded with Japanese. The deep-seated and often outspoken resentment of our white mothers at this situation can only be appreciated by those people who have struggled with similar problems.

It is with great pride that I am able to state that the people of California have borne this situation and seen its developing menace with a patience and self-restraint beyond all praise. California is proud to proclaim to the nation that despite this social situation her people have been guilty of no excesses and no indignities upon the Japanese within our borders. No outrage, no violence, no insult and no ignominy have been offered to the Japanese people within California. . . .

But with all this the people of California are determined to repress a developing Japanese community within our midst. They are determined to exhaust every power in keeping to maintain this state for its own people. This determination is based fundamentally upon the ethnological impossibility of assimilating the Japanese people and the consequential alternative of increasing a population whose very race isolation must be fraught with the gravest consequences.

2. Reverend Amzi Clarence Dixon Preaches on the Evils of Darwinism and Evolution, 1922

Evolution with its "struggle for existence" and "survival of the fittest," which gives the strong and fit the scientific right to destroy the weak and unfit is responsible for the oppression and destruction of the weak and unfit by the strong and fit. It has

"Dr. Dixon Claims Evolution Started in Unscientific Age," as appeared in *Raleigh News & Observer,* December 31, 1922, p. 5. Reprinted in Escott, et al., eds., *Major Problems in the American South,* Vol. II (Boston: Houghton Mifflin, 1999), 293–295.

fostered autocratic class distinctions and is no friend to those who stand for the protection of the weak against the oppression of the strong. The greatest war in history, which has drenched the world with blood and covered it with human bones, can be traced to this source. If the strong and fit have the scientific right to destroy the weak and unfit, that human progress may be promoted, then might is right, and Germany should not be criticized for acting upon this principle.

Nietzsche, the neurotic German philosopher, hypnotized the German mind with his Pagan brute philosophy. "The weak and botched," said he, "shall perish; first principle of humanity. And they ought to be helped to perish. What is more harmful than any vice? Practical sympathy with the botched and weak Christianity." "If what I publish be true," he wrote to an invalid woman, "a feeble woman like you would have no right to exist."

"Christianity," he said, "is the greatest of all conceivable corruptions, the one immortal blemish of mankind." And he hated it because of its sympathy with the botched and weak. He glorified his ideal "blond beast" and gave to the world a "superman," one-third brute, one-third philosopher. Under the spell of his daring brutality, Germany adopted the motto, "Corsica has conquered Galilee." Nietzsche's philosophy of beastliness has its roots in the evolutionary assumption that the strong and fit, in the struggle for existence, have the scientific right to destroy the weak and unfit.

Under the spell of Nietzsche's "superman" there came into the heads of the German politicians and militarists the vision of a super nation, with the scientific right to destroy weaker nations and build its throne upon their ruins. . . .

If the home is to be preserved as a sacred institution, the Bible which teaches that marriage came down from God and not up from the beast must be believed. The jungle theory as to the origin of marriage is today keeping busy the divorce courts of the civilized world. If government came down from God, so that "the powers that be are ordained of God," law will rule in righteousness and courts will mete out justice, but if the basis of government came from the jungle where brute force prevails, the Bolshevist rule by bullet and bayonet is scientific and the scientific mind ought to accept it. This jungle origin of government is today a world-wide peril. If the Bible is a revelation from God through inspired men, its teaching is authoritative and its truths have in them an irresistible dynamic, but if the Bible is a mere record of human experience as men have struggled upward from their jungle origin, its teaching has no authority and its sayings are to be accepted or rejected by the inner consciousness of men, which is itself a product of the jungle.

If man came down from God, created in His image and has been wrecked by sin, then sin is an intrusion, an enemy that ought to be expelled; but, if man came up from the beast through the jungle, sin is "embryonic goodness," "righteousness in process of formation," even a search after good; of course such sin has no guilt and may be condoned, if not coddled. Such a delusion makes it easy to believe that sin has no existence and all things, even theft, falsehood and murder are good, because there is no evil in the world. . . .

If Christ came down from heaven, as He says He did, "the only begotten Son of God" in the sense that He is the only one in the universe begotten of God in a virgin's womb, "God manifest in the flesh," "the Word made flesh and dwelling among men," we have in Him a unique personality; God, who is a Spirit, made concrete, thinkable, approachable and lovable; God, lowering Himself to our level, that He may lift us to His level. But if Christ is the expression of humanity's struggle up from the beast through the jungle, we have in Him simply a combination and culmination of jungle life in body, soul and spirit, detached from heaven, on the same plane with others, with little power to lift or transfigure.

The Beast-Jungle theory of evolution robs a man of his dignity, marriage of its sanctity, government of its authority, the church of her power and Christ of His glory.

3. A Survey Examines the Morals of High School Students, 1924

Excerpts from a Questionnaire relative to Moral Problems in the High Schools as judged by the students, North Central Association of Colleges and Schools, covering 19 States.

The chief moral qualities exhibited by pupils:
Honesty 30%
Fellowship 12%
Clean habits 19%
Courtesy lowest with only 9%

The most regrettable practices of boys in school:
Smoking 38%
Swearing 19%
Drinking 8%
Telling vulgar stories 5%

The most regrettable practices of girls in school:
Cosmetics 17%
Flirting & petting 14%
Profane language 12%

Factors tending to develop high moral qualities among pupils:
Teacher 31%
School Organization 18%
Athletics 17%

Invidious factors tending to undermine right conduct:
Certain low-minded people 63%

Poor discipline 11%
Immoral parties 11%

How could school help to develop morality among pupils?
Course in morals 32%
Stricter Rules 21%
Talks 19%

Is a course in moral education desirable?
61% of replies said "Yes."
39% of replies said "No."

Some forces which are the most helpful:
Mother 20%
Father 17%
Teacher 11%

Things making a boy popular:
Athletics 21%
Scholarship 14%
Good looks 10%
Dependability 1%
Capability only 2%
Character only 2% & takes 12th place of 18 questions asked.

National Archives and Records Administration and National Council for the Social Studies, *Teaching with Documents: Using Primary Sources from the National Archives* (Washington, D.C.: National Archives, 1989), 124.

Things that make a girl popular:
  Appearance 17%
  Scholarship 13%
  Personality 9%
  Morality 4%
  Character only 3% & takes 15th
  place of 18 questions asked. . . .

Present causes of worry:
  Choice of vocation 27%
  Money matters 21%
  Studies 16%
  Religious matters 2%
  (lowest of ten questions).

4. Defense Attorney Clarence Darrow Interrogates Prosecutor William Jennings Bryan in the Monkey Trial, 1925

Examination of W. J. Bryan by Clarence Darrow, of counsel for the defense:

Q—You have given considerable study to the Bible, haven't you, Mr. Bryan?

A—Yes, sir, I have tried to. . . .

Q—Do you claim that everything in the Bible should be literally interpreted?

A—I believe everything in the Bible should be accepted as it is given there; some of the Bible is given illustratively. For instance: "Ye are the salt of the earth." I would not insist that man was actually salt, or that he had flesh of salt, but it is used in the sense of salt as saving God's people.

Q—But when you read that Jonah swallowed the whale—or that the whale swallowed Jonah—excuse me please—how do you literally interpret that?

A—When I read that a big fish swallowed Jonah—it does not say whale.

Q—Doesn't it? Are you sure?

A—That is my recollection of it. A big fish, and I believe it, and I believe in a God who can make a whale and can make a man and make both do what He pleases. . . .

Q—You believe the story of the flood [Noah] to be a literal interpretation?

A—Yes, sir.

Q—When was that flood?

A—I would not attempt to fix the date. The date is fixed, as suggested this morning.

Q—About 4004 B. C. ?

A—That has been the estimate of a man that is accepted today. I would not say it is accurate.

Q—That estimate is printed in the Bible?

A—Everybody knows, at least, I think most of the people know, that was the estimate given.

Q—But what do you think that the Bible, itself, says? Don't you know how it was arrived at?

A—I never made a calculation.

Q—A calculation from what?

A—I could not say.

Q—From the generations of man?

The World's Most Famous Trial: Tennessee Evolution Case (Cincinnati: National Book Co.), 284–291.

A—I would not want to say that.

Q—What do you think?

A—I do not think about things I don't think about.

Q—Do you think about things you do think about?

A—Well, sometimes. . . .

Mr. Darrow—How long ago was the flood, Mr. Bryan? . . .

The Witness—It is given here, as 2348 years B. C.

Q—Well, 2348 years B. C. You believe that all the living things that were not contained in the ark were destroyed.

A—I think the fish may have lived. . . .

Q—Don't you know there are any number of civilizations that are traced back to more than 5,000 years?

A—I know we have people who trace things back according to the number of ciphers they have. But I am not satisfied they are accurate. . . .

Mr. Darrow—You do know that there are thousands of people who profess to be Christians who believe the earth is much more ancient and that the human race is much more ancient?

A—I think there may be.

Q—And you never have investigated to find out how long man has been on the earth?

A—I have never found it necessary. . . .

Q—Don't you know that the ancient civilizations of China are 6,000 or 7,000 years old, at the very least?

A—No; but they would not run back beyond the creation, according to the Bible, 6,000 years.

Q—You don't know how old they are, is that right?

A—I don't know how old they are, but probably you do. (Laughter in the court-yard.) I think you would give the preference to anybody who opposed the Bible, and I give the preference to the Bible.

5. Novelist F. Scott Fitzgerald Reveals Attitudes About Gender and Race in *The Great Gatsby,* 1925

Tom Buchanan who had been hovering restlessly about the room stopped and rested his hand on my shoulder.

"What you doing, Nick?"

"I'm a bond man."

"Who with?"

I told him.

"Never heard of them," he remarked decisively.

This annoyed me.

"You will," I answered shortly. "You will if you stay in the East."

"Oh, I'll stay in the East, don't you worry," he said, glancing at Daisy and then back at me as if he were alert for something more. "I'd be a God Damn fool to live anywhere else."

At this point Miss Baker said "Absolutely!" with such suddenness that I started—it was the first word she had uttered since I came into the room. Evidently it surprised her as much as it did me, for she yawned and with a series of rapid, deft movements stood up into the room.

"I'm stiff," she complained. "I've been lying on that sofa for as long as I can remember."

"Don't look at me," Daisy retorted. "I've been trying to get you to New York all afternoon."

"No thanks," said Miss Baker to the four cocktails just in from the pantry, "I'm absolutely in training."

Her host looked at her incredulously.

"You are?" He took down his drink as if it were a drop in the bottom of a glass. "How you ever get anything done is beyond me."

I looked at Miss Baker wondering what it was she "got done." I enjoyed looking at her. She was a slender, small-breasted girl with an erect carriage which she accentuated by throwing her body backward at the shoulders like a young cadet. Her grey sun-strained eyes looked back at me with polite reciprocal curiosity out of a wan, charming discontented face. It occurred to me now that I had seen her, or a picture of her, somewhere before.

"You live in West Egg," she remarked contemptuously. "I know somebody there."

"I don't know a single——"

"You must know Gatsby."

"Gatsby?" demanded Daisy. "What Gatsby?"

Before I could reply that he was my neighbor dinner was announced; wedging his tense arm imperatively under mine Tom Buchanan compelled me from the room as though he were moving a checker to another square.

Slenderly, languidly, their hands set lightly on their hips the two young women preceded us out onto a rosy-colored porch open toward the sunset where four candles flickered on the table in the diminished wind. . . .

"Civilization's going to pieces," broke out Tom violently. "I've gotten to be a terrible pessimist about things. Have you read 'The Rise of the Coloured Empires' by this man Goddard?"

"Why, no," I answered, rather surprised by his tone.

"Well, it's a fine book and everybody ought to read it. The idea is if we don't look out the white race will be—will be utterly submerged. It's all scientific stuff, it's been proved."

"Tom's getting very profound," said Daisy with an expression of unthought-ful sadness. "He reads deep books with long words in them. What was that word we——"

"Well, these books are all scientific," insisted Tom, glancing at her impatiently. "This fellow has worked out the whole thing. It's up to us who are the dominant race to watch out or these other races will have control of things."

"We've got to beat them down," whispered Daisy, winking ferociously toward the fervent sun.

"You ought to live in California——" began Miss Baker but Tom interrupted her by shifting heavily in his chair.

"This idea is that we're Nordics. I am and you are and you are and——" After an infinitesimal hesitation he included Daisy with a slight nod and she winked at me again, "——and we've produced all the things that go to make civilization—oh, science and art and all that. Do you see?"

There was something pathetic in his concentration as if his complacency, more acute than of old, was not enough to him any more. . . .

There was dancing now on the canvas in the garden, old men pushing young girls backward in eternal graceless circles, superior couples holding each other tortuously, fashionably and keeping in the corners—and a great number of single girls dancing individualistically or relieving the orchestra for a moment of the burden of the banjo or the traps. By midnight the hilarity had increased. A celebrated tenor had sung in Italian and a notorious contralto had sung in jazz and between the numbers people were doing "stunts" all over the garden while happy vacuous bursts of laughter rose toward the summer sky. A pair of stage "twins"—who turned out to be the girls in yellow—did a baby act in costume and champagne was served in glasses bigger than finger bowls. The moon had risen higher, and floating in the Sound was a triangle of silver scales, trembling a little to the stiff, tinny drip of the banjoes on the lawn.

I was still with Jordan Baker. We were sitting at a table with a man of about my age and a rowdy little girl who gave way upon the slightest provocation to uncontrollable laughter. I was enjoying myself now. I had taken two finger bowls of champagne and the scene had changed before my eyes into something significant, elemental and profound. . . .

Gatsby's butler was suddenly standing beside us.

"Miss Baker?" he inquired. "I beg your pardon but Mr. Gatsby would like to speak to you alone."

"With me?" she exclaimed in surprise.

"Yes, madame."

She got up slowly, raising her eyebrows at me in astonishment, and followed the butler toward the house. I noticed that she wore her evening dress, all her dresses, like sports clothes—there was a jauntiness about her movements as if she had first learned to walk upon golf courses on clean, crisp mornings.

6. The Ku Klux Klan Defines Americanism, 1926

The Klan . . . has now come to speak for the great mass of Americans of the old pioneer stock. We believe that it does fairly and faithfully represent them, and our proof lies in their support. To understand the Klan, then, it is necessary to understand the

"The Ku Klux Klan's Fight for Americanism" by Hiram Wesley Evans from *North American Review* (March–May 1926), 38–39, 52–54. Copyright 1926 by *North American Review*. Reprinted with permission of *North American Review* in the format Textbook via Copyright Clearance Center.

character and present mind of the mass of old-stock Americans. The mass, it must be remembered, as distinguished from the intellectually mongrelized "Liberals."

These are, in the first place, a blend of various peoples of the so-called Nordic race, the race which, with all its faults, has given the world almost the whole of modern civilization. The Klan does not try to represent any people but these. . . .

. . . The Nordic American today is a stranger in large parts of the land his fathers gave him. Moreover, he is a most unwelcome stranger, one much spit upon, and one to whom even the right to have his own opinions and to work for his own interests is now denied with jeers and revilings. "We must Americanize the Americans," a distinguished immigrant said recently. Can anything more clearly show the state to which the real American has fallen in this country which was once his own? . . .

Thus the Klan goes back to the American racial instincts, and to the common sense which is their first product, as the basis of its beliefs and methods. . . .

There are three of these great racial instincts, vital elements in both the historic and the present attempts to build an America which shall fulfill the aspirations and justify the heroism of the men who made the nation. These are the instincts of loyalty to the white race, to the traditions of America, and to the spirit of Protestantism, which has been an essential part of Americanism ever since the days of Roanoke and Plymouth Rock. They are condensed into the Klan slogan: "Native, white, Protestant supremacy."

First in the Klansman's mind is patriotism—America for Americans. He believes religiously that a betrayal of Americanism or the American race is treason to the most sacred of trusts, a trust from his fathers and a trust from God. He believes, too, that Americanism can only be achieved if the pioneer stock is kept pure. There is more than one race pride in this. Mongrelization has been proven bad. It is only between closely related stocks of the same race that interbreeding has improved men; the kind of interbreeding that went on in the early days of America between English, Dutch, German, Hugenot, Irish and Scotch. . . .

The second word in the Klansman's trilogy is "white." The white race must be supreme, not only in America but in the world. This is equally undebatable, except on the ground that the races might live together, each with full regard for the rights and interests of others, and that those rights and interests would never conflict. Such an idea, of course, is absurd; the colored races today, such as Japan, are clamoring not for equality but for their supremacy. The whole history of the world, on its broader lines, has been one of race conflicts, wars, subjugation or extinction. This is not pretty, and certainly disagrees with the maudlin theories of cosmopolitanism, but it is truth. The world has been so made that each race must fight for its life, must conquer, accept slavery or die. The Klansman believes that the whites will not become slaves, and he does not intend to die before his time. . . .

The third of the Klan principles is that Protestantism must be supreme; that Rome shall not rule America. The Klansman believes this not merely because he is a Protestant, nor even because the Colonies that are now our nation were settled for the purpose of wresting America from the control of Rome and establishing a land of free conscience. He believes it also because Protestantism is an essential part of Americanism; without it America could never have been created and without it she cannot go forward.

7. The Automobile Comes to Middletown, U.S.A., 1929

The first real automobile appeared in Middletown in 1900. About 1906 it was estimated that "there were probably 200 in the city and county." At the close of 1923 there were 6,221 passenger cars in the city, one for every 6.1 persons, or roughly two for every three families. . . . For some of the workers and some of the business class, use of the automobile is a seasonal matter, but the increase in surfaced roads and in closed cars is rapidly making the car a year-round tool for leisure-time as well as getting-a-living activities. As, at the turn of the century, business class people began to feel apologetic if they did not have a telephone, so ownership of an automobile has now reached the point of being an accepted essential of normal living. . . .

Group-sanctioned values were disturbed by the inroads of the automobile upon the family budget. A case in point is the not uncommon practice of mortgaging a home to buy an automobile. Data on automobile ownership were secured from 123 working class families. Of these, sixty have cars. Forty-one of the sixty own their homes. Twenty-six of these forty-one families have mortgages on their homes. . . .

Many families feel that an automobile is justified as an agency holding the family group together. "I never feel as close to my family as when we are all together in the car," said one business class mother, and one or two spoke of giving up Country Club membership or other recreations to get a car for this reason. "We don't spend anything on recreation except for the car. We save every place we can and put the money into the car. It keeps the family together," was an opinion voiced more than once. Sixty-one per cent of 337 boys and 60 per cent of 423 girls in the three upper years of the high school say that they motor more often with their parents than without them.

But this centralizing tendency of the automobile may be only a passing phase; sets in the other direction are almost equally prominent. "Our daughters [eighteen and fifteen] don't use our car much because they are always with somebody else in their car when we go out motoring," lamented one business class mother. And another said, "The two older children [eighteen and sixteen] never go out when the family motors. They always have something else on." "In the nineties we were all much more together," said another wife. "People brought chairs and cushions out of the house and sat on the lawn evenings. We rolled out a strip of carpet and put cushions on the porch step to take care of the unlimited overflow of neighbors that dropped by. We'd sit out so all evening. The younger couples perhaps would wander off for half an hour to get a soda but come back to join in the informal singing or listen while somebody strummed a mandolin or guitar." "What on earth *do* you want me to do? Just sit around home all evening!" retorted a popular high school girl of today when her father discouraged her going out motoring for the evening with a young blade in a rakish car waiting at the curb. The fact that 348 boys and 382 girls in the three upper years of the high school placed "use of automobile" fifth and fourth respectively in a list of twelve possible sources of disagreement between them and their parents suggests that this may be an increasing decentralizing agent. . . .

---

8. Langston Hughes: Poet of the 1920s Harlem Renaissance

One-Way Ticket

I pick up my life
And take it with me
And I put it down in
Chicago, Detroit,
Buffalo, Scranton,
Any place that is
North and East—
And not Dixie.

I pick up my life
And take it on the train
To Los Angeles, Bakersfield,
Seattle, Oakland, Salt Lake,
Any place that is
North and West—
And not South.

I am fed up
With Jim Crow laws,
People who are cruel
And afraid,
Who lynch and run,
Who are scared of me
And me of them.

I pick up my life
And take it away
On a one-way ticket—
Gone up North,
Gone out West,
Gone!

E S S A Y S

Like most periods characterized by rapid cultural change, the twenties are a bundle of contradictions. Paula S. Fass of the University of California, Berkeley, examines the social behavior of college youth in the 1920s, who, she asserts, changed gender roles and relationships between men and women. They invented "dating" (courtship not tied to marriage), "petting" (erotic interactions not tied to intercourse), and provocative fashions not expected to provoke outrage. The author looks at the range of behaviors that young people redefined as socially acceptable, from petting to smoking to drinking. What gave college youth this much power and influence? In the second essay, Edward J. Larson of the University of Georgia places the Scopes trial—too easily caricatured as a clash between "backward" yokels and sophisticated city slickers—in the context of the struggle to reconcile science with faith. The term *fundamentalism* was coined in the 1920s to symbolize the fight against theological liberalism and the "updating" (or diluting) of the old-time religion in view of new scientific information. Both Fass and Larson look at phenomena linked to schools: textbook controversies and the attitudes of college undergraduates. Why did education emerge as a battleground? The State of Tennessee won its battle against teacher John Scopes, but who won the culture war?

Sex and Youth in the Jazz Age

PAULA S. FASS

"Most of 'em pet, I guess."
"All the pretty ones."
"Some do one night and don't the next—goddam funny."
"ALL of 'em pet. Good women. Poor women. All of 'em."
"If a girl doesn't pet, a man can figure he didn't rush 'er right."

Lynn Montross and Lois Montross, Town and Gown *(1923)*

Students of modern sexual behavior have quite correctly described the twenties as a turning point, a critical juncture between the strict double standard of the age of Victoria and the permissive sexuality of the age of Freud. Too often, however, the sexual revolution of the twenties has been described exclusively in terms of scattered data suggesting an increase in premarital sexual intercourse on the part of women. One is tempted to picture investigators hunting for that special morning between 1919 and 1929 when 51% of the young unmarried women in America awoke to find that they were no longer virgins. Instead, of course, investigators are forced to deduce revolutionary changes from small, though important, increases in what remained a minority pattern of behavior. This kind of thinking, not unlike the Victorian concept of all or nothing, overlooks the fact that changes in sexual habits, as in most other areas of social relations, are evolutionary. . . .

College youth of the 1920's redefined the relationship between men and women. In good part this resulted from a simple rediscovery—love is erotic. The remainder drew on an old assumption—that the goal of relations between men and women was marriage. Together the new insight and the old tradition resulted in a significant restructuring of premarital forms of sexual behavior as relationships were charged by a new sexual dynamism and a vigorous experimentalism. Sex for middle-class youths of the 1920's had become a significant premarital experience, but it continued to be distinctly marriage-oriented and confined by stringent etiquettes and sharply etched definitions. In the process of defining their future roles in the new society and within the context of already potent changes, the young helped to create the sexual manners of the twentieth century. . . .

Paula S. Fass, *The Damned and the Beautiful: American Youth in the 1920s* (New York: Oxford University Press, 1977). Excerpts from Ch. 6, pp. 260–68, 271–72. Copyright © 1977 by Oxford University Press. Used by permission of Oxford University Press, Inc.

Dating was something definitely new in the ritual of sexual interaction. It was unlike the informal get-togethers that characterized youth socializing in the village or small town of the nineteenth century, for at such events there was no pairing early in an acquaintance. It was also unlike courting, which implied a commitment between two people. Dating permitted a paired relationship without implying a commitment to marriage and encouraged experimental relations with numerous partners. Dating emerged in response to a modern environment in which people met casually and irregularly, and in response to new kinds of recreations like movies, dance halls, and restaurants, where pairing was the most convenient form of boy-girl relation. Moreover, it developed as youths were increasingly freed from the direct supervision of family and community and allowed the freedom to develop private, intimate, and isolated associations. Dating opened the way for experimentation in mate compatibility. The lack of commitment permitted close and intimate associations and explorations of personality, and isolation and privacy laid the ground for sexual experimentation, both as a means for testing future compatibility and as an outlet for present sexual energies.

With the isolation of relations, the young were forced to rely on their own judgment in determining the degree and limits of permissible eroticism. It was this latitude for self-determination that produced the haunting fear of sexual promiscuity in the jeremiads of the twenties. The fear was unfounded. The young were thrown back on their own resources, but they were not free, either from the influence of childhood training or, more immediately, from the controls and sanctions of their peers. Basing their actions on an unyielding taboo against sexual intercourse and an elaborate network of peer norms and standards, they proceeded to open up the possibilities of sexual play without overstepping the bounds of family prohibition and peer propriety. After investigating female conduct in the late twenties, Phyllis Blanchard and Carlyn Manasses concluded that "very many girls draw a distinct line between the exploratory activities of the petting party and complete yielding of sexual favors to men." In the behavior of young men and women in the twenties, this charting of distinctions was as important as the exploration. The two ran a parallel course, for the young experimented with eroticism within a clear sense of limits, thus tasting a little of the fruit and enjoying the naughtiness of their bravery without seriously endangering the crop.

"Petting" described a broad range of potentially erotic physical contacts, from a casual kiss to more intimate caresses and physical fondling. Even such limited eroticism would have automatically defined a woman as loose and disreputable in the nineteenth century. To the Victorians, who divided good women from bad, revered ideal purity, and were suspicious of female sexuality, all forms of eroticism on the part of women could be equated with total submission. Even in the twenties, it was not unknown for reformers to introduce legislation that would prohibit petting and define it along with fornication as illegal as well as immoral. But the young drew distinct boundaries between what was acceptable erotic behavior and what was not. Petting was the means to be safe and yet not sorry, and around this form of sexual activity they elaborated a code of permissible eroticism. . . . A casual first date might thus entail a good-night kiss, but greater intimacies and a certain amount of erotic play were permitted and expected of engaged couples. "Erotic play," as Ira Wile rightfully observed, had "become an end rather than a means," and the strong "distinctions made in petting recognize that erotic activity may or may not have coitus as a goal." The young first sanctioned eroticism and then imposed degrees and standards of acceptability. . . .

Dating and petting were, moreover, distinctly marriage-oriented in the twenties. Since mating was one of the chief aims of both rituals, immediate sexual satisfactions had to be carefully weighed in view of long-term goals. And while virginity in a bride was no longer an absolute prerequisite for most men, it was still considered desirable. For men, female chastity appears to have taken a back seat to considerations of compatibility, but there was still some ambiguity on this point, and the devaluation of virginity in the bride was probably related to a growing acceptance of intercourse among engaged couples rather than to a tolerance of casual promiscuity. Women too continued to display considerable anxiety about the consequences of lost virginity. These multiple ambivalences reinforced the sense of acceptable limitations on sexual indulgence.

For most youths, this meant an acceptance of eroticism with very clear limits of permissible expression. Petting established a norm that deviated from that of the family but was still not antagonistic to its basic taboo. The majority could pet because it filled the need for response in a specific relationship, and in filling that need they believed they had the security of peer-group opinion. Of course, many ambivalences remained. But by the 1930's these sexual definitions had congealed into a dependable norm, a norm which, in the words of one investigation, provided ample room for "spontaneous demonstrations of affection." In their study of sexual behavior on the thirties campus, Dorothy Bromley and Florence Britten discovered that the fact "that a girl should feel she can give within limits or permit exploratory intimacies without compromising her essential virginity is one of the phenomena of the contemporary younger generation's mores." During the twenties, peer pressure to pet was still strong, and behavior patterns were, as a result, less stable, more inhibiting, altogether more full of anxieties. Probably many youths petted less to express personal needs than to conform to group standards and to demonstrate what Ernest Burgess called "the outstanding attitude of modern youth"—their "self-consciousness and sophistication about sex." . . .

Not surprisingly, the new attention to sexuality colored a whole range of related behavior. Language became more candid and conversations more frank as the fact of freer association between the sexes was accompanied by a basic commitment to freedom of expression. As women became companions to men in work and play, it was easier to see them as "pals" and partners, and the informal access between the sexes radically affected ideas of *de facto* equality and the manners that reflected that equality. At the same time, this access encouraged a pronounced attention to sexual attractiveness and to the cultivation of styles that operated on a purely sexual level.

What is at first glance enigmatic in the fashions and manners of young women in the twenties—the apparent conflict between those modes that emphasized her boyish characteristics, her gamin quality, and those that consciously heightened her sexual piquancy—must be understood in terms of the two distinct but related consequences of this new access between the sexes. They express not conflict but a well-poised tension between the informal boyish companion and the purposefully erotic vamp. They served at once a symbolic and a functional role in the new variety of relationships between the sexes. Bobbed hair, for example, which was the prevailing style for women on all campuses, was enthusiastically defended on the grounds that it was carefree and less troublesome to care for than the long ponderous mane, which was *de rigueur* in the prewar period. It facilitated indulgence in ad-hoc and informal activities like sports and made it easier for women to remain well-groomed during an increasingly busy campus or work day. It was indeed liberating, as it emphasized the woman's more informal existence and behavior. It allowed her to feel equal with men and unencumbered by a traditional symbol of her different role.

At the same time, the short hair was carefully marcelled, a process that occasioned no end of campus humor. The well-sculpted head was, in fact, in the context of the twenties, more self-consciously erotic than fluffy long hair that was girlish and young. Long hair was often inimical to real sexual allure because it was necessary to wear it carefully tied in a bun or chignon. Hair worn loose had for a long time been restricted to very young girls. Older girls, forced to compose it because it was improper to wear hair so informally and because it was unmanageable in an active day, often appeared staid and sedate. Short hair, on the other hand, could be worn freely and the possibility of prudish compactness averted. Bobbed hair was often attacked as a symbol of female promiscuity, of explicit sexuality, and of a self-conscious denial of respectability and the domestic ideal. Once we suspend absolute definitions of sexual attractiveness, we can begin to see the sexuality implicit in bobbed hair in the context of the period. It was not mannish but liberating, and that liberation implied a renunciation of sexual stereotypes. . . .

Short skirts, which became increasingly abbreviated as the decade progressed, were defined on the same grounds of comfort and practicality. Again, women could feel less encumbered and freer to engage in all the purportedly male activities. But the provocation of bared calves and knees was not overlooked. One outraged observer, a divinity student at Duke University, was so repelled by the bared knees of coeds that he was provoked to write a disgusted letter to the school paper. What really offended him, more even than the fashion, was the women's manipulation of the fashions. The coed, he observed, "would look every now and then to assure herself that they [her knees] were exposed to the nth degree." . . .

. . . To accompany the trend in skirt lengths and form-revealing silhouettes, there was a keen calorie-consciousness among young women. Dieting became so popular that newspapers often cited the calorie value of foods and gave nutritional advice about the amount of food intake that would help to sustain or shed weight. Young women were conscious of the new vamp silhouette and sought to imitate the lean, honed-down proportions of the movie queens. . . .

Cosmetics were used to increase attractiveness, but they were more than that—they were provocative. The use of cosmetics symbolized the woman's open acceptance of her own sexuality. Whatever the long history of cosmetics and their general use, the reference point for women in the twenties was not ancient Egypt or India but the America of the late nineteenth and early twentieth centuries. And by the mores of that period, cosmetics were immoral. They were associated with prostitutes. By appropriating the right to use such sexual aids, respectable women proclaimed that they too were endowed with a sexual personality. They had taken on themselves as potential wives all the characteristics of lovers. The two kinds of women were no longer separate and distinguishable at first glance but one and the same.

Young women did not generally abuse their new-found cosmetic allies. They used powder, rouge, and lip color in moderation with an eye to increasing allure without offending propriety. The moderate use was in conformity with the standards and expectations of their peers, who had incorporated cosmetics as a permissible part of fashion. That the peer group that encouraged the use of cosmetics also limited its over-indulgence was lost on adults. The adult world, its eyes still fixed on an older standard, stood aghast. But among the young the moderate use of cosmetics was encouraged and recognized for what it was, an attempt to increase physical attractiveness and to score points in the game of rating within the rules set by the peer group. . . .

So too, the male "line" was a conscious extension of the cultivated attention to sexual manners. A line was a well-rehearsed and oft-repeated set of phrases used by men when introduced to women. The line was a mark of sophistication, a demonstration of worldliness, a touch of cynicism that made a man more attractive by making him more dangerous. "As for the co-eds," remarked a solicitous Trinity editor, "don't the young sweet things know that the senior law students have a line so long and slippery that it can't be caught?" But it was the very slipperiness that made the line effective. It was a staged ritual, a self-conscious and even a self-protective form of sexual aggression in the new and potentially dangerous sexual explorations in which the young were engaged. It was well known that the line was not spontaneous but used as a staged approach in meeting and cultivating female company. It identified a man as experienced, so the approval of the line reflected the desirability of "experience" in meeting respectable women. A man without a line was an innocent, basically not savvy in the ways of the world. Like a woman without her cosmetics, a man without his line went out naked into the frightening wilderness of a newly sexual world. With its barely veiled sexual naughtiness, the line pointed up the ways in which conscious sexuality had been incorporated into the rituals of attack and protection that governed male and female interaction. . . .

Smoking was perhaps the one most potent symbol of young woman's testing of the elbow room provided by her new sense of freedom and equality. Prostitutes and women in liberated bohemian and intellectual sets had been known to flaunt their cigarettes publicly and privately before the twenties. But in respectable middle-class circles, and especially among young women, smoking, like rouging, was simply not done. Throughout the twenties, smoking could still provoke heated commentary, and for many young women, to smoke in public was a welcome form of notoriety. Although young women in college did not initiate the smoking habit, they increasingly took advantage of the cigarette as a symbol of liberation and as a means of proclaiming their equal rights with men. More importantly, within the college community they had the support of peer-group opinion. Among the young, smoking for women became widely accepted during the twenties, and while smoking remained an issue, as the decade wore on it became an acceptable and familiar habit among college women.

Smoking is not a sexual activity in itself. In the abstract, it is morally neutral. In the context of the specific values of American society, however, it was both morally value-laden and sexually related. Like cosmetics, smoking was sexually suggestive and associated with disreputable women or with bohemian types who self-consciously rejected traditional standards of propriety and morality. College administrators objected to smoking because it undermined an ideal of proper female behavior and decency. As the Dean of Women at Ohio State University noted, smoking was simply not "done in the best circles," and it was, in the words of the Dean of Rhode Island State College, "an unladylike act." . . .

Women and men on the campuses of the twenties proclaimed that women had a right to smoke if they pleased: "If a man can enjoy his coke more by smoking as he drinks it, why isn't it logical to assume that a woman can enjoy hers more when it is accompanied by a cigarette?" asked one woman correspondent at Illinois. "Why shouldn't a woman have a taste for cigarettes just as a man has? It is not the smoking that breaks down the bonds of convention between men and women . . . a woman can command just as much respect with a cigarette in her mouth as without." At New York University women claimed their rights by announcing that they would hold a smoker rather than a traditional tea. The Dean was outraged and prohibited the event, but the women went ahead with their plans anyway. Blanchard and Manasses found that 80% of the young women they questioned approved of smoking for women. In marked contrast, only 26% of the parents approved. . . .

In the twenties, young men and women danced whenever the opportunity presented itself. Unquestionably the most popular social pastime, dancing was, of all potentially questionable and morally related behaviors, the least disreputable in the view of the young. For most youths dancing was not even questionable but a thoroughly respectable and almost compulsory form of socializing. Even at denominational schools, where dancing continued to be regarded as morally risky by officials, students clamored for a relaxation of the older bans as they asked officials to give up outdated "prejudiced feelings" and respond to "the bending of current public opinion." A dance was an occasion. It was a meeting ground between young men and women. It was a pleasurable recreation. But above all it was a craze.

The dancers were close, the steps were fast, and the music was jazz. And because popular forms of dancing were intimate and contorting, and the music was rhythmic and throbbing, it called down upon itself all the venom of offended respectability. Administrative officials as well as women's clubs and city fathers found the dancing provocative and indecent and tried at least to stop the young from engaging in its most egregious forms, if not from the dances entirely. But the young kept on dancing.

They started during the war years, and they danced through the decade. Dancing would leave its stamp on the twenties forever, and jazz would become the lingering symbol for an era. But whatever its symbolic value during the twenties and thereafter, dancing and jazz were forms of recreation, even a means of peer-group communication, that youth appropriated to itself. . . .

Drinking for youth in the twenties was unlike sex, smoking, or dancing, because the young labored under a specific legal ordinance forbidding alcoholic indulgence of any kind. Prohibition was an anomaly in an age of increasing freedoms. Students had been permitted to drink at least off-campus before the passage of the Eighteenth Amendment and the Volstead Act, and beer drinking had been a regular form of celebration and socializing among male students. Prohibition cut off a former freedom.

Moreover, unlike the other moral issues of the twenties, drinking was a male-centered problem that secondarily involved women. Drinking had always been a male prerogative. Respectable women were effectively barred from indulgence by tradition. Drinking among youths during the twenties therefore involved a number of distinct issues: the attitude toward the moral code, the attitude toward the law, and the question of female roles. . . .

It is difficult to determine how many students actually drank during the twenties and what the significance of their behavior was. By the end of the decade, the polls of the Congressional Hearing on the Repeal of the Prohibition Amendment presented overwhelming evidence that men and women students drank in a proportion close to two drinkers to every non-drinker. This was the case in all parts of the nation. . . . Of the total number of ballots cast in the nationwide congressional poll, 29,794 in all, only 34% of the students claimed not to be drinkers. By 1930, at least, drinking appears to have been very common among the majority of all students.

Coming to the end of the decade, the Congressional survey reflected the campus situation when anti-Prohibition sentiment had reached a peak. But the college newspapers suggest that there were changes over the course of the decade in the amount and style of drinking. Drinking among the young appears to have been greatest at the very beginning and again in the second half of the twenties. There was a short period between 1921 and 1924 when the amount of drinking was kept to a minimum, the result of initial attempts by the young spurred on by the administration to control drinking, especially at official university parties and at fraternity dances. At this time, the papers, after important events like proms and homecomings, were filled with self-congratulations on the commendable way in which the students were controlling the drinking problem and enforcing the national and school anti-drinking laws. In 1921, the *Cornell Sun,* for example, which noted that the previous year had been especially wet, observed, "The low point has been passed in regard to the liquor situation, and the upward swing is beginning. All evidence, at least, points to a slowly growing public sentiment against drinking at dances—which is the crux of the whole matter. The parties in the last three or four weeks have had a different tone from those of a year ago." Even homecomings, usually the wettest weekends of the year because returning alumni brought liquor in abundance, were reported to be relatively dry. At Madison, Wisconsin, as at most schools, there was reported to be "a determined effort . . . to stamp out drinking." In the second half of the decade, however, there was a marked increase in the agitation for repeal or modification of Prohibition and a general decrease in the commitment with which the now formal injunctions against drinking were issued. This happened first at the Eastern schools, which appear to have had a shorter dry spell, and gradually affected the Midwest.

In the early period, some editors observed that Prohibition needed time to prove its efficacy and that slowly the public would be educated toward a self-imposed abstinence. On this assumption, students were urged to give Prohibition a chance. But most arguments supporting Prohibition were based on the law rather than on the social or moral objection to drinking. The injunction that the law should be obeyed was a constant aspect of the formally expressed attitudes toward drinking. This remained true throughout the decade. At Cornell, where editorial comment was consistently hostile to Prohibition and to all attempts to impose morality, the editor of the *Sun* nevertheless maintained that in respect to the law, there was but one answer, "to enforce the law . . . it is one thing for a citizen of the United States to be in doubt on the question of prohibition and it is another for him to be in doubt on the question of the dignity and power of the Constitution." . . .

At the same time, students were openly contemptuous of the kind of moral reformers who had succeeded in passing Prohibition. Self-righteous moralists trying to impose their own standards on everyone were the butt of derision. The *Daily Princetonian* struck just the right tone of contempt: "If the projects of the crusaders for virtue and purity are realized . . . once more the tottering world and western civilization will be made safe for unsullied virgins and old ladies above sixty. The absurdity of such efforts is second only to the presumption with which they are undertaken by . . . certain self-styled upholders of public morals. . . . To presume that one can define decency or legislate virtue is folly." . . .

These two very distinct and clearly articulated attitudes—the strong sentiment supporting the law and the hostility toward the idea of Prohibition—were accompanied by a less clearly enunciated ethic that made drinking an unofficially sanctioned peer activity. The editorials reflected this view. While always serious when denouncing law-breaking, editors were rarely serious about drinking. Usually drinking and Prohibition were fair game for humor and "smartness." The informal approval demonstrated by making Prohibition a joke cannot possibly have done other than undercut the effectiveness of the formal injunctions to obey the law contained in the very same papers. In this sense the spirit of Prohibition, if not the letter of the law, was officially denied. Drinking jokes were a staple of the humor columns and, more insidiously, of the side comments of the purportedly serious editorial columns. Even when intending to scold, editorials came off as shoulder-shrugging at the antics of college youths. . . .

In the early twenties, there was a clear code of limitations on drinking that reflected traditional attitudes toward propriety in drinking. Thus, drinking at athletic events and with other men was permissible, but drinking at dances and in the presence of women was not. When editors denounced drinking with alumni or at athletic events, for example, they usually invoked the law rather than the moral code. But the same editors were disturbed by drinking at dances, where it was believed to be improper because it was public and in the presence of women. The *Cornell Sun* called such drinking "an offense to good manners and against decency," and the *Sun* noted that while there was never a time in Cornell history when students did not drink, "there are times, when it is considered bad manners." So too, at the University of Wisconsin 2000 women students signed a pledge to boycott any social function where men were under the influence of liquor. The action reflected the prevailing ethic that drinking in the presence of women was improper.

The code also drew a fundamental distinction between drinking and drunkenness. In 1921, the editor of the *Daily Illini* noted that "The number of persons who object to an individual taking a drink of intoxicating liquor is probably in the minority," but that the student public strenuously objected to drinking to the point of intoxication. The editor concluded his message by advising that drinking "must not become open or offensive to student society." When the young drank according to these self-limiting rules, they were, in effect, conforming to the traditional standard of adult society that operated in the days before the Prohibition law went into effect.

During the twenties, however, the young increasingly deviated from these unofficial codes of conduct. There was a subterranean ethic developing that worked counter to these self-limiting rules. In this ethic, one drank to become drunk or, failing that, to appear drunk. Thus the *Cornell Sun* noted that where once it had been the aim to see how much one could drink without appearing drunk, it had now become part of "the game" to get as drunk as possible on whatever drink was available and to see who "can get the Greatest Publicity while in a state of Pseudo Ginification." "Contrary to the rabid assertions of matronly sewing circles and pessimistic male reformers," the *Dartmouth* declared, "the college student of today is sober ninety-nine one hundredths of the time. When he does drink, it is usually to parade his drunkenness—at a football game, at a dance, during a vacation, at a social gathering—and it is on such occasions that a shocked older generation is most liable to see youth in action." In addition, one drank in the company and together with women. It was not until the middle of the decade when this new ethic began to jell that drinking among women became an issue. Before then it was considered a strictly male-centered problem. Drinking at dances, with women, and to excess had become, by the latter twenties, a new code of permissible behavior among college students because it was sanctioned by peer opinion.

"Terpsichordian tippling," as the *Cornell Sun* called it, had become commonplace on most campuses and the editor explained quite accurately why this was so. " 'Is it the smart thing to be drunk at a college function?' 'Yes,' reply the undergraduates by their indulgence in liquor consumption at dances, house parties and the like, and by their tolerance of it by others. Right there we believe lies the solution of the drinking problem at colleges in general. . . . Campus leaders set the style by drinking openly and laughingly approving the drunken actions of fellow students." A similar situation prevailed at Duke, where "a dance among the younger set can hardly be called a success nowadays unless most of the boys get 'high,' not to mention the occasional girl who cannot be outdone by her masculine companions." . . .

Did the young use sex and morals as a basis for conscious generational revolt? On the whole the answer would appear to be no, although their sexual attitudes and practices did distinguish them from their elders and made them appear rebellious. They welcomed the lingering naughtiness of which they were accused, but more in the spirit of play than with any serious display of anger. As eager capitalists, the young were anything but rebellious in social and political questions. They emphasized style in personal matters and severely demarcated the personal from the social sphere. In so doing they were in the advance guard of twentieth-century American culture.

Religious Traditionalists Battle Modernism (and Evolution) in the Roaring Twenties

EDWARD J. LARSON

Fossil discoveries provided persuasive new evidence for human evolution and as such provoked a response from antievolutionists. Henry Fairfield Osborn threw down the gauntlet in his reply to [William Jennings] Bryan's 1922 plea in the *New York Times* for restrictions on teaching evolution. Bryan had argued that "neither

Excerpts from *Summer for the Gods: The Scopes Trial and America's Continuing Debate over Science and Religion* by Edward J. Larson, pp. 31, 33–41, 43, 45, 49–50, 56–58, 60–61, 63–65, 74–75, 83. Copyright © 1997 by Edward J. Larson. Reprinted by permission of Basic Books, a member of Perseus Books, L.L.C.

Darwin nor his supporters have been able to find a fact in the universe to support their hypothesis," prompting Osborn to cite "the Piltdown man" and other recent hominid fossil finds. "All this evidence is today within reach of every schoolboy," Osborn wrote. "It will, we are convinced, satisfactorily answer in the negative [Bryan's] question, 'Is it not more rational to believe in the creation of man by separate act of God than to believe in evolution without a particle of evidence?'" Of course, the fact that all this evidence *was* within the reach of every public-school student constituted the nub of Bryan's concern, and Osborn further baited antievolutionists by stressing how it undermined belief in the special creation of humans.

During the years leading up to the Scopes trial, antievolutionists responded to such evidence in various ways. . . .

The culprit, they all agreed, was a form of theological liberalism known as "modernism" that was gaining acceptance within most mainline Protestant denominations. Modernists viewed their creed as a means to save Christianity from irrelevancy in the face of recent developments in literary higher criticism and evolutionary thinking in the social sciences. Higher criticism, especially as applied by German theologians, subjected the Bible to the same sort of literary analysis as any other religious text, interpreting its "truths" in light of its historical and cultural context. The new social sciences, particularly psychology and anthropology, assumed that Judaism and Christianity were natural developments in the social evolution of the Hebrew people. Modernists responded to these intellectual developments by viewing God as immanent in history. Conceding human (rather than divine) authorship for scripture and evolutionary development (rather than revelational truth) for Christianity, modernists nevertheless claimed that the Bible represented valid human perceptions of how God acted. Under this view, the precise historical and scientific accuracy of scripture did not matter. Judeo–Christian ethical teachings and individual religious sentiments could still be "true" in a realm beyond the "facts" of history and science. "In belief," the modernist leader Shailer Mathews of the University of Chicago divinity school wrote in 1924, "the use of scientific, historical, and social methods in understanding and applying evangelical Christianity to the needs of living persons, is Modernism."

Conservative Christians drew together across denominational lines to fight for the so-called fundamentals of their traditional faith against the perceived heresy of modernism, and in so doing gave birth to the fundamentalist movement and anti-evolution crusade. Certainly modernism had made significant inroads within divinity schools and among the clergy of mainline Protestant denominations in the North and West, and fundamentalism represented a legitimate theological effort to counter these advances. Biblical higher criticism and an evolutionary world view, as twin pillars of this opposing creed, stood as logical targets of a conservative counterattack. A purely theological effort, however, rarely incites a mass movement, at least in pluralistic America; much more stirred up fundamentalism—and turned its fury against teaching evolution in public schools.

The First World War played a pivotal role. American intervention, as part of a progressive effort to defeat German militarism and make the world "safe for democracy," was supported by many of the modernists, who revered the nation's wartime leader, Woodrow Wilson, himself a second-generation modernist academic. A passionate champion of peace, William Jennings Bryan opposed this position and in 1915 resigned his post as Wilson's secretary of state in protest over the drift toward war. He spent the next two years criss-crossing the country campaigning against American intervention. . . .

When a horribly brutal war led to an unjust and uneasy peace, the rise of international communism, worldwide labor unrest, and an apparent breakdown of traditional values, the cultural crisis worsened for conservative Christians in the United States. "One indication that many premillennialists were shifting their emphasis— away from just evangelizing, praying, and waiting for the end time, toward more intense concern with retarding [social] degenerative trends—was the role they played in the formation of the first explicitly fundamentalist organization," [historian of religion George M.] Marsden noted. "In the summer of 1918, under the guidance of William B. Riley, a number of leaders in the Bible school and prophetic conference movement conceived of the idea of the World's Christian Fundamentals Association."

During the preceding two decades, Riley had attracted a 3,000-member congregation to his aging Baptist church in downtown Minneapolis through a distinctive combination of conservative dispensational-premillennialist theology and politicized social activism. "When the Church is regarded as the body of God-fearing, righteous-living men, then, it ought to be in politics, and as a powerful influence," he proclaimed in a 1906 book that urged Christians to promote social justice for the urban poor and workers. During the next decade, Riley focused his social activism on outlawing liquor, which he viewed as a key source of urban problems. By the twenties, he turned against teaching evolution in public schools. Later, he concentrated on attacking communism. Following the First World War and flushed with success upon ratification of the Eighteenth Amendment authorizing Prohibition, he was ideally suited to lead premillennialists into the cultural wars of the twenties.

In 1919, Riley welcomed some 6,000 conservative Christians to the World's Christian Fundamentals Association (WCFA) inaugural conference with the warning that their Protestant denominations were "rapidly coming under the leadership of the new infidelity, known as 'modernism.'" One by one, seventeen prominent ministers from across the country—the future high priests of fundamentalism—took the podium to denounce modernism as, in the words of one speaker, "the product of Satan's lie," and to call for a return to biblical fundamentals in church and culture. "It is ours to stand by our guns," Riley proclaimed in closing the conference. "God forbid that we should fail him in the hour when the battle is heavy." Participants then returned to their separate denominations, ready to battle the modernists. . . . Indeed, it was during the ensuing intradenominational strife within the Northern Baptist Convention that conservative leader Curtis Lee Laws coined the word *fundamentalist* to identify those willing "to do battle royal for the Fundamentals." Use of the term quickly spread to include all conservative Christians militantly opposed to modernism. . . .

Bryan's crusade against teaching evolution capped a remarkable thirty-five-year-long career in the public eye. He entered Congress in 1890 as a 30-year-old populist Democratic politician committed to roll back the Republican tariff for the dirt farmers of his native Nebraska. His charismatic speaking ability and youthful enthusiasm quickly earned him the nickname The Boy Orator of the Platte. Bryan's greatest speech occurred at the 1896 Democratic National Convention, where he defied his party's conservative incumbent president, Grover Cleveland, and the eastern establishment that dominated both political parties by demanding an alternative silver-based currency to help debtors cope with the crippling deflation caused by exclusive reliance on limited gold-backed money. Using a potent mix of radical majoritarian arguments and traditional religious oratory, he demanded, "You shall not press down upon the brow of labor this crown of thorns, you shall not crucify mankind upon a cross of gold." The speech electrified the convention and secured the party's presidential nomination for Bryan. For many, he became known as the Great Commoner; for some, the Peerless Leader.

. . . After helping Woodrow Wilson secure the White House in 1912, Bryan became secretary of state and idealistically (some said naively) set about negotiating a series of international treaties designed to avert war by requiring the arbitration of disputes among nations. This became more of a religious mission than a political task for Bryan, who called on America to "exercise Christian forbearance" in the face of increasing German aggression and vowed, "There will be no war while I am Secretary of State." Of course, he had to resign from office to keep this promise. . . .

Bryan's antievolutionism was compatible with his progressive politics because both supported reform, appealed to majoritarianism, and sprang from his Christian convictions. Bryan alluded to these issues in his first public address dealing with Darwinism, which he composed in 1904 at the height of his political career. From this earliest point, he described Darwinism as "dangerous" for both religious and social reasons. "I object to the Darwinian theory," Bryan said with respect to the religious implications of a naturalistic explanation for human development, "because I fear we shall lose the consciousness of God's presence in our daily life, if we must accept the theory that through all the ages no spiritual force has touched the life of man and shaped the destiny of nations." Turning to the social consequences of the theory, Bryan added, "But there is another objection. The Darwinian theory represents man as reaching his present perfection by the operation of the law of hate—the merciless law by which the strong crowd out and kill off the weak."

The Great Commoner was no more willing to defer to ivy tower scientists on this issue than to Wall Street bankers on monetary matters. "I have a right to assume," he declared in this early speech, "a Designer back of the design [in nature]—a Creator back of the creation; and no matter how long you draw out the process of creation; so long as God stands back of it you can not shake my faith in Jehovah." This last comment allowed for an extended geologic history and even for limited theistic evolution; but Bryan dug in his heels regarding the supernatural creation of humans and described it as "one of the test questions with the Christian." Although Bryan regularly delivered this speech on the Chautauqua circuit during the early years of the century, he said little else against Darwinism until the twenties, when he began blaming it for the First World War and an apparent decline in religious faith among educated Americans.

As a devout believer in peace, Bryan could scarcely understand how supposedly Christian nations could engage in such a brutal war until two scholarly books attributed it to misguided Darwinian thinking. In *Headquarters Nights,* the renowned Stanford University zoologist Vernon Kellogg, who went to Europe as a peace worker, recounted his conversations with German military leaders. "Natural selection based on violent and fatal competitive struggle is the gospel of the German intellectuals," he reported, and served as their justification "why, for the good of the world, there should be this war." Whereas Kellogg used this evidence to promote his own non-Darwinian view of evolutionary development through mutual aid, Bryan saw it as a reason to suppress Darwinian teaching. The philosopher Benjamin Kidd's *The Science of Power* further explored the link between German militarism and Darwinian thinking by examining Darwin's influence on the German philosopher Friedrich Nietzsche. Bryan regularly referred to both books when speaking and writing against teaching evolution. . . .

A third book had an even greater impact on Bryan and touched an even more sensitive nerve. In 1916, the Bryn Mawr University psychologist James H. Leuba published an extensive survey of religious belief among college students and professors. The result confirmed Bryan's worst fears. "The deepest impression left by these records," Leuba concluded, "is that . . . Christianity, as a system of belief, has utterly broken down." Among students, Leuba reported, "the proportion of disbelievers in immortality increases considerably from the freshman to the senior year in college." Among scientists, he found disbelief higher among biologists than physicists, and higher among scientists of greater than lesser distinction, such that "the smallest percentage of believers is found among the greatest biologists; they count only 16.9 per cent of believers in God." Leuba did not identify teaching evolution as the cause for this rising tide of disbelief among educated Americans, but Bryan did. "Can Christians be indifferent to such statistics?" Bryan asked in one speech. "What shall it profit a man if he shall gain all the learning of the schools and lose his faith in God?" This became his ultimate justification for the Scopes trial. . . .

The campaign for restrictive legislation spread quickly and all but commandeered the antievolution movement. Fundamentalist leader John Roach Straton began advocating antievolution legislation for his home state of New York in February 1922. J. Frank Norris, pastor of the largest church in the Dallas-Fort Worth area, soon took up the cause in Texas. The evangelist T. T. Martin carried the message throughout the South. By fall 1922, William Bell Riley was offering to debate evolutionists on the issue as he traveled around the nation battling modernism in the church. "The whole country is seething on the evolution question," he reported to Bryan in early 1923. Three years later, these same four ministers became the most prominent church figures to actively support the prosecution of John Scopes. . . .

Individual rights lost out under this political philosophy. "If it is contended that an instructor has a right to teach anything he likes, I reply that the parents who pay the salary have a right to decide what shall be taught," Bryan maintained. "A scientific soviet is attempting to dictate what is taught in our schools," he warned. "It is the smallest, the most impudent, and the most tyrannical oligarchy that ever attempted to exercise arbitrary power." He gave a similarly facile response to charges that antievolution laws infringed on the rights of nonfundamentalist parents and students. Protestants, Catholics, and Jews shared a creationist viewpoint, Bryan believed, and he sought to enlist all of them into his crusade. As for nontheists, he asserted, "The Christians who want to teach religion in their schools furnish the money for denominational institutions. If atheists want to teach atheism, why do they not build their own schools and employ their own teachers?" Such a position assumed that the separation of church and state precluded teaching the Genesis account in public schools. "We do not ask that teachers paid by taxpayers shall teach the Christian religion to students," Bryan told West Virginia lawmakers, "but we do insist that they shall not, under the guise of either science or philosophy, teach evolution as a fact." He apparently expected them to skip the topic of organic origins altogether, or to teach evolution as a hypothesis. . . .

"Fundamentalism drew first blood in Tennessee today," a January 20, 1925 article in the *Commercial Appeal* reported, "in the introduction of a bill in the Legislature by Senator [John A.] Shelton of Savannah to make it a felony to teach evolution in the public schools of the state." A day later, John W. Butler offered similar legislation in the House of Representatives. Both legislators had campaigned on the issue and their actions were predictable. Butler justified his proposal on Bryanesque grounds: "If we are to exist as a nation the principles upon which our Government is founded must not be destroyed, which they surely would be if . . . we set the Bible aside as being untrue and put evolution in its place." Butler was a little-known Democratic farmer-legislator and Primitive Baptist lay leader. For him, public schools served to promote citizenship based on biblical concepts of morality. Evolutionary beliefs undermined those concepts. Driven by such reasoning, Butler proposed making it a misdemeanor, punishable by a maximum fine of $500, for a public school teacher "to teach any theory that denies the story of the Divine Creation of man as taught in the Bible, and to teach instead that man had descended from a lower order of animal." Most of Butler's colleagues apparently agreed with this proposal, because six days later the House passed it without any amendments. The vote was seventy-one to five. Although three of the dissenters came from Memphis and one from Nashville, the bill gained the support of both rural and urban representatives, including most delegates from every major city in the state. . . .

Outnumbered Senate opponents of the legislation countered with pleas for individual rights. "It isn't a question of whether you believe in the Book of Genesis, but whether you think the church and state should be kept separate," one senator asserted. "No law can shackle human thought," another declared. A Republican lawmaker quoted passages on religious freedom from the state constitution, and blamed the entire controversy on "that greatest of all disturbers of the political and public life from the last twenty-eight or thirty years, I mean William Jennings Bryan." But a proponent countered, "This bill does not attempt to interfere with religious freedom or dictate the beliefs of any man, for it simply endeavors to carry out the wishes of the great majority of the people." Such sentiments easily carried the Senate.

State and national opponents of antievolution laws appealed to Governor Peay to veto the legislation. Owing to the governor's national reputation as a progressive who championed increased support for public education and a longer school year—efforts that later led to the naming of a college in his honor—those writing from out of state probably entertained some hope for success. Urged on by the California science writer Maynard Shipley and his Science League of America, a new organization formed to oppose antievolutionism, letters of protest poured in from across America. For example, taking the line of Draper and White, a New Yorker asked, "The Middle Ages gave us heretics, witches burnt at the stake, filth and ignorance. Do we want to return to the same?" From within Tennessee, some concerned citizens appealed for a veto. The dean of the state's premiere African-American college, Fisk University, wrote, "As a clergyman and educator, I hope that you will refuse to give your support to the Evolution Bill. It would seem most unfortunate to me should the

State of Tennessee legislate against the beliefs of liberal Christianity." The Episcopal bishop of Tennessee added, "I consider such restrictive legislation not only unfortunate but calamitous."

Yet most letters to the governor from Tennesseans supported the measure, and two potentially significant opponents kept silent. The University of Tennessee's powerful president Harcourt A. Morgan, who privately opposed the antievolution bill, held his tongue so long as Peay's proposal for expanding the university still awaited action in the state legislature—and admonished his faculty to do likewise. In a confidential note, he assured the governor, "The subject of Evolution so intricately involves religious belief, which the University has no disposition to dictate, that the University declines to engage in the controversy." Only after the legislature adjourned and the new law became the primary subject of ridicule at the annual student parade did the depth of university opposition to it become apparent. . . .

The governor explained his decision to sign the bill in a curious message to the legislature. On one hand, Peay firmly asserted for proponents, "It is the belief of our people and they say in this bill that any theory of man's descent from lower animals, . . . because a denial of the Bible, shall not be taught in our public schools." On the other hand, he assured opponents that this law "will not put our teachers in any jeopardy." Indeed, even though the most cursory review of Tennessee high school biology textbooks should have shown him otherwise, Peay wrote, "I can find nothing of consequence in the books now being taught in our schools with which this bill will interfere in the slightest manner." Nevertheless, he went on to hail the measure as "a distinct protest against an irreligious tendency to exalt *so-called* science, and deny the Bible in some schools and quarters—a tendency fundamentally wrong and fatally mischievous in its effects on our children, our institutions and our country."

Peay, whose progressivism grew out of his traditional religious beliefs, simply could not accept a conflict between public education and popular religion. . . . Yet he could not totally ignore the tension between a fundamentalist's fear of modern education and a progressive's faith in it. In his message to the legislature on the antievolution bill, he fell back on Bryan's populist refrain: "The people have a right and must have the right to regulate what is taught in their schools." Trapped between fundamentalism and progressivism, Peay may have viewed majoritarianism as an excuse for the law. Caught in the same bind, Bryan saw it as the law's ultimate justification. . . .

Activists with the American Civil Liberties Union did not dismiss the enactment of the Tennessee law against teaching evolution as an insignificant occurrence in some remote intellectual backwater. More critically, they did not view the antievolution crusade in isolation; if they had, they probably would have ignored it along with countless other laws and movements to advance Protestant culture then prevalent throughout the United States. Prior to the Scopes trial, the ACLU did not display any particular interest in challenging government efforts to protect or promote religious beliefs. To the contrary, Quakers played a major role in founding and financing the organization during the First World War as a vehicle to protect religiously motivated pacifists from compulsory military service. Yet ACLU leaders saw the new Tennessee statute in a different light, one that made it stand out as a threat to freedom and individual liberty in the broader American society.

A fashionable new book of the era, *The Mind in the Making* by James Harvey Robinson of the left-wing New School for Social Research in New York City, captured the reactionary mood of the times as perceived by many of the socially prominent, politically radical New Yorkers who led the ACLU during the early twenties. According to this book, which incorporated an evolutionary view of intellectual and social history, a systematic assault on personal liberty in the United States began during the First World War; various state and local authorities had limited freedom prior to this period, to be sure, but these earlier restrictions represented isolated incidents and could be dealt with accordingly. The war changed everything.

"It is a terrible thing to lead this great and peaceful people into war," President Wilson declared in his 1917 war message to Congress. He then added to the terror of some by warning that "a firm hand of stern repression" would curtail domestic disloyalty during wartime. At Wilson's request, Congress imposed a military draft, enacted an Espionage Act that outlawed both obstructing the recruitment of troops and causing military insubordination, and authorized the immigration service to denaturalize and deport foreign-born radicals. The federal Justice Department broadly construed the Espionage Act to cover statements critical of the war effort, while the postal service revoked mailing privileges for publications it considered to "embarrass or hamper the government in conducting the war." . . .

Proponents of civil liberties expected conditions to improve after the armistice in 1918, but to them the repression appeared only to intensify. "The war brought with it a burst of unwanted and varied animation. . . . It was common talk that when the foe, whose criminal lust for power had precipitated the mighty tragedy, should be vanquished, things would 'no longer be the same,'" Robinson wrote. "Never did bitter disappointment follow such high hopes. All the old habits of nationalistic policy reasserted themselves at Versailles. . . . Then there emerged from the autocracy of the Tsars the dictatorship of the proletariat, and in Hungary and Germany various startling attempts to revolutionize hastily and excessively." From these developments the so-called Red Scare ensued. "War had naturally produced its machinery for dealing with dissenters, . . . and it was the easiest thing in the world to extend the repression to those who held exceptional or unpopular views, like the Socialists and members of the I.W.W.," Robinson reasoned. . . .

The government reacted swiftly. Most states outlawed the possession or display of either the red flag of communism or the black flag of anarchism. They also enacted the strictly enforced tough new "criminal syndicalism" laws against organized violent or unlawful activities designed to disrupt commercial or governmental activities. . . .

"Well, of course, it was a time of tremendous labor unrest, highlighted by the two general strikes in the steel mills and coal mines. And it was also, and I guess above all, a time of intense radical agitation, brought on by the Russian Revolution," Roger Baldwin later recalled. "So by the time the World War was over we had a new war on our hands—a different one. Then, instead of arresting and persecuting opponents of the war, we were arresting and persecuting friends of Russia." Thus events stood when Baldwin . . . reassumed leadership of the National Civil Liberties Bureau. He promptly concluded, as he stated in a memorandum to the executive committee, that the bureau should be "reorganized and enlarged to cope more adequately with the invasions of civil liberties incident to the industrial struggle which had followed the war." Direct action to protect labor unions would replace legal maneuvers on behalf of pacifists as the bureau's principal focus. The bureau assumed a new name to go with its new mission: the American Civil Liberties Union. "The cause we now serve is labor," Baldwin proclaimed at the time, and labor included public school teachers. . . .

Academic freedom had been an ongoing concern of the ACLU from the organization's inception; naturally, it related to free speech, yet the interest ran even deeper. The pacifists who helped form the National Civil Liberties Bureau abhorred wartime efforts to promote patriotism and militarism in the schools. They defended teachers fired for opposing American involvement in the war and fought against efforts to purge the public school curriculum of German influences. After the war, when the ACLU turned its attention to defending unpopular speakers, its efforts widened to include fighting classroom restrictions on unpopular ideas. "The attempts to maintain a uniform orthodox opinion among teachers should be opposed," the ACLU's initial position statement declared. "The attempts of education authorities to inject into public schools and colleges instruction propaganda in the interest of any particular theory of society to the exclusion of others should be opposed."

This statement primarily reflected the ACLU's opposition to school patriotism programs. Building on wartime developments in New York, the Lusk Committee proposed legislation in 1920 to dismiss public school teachers who "advocated, either by word of mouth or in writing, a form of government other than the government of the United States." The ACLU helped persuade New York governor Al Smith to veto this bill in 1921, but Smith's successor signed similar legislation into law a year later. Dozens of other states required public school teachers and college professors to sign loyalty oaths. Powerful patriotic organizations, including the American Legion, lobbied for promoting "Americanism" in the public schools by mandatory patriotic exercises (typically a flag salute) and through classroom use of education materials that praised the military and disparaged all things "foreign" (often including the international labor movement). Publicity generated by the ACLU forestalled these programs in some places, but an ACLU lawsuit challenging compulsory military training for male students attending the state University of California at Los Angeles failed. The rise of a militantly anti-Catholic Ku Klux Klan during the early 1920s led to ACLU efforts to protect both Catholic teachers from mass firings in Klan-dominated school districts and the free-speech rights of the Klan in Catholic communities. Repeatedly, the ACLU was drawn into courtrooms over education. Indeed, during the 1920s, it had to go to court to protect its own right to sponsor programs in New York City schools after the local board of education barred all ACLU representatives from "talking in school buildings" under a general regulation requiring classroom speakers to "be loyal to American institutions." . . .

This approach to education led to a de facto establishment of Christianity within American public schools. About the time of the Scopes trial, for example, the Georgia Supreme Court dismissed a Jewish taxpayer's complaint against Christian religious exercises in public schools with the observation, "The Jew may complain to the court as a taxpayer just exactly when and only when a Christian may complain to the court as a taxpayer, *i.e.,* when the Legislature authorizes such reading of the Bible or such instruction in the Christian religion in the public schools as give one Christian sect a preference over others." The Tennessee legislature codified a similar practice in 1915 when it mandated the daily reading of ten Bible verses in public schools but prohibited any comment on the readings. This suggestion that constitutional limits on the establishment of religion simply forbad the government from giving preference to any one church denomination reflected a traditional view of religious freedom that dated at least as far back as the great federalist U.S. Supreme Court justice Joseph Story. By the 1920s, however, an increasing number of liberally educated Americans, including leaders of the ACLU, rejected the idea that public education should promote any particular political, economic, or religious viewpoint—even one broadly defined as democratic, capitalistic, or Christian. . . .

The ACLU press release offering to challenge the Tennessee law appeared in its entirety on May 4 in the *Chattanooga Times,* which had opposed enactment of the antievolution statute. "We are looking for a Tennessee teacher who is willing to accept our services in testing this law in the courts," the release stated. "Our lawyers think a friendly test case can be arranged without costing a teacher his or her job. Distinguished counsel have volunteered their services. All we need now is a willing client." Pursuing the story, a *Chattanooga Times* reporter inquired whether city schools taught evolution. "That depends on what is meant by evolution. If you have reference to the Darwinian theory, which, I suppose, was aimed at in the law passed by the Tennessee legislature, it is not," the city school superintendent assured the reporter. "It is recognized by all our teachers that this is a debatable theory and, as such, has no place in our curriculum." Earlier, in making similar assurances regarding his schools, the Knoxville superintendent had noted, "Our teachers have a hard enough time teaching the children how to distinguish between plant and animal life." These urban school officials clearly did not want to test the new law, but midway between these cities enterprising civic boosters in Dayton craved some attention for their struggling community, and accepted the ACLU offer. They got more than they bargained for. Powerful social forces converged on Dayton that summer: populist majoritarianism and traditional evangelical faith versus scientific secularism and modern concepts of individual liberty. America would never be the same again—or perhaps it had changed already from the country that had nurtured Bryan and Darrow in its heartland.

FURTHER   READING

Paul Avrich, *Sacco and Vanzetti: The Anarchist Background* (1991).
Kathleen M. Blee, *Women of the Klan: Racism and Gender in the 1920s* (1991).
Lendol Calder, *Financing the American Dream: A Cultural History of Consumer Credit* (1995).
Stanley Coben, *Rebellion Against Victorianism: The Impetus for Cultural Change in 1920s America* (1991).
David Gutierrez, *Walls and Mirrors: Mexican Americans, Mexican Immigrants, and the Politics of Ethnicity* (1995).
John Higham, *Strangers in the Land: Patterns of American Nativism* (1963).
George Hutchinson, *The Harlem Renaissance in Black and White* (1995).
David Levering Lewis, *When Harlem Was in Vogue* (1989).
Roland Marchand, *Advertising the American Dream: Making Way for Modernity* (1985).
Joan Shelley Rubin, *The Making of Middlebrow Culture* (1992).
Virginia Scharff, *Taking the Wheel: Women and the Coming of the Motor Age* (1991).
Ronald Takaki, *Strangers from a Different Shore: A History of Asian Americans* (1989).

The Depression, the New Deal, and Franklin D. Roosevelt

In the "Dirty Thirties," as sufferers of the Dust Bowl called the decade, it seemed that everything that could go wrong, did go wrong. The stock market crash of 1929, terrifying as it was to investors, who saw their shares fall by 40 percent, was only a harbinger of the international economic collapse and natural calamities to come. The run on banks that began in 1930 ultimately forced more than five thousand financial institutions to shut their doors. With no insurance on deposits, families lost their life savings. Industrial production fell to 20 percent of capacity. Unemployment zoomed to nearly 25 percent in the worst year. With no money to make mortgage payments, millions lost their homes. Local governments that tried to provide relief quickly exhausted their resources, and some went bankrupt. The federal government, which could have provided broad relief, largely refused to do so, as President Herbert Hoover feared creating a welfare-dependent class. Mismanagement by banks, corporations, and the titans of the stock market—combined with a lack of management by government— created the fear that capitalism had rotted from within, and the nation with it.

Farmers were the first to see the Depression coming. Economic stagnation had afflicted agriculture throughout the twenties. To feed the hungry of World War I, farmers had broken the sod of millions of acres of prairie soil in areas with unreliable rainfall. An end to the war and economic instability in Europe in the twenties lessened the demand for their bountiful crops. A persistent drought beginning in 1932, combined with poor farming practices, left soil exposed. Farmers everywhere saw prices for their products plummet as the Depression deepened, but few were more deeply afflicted than those who inhabited the five states making up the "Dust Bowl" (Oklahoma, Texas, Kansas, Colorado, and New Mexico). Winds caught at the dry, loosened dirt, blowing up storms of topsoil that blacked out the sky, asphyxiated animals, choked children and old people, and swept grit all the way to New York City. Foreclosures on desolated lands stimulated an exodus of desperate, starving families to more fertile areas, particularly California. And even where crops would still grow, they rotted on the ground for a lack of buyers. Angry farmers, angry workers, and angry veterans cried out for relief.

Franklin D. Roosevelt came into office prepared to experiment broadly with measures to "fix" some of the most egregious failings of the nation's economic system. The New Deal, as Roosevelt called his programs, aimed at all elements of the crisis, from the stock market on Wall Street to hog markets in Nebraska. The New Deal established the first federal minimum wage, the first government system of unem- ployment compensation, the first system of old-age pensions (Social Security), the first protections for labor unions, the first regulatory agency for stocks and bonds (the Securities and Exchange Commission), and a host of other institutions. Some of the Roosevelt administration's relief programs were fleeting, but many endure today. The New Deal did not end the Depression, which continued until World War II, nor did it eliminate all the social inequities; these had existed long before the thirties and continued after them. But the New Deal did dramatically recast the role of Washington by giving it a responsibility for the general social welfare. "Big government," like big business, was here to stay.

🇺🇸 Q U E S T I O N S   T O   T H I N K   A B O U T

Who was Franklin D. Roosevelt? Was he a compassionate man of the people, or was he a political opportunist who irresponsibly expanded the power of government to the detriment of society? What were the strengths and what were the shortcomings of the New Deal?

🇺🇸 D O C U M E N T S

The documents in this chapter illustrate the various ways in which people experienced the Depression and some of the responses to it. In Document 1, President Herbert Hoover warns the American people that too great a federal role in fighting the Depres- sion might destroy the moral character of the nation's citizens and undermine their freedom. In Document 2, the editors of *The Nation* scathingly denounce Hoover's con- cern for citizens' moral character when many of them were near starvation. In Docu- ment 3, auto manufacturer Henry Ford agrees with President Hoover that "self-help" is the best remedy for unemployment, assuming that private Americans will volunteer to help one another out. Document 4 is Roosevelt's second inaugural address, which he gave at the Capitol on January 20, 1937. In it he called for government action to meet the needs of every citizen, especially the poorest. Some business leaders foresaw that corporations would also have to become more socially responsible if they were to sur- vive the New Deal era. Document 5 is a speech by Nelson Rockefeller, wealthy heir to Standard Oil, lecturing corporate executives on the need to revamp their thinking and embrace Roosevelt's reforms. One of these key reforms was the 1935 Social Security Act, designed to provide an old-age pension to all working Americans. But as Docu- ment 6 shows, the benefits were not evenly distributed, reflecting the authors' assump- tions about gender. The architects of the plan believed that widows needed less money than widowers because women could live more easily on a tight budget than men. Another New Deal reform was the 1935 National Labor Relations Act (also called the Wagner Act for its Congressional sponsor, Senator Robert Wagner), which protected the right of workers to unionize. As Document 7 shows, union members could and did use the new law to reclaim their jobs when they were fired for organizing. Document 8 is a selection from John Steinbeck's epic novel, *The Grapes of Wrath*. In it, the fictional Joad family is forced to migrate to California, where they learn a hard lesson about being unwelcome in their own country. Steinbeck's novel publicized the plight of the "Okies," landless refugees from Oklahoma and other parts of the Dust Bowl. This excerpt makes plain the limits of neighborly compassion, and it appears to counter the blithe optimism of industrial leaders like Henry Ford. The last selection (Document 9) is folk singer Woody Guthrie's famous protest song of the Great Depression, "This Land Is Your Land, This Land Is My Land." It speaks to the frustration of people like the Joads, who starved in the midst of America's "amber waves of grain."

1. President Herbert Hoover Applauds Limited Government, 1931

The Federal Government has assumed many new responsibilities since Lincoln's time, and will probably assume more in the future when the states and local communities can not alone cure abuse or bear the entire cost of national programs, but there is an essential principle that should be maintained in these matters. I am convinced that where Federal action is essential then in most cases it should limit its responsibilities to supplement the states and local communities, and that it should not assume the major role or the entire responsibility, in replacement of the states or local government. To do otherwise threatens the whole foundation of local government, which is the very basis of self-government.

The moment responsibilities of any community, particularly in economic and social questions, are shifted from any part of the Nation to Washington, then that community has subjected itself to a remote bureaucracy with its minimum of understanding and of sympathy. It has lost a large part of its voice and its control of its own destiny. Under Federal control the varied conditions of life in our country are forced into standard molds, with all their limitations upon life, either of the individual or the community. Where people divest themselves of local government responsibilities they at once lay the foundation for the destruction of their liberties.

And buried in this problem lies something even deeper. The whole of our governmental machinery was devised for the purpose that through ordered liberty we give incentive and equality of opportunity to every individual to rise to that highest achievement of which he is capable. At once when government is centralized there arises a limitation upon the liberty of the individual and a restriction of individual opportunity. The true growth of the Nation is the growth of character in its citizens. The spread of government destroys initiative and thus destroys character. Character is made in the community as well as in the individual by assuming responsibilities, not by escape from them. Carried to its logical extreme, all this shouldering of individual and community responsibility upon the Government can lead but to the superstate where every man becomes the servant of the State and real liberty is lost. Such was not the government that Lincoln sought to build.

There is an entirely different avenue by which we may both resist this drift to centralized government and at the same time meet a multitude of problems. That is to strengthen in the Nation a sense and an organization of self-help and cooperation to solve as many problems as possible outside of government. We are today passing through a critical test in such a problem arising from the economic depression.

Due to lack of caution in business and to the impact of forces from an outside world, one-half of which is involved in social and political revolution, the march of

Herbert Hoover, "Radio Address on Lincoln's Birthday" (February 12, 1931), in *The State Papers and Other Public Writings of Herbert Hoover,* collected and edited by William Starr Myers (Garden City, N.Y.: Doubleday, 1934), Vol. 1, 503–505.

our prosperity has been retarded. We are projected into temporary unemployment, losses, and hardships. In a Nation rich in resources, many people were faced with hunger and cold through no fault of their own. Our national resources are not only material supplies and material wealth but a spiritual and moral wealth in kindliness, in compassion, in a sense of obligation of neighbor to neighbor and a realization of responsibility by industry, by business, and the community for its social security and its social welfare.

The evidence of our ability to solve great problems outside of Government action and the degree of moral strength with which we emerge from this period will be determined by whether the individuals and the local communities continue to meet their responsibilities.

Throughout this depression I have insisted upon organization of these forces through industry, through local government and through charity, that they should meet this crisis by their own initiative, by the assumption of their own responsibilities. The Federal Government has sought to do its part by example in the expansion of employment, by affording credit to drought sufferers for rehabilitation, and by cooperation with the community, and thus to avoid the opiates of Government charity and stifling of our national spirit of mutual self-help. . . .

We are going through a period when character and courage are on trial, and where the very faith that is within us is under test. Our people are meeting this test. And they are doing more than the immediate task of the day. They are maintaining the ideals of our American system. By their devotion to these ideals we shall come out of these times stronger in character, in courage, and in faith.

2. *The Nation* Asks, "Is It to Be Murder, Mr. Hoover?" 1932

Is it to be mass murder, Herbert Hoover? Murder by starvation, murder by disease, murder by killing all hope—and the soul? We ask, Mr. President, because this terrible fate is now staring multitudes in the face in the sight of plenty and because the responsibility now rests entirely upon you. Congress has adjourned after voting only $300,000,000 for direct relief—and that only for the States. No one can call it together again for five months except you. Day by day more cities approach the line of bankruptcy; day by day the plight of the individual States of the Union gets worse. In community after community the authorities and the leading citizens can see no hope whatever of heading off the starvation of innocents. And that is murder, Mr. President, cold-blooded and utterly unnecessary murder, far worse than if the victims were to be stood up against a wall and shot down by firing squads. Every death by starvation today—and there are men, women, and children perishing daily because of plain lack of food and undernourishment—must be charged up against the government of the United States, and in the last analysis against *you*. That is not merely because you are President, but because you as an individual have from the first set your face against direct federal relief to those who through no fault of their own are without work and food. You are deeply and sincerely convinced

"Is It to Be Murder, Mr. Hoover?" by *The Nation*'s editors, is reprinted with permission from the August 3, 1932 issue of *The Nation*. For subscription information, call 1-800-333-8536. Portions of each week's *Nation* magazine can be accessed at http://www.thenation.com. Cartoon by Edmund Duffy. Text and cartoon reproduced with permission.

that if necessary it is better that some should starve than that multitudes should have their characters wrecked and their initiative killed by a dole.

But Mr. President, are you living in the United States? Do you know what is happening? Do you know that it is no longer starvation of a few which is at hand? We ask these questions because your statement to the press on July 17 indicates that you are living entirely detached from the actual situation, that you do not know what is happening under the flag of which you are the chief guardian. You stated on that day that you would sign the so-called relief bill granting $300,000,000 for temporary loans by the Reconstruction Finance Corporation "to such States as are absolutely unable to finance the relief of distress." You then went on to say that, through this provision, "We have a solid back log of assurance that there need be no hunger and cold in the United States." You added that these loans were to be based only upon "absolute need and evidence of financial exhaustion," and concluded with the statement: "I do not expect any State to resort to it except as a last extremity." . . . Is it any wonder that we ask you if you know what is happening in the United States today?

. . . Have you not heard that city authorities in St. Louis and the charitable agencies have just turned adrift 13,000 families which they can no longer support, while the city of Detroit has dropped 18,000 who now have nowhere to turn, no assurance that even a single crust of bread will be forthcoming for their support? Have you not learned that the city of Bridgeport, and other cities and towns in Connecticut have let

it be known that if the State does not come to their aid at once they have no hope whatever of caring further for their unemployed, their own resources being entirely exhausted? Did you read that eight hundred men marched into the Indiana State Capitol last week demanding food, declaring that if they were not given help they would return 300,000 strong? Have you learned that the police in St. Louis have already fired on a mob demanding bread? Have you not read of the town of Clinton, Mass., where on July 7 "more than three hundred men, women, and crying children crowded the corridors of the Town Hall appealing for food"—only to learn that the town treasury has been exhausted, that it is unable to borrow a cent from any bank, and that it has been, and still is, trying to support one out of every six residents of the town who are destitute? These are not exceptional cases; they can be multiplied a hundredfold and from almost every section of the country. Is it any wonder, Mr. President, that thirty States moved at once? And how long do you think the $300,000,000 is going to last in the face of this?

3. Business Leader Henry Ford Advocates Self-Help, 1932

I have always had to work, whether any one hired me or not. For the first forty years of my life, I was an employe. When not employed by others, I employed myself. I found very early that being out of hire was not necessarily being out of work. The first means that your employer has not found something for you to do; the second means that you are waiting until he does.

We nowadays think of work as something that others find for us to do, call us to do, and pay us to do. No doubt our industrial growth is largely responsible for that. We have accustomed men to think of work that way. . . .

But something entirely outside the workshops of the nation has affected this hired employment very seriously. The word "unemployment" has become one of the most dreadful words in the language. The condition itself has become the concern of every person in the country. . . .

I do not believe in routine charity. I think it a shameful thing that any man should have to stoop to take it, or give it. I do not include human helpfulness under the name of charity. My quarrel with charity is that it is neither helpful nor human. The charity of our cities is the most barbarous thing in our system, with the possible exception of our prisons. What we call charity is a modern substitute for being personally kind, personally concerned and personally involved in the work of helping others in difficulty. True charity is a much more costly effort than money-giving. . . .

Methods of self-help are numerous and great numbers of people have made the stimulating discovery that they need not depend on employers to find work for them—they can find work for themselves. I have more definitely in mind those who have not yet made that discovery, and I should like to express certain convictions I have tested.

The land! That is where our roots are. There is the basis of our physical life. The farther we get away from the land, the greater our insecurity. From the land comes everything that supports life, everything we use for the service of physical

Literary Digest, June 18, 1932. Reprinted courtesy of Ford Motor Company.

life. The land has not collapsed or shrunk in either extent or productivity. It is there waiting to honor all the labor we are willing to invest in it, and able to tide us across any dislocation of economic conditions.

No unemployment insurance can be compared to an alliance between a man and a plot of land. With one foot in industry and another foot in the land, human society is firmly balanced against most economic uncertainties. With a job to supply him with cash, and a plot of land to guarantee him support, the individual is doubly secure. Stocks may fall, but seedtime and harvest do not fail.

I am not speaking of stop-gaps or temporary expedients. Let every man and every family at this season of the year cultivate a plot of land and raise a sufficient supply for themselves or others. Every city and village has vacant space whose use would be permitted. Groups of men could rent farms for small sums and operate them on the co-operative plan. Employed men, in groups of ten, twenty or fifty, could rent farms and operate them with several unemployed families. Or, they could engage a farmer with his farm to be their farmer this year, either as employe or on shares. There are farmers who would be glad to give a decent indigent family a corner of a field on which to live and provide against next winter. Industrial concerns every-where would gladly make it possible for their men, employed and unemployed, to find and work the land. Public-spirited citizens and institutions would most willingly assist in these efforts at self-help.

I do not urge this solely or primarily on the ground of need. It is a definite step to the restoration of normal business activity. Families who adopt self-help have that amount of free money to use in the channels of trade. That in turn means a flow of goods, an increase in employment, a general benefit.

4. President Franklin Roosevelt Seeks Justice for "One-Third of a Nation," 1937

In this nation I see tens of millions of its citizens—a substantial part of its whole population—who at this very moment are denied the greater part of what the very lowest standards of today call the necessities of life.

I see millions of families trying to live on incomes so meager that the pall of family disaster hangs over them day by day.

I see millions whose daily lives in city and on farm continue under conditions labeled indecent by a so-called polite society half a century ago.

I see millions denied education, recreation, and the opportunity to better their lot and the lot of their children.

I see millions lacking the means to buy the products of farm and factory and by their poverty denying work and productiveness to many other millions.

I see one-third of a nation ill-housed, ill-clad, ill-nourished.

It is not in despair that I paint you that picture. I paint it for you in hope—because the Nation, seeing and understanding the injustice in it, proposes to paint it out. We are determined to make every American citizen the subject of his country's interest and concern; and we will never regard any faithful law-abiding group within

The Public Papers and Addresses of Franklin Delano Roosevelt (New York: Random House, 1937), 1–6.

our borders as superfluous. The test of our progress is not whether we add more to the abundance of those who have much; it is whether we provide enough for those who have too little.

5. Nelson Rockefeller Lectures Standard Oil on Social Responsibility, 1937

The Standard Oil Company of New Jersey has established a unique record by maintaining its supremacy throughout the world despite constantly changing conditions. The adaptability and elasticity of the various departments in devising improved methods of research, production, refining, transportation, and marketing, with constantly increasing efficiency and lower cost is a wonderful tribute to the ability of the management. Unfortunately, today this is no longer enough. . . .

Throughout the world today the rights of the individual or corporation to possess property are being challenged. In many areas here and abroad these rights have already been destroyed. While their defense may rest in legal process fundamentally the preservation of these property rights will be established only by the demonstration of their value to the people. If, as and when the people become convinced—rightly or wrongly—that the owners have disregarded the responsibilities of their stewardship, they can withdraw through legislative action or otherwise these privileges of private ownership. This can apply to corporations individually or industry as a whole. Therefore, if we wish to continue our present system of individual initiative and private ownership, management must conduct its affairs with a sense of moral and social responsibility in such a way as to contribute to the general welfare of society. . . .

. . . When the collapse came in 1929, industry was not sufficiently established in the good will of the country to receive credit for the constructive things it had done and it became a target for public indignation. President Roosevelt and his administration have taken advantage of this opportunity to enact measures to correct some of the situations which industry should never have permitted to develop. Many of the fundamentally important reforms which have been enacted have been the subject of political regulation but should have come as a natural outgrowth of industry's own recognition and acceptance of economic and social changes. If these reforms are to last and become a permanent part of our democratic system they must be accepted wholeheartedly by industry and put on a practical and workable basis.

6. Social Security Advisers Consider Male and Female Pensioners, 1938

Mr. Myers One very good solution would be to require that the woman must be married to an annuitant for at least five years before she receives any benefits. If a man who is 65 retires and he has been married for three years, he receives 110% for the next two years and following that they will be married five years and they will

---

Speech of Nelson A. Rockefeller, Rockefeller Archive Center, RFA, R.G. 2, Business Interests Series, box 134, folder 1004. Reprinted by permission of the Rockefeller Archive Center.

Federal Advisory Council Minutes (April 29, 1938), morning session, 18. File 025, Box 12, Chairman's Files, RG 47, Records of the Social Security Administration, National Archives.

receive 150% thereafter. Under the plan as it is here they are supposed to be married five years and would receive 100%. Under the plan she would have to be married five years before he retired. He would receive nothing for two years and after that he would receive 150%. Under this plan he would receive 100% for the two-year period and then 150%. . . .

Mr. Mowbray It seems to me that the restriction on the marital period and the period of waiting is only desirable to keep out the designing woman. That wouldn't affect things at all. I made the remark that I thought a two-year period was long enough in a life insurance policy, but I was not at all sure that a five-year period was long enough as a defense against a designing woman.

Mr. Brown How far should those in need be kept in need to protect the system against designing women and old fools? Do you think it ought to be longer than five years? . . .

Miss Dewson I am confused about one point. The single man or single person gets less than the married person. Supposing that the man who is married, say at 66, loses his wife and becomes a single man, would that change his annuity?

Mr. Brown He would drop back. He drops back to the 100%. He no longer gets wife allowance, whereas if the wife survives him it would drop back to the 75%.

Miss Dewson That is what makes it more for the married man?

Mr. Brown Yes, on the principle that it is more costly for the single man to live than for the single woman if she is able to avail herself of the home of the child. A woman is able to fit herself into the economy of the home of the child much better than the single man; that is, the grandmother helps in the raising of the children and helps in home affairs, whereas the aged grandfather is the man who sits out on the front porch and can't help much in the home. . . .

Mr. Brown Are there any other points? In regard to the widows' benefits at 75% of the base we could put in a corollary as to whether 75% of the base is proper.

Mr. Linton I wonder why we didn't make the widows' benefit the regular individual annuity without cutting it down 25%. . . . Why not cut it 50%. Why should you pay the widow less than the individual himself gets if unmarried?

Mr. Williamson She can look after herself better than he can.

Mr. Linton Is that a sociological fact?

Mr. Brown Can a single woman adjust herself to a lower budget on account of the fact that she is used to doing her own housework whereas the single man has to go out to a restaurant?

7. A Union Man Gets His Job Back Under New Labor Law, 1938

Pursuant to notice, a hearing was held in Greenville, South Carolina, on October 4 and 5, 1937, before D. Lacy McBryde, the Trial Examiner duly designated by the Board. The Board and the respondent were represented by counsel and participated in the hearing. Full opportunity to be heard, to examine and cross-examine witnesses, and to produce evidence bearing upon the issues was afforded all parties. . . .

From *National Labor Relations Board Report,* vol. 5, 1938. Reprinted in Eileen Boris and Nelson Lichtenstein, eds., *Major Problems in the History of American Workers,* 2nd ed. (Boston: Houghton Mifflin, 2003), 292–295.

The respondent, a South Carolina corporation, is engaged in the manufacture of cotton cloth. It operates three plants, all in Greenville County, South Carolina. The main plant, known as the Woodside plant, with which this case is concerned, is located at Greenville while the other two are located at Simpsonville and Fountain Inn. . . .

Textile Workers Organizing Committee is a labor organization affiliated with the Committee for Industrial Organization and admits to membership employees of the respondent at its Woodside plant. The predecessor of the unit of the Textile Workers Organizing Committee here involved was known as United Textile Workers of America, Local 1684, and was affiliated with the American Federation of Labor. In 1936 the local was absorbed by the Textile Workers Organizing Committee. . . .

On October 10, 1935, John R. Kirby, an employee of the respondent at the Woodside plant, was discharged. Kirby had been a member of the Union since 1934, then holding the office of warden. During September of that year there was a general strike in the cotton textile industry, affecting also the Woodside plant. At that time Kirby acted as captain of the pickets around the Woodside plant. In November 1934, following the strike, Kirby was elected president of the Union for 1 year, an office he held at the time of his discharge. Avery Hall, an employee at the Woodside plant, in response to the question whether he knew Kirby to be an active Union man replied, "I sure did." And when asked whether this fact was generally known in the plant Hall testified, "Most all the hands knowed it." Another witness, Roy Dryman, an employee at the Woodside plant, when asked whether and how he knew Kirby was a Union man testified, "Because he told me he was and he asked me I guess fifty times to join." Dryman further testified, "I don't guess there was a half dozen people in the mill who didn't know he was an active Union man." From the record it is clear that Kirby was an active Union member and that this fact was generally known throughout the plant.

The Woodside plant was divided into two sections, known as Mill No. 1 and Mill No. 2, though both were in the same building. Prior to Kirby's discharge each section had worked on a day and night shift. In February 1935, pursuant to a predetermined plan, the respondent commenced to make alterations in the plant by which the production would be so changed that the night shift in Mill No. 2, as well as 22 jobs, including those of 15 frame hands, would be eliminated. . . .

On Monday, September 23, 1935, which was the next working day, Kirby started at his regular job when S. N. McConnell, at that time the second hand in Mill No. 1, told Kirby he was wanted by Bray. Grover Hardin, until then employed on the night shift in Mill No. 2, was placed in Kirby's position. Kirby reported to Bray and was told that he was to be transferred to the night shift in Mill No. 2, that being the shift which was to be eliminated as soon as the improvements had been completed. Kirby asked Bray why this was being done, and when no reason was given said, "Mr. Bray, I know why you are transferring me out there. It is because I belong to the Union." From the inception of the improvements in the plant the night shift in Mill No. 2 had been continually reduced until at the time of the transfer only three employees were working there. Kirby was the only man to be transferred from the carding room in Mill No. 1 to the carding room in Mill No. 2, where he took Hardin's place. The Monday following his transfer Kirby was notified by the respondent that his services would be terminated at the end of that week, as the particular set of frames on which he was working were not to be used longer. Accordingly, about 2 weeks after his transfer Kirby was discharged. Shortly thereafter the night shift in Mill No. 2 ceased operating.

Bray testified that in eliminating the night shift in Mill No. 2 he tried to retain the best men. He testified he tried "to pick out the people [he] thought would fit better . . . from an efficiency standpoint, and the people that could get along with people, and cause no confusion in the mill . . . regardless of the time they have been there." Bray testified that neither the pay nor the employment was regulated by seniority, but "everything being equal we try to take care of the people that has been there." . . .

The respondent tried to imply that Kirby did not work regularly by endeavoring to show in his cross-examination that he was not regular in his attendance at the plants at which he had worked since his discharge by the respondent. But if any conclusion is to be drawn from the only record available, the pay-roll record . . . , it would seem that Kirby was rarely absent. For the period of 16 weeks noted in the record he was absent but 2 days. . . .

On the basis of his efficiency, his ability to "get along with people," and his attendance at the plant, it appears that Kirby was one of the better frame hands of the 16 on the night shift in Mill No. 1. This being so, and "everything" not "being equal" as to this group of 16, the question of seniority need not be considered. It must be noted that Kirby was the only man to be transferred from the carding room in Mill No. 1 to the carding room in Mill No. 2. On the basis of the respondent's own test it is clear that if anyone were to be transferred Kirby should not have been that one. . . .

The respondent contended that it never knew Kirby was president of the Union and did not even know he belonged to it until his comment to Bray at the time of the transfer. We find, however, in view of the clear testimony that Kirby took an active part in the 1934 strike, and that almost everyone about the plant knew Kirby was active in Union affairs, that the respondent must have been aware of his Union activities. From the record it is clear that Kirby was discharged for his activities in behalf of the Union and the employees of the respondent at the Woodside plant.

We find that by the above acts the respondent has discriminated in regard to the hire and tenure of employment of Kirby, and that it has thereby discouraged membership in the Union. We also find that by the above acts the respondent has interfered with, restrained, and coerced its employees at the Woodside plant in the exercise of the rights guaranteed in Section 7 of the Act. . . .

Upon the basis of the findings of fact and conclusions of law and pursuant to Section 10(c) of the National Labor Relations Act, the National Labor Relations Board hereby orders that the respondent, Woodside Cotton Mills Co., Greenville, South Carolina, and its officers, agents, successors, and assigns shall:

1. Cease and desist from:

(a) Discouraging membership in Textile Workers Organizing Committee or any other labor organization of its employees at its plant in Greenville, South Carolina, by discrimination in regard to hire or tenure of employment or any terms or conditions of employment; . . .

2. Take the following affirmative action which the Board finds will effectuate the policies of the Act:

(a) Offer to John R. Kirby immediate and full reinstatement to his former position or to a position corresponding to that formerly held by him at the plant in Greenville, South Carolina, with all rights and privileges previously enjoyed; . . .

8. John Steinbeck Portrays the Outcast Poor in *The Grapes of Wrath,* 1939

Two men dressed in jeans and sweaty blue shirts came through the willows and looked toward the naked men. They called, "How's the swimmin'?"

"Dunno," said Tom. "We ain't tried none. Sure feels good to set here, though."

"Mind if we come in an' set?"

"She ain't our river. We'll len' you a little piece of her."

The men shucked off their pants, peeled their shirts, and waded out. The dust coated their legs to the knee; their feet were pale and soft with sweat. They settled lazily into the water and washed listlessly at their flanks. Sun-bitten, they were, a father and a boy. They grunted and groaned with the water.

Pa asked politely, "Goin' west?"

"Nope. We come from there. Goin' back home. We can't make no livin' out there."

"Where's home?" Tom asked.

"Panhandle, come from near Pampa."

Pa asked, "Can you make a livin' there?"

"Nope. But at leas' we can starve to death with folks we know. Won't have a bunch a fellas that hates us to starve with."

Pa said, "Ya know, you're the second fella talked like that. What makes 'em hate you?"

"Dunno," said the man. He cupped his hands full of water and rubbed his face, snorting and bubbling. Dusty water ran out of his hair and streaked his neck.

"I like to hear some more 'bout this," said Pa.

"Me too," Tom added. "Why these folks out west hate ya?"

The man looked sharply at Tom. "You jus' goin' wes'?"

"Jus' on our way."

"You ain't never been in California?"

"No, we ain't."

"Well, don' take my word. Go see for yourself."

"Yeah," Tom said, "but a fella kind a likes to know what he's gettin' into."

"Well, if you truly wanta know, I'm a fella that's asked questions an' give her some thought. She's a nice country. But she was stole a long time ago. You git acrost the desert an' come into the country aroun' Bakersfield. An' you never seen such purty country—all orchards an' grapes, purtiest country you ever seen. An' you'll pass lan' flat an' fine with water thirty feet down, and that lan's layin' fallow. But you can't have none of that lan'. That's a Lan' and Cattle Company. An' if they don't want ta work her, she ain't gonna git worked. You go in there an' plant you a little corn, an' you'll go to jail!"

"Good lan', you say? An' they ain't workin' her?"

"Yes, sir. Good lan' an' they ain't! Well, sir, that'll get you a little mad, but you ain't seen nothin'. People gonna have a look in their eye. They gonna look at you an' their face says, 'I don't like you, you son-of-a-bitch.' Gonna be deputy sheriffs, an' they'll push you aroun'. You camp on the roadside, an' they'll move you on. You gonna see in people's face how they hate you. An'—I'll tell you somepin. They hate you 'cause they're scairt. They know a hungry fella gonna get food even if he got to take it. They know that fallow lan's a sin an' somebody' gonna take it. What the hell! You never been called 'Okie' yet."

Tom said, "Okie? What's that?"

"Well, Okie use' ta mean you was from Oklahoma. Now it means you're a dirty son-of-a-bitch. Okie means you're scum. Don't mean nothing itself, it's the way they say it. But I can't tell you nothin'. You got to go there. I hear there's three hunderd thousan' of our people there—an' livin' like hogs, 'cause ever'thing in California is owned. They ain't nothin' left. An' them people that owns it is gonna hang on to it if they got ta kill ever'body in the worl' to do it. An' they're scairt, an' that makes 'em mad. You got to see it. You got to hear it. Purtiest goddamn country you ever seen, but they ain't nice to you, them folks. They're so scairt an' worried they ain't even nice to each other."

Tom looked down into the water, and he dug his heels into the sand. "S'pose a fella got work an' saved, couldn' he get a little lan'?"

The older man laughed and he looked at his boy, and his silent boy grinned almost in triumph. And the man said, "You ain't gonna get no steady work. Gonna scrabble for your dinner ever' day. An' you gonna do her with people lookin' mean at you." . . .

. . . Ma turned over on her back and crossed her hands under her head. She listened to Granma's breathing and to the girl's breathing. She moved a hand to start a fly from her forehead. The camp was quiet in the blinding heat, but the noises of hot grass—of crickets, the hum of flies—were a tone that was close to silence. Ma sighed deeply and then yawned and closed her eyes. In her half-sleep she heard footsteps approaching, but it was a man's voice that started her awake.

"Who's in here?"

Ma sat up quickly. A brown-faced man bent over and looked in. He wore boots and khaki pants and a khaki shirt with epaulets. On a Sam Browne belt a pistol holster hung, and a big silver star was pinned to his shirt at the left breast. A loose-crowned military cap was on the back of his head. He beat on the tarpaulin with his hand, and the tight canvas vibrated like a drum.

"Who's in here?" he demanded again.

Ma asked, "What is it you want, mister?"

"What you think I want? I want to know who's in here."

"Why, they's jus' us three in here. Me an' Granma an' my girl."

"Where's your men?"

"Why, they went down to clean up. We was drivin' all night."

"Where'd you come from?"

"Right near Sallisaw, Oklahoma."

"Well, you can't stay here."

"We aim to get out tonight an' cross the desert, mister."

"Well, you better. If you're here tomorra this time I'll run you in. We don't want none of you settlin' down here."

Ma's face blackened with anger. She got slowly to her feet. She stooped to the utensil box and picked out the iron skillet. "Mister," she said, " you got a tin button an' a gun. Where I come from, you keep your voice down." She advanced on him with the skillet. He loosened the gun in the holster. "Go ahead," said Ma. "Scarin' women. I'm thankful the men folks ain't here. They'd tear ya to pieces. In my country you watch your tongue."

The man took two steps backward. "Well, you ain't in your country now. You're in California, an' we don't want you god-damn Okies settlin' down."

Ma's advance stopped. She looked puzzled. "Okies?" she said softly. "Okies." "Yeah, Okies! An' if you're here when I come tomorra, I'll run ya in."

9. Woody Guthrie Sings "This Land Is Your Land," 1940

This land is your land, This land is my land,
From California to the New York island;
From the redwood forest to the Gulf Stream waters:
This land was made for you and me.

As I was walking that ribbon of highway,
I saw above me that endless skyway:
I saw below me that golden valley:
This land was made for you and me.

I've roamed and rambled and I followed my footsteps
To the sparkling sands of her diamond deserts;
And all around me a voice was sounding:
This land was made for you and me.

When the sun came shining, and I was strolling,
And the wheat fields waving and the dust clouds rolling,
As the fog was lifting a voice was chanting:
This land was made for you and me.

As I went walking, I saw a sign there,
And on the sign it said "No Trespassing."
But on the other side it didn't say nothing,
That side was made for you and me.

In the shadow of the steeple I saw my people,
By the relief office I seen my people;
As they stood there hungry, I stood there asking
Is this land made for you and me?

Nobody living can ever stop me,
As I go walking that freedom highway;
Nobody living can ever make me turn back,
This land was made for you and me.

⬤ E S S A Y S

Franklin D. Roosevelt excited both admirers and detractors in his own day, and still does. Herbert Hoover called him a "chameleon on plaid," implying that Roosevelt adjusted his temperament and policies as the situation dictated, without regard to any core values or personal vision. David M. Kennedy of Stanford University, whose book on this era won the Pulitzer Prize, describes a man of immense complexity, whose own experience of crippling disease gave him exceptional fortitude and empathy for others' plight. Roosevelt's leadership, Kennedy states, contrasted markedly with that of Hoover and made the New Deal what it was. Robert Higgs, a senior research fellow at the Independent Institute in Oakland, California, sees Roosevelt very differently. Higgs scorns the president as a political opportunist whose programs delayed economic recovery while vastly increasing governmental control over all aspects of American life. The New Deal legacy is a negative one, in his opinion. Which description of the president and his programs is most convincing? Did the New Deal rewrite government's contract with the people, or not?

FDR: Advocate for the American People

DAVID M. KENNEDY

Hoover brought a corporate executive's sensibility to the White House. Roosevelt brought a politician's. Hoover as president frequently dazzled visitors with his detailed knowledge and expert understanding of American business. "His was a mathematical brain," said his admiring secretary, Theodore Joslin. "Let banking officials, for instance, come into his office and he would rattle off the number of banks in the country, list their liabilities and assets, describe the trend of fiscal affairs, and go into the liquidity, or lack of it, of individual institutions, all from memory." Roosevelt, in contrast, impressed his visitors by asking them to draw a line across a map of the United States. He would then name, in order, every county through which the line passed, adding anecdotes about each locality's political particularities. Where Hoover had a Quaker's reserve about the perquisites of the presidency, Roosevelt savored them with gusto. By 1932 Hoover wore the mantle of office like a hair shirt that he could not wait to doff. Roosevelt confided to a journalist his conviction that "no man ever willingly gives up public life—no man who has ever tasted it." Almost preternaturally self-confident, he had no intimidating image of the presidential office to live up to, it was said, since his untroubled conception of the presidency consisted quite simply of the thought of himself in it.

Hoover's first elected office was the presidency. Roosevelt had been a professional politician all his life. He had spent years charting his course for the White House. To a remarkable degree, he had followed the career path blazed by his cousin Theodore Roosevelt—through the New York legislature and the office of assistant secretary of the navy to the governor's chair in Albany. In 1920 he had been the vice-presidential candidate on the losing Democratic ticket.

David M. Kennedy, *Freedom from Fear: The American People in Depression and War* (New York: Oxford University Press, 1999), 94–96, 115–117, 133–137, 144–146, 160–163, 168, 258, 261–263, 372, 377–379. Copyright © 1999 by David Kennedy. Used by permission of Oxford University Press, Inc.

The following year, while vacationing at his family's summer estate on Campobello Island, in the Canadian province of New Brunswick, he had been stricken with poliomyelitis. He was thirty-nine years of age. He would never again be able to stand without heavy steel braces on his legs. Through grueling effort and sheer will power, he eventually trained himself to "walk" a few steps, an odd shuffle in which, leaning on the strong arm of a companion, he threw one hip, then the other, to move his steel-cased legs forward. His disability was no secret, but he took care to conceal its extent. He never allowed himself to be photographed in his wheelchair or being carried.

Roosevelt's long struggle with illness transformed him in spirit as well as body. Athletic and slim in his youth, he was now necessarily sedentary, and his upper body thickened. He developed, in the manner of many paraplegics, a wrestler's torso and big, beefy arms. His biceps, he delighted in telling visitors, were bigger than those of the celebrated prizefighter Jack Dempsey. Like many disabled persons, too, he developed a talent for denial, a kind of forcefully willed optimism that refused to dwell on life's difficulties. Sometimes this talent abetted his penchant for duplicity, as in the continuing love affair he carried on with Lucy Mercer, even after he told his wife in 1918 that the relationship was ended. At other times it endowed him with an aura of radiant indomitability, lending conviction and authority to what in other men's mouths might have been banal platitudes, such as "all we have to fear is fear itself." Many of Roosevelt's acquaintances also believed that his grim companionship with paralysis gave to this shallow, supercilious youth the precious gift of a purposeful manhood. . . .

Though Roosevelt was never a systematic thinker, the period of lonely reflection imposed by his convalescence allowed him to shape a fairly coherent social philosophy. By the time he was elected governor, the distillate of his upbringing, education, and experience had crystallized into a few simple but powerful political principles. [Raymond] Moley summarized them this way: "He believed that government not only could, but should, achieve the subordination of private interests to collective interests, substitute co-operation for the mad scramble to selfish individualism. He had a profound feeling for the underdog, a real sense of the critical imbalance of economic life, a very keen awareness that political democracy could not exist side by side with economic plutocracy." As Roosevelt himself put it:

> [O]ur civilization cannot endure unless we, as individuals, realize our responsibility to and dependence on the rest of the world. For it is literally true that the "self-supporting" man or woman has become as extinct as the man of the stone age. Without the help of thousands of others, any one of us would die, naked and starved. Consider the bread upon our table, the clothes upon our backs, the luxuries that make life pleasant; how many men worked in sunlit fields, in dark mines, in the fierce heat of molten metal, and among the looms and wheels of countless factories, in order to create them for our use and enjoyment. . . . In the final analysis, the progress of our civilization will be retarded if any large body of citizens falls behind.

Perhaps deep within himself Roosevelt trembled occasionally with the common human palsies of melancholy or doubt or fear, but the world saw none of it. On February 15, 1933, he gave a memorable demonstration of his powers of self-control. Alighting in Miami from an eleven-day cruise aboard Vincent Astor's yacht

Nourmahal, FDR motored to Bay Front Park, where he made a few remarks to a large crowd. At the end of the brief speech, Mayor Anton J. Cermak of Chicago stepped up to the side of Roosevelt's open touring car and said a few words to the president-elect. Suddenly a pistol barked from the crowd. Cermak doubled over. Roosevelt ordered the Secret Service agents, who were reflexively accelerating his car away from the scene, to stop. He motioned to have Cermak, pale and pulseless, put into the seat beside him. "Tony, keep quiet—don't move. It won't hurt you if you keep quiet," Roosevelt repeated as he cradled Cermak's limp body while the car sped to the hospital.

Cermak had been mortally wounded. He died within weeks, the victim of a de-ranged assassin who had been aiming for Roosevelt. On the evening of February 15, after Cermak had been entrusted to the doctors, Moley accompanied Roosevelt back to the *Nourmahal,* poured him a stiff drink, and prepared for the letdown now that Roosevelt was alone among his intimates. He had just been spared by inches from a killer's bullet and had held a dying man in his arms. But there was nothing—"not so much as the twitching of a muscle, the mopping of a brow, or even the hint of a false gaiety—to indicate that it wasn't any other evening in any other place. Roosevelt was simply himself—easy, confident, poised, to all appearances unmoved." The episode contributed to Moley's eventual conclusion "that Roosevelt had no nerves at all." He was, said Frances Perkins, "the most complicated human being I ever knew." . . .

Roosevelt began inaugural day by attending a brief service at St. John's Episcopal Church. His old Groton School headmaster, Endicott Peabody, prayed the Lord to "bless Thy servant, Franklin, chosen to be president of the United States." After a quick stop at the Mayflower Hotel to confer urgently with his advisers on the still-worsening banking crisis, Roosevelt donned his formal attire and motored to the White House. There he joined a haggard and cheerless Hoover for the ride down Pennsylvania Avenue to the inaugural platform on the east side of the Capitol.

Braced on his son's arm, Roosevelt walked his few lurching steps to the rostrum. Breaking precedent, he recited the entire oath of office, rather than merely repeating "I do" to the chief justice's interrogation. Then he began his inaugural address, speaking firmly in his rich tenor voice. Frankly acknowledging the crippled condi-tion of the ship of state he was now to captain, he began by reassuring his country-men that "this great nation will endure as it had endured, will revive and will prosper. . . . The only thing we have to fear," he intoned, "is fear itself." The nation's distress, he declared, owed to "no failure of substance." Rather, "rulers of the ex-change of mankind's goods have failed through their own stubbornness and their own incompetence, have admitted their failure, and have abdicated. . . . The money changers have fled from their high seats in the temple of our civilization. We may now restore that temple to the ancient truths." The greatest task, he went on, "is to put people to work," and he hinted at "direct recruiting by the Government" on public works projects as the means to do it. . . .

Just weeks before his inaugural, while on his way to board the *Nourmahal* in Florida, Roosevelt had spoken restlessly of the need for "action, action." President at last, he now proceeded to act with spectacular vigor.

The first and desperately urgent item of business was the banking crisis. Even as he left the Mayflower Hotel to deliver his inaugural condemnation of the "money changers," he approved a recommendation originating with the outgoing treasury secretary, Ogden Mills, to convene an emergency meeting of bankers from the leading financial centers. The next day, Sunday, March 5, Roosevelt issued two proclamations, one calling Congress into special session on March 9, the other invoking the Trading with the Enemy Act to halt all transactions in gold and declare a four-day national banking holiday—both of them measures that Hoover had vainly urged him to endorse in the preceding weeks. Hoover's men and Roosevelt's now began an intense eighty hours of collaboration to hammer out the details of an emergency banking measure that could be presented to the special session of Congress. Haunting the corridors of the Treasury Department day and night, private bankers and government officials both old and new toiled frantically to rescue the moribund corpse of American finance. In that hectic week, none led normal lives, Moley remembered. "Confusion, haste, the dread of making mistakes, the consciousness of responsibility for the economic well-being of millions of people, made mortal inroads on the health of some of us . . . and left the rest of us ready to snap at our images in the mirror. . . . Only Roosevelt," Moley observed, "preserved the air of a man who'd found a happy way of life."

Roosevelt's and Hoover's minions "had forgotten to be Republicans or Democrats," Moley commented. "We were just a bunch of men trying to save the banking system." William Woodin, the new treasury secretary, and Ogden Mills, his predecessor, simply shifted places on either side of the secretary's desk in the Treasury Building. Otherwise, nothing changed in the room. The kind of bipartisan collaboration for which Hoover had long pleaded was now happening, but under Roosevelt's aegis, not Hoover's—and not, all these men hoped, too late. When the special session of Congress convened at noon on March 9, they had a bill ready—barely.

The bill was read to the House at 1:00 P.M., while some new representatives were still trying to locate their seats. Printed copies were not ready for the members. A rolled-up newspaper symbolically served. After thirty-eight minutes of "debate," the chamber passed the bill, sight unseen, with a unanimous shout. The Senate approved the bill with only seven dissenting votes—all from agrarian states historically suspicious of Wall Street. The president signed the legislation into law at 8:36 in the evening. "Capitalism," concluded Moley, "was saved in eight days." . . .

On Monday the thirteenth the banks reopened, and the results of Roosevelt's magic with the Congress and the people were immediately apparent. Deposits and gold began to flow back into the banking system. The prolonged banking crisis, acute since at least 1930, with roots reaching back through the 1920s and even into the days of Andrew Jackson, was at last over. And Roosevelt, taking full credit, was a hero. William Randolph Hearst told him: "I guess at your next election we will make it unanimous." Even Henry Stimson, who so recently had thought FDR a "peanut," sent his "heartiest congratulations."

The common people of the country sent their congratulations as well—and their good wishes and suggestions and special requests. Some 450,000 Americans wrote to their new president in his first week in office. Thereafter mail routinely poured in at a rate of four to seven thousand letters per day. The White House mailroom, staffed by a single employee in Hoover's day, had to hire seventy people to handle the flood of correspondence. Roosevelt had touched the hearts and imaginations of his countrymen like no predecessor in memory. . . .

Meanwhile, the steady legislative drumbeat of the Hundred Days continued. Relishing power and wielding it with gusto, Roosevelt next sent to Congress, on March 21, a request for legislation aimed at unemployment relief. Here he departed most dramatically from Hoover's pettifogging timidity, and here he harvested the greatest political rewards. He proposed a Civilian Conservation Corps (CCC) to employ a quarter of a million men on forestry, flood control, and beautification projects. Over the next decade, the CCC became one of the most popular of all the New Deal's innovations. By the time it expired in 1942, it had put more than three million idle youngsters to work at a wage of thirty dollars a month, twenty-five of which they were required to send home to their families. CCC workers built firebreaks and lookouts in the national forests and bridges, campgrounds, trails, and museums in the national parks. Roosevelt also called for a new agency, the Federal Emergency Relief Administration (FERA), to coordinate and eventually increase direct federal unemployment assistance to the states. And he served notice, a bit half-heartedly, that he would soon be making recommendations about a "broad public works labor-creating program."

The first two of these measures—CCC and FERA—constituted important steps along the road to direct federal involvement in unemployment relief, something that Hoover had consistently and self-punishingly resisted. Roosevelt showed no such squeamishness, just as he had not hesitated as governor of New York to embrace relief as a "social duty" of government in the face of evident human suffering. As yet, Roosevelt did not think of relief payments or public works employment as means of significantly increasing purchasing power. He proposed them for charitable reasons, and for political purposes as well, but not principally for economic ones. . . .

These first modest steps at a direct federal role in welfare services also carried into prominence another of Roosevelt's associates from New York, Harry Hopkins, whom Roosevelt would soon name as federal relief administrator. A chain-smoking, hollow-eyed, pauper-thin social worker, a tough-talking, big-hearted blend of the sardonic and sentimental, Hopkins represented an important and durable component of what might be called the emerging political culture of the New Deal. In common with Brain Truster Adolf Berle, future treasury secretary Henry Morgenthau Jr., and Labor Secretary Frances Perkins, Hopkins was steeped in the Social Gospel tradition. Ernest, high-minded, and sometimes condescending, the Social Gospelers were middle-class missionaries to America's industrial proletariat. Inspired originally by late nineteenth-century Protestant clergymen like Walter Rauschenbusch and Washington Gladden, they were committed to the moral and material uplift of the poor, and they had both the courage and the prejudices of their convictions. Berle and Morgenthau had worked for a time at Lillian Wald's Henry Street settlement house in New York, Perkins at Jane Addams's Hull House in Chicago, and Hopkins himself at New York's Christadora House. Amid the din and squalor of thronged immigrant neighborhoods, they had all learned at first hand that poverty could be an exitless way of life, that the idea of "opportunity" was often a mockery in the precarious, threadbare existence of the working class. Together with Franklin Roosevelt, they meant to do something about it. . . .

"What I want you to do," said Harry Hopkins to Lorena Hickok in July 1933, "is to go out around the country and look this thing over. I don't want statistics from you. I don't want the social-worker angle. I just want your own reaction, as an ordinary citizen.

"Go talk with preachers and teachers, businessmen, workers, farmers. Go talk with the unemployed, those who are on relief and those who aren't. And when you talk with them don't ever forget that but for the grace of God you, I, any of our friends might be in their shoes. Tell me what you see and hear. All of it. Don't ever pull your punches."

The Depression was now in its fourth year. In the neighborhoods and hamlets of a stricken nation millions of men and women languished in sullen gloom and looked to Washington with guarded hope. Still they struggled to comprehend the nature of the calamity that had engulfed them. Across Hopkins's desk at the newly created Federal Emergency Relief Administration flowed rivers of data that measured the Depression's impact in cool numbers. But Hopkins wanted more—to touch the human face of the catastrophe, taste in his mouth the metallic smack of the fear and hunger of the unemployed, as he had when he worked among the immigrant poor at New York's Christadora settlement house in 1912. Tied to his desk in Washington, he dispatched Lorena Hickok in his stead. In her he chose a uniquely gutsy and perceptive observer who could be counted on to see without illusion and to report with candor, insight, and moxie. . . .

From the charts and tables accumulating on his desk even before Hickok's letters began to arrive, Hopkins could already sketch the grim outlines of that history. Stockholders, his figures confirmed, had watched as three-quarters of the value of their assets had simply evaporated since 1929, a colossal financial meltdown that blighted not only the notoriously idle rich but struggling neighborhood banks, hard-earned retirement nest eggs, and college and university endowments as well. The more than five thousand bank failures between the Crash and the New Deal's rescue operation in March 1933 wiped out some $7 billion in depositors' money. Accelerating foreclosures on defaulted home mortgages—150,000 homeowners lost their property in 1930, 200,000 in 1931, 250,000 in 1932—stripped millions of people of both shelter and life savings at a single stroke and menaced the balance sheets of thousands of surviving banks. Several states and some thirteen hundred municipalities, crushed by sinking real estate prices and consequently shrinking tax revenues, defaulted on their obligations to creditors, pinched their already scant social services, cut payrolls, and slashed paychecks. Chicago was reduced to paying its teachers in tax warrants and then, in the winter of 1932–33, to paying them nothing at all.

Gross national product had fallen by 1933 to half its 1929 level. Spending for new plants and equipment had ground to a virtual standstill. Businesses invested only $3 billion in 1933, compared with $24 billion in 1929. . . . Residential and industrial construction shriveled to less than one-fifth of its pre-Depression volume, a wrenching contraction that spread through lumber camps, steel mills, and appliance factories, disemploying thousands of loggers, mill hands, sheet-metal workers, engineers, architects, carpenters, plumbers, roofers, plasterers, painters, and electricians. Mute shoals of jobless men drifted through the streets of every American city in 1933.

Nowhere did the Depression strike more savagely than in the American countryside. On America's farms, income had plummeted from $6 billion in what for farmers was the already lean year of 1929 to $2 billion in 1932. The net receipts from the wheat harvest in one Oklahoma county went from $1.2 million in 1931 to just $7,000 in 1933. Mississippi's pathetic $239 per capita income in 1929 sank to $117 in 1933.

Unemployment and its close companion, reduced wages, were the most obvious and the most wounding of all the Depression's effects. The government's data showed that 25 percent of the work force, some thirteen million workers, including nearly four hundred thousand women, stood idle in 1933. . . .

Hickok set out in quest of the human reality of the Depression. She found that and much more besides. In dingy working-class neighborhoods in Philadelphia and New York, in unpainted clapboard farmhouses in North Dakota, on the ravaged cotton farms of Georgia, on the dusty mesas of Colorado, Hickok uncovered not just the effects of the economic crisis that had begun in 1929. She found herself face to face as well with the human wreckage of a century of pell-mell, buccaneering, no-holds-barred, free-market industrial and agricultural capitalism. As her travels progressed, she gradually came to acknowledge the sobering reality that for many Americans the Great Depression brought times only a little harder than usual. She discovered, in short, what historian James Patterson has called the "old poverty" that was endemic in America well before the Depression hit. By his estimate, even in the midst of the storied prosperity of the 1920s some forty million Americans, including virtually all nonwhites, most of the elderly, and much of the rural population, were eking out unrelievedly precarious lives that were scarcely visible and practically unimaginable to their more financially secure countrymen. "The researches we have made into standards of living of the American family," Hopkins wrote, "have uncovered for the public gaze a volume of chronic poverty, unsuspected except by a few students and by those who have always experienced it." From this perspective, the Depression was not just a passing crisis but an episode that revealed deeply rooted structural inequities in American society.

The "old poor" were among the Depression's most ravaged victims, but it was not the Depression that had impoverished them. They were the "one-third of a nation" that Franklin Roosevelt would describe in 1937 as chronically "ill-housed, ill-clad, ill-nourished." By suddenly threatening to push millions of other Americans into their wretched condition, the Depression pried open a narrow window of political opportunity to do something at last on behalf of that long-suffering one-third, and in the process to redefine the very character of America. . . .

. . . The Emergency Relief Appropriation Act addressed only the most immediate of his [FDR's] goals. Most of the agencies it spawned were destined to survive less than a decade. The longer-term features of Roosevelt's grand design—unemployment insurance and old-age pensions—were incorporated in a separate piece of legislation, a landmark measure whose legacy endured and reshaped the texture of American life: the Social Security Act.

No other New Deal measure proved more lastingly consequential or more emblematic of the very meaning of the New Deal. Nor did any other better reveal the tangled skein of human needs, economic calculations, idealistic visions, political pressures, partisan maneuverings, actuarial projections, and constitutional constraints out of which Roosevelt was obliged to weave his reform program. Tortuously threading each of those filaments through the needle of the legislative process, Roosevelt began with the Social Security Act to knit the fabric of the modern welfare state. It would in the end be a peculiar garment, one that could have been fashioned only in America and perhaps only in the circumstances of the Depression era.

No one knew better the singular possibilities of that place and time than Secretary of Labor Frances Perkins. To her the president in mid-1934 assigned the task of chairing a cabinet committee to prepare the social security legislation for submission to Congress. (Its other members were Treasury Secretary Henry Morgenthau, Attorney General Homer Cummings, Agriculture Secretary Henry Wallace, and Relief Administrator Harry Hopkins.) "[T]his was the time, above all times," Perkins wrote, "to be foresighted about future problems of unemployment and unprotected old age." The president shared this sense of urgency—and opportunity. Now is the time, he said to Perkins in 1934, when "we have to get it started, or it will never start." . . .

At the outset the president entertained extravagantly far-reaching ideas about the welfare system he envisioned. "[T]here is no reason why everybody in the United States should not be covered," he mused to Perkins on one occasion. "I see no reason why every child, from the day he is born, shouldn't be a member of the social security system. When he begins to grow up, he should know he will have old-age benefits direct from the insurance system to which he will belong all his life. If he is out of work, he gets a benefit. If he is sick or crippled, he gets a benefit. . . . And there is no reason why just the industrial workers should get the benefit of this," Roosevelt went on. "Everybody ought to be in on it—the farmer and his wife and his family. I don't see why not," Roosevelt persisted, as Perkins shook her head at this presidential woolgathering. "I don't see why not. Cradle to the grave—from the cradle to the grave they ought to be in a social insurance system."

That may have been the president's ideal outcome, but he knew as well as anyone that he would have to temper that vision in the forge of political and fiscal reality. Much of the country, not least the southern Democrats who were essential to his party's congressional majority, remained suspicious about all forms of social insurance. So Perkins, with dour Yankee prudence, went to work in a more practical vein. In the summer of 1934 she convened the Committee on Economic Security (CES), an advisory body of technical experts who would hammer out the precise terms of the social security legislation. She instructed the CES in words that spoke eloquently about her sensitivity to the novelties and difficulties of what they were about to undertake. "I recall emphasizing," she later wrote, "that the President was already in favor of a program of social insurance, but that it remained for them to make it practicable. We expected them," she recollected, in a passage that says volumes about her shrewd assessment of American political culture in the 1930s, "to remember that this was the United States in the years 1934–35. We hoped they would make recommendations based upon a practical knowledge of the needs of our country, the prejudices of our people, and our legislative habits."

The needs of the country were plain enough. But what of those prejudices and habits? What, in particular, of that phrase "under state laws" in the Democratic platform? Few items more deeply vexed the CES planners. Given the mobility of American workers and the manifest desirability of uniformity in national laws, most of the CES experts insisted that a centralized, federally administered system of social insurance would be the most equitable and the easiest to manage. They deemed a miscellany of state systems to be utterly impractical. Yet deeply ingrained traditions of states' rights challenged that commonsense approach, as did pervasive doubts about the federal government's constitutional power to act in this area.

Thomas Eliot, the young, Harvard-educated general counsel to the CES who played a major role in drafting the final bill, worried above all about "the omnipresent question of constitutionality." The lower federal courts, Eliot knew, had already handed down hundreds of injunctions against other New Deal measures. Constitutional tests of NRA and AAA were working their way to the Supreme Court. There, four justices—the "Battalion of Death" that included Justices McReynolds, Butler, VanDevanter, and Sutherland—were notoriously hostile to virtually any expansion of federal power over industry and commerce, not to mention the far bolder innovation of federal initiatives respecting employment and old age. Eliot brooded that "I could not honestly assure the committee that a national plan . . . would be upheld by the Supreme Court." . . .

Against their better judgment, the CES experts therefore resigned themselves to settling for a mixed federal-state system. Perkins took what comfort she could from the reflection that if the Supreme Court should declare the federal aspects of the law to be unconstitutional, at least the state laws would remain. Though they would not be uniform, they would be better than nothing. . . .

The pattern of economic reforms that the New Deal wove arose out of concrete historical circumstances. It also had a more coherent intellectual underpinning than is customarily recognized. Its cardinal aim was not to destroy capitalism but to devolatilize it, and at the same time to distribute its benefits more evenly. . . .

. . . And ever after, Americans assumed that the federal government had not merely a role, but a major responsibility, in ensuring the health of the economy and the welfare of citizens. That simple but momentous shift in perception was the newest thing in all the New Deal, and the most consequential too.

Humankind, of course, does not live by bread alone. Any assessment of what the New Deal did would be incomplete if it rested with an appraisal of New Deal economic policies and failed to acknowledge the remarkable array of social innovations nourished by Roosevelt's expansive temperament. . . .

For all his alleged inscrutability, Franklin Roosevelt's social vision was clear enough. "We are going to make a country," he once said to Frances Perkins, "in which no one is left out." In that unadorned sentence Roosevelt spoke volumes about the New Deal's lasting historical meaning. Like his rambling, comfortable, and unpretentious old home on the bluff above the Hudson River, Roosevelt's New Deal was a welcoming mansion of many rooms, a place where millions of his fellow citizens could find at last a measure of the security that the patrician Roosevelts enjoyed as their birthright.

Perhaps the New Deal's greatest achievement was its accommodation of the maturing immigrant communities that had milled uneasily on the margins of American society for a generation and more before the 1930s. In bringing them into the Democratic Party and closer to the mainstream of national life, the New Deal, even without fully intending to do so, also made room for an almost wholly new institution, the industrial union. To tens of millions of rural Americans, the New Deal offered the modern comforts of electricity, schools, and roads, as well as unaccustomed financial stability. To the elderly and the unemployed it extended the promise of income security, and the salvaged dignity that went with it.

To black Americans the New Deal offered jobs with CCC, WPA, and PWA and, perhaps as important, the compliment of respect from at least some federal officials. The time had not come for direct federal action to challenge Jim Crow and put right at last the crimes of slavery and discrimination, but more than a few New Dealers made clear where their sympathies lay and quietly prepared for a better future. Urged on by Eleanor Roosevelt, the president brought African-Americans into the government in small but unprecedented numbers. By the mid-1930s they gathered periodically as an informal "black cabinet," guided often by the redoubtable Mary McLeod Bethune. Roosevelt also appointed the first black federal judge, William Hastie. Several New Deal Departments and agencies, including especially Ickes's Interior Department and Aubrey Williams's National Youth Administration, placed advisers for "Negro affairs" on their staffs. . . .

Above all, the New Deal gave to countless Americans who had never had much of it a sense of security, and with it a sense of having a stake in their country. And it did it all without shredding the American Constitution or sundering the American people. At a time when despair and alienation were prostrating other peoples under the heel of dictatorship, that was no small accomplishment.

FDR: Opportunistic Architect of Big Government

ROBERT HIGGS

The Great Depression was a watershed in U.S. history. Soon after Herbert Hoover assumed the presidency in 1929, the economy began to decline, and between 1930 and 1933 the contraction assumed catastrophic proportions never experienced before or since in the United States. Disgusted by Hoover's inability to stem the collapse, the voters elected Franklin Delano Roosevelt as president, along with a heavily Democratic Congress, in 1932 and thereby set in motion the radical restructuring of government's role in the economy known as the New Deal.

With few exceptions, historians have taken a positive view of the New Deal. They have generally praised such measures as the massive relief programs for the unemployed; the expanded federal regulation of agriculture, industry, finance, and labor relations; the establishment of a legal minimum wage; and the creation of the Social Security program with its old-age pensions, unemployment insurance, and income supplements for the aged poor, the physically disabled, the blind, and dependent children in single-parent families. In the construction of the U.S. regulatory-and-welfare state, no one looms larger than Roosevelt.

For this accomplishment, along with his wartime leadership, historians and the general public alike rank Franklin D. Roosevelt among the greatest of U.S. presidents. Roosevelt, it is repeatedly said, restored hope to the American people when they had fallen into despair because of the seemingly endless depression, and his policies "saved capitalism" by mitigating its intrinsic cruelties and inequalities. The very title of the volume in the *Oxford History of the United States* that deals with the Roosevelt era—*Freedom from Fear*—encapsulates the popular as well as the academic understanding of what the New Deal achieved. The author of that volume, David M. Kennedy of Stanford University, concludes that "achieving security was

Robert Higgs, *Against Leviathan: Government Power and a Free Society* (Oakland, Calif.: The Independent Institute, 2004), pp. 33–40. Reprinted with permission.

the leitmotif of virtually everything the New Deal attempted. . . . Its cardinal aim was not to destroy capitalism but to devolatilize it, and at the same time to distribute its benefits more evenly."

This view of Roosevelt and the New Deal amounts to a myth compounded of ideological predisposition and historical misunderstanding. In a 1936 book called *The Menace of Roosevelt and His Policies,* Howard E. Kershner came closer to the truth when he wrote that Roosevelt "took charge of our government when it was comparatively simple, and for the most part confined to the essential functions of government, and transformed it into a highly complex, bungling agency for throttling business and bedeviling the private lives of free people. It is no exaggeration to say that he took the government when it was a small racket and made a large racket out of it."

As this statement illustrates, not everyone admired Roosevelt during the 1930s. Although historians have tended to view his opponents as self-interested reactionaries, the legions of these "Roosevelt haters" actually had a clearer view of the economic consequences of the New Deal. The nearly 17 million men and women who, even in Roosevelt's moment of supreme triumph in 1936, voted for Alfred Landon could not all have been plutocrats.

Prolonging the Depression

The irony is that even if Roosevelt had helped to lift the spirits of the American people in the depths of the depression—an uplift for which no compelling documentation exists—that achievement only led the public to labor under an illusion. After all, the root cause of the prevailing malaise was the continuation of the depression. Had the masses understood that the New Deal was only prolonging the depression, they would have had good reason to reject it and its vaunted leader.

In fact, as many observers claimed at the time, the New Deal did prolong the depression. Had Roosevelt only kept his inoffensive campaign promises of 1932— promises to cut federal spending, balance the budget, maintain a sound currency, and rein in the bureaucratic centralization in Washington—the depression might have passed into history before his next campaign in 1936. Instead, Roosevelt and Congress, especially during the congressional sessions of 1933 and 1935, embraced interventionist policies on a wide front. With its bewildering, incoherent mass of new expenditures, taxes, subsidies, regulations, and direct government participation in productive activities, the New Deal created so much confusion, fear, uncertainty, and hostility among businessmen and investors that private investment and hence overall private economic activity never recovered enough to restore the high levels of production and employment enjoyed during the 1920s.

In the face of the interventionist onslaught, the U.S. economy between 1930 and 1940 failed to add anything to its capital stock: net private investment for that eleven-year period totaled *minus* $3.1 billion. Without ongoing capital accumulation, no economy can grow. Between 1929 and 1939, the economy sacrificed an entire decade of normal economic growth, which would have increased the national income by 30–40 percent.

The government's own greatly enlarged economic activity did not compensate for the private shortfall. Apart from the mere insufficiency of the dollars spent, the government's spending tended, as contemporary critics aptly noted, to purchase a high proportion of sheer boondoggle. In the words of the common man's poet Berton Braley,

> A dollar for the services
> A true producer renders—
> (And a dollar for experiments
> Of Governmental spenders!)
> A dollar for the earners
> And the savers and the thrifty—
> (And a dollar for the wasters,
> It's a case of fifty-fifty!).

Under heavy criticism, Roosevelt himself eventually declared that he was "not willing that the vitality of our people be further sapped by the giving of doles, of market baskets, by a few hours of weekly work cutting grass, raking leaves, or picking up papers in the public parks." Nevertheless, the dole did continue.

Buying Votes

In this madness, the New Dealers had a method. Notwithstanding its economic illogic and incoherence, the New Deal served as a highly successful vote-buying scheme. Coming into power at a time of widespread destitution, high unemployment, and business failures, the Roosevelt administration recognized that the president and his Democratic allies in Congress could appropriate unprecedented sums of money and channel them into the hands of recipients who would respond by giving political support to their benefactors. As John T. Flynn said of Roosevelt, "it was always easy to interest him in a plan which would confer some special benefit upon some special class in the population in exchange for their votes," and eventually "no political boss could compete with him in any county in America in the distribution of money and jobs."

In buying votes, the relief programs for the unemployed—especially the Federal Emergency Relief Administration, the Civilian Conservation Corp, and the Works Progress Administration—loomed largest, though many other programs fostered achievement of the same end. Farm subsidies, price supports, credit programs, and related measures won over much of the rural middle class. The labor provisions of, first, the National Industrial Recovery Act, then later the National Labor Relations Act, and finally the Fair Labor Standards Act purchased support from the burgeoning ranks of the labor unions. Homeowners supported the New Deal out of gratitude for the government's refinancing of their mortgages and its provision of home loan guarantees. Even blacks, loyal to the Republican Party every since the Civil War, abandoned it in exchange for the pittances of relief payments and the tag ends of employment in the federal work-relief programs. Put it all together and you have what political scientists call the New Deal Coalition—a potent political force that remained intact until the 1970s.

Inept, Arrogant Advisers

Journalists titillated the public with talk of Roosevelt's "Brains Trust"—his coterie of policy advisers just before and shortly after his election in 1932, of whom the most prominent were Columbia University professors Raymond Moley, Rexford Guy

Tugwell, and Adolph A. Berle. In retrospect, it is obvious that these men's ideas about the causes and cure of the depression ranged from merely wrongheaded to completely crackpot.

Many of the early New Dealers viewed the collapse of prices as the cause of the depression, so they regarded various means of raising prices, especially cartelization of industry and other measures to restrict market supplies, as appropriate in the circumstances. Raise farm prices, raise industrial prices, raise wage rates, raise the price of gold. Only one price should fall—namely, the price (that is, the purchasing power) of money. Thus, they favored inflation and, as a means to this end, the abandonment of the gold standard, which had previously kept inflation more or less in check.

Later advisers, the "happy hot dogs" (after their mentor and godfather Harvard law professor Felix Frankfurter), such as Tom Corcoran, Ben Cohen, and James Landis, who rose to prominence during the mid-1930s, had no genuine economic expertise but contributed mightily to Roosevelt's swing away from accommodating business interests and toward assaulting investors as a class, whom he dubbed "economic royalists" and blamed for the depression and other social evils.

Early and late, the president's advisers shared at least one major opinion: that the federal government should intervene deeply and widely in economic life; or, in other words, that government spending, employing, and regulating, all directed by "experts" such as themselves, could repair the various perceived defects of the market system and restore prosperity while achieving greater social justice. As Garet Garrett perceived as early as August 1933, the president's academic advisers sought not merely to deal with the emergency. Theirs was "a complex intention, not restoration, not prosperity again as it had been before, but a complete new order, scientifically planned and managed, the individual profit motive tamed by government wisdom, human happiness ascendant on a plotted curve. Even at the time, the overweening haughtiness of these incompetent policy advisers struck many thoughtful onlookers as their most distinctive trait. As James Burnham wrote of them in his 1941 book *The Managerial Revolution,* "they are, sometimes openly, scornful of capitalists and capitalist ideas. . . . They believe that they can run things, and they like to run things." More recently, even a sympathetic left-liberal historian, Alan Brinkley, wrote that the hardcore New Dealers embraced government planning "with almost religious veneration."

The Misleading Analogy of War

Many of the New Dealers, including Roosevelt himself (as assistant secretary of the navy), had been active in the wartime administration of Woodrow Wilson. Ruminating on how to deal with the depression, they seized on an analogy: the war was a national emergency, and we dealt with it by creating government agencies to control and mobilize the private economy; the depression is a national emergency, and therefore we can deal with it by creating similar agencies. From that reasoning arose a succession of government organizations modeled on wartime precedents. The Agricultural Adjustment Administration resembled the Food Administration; the National Recovery Administration resembled the War Industries Board; the Reconstruction Finance Corporation (created under Hoover but greatly expanded under

Roosevelt) resembled the War Finance Corporation; the National Labor Relations Board resembled the War Labor Board; the Tennessee Valley Authority resembled the Muscle Shoals project; the Civilian Conservation Corp resembled the army itself; and the list went on and on.

In his first inaugural speech, Roosevelt declared, "we must move as a trained and loyal army willing to sacrifice for the good of a common discipline." He warned that should Congress fail to act to his satisfaction, he would seek "broad executive power to wage a war against the emergency as great as the power that would be given me if we were in fact invaded by a foreign foe." However stirring the rhetoric, this approach to dealing with the depression rested on a complete misapprehension. The requisites of successfully prosecuting a war had virtually nothing in common with the requisites of getting the economy out of a depression. (Moreover, the president and his supporters greatly overestimated how successful their wartime measures had been—World War I had ended before the many defects of those measures became widely appreciated.)

A Pure Political Opportunist

Roosevelt did not trouble himself with serious thinking. Flynn referred to an aspect of his character as "the free and easy manner in which he could confront problems about which he knew very little." Nor did he apparently care that he knew very little; his mind sailed strictly on the surface: "Fundamentally he was without any definite political or economic philosophy. He was not a man to deal in fundamentals. . . . The positions he took on political and economic questions were not taken in accordance with deeply rooted political beliefs but under the influence of political necessity. . . . He was in every sense purely an opportunist." Raymond Moley flaunted "the superb assurances that the President has given the country in connection with some of this [1933] legislation . . . that it is frankly experimental." In other words, Roosevelt had no idea how to deal with the situation he confronted, but he determined to launch a thousand ships anyhow in the hope that one of them might reach the promised land and in the conviction that he would be rewarded politically for such mindless activism.

An indifferent student and then a wealthy, handsome, and popular young man about town, Roosevelt had distinguished himself in his early days mainly by his amiable and charming personality. A born politician—which is to say, he was devious, manipulative, and mendacious—he had a flair for campaigning and for posturing before and propagandizing the public. His "first instinct," according to *New York Times* report Turner Catledge, "was always to lie," although "sometimes in mid-sentence he would switch to accuracy because he realized he could get away with the truth in that particular instance." Though millions hated him with a white-hot passion, there is no gainsaying that far more loved him, and millions regarded him as a savior—"the Heaven-sent man of the hour," as the *New York Times* editorialized on June 18, 1933.

If demagoguery were a powerful means of creating prosperity, then Roosevelt might have lifted the country out of the depression in short order. But in 1939, ten years after the onset of the depression and six years after the commencement of the New Deal, 9.5 million persons, or 17.2 percent of the labor force, still remained officially unemployed (of whom more than 3 million were enrolled in emergency government make-work projects). Roosevelt proved himself to be a masterful politician, but, unfortunately for the American people subjected to his policies, he had no idea how to end the depression other than to "try something" and, when that didn't work, to try something else. His ill-conceived, politically shaped experiments so disrupted the operation of the market economy and so discouraged the accumulation of capital that they thwarted the full recovery that otherwise would have occurred—after all, the capitalist machine was not irreparably broken, despite what an emergent school of "stagnationist" economists was saying in the late 1930s. Roosevelt's followers revered him as a great leader then, and many people revere him still, but except for the members of the planner class and their private-sector pets, wrongheaded leadership turned out to be worse than no leadership at all.

Legacies

Although Roosevelt and the New Dealers failed to end the depression, they succeeded in revolutionizing the institutions of U.S. political and economic life and in changing the country's dominant ideology. Even today, sixty-five years after the New Deal ran out of steam, its legacies remain and continue to hamper the successful operation of the market economy and to diminish individual liberties.

One need look no further than an organization chart of the federal government. There one finds agencies such as the Export-Import Bank, the Farm Credit Administration, the Rural Housing and Community Development Service (formerly part of the Farmers Home Administration), the Federal Deposit Insurance Corporation, the Federal Housing Administration, the National Labor Relations Board, the Rural Utilities Service (formerly the Rural Electrification Administration), the Securities and Exchange Commission, the Social Security Administration, and the Tennessee Valley Authority—all of them the offspring of the New Deal. Each in its own fashion interferes with the effective operation of the free-market system. By subsidizing, financing, insuring, regulating, and thereby diverting resources from the uses most valued by consumers, each renders the economy less productive than it could be—in the service of one special interest or another.

Once the New Deal had burst the dam between 1933 and 1938, ample precedent had been set for virtually any government program that could gain sufficient political support in Congress. Limited constitutional government, especially after the Supreme Court revolution that began in 1937, became little more than an object of nostalgia for classical liberals.

Indeed, in the wake of the New Deal, the ranks of the classical liberals diminished so greatly that they became an endangered species. The legacy of the New Deal was, more than anything else, a matter of ideological change. Henceforth, nearly everyone would look to the federal government for solutions to problems great and small, real and imagined, personal as well as social. After the 1930s, the opponents of any proposed federal program might object to its structure, its personnel, or its cost, but hardly anyone objected on the grounds that the program was by its very nature improper to undertake at the federal level of government.

"People in the mass," wrote H. L. Mencken, "soon grow used to anything, including even being swindled. There comes a time when the patter of the quack becomes as natural and as indubitable to their ears as the texts of Holy Writ, and when that time comes it is a dreadful job debamboozling them." Sixty-five years after the New Deal itself petered out, Americans overwhelmingly take for granted the expansive, something-for-nothing character of the federal government established by the New Dealers. For Democrats and Republicans alike, Franklin Delano Roosevelt looms as the most significant political figure of the twentieth century.

However significant his legacies, though, Roosevelt deserves no reverence. He was no hero. Rather, he was an exceptionally resourceful political opportunist who harnessed the extraordinary potential for personal and party aggrandizement inherent in a uniquely troubled and turbulent period of U.S. history. By wheeling and dealing, by taxing and spending, by ranting against "economic royalists" and posturing as the friend of the common man, he got himself elected time after time. For all his undeniable political prowess, however, he prolonged the depression and greatly fostered a bloated, intrusive government that has been trampling on the people's liberties every since.

F U R T H E R   R E A D I N G

Alan Brinkley, *Voices of Protest: Huey Long, Father Coughlin, and the Great Depression* (1982).

Lizabeth Cohen, *Making a New Deal: Industrial Workers in Chicago* (1990).

Blanche D. Coll, *Safety Net: Welfare and Social Security* (1995).

Lewis A. Erenberg, *Swingin' the Dream: Big Band Jazz and the Rebirth of American Culture* (1998).

Colin Gordon, *New Deals: Business, Labor, and Politics in America* (1994).

James N. Gregory, *American Exodus: The Dust Bowl Migration and Okie Culture in California* (1989).

George T. McJimsey, *The Presidency of Franklin Delano Roosevelt* (2000).

Guiliana Muscio, *Hollywood's New Deal* (1997).

Harvard Sitkoff, *Fifty Years Later: The New Deal Evaluated* (1985).

Patricia Sullivan, *Days of Hope: Race and Democracy in the New Deal Era* (1996).

Studs Terkel, *Hard Times: An Oral History of the Great Depression* (1970).

Donald Worster, *Dustbowl* (1979).

The Ordeal of World War II

The Japanese bombing of American warships at Pearl Harbor, Hawaii, on December 7, 1941, brought the United States into a series of wars that had been under way, first in Asia and then in Europe, for nearly a decade. In 1931, the Japanese Imperial Army began a program of expansion and conquest that eventually reached from the cold far north of China down to the tropical jungles of Indochina. The United States consistently opposed Japan's military aggressiveness. Then, in 1933, Adolf Hitler seized dictatorial power in Germany, determined to rebuild his country. This would require, he decided, eliminating what he called the "parasites" within the nation (Jews), putting "inferior human material" (Poles, Russians, and other Slavs) to work for Germany, and obtaining the territory of other European nations for the enlargement of what he named the Third Reich. England and France went to war against Germany when Hitler invaded and occupied Poland in September 1939, following his previous annexation of Austria and Czechoslovakia. The following spring, Hitler's massive army and air force attacked Norway, Denmark, Holland, Belgium, and France, all of which fell within a few weeks and remained occupied until the Allied invasion, which began on the French beaches of Normandy four years later. The bombing of Pearl Harbor finally brought the United States into the war on the side of Britain and Russia, the last nations with any capacity to resist Hitler, who had allied himself with both Japan and the fascist government of Italy in a "Triple Axis." The United States, Britain, and Soviet Russia formed the nucleus of a worldwide, fifty-nation Grand Alliance, which eventually forced the Axis to surrender. The war culminated in the discovery of the Nazi death camps, where 6 million Jews and millions of Slavs had perished, and in the dropping of atomic bombs by the United States on the Japanese cities of Hiroshima and Nagasaki.

The war transformed America and the world. Great Britain and France witnessed the collapse of their overseas empires. The Soviet Union found itself in control of nations that had been traditionally hostile to it, and used the process of liberating central Europe from the Nazis to create a new security zone. The United States, which had entered both world wars late, emerged as the most powerful and wealthy nation on earth following the war, blessed with the opportunity and burdened with the responsibility of restructuring world politics, resurrecting the world economy, and preventing future wars. The Grand Alliance created a new organization called the United Nations designed to mediate all subsequent conflicts. The task was Herculean, but the effort to find rational alternatives to global self-destruction had begun.

Franklin D. Roosevelt and the Grand Alliance announced at the start of American participation in World War II that the war was being fought on behalf of elemental human freedoms—the "four freedoms." Hitler's deliberate slaughter of peoples who did not belong to the Aryan "race" helped to stir revulsion toward racism. One of the unforeseen consequences of the war for the United States was to highlight the extent to which the "land of the free" itself violated the dignity of citizens who were not from European or Protestant backgrounds. The war reinforced American liberalism, strengthened the hand of advocates for civil rights, brought women into the work force in greater numbers than ever before, ended the Great Depression, and heralded the onset of what the publisher of Time *and* Life *called "the American Century."*

Q U E S T I O N S   T O   T H I N K   A B O U T

How did the war change Americans' expectations of their nation's role in the world? In what ways did participation in World War II differ from participation in World War I, and what were the consequences of these differences? How did the war transform the nation internally?

D O C U M E N T S

The documents in this chapter reflect the global character of the war. What people said and did thousands of miles away from the United States mattered deeply to the history of the nation. German and Japanese actions not only brought the United States into the war but cast a new light on issues of human rights in the United States. Document 1 is drawn from *Mein Kampf* (My Battle), Hitler's blueprint for the resurgence of German power. Race and nationality were inseparable, he argued, eerily echoing sentiments that had been expressed in the United States in the twenties. Only the Aryan race could be true Germans. This book set the stage not only for German aggression and the Holocaust of the European Jews, but also for a new global definition of human rights after the war. In Document 2, President Franklin D. Roosevelt calls for war following the surprise bombing of Pearl Harbor, the Philippines and other targets by the Japanese on December 7, 1941, a "date which will live in infamy." In Document 3, British Prime Minister Winston Churchill recounts the moment at which he learned of the attack on Hawaii. American entry into the war marked the end of a lonely and desperate vigil for Great Britain, the only western European nation that had not yet been conquered by or allied itself with Nazi Germany. The alliance with Britain proved crucial to Allied victory, as the final great assault was launched from its shores. Early in the war, Roosevelt declared that the United States was fighting on behalf of what he called the "four freedoms." His statements in Document 4 helped to raise expectations at home and abroad that the nation struggled to measure up to in following decades. Document 5 reveals the ways in which the war curtailed freedoms, however, especially for Japanese Americans who found themselves the target of suspicion and discrimination. The United States government imprisoned most Japanese residing in the western states for the duration of the war, as did the government of Canada. In this selection, a girl recalls how dormitory life during internment gradually undermined the coherence and closeness of her nuclear family. Document 6 reveals the strategic complexities of the global conflict and the compromises President Roosevelt made between an ideal world and the real world. In addition to creating a United Nations, he and Soviet Premier Josef Stalin agreed that the largest nations would have to act as "policemen" after the war to ensure future peace. Document 7 shows the connection that African American citizens drew between Roosevelt's goals for the world and their own aspirations for greater freedom. Blacks stationed at segregated bases and consigned to nonfighting units complained there was a "lack of democracy" right at home. Document 8 shows another side of the war: the personal insecurities of soldiers stationed thousands of miles from home. The war disrupted familial relationships at many levels. In this selection, a platoon officer begs his wife to be faithful. In the final excerpt (Document 9), General Dwight D. Eisenhower reports to General George C. Marshall about his discoveries at the German concentration camps. The Holocaust of the Jews later contributed to American support for the creation of Israel, and came to symbolize the worst excesses of demagogic racism and unchecked aggression.

1. Nazi Leader Adolf Hitler Links Race and Nationality, 1927

There are numberless examples in history, showing with terrible clarity how each time Aryan blood has become mixed with that of inferior peoples the result has been an end of the culture-sustaining race. North America, the population of which consists for the most part of Germanic elements, which mixed very little with inferior coloured nations, displays humanity and culture very different from that of Central and South America, in which the settlers, mainly Latin in origin, mingled their blood very freely with that of the aborigines. Taking the above as an example, we clearly recognize the effects of racial intermixture. The man of Germanic race on the continent of America having kept himself pure and unmixed, has risen to be its master; and he will remain master so long as he does not fall into the shame of mixing the blood.

Perhaps the pacifist-humane idea is quite a good one in cases where the man at the top has first thoroughly conquered and subdued the world to the extent of making himself sole master of it. Then the principle when applied in practice, will not affect the mass of the people injuriously. Thus first the struggle and then pacifism. Otherwise, it means that humanity has passed the highest point in its development, and the end is not domination by any ethical idea, but barbarism, and chaos to follow. Some will naturally laugh at this, but this planet travelled through the ether for millions of years devoid of humanity, and it can only do so again if men forget that they owe their higher existence, not to the ideas of a mad ideologue, but to understanding and ruthless application of age-old natural laws.

All that we admire on this earth—science, art, technical skill and invention— is the creative product of only a small number of nations, and originally, perhaps, of one single race. All this culture depends on them for its very existence. If they are ruined, they carry with them all the beauty of this earth into the grave.

If we divide the human race into three categories—founders, maintainers, and destroyers of culture—the Aryan stock alone can be considered as representing the first category.

The Aryan races—often in absurdly small numbers—overthrow alien nations, and, favoured by the numbers of people of lower grade who are at their disposal to aid them, they proceed to develop, according to the special conditions for life in the acquired territories—fertility, climate, etc.—the qualities of intellect and organization which are dormant in them. In the course of a few centuries they create cultures, originally stamped with their own characteristics alone, and develop them to suit the special character of the land and the people which they have conquered. As time goes on, however, the conquerors sin against the principle of keeping the blood pure (a principle which they adhered to at first), and begin to blend with the original inhabitants whom they have subjugated, and end their own existence as a peculiar people; for the sin committed in Paradise was inevitably followed by expulsion. . . .

For the development of the higher culture it was necessary that men of lower civilization should have existed, for none but they could be a substitute for the technical instruments, without which higher development was inconceivable. In its beginnings human culture certainly depended less on the tamed beast and more on employment of inferior human material. . . .

The exact opposite of the Aryan is the Jew. . . .

The Jew's intellectual qualities were developed in the course of centuries. Today we think him "cunning," and in a certain sense it was the same at every epoch. But his intellectual capacity is not the result of personal development, but of education by foreigners.

Thus, since the Jew never possessed a culture of his own, the bases of his intellectual activity have always been supplied by others. His intellect has in all periods been developed by contact with surrounding civilizations. Never the opposite.

. . . His propagation of himself throughout the world is a typical phenomenon with all parasites; he is always looking for fresh feeding ground for his race.

His life within other nations can be kept up in perpetuity only if he succeeds in convincing the world that with him it is not a question of a race, but of a 'religious bond,' one however peculiar to himself. This is the first great lie!

In order to continue existing as a parasite within the nation, the Jew must set to work to deny his real inner nature. The more intelligent the individual Jew is, the better will he succeed in his deception—to the extent of making large sections of the population seriously believe that the Jew genuinely is a Frenchman or an Englishman, a German or an Italian, though of a different religion. . . .

It was clear to us, even in 1919, that the chief aim of the new movement must be to awaken a sentiment of nationality in the masses. From the tactical standpoint a number of requirements arise out of this.

1. No social sacrifice is too great in order to win the masses over to the national movement. But a movement whose aim is to recover the German worker for the German nation must realize that economic sacrifices are not an essential factor in it, so long as the maintenance and independence of the nation's economic life are not menaced by them.

2. Nationalizing of the masses can never be effected by half-measures or by mild expression of an 'objective standpoint,' but by determined and fanatical concentration

on the object aimed at. The mass of the people do not consist of professors or diplomats. A man who desires to win their adherence must know the key which will unlock the door to their hearts. This is not objectivity—i.e., weakness—but determination and strength.

3. There can only be success in winning the soul of the people if, while we are conducting the political struggle for our own aim, we also destroy those who oppose it.

The masses are but a part of nature, and it is not in them to understand mutual hand-shakings between men whose desires are nominally in direct opposition to each other. What they wish to see is victory for the stronger and destruction of the weaker.

2. President Franklin D. Roosevelt Asks Congress to Declare War, 1941

Yesterday, December 7, 1941—a date which will live in infamy—the United States of America was suddenly and deliberately attacked by naval and air forces of the Empire of Japan.

The United States was at peace with that Nation and, at the solicitation of Japan, was still in conversation with its Government and its Emperor looking toward the maintenance of peace in the Pacific. Indeed, one hour after Japanese air squadrons had commenced bombing in Oahu, the Japanese Ambassador to the United States and his colleague delivered to the Secretary of State a formal reply to a recent American message. While this reply stated that it seemed useless to continue the existing diplomatic negotiations, it contained no threat or hint of war or armed attack.

It will be recorded that the distance of Hawaii from Japan makes it obvious that the attack was deliberately planned many days or even weeks ago. During the intervening time the Japanese Government has deliberately sought to deceive the United States by false statements and expressions of hope for continued peace.

The attack yesterday on the Hawaiian Islands has caused severe damage to American naval and military forces. Very many American lives have been lost. In addition American ships have been reported torpedoed on the high seas between San Francisco and Honolulu.

Yesterday the Japanese Government also launched an attack against Malaya.

Last night Japanese forces attacked Hong Kong.

Last night Japanese forces attacked Guam.

Last night Japanese forces attacked the Philippine Islands.

Last night the Japanese attacked Wake Island.

This morning the Japanese attacked Midway Island.

Japan has, therefore, undertaken a surprise offensive extending throughout the Pacific area. The facts of yesterday speak for themselves. The people of the United States have already formed their opinions and well understand the implications to the very life and safety of our Nation.

As Commander-in-Chief of the Army and Navy I have directed that all measures be taken for our defense.

Always will we remember the character of the onslaught against us.

U.S. Department of State, *Papers Relating to the Foreign Relations of the United States, Japan: 1931–1941* (Washington, D.C.: Government Printing Office, 1943), II, 793–794.

No matter how long it may take us to overcome this premeditated invasion, the American people in their righteous might will win through to absolute victory.

I believe I interpret the will of the Congress and of the people when I assert that we will not only defend ourselves to the uttermost but will make very certain that this form of treachery shall never endanger us again.

Hostilities exist. There is no blinking at the fact that our people, our territory, and our interests are in grave danger.

With confidence in our armed forces—with the unbounded determination of our people—we will gain the inevitable triumph—so help us God.

I ask that the Congress declare that since the unprovoked and dastardly attack by Japan on Sunday, December seventh, a state of war has existed between the United States and the Japanese Empire.

3. British Prime Minister Winston Churchill Reacts to Pearl Harbor, 1941

It was Sunday evening, December 7, 1941. Winant and Averell Harriman were alone with me at the table at Chequers. I turned on my small wireless set shortly after the nine o'clock news had started. There were a number of items about the fighting on the Russian front and on the British front in Libya, at the end of which some few sentences were spoken regarding an attack by the Japanese on American shipping at Hawaii, and also Japanese attacks on British vessels in the Dutch East Indies. There followed a statement that after the news Mr. Somebody would make a commentary, and that the Brains Trust programme would then begin, or something like this. I did not personally sustain any direct impression, but Averell said there was something about the Japanese attacking the Americans, and, in spite of being tired and resting, we all sat up. By now the butler, Sawyers, who had heard what had passed, came into the room, saying, "It's quite true. We heard it ourselves outside. The Japanese have attacked the Americans." There was a silence. At the Mansion House luncheon on November 11 I had said that if Japan attacked the United States a British declaration of war would follow "within the hour." I got up from the table and walked through the hall to the office, which was always at work. I asked for a call to the President. The Ambassador followed me out, and, imagining I was about to take some irrevocable step, said, "Don't you think you'd better get confirmation first?"

In two or three minutes Mr. Roosevelt came through. "Mr. President, what's this about Japan?" "It's quite true," he replied. "They have attacked us at Pearl Harbour. We are all in the same boat now." I put Winant onto the line and some interchanges took place, the Ambassador at first saying, "Good," "Good"—and then, apparently graver, "Ah!" I got on again and said, "This certainly simplifies things. God be with you," or words to that effect. We then went back into the hall and tried to adjust our thoughts to the supreme world event which had occurred, which was of so startling a nature as to make even those who were near the centre gasp. My two American friends took the shock with admirable fortitude. We had no idea that any serious losses had been inflicted on the United States Navy. They did not wail or lament that their country was at war. They wasted no words in reproach or sorrow. In fact, one might almost have thought they had been delivered from a long pain. . . .

No American will think it wrong of me if I proclaim that to have the United States at our side was to me the greatest joy. I could not foretell the course of events. I do not pretend to have measured accurately the martial might of Japan, but now at this very moment I knew the United States was in the war, up to the neck and in to the death. So we had won after all! Yes, after Dunkirk; after the fall of France; after the horrible episode of Oran; after the threat of invasion, when, apart from the Air and the Navy, we were an almost unarmed people; after the deadly struggle of the U-boat war—the first Battle of the Atlantic, gained by a hand's-breadth; after seventeen months of lonely fighting and nineteen months of my responsibility in dire stress. We had won the war. England would live; Britain would live; the Commonwealth of Nations and the Empire would live. How long the war would last or in what fashion it would end no man could tell, nor did I at this moment care. Once again in our long island history we should emerge, however mauled or mutilated, safe and victorious. We should not be wiped out. Our history would not come to an end. We might not even have to die as individuals. Hitler's fate was sealed. Mussolini's fate was sealed. As for the Japanese, they would be ground to powder. All the rest was merely the proper application of overwhelming force. The British Empire, the Soviet Union, and now the United States, bound together with every scrap of their life and strength, were, according to my lights, twice or even thrice the force of their antagonists. . . .

Silly people, and there were many, not only in enemy countries, might discount the force of the United States. Some said they were soft, others that they would never be united. They would fool around at a distance. They would never come to grips. They would never stand blood-letting. Their democracy and system of recurrent elections would paralyse their war effort. They would be just a vague blur on the horizon to friend or foe. Now we should see the weakness of this numerous but remote, wealthy, and talkative people. But I had studied the American Civil War, fought out to the last desperate inch. American blood flowed in my veins. I thought of a remark which Edward Grey had made to me more than thirty years before—that the United States is like "a gigantic boiler. Once the fire is lighted under it there is no limit to the power it can generate." Being saturated and satiated with emotion and sensation, I went to bed and slept the sleep of the saved and thankful.

4. Roosevelt Identifies the "Four Freedoms" at Stake in the War, 1941

. . . There is nothing mysterious about the foundations of a healthy and strong democracy. The basic things expected by our people of their political and economic systems are simple. They are:

Equality of opportunity for youth and for others.

Jobs for those who can work.

The Public Papers and Addresses of Franklin D. Roosevelt (New York: Macmillan, 1941), Vol. 9, 671–672.

Security for those who need it.

The ending of special privilege for the few.

The preservation of civil liberties for all.

The enjoyment of the fruits of scientific progress in a wider and constantly rising standard of living.

These are the simple, basic things that must never be lost sight of in the turmoil and unbelievable complexity of our modern world. The inner and abiding strength of our economic and political systems is dependent upon the degree to which they fulfill these expectations.

Many subjects connected with our social economy call for immediate improvement.

As examples:

We should bring more citizens under the coverage of old-age pensions and unemployment insurance.

We should widen the opportunities for adequate medical care.

We should plan a better system by which persons deserving or needing gainful employment may obtain it.

I have called for personal sacrifice. I am assured of the willingness of almost all Americans to respond to that call.

A part of the sacrifice means the payment of more money in taxes. In my Budget Message I shall recommend that a greater portion of this great defense program be paid for from taxation than we are paying today. No person should try, or be allowed, to get rich out of this program; and the principle of tax payments in accordance with ability to pay should be constantly before our eyes to guide our legislation.

If the Congress maintains these principles, the voters, putting patriotism ahead of pocketbooks, will give you their applause.

In the future days, which we seek to make secure, we look forward to a world founded upon four essential human freedoms.

The first is freedom of speech and expression—everywhere in the world.

The second is freedom of every person to worship God in his own way—everywhere in the world.

The third is freedom from want—which, translated into world terms, means economic understandings which will secure to every nation a healthy peacetime life for its inhabitants—everywhere in the world.

The fourth is freedom from fear—which, translated into world terms, means a world-wide reduction of armaments to such a point and in such a thorough fashion that no nation will be in a position to commit an act of physical aggression against any neighbor—anywhere in the world.

That is no vision of a distant millennium. It is a definite basis for a kind of world attainable in our own time and generation. That kind of world is the very antithesis of the so-called new order of tyranny which the dictators seek to create with the crash of a bomb.

To that new order we oppose the greater conception—the moral order. A good society is able to face schemes of world domination and foreign revolutions alike without fear.

Since the beginning of our American history, we have been engaged in change—in a perpetual peaceful revolution—a revolution which goes on steadily, quietly adjusting itself to changing conditions—without the concentration camp or the quicklime in the ditch. The world order which we seek is the cooperation of free countries, working together in a friendly, civilized society.

This nation has placed its destiny in the hands and heads and hearts of millions of free men and women; and its faith in freedom under the guidance of God. Freedom means the supremacy of human rights everywhere. Our support goes to those who struggle to gain those rights or keep them. Our strength is our unity of purpose.

To that high concept there can be no end save victory.

5. A Japanese American Recalls the Effect of Internment on Family Unity, 1942

. . . The War Department was in charge of all the camps at this point. They began to issue military surplus from the First World War—olive-drab knit caps, earmuffs, peacoats, canvas leggings. Later on, sewing machines were shipped in, and one barracks was turned into a clothing factory. An old seamstress took a peacoat of mine, tore the lining out, opened and flattened the sleeves, added a collar, put arm holes in and handed me back a beautiful cape. By fall dozens of seamstresses were working full-time transforming thousands of these old army clothes into capes, slacks and stylish coats. But until that factory got going and packages from friends outside began to fill out our wardrobes, warmth was more important than style. I couldn't help laughing at Mama walking around in army earmuffs and a pair of wide-cuffed, khaki-colored wool trousers several sizes too big for her. Japanese are generally smaller than Caucasians, and almost all these clothes were oversize. They flopped, they dangled, they hung.

It seems comical, looking back; we were a band of Charlie Chaplins marooned in the California desert. But at the time, it was pure chaos. That's the only way to describe it. The evacuation had been so hurriedly planned, the camps so hastily thrown together, nothing was completed when we got there, and almost nothing worked.

I was sick continually, with stomach cramps and diarrhea. At first it was from the shots they gave us for typhoid, in very heavy doses and in assembly-line fashion; swab, jab, swab, *Move along now,* swab, jab, swab, *Keep it moving.* That knocked all of us younger kids down at once, with fevers and vomiting. Later, it was the food that made us sick, young and old alike. The kitchens were too small and badly ventilated. . . .

"The Manzanar runs" became a condition of life, and you only hoped that when you rushed to the latrine, one would be in working order.

That first morning, on our way to the chow line, Mama and I tried to use the women's latrine in our block. The smell of it spoiled what little appetite we had. Outside, men were working in an open trench, up to their knees in muck—a common sight in the months to come. Inside, the floor was covered with excrement, and all twelve bowls were erupting like a row of tiny volcanoes.

Mama stopped a kimono-wrapped woman stepping past us with her sleeve pushed up against her nose and asked, "What do you do?"

"Try Block Twelve," the woman said, grimacing. "They have just finished repairing the pipes."

It was about two city blocks away. We followed her over there and found a line of women waiting in the wind outside the latrine. We had no choice but to join the line and wait with them.

Inside it was like all the other latrines. Each block was built to the same design, just as each of ten camps, from California to Arkansas, was built to a common master plan. It was an open room, over a concrete slab. The sink was a long metal trough against one wall, with a row of spigots for hot and cold water. Down the center of the room twelve toilet bowls were arranged in six pairs, back to back, with no partitions. My mother was a very modest person, and this was going to be agony for her, sitting down in public, among strangers.

One old woman had already solved the problem for herself by dragging in a large cardboard carton. She set it up around one of the bowls, like a three-sided screen. OXYDOL was printed in large black letters down the front. I remember this well, because that was the soap we were issued for laundry; later on, the smell of it would permeate these rooms. The upended carton was about four feet high. The old woman behind it wasn't much taller. When she stood, only her head showed over the top.

She was about Granny's age. With great effort she was trying to fold the sides of the screen together. Mama happened to be at the head of the line now. As she approached the vacant bowl, she and the old woman bowed to each other from the waist. Mama then moved to help her with the carton, and the old woman said very graciously, in Japanese, "Would you like to use it?"

Happily, gratefully, Mama bowed again and said, *"Arigato"* (Thank you). *"Arigato gozaimas"* (Thank you very much). "I will return it to your barracks."

"Oh, no. It is not necessary. I will be glad to wait."

The old woman unfolded one side of the cardboard, while Mama opened the other; then she bowed again and scurried out the door.

Those big cartons were a common sight in the spring of 1942. Eventually sturdier partitions appeared, one or two at a time. The first were built of scrap lumber. Word would get around that Block such and such had partitions now, and Mama and my older sisters would walk halfway across the camp to use them. Even after every latrine in camp was screened, this quest for privacy continued. Many would wait until late at night. Ironically, because of this, midnight was often the most crowded time of all.

Like so many of the women there, Mama never did get used to the latrines. It was a humiliation she just learned to endure: *shikata ga nai,* this cannot be helped. . . .

At seven I was too young to be insulted. The camp worked on me in a much different way. I wasn't aware of this at the time, of course. No one was, except maybe Mama, and there was little she could have done to change what happened.

It began in the mess hall. Before Manzanar, mealtime had always been the center of our family scene. In camp, and afterward, I would often recall with deep yearning the old round wooden table in our dining room in Ocean Park, the biggest piece of furniture we owned, large enough to seat twelve or thirteen of us at once. A tall row of elegant, lathe-turned spindles separated this table from the kitchen, allowing talk to pass from one room to other. Dinners were always noisy, and they were always abundant with great pots of boiled rice, platters of home-grown vegetables, fish Papa caught.

He would sit at the head of this table, with Mama next to him serving and the rest of us arranged around the edges according to age, down to where Kiyo and I sat, so far away from our parents, it seemed at the time, we had our own enclosed nook inside this world. The grownups would be talking down at their end, while we two played our secret games, making eyes at each other when Papa gave the order to begin to eat, racing with chopsticks to scrape the last grain from our rice bowls, eyeing Papa to see if he had noticed who won.

Now, in the mess halls, after a few weeks had passed, we stopped eating as a family. Mama tried to hold us together for a while, but it was hopeless. Granny was too feeble to walk across the block three times a day, especially during heavy weather, so May brought food to her in the barracks. My older brothers and sisters, meanwhile, began eating with their friends, or eating somewhere blocks away, in the hope of finding better food. The word would get around that the cook over in Block 22, say, really knew his stuff, and they would eat a few meals over there, to test the rumor. Camp authorities frowned on mess hall hopping and tried to stop it, but the good cooks liked it. They liked to see long lines outside their kitchens and would work overtime to attract a crowd.

Younger boys, like Ray, would make a game of seeing how many mess halls they could hit in one meal period—be the first in line at Block 16, gobble down your food, run to 17 by the middle of the dinner hour, gulp another helping, and hurry to 18 to make the end of the chow line and stuff in the third meal of the evening. They didn't *need* to do that. No matter how bad the food might be, you could always eat till you were full.

Kiyo and I were too young to run around, but often we would eat in gangs with other kids, while the grownups sat at another table. I confess I enjoyed this part of it at the time. We all did. A couple of years after the camps opened, sociologists studying the life noticed what had happened to the families. They made some recommendations, and edicts went out that families *must* start eating together again. Most people resented this; they griped and grumbled. They were in the habit of eating with their friends. And until the mess hall system itself could be changed, not much could really be done. It was too late.

My own family, after three years of mess hall living, collapsed as an integrated unit. Whatever dignity or feeling of filial strength we may have known before

December 1941 was lost, and we did not recover it until many years after the war, not until after Papa died and we began to come together, trying to fill the vacuum his passing left in all our lives. . . .

6. Roosevelt and Soviet Premier Josef Stalin Plan the United Nations, 1943

The President then said the question of a post-war organization to preserve peace had not been fully explained and dealt with and he would like to discuss with the Marshal the prospect of some organization based on the United Nations.

The President then outlined the following general plan:

1. There would be a large organization composed of some 35 members of the United Nations which would meet periodically at different places, discuss and make recommendations to a smaller body.

Marshal Stalin inquired whether this organization was to be world-wide or European, to which the President replied, world-wide.

The President continued that there would be set up an executive committee composed of the Soviet Union, the United States, United Kingdom and China, together with two additional European states, one South American, one Near East, one Far Eastern country, and one British Dominion. He mentioned that Mr. Churchill did not like this proposal for the reason that the British Empire only had two votes. This Executive Committee would deal with all non-military questions such as agriculture, food, health, and economic questions, as well as the setting up of an International Committee. This Committee would likewise meet in various places.

Marshal Stalin inquired whether this body would have the right to make decisions binding on the nations of the world.

The President replied, yes and no. It could make recommendations for settling disputes with the hope that the nations concerned would be guided thereby, but that, for example, he did not believe the Congress of the United States would accept as binding a decision of such a body. The President then turned to the third organization which he termed "The Four Policemen," namely, the Soviet Union, United States, Great Britain, and China. This organization would have the power to deal immediately with any threat to the peace and any sudden emergency which requires this action. He went on to say that in 1935, when Italy attacked Ethiopia, the only machinery in existence was the League of Nations. He personally had begged France to close the Suez Canal, but they instead referred it to the League which disputed the question and in the end did nothing. The result was that the Italian Armies went through the Suez Canal and destroyed Ethiopia. The President pointed out that had the machinery of the Four Policemen, which he had in mind, been in existence, it would have been possible to close the Suez Canal. The President then summarized briefly the idea that he had in mind.

U.S. Department of State, *Foreign Relations of the United States: Diplomatic Papers, The Conferences at Cairo and Teheran, 1943* (Washington, D.C.: U.S. Government Printing Office, 1961), 530–532.

Marshal Stalin said that he did not think that the small nations of Europe would like the organization composed of the Four Policemen. He said, for example, that a European state would probably resent China having the right to apply certain machinery to it. And in any event, he did not think China would be very powerful at the end of the war. He suggested as a possible alternative, the creation of a European or a Far Eastern Committee and a European or a Worldwide organization. He said that in the European Commission there would be the United States, Great Britain, the Soviet Union and possibly one other European state.

The President said that the idea just expressed by Marshal Stalin was somewhat similar to Mr. Churchill's idea of a Regional Committee, one for Europe, one for the Far East, and one for the Americas. Mr. Churchill had also suggested that the United States be a member of the European Commission, but he doubted if the United States Congress would agree to the United States' participation in an exclusively European Committee which might be able to force the dispatch of American troops to Europe.

The President added that it would take a terrible crisis such as at present before Congress would ever agree to that step.

Marshal Stalin pointed out that the world organization suggested by the President, and in particular the Four Policemen, might also require the sending of American troops to Europe.

The President pointed out that he had only envisaged the sending of American planes and ships to Europe, and that England and the Soviet Union would have to handle the land armies in the event of any future threat to the peace. He went on to say that if the Japanese had not attacked the United States, he doubted very much if it would have been possible to send any American forces to Europe.

7. An African American Soldier Notes the "Strange Paradox" of the War, 1944

33rd AAF Base Unit (CCTS(H))
Section C
President Franklin Delano Roosevelt   DAVIS-MONTHAN FIELD
White House   Tucson, Arizona
Washington, D.C.   9 May 1944.

Dear President Roosevelt:

It was with extreme pride that I, a soldier in the Armed Forces of our country, read the following affirmation of our war aims, pronounced by you at a recent press conference:

"The United Nations are fighting to make a world in which tyranny, and aggression cannot exist; a world based upon freedom, equality, and justice; a world in which all persons, regardless of race, color and creed, may live in peace, honor and dignity." . . .

Taps for a Jim Crow Army: Letters from Black Soldiers in World War II, ABC-CLIO, © 1983, 134–139. Reprinted by permission of The University Press of Kentucky.

But the picture in our country is marred by one of the strangest paradoxes in our whole fight against world fascism. The United States Armed Forces, to fight for World Democracy, is within itself undemocratic. The undemocratic policy of jim crow and segregation is practiced by our Armed Forces against its Negro members. Totally inadequate opportunities are given to the Negro members of our Armed Forces, nearly one tenth of the whole, to participate with "equality" . . . "regardless of race and color" in the fight for our war aims. In fact it appears that the army intends to follow the very policy that the FEPC [Fair Employment Practices Commission] is battling against in civilian life, the pattern of assigning Negroes to the lowest types of work.

Let me give you an example of the lack of democracy in our Field, where I am now stationed. Negro soldiers are completely segregated from the white soldiers on the base. And to make doubly sure that no mistake is made about this, the barracks and other housing facilities (supply room, mess hall, etc.) of the Negro Section C are covered with black tar paper, while all other barracks and housing facilities on the base are painted white.

It is the stated policy of the Second Air Force that "every potential fighting man must be used as a fighting man. If you have such a man in a base job, you have no choice. His job must be eliminated or be filled by a limited service man, WAC, or civilian." And yet, leaving out the Negro soldiers working with the Medical Section, fully 50% of the Negro soldiers are working in base jobs, such as, for example, at the Resident Officers' Mess, Bachelor Officers' Quarters, and Officers' Club, as mess personnel, BOQ orderlies, and bar tenders. Leaving out the medical men again, based on the section C average only 4% of this 50% would not be "potential fighting men." . . .

How can we convince nearly one tenth of the Armed Forces, the Negro members, that your pronouncement of the war aims of the United Nations means what it says, when their experience with one of the United Nations, the United States of America, is just the opposite? . . .

With your issuance of Executive Order 8802, and the setting up of the Fair Employment Practices Committee, you established the foundation for fighting for democracy in the industrial forces of our country, in the interest of victory for the United Nations. In the interest of victory for the United Nations, another Executive Order is now needed. An Executive Order which will lay the base for fighting for democracy in the Armed Forces of our country. An Executive Order which would bring about the result here at Davis-Monthan Field whereby the Negro soldiers would be integrated into all of the Sections on the base, as fighting men, instead of in the segregated Section C as housekeepers.

Then and only then can your pronouncement of the war aims of the United Nations mean to *all* that we "are fighting to make a world in which tyranny, and aggression cannot exist; a world based upon freedom, equality and justice; a world in which all persons, regardless of race, color and creed, may live in peace, honor and dignity."

Respectfully yours,

Charles F. Wilson, 36794590
Private, Air Corps.

8. An American Officer Worries
About His Wife's Loyalty, 1944

Paris, France, 15 November 1944

My Dearest Darling:

. . . I have no idea what my boys are doing tonight, but they are fighting like hell and I am a damn yellow so-and-so to be here and not with them. After all, an officer is not supposed to be ill or ever feel bad. Guess I should have more intestinal fortitude so as to be able to have a sick headache and still do my duty as a machine gun platoon leader, don't you think? Why do I have to get sick and at a time that they need me, too. . . . I don't guess I have told you enough of why I am here, have I? Well, before I came overseas and a month after I came over, I had a bad headache nearly every month, then they began to come twice, then, three or four per month, and now, from one to two each week. The only thing that seems to relieve them is for me to lose all I have eaten and sleep it off. Also in the past month I have had frequent stomach aches and a tremendous amount of gas on my stomach. We had a few dull days so I came back to get checked over. The day I came back I had a bad headache and that nite I lost all I had eaten. Soo, that started it, they have taken x-rays of my sinus, my stomach, both negative and this a.m. they took one of my skull—you should see my skull, it sure is pretty, no brains at all—ha! Anyway, this is my fourth hospital, I hope they get on the ball and do one thing or the other, fix me up or tell me to get the hell back to the front. I am not sick, so don't get to doing any worrying—they are just trying to trace down the headaches which was sinus and now is migraine. One doc says one thing—another says another. . . .

If there was ever anything that you had done that you knew was not right while I've been away, you would be decent enough to tell me, wouldn't you, Barbie? Answer that. You would tell me those things even though you knew I'd hate you, wouldn't you? had you failed me. We are so far apart and I know how all the stories get to the soldiers about how their wives back in the States are roving around, too, I know what all the people back there think about the boys over here. Either one of us has a bad thing in us called jealousy, and we are too often doing too much wondering about each other's actions while we are apart.

Now, let's just stop and face this sexual situation for a minute: we are both very passionate and you might say always ready to do something when we are together, but I am quite certain we, neither one, could ever think of sexual relations or any other type relations as long as we are apart. No one could fill your sexual station with me. Sexual relations are no good unless you feel that the person you do them with is clean, above reproach, and to me you are the only clean woman in the whole wide world. I am true to you because I want to be, not because you want me to be. I love you because I want to love you, not because you want me to. I hope you are the same way, I mean, I hope you are true to me because you want to, not because you think I'd want you to be true. You know I'd want you to be true, but you get what I mean, don't you? . . .

Your Charlie

P.S. Give Miss T. a big hug and a kiss from her Dad.

9. General Dwight Eisenhower Reports to General George Marshall on the German Concentration Camps, 1945

To GEORGE CATLETT MARSHALL   *April 15, 1945*
Secret

Dear General: . . .

On a recent tour of the forward areas in First and Third Armies, I stopped momentarily at the salt mines to take a look at the German treasure. There is a lot of it. But the most interesting—although horrible—sight that I encountered during the trip was a visit to a German internment camp near Gotha. The things I saw beggar description. While I was touring the camp I encountered three men who had been inmates and by one ruse or another had made their escape. I interviewed them through an interpreter. The visual evidence and the verbal testimony of starvation, cruelty and bestiality were so overpowering as to leave me a bit sick. In one room, where they [there] were piled up twenty or thirty naked men, killed by starvation, George Patton would not even enter. He said he would get sick if he did so. I made the visit deliberately, in order to be in position to give *first-hand* evidence of these things if ever, in the future, there develops a tendency to charge these allegations merely to "propaganda." . . .

April 19, 1945

From Eisenhower to General Marshall for eyes only: We continue to uncover German concentration camps for political prisoners in which conditions of inde-scribable horror prevail. I have visited one of these myself and I assure you that whatever has been printed on them to date has been understatement. If you would see any advantage in asking about a dozen leaders of Congress and a dozen prominent editors to make a short visit to this theater in a couple of C-54's, I will arrange to have them conducted to one of these places where the evidence of bes-tiality and cruelty is so overpowering as to leave no doubt in their minds about the normal practices of the Germans in these camps. I am hopeful that some British individuals in similar categories will visit the northern area to witness similar evidence of atrocity.

The Papers of Dwight D. Eisenhower, vol. 4, *The War Years,* ed. Alfred D. Changler, Jr. (Baltimore: Johns Hopkins Press, 1970), 2615–2617, 2623.

World War II is sometimes called "the good war"—even though it is widely recognized that all war is "hell." The bombing of Pearl Harbor created a broader consensus of support for this war than for any other war in the nation's history, including the Revolution. Historians have thus tended to debate the consequences of the war more than its origins. The following two essays look at the experience of the war from different vantage points: that of the soldier fighting for his own elemental survival as well as for his country, and that of the society back home. John Morton Blum, retired from Yale University, depicts combat soldiers as largely disconnected from the geopolitical goals articulated by President Roosevelt. When they said they were fighting for America and apple pie, they were mostly thinking of the pie—in other words, about getting home. Place yourself in their boots: think about how might the war have affected that generation's view of life afterward, and of their nation's role in the world. In the second essay, Alan Brinkley of Columbia University discusses the effects of World War II on the domestic character of the United States. The war, he shows, not only brought the Great Depression to an end and established the nation as a superpower, but it helped to reshape race relations, gender roles, and the ideology of liberalism itself. Brinkley emphasizes that Americans fought, at least to some extent, to advance liberal values and social justice. Reading Blum and Brinkley together may lead you to wonder whom the war affected most: the soldiers who fought it, or the society they left behind at home.

G.I. Joe: Fighting for Home

JOHN MORTON BLUM

On September 21, 1943, War Bond Day for the Columbia Broadcasting System, Miss Kate Smith spoke over the radio at repeated intervals, in all, sixty-five times, from eight o'clock in the morning until two in the morning the next day. Her pleas to her listeners, some 20 million Americans, resulted in the sale of about $39 million worth of bonds. The content of her messages, according to a convincing analysis of her marathon, was less important than her person. Her listeners responded as they did in large part because for them she symbolized, in heroic proportions, values they honored: patriotism, sincerity, generosity. In that, of course, she was not alone. Edward L. Bernays, the premier public-relations counselor in the United States, accepted a commission during the war from the Franklin Institute "to give Benjamin Franklin greater fame and prestige in the hierarchy of American godhead symbols." As Bernays went about his business of persuading local communities to name streets, buildings, even firehouses after his subject, he found his task easy, for, as he put it, "our society craves heroes."

War accentuated that craving, especially for those at home who sought symbols on which to focus the sentiments they felt or were, they knew, supposed to feel—symbols that would assist the imagination in converting daily drabness into a sense of vicarious participation in danger. The battlefield provided a plenitude of such symbols, of genuine heroes who were then ordinarily clothed, whether justly or not,

"The GI's: American Boys" and "In Foreign Foxholes" from *V Was For Victory: Politics and American Culture During World War II,* copyright © 1976 by John Morton Blum, reprinted by permission of Harcourt, Inc.

with characteristics long identified with national virtue. The profiles of the heroes of the war followed reassuring lines, some of them perhaps more precious than ever before because they had become less relevant, less attainable than they had been in a simpler, more bucolic past. Some others, less sentimental, were no less reassuring, for they displayed the hero as a man like other men, not least the man who wanted to admire someone whose place and ways might have been his own, had chance so ruled.

No leap of a reader's imagination, however, could easily find believable heroes in the Army's official communiqués. Though they sometimes mentioned names, those accounts supplied only summaries of action that generally obliterated both the brutality and the agony of warfare. Robert Sherrod, who landed with the marines at Tarawa and wrote a piercing description of that ghastly operation, deplored the inadequacy of American information services. "Early in the war," he commented, "one communiqué gave the impression that we were bowling over the enemy every time our handful of bombers dropped a few pitiful tons from 3,000 feet. The stories . . . gave the impression that any American could lick any twenty Japs. . . . The communiqués . . . were rewritten by press association reporters who waited for them back at rear headquarters. The stories almost invariably came out liberally sprinkled with 'mash' and 'pound' and other 'vivid' verbs. . . . It was not the correspondents' fault. . . . The stories which . . . deceived . . . people back home were . . . rewritten . . . by reporters who were nowhere near the battle." Bill Mauldin, the incomparable biographer of the GI, made a similar complaint about reporting from Italy. Newspapers, he recommended, should "clamp down . . . on their rewrite men who love to describe 'smashing armored columns,' the 'ground forces sweeping ahead,' 'victorious cheering armies,' and 'sullen supermen.'" W. L. White, who interviewed the five survivors of Motor Torpedo Boat Squadron 3, the group that evacuated MacArthur from Corregidor, quoted Lieutenant Robert B. Kelly to the same point: "The news commentators . . . had us all winning the war. . . . It made me very sore. We were out here where we could see these victories. There were plenty of them. They were all Japanese. . . . Yet if even at one point we are able to check . . . an attack, the silly headlines chatter of a victory."

The resulting deception was not inadvertent. While the Japanese early in 1942 were overpowering the small, ill-equipped American garrisons on Pacific islands, the armed services invented heroic situations, presumably to encourage the American people, who might better have been allowed to face depressing facts. So it was with the mythic request of the embattled survivors on Wake Island: "Send us more Japs." That phrase, which the motion pictures tried later to immortalize, had originated merely as padding to protect the cryptographic integrity of a message from Wake to Pearl Harbor describing the severity of the American plight. So, too, in the case of Colin Kelly, a brave pilot stationed in the Philippines, who died in action when the Japanese attacked. The Army exploited his valor by exaggerating his exploits, a ruse soon exposed to the desecration of Kelly's memory. His heroism, like that of the marines on Wake Island, deserved better treatment than it received. It deserved the truth.

The truth about American soldiers, heroic or not, centered in their experience in the Army, in training, in the field, under fire. In contrast to the official communiqués, the best independent reporting revealed that truth, which was often comic or poignant when it was not triumphant or glorious. It was harder to find out much about the men themselves, their lives before they had become soldiers, their homes and parents, rearing and calling, character and hopes. About those matters even the best reporters had ordinarily to work from partial evidence and had to write, given the wartime limits of time and space, selectively.

In the first instance, from among all the men in arms, the heroes selected themselves. Their bravery, self-sacrifice, and sheer physical endurance earned them a martial apotheosis. Usually that was the end of the story, except for a parenthesis identifying the hero's home town. But on occasion, moving to a next stage, correspondents at the front used what data they had to endow the soldiers they knew with recognizable qualities of person and purpose. In the process, truth became selective. Whether consciously or inadvertently, the reporters tended to find in the young men they described the traits that Americans generally esteemed. Those in uniform shared with their countrymen a common exposure to values dominant in the United States and to the special circumstances of the Great Depression, just ended. They had a sameness that in some degree set them apart from servicemen of other countries. But the necessarily selective reporting about them, governed as it was by the comfortable conventions of American culture, made the GI's and their officers more than merely representative Americans. It freed them from the sterile anonymity of official communiqués, but it also made them exemplars of national life, heroic symbols that satisfied the normal social preferences and the wartime psychological needs of American civilians. . . .

"The range of their background was as broad as America," Robert Sherrod wrote of the marines at Tarawa, but his "hard-boiled colonel," he noted, was "born on a farm" and his bravest captain came from a small town. Ira Wolfert, in *Battle for the Solomons,* provided background information about only two of the dozens of men he mentioned. One was an accountant who loved the blues; the other "a farm boy out in Wisconsin." Of the relatively few heroes whom *Time* chose for special attention in 1944, one was a sharecropper, another "a big, silent farm hand."

The strains in American culture that related the virtuous to the rural or the outdoors or the gridiron recalled the images of the early twentieth century, of the Rough Riders and Theodore Roosevelt's "strenuous life." Similarly, *Life* and the New York *Times,* commenting upon the long odds against victorious GI's, evoked the cult of the underdog, the sentiments that in times of peace had often given an allure to the antitrust laws or, for the apolitical, to the Brooklyn Dodgers. The victory of character over hard work, over the long odds of the society or the economy, had provided, too, the stuff of the folklore of success, the scenario for the poor boy whose struggle to overcome the handicaps of his background won him fortune and fame. That kind of struggle, though rarely successful, had particularly marked American experience and consciousness during the 1930's. It was a part of the civilian past of most soldiers, and, naturally enough, a part frequently remarked by war correspondents.

The habit of joyful hard work, one ingredient of the cult of success, had always beguiled *The Saturday Evening Post,* which build its circulation not the least upon continual publication of updated Alger stories. The *Post* found an illustrious example of its favorite theme in Dwight David Eisenhower. As a boy in a household of modest means, he had "always had plenty to do. They had an orchard, a large garden, a cow, a horse, and always a dog. The boys did all the outdoor work, milked the cow and . . . helped with the housework. . . . They also all found additional jobs. . . ." Dwight pulled ice in the local ice plant, or helped near-by farmers. "It taught them a lot," their mother said. By implication, Sherrod and Hersey said as much about their young heroes on the Pacific islands who had faced the vicissitudes of the Depression as they faced the ordeals of the jungle. There was, for one, "Hawk," a marine captain, promoted from the ranks, killed at Tarawa. Before the war, "he . . . was awarded a scholarship to the Texas College of Mines. . . . Like most sons of the poor, he worked. . . . He sold magazines and delivered newspapers. . . . He was a ranchhand, a railroadhand, and a bellhop." . . .

Aviators, when they won attention as heroes, shared many attributes of the foot soldiers but also represented uncommon qualities, those of a glamorous elite. The pilots and navigators, bombardiers and gunners were special men. They had to pass rigorous physical and mental tests. They received rapid promotion and high hazardous-duty pay. Instead of mud or jungle heat or desert cold, they enjoyed, at least part of the time, the amenities of an air base and always the romantic environment of the sky. There, exploring a vertical frontier, operating complex, powerful machinery, they flew into sudden and explosive danger. As Ernie Pyle observed: "A man approached death rather decently in the Air Force. He died well-fed and clean-shaven." . . .

Of all the war correspondents, Pyle, Hersey, and Mauldin wrote most intimately and extensively about the men they knew, about their hopes and dreams in the context of their fright and hardship. "In the magazines," Pyle wrote, "war seemed romantic and exciting, full of heroics and vitality . . . yet I didn't seem capable of feeling it. . . . Certainly there were great tragedies, unbelievable heroism, even a constant undertone of comedy. But when I sat down to write, I saw instead men . . . suffering and wishing they were somewhere else . . . all of them desperately hungry for somebody to talk to besides themselves, no women to be heroes in front of, damned little wine to drink, precious little song, cold and fairly dirty, just toiling from day to day in a world full of insecurity, discomfort, homesickness and a dulled sense of danger. The drama and romance were . . . like the famous falling tree in the forest—they were no good unless there was somebody around to hear. I knew of only twice that the war would be romantic to the men: once when they could see the Statue of Liberty and again on their first day back in the home town with the folks."

The GI's shared, in Pyle's words, "the one really profound goal that obsessed every . . . American." That goal was home. Before the landing in Sicily they talked to Pyle about their plans: "These gravely yearned-for futures of men going into battle include so many things—things such as seeing the 'old lady' again, of going to college . . . of holding on your knee just once your own kid . . . of again becoming champion salesman of your territory, of driving a coal truck around the streets of Kansas City once more and, yes, of just sitting in the sun once more on the south side of a house in New Mexico. . . . It was these little hopes . . . that made up the sum total of our worry . . . rather than any visualization of physical agony to come." . . .

Soldiers in the armies of all nations in all wars have yearned to go home, but the GI's sense of home was especially an American sense. "Our men," Pyle wrote, ". . . are impatient with the strange peoples and customs of the countries they now inhabit. They say that if they ever get home they never want to see another foreign country."

Home for the soldier, according to the New York *Times,* was "where the thermometer goes below 110° at night . . . where there are chocolate milk shakes, cokes, iced beer, and girls." The GI had had enough of crumpets and croissants: "Tea from the British and vin rouge from the French . . . have only confirmed his original convictions: that America is home, that home is better than Europe." Even the sophisticated missed homely American fare. Richard L. Tobin, a correspondent for the New York *Herald Tribune,* had arrived in London only a few days before he complained, like the GI's, about English food: "What wouldn't I give right now for a piece of bread spread with soft butter, heaped with American peanut butter, and accompanied by a big glass of ice-cold milk!"

Food of course, was metaphor. Its full meaning was best expressed when John Hersey went into that Guadalcanal valley with a company of marines. "Many of them," Hersey wrote, "probably had brief thoughts, as I did, of home. But what I really wondered was whether any of them gave a single thought to what the hell this was all about. Did these men, who might be about to die, have any war aims? What were they fighting for, anyway?" Far along the trail into the jungle, "these men . . . not especially malcontents" gave Hersey his answer. "What would you say you were fighting for?" he asked. "Today, here in this valley, what are you fighting for?"

> . . . Their faces became pale. Their eyes wandered. They looked like men bothered by a memory. They did not answer for what seemed a very long time.
>
> Then one of them spoke, but not to me. He spoke to the others, and for a second I thought he was changing the subject or making fun of me, but of course he was not. He was answering my question very specifically.
>
> He whispered: "Jesus, what I'd give for a piece of blueberry pie."
>
> . . . Fighting for pie. Of course that is not exactly what they meant . . . here pie was their symbol of home.
>
> In other places there are other symbols. For some men, in places where there is plenty of good food but no liquor, it is a good bottle of Scotch whiskey. In other places, where there's drink but no dames, they say they'd give their left arm for a blonde. For certain men, books are the things; for others, music; for others, movies. But for all of them, these things are just badges of home. When they say they are fighting for these things, they mean they are fighting for home—"to get the goddam thing over and get home."
>
> Perhaps this sounds selfish. . . . But home seems to most marines a pretty good thing to be fighting for. Home is where the good things are—the generosity, the good pay, the comforts, the democracy, the pie.

Hersey, a decent man, listed democracy, but soldiers usually talked about creature comforts, secure routines, even affluence. There were three sailors Ernie Pyle knew. One wanted to build a cabin on five acres of his own in Oregon. Another wanted to return to earning bonuses as a salesman for Pillsbury flour. As for a third, a photographer before the war: "His one great postwar ambition . . . was to buy a cabin cruiser big enough for four, get another couple, and cruise down the Chattahoochee River to the Gulf of Mexico, then up the Suwannee, making color photos of the whole trip." A marine lieutenant colonel in the South Pacific had simpler fancies: "I'm going to start wearing pajamas again. . . . I'm going to polish off a few eggs and several quarts of milk. . . . A few hot baths are also in order. . . . But I'm saving the best for last—I'm going to spend a whole day flushing a toilet, just to hear the water run."

Home spurred the troops to fight. Even the self-consciously reflective soldiers, who linked the real and the ideal as Hersey did, stressed the palpable. *The Saturday Evening Post* ran a series by GI's on "What I am Fighting For." One characteristic article began: "I am fighting for that big house with the bright green roof and the big front lawn." The sergeant-author went on to include his "little sister," his gray-haired parents, his "big stone church" and "big brick schoolhouse," his "fine old college" and "nice little roadster," his piano, tennis court, black cocker spaniel, the two houses of Congress, the "magnificent Supreme Court," "that President who has led us," "everything America stands for." It was a jumble: he mentioned "freedom" one sentence after he wrote about "that girl with the large brown eyes and the red-dish tinge in her hair, that girl who is away at college right now, preparing herself for her part in the future of America and Christianity." The jumble satisfied the *Post* and its readers, who would have liked less the findings of the Army Air Corps Redistribution Center at Atlantic City. Returnees there in 1944, a representative group of men, "surprisingly normal physically and psychologically," in the opinion of the physicians who examined them, felt contempt for civilians, distrusted "politicians," and resented labor unions. According to the Assistant Secretary of War for Air, "there is very little idealism. Most regard the war as a job to be done and there is not much willingness to discuss what we are fighting for."

The Assistant Secretary thought indoctrination lectures would help. On the basis of his own experience, Ernie Pyle would probably have disagreed:

> Awhile back a friend of mine . . . wrote me an enthusiastic letter telling of the . . . Resolution in the Senate calling for the formation of a United Nations organization to coordinate the prosecution of the war, administer reoccupied countries, feed and economically re-establish liberated nations, and to assemble a . . . military force to suppress any future military aggression.
>
> My friend . . . ordered me . . . to send back a report on what the men at the front thought of the bill.
>
> I didn't send my report, because the men at the front thought very little about it one way or the other. . . . It sounded too much like another Atlantic Charter. . . .
>
> The run-of-the-mass soldiers didn't think twice about this bill if they heard of it at all. . . .
>
> We see from the worm's eye view, and our segment of the picture consists only of tired and dirty soldiers who are alive and don't want to die . . . of shocked men wandering back down the hill from battle . . . of . . . smelly bed rolls and C rations . . . and blown bridges and dead mules . . . and of graves and graves and graves. . . .

The mood of the soldiers conformed in large measure to the mood of Washington. There was, as Henry Morgenthau had said, "little inspirational" for young men and women. The President, deliberately avoiding talk about grand postwar plans, concentrated on victory first and almost exclusively. So did the GI, for he knew that he had to win the war before he could get home, his ultimate objective. He felt, the New York *Times* judged, "that the war must be finished quickly so that he can return to take up his life where he left it." There was not "any theoretical proclamation that the enemy must be destroyed in the name of freedom," Pyle wrote after the Tunisian campaign; "it's just a vague but growing individual acceptance of the bitter fact that we must win the war or else. . . . The immediate goal used to be the Statue of Liberty; more and more it is becoming Unter den Linden."

Winning the war, his intermediate goal, turned the soldier to his direct task, combat. There impulses for friendship and generosity had to surrender to instincts for killing and hate. "It would be nice . . . to get home," one pilot told Bob Hope, ". . . and stretch my legs under a table full of Mother's cooking. . . . But all I want to do is beat these Nazi sons-of-bitches so we can get at those little Jap bastards." The hardening process of training and danger, in Marion Hargrove's experience, made "a civilian into a soldier, a boy into a man." "Our men," Pyle concluded, "can't . . . change from normal civilians into warriors and remain the same people. . . . If they didn't toughen up inside, they simply wouldn't be able to take it." The billboard overlooking Tulagi harbor carried the message: "Kill Japs; kill more Japs; you will be doing your part if you help to kill those yellow bastards."

Bill Mauldin was more reflective: "I read someplace that the American boy is not capable of hate . . . but you can't have friends killed without hating the men who did it. It makes the dogfaces sick to read articles by people who say, 'It isn't the Germans, it's the Nazis.' . . . When our guys cringe under an 88 barrage, you don't hear them say 'Those dirty Nazis.' You hear them say, 'Those goddam Krauts.' " Mauldin understood hate and hated war:

> Some say the American soldier is the same clean-cut young man who left his home; others say morale is sky-high at the front because everybody's face is shining for the great Cause.
>
> They are wrong. The combat man isn't the same clean-cut lad because you don't fight a Kraut by Marquis of Queensberry rules. You shoot him in the back, you blow him apart with mines, you kill or maim him . . . with the least danger to yourself. He does the same to you . . . and if you don't beat him at his own game you don't live to appreciate your own nobleness.
>
> But you don't become a killer. No normal man who has smelled and associated with death ever wants to see any more of it. . . . The surest way to become a pacifist is to join the infantry.

War, Bob Hope thought, made "a lot of guys appreciate things they used to take for granted," and Pyle believed that "when you've lived with the unnatural mass cruelty that man is capable of . . . you find yourself dispossessed of the faculty for blaming one poor man for the triviality of his faults. I don't see how any survivor of war can ever again be cruel." Mauldin put it more bluntly: "The vast majority of combat men are going to be no problem at all. They are so damned sick and tired of having their noses rubbed in a stinking war that their only ambition will be to forget it." Consequently Mauldin was not much worried about the adaptability of the veteran:

> I've been asked if I have a postwar plan for Joe and Willie. I do. . . . Joe and Willie are very tired of war. . . . While their buddies are . . . trying to learn to be civilians again, Joe and Willie are going to do the same. . . . If their buddies find their girls have married somebody else, and if they have a hard time getting jobs back, and if they run into difficulties in the new, strange life of a free citizen, then Joe and Willie are going to do the same. And if they finally get settled and drop slowly into the happy obscurity of a humdrum job and a little wife and a household of kids, Joe and Willie will be happy to settle down too. They might even shave and become respectable. . . .

Indeed they might. The GI, a homely hero, naturally decent and generous, inured slowly to battle and danger, would be in the end still generous, still trusting, wiser but still young, dirtier but still more content in his office or factory or on his sun-swept farm. He was as plain, as recognizable, as American as the militiamen of the past, he was the conscript citizen—competent enough but fundamentally an amateur, a transient, and an unhappy warrior. He was the essential republican, the common good man. He was the people's hero.

Like them, he had little visible purpose but winning the war so that he could return to a familiar, comfortable America, to what an earlier generation meant, more or less, by "normalcy." . . .

American Liberals: Fighting for a Better World

ALAN BRINKLEY

Few would disagree that World War II changed the world as profoundly as any event of this century, perhaps any century. What is less readily apparent, perhaps, is how profoundly the war changed America—its society, its politics, and . . . its image of itself. Except for the combatants themselves, Americans experienced the war at a remove of several thousand miles. They endured no bombing, no invasion, no massive dislocations, no serious material privations. Veterans returning home in 1945 and 1946 found a country that looked very much like the one they had left—something that clearly could not be said of veterans returning home to Britain, France, Germany, Russia, or Japan.

But World War II did transform America in profound, if not immediately visible, ways. Not the least important of those transformations was in the nature of American liberalism, a force that would play a central role in shaping the nation's postwar political and cultural life. Liberalism in America rests on several consistent and enduring philosophical assumptions: the high value liberals believe society should attribute to individual rights and freedoms and the importance of avoiding rigid and immutable norms and institutions. But in the half century since the New Deal, liberalism in America has also meant a prescription for public policy and political action; and in the 1940s this "New Deal liberalism" was in a state of considerable uncertainty and was undergoing significant changes. Several broad developments of the war years helped lay the foundations for the new liberal order that followed the war.

Among those developments was a series of important shifts in the size, distribution, and character of the American population. Not all the demographic changes of the 1940s were a result of the war, nor were their effects on liberal assumptions entirely apparent until well after 1945. But they were a crucial part of the process that would transform American society and the way liberals viewed their mission in that society.

Perhaps the most conspicuous demographic change was the single biggest ethnic migration in American history: the massive movement of African Americans from the rural South to the urban North, a migration much larger than the "great migration" at the time of World War I. Between 1910 (when the first great migration began) and 1940, approximately 1.5 million blacks moved from the South to the

Excerpts from Brinkley, A., "World War II and American Liberalism" in *The War in American Culture*, Erenberg & Hirsch, eds., pp. 314–323, 326–327. Copyright © 1996 by The University of Chicago. Reprinted by permission of the University of Chicago.

North. In the 1940s alone, 2 million African Americans left the South, and 3 million more moved in the twenty years after that. The migration brought substantial numbers of them closer to the center of the nation's economic, cultural, and institutional life. The number of blacks employed in manufacturing more than doubled during the war. There were major increases in the number of African Americans employed as skilled craftsmen or enrolled in unions. There was a massive movement of African American women out of domestic work and into the factory and the shop. Much of this would have occurred with or without World War II, but the war greatly accelerated the movement by expanding industrial activity and by creating a labor shortage that gave African American men and women an incentive to move into industrial cities.

This second great migration carried the question of race out of the South and into the North, out of the countryside and into the city, out of the field and into the factory. African American men and women encountered prejudice and discrimination in the urban, industrial world much as they had in the agrarian world; but in the city they were far better positioned to organize and protest their condition, as some were beginning to do even before the fighting ended. World War II therefore began the process by which race would increase its claim on American consciousness and, ultimately, transform American liberalism.

Just as the war helped lay the groundwork for challenges to racial orthodoxies, so it contributed to later challenges to gender norms. Three million women entered the paid workforce for the first time during the war, benefiting—like black workers—from the labor shortage military conscription had created. Many women performed jobs long considered the exclusive province of men. Women had been moving into the workforce in growing numbers before the war began, to be sure, and almost certainly they would have continued to do so even had the United States remained at peace. Many of their wartime gains, moreover, proved short lived. Female factory workers in particular were usually dismissed as soon as male workers returned to take their places, even though many wanted to remain in their jobs.

Still, most women who had begun working during the war continued working after 1945 (if not always in the same jobs). And while popular assumptions about women's roles (among both women and men) were slow to change, the economic realities of many women's lives were changing dramatically and permanently—in ways that would eventually help raise powerful challenges to ideas about gender. The war, in short, accelerated a critical long-term shift in the role of women in society that would produce, among other things, the feminist movements of the 1960s and beyond.

Similar, if less dramatic, changes were affecting other American communities during the war. Men and women who had long lived on the margins of American life—because of prejudice or geographical isolation or both—found their lives transformed by the pressures of war. Asian Americans, Latino Americans, Native Americans, and others served in the military, worked in factories, moved into diverse urban neighborhoods, and otherwise encountered the urban-industrial world of the midtwentieth century. Life was not, perhaps, much better for many such people in their new roles than it had been in traditional ones. For Japanese Americans on the West Coast, who spent much of the war in internment camps, victims of popular and official hysteria, it was considerably worse. But for many such communities the changes helped erode the isolation that had made it difficult to challenge discrimination and demand inclusion.

No one living in the era of multiculturalism will be inclined to argue with the proposition that the changing composition of the American population over the past fifty years—and the changing relations among different groups within the population—is one of the most important events in the nation's recent history. Those changes have reshaped America's economy, its culture, its politics, and its intellectual life. They have forced the nation to confront its increasing diversity in more direct and painful ways than at any time since the Civil War. They have challenged America's conception of itself as a nation and a society. And they have transformed American liberalism. In the 1930s, most liberals considered questions of racial, ethnic, or gender difference of distinctly secondary importance (or in the case of gender, virtually no importance at all). Liberal discourse centered much more on issues of class and the distribution of wealth and economic power. By 1945 that was beginning to change. One sign of that change was the remarkable reception among liberals of Gunnar Myrdal's *An American Dilemma,* published in 1944. Myrdal identified race as the one issue most likely to shape and perplex the American future. The great migration of the 1940s helped ensure that history would vindicate Myrdal's prediction and that American liberals would adjust their outlook and their goals in fundamental ways in the postwar years.

Perhaps the most common and important observation about the domestic impact of World War II is that it ended the Great Depression and launched an era of unprecedented prosperity. Between 1940 and 1945 the United States experienced the greatest expansion of industrial production in its history. After a decade of depression, a decade of growing doubts about capitalism, a decade of high unemployment and underproduction, suddenly, in a single stroke, the American economy restored itself and—equally important—seemed to redeem itself. Gross national product in the war years rose from $91 billion to $166 billion; 15 million new jobs were created, and the most enduring problem of the depression—massive unemployment—came to an end; industrial production doubled; personal incomes rose (depending on location) by as much as 200 percent. The revival of the economy is obviously important in its own right. But it also had implications for the future of American political economy, for how liberals in particular conceived of the role of the state in the postwar United States.

One of the mainstays of economic thought in the late 1930s was the belief that the United States had reached what many called "economic maturity": the belief that the nation was approaching, or perhaps had reached, the end of its capacity to grow, that America must now learn to live within limits. This assumption strengthened the belief among many reformers that in the future it would be necessary to regulate the economy much more closely and carefully for the benefit of society as a whole. America could not rely any more on a constantly expanding pie; it would have to worry about how the existing pie was to be divided.

The wartime economic experience—the booming expansion, the virtual elimination of unemployment, the creation of new industries, new "frontiers"—served as a rebuke to the "mature economy" idea and restored the concept of growth to the center of liberal hopes. The capitalist economy, liberals suddenly discovered, was not irretrievably stagnant. Economic expansion could achieve, in fact had achieved, dimensions beyond the wildest dreams of the 1930s. Social and economic advancement could proceed, therefore, without structural changes in capitalism, without continuing, intrusive state management of the economy. It could proceed by virtue of growth.

Assaults on the concept of economic maturity were emerging as early as 1940 and gathered force throughout the war. Alvin Hansen, one of the most prominent champions in the 1930s of what he called "secular stagnation," repudiated the idea in 1941. "All of us had our sights too low," he admitted. The *New Republic* and the *Nation,* both of which had embraced the idea of economic maturity in 1938 and 1939, openly rejected it in the 1940s—not only rejected it, but celebrated its demise. The country had achieved a "break," exulted the *Nation,* "from the defeatist thinking that held us in economic thraldom through the thirties, when it was assumed that we could not afford full employment or full production in this country."

But along with this celebration of economic growth came a new and urgent fear: that the growth might not continue once the war was over. What if the depression came back? What if there was a return to massive unemployment? What could be done to make sure that economic growth continued? That was the great liberal challenge of the war years—not to restructure the economy, not to control corporate behavior, not to search for new and more efficient forms of management, but to find a way to keep things going as they were.

And in response to that challenge, a growing number of liberal economists and policymakers became interested in a tool that had begun to attract their attention in the 1930s and that seemed to prove itself during the war: government spending. That was clearly how the economy had revived—in response to the massive increase in the federal budget in the war years, from $9 billion in 1939 to $100 billion in 1945. And that was how the revival could be sustained—by pumping more money into the economy in peacetime. What government needed to do, therefore, was to "plan" for postwar full employment.

Those who called themselves "planners" in the 1940s did not talk much anymore, as planners had talked in earlier years, about the need for an efficient, centrally planned economy in which the government would help direct the behavior of private institutions. They talked instead about fiscal planning—about public works projects, about social welfare programs, about the expansion of the Social Security system. The National Resource Planning Board, the central "planning" agency of the New Deal since 1933, issued a report in 1942 called *Security, Work, and Relief Policies.* In the past, the NRPB had been preoccupied largely with older ideas of planning—regional planning, resource management, government supervision of production and investment. Now, in their 1942 report, the members turned their attention to the new kind of planning. The government should create a "shelf" of public works projects, so that after the war—whenever the economy showed signs of stagnating—it could pull projects off the shelf and spend the money on them to stimulate more growth. The government should commit itself to more expansive Social Security measures so that after the war—if the economy should slow down—there would be welfare mechanisms in place that would immediately pick up the slack and start paying out benefits, which would increase purchasing power and stimulate growth.

All of this reflected, among other things, the increasing influence in American liberal circles of Keynesian economics. The most important liberal economist of the war years—Alvin Hansen of Harvard, who contributed to many NRPB reports—was also the leading American exponent of Keynesianism. Keynesianism provided those concerned about the future of the American economy with an escape from their fears of a new, postwar depression. Economic growth, it taught them, did not require constant involvement in the affairs of private institutions—which the 1930s (and the war itself) had shown to be logistically difficult and politically controversial. Growth could be sustained through the *indirect* manipulation of the economy by fiscal and monetary levers.

The wartime faith in economic growth led, in other words, to several developments of great importance to the future of American liberalism. It helped relegitimize capitalism among people who had, in the 1930s, developed serious doubts about its viability. It helped rob the "administrative" reform ideas of the late 1930s—the belief in ever greater regulation of private institutions—of their urgency. It helped elevate Keynesian ideas about indirect management of the economy to the center of reform hopes. And it made the idea of the welfare state—of Social Security and public works and other social welfare efforts—come to seem a part of the larger vision of sustaining economic growth by defining welfare as a way to distribute income and stimulate purchasing power. It helped channel American liberalism into a new, less confrontational direction—a direction that would produce fewer clashes with capitalist institutions; that tried to define the interests of capitalists and the interests of the larger public in identical terms; that emphasized problems of consumption over problems of production; that shaped the liberal agenda for more than a generation and helped shape the next great episode in liberal policy experiments: the Great Society of the 1960s.

World War II had other important and more purely ideological effects on American liberalism—some of them in apparent conflict with others, but all of them important in determining the permissible range of liberal aspirations for the postwar era. First, the war created, or at least greatly reinforced, a set of anxieties and fears that would become increasingly central to liberal thought in the late 1940s and 1950s. It inflamed two fears in particular: a fear of the state and a fear of the people. Both were a response, in large part, to the horror with which American liberals (and most other Americans as well) regarded the regimes the United States was fighting in World War II. Both would be sustained and strengthened by the similar horror with which most Americans came to view the regime the nation was beginning to mobilize against in peacetime even before the end of the war: the Soviet Union.

The fear of the state emerged directly out of the way American liberals (and the American people generally) defined the nature of their enemy in World War II. During World War I many Americans had believed the enemy was a race, a people: the Germans, the beastlike "Huns," and their presumably savage culture. In World War II racial stereotypes continued to play an important role in portrayals of the Japanese; but in defining the enemy in Europe—always the principal enemy in the 1940s to most Americans—the government and most of the media relied less on racial or cultural images than on political ones. Wartime propaganda in World War II did not personify the Germans and Italians as evil peoples. It focused instead on the Nazi and fascist states.

The war, in other words, pushed a fear of totalitarianism (and hence a general wariness about excessive state power) to the center of American liberal thought. In particular, it forced a reassessment of the kinds of associational and corporatist arrangements that many had found so attractive in the aftermath of World War I. Those, after all, were the kinds of arrangements Germany and Italy had claimed to be creating. But it also created a less specific fear of state power that made other kinds of direct planning and management of the economy of society seem unappealing as well. "The rise of totalitarianism," Reinhold Niebuhr noted somberly in 1945, "has prompted the democratic world to view all collectivist answers to our social problems with increased apprehension." Virtually all experiments in state supervision of private institutions, he warned, contained "some peril of compounding economic and political power." Hence "a wise community will walk warily and test the effect of each new adventure before further adventures." To others the lesson was even starker. *Any* steps in the direction of state control of economic institutions were (to use the title of Friedrich A. Hayek's celebrated antistatist book of 1944) steps along "the road to serfdom." This fear of the state was one of many things that lent strength to the emerging Keynesian–welfare state liberal vision of political economy, with its much more limited role for government as a manager of economic behavior.

Along with this fear of the state emerged a related fear: a fear of "mass politics" or "mass man"; a fear, in short, of the people. Nazi Germany, facist Italy, even the Soviet Union, many liberals came to believe, illustrated the dangers inherent in trusting the people to control their political life. The people, the "mass," could too easily be swayed by demagogues and tyrants. They were too susceptible to appeals to their passions, to the dark, intolerant impulses that in a healthy society remained largely repressed and subdued. Fascism and communism were not simply the products of the state or of elite politics, many liberals believed; they were the products of mass movements, of the unleashing of the dangerous and irrational impulses within every individual and every society.

This fear of the mass lay at the heart of much liberal cultural and intellectual criticism in the first fifteen years after World War II. It found expression in the writings of Hannah Arendt, Theodor Adorno, Richard Hofstadter, Lionel Trilling, Daniel Bell, Dwight Macdonald, and many others. Like the fear of the state, with which it was so closely associated, it reinforced a sense of caution and restraint in liberal thinking; a suspicion of ideology, a commitment to pragmatism, a wariness about moving too quickly to encourage or embrace spontaneous popular movements; a conviction that one of the purposes of politics was to defend the state against popular movements and their potentially dangerous effects.

There were, in short, powerful voices within American liberalism during and immediately after World War II arguing that the experience of the war had introduced a dark cloud of doubt and even despair to human society. A world that could produce so terrible a war; a world that could produce Hiroshima, Nagasaki, the Katyn Forest, Auschwitz; a world capable of profound evil and inconceivable destruction: such a world, many American liberals argued, must be forever regarded skeptically and suspiciously. Humankind must move cautiously into its uncertain future, wary of unleashing the dark impulses that had produced such horror.

Some liberal intellectuals went further. Americans, they argued, must resist the temptation to think of themselves, in their hour of triumph, as a chosen people. No people, no nation, could afford to ignore its own capacity for evil. Reinhold Niebuhr spoke for many liberals when he wrote of the dangers of the "deep layer of

Messianic consciousness in the mind of America" and warned of liberal culture's "inability to comprehend the depth of evil to which individuals and communities may sink, particularly when they try to play the role of God in history." Americans, he said, would do well to remember that "no nation is sacred and unique. . . . Providence has not set Americans apart from lesser breeds. We too are part of history's seamless web."

But Niebuhr's statements were obviously written to refute a competing assumption. And as it suggests, there was in the 1940s another, very different ideological force at work in America, another form of national self-definition that affected liberal thought and behavior, at home and in the world, at least as much as the somber assessments of Niebuhr and others. Indeed even many liberal intellectuals attracted to Niebuhr's pessimistic ideas about human nature and mass politics were simultaneously drawn to this different and, on the surface at least, contradictory assessment of the nation's potential. For in many ways the most powerful ideological force at work in postwar American liberalism, and in the postwar United States generally, was the view of America as an anointed nation; America as a special moral force in the world; America as a society with a unique mission, born of its righteousness. This is an ideological tradition that is often described as the tradition of American innocence. But innocence is perhaps too gentle a word for what has often been an aggressive and intrusive vision, a vision that rests on the belief that America is somehow insulated from the sins and failures and travails that affect other nations, that America stands somehow outside of history, protected from it by its own strength and virtue.

World War II did not create those beliefs. They are as old as the nation itself. But the American experience in the conflict, and the radically enhanced international stature and responsibility of the United States in the aftermath of the war, strengthened such ideas and gave them a crusading quality that made them as active and powerful as they had been at any moment in the nation's history. . . .

The war left other ideological legacies for American liberalism as well. In the glow of the nation's victory, in the sense of old orders shattered and a new world being born, came an era of exuberant innovation, an era in which, for a time, nothing seemed more appealing than the new. The allure of the new was visible in the brave new world of architectural modernism, whose controversial legacy is so much a part of the postwar American landscape. It was visible in the explosive growth of the innovative and iconoclastic American art world, which made New York in the 1940s and 1950s something of what Paris had been in the nineteenth century. It was visible in the increased stature and boldness of the American scientific community, and in the almost religious faith in technological progress that came to characterize so much of American life.

Above all, perhaps, it was visible in the way it excited, and then frustrated, a generation of American liberals as they imagined new possibilities for progress and social justice. That is what Archibald MacLeish meant in 1943 when he spoke about the America of the imagination, the society that the war was encouraging Americans to create:

> We have, and we know we have, the abundant means to bring our boldest dreams to pass—to create for ourselves whatever world we have the courage to desire. . . . We have the tools and the skill and the intelligence to take our cities apart and put them together,

to lead our roads and rivers where we please to lead them, to build our houses where we want our houses, to brighten the air, to clean the wind, to live as men in this Republic, free men, should be living. We have the power and the courage and the resources of good-will and decency and common understanding . . . to create a nation such as men have never seen. . . . We stand at the moment of the building of great lives, for the war's end and our victory in the war will throw that moment and the means before us.

There was, of course, considerable naïveté, and even arrogance, in such visions. But there was also an appealing sense of hope and commitment—a belief in the possibility of sweeping away old problems and failures, of creating "great lives." Out of such visions came some of the postwar crusades of American liberals—the battle for racial justice, the effort to combat poverty, the expansion of individual rights. And although all of those battles had some ambiguous and even unhappy consequences, they all reflected a confidence in the character and commitment of American society—and the possibility of creating social justice within it—that few people would express so blithely today. Postwar liberalism had suffered many failures and travails in the half century since 1945. But surely its postwar faith in the capacity of America to rebuild—and perhaps even redeem—itself remains one of its most appealing legacies.

FURTHER READING

Michael C. C. Adams, *The Best War Ever: America and World War II* (1994).

Elizabeth Borgwardt, *A New Deal for the World: America's Vision for Human Rights* (2005).

Joanna Bourke, *The Second World War: A People's History* (2002).

Steven Casey, *Cautious Crusade: Franklin D. Roosevelt, American Public Opinion, and the War Against Nazi Germany* (2001).

Iris Chang, *The Rape of Nanking: The Forgotten Holocaust of World War II* (1997).

Robert Dallek, *Franklin D. Roosevelt and American Foreign Policy, 1932–1945* (1979).

Michael Doubler, *Closing with the Enemy: How GIs Fought the War in Europe* (1994).

John W. Dower, *War Without Mercy: Race and Power in the Pacific War* (1986).

Marilyn S. Johnson, *The Second Gold Rush: Oakland and the East Bay in World War II* (1993).

David M. Kennedy, *Freedom from Fear: The American People in Depression and War* (1999).

Warren F. Kimball, *The Juggler: Franklin Roosevelt as Wartime Statesman* (1991).

Martin J. Sherwin, *A World Destroyed: The Atomic Bomb and the Grand Alliance* (1975).

John Tateishi, *And Justice for All: An Oral History of the Japanese American Detention Camps* (1984).

C H A P T E R
10

The Cold War and the Nuclear Age

Winning the peace can be more difficult than winning the war, as both the United States and the Soviet Union learned in the decade following V-E Day (Victory-Europe). "We may not get 100 percent of what we want in the postwar world, but I think we can get 85 percent," President Harry Truman optimistically told his advisers. Yet the United States was not the only victor, and more importantly not the only superpower, to arise from the ashes. The Soviet Union had lost more than 20 million of its people, compared with American losses of less than half a million. The Soviet resolve to maintain a security zone in eastern Europe after the war clashed with American expectations, as well as with the wishes of most eastern Europeans. Some historians contend that the Cold War began with the initial American decision to keep the atomic bomb a secret from its Soviet ally, stirring Stalin's suspicions. Others cite the influence of people like diplomat George Kennan, who saw no end to Soviet ambition and gave advice that helped to crystallize the policy called containment. Still other historians cite the actions of the Russian army, which made the Soviet Union thoroughly unpopular in the zones where the USSR hoped to maintain a sphere of influence.

Whatever its causes, discord between the two most powerful members of the former Grand Alliance created a Cold War that lasted more than forty years. With the Truman Doctrine of 1947, the United States adopted the role of "global policeman." With the Marshall Plan of 1948, the United States adopted the role of economic caretaker of Europe. Both actions originated as attempts to stop the perceived communist threat to world peace and stability. When the Korean War broke out in 1950, the Truman administration approved a policy drafted by the National Security Council (NSC), NSC-68. This policy drastically expanded American defense expenditures, placed the nation on a permanent war footing, and created what President Eisenhower later dubbed "the military-industrial complex."

Two of the most important effects of the Cold War for the United States were the "Red Scare" at home and the nuclear arms race. Unable to understand why the United States could not better control the outcomes of World War II, many Americans readily believed critics who charged that traitors in government were responsible. Senator Joseph McCarthy was not the first to make these claims, but he became the most famous. McCarthy's subcommittee in the Senate publicly interrogated citizens on their loyalty, as did the Un-American Activities Committee of the House of Representatives. These congressional initiatives coincided with the prosecution of suspected communists under a new federal loyalty program created by Truman in 1947. Between 1947 and 1952, 6.6 million federal employees were investigated for disloyalty. Thousands of people lost their jobs and sometimes their freedom as a result of tenuous connections to leftist causes or ideas.

The nuclear buildup went into full swing when the Soviet Union tested its first nuclear weapon in 1949. The United States immediately began construction of the more powerful hydrogen bomb, and scientists who opposed the arms race, including J. Robert Oppenheimer, the "father" of the atom bomb, were run out of government on grounds of disloyalty. Under President Dwight D. Eisenhower, the U.S. government gradually developed a policy of nuclear deterrence—backed up by immense lethal arsenals—which later developed into MAD, or mutual assured destruction. The potential for nuclear annihilation contrasted bizarrely with a booming economy and with the happy families portrayed on television in the 1950s. Some Americans wondered what to believe: that life was wonderful, or that the world might be destroyed the next day. Ironically, both things could be true.

QUESTIONS TO THINK ABOUT

Why was there a Cold War? Did Soviet aggression make conflict inevitable, or did the United States overreact to the battered Soviet Union's quest for security? What was the effect of the Cold War on the worldview and psychology of American citizens?

DOCUMENTS

The documents in this chapter provide various perspectives on the Cold War. At the end of World War II, the United States was the only nation with atomic bombs. Document 1 is American diplomat George Kennan's famous 1946 telegram from Moscow to Washington, in which he states that the Russians could not be trusted and must be met with force before they destroyed "our traditional way of life." In Document 2, Henry Wallace, secretary of commerce and former vice president, states that Americans should try to understand how their attempts to reshape the world order (and build an atomic arsenal) might appear to the Soviets. Soon thereafter Wallace, the last of the New Dealers in Truman's cabinet, was forced to resign. Document 3 gives a Soviet perspective: that of Ambassador Nikolai Novikov, who tells his superiors that the United States seems bent on world dominance. In Document 4, the president outlines to Congress what came to be known as the Truman Doctrine: the commitment of the United States to police the world to ensure that free peoples are able to "work out their own destinies in their own way." Although the Truman Doctrine initially authorized the government to aid only Greece and Turkey, the commitment soon spread to all areas of the globe. Document 5 outlines the Marshall Plan, a $12 billion program to reconstruct the economies of western Europe after the war to ensure that these countries remained allied with the United States. The last three documents show some of the consequences of Truman's campaign to enlist Americans in fighting communism worldwide. In his famous Wheeling, West Virginia, speech (Document 6), Senator Joseph McCarthy claimed that the international communist threat was actually the result of treason at home, especially within the U.S. Department of State. The Truman administration's own campaign against subversion lent credence to McCarthy's claims, having stirred up doubts about numerous federal employees, often on the basis of flimsy evidence. In Document 7, a temporary postal clerk loses his job because, among other things, a college professor once required him to read *Das Kapital,* the nineteenth-century economics book by Karl Marx. Document 8 illustrates the fear of nuclear war that gradually permeated the popular psyche, as the arms race escalated between the United States and the Soviet Union. *Life* magazine praises Republican Governor Nelson Rockefeller for urging the development of fallout shelters for those living outside "the blast area" of likely targets like New York City. After all, not everyone needed to die in World War III, should it come.

1. Diplomat George F. Kennan
Advocates Containment, 1946

At bottom of Kremlin's neurotic view of world affairs is traditional and instinctive Russian sense of insecurity. Originally, this was insecurity of a peaceful agricultural people trying to live on vast exposed plain in neighborhood of fierce nomadic peoples. To this was added, as Russia came into contact with economically advanced West, fear of more competent, more powerful, more highly organized societies in that area. . . . For this reason they have always feared foreign penetration, feared direct contact between Western world and their own, feared what would happen if Russians learned truth about world without or if foreigners learned truth about world within. And they had learned to seek security only in patient but deadly struggle for total destruction of rival power, never in compacts and compromises with it.

It was no coincidence that Marxism, which had smouldered ineffectively for half a century in Western Europe, caught hold and blazed for first time in Russia. Only in this land which had never known a friendly neighbor or indeed any tolerant equilibrium of separate powers, either internal or international, could a doctrine thrive which viewed economic conflicts of society as insoluble by peaceful means. After establishment of Bolshevist regime, Marxist dogma, rendered even more truculent and intolerant by Lenin's interpretation, became a perfect vehicle for sense of insecurity with which Bolsheviks, even more than previous Russian rulers, were afflicted. In this dogma, with its basic altruism of purpose, they found justification for their instinctive fear of outside world, for the dictatorship without which they did not know how to rule, for cruelties they did not dare not to inflict, for sacrifices they felt bound to demand. In the name of Marxism they sacrificed every single ethical value in their methods and tactics. Today they cannot dispense with it. It is fig leaf of their moral and intellectual respectability. . . .

In summary, we have here a political force committed fanatically to the belief that with US there can be no permanent *modus vivendi,* that it is desirable and necessary that the internal harmony of our society be disrupted, our traditional way of life be destroyed, the international authority of our state be broken, if Soviet power is to be secure. This political force has complete power of disposition over energies of one of world's greatest peoples and resources of world's richest national territory, and is

U.S. Department of State, *Foreign Relations of the United States, 1946, Eastern Europe: The Soviet Union* (Washington, D.C.: U.S. Government Printing Office, 1969), VI, 699–701, 706–707.

borne along by deep and powerful currents of Russian nationalism. In addition, it has an elaborate and far flung apparatus for exertion of its influence in other countries, an apparatus of amazing flexibility and versatility, managed by people whose experience and skill in underground methods are presumably without parallel in history. . . . Problem of how to cope with this force [is] undoubtedly greatest task our diplomacy has ever faced and probably greatest it will ever have to face. It should be point of departure from which our political general staff work at present juncture should proceed. It should be approached with same thoroughness and care as solution of major strategic problem in war, and if necessary, with no smaller outlay in planning effort. I cannot attempt to suggest all answers here. But I would like to record my conviction that problem is within our power to solve—and that without recourse to any general military conflict. And in support of this conviction there are certain observations of a more encouraging nature I should like to make:

1. Soviet power, unlike that of Hitlerite Germany, is neither schematic nor adventuristic. It does not work by fixed plans. It does not take unnecessary risks. Impervious to logic of reason, and it is highly sensitive to logic of force. For this reason it can easily withdraw—and usually does—when strong resistance is encountered at any point. Thus, if the adversary has sufficient force and makes clear his readiness to use it, he rarely has to do so. If situations are properly handled there need be no prestige-engaging showdowns.
2. Gauged against Western World as a whole, Soviets are still by far the weaker force. Thus, their success will really depend on degree of cohesion, firmness and vigor which Western World can muster. And this is factor which it is within our power to influence.
3. Success of Soviet system, as form of internal power, is not yet finally proven. It has yet to be demonstrated that it can survive supreme test of successive transfer of power from one individual group to another.

2. Secretary of Commerce Henry A. Wallace Questions the "Get Tough" Policy, 1946

How do American actions since V-J Day appear to other nations? I mean by actions the concrete things like $13 million for the War and Navy Departments, the Bikini tests of the atomic bomb and continued production of bombs, the plan to arm Latin America with our weapons, production of B-29s and planned production of B-36s, and the effort to secure air bases spread over half the globe from which the other half of the globe can be bombed. I cannot but feel that these actions must make it look to the rest of the world as if we were only paying lip service to peace at the conference table. These facts rather make it appear either (1) that we are preparing ourselves to win the war which we regard as inevitable or (2) that we are trying to build up a predominance of force to intimidate the rest of mankind. How would it look to us if

Henry A. Wallace, "The Path to Peace with Russia," *New Republic,* 115 (1946), 401–406.

Russia had the atomic bomb and we did not, if Russia had ten thousand-mile bombers and air bases within a thousand miles of our coast lines and we did not?

Some of the military men and self-styled "realists" are saying: "What's wrong with trying to build up a predominance of force? The only way to preserve peace is for this country to be so well armed that no one will dare attack us. We know that America will never start a war."

The flaw in this policy is simply that it will not work. In a world of atomic bombs and other revolutionary new weapons, such as radioactive poison gases and biological warfare, a peace maintained by a predominance of force is no longer possible. . . .

Insistence on our part that the game must be played our way will only lead to a deadlock. The Russians will redouble their efforts to manufacture bombs, and they may also decide to expand their "security zone" in a serious way. Up to now, despite all our outcries against it, their efforts to develop a security zone in Eastern Europe and in the Middle East are small change from the point of view of military power as compared with our air bases in Greenland, Okinawa and many other places thousands of miles from our shores. We may feel very self-righteous if we refuse to budge on our plan and the Russians refuse to accept it, but that means only one thing—the atomic armament race is on in deadly earnest. . . .

I should list the factors which make for Russian distrust of the United States and of the Western world as follows: The first is Russian history, which we must take into account because it is the setting in which Russians see all actions and policies of the rest of the world. Russian history for over a thousand years has been a succession of attempts, often unsuccessful, to resist invasion and conquest—by the Mongols, the Turks, the Swedes, the Germans and the Poles. The scant thirty years of the existence of the Soviet government has in Russian eyes been a continuation of their historical struggle for national existence. . . .

Second, it follows that to the Russians all of the defense and security measures of the Western powers seem to have an aggressive intent. Our actions to expand our military security system—such steps as extending the Monroe Doctrine to include the arming of the Western Hemisphere nations, our present monopoly of the atomic bomb, our interest in outlying bases and our general support of the British Empire—appear to them as going far beyond the requirements of defense. . . .

Finally, our resistance to her attempts to obtain warm water ports and her own security system in the form of "friendly" neighboring states seems, from the Russian point of view, to clinch the case. After twenty-five years of isolation and after having achieved the status of a major power, Russia believes that she is entitled to recognition of her new status. Our interest in establishing democracy in Eastern Europe, where democracy by and large has never existed, seems to her an attempt to reestablish the encirclement of unfriendly neighbors which was created after the last war and which might serve as a springboard of still another effort to destroy her.

If this analysis is correct, and there is ample evidence to support it, the action to improve the situation is clearly indicated. The fundamental objective of such action should be to allay any reasonable Russian grounds for fear, suspicions and distrust. We must recognize that the world has changed and that today there can be no "one world" unless the United States and Russia can find some way of living together.

3. Soviet Ambassador Nikolai Novikov Sees a U.S. Bid for World Supremacy, 1946

The foreign policy of the United States, which reflects the imperialist tendencies of American monopolistic capital, is characterized in the postwar period by a striving for world supremacy. This is the real meaning of the many statements by President Truman and other representatives of American ruling circles: that the United States has the right to lead the world. All the forces of American diplomacy—the army, the air force, the navy, industry and science—are enlisted in the service of this foreign policy. . . .

The foreign policy of the United States is not determined at present by the circles in the Democratic party that (as was the case during Roosevelt's lifetime) strive to strengthen the cooperation of the three great powers that constituted the basis of the anti-Hitler coalition during the war. The ascendance to power of President Truman, a politically unstable person but with certain conservative tendencies, and the subsequent appointment of [James F.] Byrnes as Secretary of State meant a strengthening of the influence on U.S. foreign policy of the most reactionary circles of the Democratic party. . . .

At the same time, there has been a decline in the influence on foreign policy of those who follow Roosevelt's course for cooperation among peace-loving countries. Such persons in the government, in Congress, and in the leadership of the Democratic party are being pushed farther and farther into the background. The contradictions in the field of foreign policy existing between the followers of [Henry] Wallace and [Claude] Pepper, on the one hand, and the adherents of the reactionary "bi-partisan" policy, on the other, were manifested with great clarity recently in the speech by Wallace that led to his resignation from the post of Secretary of Commerce. . . .

In the summer of 1946, for the first time in the history of the country, Congress passed a law on the establishment of a peacetime army, not on a volunteer basis but on the basis of universal military service. The size of the army, which is supposed to amount to about one million persons as of July 1, 1947, was also increased significantly. The size of the navy at the conclusion of the war decreased quite insignificantly in comparison with wartime. At the present time, the American navy occupies first place in the world, leaving England's navy far behind, to say nothing of those of other countries.

Expenditures on the army and navy have risen colossally, amounting to 13 billion dollars according to the budget for 1946–47 (about 40 percent of the total budget of 36 billion dollars). This is more than ten times greater than corresponding expenditures in the budget for 1938, which did not amount to even one billion dollars. . . .

The "hard-line" policy with regard to the USSR announced by [Secretary of State James F.] Byrnes after the rapprochement of the reactionary Democrats with the Republicans is at present the main obstacle on the road to cooperation of the Great Powers. It consists mainly of the fact that in the postwar period the United

Origins of the Cold War: The Novikov, Kennan, and Roberts 'Long Telegram' of 1946. Kenneth M. Jensen, editor. Copyright © 1991 by the Endowment of the United States Institute of Peace. Used with permission by the United States Institute of Peace, Washington, D.C.

States no longer follows a policy of strengthening cooperation among the Big Three (or Four) but rather has striven to undermine the unity of these countries. The objective has been to impose the will of other countries on the Soviet Union.

4. The Truman Doctrine Calls for the United States to Become the World's Police, 1947

The gravity of the situation which confronts the world today necessitates my appearance before a joint session of the Congress.

The foreign policy and the national security of this country are involved.

One aspect of the present situation, which I present to you at this time for your consideration and decision, concerns Greece and Turkey.

The United States has received from the Greek Government an urgent appeal for financial and economic assistance. Preliminary reports from the American Economic Mission now in Greece and reports from the American Ambassador in Greece corroborate the statement of the Greek Government that assistance is imperative if Greece is to survive as a free nation. . . .

The British Government has informed us that, owing to its own difficulties, it can no longer extend financial or economic aid to Turkey.

As in the case of Greece, if Turkey is to have the assistance it needs, the United States must supply it. We are the only country able to provide that help.

I am fully aware of the broad implications involved if the United States extends assistance to Greece and Turkey, and I shall discuss these implications with you at this time.

One of the primary objectives of the foreign policy of the United States is the creation of conditions in which we and other nations will be able to work out a way of life free from coercion. This was a fundamental issue in the war with Germany and Japan. Our victory was won over countries which sought to impose their will, and their way of life, upon other nations. . . .

The peoples of a number of countries of the world have recently had totalitarian regimes forced upon them against their will. The Government of the United States has made frequent protests against coercion and intimidation, in violation of the Yalta agreement, in Poland, Rumania, and Bulgaria. I must also state that in a number of other countries there have been similar developments. . . .

I believe that it must be the policy of the United States to support free peoples who are resisting attempted subjugation by armed minorities or by outside pressures.

I believe that we must assist free peoples to work out their own destinies in their own way.

I believe that our help should be primarily through economic and financial aid which is essential to economic stability and orderly political processes. . . .

I therefore ask the Congress to provide authority for assistance to Greece and Turkey in the amount of $400,000,000 for the period ending June 30, 1948. . . .

Public Papers of the Presidents of the United States: Harry S Truman, 1947 (Washington, D.C.: U.S. Government Printing Office, 1963), 176–180.

In addition to funds, I ask the Congress to authorize the detail of American civilian and military personnel to Greece and Turkey, at the request of those countries, to assist in the tasks of reconstruction, and for the purpose of supervising the use of such financial and material assistance as may be furnished. I recommend that authority also be provided for the instruction and training of selected Greek and Turkish personnel. . . .

This is a serious course upon which we embark.

I would not recommend it except that the alternative is much more serious. The United States contributed $341,000,000,000 toward winning World War II. This is an investment in world freedom and world peace.

The assistance that I am recommending for Greece and Turkey amounts to little more than 1/10 of 1 percent of this investment. It is only common sense that we should safeguard this investment and make sure that it was not in vain.

5. The Marshall Plan Seeks to Rebuild Europe, 1948

Recognizing the intimate economic and other relationships between the United States and the nations of Europe, and recognizing that disruption following in the wake of war is not contained by national frontiers, the Congress finds that the existing situation in Europe endangers the establishment of a lasting peace, the general welfare and national interest of the United States, and the attainment of the objectives of the United Nations. The restoration or maintenance in European countries of principles of individual liberty, free institutions, and genuine independence rests largely upon the establishment of sound economic conditions, stable international economic relationships, and the achievement by the countries of Europe of a healthy economy independent of extraordinary outside assistance. The accomplishment of these objectives calls for a plan of European recovery, open to all such nations which cooperate in such plan, based upon a strong production effort, the expansion of foreign trade, the creation and maintenance of internal financial stability, and the development of economic cooperation, including all possible steps to establish and maintain equitable rates of exchange and to bring about the progressive elimination of trade barriers. Mindful of the advantages which the United States has enjoyed through the existence of a large domestic market with no internal trade barriers, and believing that similar advantages can accrue to the countries of Europe, it is declared to be the policy of the people of the United States to encourage these countries through a joint organization to exert sustained common efforts as set forth in the report of the Committee of European Economic Cooperation signed at Paris on September 22, 1947, which will speedily achieve that economic cooperation in Europe which is essential for lasting peace and prosperity. It is further declared to be the policy of the people of the United States to sustain and strengthen principles of individual liberty, free institutions, and genuine independence in Europe through assistance to those countries of Europe which participate in a joint recovery program based upon self-help and mutual cooperation.

United States Statutes at Large, 1948 (Washington, D.C.: U.S. Government Printing Office, 1949), Vol. 62, p. 137.

6. Senator Joseph McCarthy Describes the Internal Communist Menace, 1950

Five years after a world war has been won, men's hearts should anticipate a long peace, and men's minds should be free from the heavy weight that comes with war. But this is not such a period—for this is not a period of peace. This is a time of the "cold war." This is a time when all the world is split into two vast, increasingly hostile armed camps—a time of a great armaments race. . . .

Six years ago, at the time of the first conference to map out the peace—Dumbarton Oaks—there was within the Soviet orbit 180,000,000 people. Lined up on the antitotalitarian side there were in the world at that time roughly 1,625,000,000 people. Today, only 6 years later, there are 800,000,000 people under the absolute domination of Soviet Russia—an increase of over 400 percent. On our side, the figure has shrunk to around 500,000,000. In other words, in less than 6 years the odds have changed from 9 to 1 in our favor to 8 to 5 against us. This indicates the swiftness of the tempo of Communist victories and American defeats in the cold war. As one of our outstanding historical figures once said, "When a great democracy is destroyed, it will not be because of enemies from without, but rather because of enemies from within." . . .

The reason why we find ourselves in a position of impotency is not because our only powerful potential enemy has sent men to invade our shores, but rather because of the traitorous actions of those who have been treated so well by this Nation. It has not been the less fortunate or members of minority groups who have been selling this Nation out, but rather those who have had all the benefits that the wealthiest nation on earth has had to offer—the finest homes, the finest college education, and the finest jobs in Government we can give.

This is glaringly true in the State Department. There the bright young men who are born with silver spoons in their mouths are the ones who have been the worst. . . . In my opinion the State Department, which is one of the most important government departments, is thoroughly infested with Communists.

I have in my hand 57 cases of individuals who would appear to be either card carrying members or certainly loyal to the Communist Party, but who nevertheless are still helping to shape our foreign policy. . . .

As you know, very recently the Secretary of State proclaimed his loyalty to a man guilty of what has always been considered as the most abominable of all crimes—of being a traitor to the people who gave him a position of great trust. The Secretary of State in attempting to justify his continued devotion to the man who sold out the Christian world to the atheistic world, referred to Christ's Sermon on the Mount as a justification and reason therefore, and the reaction of the American people to this would have made the heart of Abraham Lincoln happy.

When this pompous diplomat in striped pants, with a phony British accent, proclaimed to the American people that Christ on the Mount endorsed communism, high treason, and betrayal of a sacred trust, the blasphemy was so great that it awakened the dormant indignation of the American people.

Congressional Record, 81 Cong., 2d Sess., pp. 1954–1957.

He has lighted the spark which is resulting in a moral uprising and will end only when the whole sorry mess of twisted, warped thinkers are swept from the national scene so that we may have a new birth of national honesty and decency in government.

7. The Federal Loyalty-Security Program Expels a Postal Clerk, 1954

In late February 1954, the employee was working in a clerical capacity as a substitute postal employee. He performed no supervisory duties. His tasks were routine in nature.

One year prior to the initiation of proceedings, the employee had resigned from his position as an executive officer of a local union whose parent union had been expelled from the CIO in 1949 as Communist dominated. The employee had served as an officer for one year prior to the expulsion, had helped to lead his local out of the expelled parent and back into the CIO, and had thereafter remained in an executive capacity until his resignation in 1953. He resigned from that position upon being appointed a substitute clerk with the United States Post Office in early 1953. . . .

In the last week of February 1954, the employee received notice, by mail, that he was under investigation by the Regional Office of the United States Civil Service Commission. . . .

[The employee immediately answered the first set of charges against him only to be suspended without pay at the end of March on the following charges.————Ed.]

"3. In January 1948, your name appeared on a general mailing list of the Spanish Refugee Appeal of the Joint Anti-Fascist Refugee Committee. . . .
"5. Your wife . . . was a member of the . . . Club of the Young Communist League.
"6. In 1950, Communist literature was observed in the bookshelves and Communist art was seen on the walls of your residence in ————.
"7. Your signature appeared on a Communist Party nominating petition in the November 1941 Municipal Elections in ————." . . .

The employee had a hearing four months later, in July 1954. The members of the Board were three (3) civilian employees of military installations. None of them were attorneys. The Post Office establishment was represented by an Inspector, who administered the oath to the employee and his witnesses, but did not otherwise participate in the proceedings. There was no attorney-adviser to the Board. There was no testimony by witnesses hostile to the employee, nor was any evidence introduced against him. . . .

. . . Before the employee testified, he submitted a nine-page autobiography to the Hearing Board. . . .

. . . The autobiography set forth in some detail the employee's activities as an officer of his local union, and discussed particularly his role therein as an anti-Communist, and his opposition to the pro-Communist policies of the National

Case Studies in Personnel Security, ed. Adam Yarmolinsky (Washington, D.C.: Bureau of National Affairs, 1955), 142–149.

Organization with which his local was affiliated. The autobiography recited that when his National Union was expelled from the CIO, he and his supporters successfully won a struggle within his local and as a direct result thereof, caused the said local to disaffiliate from the expelled parent, and affiliate with a new organization established within the CIO. The employee's autobiography recited that the aforesaid struggle directly involved the question of Communist domination of the local's parent union, that the victory of the employee and his supporters represented a victory over Communist adherents in the local, and that the employee was the frequent target of threats and slander by the pro-Communist faction of his local. . . .

With respect to the third charge against the employee (that his name had been on a general mailing list of the Spanish Refugee Appeal of the Joint Anti-Fascist Refugee Committee), the employee reiterated his denial of any knowledge concerning it, and his counsel reminded the Board that no Attorney General's list existed in January 1948—the date contained in the charge. The employee testified, further, that he had no recollection of ever having received any mail from the organization involved. . . .

With respect to charge No. 5 against the employee (that his wife had been a member of the Young Communist League), the Chairman of the Hearing Board advised the employee that the date involved was March 1944. The employee testified that he and his wife were married in February 1944, and that the charge was ridiculous. He testified, further, that he had no independent recollection that his wife was ever a member of the said organization. In addition, the employee testified that he had never lived in the neighborhood in which the organization was alleged to have existed, and that he had never heard of said organization. . . .

The Chairman then read charge No. 6 in which it was alleged that Communist literature was observed in the employee's bookshelves at home. . . .

Counsel for the employee then questioned him concerning his courses in college, and the books which he was there required to read for those courses. In this connection, counsel for the employee asked whether books had been recommended as part of study courses by instructors, and whether one of these books had been *Das Kapital* by Karl Marx, and whether the employee had bought *Das Kapital,* following such a recommendation. The employee responded that certain books had been recommended by his instructors, that *Das Kapital* was one, and that he had bought the Modern Library Giant Edition of *Das Kapital.* . . .

Thereafter, in response to counsel's question, the employee testified that he had not read *Das Kapital* in its entirety, that he had been required to read "a chapter or two for classwork," and that "he had found it a little dull and tedious." . . .

The Chairman read charge No. 7, in which it was alleged that the employee's signature appeared on a Communist Party nominating petition in 1941 municipal elections in the employee's home city.

The employee had answered this charge by stating that he had signed such a petition; that in 1941, the Communist Party appeared on the initial ballot; that his recollection was that on the cover page of the petition it stated that the signers were not members of the Communist Party, and that prior to 1941 and at all times thereafter, the employee had been registered as a member of one of the two major political parties, and that he had no recollection of voting for any political party other than one of the two major political parties. . . .

Thereafter, counsel for the employee objected to the charge on the ground that the signing of a petition for a party which had a legal place on the ballot in 1941 had no relationship to present security. The Chairman then asked the employee to recall the circumstances in which his signature had been solicited in 1941. The employee responded by stating that, so far as he could recall, someone came down the street and seeing him working on the premises asked him to sign the petition, after explaining the petition to him. In response to a question by a member of the Board, the employee stated that he did not know the person who had solicited his signature, and that he had never seen or heard from him thereafter, nor had he thereafter heard from the Communist Party. . . .

. . . In early September, 1954, and without notice as to whether the Board had reached a decision in his case, the employee received notice from the Post Office Department that the Postmaster General had ordered the employee's removal. . . . The employee [also] received a letter from the Regional Office of the United States Civil Service Commission. This letter advised the employee that he had been rated ineligible for Civil Service appointment, and that he was barred from competing in Federal Civil Service Examinations for a period of three years.

8. *Life* Magazine Reassures Americans "We Won't All Be Dead" After Nuclear War, 1959

The governor of New York last week became the first important elected official to espouse a mandatory fallout shelter program, one which may become law for the people of his state. Nelson Rockefeller has thus identified himself with the least popular issue in the U.S. today. He has done the whole country a political service. For if his example succeeds and is copied by other states, it could be the means of saving anywhere from 20 to 100 million American lives.

Why do most Americans go deaf or change the subject when asked to think about defending themselves against a possible nuclear attack? There has been a federal civilian defense office since 1951, but it has neither carried conviction nor made itself heard. It has spent $500 million on studies, pamphlets, volunteers, overhead, etc., yet our population is almost totally ignorant of how to behave in case Khrushchev should carry out his repeated threat. We don't even recognize the alarm signals. It is U.S. government policy that every surviving American family should be prepared to feed and protect itself without help for two weeks after a nuclear attack. How many Americans have even heard that—let alone made any preparations?

Most of us evidently either hope to die quickly or expect some authority or other to keep us alive. One New York paper greeted Rocky's program with the scornful determination to "die gaily but not daily." That is nonsense. It is as if we had adopted a couple of new national vices from our late enemies—the shrug from Italy and the kamikaze spirit (though of a strangely passive variety) from Japan. Our military policy is based on the possibility of a nuclear war in which we expect to receive—not to strike—the first blow. Yet the defensive preparedness this strategy obviously calls for is zero. Its lack saps the deterrent power of SAC and our bargaining power with Russia.

Helplessness is not a sound reason for the general apathy. The fact is that nuclear war, though a catastrophe, would be a catastrophe with limits which can be narrowed in advance. A full shelter program against blast and heat, as described by Willard Bascom in LIFE (March 18, 1957), would cost at least $20 billion and for that reason alone arouses little interest. But according to the latest government studies, blast and heat would account for only a quarter of the total deaths (even in a fat-target state like New York) if we were attacked tomorrow. The other three quarters would die more slowly from "the silent killer," called radioactive fallout. This would threaten the remotest farm, but anyone outside the blast area could, by *taking the right precautions,* expect to survive.

These precautions need not cost much. You probably would have some protection now if you knew how to use it. According to a committee of Governor Rockefeller's, present houses with cellars can be made fallout-proof for the critical two weeks for $150 to $200. In addition each member of the family needs a "survival kit" (dehydrated food, water container) costing about $7. Above all you need instruction on how to wash, measure radiation, etc. The place to get that is from your local CD director. He may be the least popular man in town, but he is in business for your health.

Yours and the nation's. The number of individual survivors and their morale will determine whether or not the U.S.A. can survive a nuclear war. All we can assume about Russian military planning, target dispersion and CD instructions to the people indicates that they are much better prepared for D+1 and D+14 *et seq.* than we are. Russia has survived a high order of casualties before. Our national preoccupation with an eight-hour war, which we also think of as the end of the world, could easily condemn us to lose the negotiations that would prevent such a war, or once it has started, cause us to succumb to "post-attack blackmail" on a day we had wrongly expected to be dead.

We won't all be dead, that's sure. It is also sure that we can ourselves limit the casualties by taking thought now about this dreadful subject. Since when has survival been too dreadful to think about? It's a complex subject, but not an unmanageable one. Governor Rockefeller has done quite right to open it up. Let it stay open until all of us—Washington, the states and the people—have faced up to what needs to be done.

☛ E S S A Y S

The Cold War had tremendous costs for both the United States and the Soviet Union. It helped justify domestic repression in both nations, led to enormous expenditures on weapons that could destroy the earth many times over, and involved both countries in costly "proxy" wars at the margins of their spheres of influence. (For the United States, Korea and Vietnam are the best examples.) Thus, for many scholars, the question of who started the Cold War prompts passionate debate about which nation should bear primary responsibility.

Walter LaFeber of Cornell University makes the argument that the United States unintentionally, but quite clearly, provoked the conflict. President Harry Truman came

into office an insecure and uninformed man who was determined not to appear soft
and therefore took the advice of hard-liners in his administration. Strategists who held
opposite views and who had earlier advised President Roosevelt were largely shunted
aside. John Lewis Gaddis of Yale University takes a different tack. Gaddis acknowledges
that both superpowers sought to mold the world in their own images, but that the system
advocated by the United States was inherently more benign. In this essay he contrasts
the ways in which Soviets and Americans acted abroad. He argues that the American
"empire" was more enduring and attractive because it consulted its allies and promised
security. The Soviets provoked the Cold War by treating their neighbors in eastern
Europe so harshly that they could be kept "friendly" only through coercion, and by
scaring western Europeans into a military alliance with the United States. Soviet
behavior, far more than American, gradually led to the creation of two hostile blocs.

Truman's Hard Line Prompted the Cold War

WALTER LAFEBER

. . . Truman entered the White House a highly insecure man. ("I felt like the moon,
the stars, and all the planets had fallen on me," he told reporters.) And he held the
world's most responsible job in a world that was changing radically. Truman tried
to compensate for his insecurity in several ways. First, he was extremely jealous of
his presidential powers and deeply suspicious of anyone who challenged those
powers. Truman made decisions rapidly not only because that was his character but
also because he determined "the buck stopped" at his desk. There would be no more
sloppy administration or strong, freewheeling bureaucrats as in FDR's later years.

Second, and more dangerously, Truman was determined that these decisions
would not be tagged as "appeasement." He would be as tough as the toughest. After
only twenty-four hours in the White House, the new President confidently informed
his secretary of state, "We must stand up to the Russians," and he implied "We had
been too easy with them." In foreign-policy discussions during the next two weeks,
Truman interrupted his advisers to assure them he would certainly be "tough."

His determination was reinforced when he listened most closely to such advisers
as Harriman, Leahy, and Secretary of the Navy James Forrestal, who urged him to
take a hard line. Warning of a "barbarian invasion of Europe," Harriman declared that
postwar cooperation with the Soviets, especially economically, must depend on their
agreement to open Poland and Eastern Europe. In a decisive meeting on April 23,
Secretary of War Henry Stimson argued with Harriman. Stimson declared that peace
must never be threatened by an issue such as Poland, for free elections there were
impossible, Russia held total control, and Stalin was "not likely to yield . . . in substance." Stimson was not an amateur; he had been a respected Wall Street lawyer and
distinguished public servant for forty years, including a term as Herbert Hoover's
secretary of state.

But Truman dismissed Stimson's advice, accepted Harriman's, and later that day
berated Soviet Foreign Minister Molotov "in words of one syllable" for breaking the

Walter LaFeber, *America, Russia, and the Cold War, 1945–2000* (New York: McGraw-Hill, 2001)
pp. 17–20, 22–26, 29–30, 42–43, 48, 55, 62–65, 67–68, 74, 76–77, 81, 88, 91, 101–103. Reproduced
with permission of The McGraw-Hill Companies.

Yalta agreements on Poland. Truman demanded that the Soviets agree to a "new" (not merely "reorganized") Polish government. An astonished Molotov replied, "I have never been talked to like that in my life." "Carry out your agreements," Truman supposedly retorted, "and you won't get talked to like that."

The next day Stalin rejected Truman's demand by observing that it was contrary to the Yalta agreement. The dictator noted that "Poland borders with the Soviet Union, what [*sic*] cannot be said of Great Britain and the United States." After all, Stalin continued, the Soviets do not "lay claim to interference" in Belgium and Greece where the Americans and British made decisions without consulting the Russians. . . . Stimson had been correct. Truman's toughness had only stiffened Russian determination to control Poland.

An "iron fence" was falling around Eastern Europe, Churchill blurted out to Stalin in mid-1945. "All fairy-tales," the Soviet leader blandly replied. But it was partly true. The crises over Rumania and Poland only raised higher the fence around those two nations. In other areas, however, the Soviet approach varied. A Russian-sponsored election in Hungary produced a noncommunist government. In Bulgaria the Soviet-conducted elections satisfied British observers, if not Americans. Stalin agreed to an independent, noncommunist regime in Finland if the Finns would follow a foreign policy friendly to Russia. An "iron fence" by no means encircled all of Eastern Europe. There was still room to bargain if each side wished to avoid a confrontation over the remaining areas.

But the bargaining room was limited. Stalin's doctrine and his determination that Russia would not again be invaded from the west greatly narrowed his diplomatic options. So too did the tremendous devastation of the war. Rapid rebuilding under communism required security, required access to resources in Eastern and Central Europe, and continued tight control over the Russian people. The experience of war was indelible. Russians viewed almost everything in their lives through their "searing experience of World War II," as one psychologist has phrased it. The conflict had destroyed 1700 towns, 70,000 villages and left 25 million homeless. Twenty million died; 600,000 starved to death at the single siege of Leningrad. . . .

Some scholars have examined Stalin's acts of 1928–1945, pronounced them the work of a "paranoid," and concluded that the United States had no chance to avoid a cold war since it was dealing with a man who was mentally ill. That interpretation neatly avoids confronting the complex causes of the Cold War but is wholly insufficient to explain those causes. However Stalin acted inside Russia, where he had total control, in his foreign policy during 1941–1946 he displayed a realism, a careful calculation of forces, and a diplomatic finesse that undercut any attempt to explain away his actions as paranoid. If he and other Soviets were suspicious of the West, they were realistic, not paranoid: the West had poured thousands of troops into Russia between 1917 and 1920, refused to cooperate with the Soviets during the 1930s, tried to turn Hitler against Stalin in 1938, reneged on promises about the second front, and in 1945 tried to penetrate areas Stalin deemed crucial to Soviet security.

American diplomats who frequently saw Stalin understood this background. In January 1945 Harriman told the State Department, "The overriding consideration in Soviet foreign policy is the preoccupation with 'security,' as Moscow sees it." The problem was that Americans did not see "security" the same way. They believed their security required an open world, including an open Eastern Europe. . . .

By mid-1945 Stalin's policies were brutally consistent, while Truman's were confused. The confusion became obvious when the United States, opposed to a sphere of interest in Europe, strengthened its own sphere in the Western Hemisphere. Unlike its policies elsewhere, however, the State Department did not use economic weapons. The economic relationship with Latin America and Canada could simply be assumed. . . .

But Latin America was not neglected politically. A young assistant secretary of state for Latin American affairs, Nelson Rockefeller, and Senator Arthur Vandenberg (Republican from Michigan) devised the political means to keep the Americas solidly within Washington's sphere. Their instrument was Article 51 of the U.N. Charter. This provision was largely formulated by Rockefeller and Vandenberg at the San Francisco conference that founded the United Nations in the spring of 1945. The article allowed for collective self-defense through special regional organizations to be created outside the United Nations but within the principles of the charter. In this way, regional organizations would escape Russian vetoes in the Security Council. The United States could control its own sphere without Soviet interference. . . .

The obvious confusion in that approach was pinpointed by Secretary of War Stimson when he condemned Americans who were "anxious to hang on to exaggerated views of the Monroe Doctrine [in the Western Hemisphere] and at the same time butt into every question that comes up in Central Europe." Almost alone, Stimson argued for an alternative policy. Through bilateral U.S.-U.S.S.R. negotiations (and not negotiations within the United Nations, where the Russians would be defensive and disagreeable because the Americans controlled a majority), Stimson hoped each side could agree that the other should have its own security spheres. But as he had lost the argument over Poland, so Stimson lost this argument. Truman was prepared to bargain very little. He might not get 100 percent, the President told advisers, but he would get 85 percent. Even in Rumania, where the Russians were particularly sensitive, the State Department secretly determined in August 1945, "It is our intention to attain a position of equality with the Russians." When, however, the Americans pressed, the Soviets only tightened their control of Rumania. . . .

Although Truman did not obtain his "85 percent" at Potsdam, en route home he received the news that a weapon of unimaginable power, the atomic bomb, had obliterated Hiroshima, Japan, on August 6. Eighty thousand had died. This was some 20,000 fewer than had been killed by a massive American fire bombing of Tokyo earlier in the year, but it was the newly opened secret of nature embodied in a single bomb that was overwhelming. Roosevelt had initiated the atomic project in 1941. He had decided at least by 1944 not to share information about the bomb with the Soviets, even though he knew Stalin had learned about the project. By the summer of 1945 this approach, and the growing Soviet-American confrontation in Eastern Europe, led Truman and Byrnes to discuss securing "further *quid pro quos*" in Rumania, Poland, and Asia from Stalin before the Russians could share the secret of atomic energy. . . .

. . . Stimson, about to retire from the War Department, made one final attempt to stop an East-West confrontation. In a September 11 memorandum to Truman,

Stimson prophesied "that it would not be possible to use our possession of the atomic bomb as a direct lever to produce the change" desired inside Eastern Europe. If Soviet-American negotiations continue with "this weapon rather ostentatiously on our hip, their suspicions and their distrust of our purposes and motives will increase." He again urged direct, bilateral talks with Stalin to formulate control of the bomb and to write a general peace settlement. Stimson's advice was especially notable because several months before he himself had hoped to use the bomb to pry the Soviets out of Eastern Europe. Now he had changed his mind.

Truman again turned Stimson's advice aside. A month later the President delivered a speech larded with references to America's monopoly of atomic power, then attacked Russia's grip on Eastern Europe. Molotov quickly replied that peace could not be reconciled with an armaments race advocated by "zealous partisans of the imperialist policy." In this connection, he added, "We should mention the discovery of . . . the atomic bomb."

With every utterance and every act, the wartime alliance further disintegrated. . . .

During early 1946 Stalin and Churchill issued their declarations of Cold War. In an election speech of February 9, the Soviet dictator announced that Marxist-Leninist dogma remained valid, for "the unevenness of development of the capitalist countries" could lead to "violent disturbance" and the consequent splitting of the "capitalist world into two hostile camps and war between them." War was inevitable as long as capitalism existed. The Soviet people must prepare themselves for a replay of the 1930s by developing basic industry instead of consumer goods and, in all, making enormous sacrifices demanded in "three more Five-Year Plans, I should think, if not more." There would be no peace, internally or externally. These words profoundly affected Washington. Supreme Court Justice William Douglas, one of the reigning American liberals, believed that Stalin's speech meant "The Declaration of World War III." The *New York Times* front-page story of the speech began by declaring that Stalin believed "the stage is set" for war.

Winston Churchill delivered his views at Fulton, Missouri, on March 5. The former prime minister exalted American power with the plea that his listeners recognize that "God has willed" the United States, not "some Communist or neo-Fascist state" to have atomic bombs. To utilize the "breathing space" provided by these weapons, Churchill asked for "a fraternal association of the English-speaking peoples" operating under the principles of the United Nations, but not inside that organization, to reorder the world. This unilateral policy must be undertaken because "from Stettin in the Baltic to Trieste in the Adriatic, an iron curtain has descended across the Continent" allowing "police government" to rule Eastern Europe. The Soviets, he emphasized, did not want war: "What they desire is the fruits of war and the indefinite expansion of their power and doctrines."

The "iron curtain" phrase made the speech famous. But, as Churchill himself observed, the "crux" of the message lay in the proposal that the Anglo-Americans, outside the United Nations and with the support of atomic weaponry (the title of the address was "The Sinews of Peace"), create "a unity in Europe from which no nation should be permanently outcast." The Soviets perceived this as a direct challenge to their power in Eastern Europe. Within a week Stalin attacked Churchill and his "friends" in America, whom he claimed resembled Hitler by holding a "racial theory" that those who spoke the English language "should rule over the remaining nations of the world." This, Stalin warned, is "a set-up for war, a call to war with the Soviet Union."

Within a short period after the Churchill speech, Stalin launched a series of policies which, in retrospect, marks the spring and summer of 1946 as a milestone in the Cold War. During these weeks the Soviets, after having worked for a loan during the previous fifteen months, finally concluded that Washington had no interest in loaning them $1 billion, or any other amount. They refused to become a member of the World Bank and the International Monetary Fund. These rejections ended the American hope to use the lure of the dollar to make the Soviets retreat in Eastern Europe and join the capitalist-controlled bank and IMF.

Actually there had never been reason to hope. Control of their border areas was worth more to the Russians than $1 billion, or even $10 billion. . . .

. . . Truman's difficulties came into the open during the autumn of 1946, when he was attacked by liberals for being too militaristic and by conservatives for his economic policies.

The liberal attack was led by Henry Agard Wallace, a great secretary of agriculture during the early New Deal, Vice President from 1941–1945, maneuvered out of the vice-presidential nomination in 1944 so that Harry Truman could be FDR's running mate, and finally secretary of commerce in 1945. Here he devoted himself to the cause of what he liked to call the "Common Man," by extending increased loans to small businessmen and, above all, enlarging the economic pie by increasing foreign trade. Wallace soon discovered that Truman threatened to clog the trade channels to Russia, Eastern Europe, perhaps even China, with his militant attitude toward the Soviets.

At a political rally in New York on September 12, 1946, Wallace delivered a speech, cleared personally, and too rapidly, by Truman. The address focused on the necessity of a political understanding with Russia. This, Wallace declared, would require guaranteeing Soviet security in Eastern Europe. . . . At that moment Byrnes and Vandenberg were in Paris, painfully and unsuccessfully trying to negotiate peace treaties with Molotov. They immediately demanded Wallace's resignation. On September 20, Truman complied. . . .

On March 12, 1947, President Truman finally issued his own declaration of Cold War. Dramatically presenting the Truman Doctrine to Congress, he asked Americans to join in a global commitment against communism. The nation responded. A quarter of a century later, Senator J. William Fulbright declared, "More by far than any other factor the anti-communism of the Truman Doctrine has been the guiding spirit of American foreign policy since World War II." . . .

The Truman Doctrine was a milestone in American history for at least four reasons. First, it marked the point at which Truman used the American fear of communism both at home and abroad to convince Americans they must embark upon a Cold War foreign policy. This consensus would not break apart for a quarter of a century. Second . . . , Congress was giving the President great powers to wage this Cold War as he saw fit. Truman's personal popularity began spiraling upward after his speech. Third, for the first time in the postwar era, Americans massively intervened in another nation's civil war. Intervention was justified on the basis of anticommunism.

In the future, Americans would intervene in similar wars for supposedly the same reason and with less happy results. . . .

Finally, and perhaps most important, Truman used the doctrine to justify a gigantic aid program to prevent a collapse of the European and American economies. Later such programs were expanded globally. The President's arguments about the need to fight communism now became confusing, for the Western economies would have been in grave difficulties whether or not communism existed. The complicated problems of reconstruction and U.S. dependence on world trade were not well understood by Americans, but they easily comprehended anticommunism. So Americans embarked upon the Cold War for the good reasons given in the Truman Doctrine, which they understood, and for real reasons, which they did not understand. . . .

The President's program evolved naturally into the Marshall Plan. Although the speech did not limit American effort, Secretary of State Marshall did by concentrating the administration's attention on Europe. Returning badly shaken from a Foreign Ministers conference in Moscow, the secretary of state insisted in a nationwide broadcast that Western Europe required immediate help. "The patient is sinking," he declared, "while the doctors deliberate." Personal conversations with Stalin had convinced Marshall that the Russians believed Europe would collapse. Assuming that the United States must lead in restoring Europe, Marshall appointed a policy-planning staff under the direction of George Kennan to draw up guidelines. . . .

Building on this premise, round-the-clock conferences in May 1947 began to fashion the main features of the Marshall Plan. The all-important question became how to handle the Russians. Ostensibly, Marshall accepted Kennan's advice to "play it straight" by inviting the Soviet bloc. In reality the State Department made Russian participation improbable by demanding that economic records of each nation be open for scrutiny. For good measure Kennan also suggested that the Soviets' devastated economy, weakened by the war and at that moment suffering from drought and famine, participate in the plan by shipping Soviet goods to Europe. Apparently no one in the State Department wanted the Soviets included. Russian participation would vastly multiply the costs of the program and eliminate any hope of its acceptance by a purse-watching Republican Congress, now increasingly convinced by Truman that communists had to be fought, not fed. . . .

The European request for a four-year program of $17 billion of American aid now had to run the gauntlet of a Republican Congress, which was dividing its attention between slashing the budget and attacking Truman, both in anticipation of the presidential election only a year away. In committee hearings in late 1947 and early 1948, the executive presented its case. Only large amounts of government money which could restore basic facilities, provide convertibility of local currency into dollars, and end the dollar shortage would stimulate private investors to rebuild Europe, administration witnesses argued. . . .

The Marshall Plan now appears to have signaled not the beginning but the end of an era. It marked the last phase in the administration's use of economic tactics as the primary means of tying together the Western world. The plan's approach . . . soon evolved into military alliances. Truman proved to be correct in saying that the Truman Doctrine and the Marshall Plan "are two halves of the same walnut." Americans willingly acquiesced as the military aspects of the doctrine developed into quite the larger part. . . .

The military and personal costs of the Truman Doctrine . . . were higher than expected. And the cost became more apparent as Truman and J. Edgar Hoover (director of the Federal Bureau of Investigation) carried out the President's Security Loyalty program. Their search for subversives accelerated after Canadians uncovered a Soviet spy ring.

The House Un-American Activities Committee began to intimate that Truman was certainly correct in his assessment of communism's evil nature but lax in destroying it. In March 1948 the committee demanded the loyalty records gathered by the FBI. Truman handled the situation badly. Unable to exploit the committee's distorted view of the internal communist threat, he accused it of trying to cover up the bad record of the Republican Congress. He refused to surrender the records, ostensibly because they were in the exclusive domain of the executive, more probably because of his fear that if the Republicans saw the FBI reports, which accused some federal employees of disloyalty on the basis of hearsay, unproven allegations, and personal vendettas, November might be an unfortunate month for Truman's political aspirations. Unable to discredit the loyalty program he had set in motion, trapped by his own indiscriminating anticommunist rhetoric designed to "scare hell" out of the country, Truman stood paralyzed as the ground was carefully plowed around him for the weeds of McCarthyism. . . .

And then came the fall of Czechoslovakia. The Czechs had uneasily coexisted with Russia by trying not to offend the Soviets while keeping doors open to the West. This policy had started in late 1943, when Czech leaders signed a treaty with Stalin that, in the view of most observers, obligated Czechoslovakia to become a part of the Russian bloc. President Edvard Beneš and Foreign Minister Jan Masaryk, one of the foremost diplomatic figures in Europe, had nevertheless successfully resisted complete communist control. Nor had Stalin moved to consolidate his power in 1946 after the Czech Communist party emerged from the parliamentary elections with 38 percent of the vote, the largest total of any party. By late 1947 the lure of Western aid and internal political changes began to pull the Czech government away from the Soviets. At this point Stalin, who like Truman recalled the pivotal role of Czechoslovakia in 1938, decided to put the 1943 treaty into effect. Klement Gottwald, the Czech Communist party leader, demanded the elimination of independent parties. In mid-February 1948 Soviet armies camped on the border as Gottwald ordered the formation of a wholly new government. A Soviet mission of top officials flew to Prague to demand Beneš's surrender. The communists assumed full control on February 25. Two weeks later Masaryk either committed suicide, or, as Truman believed, was the victim of "foul play."

Truman correctly observed that the coup "sent a shock throughout the civilized world." He privately believed "We are faced with exactly the same situation with which Britain and France were faced in 1938–9 with Hitler." . . . Two days before, on March 14, the Senate had endorsed the Marshall Plan by a vote of 69 to 17. As it went to the House for consideration, Truman, fearing the "grave events in Europe [which] were moving so swiftly," decided to appear before Congress.

In a speech remarkable for its repeated emphasis on the "increasing threat" to the very "survival of freedom," the President proclaimed the Marshall Plan "not enough."

Europe must have "some measure of protection against internal and external aggression." He asked for Universal Training, the resumption of Selective Service (which he had allowed to lapse a year earlier), and speedy passage of the Marshall Plan. Within twelve days the House approved authorization of the plan's money. . . .

During the spring of 1948 a united administration, enjoying strong support on foreign policy from a Republican Congress, set off with exemplary single-mindedness to destroy the communist threat that loomed over Europe. Within two years this threat had been scotched. But the officials who created the policy had split, the Congress that ratified the policy had turned against the executive, the administration had fought off charges that it had been infiltrated by communists, and the United States found itself fighting a bloody war not in Europe but in Asia. These embarrassments did not suddenly emerge in 1950 but developed gradually from the policies of 1948–1949. . . .

The world in which NATO was to be born was undergoing rapid change. . . .

The Senate ratified the [NATO] treaty 82 to 13. On the day he added his signature in mid-July 1949, Truman sent Congress a one-year Mutual Defense Assistance (MDA) bill providing for $1.5 billion for European military aid. This was the immediate financial price for the NATO commitment. A memorandum circulating through the executive outlined the purpose of MDA: "to build up our own military industry," to "create a common defense frontier in Western Europe" by having the Allies pool "their industrial and manpower resources," and particularly, to subordinate "nationalistic tendencies." In the House, however, the bill encountered tough opposition from budget-cutting congressmen. On September 22 President Truman announced that Russia had exploded an atomic bomb. Within six days the NATO appropriations raced through the House and went to the President for approval.

Although publicly playing down the significance of the Russian bomb, the administration painfully realized that, in Vandenberg's words, "This is now a different world." Few American officials had expected the Soviet test this early. Because it was simultaneous with the fall of China, the American diplomatic attitude further stiffened. . . .

. . . A grim President, pressed by domestic critics and the new Soviet bomb, demanded a wide-ranging reevaluation of American Cold War policies. In early 1950 the National Security Council began work on a highly secret document (declassified only a quarter of a century later, and then through an accident) that would soon be known as NSC-68. Truman examined the study in April, and it was ready for implementation when Korea burst into war.

NSC-68 proved to be the American blueprint for waging the Cold War. It began with two assumptions that governed the rest of the document. First, the global balance of power had been "fundamentally altered" since the nineteenth century so that the Americans and Russians now dominated the world: "What is new, what makes the continuing crisis, is the polarization of power which inescapably confronts the slave society with the free." It was us against them. Second, "the Soviet Union, unlike previous aspirants to hegemony, is animated by a new fanatic faith, antithetical to our own, and seeks to impose its absolute authority," initially in "the Soviet Union and second in the area now under [its] control." Then the crucial sentence: "In the minds of the Soviet leaders, however, achievement of this design requires the dynamic extension of their authority and the ultimate elimination of any effective opposition to their authority. . . . To that end Soviet efforts are now directed toward the domination of the Eurasian land mass." . . .

In conclusion, therefore, NSC-68 recommended (1) against negotiations with Russia since conditions were not yet sufficient to force the Kremlin to "change its policies drastically"; (2) development of hydrogen bombs to offset possible Soviet possession of an effective atomic arsenal by 1954; (3) rapid building of conventional military forces to preserve American interests without having to wage atomic war; (4) a large increase in taxes to pay for this new, highly expensive military establishment; (5) mobilization of American society, including a government-created "consensus" on the necessity of "sacrifice" and "unity" by Americans; (6) a strong alliance system directed by the United States; (7) and—as the topper—undermining the "Soviet totalitariat" from within by making "the Russian people our allies in this enterprise." How this was to be done was necessarily vague. But no matter. Truman and Acheson were no longer satisfied with containment. They wanted Soviet withdrawal and an absolute victory. . . .

Stalin's Hard Line Prompted a Defensive Response in the United States and Europe

JOHN LEWIS GADDIS

Leaders of both the United States and the Soviet Union would have bristled at having the appellation "imperial" affixed to what they were doing after 1945. But one need not send out ships, seize territories, and hoist flags to construct an empire: "informal" empires are considerably older than, and continued to exist alongside, the more "formal" ones Europeans imposed on so much of the rest of the world from the fifteenth through the nineteenth centuries. During the Cold War years Washington and Moscow took on much of the character, if never quite the charm, of old imperial capitals like London, Paris, and Vienna. And surely American and Soviet influence, throughout most of the second half of the twentieth century, was at least as ubiquitous as that of any earlier empire the world had ever seen. . . .

Let us begin with the structure of the Soviet empire, for the simple reason that it was, much more than the American, deliberately designed. It has long been clear that, in addition to having had an authoritarian vision, [Joseph] Stalin also had an imperial one, which he proceeded to implement in at least as single-minded a way. No comparably influential builder of empire came close to wielding power for so long, or with such striking results, on the Western side.

It was, of course, a matter of some awkwardness that Stalin came out of a revolutionary movement that had vowed to smash, not just tsarist imperialism, but all forms of imperialism throughout the world. The Soviet leader constructed his own logic, though, and throughout his career he devoted a surprising amount of attention to showing how a revolution and an empire might coexist. Bolsheviks could never

John Lewis Gaddis, *We Now Know: Rethinking Cold War History* (New York: Oxford University Press, 1997). Reprinted by permission of Oxford University Press.

be imperialists, Stalin acknowledged in one of his earliest public pronouncements on this subject, made in April 1917. But surely in a *revolutionary* Russia nine-tenths of the non-Russian nationalities would not *want* their independence. Few among those minorities found Stalin's reasoning persuasive after the Bolsheviks did seize power later that year, however, and one of the first problems [Vladimir] Lenin's new government faced was a disintegration of the old Russian empire not unlike what happened to the Soviet Union after communist authority finally collapsed in 1991.

Whether because of Lenin's own opposition to imperialism or, just as plausibly, because of Soviet Russia's weakness at the time, Finns, Estonians, Latvians, Lithuanians, Poles, and Moldavians were allowed to depart. Others who tried to do so— Ukrainians, Belorussians, Caucasians, Central Asians—were not so fortunate, and in 1922 Stalin proposed incorporating these remaining (and reacquired) nationalities into the Russian republic, only to have Lenin as one of his last acts override this recommendation and establish the multi-ethnic Union of Soviet Socialist Republics. After Lenin died and Stalin took his place it quickly became clear, though, that whatever its founding principles the USSR was to be no federation of equals. Rather, it would function as an updated form of empire even more tightly centralized than that of the Russian tsars. . . .

Stalin's fusion of Marxist internationalism with tsarist imperialism could only reinforce his tendency, in place well before World War II, to equate the advance of world revolution with the expanding influence of the Soviet state. . . .

Stalin had been very precise [after World War II] about where he wanted Soviet boundaries changed; he was much less so on how far Moscow's sphere of influence was to extend. He insisted on having "friendly" countries around the periphery of the USSR, but he failed to specify how many would have to meet this standard. He called during the war for dismembering Germany, but by the end of it was denying that he had ever done so: that country would be temporarily divided, he told leading German communists in June 1945, and they themselves would eventually bring about its reunification. He never gave up on the idea of an eventual world revolution, but he expected this to result—as his comments to the Germans suggested—from an expansion of influence emanating from the Soviet Union itself. "[F]or the Kremlin," a well-placed spymaster recalled, "the mission of communism was primarily to consolidate the might of the Soviet state. Only military strength and domination of the countries on our borders could ensure us a superpower role."

But Stalin provided no indication—surely because he himself did not know— of how rapidly, or under what circumstances, this process would take place. He was certainly prepared to stop in the face of resistance from the West: at no point was he willing to challenge the Americans or even the British where they made their interests clear. . . .

What all of this suggests, though, is not that Stalin had limited ambitions, only that he had no timetable for achieving them. [Foreign minister Vyacheslav] Molotov retrospectively confirmed this: "Our ideology stands for offensive operations when possible, and if not, we wait." Given this combination of appetite with aversion to risk, one cannot help but wonder what would have happened had the West tried containment earlier. To the extent that it bears partial responsibility for the coming of the Cold War, the historian Vojtech Mastny has argued, that responsibility lies in its failure to do just that. . . .

. . . The fact that Stalin was able to *expand* his empire when others were contracting and while the Soviet Union was as weak as it was required explanation. Why did opposition to this process, within and outside Europe, take so long to develop?

One reason was that the colossal sacrifices the Soviet Union had made during the war against the Axis had, in effect, "purified" its reputation: the USSR and its leader had "earned" the right to throw their weight around, or so it seemed. Western governments found it difficult to switch quickly from viewing the Soviet Union as a glorious wartime ally to portraying it as a new and dangerous adversary. President Harry S Truman and his future Secretary of State Dean Acheson—neither of them sympathetic in the slightest to communism—nonetheless tended to give the Soviet Union the benefit of the doubt well into the early postwar era. . . .

Resistance to Stalin's imperialism also developed slowly because Marxism-Leninism at the time had such widespread appeal. It is difficult now to recapture the admiration revolutionaries outside the Soviet Union felt for that country before they came to know it well. "[Communism] was the most rational and most intoxicating, all-embracing ideology for me and for those in my disunited and desperate land who so desired to skip over centuries of slavery and backwardness and to bypass reality itself," [Milovan] Djilas recalled, in a comment that could have been echoed throughout much of what came to be called the "third world." Because the Bolsheviks themselves had overcome one empire and had made a career of condemning others, it would take decades for people who were struggling to overthrow British, French, Dutch, or Portuguese colonialism to see that there could also be such a thing as Soviet imperialism. European communists—notably the Yugoslavs—saw this much earlier, but even to most of them it had not been apparent at the end of the war. . . .

One has the impression that Stalin and the Eastern Europeans got to know one another only gradually. The Kremlin leader was slow to recognize that Soviet authority would not be welcomed everywhere beyond Soviet borders; but as he did come to see this he became all the more determined to impose it everywhere. The Eastern Europeans were slow to recognize how confining incorporation within a Soviet sphere was going to be; but as they did come to see this they became all the more determined to resist it, even if only by withholding, in a passive but sullen manner, the consent any regime needs to establish itself by means other than coercion. Stalin's efforts to consolidate his empire therefore made it at once more repressive and less secure. Meanwhile, an alternative vision of postwar Europe was emerging from the other great empire that established itself in the wake of World War II, that of the United States, and this too gave Stalin grounds for concern.

The first point worth noting, when comparing the American empire to its Soviet counterpart, is a striking reversal in the sequence of events. Stalin's determination to create his empire preceded by some years the conditions that made it possible: he had first to consolidate power at home and then defeat Nazi Germany, while at the same time seeing to it that his allies in that enterprise did not thwart his long-term objectives. With the United States, it was the other way around: the conditions for establishing an empire were in place long before there was any clear intention on the part of its leaders to do so. Even then, they required the support of a skeptical electorate, something that could never quite be taken for granted.

The United States had been poised for global hegemony at the end of World War I. Its military forces played a decisive role in bringing that conflict to an end. Its economic predominance was such that it could control both the manner and the rate of European recovery. Its ideology commanded enormous respect, as Woodrow Wilson found when he arrived on the Continent late in 1918 to a series of rapturous public receptions. The Versailles Treaty fell well short of Wilson's principles, to be sure, but the League of Nations followed closely his own design, providing an explicit legal basis for an international order that was to have drawn, as much as anything else, upon the example of the American constitution itself. If there was ever a point at which the world seemed receptive to an expansion of United States influence, this was it.

Americans themselves, however, were not receptive. The Senate's rejection of membership in the League reflected the public's distinct lack of enthusiasm for international peace-keeping responsibilities. Despite the interests certain business, labor, and agricultural groups had in seeking overseas markets and investment opportunities, most Americans saw few benefits to be derived from integrating their economy with that of the rest of the world. . . .

This isolationist consensus broke down only as Americans began to realize that a potentially hostile power was once again threatening Europe: even their own hemisphere, it appeared, might not escape the consequences this time around. After September 1939, the Roosevelt administration moved as quickly as public Congressional opinion would allow to aid Great Britain and France by means short of war; it also chose to challenge the Japanese over their occupation of China and later French Indochina, thereby setting in motion a sequence of events that would lead to the attack on Pearl Harbor. . . .

It did not automatically follow, though, that the Soviet Union would inherit the title of "first enemy" once Germany and Japan had been defeated. A sense of vulnerability preceded the identification of a source of threat in the thinking of American strategists: innovations in military technology—long-range bombers, the prospect of even longer-range missiles—created visions of future Pearl Harbors before it had become clear from where such an attack might come. Neither in the military nor the political-economic planning that went on in Washington during the war was there consistent concern with the USSR as a potential future adversary. The threat, rather, appeared to arise from war itself, whoever might cause it, and the most likely candidates were thought to be resurgent enemies from World War II.

The preferred solution was to maintain preponderant power for the United States, which meant a substantial peacetime military establishment and a string of bases around the world from which to resist aggression if it should ever occur. But equally important, a revived international community would seek to remove the fundamental causes of war through the United Nations, a less ambitious version of Wilson's League, and through new economic institutions like the International Monetary Fund and the World Bank, whose task it would be to prevent another global depression and thereby ensure prosperity. The Americans and the British assumed that the Soviet Union would want to participate in these multilateral efforts to achieve military and economic security. The Cold War developed when it became clear that Stalin either could not or would not accept this framework.

Did the Americans attempt to impose their vision of the postwar world upon the USSR? No doubt it looked that way from Moscow: both the Roosevelt and Truman administrations stressed political self-determination and economic integration with sufficient persistence to arouse Stalin's suspicions—easily aroused, in any event—as to their ultimate intentions. But what the Soviet leader saw as a challenge to his hegemony the Americans meant as an effort to salvage multilateralism. At no point prior to 1947 did the United States and its Western European allies abandon the hope that the Russians might eventually come around; and indeed negotiations aimed at bringing them around would continue at the foreign minister's level, without much hope of success, through the end of that year. The American attitude was less that of expecting to impose a system than one of puzzlement as to why its merits were not universally self-evident. It differed significantly, therefore, from Stalin's point of view, which allowed for the possibility that socialists in other countries might come to see the advantages of Marxism-Leninism as practiced in the Soviet Union, but never capitalists. They were there, in the end, to be overthrown, not convinced. . . .

At the same time, though, it is difficult to see how a strategy of containment could have developed—with the Marshall Plan as its centerpiece—had there been nothing to contain. . . . The American empire arose *primarily,* therefore, not from internal causes, as had the Soviet empire, but from a perceived external danger powerful enough to overcome American isolationism.

Washington's wartime vision of a postwar international order had been premised on the concepts of political self-determination and economic integration. It was intended to work by assuming a set of *common* interests that would cause other countries to *want* to be affiliated with it rather than to resist it. The Marshall Plan, to a considerable extent, met those criteria. . . .

The test of any empire comes in administering it, for even the most repressive tyranny requires a certain amount of acquiescence among its subjects. Coercion and terror cannot everywhere and indefinitely prop up authority: sooner or later the social, economic, and psychological costs of such measures begin to outweigh the benefits. . . .

It is apparent now, even if it was not always at the time, that the Soviet Union did not manage its empire particularly well. Because of his personality and the structure of government he built around it, Stalin was—shall we say—less than receptive to the wishes of those nations that fell within the Soviet sphere. He viewed departures from his instructions with deep suspicion, but he also objected to manifestations of independent behavior where instructions had not yet been given. As a result, he put his European followers in an impossible position: they could satisfy him only by seeking his approval for whatever he had decided they should do— even, at times, before he had decided that they should do it.

An example occurred late in 1944 when the Yugoslavs—then the most powerful but also the most loyal of Stalin's East European allies—complained politely to Soviet commanders that their troops had been raping local women in the northern corner of the country through which they were passing. Stalin himself took note of this matter, accusing the Yugoslavs—at one point tearfully—of showing insufficient respect for Soviet military sacrifices and for failing to sympathize when "a soldier who has crossed thousands of kilometers through blood and fire and death has fun with a woman or takes some trifle." The issue was not an insignificant one: the Red Army's behavior was a problem throughout the territories it occupied, and did much to alienate those who lived there. . . .

The United States, in contrast, proved surprisingly adept at managing an empire. Having attained their authority through democratic processes, its leaders were experienced—as their counterparts in Moscow were not—in the arts of persuasion, negotiation and compromise. Applying domestic political insights to foreign policy could produce embarrassing results, as when President Truman likened Stalin to his old Kansas City political mentor, Tom Pendergast, or when Secretary of State James F. Byrnes compared the Russians to the US Senate: "You build a post office in their state, and they'll build a post office in our state." But the habits of democracy had served the nation well during World War II: its strategists had assumed that their ideas would have to reflect the interests and capabilities of allies; it was also possible for allies to advance proposals of their own and have them taken seriously. That same pattern of mutual accommodation persisted after the war, despite the fact that all sides acknowledged—as they had during most of the war itself—the disproportionate power of the United States could ultimately bring to bear.

Americans so often deferred to the wishes of allies during the early Cold War that some historians have seen the Europeans—especially the British—as having managed *them*. The new Labour government in London did encourage the Truman administration to toughen its policy toward the Soviet Union; Churchill—by then out of office—was only reinforcing these efforts with his March 1946 "Iron Curtain" speech. The British were ahead of the Americans in pressing for a consolidation of Western occupation zones in Germany, even if this jeopardized prospects for an overall settlement with the Russians. Foreign Secretary Ernest Bevin determined the timing of the February 1947 crisis over Greece and Turkey when he ended British military and economic assistance to those countries. . . .

But one can easily make too much of this argument. Truman and his advisers were not babes in the woods. They knew what they were doing at each stage, and did it only because they were convinced their actions would advance American interests. They never left initiatives entirely up to the Europeans: they insisted on an integrated plan for economic recovery and quite forcefully reined in prospective recipients when it appeared that their requests would exceed what Congress would approve. "[I]n the end we would not *ask* them," Kennan noted, "we would just *tell* them, what they would get." The Americans were flexible enough, though, to accept and build upon ideas that came from allies; they also frequently let allies determine the timing of actions taken. . . .

The Americans simply did not find it necessary, in building a sphere of influence, to impose unrepresentative governments or brutal treatment upon the peoples that fell within it. . . . It was as if the Americans were projecting abroad a tradition they had long taken for granted at home: that civility made sense; that spontaneity, within a framework of minimal constraint, was the path to political and economic robustness; that to intimidate or to overmanage was to stifle. The contrast to Stalin's methods of imperial administration could hardly have been sharper.

Stalin saw the need, after learning of the Marshall Plan, to improve his methods of imperial management. He therefore called a meeting of the Soviet and East European communist parties, as well as the French and the Italian communists, to be held in Poland in September 1947, ostensibly for the purpose of exchanging ideas on fraternal cooperation. Only after the delegations had assembled did he reveal his real objective, which was to organize a new coordinating agency for the international communist movement. . . .

Even with the Cominform in place, the momentary independence Czechoslovakia demonstrated must have continued to weigh on Stalin's mind. That country, more than any other in Eastern Europe, had sought to accommodate itself to Soviet hegemony. Embittered by how easily the British and French had betrayed Czech interests at the Munich conference in 1938, President Eduard Beneš welcomed the expansion of Soviet influence while reassuring Marxist-Leninists that they had nothing to fear from the democratic system the Czechs hoped to rebuild after the war. "If you play it well," he told Czech Communist Party leaders in 1943, "you'll win."

But Beneš meant "win" by democratic means. Although the Communists had indeed done well in the May 1946 parliamentary elections, their popularity began to drop sharply after Stalin forbade Czech participation in the Marshall Plan the following year. Convinced by intelligence reports that the West would not intervene, they therefore took advantage of a February 1948 government crisis to stage a *coup d'état*—presumably with Stalin's approval—that left them in complete control, with no further need to resort to the unpredictabilities of the ballot box. . . .

Because of its dramatic impact, the Czech coup had consequences Stalin could hardly have anticipated. It set off a momentary—and partially manufactured—war scare in Washington. It removed the last Congressional objections to the Marshall Plan, resulting in the final approval of that initiative in April 1948. It accelerated plans by the Americans, the British, and the French to consolidate their occupation zones in Germany and to proceed toward the formation of an independent West German state. And it caused American officials to begin to consider, much more seriously than they had until this point, two ideas Bevin had begun to advance several months earlier: that economic assistance alone would not restore European self-confidence, and that the United States would have to take on direct military responsibilities for defending that portion of the Continent that remained outside Soviet control.

Stalin then chose the late spring of 1948 to attempt a yet further consolidation of the Soviet empire, with even more disastrous results. . . .

West Europeans were meanwhile convincing themselves that they had little to lose from living within an American sphere of influence. The idea of a European "third force" soon disappeared, not because Washington officials lost interest in it, but because the Europeans themselves rejected it. The North Atlantic Treaty Organization, which came into existence in April 1949, had been a European initiative from the beginning: it was as explicit an invitation as has ever been extended from smaller powers to a great power to construct an empire and include them within it. When Kennan, worried that NATO would divide Europe permanently, put forward a plan later that spring looking toward an eventual reunification and neutralization of Germany as a way of ending both the Soviet and American presence on the continent, British and French opposition quickly shot it down. . . .

. . . Why were allies of the United States willing to give up so much autonomy in order to enhance their own safety? How did the ideas of sovereignty and security, which historically have been difficult to separate, come to be so widely seen as divisible in this situation?

The answer would appear to be that despite a postwar polarization of authority quite at odds, in its stark bilateralism, from what wartime planners had expected, Americans managed to retain the multilateral conception of security they had developed during World War II. They were able to do this because Truman's foreign policy—like Roosevelt's military strategy—reflected the habits of domestic democratic politics. Negotiation, compromise, and consensus building abroad came naturally to statesmen steeped in the uses of such practices at home: in this sense, the American political tradition served the country better than its realist critics— Kennan definitely among them—believed it did. . . .

It would become fashionable to argue, in the wake of American military intervention in Vietnam, the Soviet invasions of Czechoslovakia and Afghanistan, and growing fears of nuclear confrontation that developed during the early 1980s, that there were no significant differences in the spheres of influence Washington and Moscow had constructed in Europe after World War II: these had been, it was claimed, "morally equivalent," denying autonomy quite impartially to all who lived under them. Students of history must make their own judgments about morality, but even a cursory examination of the historical record will show that these imperial structures could hardly have been more different in their origins, their composition, their tolerance of diversity, and as it turned out their durability. It is important to specify just what these differences were. . . .

One empire arose . . . by invitation, the other by imposition. *Europeans* made this distinction, very much as they had done during the war when they welcomed armies liberating them from the west but feared those that came from the east. They did so because they saw clearly at the time—even if a subsequent generation would not always see—how different American and Soviet empires were likely to be. It is true that the *extent* of the American empire quickly exceeded that of its Soviet counterpart, but this was because *resistance* to expanding American influence was never as great. The American empire may well have become larger, paradoxically, because the American *appetite* for empire was less that of the USSR. The United States had shown, throughout most of its history, that it could survive and even prosper without extending its domination as far as the eye could see. The logic of Lenin's ideological internationalism, as modified by Stalin's Great Russian nationalism and personal paranoia, was that the Soviet Union could not.

◥ F U R T H E R   R E A D I N G

Paul S. Boyer, *By the Bomb's Early Light: American Thought and Culture at the Dawn of the Atomic Age* (1985).

Richard M. Fried, *The Russians Are Coming! The Russians Are Coming! Pageantry and Patriotism in the Cold War* (1998).

John Earl Haynes and Harvey Klehr, *Venona: Decoding Soviet Espionage in the United States* (1999).

Margot Henriksen, *Dr. Strangelove's America: Society and Culture in the Atomic Age* (1997).

Michael J. Hogan, *A Cross of Iron: Harry S Truman and the Origins of the National Security State* (1998).

Robbie Lieberman, *The Strangest Dream: Communism, Anticommunism, and the U.S. Peace Movement, 1945–1963* (2000).

Vojtech Mastny, *The Cold War and Soviet Insecurity* (1996).

Thomas G. Paterson, *On Every Front: The Making and Unmaking of the Cold War* (1992).

Stanley Sandler, *The Korean War: No Victors, No Vanquished* (1999).

Ellen Schrecker, *Many Are the Crimes: McCarthyism in America* (1998).

Reinhold Wagnleitner, *Coca-Colonization and the Cold War: The Cultural Mission of the United States in Austria After the Second World War* (1994).

Vladislav Zubok and Constantine Pleshakov, *Inside the Kremlin's Cold War* (1996).

CHAPTER
11

The 1950s "Boom":
Affluence and Anxiety

In the 1950s, everything about America seemed to get bigger: families, towns, highways, shopping centers, corporations, and government. Americans' wealth grew along with the domestic economy, and American power expanded with the Cold War. After the trials of the Great Depression and World War II, Americans appeared to revel in the stability and normalcy of the fifties. The G.I. Bill, passed by Congress in 1944, paid millions of former soldiers to go to college, lent them money to buy homes, and helped finance their new careers. Although some people thought President Eisenhower bland, many more embraced the cheerful Republican slogan "I Like Ike." Patriotism soared, along with belief in the superiority of the so-called American Way. With political and economic confidence high, well-off consumers fueled a spectacular economic expansion. Middle-class families could afford to, and did, purchase most of the conveniences offered by mass production—including mass-produced homes in sprawling new suburbs. They had more babies than their parents' generation to fill these homes, and affluence enabled women to stay home in droves to take care of this special "baby-boom" generation. Parents sought to give their children all the things they had not had growing up in the Depression and during the war.

Affluence sparked anxiety, however. Some critics asserted that the United States was becoming too complacent, and its citizens too coddled. Parents especially worried about the effect of abundance on their children's character development. Novelists and social commentators harped on the emergence of a new phenomenon that some called "juvenile delinquency." Blockbuster films such as Rebel Without a Cause, West Side Story, Splendor in the Grass, *and* Blackboard Jungle *told of a generation run wild: sophisticated, perhaps, but lost. Adult roles also occasioned commentary. The fifties witnessed an ongoing preoccupation with the lack of creative or "manly" jobs for men in mass society, and with women's place in the family.*

Television contributed to the social ferment. At the start of the decade, only a small fraction of the population (roughly 3 million Americans) owned the new technology. By 1960, 50 million households had TV sets. More Americans had TVs than had running water and indoor toilets. Television helped to create a more uniform culture than had ever before existed in the United States. Coal miners in rural Appalachia could hear the bubbling Cuban accent of Desi Arnaz on I Love Lucy. *Schoolchildren in southern California could identify the nasal twang of the Boston Irish in the 1960 TV appearances of John Kennedy. Overtaking all of these regional speech patterns was the uniform, "accentless" cadence of a new generation of television performers and news announcers, whose dialect and appearance set the norm for "middle America." The new television shows also brought regions, classes, and ethnic groups together by giving them a common subject: 50 million households could laugh at the same jokes and pratfalls. Because the content of many shows focused on optimistic, happy portrayals of suburban life, these shows also helped to set a standard—rarely attainable—of the ideal postwar family. And, by establishing an ideal, television offered viewers a chance to compare their own lives with those of others, creating an anxiety about why they might not match the model.*

Although "traditional" by reputation, the fifties were a time of great flux. Pervasive television imagery, booming suburbs, and growing incomes dramatically changed how Americans lived and what they thought about it.

QUESTIONS TO THINK ABOUT

Were the fifties really *Happy Days,* as a television show once characterized the era, or is the period more accurately described as an era of psychological, social, and political tensions? Why do the fifties prompt (as they have) such nostalgia for poodle skirts, sock hops, hula hoops, stay-at-home moms, and Fourth of July parades?

DOCUMENTS

The documents in this chapter reveal many aspects of the postwar boom in population and prosperity. Near the close of World War II, the U.S. Congress passed a bill that transformed the lives of millions, and the American economy as well. Document 1, the Servicemens' Readjustment Act—also known as the G.I. Bill of Rights—outlines the many benefits that came to those who fought and survived World War II. Document 2 is from Ron Kovic's memoir, *Born on the Fourth of July.* The author later lost the use of his legs (and his trust in government) in Vietnam, but his fifties childhood helps to explain the boundless admiration he felt for his country growing up. In Document 3, *Science News Letter* observes a startling new trend: a sharp upswing in the birth rate among college-educated Americans. The 1950s, indeed, was the key decade of what became known as the "baby boom." Document 4 points to the conflict between some baby-boom adolescents and their "permissive" parents. Actor James Dean, who died in a high-speed car crash shortly before the release of *Rebel Without a Cause,* came to symbolize the angst of his generation, who wanted to be "men" but were treated as spoiled children. Document 5 shows that expectations for females were quite different from those for males. In this selection, Governor Adlai Stevenson addresses a class of women from Smith, an elite Massachusetts women's college. He suggests that there is nothing more fulfilling for a woman than reminding her husband of the values of Western civilization as he goes to a specialized job each day—one that, in effect, diminishes his individuality and understanding of life's broader purpose. In Document 6, famed social critic Paul Goodman talks about "growing up absurd"—the consequence of a mass society that no longer calls upon creativity, bravery, or even hard work from its young men. Combined with a growing economy, the baby boom helped to create an immense new market for retail sales: teenagers. As we see in Document 7 from *Life* magazine, some people complained that "teenagers are spoiled to death these days," but business boomed along with this new generation. In Document 8, feminist author Betty Friedan countered the assumptions of men like Adlai Stevenson and Paul Goodman. She helped start a revolution among women by raising the question, "Is this all?" Lastly, Document 9 reveals the commonplace sexism of American society during this era, while hinting at new social attitudes that rejected as absurd the notion that "fun" women were stupid.

1. Congress Passes the G.I. Bill of Rights, 1944

AN ACT

To provide Federal Government aid for the readjustment in civilian life of returning World War II veterans.

Be it enacted by the Senate and House of Representatives of the United States of America in Congress assembled, That this Act may be cited as the "Servicemen's Readjustment Act of 1944."

Title I

The Veterans' Administration is hereby declared to be an essential war agency and entitled, second only to the War and Navy Departments, to priorities in personnel, equipment, supplies, and material under any laws, Executive orders, and regulations pertaining to priorities, and in appointments of personnel from civil-service registers the Administrator of Veterans' Affairs is hereby granted the same authority and discretion as the War and Navy Departments and the United States Public Health Service: *Provided,* That the provisions of this section as to priorities for materials shall apply to any State institution to be built for the care or hospitalization of veterans.

Sec. 101. The Administrator of Veterans' Affairs and the Federal Board of Hospitalization are hereby authorized and directed to expedite and complete the construction of additional hospital facilities for war veterans, and to enter into agreements and contracts for use by or transfer to the Veterans' Administration of suitable Army and Navy hospitals after termination of hostilities in the present war or after such institutions are no longer needed by the armed services; and the Administrator of Veterans' Affairs is hereby authorized and directed to establish necessary regional offices, suboffices, branch offices, contact units, or other subordinate offices in centers of population where there is no Veterans' Administration. . . .

Title II—Education of Veterans

Any person who served in the active military or naval service on or after September 16, 1940, and prior to the termination of the present war, and who shall have been discharged or released therefrom under conditions other than dishonorable, and whose education or training was impeded, delayed, interrupted, or interfered with by reason of his entrance into the service, . . . shall be eligible for and entitled to receive education or training under this part: *Provided,* That such course shall be initiated not later than two years after either the date of discharge or the termination of the present war, whichever is the later: *Provided further,* That no such education or training shall be afforded beyond seven years after the termination of the present war: *And provided further,* That any such person who was not over 25 years of age at the time he entered the service shall be deemed to have had his education or training impeded, delayed, interrupted, or interfered with. . . .

The Administrator shall pay to the education or training institution, for each person enrolled in full time or part time course of education or training, the customary cost of tuition, and such laboratory, library, health, infirmary, and other similar fees as are customarily charged, and may pay for books, supplies, equipment, and other necessary expenses, exclusive of board, lodging, other living expenses, and travel, as are generally required for the successful pursuit and completion of the course by other students in the institution. . . .

While enrolled in and pursuing a course under this part, such person, upon application to the Administrator, shall be paid a subsistence allowance of $50 per month, if without a dependent or dependents, or $75 per month, if he has a dependent or dependents, including regular holidays and leave not exceeding thirty days in a calendar year. . . .

Title III—Loans for the Purchase or Construction of Homes, Farms, and Business Property

Any person who shall have served in the active military or naval service of the United States at any time on or after September 16, 1940, and prior to the termination of the present war . . . shall be eligible for the benefits of this title. Any such veteran may apply within two years after separation from the military or naval forces, or two years after termination of the war, whichever is the later date, but in no event more than five years after the termination of the war, to the Administrator of Veterans' Affairs for the guaranty by the Administrator of not to exceed 50 per centum of a loan or loans for any of the purposes specified in sections 501, 502 and 503. . . .

Purchase or Construction of Homes.   Sec. 501. (a) Any application made by a veteran under this title for the guaranty of a loan to be used in purchasing residential property, or in constructing a dwelling on unimproved property owned by him to be occupied as his home may be approved by the Administrator of Veterans' Affairs. . . .

Purchase of Farms and Farm Equipment.   Sec. 502. Any application made under this title for the guaranty of a loan to be used in purchasing any land, buildings, livestock, equipment, machinery, or implements, or in repairing, altering, or improving any building or equipment, to be used in farming operations conducted by the applicant, may be approved by the Administrator of Veterans' Affairs. . . .

Purchase of Business Property.   Sec. 503. Any application made under this title for the guaranty of a loan to be used in purchasing any business, land, buildings, supplies, equipment, machinery, or tools, to be used by the applicant in pursuing a gainful occupation (other than farming) may be approved by the Administrator of Veterans' Affairs. . . .

Title IV—Employment of Veterans

Sec. 600. (a) In the enactment of the provisions of this title Congress declares as its intent and purpose that there shall be an effective job counseling and employment placement service for veterans and that, to this end, policies shall be promulgated and administered, so as to provide for them the maximum of job opportunity in the field of gainful employment. For the purpose there is hereby created to cooperate with and assist the United States Employment Service, as established by the provisions of the Act of June 6, 1933, a Veterans' Placement Service Board.

2. A Young American Is "Born on the Fourth of July," 1946

For me it began in 1946 when I was born on the Fourth of July. The whole sky lit up in a tremendous fireworks display and my mother told me the doctor said I was a real firecracker. Every birthday after that was something the whole country celebrated. It was a proud day to be born on. . . .

The whole block grew up watching television. There was Howdy Doody and Rootie Kazootie, Cisco Kid and Gabby Hayes, Roy Rogers and Dale Evans. The Lone Ranger was on Channel 7. We watched cartoons for hours on Saturdays—Beanie and Cecil, Crusader Rabbit, Woody Woodpecker—and a show with puppets called Kukla, Fran, and Ollie. I sat on the rug in the living room watching Captain Video take off in his spaceship and saw thousands of savages killed by Ramar of the Jungle.

I remember Elvis Presley on the Ed Sullivan Show and my sister Sue going crazy in the living room jumping up and down. He kept twanging this big guitar and wiggling his hips, but for some reason they were mostly showing just the top of him. My mother was sitting on the couch with her hands folded in her lap like she was praying, and my dad was in the other room talking about how the Church had advised us all that Sunday that watching Elvis Presley could lead to sin.

I loved God more than anything else in the world back then and I prayed to Him and the Virgin Mary and Jesus and all the saints to be a good boy and a good American. Every night before I went to sleep I knelt down in front of my bed, making the sign of the cross and cupping my hands over my face, sometimes praying so hard I would cry. I asked every night to be good enough to make the major leagues someday. With God anything was possible. I made my first Holy Communion with a cowboy hat on my head and two six-shooters in my hands. . . .

Every Saturday afternoon we'd all go down to the movies in the shopping center and watch gigantic prehistoric birds breathe fire, and war movies with John Wayne

Excerpt from R. Kovic, *Born on the Fourth of July.* © 1976, 2005 by Ron Kovic. Used by permission of Akashic Books.

and Audie Murphy. Bobbie's mother always packed us a bagful of candy. I'll never forget Audie Murphy in *To Hell and Back*. At the end he jumps on top of a flaming tank that's just about to explode and grabs the machine gun blasting it into the German lines. He was so brave I had chills running up and down my back, wishing it were me up there. There were gasoline flames roaring around his legs, but he just kept firing that machine gun. It was the greatest movie I ever saw in my life.

[My best friend Richie] Castiglia and I saw *The Sands of Iwo Jima* together. The Marine Corps hymn was playing in the background as we sat glued to our seats, humming the hymn together and watching Sergeant Stryker, played by John Wayne, charge up the hill and get killed just before he reached the top. And then they showed the men raising the flag on Iwo Jima with the marines' hymn still playing, and Castiglia and I cried in our seats. . . .

We'd go home and make up movies like the ones we'd just seen or the ones that were on TV night after night. We'd use our Christmas toys—the Matty Mattel machine guns and grenades, the little green plastic soldiers with guns and flamethrowers in their hands. My favorites were the green plastic men with bazookas. They blasted holes through the enemy. They wiped them out at thirty feet just above the coffee table. They dug in on the front lawn and survived countless artillery attacks. . . .

The Communists were all over the place back then. And if they weren't trying to beat us into outer space, Castiglia and I were certain they were infiltrating our schools, trying to take over our classes and control our minds. We were both certain that one of our teachers was a secret Communist agent and in our next secret club meeting we promised to report anything new he said during our next history class. We watched him very carefully that year. One afternoon he told us that China was going to have a billion people someday. "One billion!" he said, tightly clenching his fist. "Do you know what that means?" he said, staring out the classroom window. "Do you know what that's going to mean?" he said in almost a whisper. He never finished what he was saying and after that Castiglia and I were convinced he was definitely a Communist.

About that time I started doing push-ups in my room and squeezing rubber balls until my arms began to ache, trying to make my body stronger and stronger. . . .

I wanted to be a hero.

3. *Science News Letter* Reports a Baby Boom, 1954

The trend toward larger families among married college graduates is still continuing, the Population Reference Bureau reports.

For the last eight years, since 1946, the number of babies per graduate has been going up. The increase is greater for men graduates than for women.

"There is even a possibility," says a report in the Population Bulletin, "that members of the class of 1944 will replace themselves in the new generation." Statisticians figure that each graduate must have an average of 2.1 children to be sure that one will live to grow up, marry and have children to carry on the chain unbroken.

"Baby Boom Continues Among College Grads," *Science News Letter,* June 19, 1954. Reprinted with permission of *Science News,* the weekly magazine of science, copyright 1954.

The low was reached by men graduates in the class of 1922 with 1.70 children per graduate; by women in the class of 1926 with 1.18.

For many years in the United States the tendency among white women of child-bearing age has been for those with the most education to have the fewest children. The figure in 1940 was 1.23 for college graduates as compared with 4.33 for women who had not gone beyond fourth grade.

The institution leading in number of children per graduate, for men of both the class 1944 and the class 1929 and women for the class 1929, is Brigham Young University in Utah. But this university is outdistanced by the 1944 women graduates of St. Mary's College in Indiana.

The increasing fertility of recent college graduates is attributed to an improvement in economic conditions and to changing attitudes toward marriage. In the 20's and early 30's, marriage and birth rates were both low. People were marrying later in life.

Now that it is easier for young couples to set up their home and start families, they are marrying younger. Births are not deferred as often nor as long as they were 15 years ago.

4. Parental Indulgence Is Criticized in *Rebel Without a Cause,* 1955

[MOTHER, FATHER *and* GRANDMA *are framed in entrance, frozen. They are all well dressed in party clothes.* MOTHER *is a very chic but rather hard-faced woman.* FATHER *is a man always unsure of himself.* GRANDMA *is the smallest, also very chic and very bright-eyed.* RAY *has paused by upstage side of desk again.*]

JIM [*facing them*]. Happy Easter.

MOTHER [*as she,* FATHER, *and* GRANDMA *move toward him*].Where were you tonight? They called us at the club, and I got the fright of my life! [*Silence.*]

FATHER. Where were you tonight, Jimbo? [JIM *says nothing.* FATHER *laughs uncomfortably.*]

JIM [*nodding toward* RAY (a juvenile officer)]. Ask him.

FATHER [*to* RAY]. Was he drinking? I don't see what's so bad about taking a little drink.

RAY. You don't?

FATHER. No. I definitely don't. I did the sa——

RAY. He's a minor, Mr. Stark, and he hasn't been drinking. He was picked up on suspicion at the scene of a stomping.

FATHER. A what?

RAY. A gang of teen-agers beat up a man. . . .

FATHER. But Jim hasn't done anything. You said so.

RAY. That's right.

FATHER. After all, a little drink isn't much. I cut pretty loose in my day, too.

MOTHER. [*needling him*]. Really, Frank? When was that?

FATHER [*blowing up*]. Listen, *can't you wait till we get home?*

RAY [*holding up his hand*]. Whoa! Whoa! I know you're a little upset, but——

FATHER. Sorry.

RAY. What about you, Jim? Got anything to say for yourself? [JIM *stops humming and shrugs.*] Not interested, huh? [JIM *shakes his head.*]

MOTHER. Can't you answer? What's the matter with you?

FATHER. He's in one of his moods.

MOTHER [*to* FATHER]. I was talking to *Jim.*

FATHER. [*crossing to* RAY]. Let me explain. We just moved here, y'understand? The kid has no friends yet and——

JIM. Tell him why we moved here.

FATHER. Hold it, Jim.

JIM. You can't protect me.

FATHER. [*to* JIM]. You mind if I *try?* You have to slam the door in my face? [*To* RAY.] I try to get to him. What happens? [*To* JIM.] Don't I give you everything you want? A bicycle—you get a bicycle. A car——

JIM. You buy me many things. [*A little mock bow.*] Thank you.

FATHER. Not just buy! You hear all this talk about not loving your kids enough. We give you love and affection, don't we? [*Silence.* JIM *is fighting his emotion.*] Then what is it? I can't even touch you any more but you pull away. I want to understand you. You must have reasons. [JIM *stares straight ahead, trying not to listen.*] Was it because we went to that party? [*Silence.*] You know what kind of drunken brawls those parties turn into. It's no place for kids.

MOTHER. A minute ago you said you didn't care if *he* drinks.

GRANDMA. He said a *little* drink.

JIM [*exploding*]. Let me alone! [*Moves down right in* L *area.*]

MOTHER. What?

JIM. Stop tearing me apart! You say one thing, and he says another, and then everybody changes back——

MOTHER. That's a fine way to talk!

GRANDMA [*smiling*]. Well, you know whom he takes after! . . .

[MOTHER, JIM, FATHER, *and* GRANDMA *go out* D L, RAY *looking after them.* RAY *lights a cigarette and shakes his head as he stands in front of desk.*]

OFFICER. What a way to raise a kid.

RAY. How do you mean that?

OFFICER. Give him everything he wants and nothing he needs.

RAY. What does he need?

OFFICER. It's too late now, but instead of throwing bikes and cars at him, a strap on the behind when he got uppity would've saved them a lot of grief.

RAY. You figure he'll be back?

OFFICER. Hell, yes! He's got modern parents.

5. Governor Adlai Stevenson Tells College Women About Their Place in Life, 1955

I think there is much you can do about our crisis in the humble role of housewife.

The peoples of the West are still struggling with the problems of a free society and just now are in dire trouble. For to create a free society is at all times a precarious and audacious experiment. Its bedrock is the concept of man as an end in himself. But violent pressures are constantly battering away at this concept, reducing man once again to subordinate status, limiting his range of choice, abrogating his responsibility and returning him to his primitive status of anonymity in the social group. I think you can be more helpful in identifying, isolating and combatting these pressures, this virus, than you perhaps realize.

Let me put it this way: individualism has promoted technological advance, technology promoted increased specialization, and specialization promoted an ever closer economic interdependence between specialties. . . .

Thus this typical Western man, or typical Western husband, operates well in the realm of means, as the Romans did before him. But outside his specialty, in the realm of ends, he is apt to operate poorly or not at all. And this neglect of the cultivation of more mature values can only mean that his life, and the life of the society he determines, will lack valid purpose, however busy and even profitable it may be.

And here's where you come in: to restore valid, meaningful purpose to life in your home; to beware of instinctive group reaction to the forces which play upon you and yours, to watch for and arrest the constant gravitational pulls to which we are all exposed—your workaday husband especially—in our specialized, fragmented society, that tend to widen the breach between reason and emotion, between means and ends. . . .

Women, especially educated women, have a unique opportunity to influence us, man and boy, and to play a direct part in the unfolding drama of our free society. But I am told that nowadays the young wife or mother is short of time for such subtle arts, that things are not what they used to be; that once immersed in the very pressing and particular problems of domesticity, many women feel frustrated and far apart from the great issues and stirring debates for which their education has given them understanding and relish. Once they read Baudelaire. Now it is the Consumer's Guide. Once they wrote poetry. Now it's the laundry list. Once they discussed art and philosophy until late in the night. Now they are so tired they fall asleep as soon as the dishes are finished. There is, often, a sense of contraction, of closing horizons and lost opportunities. They had hoped to play their part in the crisis of the age. . . .

The point is that whether we talk of Africa, Islam or Asia, women "never had it so good" as you do. And in spite of the difficulties of domesticity, you have a way to participate actively in the crisis in addition to keeping yourself and those about you straight on the difference between means and ends, mind and spirit, reason and emotion—not to mention keeping your man straight on the differences between Botticelli and Chianti.

Adlai Stevenson, "A Purpose for Modern Woman," excerpted from Commencement Address, Smith College, 1955, in *Women's Home Companion* (September 1955).

6. Author Paul Goodman Describes Growing Up Absurd, 1956

In every day's newspaper there are stories about the two subjects that I have brought together in this book, the disgrace of the Organized System of semimonopolies, government, advertisers, etc., and the disaffection of the growing generation. Both are newsworthily scandalous, and for several years now both kinds of stories have come thicker and faster. It is strange that the obvious connections between them are not played up in the newspapers; nor, in the rush of books on the follies, venality, and stifling conformity of the Organization, has there been a book on Youth Problems in the Organized System.

Those of the disaffected youth who are articulate, however—for instance, the Beat or Angry young men—are quite clear about the connection: their main topic is the "system" with which they refuse to co-operate. They will explain that the "good" jobs are frauds and sells, that it is intolerable to have one's style of life dictated by Personnel, that a man is a fool to work to pay installments on a useless refrigerator for his wife, that the movies, TV, and Book-of-the-Month Club are beneath contempt, but the Luce publications make you sick to the stomach; and they will describe with accuracy the cynicism and one-upping of the "typical" junior executive. They consider it the part of reason and honor to wash their hands of all of it.

Naturally, grown-up citizens are concerned about the beatniks and delinquents. The school system has been subjected to criticism. And there is a lot of official talk about the need to conserve our human resources lest Russia get ahead of us. The question is why the grownups do not, more soberly, draw the same connections as the youth. Or, since no doubt many people *are* quite clear about the connection that the structure of society that has become increasingly dominant in our country is disastrous to the growth of excellence and manliness, why don't more people speak up and say so, and initiate a change? . . .

This brings me to another proposition about growing up, and perhaps the main theme of this book. *Growth, like any ongoing function, requires adequate objects in the environment* to meet the needs and capacities of the growing child, boy, youth, and young man, until he can better choose and make his own environment. It is not a "psychological" question of poor influences and bad attitudes, but an objective question of real opportunities for worth-while experience. . . .

(I say the "young men and boys" rather than the "young people" because the problems I want to discuss in this book belong primarily, in our society, to the boys: how to be useful and make something of oneself. A girl does not *have* to, she is not expected to, "make something" of herself. Her career does not have to be self-justifying, for she will have children, which is absolutely self-justifying, like any other natural or creative act. With this background, it is less important, for instance, what job an average young woman works at till she is married.) . . .

. . . In our society, bright lively children, with the potentiality for knowledge, noble ideals, honest effort, and some kind of worth-while achievement, are transformed into useless and cynical bipeds, or decent young men trapped or early resigned, whether in or out of the organized system. My purpose is a simple one: to show how it is desperately hard these days for an average child to grow up to be a man, for our present organized system of society does not want men. They are not safe. They do not suit.

7. *Life* Magazine Identifies the New Teen-age Market, 1959

To some people the vision of a leggy adolescent happily squealing over the latest fancy present from Daddy is just another example of the way teen-agers are spoiled to death these days. But to a growing number of businessmen the picture spells out the profitable fact that the American teen-agers have emerged as a big-time consumer in the U.S. economy. They are multiplying in numbers. They spend more and have more spent on them. And they have minds of their own about what they want.

The time is past when a boy's chief possession was his bike and a girl's party wardrobe consisted of a fancy dress worn with a string of dime-store pearls. What Depression-bred parents may still think of as luxuries are looked on as necessities by their offspring. Today teen-agers surround themselves with a fantastic array of garish and often expensive baubles and amusements. They own 10 million phonographs, over a million TV sets, 13 million cameras. Nobody knows how much parents spend on them for actual necessities nor to what extent teen-agers act as hidden persuaders on their parents' other buying habits. Counting only what is spent to satisfy their special teen-age demands, the youngsters and their parents will shell out about $10 billion this year, a billion more than the total sales of GM. . . .

8. Feminist Betty Friedan Describes the Problem That Has No Name, 1959

The problem lay buried, unspoken, for many years in the minds of American women. It was a strange stirring, a sense of dissatisfaction, a yearning that women suffered in the middle of the twentieth century in the United States. Each suburban wife struggled with it alone. As she made the beds, shopped for groceries, matched slip-cover material, ate peanut butter sandwiches with her children, chauffeured Cub Scouts and Brownies, lay beside her husband at night—she was afraid to ask even of herself the silent question—"Is this all?"

For over fifteen years there was no word of this yearning in the millions of words written about women, for women, in all the columns, books and articles by experts telling women their role was to seek fulfillment as wives and mothers. Over and over women heard in voices of tradition and of Freudian sophistication that they

"A Young $10 Billion Power: The US Teen-age Consumer Has Become a Major Factor in the Nation's Economy," *Life* (August 31, 1959), 78–84. Copyright © 1959 Time Inc. Reprinted with permission.

Betty Friedan, *The Feminine Mystique* (New York: Norton, 1963), 15–17, 19–20. Copyright © 1983, 1974, 1973, 1963 by Betty Friedan. Used by permission of W. W. Norton & Company, Inc.

could desire no greater destiny than to glory in their own femininity. Experts told them how to catch a man and keep him, how to breastfeed children and handle their toilet training, how to cope with sibling rivalry and adolescent rebellion; how to buy a dishwasher, bake bread, cook gourmet snails, and build a swimming pool with their own hands; how to dress, look, and act more feminine and make marriage more exciting; how to keep their husbands from dying young and their sons from growing into delinquents. They were taught to pity the neurotic, unfeminine, unhappy women who wanted to be poets or physicists or presidents. They learned that truly feminine women do not want careers, higher education, political rights—the independence and the opportunities that the old-fashioned feminists fought for. Some women, in their forties and fifties, still remembered painfully giving up those dreams, but most of the younger women no longer even thought about them. A thousand expert voices applauded their femininity, their adjustment, their new maturity. All they had to do was devote their lives from earliest girlhood to finding a husband and bearing children.

By the end of the nineteen-fifties, the average marriage age of women in America dropped to 20, and was still dropping, into the teens. Fourteen million girls were engaged by 17. The proportion of women attending college in comparison with men dropped from 47 per cent in 1920 to 35 per cent in 1958. A century earlier, women had fought for higher education; now girls went to college to get a husband. By the mid-fifties, 60 per cent dropped out of college to marry, or because they were afraid too much education would be a marriage bar. Colleges built dormitories for "married students," but the students were almost always husbands. A new degree was instituted for the wives—"Ph.T." (Putting Husband Through). . . .

If a woman had a problem in the 1950's and 1960's, she knew that something must be wrong with her marriage, or with herself. Other women were satisfied with their lives, she thought. What kind of a woman was she if she did not feel this mysterious fulfillment waxing the kitchen floor? She was so ashamed to admit her dissatisfaction that she never knew how many other women shared it. If she tried to tell her husband, he didn't understand what she was talking about. She did not really understand it herself. For over fifteen years women in America found it harder to talk about this problem than about sex. Even the psychoanalysts had no name for it. . . .

But on an April morning in 1959, I heard a mother of four, having coffee with four other mothers in a suburban development fifteen miles from New York, say in a tone of quiet desperation, "the problem." And the others knew, without words, that she was not talking about a problem with her husband, or her children, or her home. Suddenly they realized they all shared the same problem, the problem that has no name. They began, hesitantly, to talk about it. Later, after they had picked up their children at nursery school and taken them home to nap, two of the women cried, in sheer relief, just to know they were not alone.

9. *New Yorker* Cartoon, 1963

"You're stupid. I like that in a woman."

E S S A Y S

Was America at its best in the fifties, or is that an illusion created by hindsight? In the first reading, John Patrick Diggins of the University of California, Irvine, charts social and economic change in the fifties. He characterizes the era as one of bountiful lifestyles, traditional values, and remarkable stability for families. Diggins further argues that the fifties were not an aberration, but represent "the steady norm of America's political temper." Stephanie Coontz, a professor at Evergreen State College, articulates almost the reverse argument: the fifties remade the nuclear family, trapped men and women in roles they came to loathe, and created a stereotype of the "perfect fifties family" that clouds political debate to the present. This stereotype, she insists, is "the way we never were."

A Decade to Make One Proud

JOHN PATRICK DIGGINS

Although McCarthyism, the cold war, Korea and politics dominated front pages in the fifties, opinion polls profiled the American people as preoccupied with their own lives and largely nonpolitical. To most white, middle-class Americans the fifties meant television; bobby sox and the bunny hop; bermuda shorts and gray flannel suits; "I Love Lucy"; Marlon Brando astride a motorcycle and Elvis belting out "Hound Dog"; Lolita the nymphet; crew cut and duck's ass hairstyles; Marilyn Monroe; James Dean; cruising and panty raids; preppies and their cashmeres and two-toned saddle shoes; Willie Mays; Rocky Graziano; drive-in movies and restaurants; diners with chrome-leg tables and backless stools; suburbia; barbecued steaks; Billy Graham and the way to God without sacrifice; the Kinsey Report and the way to sex without sin. Few items in this list would strike one as serious, but many of them have proved durable. Indeed, such subjects fascinate even members of the post-fifties generation. In the seventies and eighties mass magazines like *Newsweek* and *Life* devoted special issues to the fifties as "The Good Old Days" and Hollywood produced *The Last Picture Show, American Graffiti,* and *The Way We Were.* Nostalgia even succeeded in trivializing the Korean War, as with the immensely popular "M*A*S*H."

Nostalgia is one way to ease the pain of the present. Those who survived the sixties, a decade that witnessed the turmoils of the Vietnam War and the tragedies of political assassination, looked back wistfully on the fifties as a period of peace and prosperity. Many of those who survived the fifties, however, particularly writers and professors, passed a different verdict. "Good-by to the fifties—and good riddance," wrote the historian Eric Goldman, "the dullest and dreariest in all our history." "The Eisenhower years," judged columnist William Shannon, "have been years of flabbiness and self-satisfaction and gross materialism. . . . The loudest sound in the land has been the oink-and-grunt of private hoggishness. . . . It has been the age of the slob." The socialist Michael Harrington called the decade "a moral disaster, an amusing waste of time," and the novelist Norman Mailer derided it as "one of the worst decades in the history of man." The poet Robert Lowell summed up his impatience in two lines: "These are the tranquil Fifties, and I am forty./Ought I to regret my seedtime?"

On the other side of the political spectrum, conservative writers tended to praise the fifties as "the happiest, most stable, most rational period the western world has ever known since 1914." They point to the seemingly pleasant fact that in the fifties, in contrast to the sixties, many nations like India and Burma achieved independence without resorting to armed force. The same era enjoyed a postwar prosperity and overcame a massive unemployment that had haunted the depression generation, and did it without raising inflation. Yet even conservatives conceded that the fifties were not a "creative time" in the realm of high culture. This was all right for

Reprinted from *The Proud Decades, America in War and Peace, 1941–1960,* by John Patrick Diggins, 177–178, 194–199, 204–207, 219, 348–350. Copyright © 1988 by John Patrick Diggins. Used by permission of W. W. Norton & Company, Inc.

many of them since "creative periods have too often a way of coinciding with periods of death and destruction."

Whatever the retrospective of writers and intellectuals, those who lived through the fifties looked upon them as a period of unbounded possibility. This was especially true of the beginning of the decade when the lure and novelty of material comforts seemed irresistible. Toward the end of the decade a barely noticeable undercurrent of dissatisfaction emerged and by the early sixties a minority of women and men would rebel against the conditions of the fifties and wonder what had gone wrong with their lives. A sweet decade for the many, it became a sour experience for the few who would go on to question not only the feminine mystique but the masculine as well. In dealing with the fifties one must deal with its contented and its discontents. . . .

The economic context is crucial. Between 1950 and 1958, the economy expanded enormously. A steady high growth rate of 4.7 percent heralded remarkable increases in living standards and other conditions of life. This prosperity derived from a combination of factors: (a) the lingering postwar back-up demand for consumer goods together with increased purchasing power as a result of savings; (b) the expansion of plant and machine tool capacity, and other technological advances left by the war and revived by the cold war and Korean conflict; (c) the appearance of new and modernized industries ranging from electronics to plastics; (d) population growth and the expansion of large cities; (e) increases in the productivity, or output per man-hour, of the working force; and (f) the commitment to foreign aid, which made possible overseas credits and American exports.

America experienced three mild recessions in the fifties, but through them all the rate of personal income grew and reached a record high of a 3.9 percent rise in 1960. If few became rich, the great majority lived more comfortably than ever before and enjoyed shorter hours on the job, as America moved to the five-day work week. Prior to the Second World War only 25 percent of the farming population had electricity. By the end of the fifties more than 80 percent had not only lighting but telephones, refrigerators, and televisions.

The generation that had borne the depression and the war was now eager to put politics behind and move into a bountiful new world. One strong indicator of confidence in the future was a sudden baby boom. Demographers had been predicting a postwar relative decline in fertility rates and no expansion of immigration quotas. Instead, population leaped from 130 million in 1940 to 165 million by the mid-fifties, the biggest increase in the history of the Republic. Population migrated as well as grew, spreading into the region that came to be called "the sun belt," states like Florida, Texas, Arizona, and California. Farms and small towns lost population. Many big cities, while still growing with lower-class and minority inhabitants, witnessed the flight of the middle class to the periphery. The massive phenomenon of suburbia would rip apart and remake the texture of social life in America.

Suburbia met a need and fulfilled a dream. During the depression and the war most Americans lived in apartments, flats, or small houses within an inner city. After the war, with GIs returning and the marriage rate doubling, as many as two million young couples had to share a dwelling with their relatives. Some settled for a cot in the living room, while married college students often had to live in off-campus quonset huts. Their immediate need for space in which to raise a family was answered by the almost overnight appearance of tracts, subdivisions, and other developments that sprawled across the landscape. Ironically, while suburban growth cut into the natural environment, felling trees and turning fields into asphalt streets, the emotional appeal of suburbia lay in a desire to recapture the greenness and calm of rural life. Thus eastern tracts featured such names as "Crystal Stream," "Robin Meadows," and "Stonybrook," while in the West the Spanish motif of "Villa Serena" and "Tierra Vista" conveyed the ambience of old, preindustrial California. In California the tracts were developed by Henry J. Kaiser and Henry Doelger, who drew on their war-time skills for mass production to provide ranch-style homes complete with backyards and front lawns. In the Northeast William Levitt offered New Yorkers and Pennsylvanians houses with shuttered windows and steep pitched roofs to mimic the cozy Cape Cod look. Levitt had never liked cities. Having no patience with people who did, he saw his opportunity after the war when the government agreed to guarantee to banks the entire amount of a veteran's mortgage, making it possible for him to move in with no down payment, depending on the Veteran Administration's assessment of the value of the specific property. To keep building costs down, Levitt transformed the housing industry by using prefabricated walls and frames assembled on the site. In an effort to foster community spirit, he and other builders added schools, swimming pools, tennis courts, and athletic fields with Little League diamonds. For young members of the aspiring middle class, suburbia was a paradise of comfort and convenience.

Others were not so sure. "Is this the American dream, or is it a nightmare?" asked *House Beautiful.* Architectural and cultural critics complained of the monotony of house after house with the same façade, paint, and lawn inhabited by people willing to sign an agreement to keep them the same. One song writer would call them "little boxes made of ticky-tacky." Some children who grew up in them would agree, rebelling in the following decade against all that was sterile and standardized. The most angry critic was the cultural historian Lewis Mumford, author of *The City in History.* Mumford feared that Levitt was doing more to destroy the modern city than did the World War II aerial bombings. He also feared that suburbia was transforming the American character, rendering it dreary and conformist when it should be daring and courageous. "In the mass movement into suburban areas a new kind of community was produced, which caricatured both the historic city and the archetypal suburban refuge, a multitude of uniform, unidentifiable houses, lined up inflexibly at uniform distances, on uniform roads, in a treeless communal waste, inhabited by people in the same class, the same income, the same age group, witnessing the same television performances, eating the same tasteless pre-fabricated foods from the same freezers, conforming in every outward and inward respect to a common mold."

Admonishments aside, Americans were falling in love with suburbia—at least at first; some would have second thoughts and later wonder what they had bought, the theme of the cheerless film *No Down Payment* (1957). By the end of the fifties one-fourth of the population had moved to such areas. If not beautiful, suburbia was affordable, and thousands of homeless veterans were grateful to have their place in the sun for $65 per month on a full purchase price of $6,990 that included separate bedrooms for the children and a kitchen full of glittering gadgets. Such amenities also enabled housewives to be free of some domestic chores as they became involved in community affairs while their husbands commuted to work in the cities. A frequent event was the Tupperware party, arranged by wives ostensibly to sell household conveniences but also to overcome isolation and boredom. The most serious drawback of suburbia was that its planners envisaged no need for public transportation. As a result, suburbanites became forever dependent upon the automobile. When their children reached driving age, some households became three- or even four-car families. But in the fifties, when gasoline was relatively cheap and the promising new freeways wide and uncongested, the car was seen as a solution, not a problem. Indeed, for proud teenagers it was the supreme status symbol, the one possession that with its "souped-up" carburetors and lowered chassis and various metallic colors, answered the need for freedom and diversity in a community of flatness and conformity.

In the fifties, car was king. Freeways, multilevel parking lots, shopping centers, motels, and drive-in restaurants and theaters all catered to the person behind the wheel. By 1956 an estimated seventy-five million cars and trucks were on American roads. One out of every seven workers held a job connected to the automobile industry. In suburbia the station wagon became a common sight. But really to fulfill the American dream one needed a Cadillac, or so advertisers informed the arriviste of new wealth with such effectiveness that one had to wait a year for delivery. Almost all American automobiles grew longer and wider. Their supersize and horsepower, together with more chrome and bigger tailfins, served no useful transportation purpose but were powerful enhancers of self-esteem. At the end of the decade, when many rich Texans, some country-western singers, salesmen, and even gangsters and pimps owned a Cadillac, it became what it always was, gauche, and its image declined from the sublime to the ridiculous.

In the fifties the spectacle of waste, once regarded by the older morality as a sign of sin, had become a sign of status. It was no coincidence that Americans junked almost as many cars as Detroit manufactured, thereby fulfilling Thorstein Veblen's earlier prediction that modern man would be more interested in displaying and destroying goods than in producing them. Veblen's insight into "conspicuous consumption" also took on real meaning in this era as Americans rushed out to buy the latest novelty, whether it was a convertible, TV set, deep-freeze, electric carving knife, or the "New Look" Christian Dior evening dress. The postwar splurge of consumption had been made possible by the $100 billion of savings Americans had banked during the war. Immediately after the war, household appliances were in demand, then luxuries like fashionable clothes and imported wines. For those who bought homes for $8,000 or more, luxuries were seen as necessities. The middle-class suburbanite looked out his window and "needed" what his neighbor had—a white Corvette or a swimming pool. Travel to Europe, once regarded as the "Grand Tour" only for the rich and famous, became accessible to millions of Americans in the fifties. For the masses who remained at home and took to the road, new tourist attractions sprang up, like Disneyland. Mass recreational mobility changed the nation's eating habits. In 1954 in San Bernardino, California, Ray Kroc, a high-school dropout, devised a precision stand for turning out French fries, beverages, and fifteen-cent hamburgers that grew rapidly into a fast-food empire: McDonald's.

Spending less time cooking and eating, Americans had more time for shopping. Discount houses such as Korvette's and Grant's opened up for the lower-middle class while the prestigious Neiman-Marcus catered to the needs of oil-rich Texans. Parents raised in the depression naturally felt that more was better, not only for themselves but particularly for their children. Teenagers splurged on phonograph records, bedroom decorations, cashmere sweaters, trips to Hawaii, motor scooters, and hot rods. The seemingly infinite indulgence of the young worried many parents even as they contributed to it. In a survey 94 percent of the mothers interviewed reported that their children had asked them to buy various goods they had seen on television.

Television in America, unlike in England and much of Western Europe, was supported by the advertising industry, which did more than any other institution to fill the viewer's eyes with images of abundance. Advertisers spent $10 billion a year to persuade, not to say manipulate, the people into buying products that promised to improve their lives, whether frozen peas or French perfume. Professional football, the prime target for beer ads, invented the "two-minute warning" in the last quarter to accommodate commercials. Confronted by a medical report linking smoking to lung cancer, tobacco companies increased their ad campaigns with jingles like "Be Happy Go Lucky!" Television bloomed with romantic scenes of a dashing young man offering a cigarette to a seductively beautiful woman under a full moon. As violins rose, the match was lit, and her face turned into that of a goddess—young, eager, divine. Partial takeoffs from the Bogart-Bacall films of the early forties, Madison Avenue could readily exploit such scenes, perhaps realizing that desire can always be tempted precisely because it can never be completely fulfilled.

What facilitated the illusion of fulfillment was a little rectangle of plastic dubbed the credit card. In 1950 Diner's Club distributed credit cards to select wealthy New Yorkers to give them the privilege of eating at swank restaurants without fumbling for money. By the end of the decade Sears Roebuck alone had more than ten million accounts for those who chose to live on credit or, more bluntly, to be in debt. Installment buying shot consumer indebtedness up to $196 billion, so high that certain department stores offered "debt counselors" for worried customers. One soothing nostrum was a good stiff martini, the favorite drink of suburbia and the commuters' circle. Drinking rose sharply in the fifties. So did prescription-drugs use. Sales of "tranquilizers" soared; by 1959, 1,159,000 pounds had been consumed. The following decade the Food and Drug Administration discovered that the once-popular pill "miltown" had no medicinal value. But for the fifties generation, coping with the boss's demands at work and the children's at home, popping tranquilizing drugs became a respectable adult addiction. That mental anxiety should accompany material abundance is no surprise. For centuries moralists had warned that people become unhappy when they get what they want—or think they want. Suburbia offered Americans the cleanliness and safety of a planned community, but nothing is more hopeless than planned happiness. . . .

During the forties and fifties music became widely accessible to the masses of people. Elaborate hi-fi sets replaced the simple victrola and the jukebox lifted the spirits of the lonely, the tense, and the bored. Light operas like "Oklahoma," "South Pacific," and "My Fair Lady" played to packed theaters, and Americans listened to Mary Martin and Ethel Merman belt out popular songs.

One of the most curious shifts in popular musical tastes that separated the forties and the fifties involved the careers of Frank Sinatra and Elvis Presley. During World War II Sinatra suddenly became the idol of hordes of bobby soxers who were mysteriously mesmerized by his crooning serenades, some shrieking and swooning, others fainting or possibly pretending to. . . . Yet the hysteria ended almost as suddenly as it began, and by the early fifties Sinatra could not land even a Hollywood film contract. Then another singer captured the youth's imagination and another mode of music determined the nation's sound and rhythm for years to come—Elvis and rock 'n' roll.

. . . Unlike Sinatra, who appeared so emaciated as to be starving, Presley exuded raw strength and sensuality. Parents brought up on the mawkish music of Bing Crosby tried in vain to shield their children from contamination by the new phenomenon sweeping the country. They were aghast watching "Elvis the Pelvis" with his tight pants, full, pouting lips, and shoulder-length black hair, grip the microphone and buck his hips in gestures so lewd that some TV producers would only film him from the waist up. Magnetic but aloof, self-possessed yet sad, Presley stood before screaming crowds as the icon of the fifties, charging teenagers with energy and emotion in scores like "I Want You, I Need You, I Love You," "Don't Be Cruel," and "Love Me Tender."

Commentators in the fifties often compared Presley to Marlon Brando, James Dean, and Montgomery Clift, three new film stars who revolutionized acting methods and left audiences emotionally drained and confused. . . . All were actors who conveyed complex emotions more felt than understood in an attempt to express what could not be voiced. In *On the Waterfront, East of Eden,* and *From Here to Eternity,* Brando, Dean, and Clift displayed a sensitivity and depth of pure feeling that rendered them almost defenseless against the world. Indeed the film *Rebel Without a Cause* is haunted by tragedy. All of its four stars—Dean, Natalie Wood, Sal Mineo, and Vic Morrow—would suffer tragic deaths.

To the fifties generation, James Dean communicated the emotions of a crippled romantic, a moody idealist whose dreams about the world have already been destroyed by his resentment toward it. "My mother died on me when I was nine years old," he complained of his broken home. "What does she expect me to do? Do it all myself?" Raised in Indiana by a father and step-mother, Dean had little interest in school except for basketball, track, and dramatics. After dropping out of college in California, he held a string of odd jobs before heading for New York and acting school. There he was discovered and immediately compared to Brando in *The Wild One:* the same wandering, lonely eyes, the scornful lip, the inarticulate mumblings, and the controlled rage that made being "cool" the strategy of survival. . . . Dean also played the restless, searching youth, hungering for innocence, knowing too much about the compromises and complacencies of the world. Thus in films he appeared both wiser and sadder than the older characters. Yet he would make no reconciliation with reality. To do so was to adjust and settle down, precisely what society demanded of the fifties generation. "Whoso would be a man," wrote Emerson a century earlier, "must be a nonconformist." On September 30, 1955, Dean's speeding white Porsche-Spider collided with another car; the steering wheel went right through him. Lost and lovable, the symbol of troubled youth, James Dean was dead at the age of twenty-four. . . .

"Live fast, die young, and have a good-looking corpse." The lines by the novelist Willard Motley haunted sensitive youths of the fifties generation, many of whom experienced the era with more unease than did their parents. As children they had come to know the horrors of the bomb from the media; in school they were taught "duck-and-cover" exercises in case of attack; at home some of the affluent heard their parents speak of building bomb shelters in the backyards. Teenagers often knew someone who had been killed in an auto accident or drag race. A best-selling novel, Irving Shulman's *The Amboy Dukes,* intended to expose the brutality of urban street gangs; for young males it had the opposite effect of glorifying courage in the face of violence. A similar response could be felt after watching such films as *Rebel Without a Cause, The Wild One,* and *Blackboard Jungle,* where the opening scene thunders with the theme song, "Rock-Around-the-Clock," a shrill of seething rebellion. Asked what he was rebelling against, Brando replied: "What've ya got?" Perhaps the quest for security on the part of the parents drove their children to desire risk and adventure all the more. Boys cruising in hot rods and quaffing six-packs of beer knew they were flirting with danger, as did those girls who risked pregnancy to discover the secret pleasures of the body. Why not? The fifties was the first generation in modern history to know that the world could end tomorrow. . . .

The amount of attention the media devoted to sex in the fifties may be misleading since there is reason to doubt significant changes in behavior actually occurred. Sex was then an emotion more felt than fulfilled. It was also a fantasy, and if fantasies reflect what people desire and not necessarily what they do, desires nonetheless are a large part of the human secrets of life.

During the decade, while teachers and professors were lamenting the decline in educational standards and ministers and priests the decline of morality, teenagers and college students were awakening to something stirring in their own bodies, something at once new, at least to them, and exciting and confusing, a subject more seen and felt than heard and understood. It could be seen in *Playboy,* which started publishing in 1955, exposing more naked angles to the female body than male students could ever imagine, fleshy images that aroused erotic fantasies and made one forget Somerset Maugham's witty warning about sex: the pleasure is momentary, the price damnable, and the position ridiculous. . . .

Their curiosities were met by two postwar publications, *Sexual Behavior in the Human Male* (1948) and *Sexual Behavior in the Human Female* (1953), both by Alfred Kinsey and his colleagues of the Institute for Sexual Research at Indiana University. . . .

Fifty percent of American husbands had committed adultery and 85 percent had sexual intercourse before marriage. Ninety-five percent of males had been sexually active before the age of fifteen and by the ages sixteen and seventeen the activity was at a peak. The average unmarried male had three or four orgasms a week. Nearly 90 percent of men had relationships with prostitutes by their thirty-fifth birthday, and one out of six American farm boys had copulated with farm animals. As to females, two out of three had engaged in premarital petting. Fifty percent were non-virgins before marriage. One out of every six girls had experienced orgasm prior to adolescence, and one in four by the age of fifteen. . . .

No one knew how accurate Kinsey's figures were and no one knew what to make of them. Fearing the worst, a few politicians persuaded the Rockefeller Foundation to withdraw support of Kinsey's Institute for Sexual Research. A double standard prevailed. The male study aroused relatively little objection, but when the female document emerged a few years later some Americans regarded it as a threat to women's virtue. . . . Very acceptable, however, were big breasts, and those who had them—Jayne Mansfield, Jane Russell, Mamie Van Doren, Marilyn Monroe,

Elizabeth Taylor. These desirables covered magazines in poses that defied the laws of geometry.

But even these monuments to photography could mislead by confusing fantasy for reality. Was there a sexual revolution in the fifties? Hardly. . . .

Among the lower classes uninvestigated by Kinsey and perhaps untouched by *Playboy*, sex still had more to do with having a lot of children than having multiple orgasms. Married middle-class adults probably enjoyed more sexual intimacy with their marital partners than their parents or grandparents ever contemplated. . . .

The striking thing about the fifties was not the coming crisis of the modern family but its enduring stability. True, the rising divorce rate alarmed Americans in the immediate postwar years. But it soon leveled off and then decreased so that at the end of the fifties the rate was near that of the forties—1.4 percent versus 2.5 percent. Neither marriage nor the family had been threatened by the Kinsey report. Monogamy may have been strained by the freeing effect of carnal knowledge, but most Americans remained inhibited and feared their sexual feelings as soon as they felt them. "Sex is Fun—or Hell," was how J. D. Salinger put it in one of his short stories. In the words of one memoirist, women in particular vacillated between "titillation and terror." Ultimately most married men and women accepted their situation, for better or for worse. Society said they should, and in the fifties the pressures of society, not the risqué pleasures of the body, dictated the conduct of life. . . .

The mixed messages were only part of the many paradoxes of the fifties. It was an age of stable nuclear families and marital tension, of student conformity on the campus and youth rebellion on the screen and phonograph, of erotic arousal before the visual and sexual hesitancy before the actual, of suburban contentment with lawns and station wagons and middle-class worry about money and status, of high expectations of upward mobility and later some doubts about the meaning and value of the age's own achievements. Members of the fifties generation were unique. They had more education and aspirations. They married younger and produced more babies. They possessed more buying power and enjoyed more material pleasure than any generation of men and women in American history. And it is a measure of the complexity of the fifties that its members could reach no consensus about the meaning of their accomplishments and disappointments. Looking back from the eighties, one male member, a building contractor and multimillionaire, put it this way:

> If you had a college diploma, a dark suit, and anything between the ears, it was like an escalator; you just stood there and you moved up. . . .

The Truman and Eisenhower years gave Americans a sense of pride in themselves and confidence in the future. It is questionable whether either sentiment survived the fifties intact. The America that emerged victorious from World War II was not the same America fifteen years later. The decline of confidence resulted in part from the changing nature of warfare brought by modern technology. After the Second World War Americans could take pride in the performance of their soldiers. With the increasing complexity of the cold war, which offered the possibility of either covert CIA operations or nuclear attack and retaliation, warfare seemed more and more a choice between the dishonorable and the suicidal; and if new inventions in sophisticated missile weaponry would make some Americans feel proud of their technological achievements, it was a pride born of fear.

The cold war itself, however, is not the only explanation for the decline of self-assurance that came to be felt at the end of the Eisenhower years. Equally troubling was the sense of unease and discontent. No one had predicted it. In 1950, for example, *Fortune* published a book with the curious title, *U.S.A., the Permanent Revolution.* The title, taken from Leon Trotsky, was meant to depict a new way of life founded on unlimited prosperity, active citizen participation, winning friends abroad with generous foreign aid and free-trade policies, and proudly accepting the burdens of history as a great world power. America must be understood not as a nation of definite goals but of indefinite growth. "Americans wish that other people could see their country as it really is: not as an achievement but as a *process*—a process of becoming." But can there be growth without conscious direction and meaning? "Why should we assume that America has *any* meaning?" the editors asked. "Rightly understood, the principles that embody the meaning of America are the very forces that have done most to change America."

By 1960, all confidence that America could simply be accepted as a process of continual growth and change came to be questioned and in many instances rejected. "What is wrong with America?" queried the *U.S. News and World Report.* "What shall we do with our greatness?" asked the editors of *Life.* President Eisenhower set up a "Commission on National Goals" and Walter Lippmann analyzed the "Anatomy of Discontent," which he specified as a willingness to fulfill them. The Reverend Billy Graham thought Americans overextended themselves in more concrete ways. "We overeat, overdrink, oversex, and overplay. . . . We have tried to fill ourselves with science and education, with better living and pleasure . . . but we are still empty and bored." Adlai Stevenson doubted that America's "permanent revolution" would have any impact on the rest of the world. "With the supermarket as our temple and the singing commercial as our litany, are we likely to fire the world with an irresistible vision of America's exalted purpose and inspiring way of life?" "Something has gone wrong in America," complained the novelist John Steinbeck of his fellow people. "Having too many things, they spend their hours and money on the couch searching for a soul." Everywhere Americans were engaged in the "great debate" about "the national purpose." Americans have become worried, journalists concluded, because they feel they lack inspiring ideals and because they have been led to believe that they do not need them. "The case of the missing purpose," wrote a philosopher in *The Nation,* "is a case of human beings missing the purpose of life." The proud decades were over.

Or were they? Several months before Eisenhower's farewell and Kennedy's inauguration, things were changing. Within a few years America would be addressing problems it never knew existed and some people would be singing "We Shall Overcome!" Yet even before the sixties ended America would be more divided than ever, the two Kennedys and King dead, and the Republicans back in office. Now it was Nixon who promised to bring Americans "back together again." Henceforth, the period of the fifties, once regarded as a dreadful aberration standing between the more compassionate thirties and activist sixties, would seem more and more the steady norm of America's political temper. The generation of the sixties experienced the previous decade as a burden that had to be radically transformed, and some of its worst aspects were confronted and eradicated. But as the radical sixties petered out, it became all the more clear that the two decades beginning with the Second World War shaped the nation's environment and consciousness in more enduring ways than had once been expected. The forties and perhaps especially the fifties are still living in the present, and the assumptions and values of the two decades have become ingrained in our habits and institutions. "What is the national purpose?" asked Dean Acheson in response to the great debate of the late fifties. "To survive and, perchance, to prosper." In doing both well, America still had good reason to be proud of itself.

Families in the Fifties: The Way We Never Were

STEPHANIE COONTZ

Our most powerful visions of traditional families derive from images that are still delivered to our homes in countless reruns of 1950s television sit-coms. When liberals and conservatives debate family policy, for example, the issue is often framed in terms of how many "Ozzie and Harriet" families are left in America. Liberals compute the percentage of total households that contain a breadwinner father, a full-time homemaker mother, and dependent children, proclaiming that fewer than 10 percent of American families meet the "Ozzie and Harriet" or "Leave It to Beaver" model. Conservatives counter that more than half of all mothers with preschool children either are not employed or are employed only part-time. They cite polls showing that most working mothers would like to spend more time with their children and periodically announce that the Nelsons are "making a comeback," in popular opinion if not in real numbers.

Since everyone admits that nontraditional families are now a majority, why this obsessive concern to establish a higher or a lower figure? Liberals seem to think that unless they can prove the "Leave It to Beaver" family is on an irreversible slide toward extinction, they cannot justify introducing new family definitions and social policies. Conservatives believe that if they can demonstrate the traditional family is alive and well, although endangered by policies that reward two-earner families and single parents, they can pass measures to revive the seeming placidity and prosperity of the 1950s, associated in many people's minds with the relative stability of marriage, gender roles, and family life in that decade. If the 1950s family existed today, both sides seem to assume, we would not have the contemporary social dilemmas that cause such debate.

At first glance, the figures seem to justify this assumption. The 1950s was a pro-family period if there ever was one. Rates of divorce and illegitimacy were half what they are today; marriage was almost universally praised; the family was everywhere hailed as the most basic institution in society; and a massive baby boom, among all classes and ethnic groups, made America a "child-centered" society. Births rose from a low of 18.4 per 1,000 women during the Depression to a high of 25.3 per 1,000 in 1957. "The birth rate for third children doubled between 1940 and 1960, and that for fourth children tripled."

In retrospect, the 1950s also seem a time of innocence and consensus: Gang warfare among youths did not lead to drive-by shootings; the crack epidemic had not

Stephanie Coontz, *The Way We Never Were: American Families and the Nostalgia Trap,* pp. 23–33, 36–41. Copyright © 1997 by Basic Books, a Division of HarperCollins Publishers, Inc. Reprinted by permission of Basic Books, a member of Perseus Books, LLC.

yet hit; discipline problems in the schools were minor; no "secular humanist" movement opposed the 1954 addition of the words *under God* to the Pledge of Allegiance; and 90 percent of all school levies were approved by voters. Introduction of the polio vaccine in 1954 was the most dramatic of many medical advances that improved the quality of life for children.

The profamily features of this decade were bolstered by impressive economic improvements for vast numbers of Americans. Between 1945 and 1960, the gross national product grew by almost 250 percent and per capita income by 35 percent. Housing starts exploded after the war, peaking at 1.65 million in 1955 and remaining above 1.5 million a year for the rest of the decade; the increase in single-family homeownership between 1946 and 1956 outstripped the increase during the entire preceding century and a half. By 1960, 62 percent of American families owned their own homes, in contrast to 43 percent in 1940. Eighty-five percent of the new homes were built in the suburbs, where the nuclear family found new possibilities for privacy and togetherness. While middle-class Americans were the prime beneficiaries of the building boom, substantial numbers of white working-class Americans moved out of the cities into affordable developments, such as Levittown.

Many working-class families also moved into the middle class. The number of salaried workers increased by 61 percent between 1947 and 1957. By the mid-1950s, nearly 60 percent of the population had what was labeled a middle-class income level (between $3,000 and $10,000 in constant dollars), compared to only 31 percent in the "prosperous twenties," before the Great Depression. By 1960, thirty-one million of the nation's forty-four million families owned their own home, 87 percent had a television, and 75 percent possessed a car. The number of people with discretionary income doubled during the 1950s.

For most Americans, the most salient symbol and immediate beneficiary of their newfound prosperity was the nuclear family. The biggest boom in consumer spending, for example, was in household goods. Food spending rose by only 33 percent in the five years following the Second World War, and clothing expenditures rose by 20 percent, but purchases of household furnishings and appliances climbed 240 percent. "Nearly the entire increase in the gross national product in the mid-1950s was due to increased spending on consumer durables and residential construction," most of it oriented toward the nuclear family.

Putting their mouths where their money was, Americans consistently told pollsters that home and family were the wellsprings of their happiness and self-esteem. Cultural historian David Marc argues that prewar fantasies of sophisticated urban "elegance," epitomized by the high-rise penthouse apartment, gave way in the 1950s to a more modest vision of utopia: a single-family house and a car. The emotional dimensions of utopia, however, were unbounded. When respondents to a 1955 marriage study "were asked what they thought they had sacrificed by marrying and raising a family, an overwhelming majority of them replied, 'Nothing.'" Less than 10 percent of Americans believed that an unmarried person could be happy. As one popular advice book intoned: "The family is the center of your living. If it isn't, you've gone far astray."

In fact, the "traditional" family of the 1950s was a qualitatively new phenomenon. At the end of the 1940s, all the trends characterizing the rest of the twentieth century suddenly reversed themselves: For the first time in more than one hundred years, the age for marriage and motherhood fell, fertility increased, divorce rates declined, and women's degree of educational parity with men dropped sharply. In a period of less than ten years, the proportion of never-married persons declined by as much as it had during the entire previous half century.

At the time, most people understood the 1950s family to be a new invention. The Great Depression and the Second World War had reinforced extended family ties, but in ways that were experienced by most people as stultifying and oppressive. As one child of the Depression later put it, "The Waltons" television series of the 1970s did not show what family life in the 1930s was really like: "It wasn't a big family sitting around a table radio and everybody saying goodnight while Bing Crosby crooned 'Pennies from Heaven.'" On top of Depression-era family tensions had come the painful family separations and housing shortages of the war years: By 1947, six million American families were sharing housing, and postwar family counselors warned of a widespread marital crisis caused by conflicts between the generations. A 1948 *March of Time* film, "Marriage and Divorce," declared: "No home is big enough to house two families, particularly two of different generations, with opposite theories on child training."

During the 1950s, films and television plays, such as "Marty," showed people working through conflicts between marital loyalties and older kin, peer group, or community ties; regretfully but decisively, these conflicts were almost invariably "resolved in favor of the heterosexual couple rather than the claims of extended kinship networks, . . . homosociability and friendship." Talcott Parsons and other sociologists argued that modern industrial society required the family to jettison traditional productive functions and wider kin ties in order to specialize in emotional nurturance, childrearing, and production of a modern personality. Social workers "endorsed nuclear family separateness and looked suspiciously on active extended-family networks."

Popular commentators urged young families to adopt a "modern" stance and strike out on their own, and with the return of prosperity, most did. By the early 1950s, newlyweds not only were establishing single-family homes at an earlier age and a more rapid rate than ever before but also were increasingly moving to the suburbs, away from the close scrutiny of the elder generation.

For the first time in American history, moreover, such average trends did not disguise sharp variations by class, race, and ethnic group. People married at a younger age, bore their children earlier and closer together, completed their families by the time they were in their late twenties, and experienced a longer period living together as a couple after their children left home. The traditional range of acceptable family behaviors—even the range in the acceptable number and timing of children—narrowed substantially.

The values of 1950s families also were new. The emphasis on producing a whole world of satisfaction, amusement, and inventiveness within the nuclear family had no precedents. Historian Elaine Tyler May comments: "The legendary family of the 1950s . . . was not, as common wisdom tells us, the last gasp of 'traditional' family life with deep roots in the past. Rather, it was the first wholehearted effort to create a home that would fulfill virtually all its members' personal needs through an energized and expressive personal life."

Beneath a superficial revival of Victorian domesticity and gender distinctions, a novel rearrangement of family ideals and male-female relations was accomplished.

For women, this involved a reduction in the moral aspect of domesticity and an expansion of its orientation toward personal service. Nineteenth-century middle-class women had cheerfully left housework to servants, yet 1950s women of all classes created makework in their homes and felt guilty when they did not do everything for themselves. The amount of time women spent doing housework actually *increased* during the 1950s, despite the advent of convenience foods and new, labor-saving appliances; child care absorbed more than twice as much time as it had in the 1920s. By the mid-1950s, advertisers' surveys reported on a growing tendency among women to find "housework a medium of expression for . . . [their] femininity and individuality."

For the first time, men as well as women were encouraged to root their identity and self-image in familial and parental roles. The novelty of these family and gender values can be seen in the dramatic postwar transformation of movie themes. Historian Peter Biskind writes that almost every major male star who had played tough loners in the 1930s and 1940s "took the roles with which he was synonymous and transformed them, in the fifties, into neurotics or psychotics." In these films, "men belonged at home, not on the streets or out on the prairie, . . . not alone or hanging out with other men." The women who got men to settle down had to promise enough sex to compete with "bad" women, but ultimately they provided it only in the marital bedroom and only in return for some help fixing up the house.

Public images of Hollywood stars were consciously reworked to show their commitment to marriage and stability. After 1947, for example, the Actors' Guild organized "a series of unprecedented speeches . . . to be given to civic groups around the country, emphasizing that the stars now embodied the rejuvenated family life unfolding in the suburbs." Ronald Reagan's defense of actors' family values was especially "stirring," noted one reporter, but female stars, unlike Reagan and other male stars, were obliged to *live* the new values as well as propagandize them. Joan Crawford, for example, one of the brash, tough, independent leading ladies of the prewar era, was now pictured as a devoted mother whose sex appeal and glamour did not prevent her from doing her own housework. She posed for pictures mopping floors and gave interviews about her childrearing philosophy.

The "good life" in the 1950s, historian Clifford Clark points out, made the family "the focus of fun and recreation." The ranch house, architectural embodiment of this new ideal, discarded the older privacy of the kitchen, den, and sewing room (representative of separate spheres for men and women) but introduced new privacy and luxury into the master bedroom. There was an unprecedented "glorification of self-indulgence" in family life. Formality was discarded in favor of "livability," "comfort," and "convenience." A contradiction in terms in earlier periods, "the sexually charged, child-centered family took its place at the center of the postwar American dream."

On television, David Marc comments, all the "normal" families moved to the suburbs during the 1950s. Popular culture turned such suburban families into capitalism's answer to the Communist threat. In his famous "kitchen debate" with Nikita Khrushchev in 1959, Richard Nixon asserted that the superiority of capitalism over communism was embodied not in ideology or military might but in the comforts of the suburban home, "designed to make things easier for our women."

Acceptance of domesticity was the mark of middle-class status and upward mobility. In sit-com families, a middle-class man's work was totally irrelevant to his identity; by the same token, the problems of working-class families did not lie in their economic situation but in their failure to create harmonious gender roles. Working-class and ethnic men on television had one defining characteristic: They were unable to control their wives. The families of middle-class men, by contrast, were generally well behaved.

Not only was the 1950s family a new invention; it was also a historical fluke, based on a unique and temporary conjuncture of economic, social, and political factors. During the war, Americans had saved at a rate more than three times higher than that in the decades before or since. Their buying power was further enhanced by America's extraordinary competitive advantage at the end of the war, when every other industrial power was devastated by the experience. This privileged economic position sustained both a tremendous expansion of middle-class man-agement occupations and a new honeymoon between management and organized labor: During the 1950s, real wages increased by more than they had in the entire previous half century.

The impact of such prosperity on family formation and stability was magnified by the role of government, which could afford to be generous with education benefits, housing loans, highway and sewer construction, and job training. All this allowed most middle-class Americans, and a large number of working-class ones, to adopt family values and strategies that assumed the availability of cheap energy, low-interest home loans, expanding educational and occupational opportunities, and steady employment. . . .

Even aside from the exceptional and ephemeral nature of the conditions that supported them, 1950s family strategies and values offer no solution to the discon-tents that underlie contemporary romanticization of the "good old days." The reality of these families was far more painful and complex than the situation-comedy reruns or the expurgated memories of the nostalgic would suggest. Contrary to popular opin-ion, "Leave It to Beaver" was not a documentary.

In the first place, not all American families shared in the consumer expansion that provided Hotpoint appliances for June Cleaver's kitchen and a vacuum cleaner for Donna Stone. A full 25 percent of Americans, forty to fifty million people, were poor in the mid-1950s, and in the absence of food stamps and housing programs, this poverty was searing. Even at the end of the 1950s, a third of American children were poor. Sixty percent of Americans over sixty-five had incomes below $1,000 in 1958, considerably below the $3,000 to $10,000 level considered to represent middle-class status. A majority of elders also lacked medical insurance. Only half the population had savings in 1959; one-quarter of the population had no liquid assets at all. Even when we consider only native-born, white families, one-third could not get by on the income of the household head.

In the second place, real life was not so white as it was on television. Television, comments historian Ella Taylor, increasingly ignored cultural diversity, adopting "the motto 'least objectionable programming,' which gave rise to those least objec-tionable families, the Cleavers, the Nelsons and the Andersons." Such families were so completely white and Anglo-Saxon that even the Hispanic gardener in "Father Knows Best" went by the name of Frank Smith. But contrary to the all-white lineup on the television networks and the streets of suburbia, the 1950s saw a major trans-formation in the ethnic composition of America. More Mexican immigrants entered the United States in the two decades after the Second World War than in the entire previous one hundred years. Prior to the war, most blacks and Mexican-Americans lived in rural areas, and three-fourths of blacks lived in the South. By 1960, a majority of blacks resided in the North, and 80 percent of both blacks and Mexican-Americans lived in cities. Postwar Puerto Rican immigration was so massive that by 1960 more Puerto Ricans lived in New York than in San Juan. . . .

The happy, homogeneous families that we "remember" from the 1950s were thus partly a result of the media's denial of diversity. But even among sectors of the population where the "least objectionable" families did prevail, their values and behaviors were not entirely a spontaneous, joyful reaction to prosperity. If suburban ranch houses and family barbecues were the carrots offered to white middle-class families that adopted the new norms, there was also a stick. . . .

Vehement attacks were launched against women who did not accept [the prevailing] self-definitions. In the 1947 bestseller, *The Modern Woman: The Lost Sex,* Marynia Farnham and Ferdinand Lundberg described feminism as a "deep illness," called the notion of an independent woman a "contradiction in terms," and accused women who sought educational or employment equality of engaging in symbolic "castration" of men. As sociologist David Riesman noted, a woman's failure to bear children went from being "a social disadvantage and sometimes a personal tragedy" in the nineteenth century to being a "quasi-perversion" in the 1950s. The conflicting messages aimed at women seemed almost calculated to demoralize: At the same time as they labeled women "unnatural" if they did not seek fulfillment in motherhood, psychologists and popular writers insisted that most modern social ills could be traced to domineering mothers who invested too much energy and emotion in their children. Women were told that "no other experience in life . . . will provide the same sense of fulfillment, of happiness, of complete pervading contentment" as motherhood. But soon after delivery they were asked, "Which are you first of all, Wife or Mother?" and warned against the tendency to be "too much mother, too little wife." . . .

Men were also pressured into acceptable family roles, since lack of a suitable wife could mean the loss of a job or promotion for a middle-class man. Bachelors were categorized as "immature," "infantile," "narcissistic," "deviant," or even "pathological." Family advice expert Paul Landis argued: "Except for the sick, the badly crippled, the deformed, the emotionally warped and the mentally defective, almost everyone has an opportunity [and, by clear implication, a duty] to marry."

Families in the 1950s were products of even more direct repression. Cold war anxieties merged with concerns about the expanded sexuality of family life and the commercial world to create what one authority calls the domestic version of George F. Kennan's containment policy toward the Soviet Union: A "normal" family and vigilant mother became the "front line" of defense against treason; anticommunists linked deviant family or sexual behavior to sedition. The FBI and other government agencies instituted unprecedented state intrusion into private life under the guise of investigating subversives. Gay baiting was almost as widespread and every bit as vicious as red baiting.

The Civil Service Commission fired 2,611 persons as "security risks" and reported that 4,315 others resigned under the pressure of investigations that asked leading questions of their neighbors and inquired into the books they read or the music to which they listened. In this atmosphere, movie producer Joel Schumacher recalls, "No one told the truth. . . . People pretended they weren't unfaithful. They pretended that they weren't homosexual. They pretended that they weren't horrible."

Even for people not directly coerced into conformity by racial, political, or personal repression, the turn toward families was in many cases more a defensive move than a purely affirmative act. Some men and women entered loveless marriages in order to forestall attacks about real or suspected homosexuality or lesbianism. Growing numbers of people saw the family, in the words of one husband, as the one "group that in spite of many disagreements internally always will face its external enemies together." Conservative families warned children to beware of communists who might masquerade as friendly neighbors; liberal children learned to confine their opinions to the family for fear that their father's job or reputation might be threatened. . . .

A successful 1950s family, moreover, was often achieved at enormous cost to the wife, who was expected to subordinate her own needs and aspirations to those of both her husband and her children. In consequence, no sooner was the ideal of the postwar family accepted than observers began to comment perplexedly on how discontented women seemed in the very roles they supposedly desired most. In 1949, *Life* magazine reported that "suddenly and for no plain reason" American women were "seized with an eerie restlessness." Under a "mask of placidity" and an outwardly feminine appearance, one physician wrote in 1953, there was often "an inwardly tense and emotionally unstable individual seething with hidden aggressiveness and resentment.". . .

Although Betty Friedan's bestseller *The Feminine Mystique* did not appear until 1963, it was a product of the 1950s, originating in the discontented responses Friedan received in 1957 when she surveyed fellow college classmates from the class of 1942. The heartfelt identification of other 1950s women with "the problem that has no name" is preserved in the letters Friedan received after her book was published, letters now at the Schlesinger Library at Radcliffe.

Men tended to be more satisfied with marriage than were women, especially over time, but they, too, had their discontents. Even the most successful strivers after the American dream sometimes muttered about "mindless conformity." The titles of books such as *The Organization Man,* by William Whyte (1956), and *The Lonely Crowd,* by David Riesman (1958), summarized a widespread critique of 1950s culture. Male resentments against women were expressed in the only partly humorous diatribes of *Playboy* magazine (founded in 1953) against "money-hungry" gold diggers or lazy "parasites" trying to trap men into commitment.

Happy memories of 1950s family life are not all illusion, of course—there were good times for many families. But even the most positive aspects had another side. One reason that the 1950s family model was so fleeting was that it contained the seeds of its own destruction. . . . It was during the 1950s, not the 1960s, that the youth market was first produced, then institutionalized into the youth culture. It was through such innocuous shows as "Howdy Doody" and "The Disney Hour" that advertisers first discovered the riches to be gained by bypassing parents and appealing directly to youth. It was also during this period that advertising and consumerism became saturated with sex. . . .

Whatever its other unexpected features, the 1950s family does appear, at least when compared to families in the last two decades, to be a bastion of "traditional" sexual morality. Many modern observers, accordingly, look back to the sexual values of this decade as a possible solution to what they see as the peculiarly modern "epidemic" of teen pregnancy. On closer examination, however, the issue of teen pregnancy is a classic example of both the novelty and the contradictions of the 1950s family.

Those who advocate that today's youth should be taught abstinence or deferred gratification rather than sex education will find no 1950s model for such restraint. "Heavy petting" became a norm of dating in this period, while the proportion of white brides who were pregnant at marriage more than doubled. Teen birth rates soared, reaching highs that have not been equaled since. In 1957, 97 out of every 1,000 girls aged fifteen to nineteen gave birth, compared to only 52 of every 1,000 in 1983. A surprising number of these births were illegitimate, although 1950s census codes made it impossible to identify an unmarried mother if she lived at home with her parents. The incidence of illegitimacy was also disguised by the new emphasis on "rehabilitating" the white mother (though not the black) by putting her baby up for adoption and encouraging her to "start over"; there was an 80 percent increase in the number of out-of-wedlock babies placed for adoption between 1944 and 1955.

The main reason that teenage sexual behavior did not result in many more illegitimate births during this period was that the age of marriage dropped sharply. Young people were not taught how to "say no"—they were simply handed wedding rings. In fact, the growing willingness of parents to subsidize young married couples and the new prevalence of government educational stipends and home ownership loans for veterans undermined the former assumption that a man should be able to support a family before embarking on marriage. . . .

Contemporary teenage motherhood . . . in some ways represents a *continuation* of 1950s values in a new economic situation that makes early marriage less viable. Of course, modern teen pregnancy also reflects the rejection of some of those earlier values. The values that have broken down, however, have little to do with sexual restraint. What we now think of as 1950s sexual morality depended not so much on stricter sexual control as on intensification of the sexual double standard. Elaine Tyler May argues that sexual "repression" gave way to sexual "containment." The new practice of going steady "widened the boundaries of permissible sexual activity," creating a "sexual brinksmanship" in which women bore the burden of "drawing the line," but that line was constantly changing. Popular opinion admitted, as the *Ladies' Home Journal* put it in 1956, that "sex suggestiveness" was here to stay, but insisted that it was up to women to "put the brakes on."

This double standard led to a Byzantine code of sexual conduct: "Petting" was sanctioned so long as one didn't go "too far" (though this was an elastic and ambiguous prohibition); a woman could be touched on various parts of her body (how low depended on how serious the relationship was) but "nice girls" refused to fondle the comparable male parts in return; mutual stimulation to orgasm was compatible with maintaining a "good" reputation so long as penetration did not occur.

The success of sexual containment depended on sexual inequality. Men no longer bore the responsibility of "saving themselves for marriage"; this was now exclusively a woman's job. In sharp contrast to the nineteenth century, when "oversexed" or demanding men were considered to have serious problems, it was now considered "normal" or "natural" for men to be sexually aggressive. The "average man," advice writers for women commented indulgently, "will go as far as you let him go." When women succeeded in "holding out" (a phrase charged with moral ambiguity), they sometimes experienced problems "letting go," even after marriage; when they failed, they were often reproached later by their husbands for having "given in." The contradictions of this double standard could not long withstand the period's pressures for companionate romance: By 1959, a more liberal single standard had already gained ground among older teenagers across America.

People who romanticize the 1950s, or any model of the traditional family, are usually put in an uncomfortable position when they attempt to gain popular support. The legitimacy of women's rights is so widely accepted today that only a tiny minority of Americans seriously propose that women should go back to being full-time housewives or should be denied educational and job opportunities because of their family responsibilities. Yet when commentators lament the collapse of traditional family commitments and values, they almost invariably mean the uniquely female duties associated with the doctrine of separate spheres for men and women.

Karl Zinsmeister of the American Enterprise Institute, for example, bemoans the fact that "workaholism and family dereliction have become equal-opportunity diseases, striking mothers as much as fathers." David Blankenhorn of the Institute for American Values expresses sympathy for the needs of working women but warns that "employed women do not a family make. The goals of women (and of men, too) in the workplace are primarily individualistic: social recognition, wages, opportunities for advancement, and self-fulfillment. But the family is about collective goals . . . , building life's most important bonds of affection, nurturance, mutual support, and long-term commitment."

In both statements, a seemingly gender-neutral indictment of family irresponsibility ends up being directed most forcefully against women. For Blankenhorn, it is not surprising that *men's* goals should be individualistic; this is a parenthetical aside. For Zinsmeister, the problem with the disease of family dereliction is that it has spread to women. So long as it was confined to men, evidently, there was no urgency about finding a cure.

FURTHER READING

Joel A. Carpenter, *Revive Us Again: The Reawakening of American Fundamentalism* (1997).
Michael Coyne, *The Crowded Prairie: American National Identity in the Hollywood Western* (1997).
Henry Louis Gates, Jr., *Colored People: A Memoir* (1994).
William Graebner, *Coming of Age in Buffalo: Youth and Authority in the Postwar Era* (1990).
Julia Grant, *Raising Baby by the Book: The Education of American Mothers* (1998).
Kenneth T. Jackson, *Crabgrass Frontier: The Suburbanization of America* (1985).
Elaine Tyler May, *Homeward Bound: American Families in the Cold War Era* (1988).
William L. O'Neill, *American High: The Years of Confidence* (1989).
Richard H. Pells, *The Liberal Mind in a Conservative Age: American Intellectuals in the 1940s and 1950s* (1985).
Benjamin G. Rader, *In Its Own Image: How Television Has Transformed Sports* (1985).
Jessica Weiss, *To Have and to Hold: Marriage, the Baby Boom, and Social Change* (2000).
Andrew Wiese, *Places of Their Own: African American Suburbanization in the Twentieth Century* (2004).

CHAPTER
12

Making the Great Society:
Civil Rights

The "American Way" meant something very different to blacks in the 1950s from what it did to people like Ron Kovic (Born on the Fourth of July). For blacks in the South, the American Way was "Jim Crow," a system of segregation that included separate schools, separate drinking fountains, separate beaches, separate neighborhoods, separate public accommodations: most African Americans in the South could not vote, marry whites, sit in the front of buses, attend state colleges, or even try on clothes and hats in major department stores. Beyond the inconvenience and embarrassment lurked the potential for violence. Women and men who "stepped out of line" could expect the full force of the law—and perhaps even brutal vigilantes like the Ku Klux Klan or White Citizens Council—to turn upon them. It took incalculable bravery to confront this system, and in the 1950s a grassroots movement of men, women, and children did just this.

People like Rosa Parks and Martin Luther King, Jr., helped to start the Civil Rights Movement, which led finally to the implementation of the Fourteenth and Fifteenth Amendments to the Constitution, placed on the books almost one hundred years earlier. The Civil Rights Act of 1964 outlawed segregation in public establishments and discrimination in employment. It extended equal protection under the law to all citizens, which had been the intent of the Fourteenth Amendment. The Civil Rights Act of 1965 guaranteed the right to vote, and the Civil Rights Act of 1968 prohibited discrimination in housing. But the movement did not stop at legal reforms, nor did it pertain only to African Americans. Racial prejudice itself came under attack, and other groups whose rights had been abridged grabbed hold of the new, empowering rhetoric to proclaim their inalienable right to "life, liberty, and the pursuit of happiness." Women, American Indians, Chicanos, Asian Americans, gays, the elderly, and, by 1990, the disabled all sought remedies for discrimination and inequality. They echoed one another's statements and demands, each asserting in turn that freedoms guaranteed to one group of people could not be denied to another.

Although none of these groups achieved their ultimate goal of creating a perfectly just society—what President Lyndon Baines Johnson called the Great Society—they changed many laws and practices within the United States. Legal segregation came to an end. No ethnic or racial group could be paid less than another, and women could no longer legally be paid less than men (or be beaten by their husbands). The very words that people spoke, and the jokes that they told, changed as the legacy of racism, sexism, ageism, and all the other "isms" came under attack.

Of course, the problem was as old as slavery, the solution as old as the Declaration of Independence. Almost two hundred years before the Civil Rights Movement, Jefferson had written the immortal words, "We hold these truths to be self-evident, that all men are created equal." In the 1950s and 1960s, for arguably the first time, the nation sought to put these words into practice across the board. Why then? There are many places to look for the answer to this question, including beyond the United States. The holocaust of World War II and the role of the United States as world leader helped to reshape thinking about the place of discrimination in the "land of the free, home of the brave." This new thinking was the most important legacy of the 1950s and 1960s.

◥ Q U E S T I O N S   T O   T H I N K   A B O U T

Why were Jefferson's "self-evident" truths finally adopted in practice at this time? What was more important in bringing about these fundamental changes: transcendent black leadership or the new world role of the United States? In the lingo of the Civil Rights era, how did the "white establishment" advance or hinder the cause of democracy?

◥ D O C U M E N T S

The documents in this chapter illustrate the various dimensions of the Civil Rights Movement. Document 1 is the Universal Declaration of Human Rights passed by the United Nations in 1948. Arising out of the genocide of World War II, this was the first global concord in human history that articulated the premise "All human beings are born free and equal in dignity and rights." Eleanor Roosevelt, a champion of civil rights in the United States, chaired the tumultuous U.N. committee that drafted the declaration. Document 2 is the Supreme Court's famous reversal of *Plessy v. Ferguson* (1896). Separate is not equal, the Court ruled in *Brown v. Board of Education.* Document 3 is from Martin Luther King, Jr.'s first speech on behalf of Rosa Parks at the Holt Street Baptist Church in Montgomery, Alabama. Returning home from work, Parks refused to give up her seat on a bus so that a white person would not have to occupy the same row as she. This 1955 sermon following Rosa Parks's arrest helped to launch the Montgomery bus boycott, as well as King's career as a civil rights leader. In Document 4, Henry Louis Gates, Jr., now a professor at Harvard University, remembers growing up in the segregated South and learning about civil rights on TV. This selection shows the ways in which different generations perceived the movement. Document 5 is the Civil Rights Act of 1964, one of the milestones of American history. In Document 6, black Muslim leader Malcolm X draws on the imagery of the American Revolution to encourage the nation to live up to its promises. This selection speaks sharply to the alternative to the ballot, which, as in 1776, was "the bullet." The Voting Rights Act of 1965, passed the next year, answered Malcolm X's challenge. Document 7 is the founding statement of the National Organization for Women. The women's rights movement gathered force quickly in the 1960s, spurred by the Civil Rights Movement and by female activists. Document 8 describes La Raza Unida, a third party designed to amplify the political voice of Mexican Americans. It highlights the leadership of César Chávez and the inspiration that Chicanos drew from "Negro civil rights" as well as from the Cuban Revolution. Document 9 is a satirical manifesto sent to "the Great White Father" by the founders of the American Indian Movement after their occupation of Alcatraz Island in San Francisco Bay. The Indians offered to pay $24 in glass beads and red cloth for the sixteen acres. Document 10, the Americans with Disabilities Act, is a clear outcome of the commitment made back in 1948 to respect the rights, dignity, and abilities of all humans regardless of condition. It shows how far the "minority rights revolution" ultimately spread.

1. The United Nations Approves a Universal Declaration of Human Rights, 1948

PREAMBLE

Whereas recognition of the inherent dignity and of the equal and inalienable rights of all members of the human family is the foundation of freedom, justice and peace in the world,

Whereas disregard and contempt for human rights have resulted in barbarous acts which have outraged the conscience of mankind, and the advent of a world in which human beings shall enjoy freedom of speech and belief and freedom from fear and want has been proclaimed as the highest aspiration of the common people,

Whereas it is essential, if man is not to be compelled to have recourse, as a last resort, to rebellion against tyranny and oppression, that human rights should be protected by the rule of law,

Whereas it is essential to promote the development of friendly relations between nations,

Whereas the peoples of the United Nations have in the Charter reaffirmed their faith in fundamental human rights, in the dignity and worth of the human person and in the equal rights of men and women and have determined to promote social progress and better standards of life in larger freedom,

Whereas Member States have pledged themselves to achieve, in cooperation with the United Nations, the promotion of universal respect for and observance of human rights and fundamental freedoms,

Whereas a common understanding of these rights and freedoms is of the greatest importance for the full realization of this pledge,

Now, Therefore THE GENERAL ASSEMBLY proclaims THIS UNIVERSAL DECLARATION OF HUMAN RIGHTS as a common standard of achievement

---

United Nations web site, www.un.org/Overview/rights.html.

for all peoples and all nations, to the end that every individual and every organ of society, keeping this Declaration constantly in mind, shall strive by teaching and education to promote respect for these rights and freedoms and by progressive measures, national and international, to secure their universal and effective recognition and observance, both among the peoples of Member States themselves and among the peoples of territories under their jurisdiction.

Article 1.

All human beings are born free and equal in dignity and rights. They are endowed with reason and conscience and should act towards one another in a spirit of brotherhood.

Article 2.

Everyone is entitled to all the rights and freedoms set forth in this Declaration, without distinction of any kind, such as race, colour, sex, language, religion, political or other opinion, national or social origin, property, birth or other status. . . .

Article 3.

Everyone has the right to life, liberty and security of person.

Article 4.

No one shall be held in slavery or servitude; slavery and the slave trade shall be prohibited in all their forms.

Article 5.

No one shall be subjected to torture or to cruel, inhuman or degrading treatment or punishment.

Article 6.

Everyone has the right to recognition everywhere as a person before the law.

2. The Supreme Court Rules on
Brown v. Board of Education, 1954

These cases come to us from the States of Kansas, South Carolina, Virginia, and Delaware. They are premised on different facts and different local conditions, but

Brown v. Board of Education, 324, U.S. 483–496 (1954).

a common legal question justifies their consideration together in this consolidated opinion.

In each of the cases, minors of the Negro race, through their legal representatives, seek the aid of the courts in obtaining admission to the public schools of their community on a nonsegregated basis. In each instance, they had been denied admission to schools attended by white children under laws requiring or permitting segregation according to race. This segregation was alleged to deprive the plaintiffs of the equal protection of the laws under the Fourteenth Amendment. In each of the cases other than the Delaware case, a three-judge federal district court denied relief to the plaintiffs on the so-called "separate but equal" doctrine announced by this Court in *Plessy v. Ferguson,* 163 U.S. 537. Under that doctrine, equality of treatment is accorded when the races are provided substantially equal facilities, even though these facilities be separate. . . .

The plaintiffs contend that segregated public schools are not "equal" and cannot be made "equal," and that hence they are deprived of the equal protection of the laws. . . .

In approaching this problem, we cannot turn the clock back to 1868 when the Amendment was adopted, or even to 1896 when *Plessy v. Ferguson* was written. We must consider public education in the light of its full development and its present place in American life throughout the Nation. Only in this way can it be determined if segregation in public schools deprives these plaintiffs of the equal protection of the laws.

Today, education is perhaps the most important function of state and local governments. Compulsory school attendance laws and the great expenditures for education both demonstrate our recognition of the importance of education to our democratic society. It is required in the performance of our most basic public responsibilities, even service in the armed forces. It is the very foundation of good citizenship. Today it is a principal instrument in awakening the child to cultural values, in preparing him for later professional training, and in helping him to adjust normally to his environment. In these days, it is doubtful that any child may reasonably be expected to succeed in life if he is denied the opportunity of an education. Such an opportunity, when the state has undertaken to provide it, is a right which must be made available to all on equal terms.

We come then to the question presented: Does segregation of children in public schools solely on the basis of race, even though the physical facilities and other "tangible" factors may be equal, deprive the children of the minority group of equal educational opportunities? We believe that it does.

. . . To separate them from others of similar age and qualifications solely because of their race generates a feeling of inferiority as to their status in the community that may affect their hearts and minds in a way unlikely ever to be undone. . . .

We conclude that in the field of public education the doctrine of "separate but equal" has no place. Separate educational facilities are inherently unequal. Therefore, we hold that the plaintiffs and others similarly situated for whom the actions have been brought are, by reason of the segregation complained of, deprived of the equal protection of the laws guaranteed by the Fourteenth Amendment.

3. Reverend Martin Luther King, Jr., Defends Seamstress Rosa Parks, 1955

We are here this evening for serious business. We are here in a general sense because first and foremost we are American citizens, and we are determined to apply our citizenship to the fullness of its means. We are here because of our love for democracy, because of our deep-seated belief that democracy transformed from thin paper to thick action is the greatest form of government on earth. But we are here in a specific sense, because of the bus situation in Montgomery. We are here because we are determined to get the situation corrected.

This situation is not at all new. The problem has existed over endless years. For many years now Negroes in Montgomery and so many other areas have been inflicted with the paralysis of crippling fear on buses in our community. On so many occasions, Negroes have been intimidated and humiliated and oppressed because of the sheer fact that they were Negroes. I don't have time this evening to go into the history of these numerous cases. . . . But at least one stands before us now with glaring dimensions. Just the other day, just last Thursday to be exact, one of the finest citizens in Montgomery—not one of the finest Negro citizens but one of the finest citizens in Montgomery—was taken from a bus and carried to jail and arrested because she refused to get up to give her seat to a white person. . . . Mrs. Rosa Parks is a fine person. And since it had to happen I'm happy it happened to a person like Mrs. Parks, for nobody can doubt the boundless outreach of her integrity. Nobody can doubt the height of her character, nobody can doubt the depth of her Christian commitment and devotion to the teachings of Jesus. . . .

And just because she refused to get up, she was arrested. . . . You know my friends there comes a time when people get tired of being trampled over by the iron feet of oppression. There comes a time my friends when people get tired of being flung across the abyss of humiliation where they experience the bleakness of nagging despair. There comes a time when people get tired of being pushed out of the glittering sunlight of life's July and left standing amidst the piercing chill of an Alpine November.

We are here, we are here this evening because we're tired now. Now let us say that we are not here advocating violence. We have overcome that. I want it to be known throughout Montgomery and throughout this nation that we are Christian people. We believe in the Christian religion. We believe in the teachings of Jesus. The only weapon that we have in our hands this evening is the weapon of protest. And secondly, this is the glory of America, with all its faults. This is the glory of our democracy. If we were incarcerated behind the iron curtains of a Communistic nation we couldn't do this. If we were trapped in the dungeon of a totalitarian regime we couldn't do this. But the great glory of American democracy is the right to protest for right. . . .

And as we stand and sit here this evening, and as we prepare ourselves for what lies ahead, let us go out with a grim and bold determination that we are going

Excerpt from speech delivered by Martin Luther King, Jr., at Holt Street Baptist Church, Montgomery, Alabama, December 5, 1955, as reprinted in *The Eyes on the Prize Civil Rights Reader* (New York: Viking, 1991), 48–51. Reprinted by arrangement with the Estate of Martin Luther King, Jr., c/o Writers House as agent for the proprietor. Copyright 1967 Martin Luther King, Jr., copyright renewed 1991 Coretta Scott King.

to stick together. We are going to work together. Right here in Montgomery when the history books are written in the future, somebody will have to say "There lived a race of people, black people, fleecy locks and black complexion, of people who had the moral courage to stand up for their rights." And thereby they injected a new meaning into the veins of history and of civilization. And we're gonna do that. God grant that we will do it before it's too late.

4. Author Henry Louis Gates, Jr., Remembers Civil Rights on TV, 1957

Civil rights took us all by surprise. Every night we'd wait until the news to see what "Dr. King and dem" were doing. It was like watching the Olympics or the World Series when somebody colored was on. The murder of Emmett Till was one of my first memories. He whistled at some white girl, they said; that's all he did. He was beat so bad they didn't even want to open the casket, but his mama made them. She wanted the world to see what they had done to her baby.

In 1957, when I was in second grade, black children integrated Central High School in Little Rock, Arkansas. We watched it on TV. All of us watched it. I don't mean Mama and Daddy and Rocky. I mean *all* the colored people in America watched it, together, with one set of eyes. We'd watch it in the morning, on the *Today* show on NBC, before we'd go to school; we'd watch it in the evening, on the news, with Edward R. Murrow on CBS. We'd watch the Special Bulletins at night, interrupting our TV shows.

The children were all well scrubbed and greased down, as we'd say. Hair short and closely cropped, parted, and oiled (the boys); "done" in a "permanent" and straightened, with turned-up bangs and curls (the girls). Starched shirts, white, and creased pants, shoes shining like a buck private's spit shine. Those Negroes were *clean.* The fact was, those children trying to get the right to enter that school in Little Rock looked like black versions of models out of *Jack & Jill* magazine, to which my mama had subscribed for me so that I could see what children outside the Valley were up to. "They hand-picked those children," Daddy would say. "No dummies, no nappy hair, heads not too kinky, lips not too thick, no disses and no dats." At seven, I was dismayed by his cynicism. It bothered me somehow that those children would have been chosen, rather than just having shown up or volunteered or been nearby in the neighborhood.

Daddy was jaundiced about the civil rights movement, and especially about the Reverend Dr. Martin Luther King, Jr. He'd say all of his names, to drag out his scorn. By the mid-sixties, we'd argue about King from sunup to sundown. Sometimes he'd just mention King to get a rise from me, to make a sagging evening more interesting, to see if I had *learned* anything real yet, to see how long I could think up counter arguments before getting so mad that my face would turn purple. I think he just liked the color purple on my face, liked producing it there. But he was not of two minds about those children in Little Rock. . . .

The TV was the ritual arena for the drama of race. In our family, it was located in the living room, where it functioned like a fireplace in the proverbial New England winter. I'd sit in the water in the galvanized tub in the middle of our kitchen, watching the TV in the next room while Mama did the laundry or some other chore as she waited for Daddy to come home from his second job. We watched people getting hosed and cracked over their heads, people being spat upon and arrested, rednecks siccing fierce dogs on women and children, our people responding by singing and marching and staying strong. Eyes on the prize. Eyes on the prize. George Wallace at the gate of the University of Alabama, blocking Autherine Lucy's way. Charlayne Hunter at the University of Georgia. President Kennedy interrupting our scheduled program with a special address, saying that James Meredith will *definitely* enter the University of Mississippi; and saying it like he believed it (unlike Ike), saying it like the big kids said "It's our turn to play" on the basketball court and walking all through us as if we weren't there.

5. Congress Outlaws Segregation with the Civil Rights Act of 1964

Injunctive Relief Against Discrimination in Places of Public Accommodation

Sec. 201. (a) All persons shall be entitled to the full and equal enjoyment of the goods, services, facilities, privileges, advantages, and accommodations of any place of public accommodation, as defined in this section, without discrimination or segregation on the ground of race, color, religion, or national origin.

(b) Each of the following establishments which serves the public is a place of public accommodation within the meaning of this title if its operations affect commerce, or if discrimination or segregation by it is supported by State action:

(1) any inn, hotel, motel, or other establishment which provides lodging to transient guests, other than an establishment located within a building which contains not more than five rooms for rent or hire and which is actually occupied by the proprietor of such establishment as his residence;

(2) any restaurant, cafeteria, lunchroom, lunch counter, soda fountain, or other facility principally engaged in selling food for consumption on the premises, including, but not limited to, any such facility located on the premises of any retail establishment; or any gasoline station;

(3) any motion picture house, theater, concert hall, sports arena, stadium or other place of exhibition or entertainment. . . .

Discrimination Because of Race, Color, Religion, Sex, or National Origin

Sec. 703. (a) It shall be an unlawful employment practice for an employer—

(1) to fail or refuse to hire or to discharge any individual, or otherwise to discriminate against any individual with respect to his compensation, terms,

U.S. Statutes at Large 78 (1964), pp. 243, 255.

conditions, or privileges of employment, because of such individual's race, color, religion, sex, or national origin; or

(2) to limit, segregate, or classify his employees in any way which would deprive or tend to deprive any individual of employment opportunities or otherwise adversely affect his status as an employee, because of such individual's race, color, religion, sex, or national origin.

6. Black Muslim Malcolm X Warns: The Ballot or the Bullet, 1964

Our People, 22,000,000 African-Americans, are fed up with America's hypocritical democracy and today we care nothing about the odds that are against us. Every time a black man gets ready to defend himself some Uncle Tom tries to tell us, how can you win? That's Tom talking. Don't listen to him. This is the first thing we hear: the odds are against you. You're dealing with black people who don't care anything about odds. We care nothing about odds.

Again I go right back to the people who founded and secured the independence of this country from the colonial power of England. When George Washington and the others got ready to declare or come up with the Declaration of Independence, they didn't care anything about the odds of the British Empire. They were fed up with taxation without representation. And you've got 22,000,000 black people in this country today, 1964, who are fed up with taxation without representation, and will do the same thing. Who are ready, willing and justified to do the same thing today to bring about independence for our people that your forefathers did to bring about independence for your people. . . .

So 1964 will see the Negro revolt evolve and merge into the world-wide black revolution that has been taking place on this earth since 1945. The so-called revolt will become a real black revolution. Now the black revolution has been taking place in Africa and Asia and in Latin America. Now when I say black, I mean non-white. Black, brown, red or yellow. Our brothers and sisters in Asia, who were colonized by the Europeans, our brothers and sisters in Africa, who were colonized by the Europeans, and in Latin America, the peasants, who were colonized by the Europeans, have been involved in a struggle since 1945 to get the colonialists, or the colonizing powers, the Europeans, off their land, out of their country. . . .

So in my conclusion in speaking about the black revolution, America today is at a time or in a day or at an hour where she is the first country on this earth that can actually have a bloodless revolution. In the past revolutions have been bloody. Historically you just don't have a peaceful revolution. Revolutions are bloody, revolutions are violent, revolutions cause bloodshed and death follows in their paths. America is the only country in history in a position to bring about a revolution without violence and bloodshed. But America is not morally equipped to do so.

Why is America in a position to bring about a bloodless revolution? Because the Negro in this country holds the balance of power and if the Negro in this country were given what the Constitution says he is supposed to have, the added power of the Negro in this country would sweep all of the racists and the segregationists out of office. It would change the entire political structure of the country. It would wipe out the Southern segregationism that now controls America's foreign policy, as well as America's domestic policy.

And the only way without bloodshed that this can be brought about is that the black man has to be given full use of the ballot in every one of the 50 states. But if the black man doesn't get the ballot, then you are going to be faced with another man who forgets the ballot and starts using the bullet.

7. The National Organization for Women Calls for Equality, 1966

We, men and women who hereby constitute ourselves as the National Organization for Women, believe that the time has come for a new movement toward true equality for all women in America, and toward a fully equal partnership of the sexes, as part of the world-wide revolution of human rights now taking place within and beyond our national borders.

The purpose of NOW is to take action to bring women into full participation in the mainstream of American society now, exercising all the privileges and responsibilities thereof in truly equal partnership with men. . . .

NOW is dedicated to the proposition that women first and foremost are human beings, who, like all other people in our society, must have the chance to develop their fullest human potential. We believe that women can achieve such equality only by accepting to the full challenges and responsibilities they share with all other people in our society, as part of the decision-making mainstream of American political, economic and social life. . . .

There is no civil rights movement to speak for women, as there has been for Negroes and other victims of discrimination. The National Organization for Women must therefore begin to speak.

WE BELIEVE that the power of American law, and the protection guaranteed by the U.S. Constitution to the civil rights of all individuals, must be effectively applied and enforced to isolate and remove patterns of sex discrimination, to ensure equality of opportunity in employment and education, and equality of civil and political rights and responsibilities on behalf of women, as well as for Negroes and other deprived groups. . . .

WE BELIEVE that it is as essential for every girl to be educated to her full potential of human ability as it is for every boy—with the knowledge that such education is the key to effective participation in today's economy and that, for a girl as for a boy, education can only be serious where there is expectation that it

NOW Statement of Purpose, October 1966. Excerpt reprinted by permission of the National Organization for Women. This is a historical document and may not reflect the current language or priorities of the organization.

will be used in society. We believe that American educators are capable of devising means of imparting such expectations to girl students. Moreover, we consider the decline in the proportion of women receiving higher and professional education to be evidence of discrimination. . . . We believe that the same serious attention must be given to high school dropouts who are girls as to boys.

WE REJECT the current assumptions that a man must carry the sole burden of supporting himself, his wife, and family, and that a woman is automatically entitled to lifelong support by a man upon her marriage, or that marriage, home and family are primarily woman's world and responsibility—hers, to dominate, his to support. We believe that a true partnership between the sexes demands a different concept of marriage, an equitable sharing of the responsibilities of home and children and of the economic burdens of their support. We believe that proper recognition should be given to the economic and social value of homemaking and child care. To these ends, we will seek to open a reexamination of laws and mores governing marriage and divorce, for we believe that the current state of "half-equality" between the sexes discriminates against both men and women, and is the cause of much unnecessary hostility between the sexes. . . .

WE BELIEVE THAT women will do most to create a new image of women by *acting* now, and by speaking out in behalf of their own equality, freedom, and human dignity—not in pleas for special privilege, nor in enmity toward men, who are also victims of the current half-equality between the sexes—but in an active, self-respecting partnership with men. By so doing, women will develop confidence in their own ability to determine actively, in partnership with men, the conditions of their life, their choices, their future and their society.

8. Mexican Americans Form La Raza Unida, 1968

1. What is LA RAZA UNIDA? It is a ground swell movement of Mexican-American solidarity throughout the Southwest comprising a loose fellowship of some two or three hundred civic, social, cultural, religious, and political groups.

2. What has brought it about? The need deeply felt among Mexican-Americans to dramatize their plight as a disadvantaged minority, to assert their rights as first-rate citizens, and to assume their rightful share of the social, economic, educational, and political opportunities guaranteed by the American democratic system.

3. Are Mexican-Americans a disadvantaged minority? The most recent study, the Mexican-American Study Project conducted at UCLA and funded by the Ford Foundation, has disclosed that in the Southwest, as compared to the Negro, the Mexican-American is on generally the same level economically, but substantially below educationally. As for dilapidated housing and unemployment, the Mexican-American is not too much better off than the Negro.

4. Why this sudden awakening? Actually, it is not as sudden as it looks. Its first manifestations begin in the period following the Second World War. Mexican-Americans

---

"What Is La Raza?" by Jorge Lara Braud, in *La Raza Yearbook,* Sept. 1968. This document can also be found in Luis Valdez and Stan Steiner (eds.), *Aztlan: An Anthology of Mexican-American Literature* (New York: Vintage, 1972), pp. 222–224.

emerged from that conflict with a new determination to make their sacrifice count. No ethnic group has received a larger proportion of decorations, and few had sustained as large a share of casualties. These veterans challenged in and out of court the blatant legacy of discrimination still prevailing in the Southwest, often displayed by the glaring signs or the brutal words "No Mexicans allowed." The G.I. Bill made it possible for quite a few to obtain college degrees, better jobs, and positions of leadership. . . .

Since then Latin America has been rediscovered south and north of the Rio Grande, following the tremors set off by the Cuban revolution. Spanish is once again a prestige language, and being bilingual somehow is no longer un-American. Then came the radiation fall-out of the Negro civil rights struggle which made even the most disillusioned Mexican-American begin to dream large dreams again. But if anyone thought the new vision borrowed from this struggle would give way to violence, there emerged in 1965 the most inspirational of all, Cesar Chavez. It is he, more than anyone else, who has contributed to LA RAZA UNIDA the mystique of the pursuit of justice through non-violent means. His recent 24-day penitential fast was undertaken to signify the Christian determination of himself and his followers not to be driven into acts of violence by the obdurate grape-growing firms near Delano, California, which refuse to enter into contract negotiations with his fledgling union, while using every conceivable means to discredit it.

5. Are all members of LA RAZA UNIDA non-violent? The vast majority abhor violence. Indeed, one of their most persistent criticisms is that they have been the victims of too much violence, and they are sick of it. . . . An unbiased look at this vigorous awakening of the Mexican-American will make us realize it is a tremendous affirmation of faith in the American dream. They actually believe, unlike many other sectors, that this society is still capable of undergoing a reformation of "freedom and justice for all."

9. A Proclamation from the Indians of All Tribes, Alcatraz Island, 1969

To the Great White Father and All His People—

We, the native Americans, re-claim the land known as Alcatraz Island in the name of all American Indians by right of discovery.

We wish to be fair and honorable in our dealings with the Caucasian inhabitants of this land, and hereby offer the following treaty:

We will purchase said Alcatraz Island for twenty-four dollars (24) in glass beads and red cloth, a precedent set by the white man's purchase of a similar island about 300 years ago. We know that $24 in trade goods for these 16 acres is more than was paid when Manhattan Island was sold, but we know that land values have risen over the years. Our offer of $1.24 per acre is greater than the 47 cents per acre the white men are now paying the California Indians for their land.

We will give to the inhabitants of this island a portion of the land for their own to be held in trust by the American Indian Affairs and by the bureau of Caucasian

Peter Blue Cloud, ed., *Alcatraz Is Not an Island*, by Indians of All Tribes (Berkeley, Calif.: Wingbow Press, 1972), pp. 40–42.

Affairs to hold in perpetuity—for as long as the sun shall rise and the rivers go down to the sea. We will further guide the inhabitants in the proper way of living. We will offer them our religion, our education, our life-ways, in order to help them achieve our level of civilization and thus raise them and all their white brothers up from their savage and unhappy state. We offer this treaty in good faith and wish to be fair and honorable in our dealings with all white men.

We feel that this so-called Alcatraz Island is more than suitable for an Indian reservation, as determined by the white man's own standards. By this we mean that this place resembles most Indian reservations in that:

1. It is isolated from modern facilities, and without adequate means of transportation.
2. It has no fresh running water.
3. It has inadequate sanitation facilities.
4. There are no oil or mineral rights.
5. There is no industry and so unemployment is very great.
6. There are no health care facilities.
7. The soil is rocky and non-productive, and the land does not support game.
8. There are no educational facilities.
9. The population has always exceeded the land base.
10. The population has always been held as prisoners and kept dependent upon others.

Further, it would be fitting and symbolic that ships from all over the world, entering the Golden Gate, would first see Indian land, and thus be reminded of the true history of this nation. This tiny island would be a symbol of the great lands once ruled by free and noble Indians.

What use will we make of this land?

Since the San Francisco Indian Center burned down, there is no place for Indians to assemble and carry on tribal life here in the white man's city. Therefore, we plan to develop on this island several Indian institutions:

1. A Center for Native American Studies which will educate them to the skills and knowledge relevant to improve the lives and spirits of all Indian peoples.
2. An American Indian Spiritual Center which will practice our ancient tribal religious and sacred healing ceremonies. . . .
3. An Indian Center of Ecology which will train and support our young people in scientific research and practice to restore our lands and waters to their pure and natural state. . . .
4. A Great Indian Training School will be developed to teach our people how to make a living in the world, improve our standard of living, and to end hunger and unemployment among all our people. . . .

In the name of all Indians, therefore, we re-claim this island for our Indian nations.

> Signed,
> Indians of All Tribes
> November 1969
> San Francisco, California

10. Congress Guarantees Rights of Americans with Disabilities, 1990

The Congress finds that—

(1) some 43,000,000 Americans have one or more physical or mental disabilities, and this number is increasing as the population as a whole is growing older;

(2) historically, society has tended to isolate and segregate individuals with disabilities, and, despite some improvements, such forms of discrimination against individuals with disabilities continue to be a serious and pervasive social problem;

(3) discrimination against individuals with disabilities persists in such critical areas as employment, housing, public accommodations, education, transportation, communication, recreation, institutionalization, health services, voting, and access to public services;

(4) unlike individuals who have experienced discrimination on the basis of race, color, sex, national origin, religion, or age, individuals who have experienced discrimination on the basis of disability have often had no legal recourse to redress such discrimination. . . .

It is the purpose of this Act—

(1) to provide a clear and comprehensive national mandate for the elimination of discrimination against individuals with disabilities;

(2) to provide clear, strong, consistent, enforceable standards addressing discrimination against individuals with disabilities;

(3) to ensure that the Federal Government plays a central role in enforcing the standards established in this Act on behalf of individuals with disabilities; and

(4) to invoke the sweep of congressional authority, including the power to enforce the fourteenth amendment and to regulate commerce, in order to address the major areas of discrimination faced day-to-day by people with disabilities.

ESSAYS

One might well ponder how and why Americans "woke up" when then did to the full implications of their nation's founding principles. Historians have examined conditions external to the South, as well as the vision and dedication of charismatic African Americans like Martin Luther King, Jr., who persevered despite the constant threat of violent death. David Garrow of Emory University focuses on King's leadership. In this selection from his Pulitzer Prize–winning biography, Garrow reveals the depth of King's commitment to a role he did not ask for. King's sacrifice is made more poignant by the fact that he knew full well that he was making one. The willingness of King, and many others, to "bear the cross" testifies to the critical place of individuals in history. John Skrentny of the University of California, San Diego, takes a different tack. He argues that world events made the triumph of the American civil rights movement possible. The cause that had languished since the failure of Reconstruction blossomed again as a consequence of World War II, when the United States sought, once more, to construct a new order in the midst of calamity. Skrentny's analysis encourages readers to look at the process of historical change from top down, as well as bottom up.

Statutes of the United States 104 (1990): 327–378.

Martin Luther King, Jr.: The Emergence of a Grassroots Leader

DAVID J. GARROW

Thursday had been busy and tiring for Mrs. Raymond A. Parks. Her job as a tailor's assistant at the Montgomery Fair department store had left her neck and shoulder particularly sore, and when she left work at 5:30 P.M. that December 1, 1955, she went across the street to a drugstore in search of a heating pad. Mrs. Parks didn't find one, but she purchased a few other articles before recrossing the street to her usual bus stop on Court Square. The buses were especially crowded this cold, dark evening, and when she boarded one for her Cleveland Avenue route, only one row of seats—the row immediately behind the first ten seats that always were reserved for whites only—had any vacancies. She took an aisle seat, with a black man on her right next to the window, and two black women in the parallel seat across the way.

As more passengers boarded at each of the two next stops, the blacks moved to the rear, where they stood, and the whites occupied their exclusive seats at the front of the bus. At the third stop, more passengers got on, and one, a white male, was left standing after the final front seat was taken. The bus driver, J. F. Blake, looked back and called out to Mrs. Parks and her three colleagues, "All right you folks, I want those two seats." Montgomery's customary practice of racial preference demanded that all four blacks would have to stand in order to allow one white man to sit, since no black was allowed to sit parallel with a white. No one moved at first. Blake spoke out again: "You all better make it light on yourselves and let me have those seats." At that, the two women across from Mrs. Parks rose and moved to the rear; the man beside her rose also, and she moved her legs to allow him out into the aisle. She remained silent, but shifted to the window side of the seat.

Blake could see that Mrs. Parks had not arisen. "Look, woman, I told you I wanted the seat. Are you going to stand up?" At that, Rosa Lee McCauley Parks uttered her first word to him: "No." Blake responded, "If you don't stand up, I'm going to have you arrested." Mrs. Parks told him to go right ahead, that she was not going to move. Blake said nothing more, but got off the bus and went to a phone. No one spoke to Mrs. Parks, and some passengers began leaving the bus, not wanting to be inconvenienced by the incident. . . .

Word of Mrs. Parks's arrest began to spread even before that phone call. One passenger on the bus told a friend of Mrs. Parks's about the event, and that friend, Mrs. Bertha Butler, immediately called the home of longtime black activist E. D. Nixon, a past president of Montgomery's National Association for the Advancement of Colored People (NAACP) chapter and the most outspoken figure in the black community. Nixon was not at home, but his wife, Arlet, was, and she phoned his small downtown office. Nixon was out at the moment, but when he returned a few moments later, he saw the message to call home. "What's up?" he asked his wife. She told him of Mrs. Parks's arrest, but couldn't tell him what the charge was. Nixon hung up and immediately called the police station.

The desk officer rudely told Nixon that the charges against Mrs. Parks were none of his business. Determined to pursue the matter, but knowing that Montgomery's principal black lawyer, Fred Gray, was out of town, Nixon called the home of a white lawyer, Clifford Durr, one of the city's few racial liberals. . . .

Mrs. Parks, Mr. Nixon, and the Durrs all had known each other for a number of years. Mrs. Parks, forty-two years old at the time of her arrest, had been an active member and occasional officer of Montgomery's NAACP chapter since 1943, and had worked with Nixon on a number of voter registration efforts. Nixon, a Pullman porter whose job regularly took him to Chicago and other northern cities, had been a stalwart member of A. Philip Randolph's Brotherhood of Sleeping Car Porters, as well as a local activist, since the 1920s. The Durrs, Alabama natives who had returned to the state several years earlier following Clifford's service on the Federal Communications Commission, had become friendly with Nixon through his political activism. . . .

Over the years, the Durrs had heard distressing stories of how Montgomery bus drivers regularly insulted black passengers. Mrs. Parks once told them about how she had been physically thrown off a bus some ten years earlier when, after paying her fare at the front of the bus, she had refused to get off and reenter by the back door—a custom often inflicted on black riders. . . .

On their way to the jail Nixon and the Durrs discussed the possibility of Mrs. Parks being a test case. . . .

Throughout the early 1950s the Women's Political Council, sometimes in conjunction with Nixon or Nixon's chief rival for active leadership in the black community, businessman and former Alabama State football coach Rufus Lewis, who headed the Citizens Steering Committee, repeatedly complained to Montgomery's three popularly elected city commissioners about how the municipally chartered Montgomery City Lines mistreated its black customers. The commissioners politely, but consistently, brushed aside the WPC's entreaties concerning drivers' behavior and how blacks had to stand while whites-only seats remained vacant. In early 1954 Mrs. [Jo Ann] Robinson suggested to the commissioners "a city law that would make it possible for Negroes to sit from back toward front, and whites from front toward back until all seats were taken," so that no one would have to stand over a vacant seat, but again the officials were unresponsive.

Then, on May 17, 1954, the U.S. Supreme Court handed down its widely heralded school desegregation decision in *Brown v. Board of Education of Topeka,* which explicitly held that the segregationist doctrine of "separate but equal" was unconstitutional. Her spirits lifted, Mrs. Robinson four days later sent a firm declaration to Montgomery Mayor W. A. Gayle. . . . Other Alabama cities, such as Mobile, were using the front-to-back and back-to-front seating policy without any problems, Mrs. Robinson reminded Gayle. Why could not Montgomery do the same? "Please consider this plea," she wrote him, "and if possible, act favorably upon it, for even now plans are being made to ride less, or not at all, on our buses. We do not want this."

Robinson's hints about a boycott were not supported by any unified sentiment in the black community. One mid-1954 meeting of community leaders had found a majority opposed to any boycott at that time. The stalemate continued into early 1955 as Nixon and the WPC privately discussed the possibility of mounting a legal challenge to Montgomery's bus seating practices. Then, on March 2, 1955, an incident occurred that galvanized the long-smoldering black sentiments. A fifteen-year-old high school student, Claudette Colvin, refused a driver's demand that she give up her bus seat, well toward the rear of the vehicle, to allow newly boarding whites to sit down. Policemen dragged Colvin from the bus, and word spread quickly. Mrs. Robinson and Nixon thought they might have an ideal legal test case. Colvin had been active in the NAACP Youth Council, and the group's advisor, Mrs. Rosa Parks, along with her friend Virginia Durr, began soliciting contributions toward the legal fees. Almost immediately, however, problems developed. First, Colvin's resistance to the arresting officers had resulted in her being charged with assault and battery as well as violating city and state segregation statutes. Second, both Robinson and Nixon learned in independent interviews with Colvin and her family that the young unmarried woman was several months pregnant. Both leaders concluded that Colvin would be neither an ideal candidate for symbolizing the abuse heaped upon black passengers nor a good litigant for a test suit certain to generate great pressures and publicity. . . .

When Mrs. Robinson learned of the [Rosa Parks's] arrest late that Thursday night from Fred Gray, she immediately phoned Nixon, who had just gotten home from Mrs. Parks's house. Together they agreed that this was just what they had been waiting for. "We had planned the protest long before Mrs. Parks was arrested," Mrs. Robinson emphasized years later. "There had been so many things that happened, that the black women had been embarrassed over, and they were ready to explode." Also, "Mrs. Parks had the caliber of character we needed to get the city to rally behind us." Robinson told Nixon that she and her WPC colleagues would begin producing boycott leaflets immediately, and the two agreed that the flyers would call on all black people to stay off the buses on Monday, the day of Mrs. Parks's trial. They also agreed that the black community leadership should assemble on Friday. Nixon would organize that meeting, while Robinson would see to the leafletting.

Robinson alerted several of her WPC colleagues, then sat down and drafted the leaflet. She called a friend who had access to Alabama State's mimeograph room, and they rendezvoused at the college and began running off thousands of copies. They worked all night, and when morning came, WPC members, helped by some of Robinson's students, began distributing the announcements to every black neighborhood in Montgomery. . . . The long-discussed boycott was about to get under way.

After a fitful night, E. D. Nixon arose early Friday morning to begin assembling the black leadership. Nixon knew that a mass boycott of Montgomery's buses could not be accomplished simply by the WPC and the few regular activists such as himself. Although the women had been the driving force behind all of the black community efforts of the last few years, a mass protest would succeed only if they could obtain the enthusiastic support of Montgomery's black ministers. With that in mind, Nixon made his first call to one of the youngest and most outspoken of the city's pastors, Ralph D. Abernathy.

Abernathy, the secretary of the Baptist Ministers' Alliance, told Nixon he would support the effort. . . . Abernathy also advised Nixon to phone one of Abernathy's best friends, the Reverend M. L. King, Jr., pastor of Dexter Avenue Baptist Church, and ask if the meeting could be held there. In the meantime, Abernathy would begin contacting other ministers.

Nixon quickly secured [President of the Baptist Ministers' Alliance Reverend H. H.] Hubbard's approval. He then called King. Nixon related the events of the previous evening, told King of the emerging consensus to begin a boycott on Monday, and asked if the young pastor would join in supporting the effort. King hesitated. He had a newborn daughter, less than one month old, and heavy responsibilities at his church. Only a few weeks earlier he had declined to be considered for president of the local NAACP chapter because of these other demands on his time. He wasn't sure he could handle any additional responsibilities. "Brother Nixon," he said, "let me think about it awhile, and call me back." Nixon told King that he and Abernathy already were telling people to meet at King's church that evening. "That's all right," King replied. "I just want to think about it and then you call me back." Nixon agreed.

King hadn't had long to mull over Nixon's request before Abernathy called. Abernathy had heard from Nixon about his friend's hesitation, and wanted to stress to King the opportunity that the Parks arrest represented. King acknowledged that Abernathy was correct; he had no quarrel with the boycott plan. So long as he did not have to do the organizational work, he would be happy to support the effort and host the evening meeting at Dexter church. . . .

Early Friday evening, as Mrs. Robinson's leaflets circulated throughout Montgomery, some seventy black leaders assembled in the basement meeting room of Dexter Avenue Baptist Church. After a brief prayer by Hubbard, [Reverend L. Roy] Bennett took the floor and told the influential group that he did not see much need for any extended discussion because he, Bennett, knew full well how to organize a boycott.

Bennett lectured on. As the minutes passed, more and more people became frustrated and angry. Despite repeated requests, Bennett refused to yield the floor. When Bennett's monologue reached the half-hour mark, some people began walking out. Among those to leave was Alabama State Professor James E. Pierce, one of Nixon's closest allies. Earlier that day Pierce had tried to dissuade his friend from the boycott plan on the grounds that many black citizens might not support it. This session had only strengthened Pierce's doubts about the effort, and his fear that many individual leaders, like Bennett, would be unable to put aside their rivalries and desires for self-advancement long enough to agree on a unified community effort. Heading out the door, Pierce paused and whispered to King, "This is going to fizzle out. I'm going." King was unhappy too, and told Pierce, "I would like to go too, but it's in my church."

Finally, Ralph Abernathy stood up and took over the meeting from Bennett, insisting that all of the twenty or so people who remained be given an opportunity to speak. Jo Ann Robinson seconded Abernathy's demand, and proposed that all present endorse the Monday boycott. A mass meeting would be called for Monday night at the large Holt Street Baptist Church to determine whether community sentiment would support extending the boycott beyond Monday. A new version of Robinson's leaflet would be prepared, adding the news about the mass meeting. Some ministers, hesitant about even a one-day boycott, went along so that some unity would emerge despite Bennett's performance. It was agreed that those who remained would meet again Monday afternoon, after Mrs. Parks's trial, to plan the mass meeting.

Abernathy and King stayed at Dexter church until almost midnight, mimeographing the new leaflets. Early Saturday the distribution began, with two hundred or more volunteers giving out the handbills in door-to-door visits. Meanwhile, a taxi committee headed by Rev. W. J. Powell was winning agreement from all the black cab firms to carry riders on Monday for only the standard bus fare of ten cents. Then, Saturday evening, King, Abernathy, and others visited nightclubs to spread further the news of the upcoming boycott. . . .

The first public word of the impending boycott appeared, however, in the Saturday afternoon edition of Montgomery's smaller paper, the *Alabama Journal.* It quoted the bus company's Bagley as saying he was "sorry that the colored people blame us for any state or city ordinance which we didn't have passed," and reported that he had discussed the news with company attorney Jack Crenshaw. Montgomery City Lines, Bagley stressed, felt it had no choice in the matter. "We have to obey all laws." . . .

Although happy with the public coverage, the black leaders discussed Bennett's disastrous performance and the need to move the protest out from under the mantle of his Interdenominational Ministerial Alliance. There were few options. The leadership of the Women's Political Council knew that any public revelation of their central role would cost many of them their jobs at publicly controlled Alabama State. No other existing organization, including the NAACP chapter, had sufficient breadth of membership to represent all those who already had taken a hand in organizing the boycott. A new organization, with freshly chosen leaders, would have to be formed.

Abernathy and King agreed that creating a new organization would be the best way to oust Bennett without openly insulting him. Abernathy thought that Nixon would be the obvious choice for president of the new group, but King had doubts, arguing that Rufus Lewis would be better suited for the job. Only one month earlier King had tried to persuade Abernathy to take the NAACP presidency, but he had said no. He was thinking of returning to graduate school. Abernathy knew that King also had declined the NAACP post.

In addition to King and Abernathy, . . . Rufus Lewis and one of his closest friends, P. E. Conley, spent the weekend discussing what they could do. They also wanted to be rid of Bennett, and Lewis felt that the unschooled Nixon would be equally unacceptable. An ideal candidate who should be acceptable to all the different groups, Lewis told Conley, was his own pastor, Reverend King. True, Lewis conceded, the twenty-six-year-old King did look "more like a boy than a man," but he was extremely well educated and an articulate speaker. Those qualities would appeal strongly to the wealthier, professional segment of the black community, people who otherwise might be ambivalent about conditions on public buses that they rarely patronized. Likewise, the fact that King was a minister, and a Baptist minister, should help to draw the more conservative clergy into what had begun as a secularly led effort. . . . King, he told Conley, would be an ideal choice; both men agreed to put him forward at the Monday meeting.

Early Monday morning the attention of the black leadership shifted to the question of how successful the boycott would be. Nixon, Robinson, King, and others arose early to begin their own individual surveys of bus ridership. King watched several nearly empty buses pass his South Jackson Street home and then set out by car to observe others. In one hour's worth of driving, King spied only *eight* black riders. Hundreds of others could be seen headed toward their jobs on foot, or gathering for rides with friends and acquaintances. The black leaders were pleased; the first hours of the boycott represented a grand success. . . .

That afternoon, several dozen black leaders assembled at Reverend Bennett's Mt. Zion AME Church. Bennett immediately took charge. "We are not going to have any talking. I am not going to let anybody talk; we came here to work and to outline our program." As Ralph Abernathy recalled the scene, "I tried to get the floor, but he said, 'Well, Ab, although you're my good friend, I'm not going to even let you talk—so sit down.'" At that point, an objection was raised that some "stool pigeons" representing city officials might be present, and that a smaller group should meet in private to map their course of action. That idea was adopted, and a committee of eighteen persons was chosen to meet in the pastor's study. . . .

The group also accepted Abernathy's recommendation of "Montgomery Improvement Association" as a name for the new organization. Then Bennett called for nominations for officers, beginning with president. Without a moment's pause, Rufus Lewis's voice rang out. "Mr. Chairman, I would like to nominate Reverend M. L. King for president." P. E. Conley, Lewis's friend, immediately seconded it. No other candidates were put forward, and King was asked if he would accept the position. Abernathy, seated beside him, fully expected King to decline. Instead, after a pause, King told his colleagues, "Well, if you think I can render some service, I will," and accepted the presidency. . . .

The newly chosen president returned home less than an hour before the meeting at which he would deliver the major speech. . . .

As 7:00 P.M. approached, the area around Holt Street Baptist Church became increasingly crowded with cars and people. Thousands of Montgomery's black citizens were intent upon attending the mass meeting. The building itself was full to capacity long before seven, but Reverend Wilson quickly arranged for loudspeakers to be set up outside. King and Abernathy had to make their way slowly through the growing crowd, which was solemn and dignified almost to the point of complete silence. Though perhaps unwieldy, the number of people was gratifying to the leaders, and answered the question that had been left open that afternoon. As King put it, "my doubts concerning the continued success of our venture" were dispelled by the mass turnout. "The question of calling off the protest was now academic."

When the program got under way, one thousand people were inside the church and four thousand were gathered outside for at least a block in every direction. Contrary to E. D. Nixon's desire, no speakers were introduced by name as one pastor led a prayer and a second read a selection of Scripture. Then King stepped forward to tell the people why and how they must protest the arrest and conviction of Mrs. Parks and the continuing indignities that hundreds of them regularly suffered on Montgomery's buses. King gave a lengthy testimonial to Mrs. Parks's character, and reminded his listeners that she, and they, suffered these insults only on account of their race. "First and foremost we are American citizens," he continued. "We are not here advocating violence. We have overcome that. . . . The only weapon that we have . . . is the weapon of protest," and "the great glory of American democracy is the right to protest for right." He referred twice to the commands of the U.S. Constitution, and once to the Supreme Court's prior vindication of blacks' demands for truly equal rights. But protest and legal demands were only part of what was required,

King went on. "We must keep God in the forefront. Let us be Christian in all of our action.". . . Rising to their feet, the people applauded heartily.

King's MIA colleague and subsequent biographer, L. D. Reddick, later observed that "during this early period, King's philosophy of nonviolent resistance was only gradually taking form. When he made his debut as president of the MIA at the initial mass meeting, December 5, he did not mention Gandhi or anything directly relating to the Mahatma's theory or practice of social change. His speech was just one more appeal to principles of Christianity and democracy, to fair play and compassion for those in the opposite camp." By Christmas, however, an emerging emphasis on nonviolence was clear. The statement of the MIA position, set forth in the mimeographed brochure, observed that "this is a movement of passive resistance, depending on moral and spiritual forces. We, the oppressed, have no hate in our hearts for the oppressors, but we are, nevertheless, determined to resist until the cause of justice triumphs." Though "*passive* resistance" was a misnomer, the conscious desire to combine Gandhian precepts with Christian principles was growing in both King and the MIA. . . .

Within the private councils of the MIA, there was growing appreciation both for King's ability as the boycott's principal public spokesman and for his skillful leadership of the executive board. "King knew how to get along with all types and classes of people. He also persuaded them to get along with each other," MIA historian Lawrence Reddick later recalled. King's "democratic, patient and optimistic" approach to things impressed everyone. . . .

. . . On Monday, [January 23, 1956] Mayor Gayle announced that the city was adopting a new, tougher stance. Calling the MIA "a group of Negro radicals who have split asunder the fine relationships" between Montgomery's blacks and whites, Gayle declared that "we have pussyfooted around on this boycott long enough." No further negotiations would take place while the protest remained in force. "Until they are ready to end it, there will be no more discussions." White people, Gayle emphasized, must realize that far more was at stake in the MIA's demands than merely the question of seating practices. "What they are after is the destruction of our social fabric."

The meaning of the new city policy quickly became clear. Sellers ordered policemen to disperse groups of blacks waiting for car pool rides on street corners, and Gayle asked white housewives to stop giving rides to their black domestic workers. Giving a lift to any black person would merely aid "the Negro radicals who lead the boycott." City police also began tailing drivers from the MIA car pool, issuing tickets for trivial or nonexistent traffic violations. The official harassment made some protest supporters pause. "The voluntary pick-up system began to weaken," one MIA leader reported, and "for a moment the protest movement seemed to be wavering."

One of the first motorists to fall victim to this new policy of traffic enforcement was King himself. On Thursday, January 26, King left Dexter church in midafternoon, accompanied by one of his best friends, Robert Williams, and his church secretary, Mrs. Lillie Thomas. Before heading home, King stopped at the MIA's central transportation point to give three other persons a lift. When King pulled out, two motorcycle officers began tailing him. After several blocks, King stopped to drop off the riders. The officers pulled up beside him and told him he was under arrest. . . .

King was placed in a filthy group cell with various black criminals. Several minutes later he was taken out and fingerprinted. It was the first time King had been locked in a jail, and the first time he had been fingerprinted. . . .

Meanwhile, word of King's arrest had spread rapidly through the black community. Even before Abernathy returned, several dozen others—members of Dexter, MIA colleagues, and friends—began arriving at the jail. The growing crowd worried the white jailers, and while the fingerprinting ink was still being wiped from King's hands, the chief jailer told him he was free to leave upon his own signature. His trial would be Saturday morning. In hardly a moment's time, King was escorted out and driven back to town.

The emotional trauma of the arrest heightened the growing personal tensions King was feeling. He had not wanted to be *the* focal point of the protest in the first place, and he had erroneously assumed that a negotiated settlement would be obtained in just a few weeks time. With no end in sight, and more attention coming his way, King wondered whether he was up to the rigors of the job. He stressed to everyone that he as an individual was not crucial to the protest, that if something happened to him, or should he step aside, the movement would go on. "If M. L. King had never been born this movement would have taken place," the young minister told one mass meeting. "I just happened to be here. You know there comes a time when time itself is ready for change. That time has come in Montgomery, and I had nothing to do with it."

. . . That night, for the first time in his life, King felt . . . an experience [with God] as he sought to escape the pressures the MIA presidency had placed upon him.

He thought more about how trouble-free his life had been until the movement began. . . .

> And then we started our struggle together. Things were going well for the first few days but then, about ten or fifteen days later, after the white people in Montgomery knew that we meant business, they started doing some nasty things. They started making nasty telephone calls, and it came to the point that some days more than forty telephone calls would come in, threatening my life, the life of my family, the life of my child. I took it for a while, in a strong manner.

But that night, unable to be at peace with himself, King feared he could take it no longer. It was the most important night of his life, the one he always would think back to in future years when the pressures again seemed to be too great.

"It was around midnight," he said, thinking back on it. "You can have some strange experiences at midnight." The threatening caller had rattled him deeply. "Nigger, we are tired of you and your mess now. And if you aren't out of this town in three days, we're going to blow your brains out, and blow up your house."

> I sat there and thought about a beautiful little daughter who had just been born. . . . She was the darling of my life. I'd come in night after night and see that little gentle smile. And I sat at that table thinking about that little girl and thinking about the fact that she could be taken away from me any minute. . . .
>
> And I discovered then that religion had to become real to me, and I had to know God for myself. And I bowed down over that cup of coffee. I never will forget it . . . I prayed a prayer, and I prayed out loud that night. I said, "Lord, I'm down here trying to do what's right. I think I'm right. I think the cause that we represent is right. But Lord, I must confess that I'm weak now, I'm faltering. I'm losing my courage. And I can't let

the people see me like this because if they see me weak and losing my courage, they will begin to get weak."

Then it happened:

> And it seemed at that moment that I could hear an inner voice saying to me, "Martin Luther, stand up for righteousness. Stand up for justice. Stand up for truth. And lo I will be with you, even until the end of the world." . . . I heard the voice of Jesus saying still to fight on. He promised never to leave me, never to leave me alone. No never alone. No never alone. He promised never to leave me, never to leave me alone.

That experience gave King a new strength and courage. "Almost at once my fears began to go. My uncertainty disappeared." He went back to bed no longer worried about the threats of bombings. . . .

King's sense of history and the broader meaning of the protest was striking. "Whether we want to be or not, we are caught in a great moment of history," King told one mass meeting. "It is bigger than Montgomery. . . . The vast majority of the people of the world are colored. . . . Up until four or five years ago" most of them "were exploited by the empires of the west. . . . Today many are free. . . . And the rest are on the road. . . . We are part of that great movement." The target was larger than just segregation. "We must oppose all exploitation. . . . We want no classes and castes. . . . We want to see everybody free."

The Minority Rights Revolution: Top Down and Bottom Up

JOHN D. SKRENTNY

On January 6, 1969, Senator Barry Goldwater, Republican of Arizona, sent a letter to the new presidential administration of Richard M. Nixon. Goldwater personified the right wing of the Republican Party, argued passionately for limited government, and had previously written a book entitled *The Conscience of a Conservative*. He had also famously stuck to his principles and voted against the Civil Rights Act of 1964, the landmark law that ended racial segregation. On this day, however, Goldwater offered a lesson in political savvy for dealing with a disadvantaged group. The senator reminded the new administration that Nixon had promised a White House conference on Mexican American issues during his campaign, and that Nixon wanted to have "Mexicans" serve in his administration. Goldwater explained that this group preferred to be called "Mexican-Americans" and that the administration should avoid referring to them as Latin American—save that term for South America, coached Goldwater. The White House conference should occur "at the earliest possible time because these people are watching us to see if we will treat them the way the Democrats have." He reminded them that New York was the largest Spanish-speaking city in the United States and that nationwide there were 6 million in this

Reprinted by permission of the publisher from *The Minority Rights Revolution* by John D. Skrentny, pp. 1–5, 7–9, 11–12, 19–21, 25–26, 31, 33, 35–37, 39–40, 49, 51–52, 57, Cambridge, Mass.: The Belknap Press of Harvard University Press. Copyright © 2002 by the President and Fellows of Harvard College.

category. "You will hear a lot on this subject from me," the strident states' rights conservative warned, "so the faster you move, the less bother I will be."

A few years later, Robert H. Bork, who would become a famously right-leaning federal judge and author of the 1996 book *Slouching towards Gomorrah: Modern Liberalism and American Decline,* also promoted the cause of federal recognition of disadvantaged groups. In 1974, Bork was Nixon's solicitor general, and in that year co-authored a brief to the Supreme Court arguing that the failure to provide special language education for immigrant children was racial discrimination, according to both the Constitution and the Civil Rights Act of 1964. The Supreme Court agreed with the statutory argument, though it did not wish to go as far as Bork and create constitutional language rights in schools.

Goldwater and Bork were not alone in promoting rights for minorities. The 1965–75 period was a minority rights revolution. After the mass mobilization and watershed events of the black civil rights movement, this later revolution was led by the Establishment. It was a bipartisan project, including from both parties liberals and conservatives—though it was hard to tell the difference. Presidents, the Congress, bureaucracies, and the courts all played important roles. In the signature minority rights policy, affirmative action, the federal government went beyond African Americans and declared that certain groups were indeed "minorities"—an undefined term embraced by policymakers, advocates, and activists alike—and needed new rights and programs for equal opportunity and full citizenship. In the parlance of the period, minorities were groups seen as "disadvantaged" but not defined by income or education. African Americans were the paradigmatic minority, but there were three other ethnoracial minorities: Latinos, Asian Americans, and American Indians. Immigrants, women, and the disabled of all ethnic groups were also included and won new rights during this revolutionary period.

Bipartisanship was not the only notable aspect of the minority rights revolution. Consider also the *speed* of the development of its laws and regulations. While they appeared to have global momentum on their side, it still took two decades from the first proposition in 1941 that blacks be ensured nondiscrimination in employment to the law (Title VII of the Civil Rights Act of 1964) guaranteeing that right. Similarly, it took about twenty years between the first efforts to allow expanded immigration from outside northern and western Europe and the Immigration Act of 1965, ending all national origin discrimination in immigration. Following these landmarks, however, the government passed other laws and regulations almost immediately after first proposal. In most cases, it took only a few years to have a new law passed and there was little lobbying pressure. Bilingual education for Latinos, equal rights for women in education, and equal rights for the disabled all became law within two years of first proposal. Affirmative action expanded beyond blacks almost immediately. Such rapid success in American politics is rare. It is especially rare when achieved by groups that were defined precisely by their powerlessness and disadvantage in American society.

The rapidity and ease of the minority rights revolution brings up another puzzle. If minority rights were so easy to establish, why were not more groups included? For example, government officials perceived eastern and southern European Americans (Italians, Poles, Jews, Greeks, etc.) to be discriminated against, economically disadvantaged, or both. These "white ethnics" also had strong advocates. Yet they were never made the subjects of special policies for aid, protection, or preference. Despite widespread perceptions of their oppression, gays and lesbians similarly failed to gain a federal foothold in the minority rights revolution. Some members of Congress first submitted a bill to protect Americans from discrimination on the basis of sexual orientation in 1974. There still is no law ensuring this protection.

Another curious aspect of this minority rights revolution is that the 1960s recognition of the right to be free from discrimination was not just an American phenomenon. Nondiscrimination was quite suddenly a *world* right, a *human* right. That is, the United States was anything but alone in its recognition of minority rights. Consider the dates of major American minority-rights developments and United Nations conventions and covenants guaranteeing human-rights protections. Though usually (and notoriously) unperturbed by world trends, Americans were guaranteeing nondiscrimination and other rights at the same time that much of the world was coming to a formal consensus on these same issues. Was it just a coincidence that America and many other nations traveled on parallel paths? Moreover, was it happenstance that Africans and Asians simultaneously threw off the yoke of colonialism and their new nations joined the UN while American citizens of third-world ancestry also gained more control of their destinies?

The minority rights revolution is not only an intellectual puzzle. It was an event of enormous significance. It shaped our current understanding of American citizenship, which is more inclusive than ever before, while also drawing lines of difference between Americans. It was a major part of the development of the American regulatory state, later decried by those same conservatives who joined with liberals in building it up. And it offers a unique look at American democracy. When the stars and planets line up in just the right way, politicians, bureaucrats, and judges can offer a range of efforts to help disadvantaged Americans—even if those Americans did not ask for them. . . .

Readers will almost certainly expect a book on the spread of minority rights in the 1960s and 1970s to be a study of social movements. The image that comes to most Americans' minds when they think of the period is angry protest—radical blacks, feminists, and Latinos shouting slogans, a white ethnic "backlash," newly assertive disabled and gay people, all joining Vietnam War protesters in creating a climate of upheaval. These images exist because there was, of course, a very large amount of social-movement activity. One account of the minority rights revolution might therefore emphasize the role of grassroots mobilizing. . . .

Much of what I describe does not contradict this model. But a social-movement approach also leaves many questions unanswered. Most important, because social-movement theories are mostly about the emergence of social movements, they offer little guidance on the outcomes of social movements or the *content* of reforms. Second, they cannot explain why some groups during the same time period had to exert more pressure than others, some did not have to lobby at all, and still others failed completely despite lobbying and pressure. Why are "opportunistic politicians" so selective? Groups representing white ethnics and gays and lesbians found little and no success, respectively, during the revolution. Latinos succeeded marvelously despite small numbers, weak organization, and inconsistent demands. Women, who had better organization than Latino groups and ostensibly promised greater votes to opportunistic politicians, struggled for some of their new rights. A movement seeking rights for the disabled did not exist when the first disabled-rights law was passed. . . .

The minority rights revolution could not have occurred without the prior world battle against the Nazis and Japanese and the Cold War struggle with the Soviet Union. World War II and especially the Cold War's broadly defined "national security" policy had important legacies in domestic politics. In some ways this was direct and obvious: the perceived need for national security led to great investment in the means of warfare, driving a large part of the economy and building up firms that created weapons and other equipment. But there were other, more far-reaching effects.

During this dynamic period, war threats were staggering and horrifying, and national security prompted policies that included everything from education to highways to racial and ethnic equality. The latter became part of national security because American strategy in World War II set in motion the creation of global human-rights norms that gave a cause for the Allies and a structure to the later Cold War struggle with the Soviet Union. World War II marked the beginning of an un-precedented global cultural integration and the establishment of a global public sphere, held together by the UN and a few basic premises. The sanctity of human rights was one. At the top of the rights list was nondiscrimination. Race or ethnic discrimination, especially when practiced by those of European ancestry, was wrong. In short, geopolitical developments set into motion a dynamic where policies defined as furthering the goal of national security by fighting Nazism or global communism—including equal rights policies—found bipartisan support and rapid change in political fortunes.

The legacies of black civil rights policy were complex and varied. One important legacy was the creation of new "institutional homes" (to borrow Chris Bonastia's term) for rights advocates to have positions of real policymaking power. Most important here were the Equal Employment Opportunity Commission (EEOC), the Department of Health, Education and Welfare's Office for Civil Rights, and the De-partment of Labor's Office of Federal Contract Compliance. All were created to enforce rights laws for blacks, and all attracted employees who supported equal-opportunity rights. . . .

Other policy legacies of the black civil rights movement were more cultural in character, though equally important. The Civil Rights Act of 1964, as well as other efforts to help blacks, created a tool kit or repertoire of policy models that could be extended again and again and adapted to deal with the problems of groups other than black Americans. Through their own initiative, or when pressured by nonblack minority advocates, civil-rights bureaucrats responded with affirmative action—regardless of the specific demands of the minority advocates. Policymakers some-times simply anticipated what minority constituents wanted. They created an "anticipatory politics" based on these policy tools and the new legitimacy of minor-ity targeting. Activist members of Congress used the Civil Rights Act's Title VI, barring federal funds for any program that discriminated on the basis race, national origin, or religion, as part of a policy repertoire when seeking votes or social move-ment goals. Congress thus created Title IX of the Education Amendments of 1972, barring sex discrimination on the part of educational institutions receiving federal funds, and Section 504 of the Rehabilitation Act of 1973, which addressed discrimination on the basis of disability also by using the Civil Rights Act model. . . .

. . . To attract support for the Allied side during World War II, President Franklin Delano Roosevelt strongly promoted the United States as a symbol of human rights and race equality. These efforts then invited first the Axis and then the Soviet Union's propaganda strategies highlighting American racism and ethnic inequality. Especially with the parts of government aware of this propaganda and engaged with foreign audiences, specifically presidents and State Department officials, there was a rapid recategorization of domestic nondiscrimination as part of foreign policy and national security. This is apparent in both Democratic and Republican administrations. Comprehensive policy change, however, required convincing Congress and the American public, and both government leaders and rights groups actively promoted the meaning of nondiscrimination as national security. Change was incremental and needed mass mobilization for black civil rights and lobbying campaigns for immigration reform before breakthrough victories finally came in the mid-1960s.

Other rights could not be categorized as easily as national security. Women, for example, made few gains because gender was not a dividing principle in geopolitics as was race. Gender equality was not a part of Nazi, Japanese, or Communist propaganda and therefore served no national security interest. Social rights and welfare state development similarly did not become part of national security policy, even during the Cold War when America confronted an ideology based on economic egalitarianism. This was in part because many business and professional interest groups and Republican party leaders could quite plausibly argue that excessive interference with the market economy and market-based wealth distributions would push America *toward* socialism, rather than save it from this threat.

This was not only a matter of simple voting power, lobbying, or protest strength. Success and the speed at which it was achieved in the minority rights revolution depended greatly on the meaning of the group in question. After advocates for black Americans helped break the taboo on targeting policy at disadvantaged groups, government officials quickly categorized some groups as "minorities"—a never-defined term that basically meant "analogous to blacks." These classifications were *not* based on study, but on simple, unexamined prototypes of groups. Most obviously, government officials saw the complex category of Latinos (then usually called "Spanish-surnamed" or Spanish-speaking") in terms of a simple racial prototype, obscuring the fact that many Latinos consider themselves white. Racialized in this way, Latinos needed little lobbying to win minority rights. Women, who faced ridicule like no other group, needed significant meaning entrepreneurship. Their advocates pushed hard to make the black analogy. Though Asian Americans presumably possessed a clearer group racial definition that did Latinos, the analogy between Asians and blacks was weaker than that between Latinos and blacks. Policymakers sometimes dropped Asian Americans from their lists. This was apparently just a cognitive forgetting—it required only small reminders for them to be included in minority policy, at least formally. . . .

Two cases of the failure of the minority rights revolution highlight the importance of group meanings in shaping its limits. First, white ethnics, or the immigrants from eastern and southern Europe and their descendants, organized for action and were recognized as a disadvantaged and important political constituency. They nevertheless did not gain policy recognition and remained categorized outside the minority rights revolution. Ethnic rights failed primarily because the meaning perceived in white ethnics as a group. On the one hand, government officials did not see ethnics as being within a threshold of oppression or victimhood that while unspoken, undebated, and unlegislated, nevertheless powerfully shaped policy. Additionally, politicians saw ethnics in multifaceted ways—as ethnic minorities, but also as Catholics, union members, and anti-Communists. These different perceived identities sent policy appeals off in directions other than those derived from black rights. Second, gays and lesbians, though undeniably discriminated against, victimized, oppressed, and newly organized for power, also were left out of the rights revolution during the 1965 to 1975 because of the meaning of homosexuality. The analogy with blacks again hit a wall: this group was different—too different. The basis of group difference—same-gender sexual attractions—remained taboo as a target of protective policy recognition, and gay rights bills in Congress went nowhere. . . .

Shortly before the passage of the Civil Rights Act of 1964, the Republican Senate minority leader, Everett Dirksen of Illinois, said he finally supported equal rights for blacks. He explained, "No army is stronger than an idea whose time has come." Dirksen was right. Any resistance to federally guaranteed black civil rights by a national political leader was anachronistic. The following year, Congress passed the Voting Rights Act, giving African Americans in the southern states the right to vote, and the Immigration Act, ending decades of discrimination against Asians and eastern and southern Europeans in their ability to come to the United States.

But why were federally guaranteed nondiscrimination rights such a powerful idea? The brilliant strategies and sacrifices of the black civil rights movement were certainly part of the story, as was their growing political strength in conventional electoral politics. These factors cannot explain, however, the establishment of immigration and naturalization rights for Asians, who had little political clout and no major lobbying or protest activities. Moreover, racial supremacy and blatant racial discrimination were anachronisms the world over, not just in the United States. This was not a coincidence. The development of minority rights in the United States was connected to their development elsewhere in the world. . . .

Roosevelt died in 1944 but his vision of human rights lived on in the Truman administration. Various nongovernmental organizations—notably, black civil-rights groups—played a crucial role in keeping the commitment to equal rights part of the world order. At the founding UN meeting in San Francisco, black leaders such as the NAACP's W. E. B. Du Bois and Walter White lobbied for the inclusion of a bill of human rights, as they "huddled constantly" with officials from such diverse countries as the United States, France, the Philippines, Haiti, and Liberia. They sought to equally benefit both non-American nonwhite people and their fellow citizens. Du Bois and White saw these fates as linked. For example, Du Bois told the *San Francisco Chronicle* that the world's colonies were similar to "slums," and explained that a world bill of rights would hold all nations accountable for their discriminatory treatment of human beings. The historian Brenda Gayle Plummer credits these efforts with getting "human rights" mentioned in the official UN charter. . . .

Another result was a commitment to produce a universal declaration of human rights. In 1946, President Harry Truman appointed Eleanor Roosevelt to represent the United States and chair a new UN Commission on Human Rights charged with creating the declaration. Despite conflicts (the Soviet Union was concerned by the inclusion of French- and Anglo-American-style liberties, and the State Department opposed the inclusion of socialist-style social or economic rights, such as a right to employment and health care), the UN ratified the declaration of December 10, 1948. Though unenforceable, this was a grand statement of world wide moral principles. . . .

Government advocates for civil rights used links between world opinion and national security in propaganda aimed at American citizens. The strategy was to get Americans to think of the global audience and the different policies that could help in the fight against Communism. Truman's President's Committee on Civil Rights used this strategy prominently in its high-profile report, *To Secure These Rights*. After detailing the various rights being denied to blacks, the report concluded with justifications for federal action, including the "moral reason," the "economic reason," and the "international reason." Here the report explained that "our position in the postwar world is so vital to the future that our smallest actions have far-reaching effects." The report concluded, "The United States is not so strong, the final triumph of the democratic ideal is not so inevitable that we can ignore what the world thinks of us or our record."

National-security meanings also shaped campaign strategy and political speeches at home that discussed civil rights. Nongovernmental groups representing business and religious faiths argued for the same recategorization. The Advertising Council had embarked on a publicity campaign entitled " 'United America' (Group Prejudice is a Post-War Menace)" designed to encourage Americans to respect human rights. The Institute for Religious and Social Studies—a graduate school created at the Jewish Theological Seminary of America, but which united Jewish, Catholic, and Protestant scholars—published lectures in a 1949 series called *Discrimination and National Welfare*. Leading scholars such as the sociologist Robert K. Merton as well as political activists such as Roger Baldwin of the ACLU and Adolph A. Berle, a leading member of the Roosevelt administration's "brains trust," contributed to the collected lectures. Readers encountered reasoned arguments that mostly stressed the cost of discrimination in terms of business, foreign policy, and national security. . . .

More so than during the Truman presidency, the Eisenhower years and those following saw violent civil-rights conflicts that would provide the USSR with its most powerful propaganda—photographic evidence of American racial injustice. Especially worrisome were photos of southern repression of civil-rights demonstrations that filled the pages of the world's newspapers. [Mary] Dudziak has written, for example, of Eisenhower's great distress regarding the international consequences of his order to send troops into Little Rock, Arkansas when disorder and violence threatened to engulf efforts at school desegregation. In recounting the incident in his memoirs and in private communications, Eisenhower revealed how he construed the crises in terms of national security and the moral boundaries then taken for granted in the UN. . . .

Throughout the early 1960s, civil-rights leaders continued their effective strategy of directing world attention to black inequality and linking black civil rights to national security. They traveled to Africa and seized opportunities in the UN. Martin Luther King Jr. encouraged the nation to think globally, often stressing the links between the struggles of black people in the United States to those in Africa. And any time civil-rights leaders met white repression, the story made international headlines. . . .

In this domestic and international context, and with domestic public opinion supporting civil rights at an all-time high, Kennedy sent legislation (later to become the Civil Rights Act of 1964) to Congress. Fearing more racial violence, he worked behind the scenes meeting with business leaders and other elites in an attempt to gain control of the racial situation. In a July 11, 1963 meeting with approximately seventy members of the Business Council, Kennedy, Vice President Lyndon Johnson, Attorney General Robert Kennedy, and Secretary of State Dean Rusk all urged these business leaders to help by employing more black Americans. . . .

Lyndon Johnson presided over great propaganda triumphs for the global image of the United States. His time in office saw the Civil Rights Act of 1964, the Voting Rights Act of 1965, and the Civil Rights Act of 1968 (for equal rights in housing)— all crowning jewels of the black civil rights movement. . . .

One difficulty with assessing the impact of war and geopolitics on minority rights is that in the case most often studied, that of black Americans, the impact of war coincided with growing organized black protest and increasing black voting power gained through migration to the northern states. Did national-security meanings really have any independent prorights impact? Evidence that it did comes from an examination of rights reform in the area of immigration and naturalization, a case where, at least in the early stages, there was no mass mobilization pressure and few electoral benefits for reform-minded lawmakers.

American immigration and naturalization policy used race and ethnic discrimination from the nation's founding. In 1790, Congress limited the right of naturalization to free whites. Blacks gained naturalization rights during Reconstruction, but Asians remained excluded. . . .

In 1942, the new effort at allowing Asian immigration began, led by a small but elite group of sympathetic, non-Chinese New Yorkers. Magazines such as the *Christian Century,* the *New Republic,* and Richard Walsh's *Asia and the Americas* tried to raise awareness of the issue by publishing such articles as "Our Great Wall against the Chinese," "Repeal Exclusion Laws Now," "Are We Afraid to Do Justice?" and "Justice for the Chinese." Walsh was the husband of author Pearl Buck, whose novel of China, *The Good Earth,* won a Pulitzer prize in 1932. He formed a Citizen's Committee to Repeal Chinese Exclusion, which first met on May 25, 1943. . . .

By the early 1960s, ending discrimination on the basis of national origin was a way to appeal to the ethnic groups that were disadvantaged by the current system. The success of the black civil rights movement further eroded the legitimacy of national origin discrimination in immigration. During the 1960 election, both parties supported immigration reform in their national party platforms. . . .

Like the two presidents before him, President Kennedy lent the prestige of his office to the cause of immigration reform. He was a supporter of immigration (he even published a book on the subject in 1958), and was almost certainly aware of the electoral benefits of immigration reform. The State Department pressed for change as it did with black civil rights. By 1961, various nationality groups, especially Chinese, Polish, and Italian groups, were regularly sending letters in support of immigration reform. . . .

Kennedy would not live to see reform, but his successor Lyndon Johnson maintained the pattern of past presidents in supporting reform, as did Secretary of State Dean Rusk in 1964 congressional hearings. Rusk pointed out that the national origins system "results in discrimination in our hospitality to different nationalities in a world situation which is quite different from that which existed at the time the national origins system was originally adopted. . . .

Eliminating that national-origins system, and especially the racist program for Asia, would therefore eliminate a millstone and fight enemy propaganda while only technically changing policy. Rusk explained, "We deprive ourselves of a powerful weapon in our fight against misinformation if we do not reconcile here, too, the letter of the law with the facts of immigration and thus erase the unfavorable impression made by our old quota limitation for Asian persons." . . .

The Immigration Act of 1965 is strangely neglected in studies of American politics and minority rights. Even major figures instrumental to its passage appear to think little of it. Momentous and hard fought, it is not discussed at all in Johnson's memoirs of his presidency—not a single mention. Dean Rusk, a star player in its passage, gave the topic only one paragraph in his memoirs, saying, "We at State helped promote it."

Still, it was a major policy development—much more so than was intended. . . . The point here, however, is that reform happened at about the same time as other major nondiscrimination laws and declarations in America and in the UN. By mostly benefiting Asians, it benefited a group that, in the initial stages at least, were unlike African Americans in that they were tiny parts of the population, promised few electoral benefits, and did not mass mobilize. But regardless of party, presidents and State Department officials were active players in the reform of immigration; mindful of foreign propaganda, they therefore saw nondiscrimination in immigration as they did black civil rights—as national-security policy.

◤ FURTHER READING

Taylor Branch, *Parting the Waters* (1988) and *Pillar of Fire* (1998).

Clayborne Carson, *In Struggle: SNCC and the Black Awakening of the 1960s* (1981).

George Pierre Castile, *To Show Heart: Native American Self-Determination and Federal Indian Policy* (1998).

Vine Deloria, Jr., *Custer Died for Your Sins: An Indian Manifesto* (1969).

John D'Emilio, *Sexual Politics, Sexual Communities: The Making of a Homosexual Minority in the United States, 1940–1970* (1983).

Mary L. Dudziak, *Cold War Civil Rights: Race and the Image of American Democracy* (2000).

Michael B. Friedland, *Lift Up Your Voice Like a Trumpet: White Clergy and the Civil Rights and Anti-War Movements* (1998).

Ignacio M. Garcia, *Viva Kennedy: Mexican Americans in Search of Camelot* (2000).

Alex Haley, comp., *The Autobiography of Malcolm X* (1965).

Manning Marable, *Race, Reform, and Rebellion: The Second Reconstruction in Black America, 1945–1990* (1991).

Ruth Rosen, *The World Split Open: How the Modern Women's Movement Changed America* (2000).

Douglas Rossinow, *The Politics of Authenticity: Liberalism, Christianity, and the New Left in America* (1998).

CHAPTER
13

The Sixties: Left, Right,
and the Culture Wars

Like the psychedelic music and drugs that were popular during the decade, the history of the sixties can be a mind-altering experience. Colorful reform movements shift, reshape, and overlap as in a kaleidoscope. Consumer advocacy, environmental reform, organic foods, communal living, the sexual revolution, personal growth groups, feminism, civil rights, the antiwar crusade, and dozens of other "issues" clamored for attention (and some of them still do). In fact, it was this bewildering hubbub that defined the sixties as a captivating and, for some, maddening period of time. Everything seemed open to question: politics, manners, sexual relations, and even the meaning of America.

Of course the sixties did not begin on New Year's Day 1960 and end on New Year's Eve 1969. As we have seen, the sources of unrest reached back into the 1950s for both liberals and conservatives. Liberals looked out on the political landscape and optimistically asked themselves, how can we enable the greatest nation on earth to live up to its full potential for social justice? They did not have to look far beyond the Mason-Dixon line to see one set of answers. John Kennedy, in fact, said explicitly in the campaign debates that led to his election, "I think we can do better." The president consistently emphasized the theme of citizen responsibility, exhorting Americans: "Ask not what your country can do for you—ask what you can do for your country." Conservatives posed a different question to their constituencies: where did we go wrong? Brash new leaders like Barry Goldwater, George Wallace, and Ronald Reagan repudiated moderate "Eisenhower Republicanism," seeing it as an unholy compromise with a set of disturbing trends unleashed by Roosevelt during the New Deal. They wanted "big government" out, "states' rights" in, and a return to so-called traditional values at all levels. As the decade wore on, activists on both the right and the left became more assertive in their rhetoric and more radical in their demands.

But many of the social forces at work in the period were beyond the control of any political group, liberal or conservative. The invention of the birth control pill at Stanford University in 1960, for example, fundamentally altered the behavior of millions of women and men, regardless of religion, politics, or economic privilege; the so-called Sexual Revolution had begun. And issues like civil rights were not something many politicians took up willingly—they pushed up from the grassroots. Even prosperity, as we saw in the fifties, invited discontent. Suddenly millions of

Americans became worried about their "potential." *The Human Potential Movement of the 1960s, centered in California, asked Americans not what they could do for their country, but what they could do for themselves. Gestalt therapy, encounter groups, and Transactional Analysis were so far outside the ken of official Washington that California was ridiculed as "Lala land."*

The period continues to excite debate in part because we are still not entirely sure of its legacy. By the end of the sixties, the liberal administrations of John F. Kennedy and Lyndon Johnson had implemented a number of reforms, but the Democratic Party lost the presidency. Four of the greatest reformers ended their lives in pools of blood: John Kennedy, Robert Kennedy, Martin Luther King, Jr., and Malcolm X. If liberals or leftists defined the sixties, as conservatives sometimes say, how did it end so badly for them? In the end, who really won?

QUESTIONS TO THINK ABOUT

Did the sixties, on balance, create a more liberal or a more conservative America? How and why did both the Left and Right become radical by the end of the decade? Which changes initiated in the sixties are still with us today?

DOCUMENTS

The documents in the chapter reflect the sharp divergence of views during the sixties. Document 1 articulates the goals of the Young Americans for Freedom, a group then on the "right-wing fringe" of the moderate Republican Party. The sixties are correctly remembered as a decade of liberal youth activism, but it's equally true that young conservatives struggled to make their voices heard. Document 2 is from John F. Kennedy's inaugural speech, given January 20, 1961. As journalist Bill Moyers recalls in Document 3, the president galvanized hopeful young Americans around an ideal of public service. Shortly after the inaugural, Moyers became deputy director of the Peace Corps, an organization started by Kennedy to send volunteers to the Third World. In Document 4, Students for a Democratic Society (also known as SDS) proclaim goals opposite those of Young Americans for Freedom. They express support for social experimentation to achieve a better world. Document 5 is a folk song by Malvina Reynolds that encourages young people to break out of the mass society that puts people in "little boxes." In Document 6, Alabama Governor George Wallace denounces "pseudo-liberal spokesmen" who believe that government can provide a "utopian life" for all if given enough authority. He also proclaims "segregation forever," speaking for southern traditionalists who opposed both federal activism and civil rights. In Document 7, written less than two months after Kennedy's assassination on November 22, 1963, Lyndon Baines Johnson declares a national "war on poverty" in the name of the martyred president. Document 8 reveals what was sometimes called "the generation gap." In this selection, a nineteen-year-old participant at "sit-ins" at Columbia University in 1968 recalls conversations with his father about long hair and the meaning of student protest. In Document 9, Vice President Spiro Agnew attacks student protestors as "impudent snobs" whose notion of popular democracy is "government by street carnival." In the last reading, Document 10, California psychologist Carl Rogers describes an alternative to the phoniness of mass society: focusing inward to find the "real" you. Encounter groups like those pioneered by Rogers probably had more participants than protest organizations. Their popularity reflects the transition from President Kennedy's "we" generation to the "me" generation, as Americans came to value "getting in touch with their feelings."

1. Young Americans for Freedom Draft a Conservative Manifesto, 1960

In this time of moral and political crisis, it is the responsibility of the youth of America to affirm certain eternal truths.

We, as young conservatives, believe:

That foremost among the transcendent values is the individual's use of his God-given free will, whence derives his right to be free from the restrictions of arbitrary force;

That liberty is indivisible, and that political freedom cannot long exist without economic freedom;

That the purposes of government are to protect these freedoms through the preservation of internal order, the provision of national defense, and the administration of justice;

That when government ventures beyond these rightful functions, it accumulates power which tends to diminish order and liberty;

That the Constitution of the United States is the best arrangement yet devised for empowering government to fulfill its proper role, while restraining it from the concentration and abuse of power;

That the genius of the Constitution—the division of powers—is summed up in the clause which reserves primacy to the several states, or to the people, in those spheres not specifically delegated to the Federal Government;

That the market economy, allocating resources by the free play of supply and demand, is the single economic system compatible with the requirements of personal freedom and constitutional government, and that it is at the same time the most productive supplier of human needs;

That when government interferes with the work of the market economy, it tends to reduce the moral and physical strength of the nation; that when it takes from one man to bestow on another, it diminishes the incentive of the first, the integrity of the second, and the moral autonomy of both;

That we will be free only so long as the national sovereignty of the United States is secure: that history shows periods of freedom are rare, and can exist only when free citizens concertedly defend their rights against all enemies;

That the forces of international Communism are, at present, the greatest single threat to these liberties;

That the United States should stress victory over, rather than coexistence with, this menace; and

That American foreign policy must be judged by this criterion: does it serve the just interests of the United States?

2. President John Kennedy Tells Americans to Ask "What You Can Do," 1961

We observe today not a victory of party but a celebration of freedom—symbolizing an end as well as a beginning—signifying renewal as well as change. For I have sworn before you and Almighty God the same solemn oath our forebears prescribed nearly a century and three-quarters ago.

The world is very different now. For man holds in his mortal hands the power to abolish all forms of human poverty and all forms of human life. And yet the same revolutionary beliefs for which our forebears fought are still at issue around the globe—the belief that the rights of man come not from the generosity of the state but from the hand of God.

We dare not forget today that we are the heirs of that first revolution. Let the word go forth from this time and place, to friend and foe alike, that the torch has been passed to a new generation of Americans—born in this century, tempered by war, disciplined by a hard and bitter peace, proud of our ancient heritage—and unwilling to witness or permit the slow undoing of those human rights to which this nation has always been committed, and to which we are committed today at home and around the world.

Let every nation know, whether it wishes us well or ill, that we shall pay any price, bear any burden, meet any hardship, support any friend, oppose any foe to assure the survival and the success of liberty.

This much we pledge—and more. . . .

In your hands, my fellow citizens, more than mine, will rest the final success or failure of our course. Since this country was founded, each generation of Americans has been summoned to give testimony to its national loyalty.The graves of young Americans who answered the call to service surround the globe.

Now the trumpet summons us again—not as a call to bear arms, though arms we need,—not as a call to battle, though embattled we are—but a call to bear the burden of a long twilight struggle, year in and year out, "rejoicing in hope, patient in tribulation"—a struggle against the common enemies of man: tyranny, poverty, disease, and war itself.

Can we forge against these enemies a grand and global alliance, North and South, East and West, that can assure a more fruitful life for all mankind? Will you join in that historic effort?

In the long history of the world, only a few generations have been granted the role of defending freedom in its hour of maximum danger. I do not shrink from this responsibility—I welcome it. I do not believe that any of us would exchange places with any other people or any other generation. The energy, the faith, the devotion which we bring to this endeavor will light our country and all who serve it—and the glow from that fire can truly light the world.

And so, my fellow Americans: ask not what your country can do for you—ask what you can do for your country.

Public Papers of the Presidents of the United States: John F. Kennedy, 1961 (Washington, D.C.: U.S. Government Printing Office, 1962), p. 1.

My fellow citizens of the world: ask not what America will do for you, but what together we can do for the freedom of man.

Finally, whether you are citizens of America or citizens of the world, ask of us here the same high standards of strength and sacrifice which we ask of you. With a good conscience our only sure reward, with history the final judge of our deeds, let us go forth to lead the land we love, asking His blessing and His help, but knowing that here on earth God's work must truly be our own.

3. Bill Moyers Remembers Kennedy's Effect on His Generation (1961), 1988

Of the private man John Kennedy I knew little. I saw him rarely. Once, when the 1960 campaign was over and he was ending a post-election visit to the LBJ Ranch, he pulled me over into a corner to urge me to abandon my plans for graduate work at the University of Texas and to come to Washington as part of the New Frontier. I told him that I had already signed up to teach at a Baptist school in Texas while pursuing my doctorate. Anyway, I said, "You're going to have to call on the whole faculty at Harvard. You don't need a graduate of Southwestern Baptist Theological Seminary." In mock surprise he said, "Didn't you know that the first president of Harvard was a Baptist? You'll be right at home."

And so I was.

So I remember John Kennedy not so much for what he was or what he wasn't but for what he empowered in me. We all edit history to give some form to the puzzle of our lives, and I cherish the memory of him for awakening me to a different story for myself. He placed my life in a larger narrative than I could ever have written. One test of a leader is knowing, as John Stuart Mill put it, that "the worth of the state, in the long run, is the worth of the individuals composing it." Preserving civilization is the work not of some miracle-working, superhuman personality but of each one of us. The best leaders don't expect us just to pay our taxes and abdicate, they sign us up for civic duty and insist we sharpen our skills as citizens. . . .

Public figures either make us feel virtuous about retreating into the snuggeries of self or they challenge us to act beyond our obvious capacities. America is always up for grabs, can always go either way. The same culture that produced the Ku Klux Klan, Lee Harvey Oswald, and the Jonestown massacre also produced Martin Luther King, Archibald MacLeish, and the Marshall Plan.

A desperate and alienated young man told me in 1970, after riots had torn his campus and town: "I'm just as good as I am bad. I think all of us are. But nobody's speaking to the good in me." In his public voice John Kennedy spoke to my generation of service and sharing; he called us to careers of discovery through lives open to others. . . .

. . . It was for us not a trumpet but a bell, sounding in countless individual hearts that one clear note that said: "You matter. You can signify. You can make a difference." Romantic? Yes, there was romance to it. But we were not then so callous toward romance.

Bill Moyers, *To Touch the World: The Peace Corps Experience* (Washington, D.C.: Peace Corps, 1995), pp. 152–153.

4. Students for a Democratic Society Advance a Reform Agenda, 1962

We are people of this generation, bred in at least modest comfort, housed now in universities, looking uncomfortably to the world we inherit.

When we were kids the United States was the wealthiest and strongest country in the world; the only one with the atom bomb, the least scarred by modern war, an initiator of the United Nations that we thought would distribute Western influence throughout the world. Freedom and equality for each individual, government of, by, and for the people—these American values we found good, principles by which we could live as men. Many of us began maturing in complacency.

As we grew, however, our comfort was penetrated by events too troubling to dismiss. First, the permeating and victimizing fact of human degradation, symbolized by the Southern struggle against racial bigotry, compelled most of us from silence to activism. Second, the enclosing fact of the Cold War, symbolized by the presence of the Bomb, brought awareness that we ourselves, and our friends, and millions of abstract "others" we knew more directly because of our common peril, might die at any time. We might deliberately ignore, or avoid, or fail to feel all other human problems, but not these two, for these were too immediate and crushing in their impact, too challenging in the demand that we as individuals take the responsibility for encounter and resolution.

While these and other problems either directly oppressed us or rankled our consciences and became our own subjective concerns, we began to see complicated and disturbing paradoxes in our surrounding America. The declaration "all men are created equal . . . " rang hollow before the facts of Negro life in the South and the big cities of the North. The proclaimed peaceful intentions of the United States contradicted its economic and military investments in the Cold War status quo. . . .

Our work is guided by the sense that we may be the last generation in the experiment with living. But we are a minority—the vast majority of our people regard the temporary equilibriums of our society and world as eternally-functional parts. In this is perhaps the outstanding paradox: we ourselves are imbued with urgency, yet the message of our society is that there is no viable alternative to the present. Beneath the reassuring tones of the politicians, beneath the common opinion that America will "muddle through," beneath the stagnation of those who have closed their minds to the future, is the pervading feeling that there simply are no alternatives, that our times have witnessed the exhaustion not only of Utopias, but of any new departures as well. . . .

Some would have us believe that Americans feel contentment amidst prosperity—but might it not be better called a glaze above deeply-felt anxieties about their role in the new world? And if these anxieties produce a developed indifference to human affairs, do they not as well produce a yearning to believe there *is* an alternative to the present, that something *can* be done to change circumstances in the school, the workplaces, the bureaucracies, the government? It is to this latter yearning, at once the spark and engine of change, that we direct our present appeal.

Excerpt from The Port Huron Statement, 1962. State Historical Society of Wisconsin.

The search for truly democratic alternatives to the present, and a commitment to social experimentation with them, is a worthy and fulfilling human enterprise, one which moves us and, we hope, others today.

5. Folk Singer Malvina Reynolds Sees Young People in "Little Boxes," 1963

Little boxes on the hillside, little boxes made of ticky tacky
Little boxes on the hillside, little boxes all the same
There's a green one and a pink one and a blue one and a yellow one
And they're all made out of ticky tacky and they all look just the same.

And the people in the houses
All went to the university,
Where they were put in boxes
And they came out all the same,
And there's doctors and there's lawyers,
And business executives,
And they're all made out of ticky tacky
And they all look just the same.
And they all play on the golf course
And drink their martinis dry,
And they all have pretty children
And the children go to school,
And the children go to summer camp
And then to the university,
Where they are put in boxes and they come out all the same.

And the boys go into business
and marry and raise a family
In boxes made of ticky tacky
And they all look just the same.

6. Governor George Wallace Denounces Top-Down Reform and Pledges "Segregation Forever," 1963

Today I have stood, where once Jefferson Davis stood, and took an oath to my people. It is very appropriate then that from this Cradle of the Confederacy, this very Heart of the Great Anglo-Saxon Southland, that today we sound the drum for freedom as have our generations of forebears before us done, time and time again through history. Let us rise to the call of freedom-loving blood that is in us and send our answer to the tyranny that clanks its chains upon the South. In the name of the greatest people that have ever trod this earth, I draw the line in the dust and toss the gauntlet before

---

From the song, "Little Boxes." Words and music by Malvina Reynolds. Copyright © 1962 by Schroder Music Company (ASCAP. Renewed 1990). Used with permission. All rights reserved.

Inaugural speech, January 14, 1963, Alabama Department of Historical Archives.

the feet of tyranny . . . and I say . . . segregation today . . . segregation tomorrow . . . segregation forever. . . .

Let us send this message back to Washington by our representatives who are with us today . . . that from this day we are standing up, and the heel of tyranny does not fit the neck of an upright man . . . that we intend to take the offensive and carry our fight for freedom across the nation, wielding the balance of power we know we possess in the Southland . . . that WE, not the insipid bloc of voters of some sections . . . will determine in the next election who shall sit in the White House of these United States. . . . That from this day, from this hour . . . from this minute . . . we give the word of a race of honor that we will tolerate their boot in our face no longer . . . and let those certain judges put *that* in their opium pipes of power and smoke it for what it is worth. . . .

. . . We can no longer hide our head in the sand and tell ourselves that the ideology of our free fathers is not being attacked and is not being threatened by another idea . . . for it is. We are faced with an idea that if a centralized government assumes enough authority, enough power over its people, that it can provide a utopian life . . . that if given the power to dictate, to forbid, to require, to demand, to distribute, to edict and to judge what is best and enforce that will produce only "good" . . . and it shall be our father . . . and our God. It is an idea of government that encourages our fears and destroys our faith. . . . It is a system that is the very opposite of Christ for it feeds and encourages everything degenerate and base in our people as it assumes the responsibilities that we ourselves should assume. Its pseudo-liberal spokesmen and some Harvard advocates have never examined the logic of its substitution of what it calls "human rights" for individual rights, for its propaganda play on words has appeal for the unthinking. . . .

And that is why today, I stand ashamed of the fat, well-fed whimperers who say that it is inevitable . . . that our cause is lost. I am ashamed *of* them . . . and I am ashamed *for* them. They do not represent the people of the Southland. . . .

We remind all within hearing of this Southland that a *Southerner*, Peyton Randolph, presided over the Continental Congress in our nation's beginning . . . that a *Southerner*, Thomas Jefferson, wrote the Declaration of Independence, that a *Southerner*, George Washington, is the Father of our country . . . that a *Southerner*, James Madison, authored our Constitution, that a *Southerner*, George Mason, authored the Bill of Rights and it was a Southerner who said, "Give me liberty . . . or give me death," Patrick Henry.

Southerners played a most magnificent part in erecting this great divinely inspired system of freedom . . . and as God is our witness, Southerners will save it.

7. President Lyndon B. Johnson Declares a Federal War on Poverty, 1964

Let this session of Congress be known as the session which did more for civil rights than the last hundred sessions combined; as the session which enacted the most far-reaching tax cut of our time; as the session which declared all-out war on human

Public Papers of the Presidents of the United States: Lyndon B. Johnson, 1964 (Washington, D.C.: U.S. Government Printing Office, 1965), pp. 704–707.

poverty and unemployment in these United States; as the session which finally recognized the health needs of all our older citizens; as the session which reformed our tangled transportation and transit policies; as the session which achieved the most effective, efficient foreign aid program ever; and as the session which helped to build more homes, more schools, more libraries, and more hospitals than any single session of Congress in the history of our Republic. . . .

Unfortunately, many Americans live on the outskirts of hope—some because of their poverty, and some because of their color, and all too many because of both. Our task is to help replace their despair with opportunity.

This administration today, here and now, declares unconditional war on poverty in America. I urge this Congress and all Americans to join with me in that effort. . . .

Our aim is not only to relieve the symptom of poverty, but to cure it and, above all, to prevent it. No single piece of legislation, however, is going to suffice.

We will launch a special effort in the chronically distressed areas of Appalachia.

We must expand our small but our successful area redevelopment program.

We must enact youth employment legislation to put jobless, aimless, hopeless youngsters to work on useful projects.

We must distribute more food to the needy through a broader food stamp program.

We must create a National Service Corps to help the economically handicapped of our own country as the Peace Corps now helps those abroad.

We must modernize our unemployment insurance and establish a high-level commission on automation. If we have the brain power to invent these machines, we have the brain power to make certain that they are a boon and not a bane to humanity.

We must extend the coverage of our minimum wage laws to more than 2 million workers now lacking this basic protection of purchasing power.

We must, by including special school aid funds as part of our education program, improve the quality of teaching, training, and counseling in our hardest hit areas.

We must build more libraries in every area and more hospitals and nursing homes under the Hill-Burton Act, and train more nurses to staff them.

We must provide hospital insurance for our older citizens financed by every worker and his employer under Social Security, contributing no more than $1 a month during the employee's working career to protect him in his old age in a dignified manner without cost to the Treasury, against the devastating hardship of prolonged or repeated illness.

We must, as a part of a revised housing and urban renewal program, give more help to those displaced by slum clearance, provide more housing for our poor and our elderly, and seek as our ultimate goal in our free enterprise system a decent home for every American family.

We must help obtain more modern mass transit within our communities as well as low-cost transportation between them.

Above all, we must release $11 billion of tax reduction into the private spending stream to create new jobs and new markets in every area of this land.

8. A Protester at Columbia University Defends Long Hair and Revolution, 1969

Columbia used to be called King's College. They changed the name in 1784 because they wanted to be patriotic and *Columbia* means *America.* This week we've been finding out what America means.

Every morning now when I wake up I have to run through the whole thing in my mind. I have to do that because I wake up in a familiar place that isn't what it was. I wake up and I see blue coats and brass buttons all over the campus. ("Brass buttons, blue coat, can't catch a nanny goat" goes the Harlem nursery rhyme.) I start to go off the campus but then remember to turn and walk two blocks uptown to get to the only open gate. There I squeeze through the three-foot "out" opening in the police barricade, and I feel for my wallet to be sure I've got the two I.D.'s necessary to get back into my college. I stare at the cops. They stare back and see a red armband and long hair and they perhaps tap their night sticks on the barricade. They're looking at a radical leftist. . . .

At the sundial are 500 people ready to follow Mark Rudd (whom they don't particularly like because he always refers to President Kirk as "that shithead") into the Low Library administration building to demand severance from IDA [Institute for Defense Analysis], an end to gym construction, and to defy Kirk's recent edict prohibiting indoor demonstrations. . . .

I go upstairs to reconnoiter and there is none other than Peter Behr of Linda LeClair fame* chalking on the wall, " 'Up against the wall, motherfucker, . . .' from a poem by LeRoi Jones." I get some chalk and write "I am sorry about defacing the walls, but babies are being burned and men are dying, and this University is at fault quite directly."

. . . Medical science has yet to discover any positive correlation between hair length and anything—intelligence, virility, morality, cavities, cancer—anything.

Long hair on men, however, has been known to make some people sick.

My father, for instance. On July 8, 1968, he alleged that long hair on his sons made him sick. "You look like a woman," he said. "I'll get a haircut," I said. That threw him off, but only for a moment. "If I were a girl," he continued, "I wouldn't like the way you look." "You are not a girl," I said, "and anyway, I said I'd get a haircut." "I don't see how your hair could possibly get any longer," he added. "Would you agree," I asked, "that if I let it grow for another two months, it would get longer?" "Maybe," he conceded, "but it just couldn't possibly be any longer."

My father talks about the bad associations people make when they see someone with hair. I come back with the bad associations people make when they see someone replete with a shiny new Cadillac that looks like it should have a silk-raimented coachman standing at each fender. But as for bad vibrations emanating

---

Excerpt from *The Strawberry Statement* by James S. Kunen, published by Brandywine Press. Reprinted by permission of Sll/Sterling Lord Literistic, Inc. Copyright by James S. Kunen.

*Peter Behr and Linda LeClair were students from Columbia and Barnard—both single-sex schools— who flouted university rules by living together off campus while unmarried.

from my follicles, I say great. I want the cops to sneer and the old ladies swear and the businessmen worry. I want everyone to see me and say "There goes an enemy of the state," because that's where I'm at, as we say in the Revolution biz.

Also, I like to have peace people wave me victory signs and I like to return them, and for that we've got to be able to recognize each other. And hair is an appropriate badge. Long hair should be associated with peace, because the first time American men wore short hair was after World War I, the first time great numbers of American men had been through the military. . . .

9. Vice President Spiro Agnew
Warns of the Threat to America, 1969

A little over a week ago, I took a rather unusual step for a Vice President. I said something. Particularly, I said something that was predictably unpopular with the people who would like to run the country without the inconvenience of seeking public office. I said I did not like some of the things I saw happening in this country. I criticized those who encouraged government by street carnival and suggested it was time to stop the carousel. . . .

Think about it. Small bands of students are allowed to shut down great universities. Small groups of dissidents are allowed to shout down political candidates. Small cadres of professional protestors are allowed to jeopardize the peace efforts of the President of the United States.

It is time to question the credentials of their leaders. And, if in questioning we disturb a few people, I say it is time for them to be disturbed. If, in challenging, we polarize the American people, I say it is time for a positive polarization.

It is time for a healthy in-depth examination of policies and constructive realignment in this country. It is time to rip away the rhetoric and to divide on authentic lines. It is time to discard the fiction that in a country of 200 million people, everyone is qualified to quarterback the government. . . .

Now, we have among us a glib, activist element who would tell us our values are lies, and I call them impudent. Because anyone who impugns a legacy of liberty and dignity that reaches back to Moses, is impudent.

I call them snobs for most of them disdain to mingle with the masses who work for a living. They mock the common man's pride in his work, his family and his country. . . .

Abetting the merchants of hate are the parasites of passion. These are the men who value a cause purely for its political mileage. These are the politicians who temporize with the truth by playing both sides to their own advantage. They ooze sympathy for "the cause" but balance each sentence with equally reasoned reservations. Their interest is personal, not moral. They are ideological eunuchs whose most comfortable position is straddling the philosophical fence, soliciting votes from both sides. . . .

Alexander Bloom and Wini Breines, eds., *Takin' It to the Streets: A Sixties Reader* (New York: Oxford University Press, 1995), pp. 355–358.

This is what is happening in this nation. We *are* an effete society if we let it happen here. . . .

Because on the eve of our nation's 200th birthday, we have reached the crossroads. Because at this moment totalitarianism's threat does not necessarily have a foreign accent. Because we have a home-grown menace, made and manufactured in the U.S.A. Because if we are lazy or foolish, this nation could forfeit its integrity, never to be free again.

10. Psychologist Carl Rogers Emphasizes Being "Real" in Encounter Groups, 1970

I think of one government executive, a man with high responsibility and excellent technical training as an engineer. At the first meeting of the group he impressed me, and I think others, as being cold, aloof, somewhat bitter, resentful, cynical. When he spoke of how he ran his office he appeared to administer it "by the book" without warmth or human feeling entering in. In one of the early sessions, when he spoke of his wife a group member asked him, "Do you love your wife?" He paused for a long time, and the questioner said, "OK, that's answer enough." The executive said, "No, wait a minute! The reason I didn't respond was that I was wondering if I ever loved anyone. I don't think I have *ever* really *loved* anyone." It seemed quite dramatically clear to those of us in the group that he had come to accept himself as an unloving person.

A few days later he listened with great intensity as one member of the group expressed profound personal feelings of isolation, loneliness, pain, and the extent to which he had been living behind a mask, a façade. The next morning the engineer said, "Last night I thought and thought about what Bill told us. I even wept quite a bit by myself. I can't remember how long it has been since I've cried and I really *felt* something. I think perhaps what I felt was love."

It is not surprising that before the week was over he had thought through new ways of handling his growing son, on whom he had been placing extremely rigorous demands. He had also begun genuinely to appreciate his wife's love for him, which he now felt he could in some measure reciprocate. . . .

Still another person reporting shortly after his workshop experience says, "I came away from the workshop feeling much more deeply that 'It's all right to be me with all my strengths and weaknesses.' My wife told me that I seem more authentic, more real, more genuine."

This feeling of greater realness and authenticity is a very common experience. It would appear that the individual is learning to accept and to *be* himself and is thus laying the foundation for change. He is closer to his own feelings, hence they are no longer so rigidly organized and are more open to change. . . .

. . . As the sessions continue, so many things tend to occur together that it is hard to know which to describe first. It should again be stressed that these different threads and stages interweave and overlap. One of the threads is the increasing impatience with defenses. As time goes on the group finds it unbearable that any member should live behind a mask or front. The polite words, the intellectual understanding of each other and of relationships, the smooth coin of tact and cover-up—amply satisfactory for interactions outside—are just not good enough. The expression of self by some members of the group has made it very clear that a deeper and more basic encounter is *possible,* and the group appears to strive intuitively and unconsciously, toward this goal. Gently at times, almost savagely at others, the group *demands* that the individual be himself, that his current feelings not be hidden, that he remove the mask of ordinary social intercourse. In one group there was a highly intelligent and quite academic man who had been rather perceptive in his understanding of others but revealed himself not at all. The attitude of the group was finally expressed sharply by one member when he said, "Come out from behind that lectern, Doc. Stop giving us speeches. Take off your dark glasses. We want to know *you.*"

E S S A Y S

How one assesses the legacy of the sixties depends partly on which aspect of the era one looks at. In the first essay, the late Kenneth Cmiel of the University of Iowa shows how the sixties reshaped popular notions of civility—what it meant to be "nice." How could one be polite, for instance, when being polite to white people meant yielding one's seat on a bus or quietly absorbing deliberate insults? Cmiel traces the effects of civil rights, the counterculture, the New Left, feminism, and the rulings of the Supreme Court on how Americans treated one another in the sixties and how they treat one another today. The second essay, by Dan Carter of the University of South Carolina, examines the political outcomes of the sixties. His essay helps to explain how the Republican Party triumphed in 1968, and why it continued to veer to the right for decades afterward.

Triumph of the Left: Sixties Revolution and the Revolution in Manners

KENNETH CMIEL

As the 1960s opened, civility was, quite literally, the law of the land. In 1942 the U.S. Supreme Court had declared that certain words were not protected by the First Amendment. Not only fighting words, but also the "lewd," "obscene," and "profane" were all excluded from protection. A statute declaring that "no person shall address any offensive, derisive or annoying word to any other person who is lawfully in any street" was upheld by the Court as perfectly legal. This decision, although modified in later years, was still law in 1960, and statutes like the one mentioned above continued to be on the books and enforced. They implied that free speech was possible only in what eighteenth-century writers had called "civil society." Civility, in other words, had to precede civil rights.

Kenneth Cmiel, "The Politics of Civility," in *The Sixties: From Memory to History,* ed. David Farber (Chapel Hill: University of North Carolina Press, 1994), 263–284. Copyright © 1994 by the University of North Carolina Press. Used with permission of the publisher and the author.

One part of the contentious politics of the sixties, however, was a fight over this notion. From a number of perspectives, prevailing attitudes toward social etiquette were attacked. African Americans argued that civil society as constructed by whites helped structure racial inequality. Counterculturalists insisted that civil politeness suppressed more authentic social relations. Some student radicals infused the strategic disruption of civility with political meaning. And finally, there was a moderate loosening of civil control at the center of society. Under this onslaught, the nation's courts struggled to redefine the relationship between law and civil behavior.

. . . This essay charts the shift within the United States from one sense of order to another. In reaction to various social changes and pressures, federal courts, most importantly the Supreme Court, altered the law of decorum. From the belief that civility took precedence over civil rights, the Supreme Court decided that in public forums, incivility was protected by the First Amendment. But this major change was qualified. No incivility, the Court argued, could disrupt the normal workings of a school, workplace, or courtroom. . . .

The civil rights movement's nonviolent efforts to alter the social order marked the first powerful sortie into the politics of civility during the 1960s. As the sixties opened, nonviolent direct action was the tactic of choice for organizations like the Congress of Racial Equality (CORE), the Southern Christian Leadership Conference (SCLC), and the Student Nonviolent Coordinating Committee (SNCC). . . .

Nonviolent resistance asked demonstrators to peaceably and lovingly call attention to the inequities of the social system. For those believing in direct nonviolent action, the path of protest was a complicated and patient one, moving through four distinct stages—the investigation of a problem, efforts to negotiate a solution, public protest, and then further negotiation. One never proceeded to the next stage without warrant. Henry David Thoreau's "Civil Disobedience" was often cited as a precursor to direct action. Another important source was Mahatma Gandhi. Indeed, Gandhi's 1906 campaign in South Africa was seen as the first example of a mass direct non-violent action.

But while Gandhi and Thoreau were sources, for both black and white activists committed to direct nonviolent action there was something far more important—the Gospel's injunction to love one's enemies. All the early leaders of CORE, SCLC, and SNCC were deeply influenced by the Christian message of hope and redemption. SNCC's statement of purpose on its founding in May 1960 called attention to those "Judaic-Christian traditions" that seek "a social order permeated by love." . . .

Civil rights protest took a number of characteristic forms—the boycott, the sit-in, the freedom ride, and the mass march. At all, efforts were made to keep the protest civil. In 1960, when four neatly dressed black college students sat down at a white-only lunch counter in a downtown Woolworth's in Greensboro, North Carolina, one began the protest by turning to a waitress and saying, "I'd like a cup of coffee, please." Although the students were not served, they continued to be well mannered, sitting "politely" at the counter for days on end. This first effort set off a wave of sit-ins to desegregate southern restaurants. Typical were the instructions given in Nashville: "Do show yourself friendly on the counter at all times. Do sit straight and always face the counter. Don't strike back or curse back if attacked." Candie Anderson, one of the students at the Nashville sit-in, recalled: "My friends were determined to be courteous and well-behaved. . . . Most of them read or studied while they sat at the counters, for three or four hours. I heard them remind each other not to leave cigarette ashes on the counter, to take off their hats, etc." . . .

The meaning of the polite protests was complicated. Rosa Parks, who refused to move to the back of the bus in Montgomery, Alabama, the students integrating lunch counters in Greensboro, and the marchers at Selma were all not only acting with decorum, they were also all breaking the law, calling attention to the inadequacy of the present system, and violating long-standing white/black custom of the South. The southern caste system was reinforced through an elaborate etiquette. Blacks stepped aside on the street to let whites pass, they averted their eyes from whites, and even adult African Americans were called by a diminutive first name ("Charlie" or "Missie") while addressing all whites with the formal titles of "Sir," "Ma'am," "Mr.," or "Mrs." No distinctions in economic status changed this. Black ministers tipped their hats to white tradesmen. To the overwhelming majority of white southerners, the assertion of civil equality by civil rights protesters was in fact a radical *break* in decorum.

The protest, indeed, highlights some of the complexities of civility itself. On the one hand, politeness is a means of avoiding violence and discord. It is a way of *being nice.* One of sociologist Norbert Elias's great insights was to see that the introduction of civil etiquette in the early modern West was part of an effort to reduce the amount of interpersonal violence prevalent during the Middle Ages." At some time or other, all of us are polite to people we do not like simply because we do not want to live in an overly contentious world. On the other hand, however, civility *also* reaffirms established social boundaries. And when there are huge inequities in the social order, polite custom ratifies them in everyday life.

Direct nonviolent action attempted to undermine southern etiquette. It did so not by attacking civility pure and simple but by using polite behavior to challenge social inequality. More precisely, the first function of politeness (being nice) attacked the second (the caste system). The determined civility of the protesters dramatized the inequities of the South and at the same time signaled to the nation and world the "worthiness" (that is, civility) of African Americans.

Most southern whites did not see it this way. Even those who were called moderates in the early sixties often viewed the polite protests as an attack on civility. Sit-ins, boycotts, and marches openly challenged the caste system and, moderates argued, too easily slipped into violence. To the *Nashville Banner,* the sit-ins were an "incitation to anarchy." . . .

In Greensboro, it was *white* children who were the first to be arrested for disorderly conduct, who harassed blacks at the lunch counter, who got angry. At Selma, it was the white police who waded into crowds of protesters and began clubbing them. Black activists, in fact, had expected this to happen. Martin Luther King was typical, noting that nonviolent resistance forced "the oppressor to commit his brutality openly—in the light of day—with the rest of the world looking on." . . .

This style of protest was under assault almost as the sixties started. As early as 1961, and certainly by 1964, those partisans of "civil" protest were faced with a growing mass movement that was more assertive, less polite, and more willing to defend itself. A host of reasons explain this shift. The fiercely violent reaction of so many whites made nonviolent decorum extremely hard and dangerous to maintain. Black nationalism, grass roots activism, a growing sense of frustration, and burgeoning antiestablishment sentiment in the culture at large all helped throw bourgeois misrule on the defensive. It would be just a few more steps to the Black Panther party or the calls to violence by people like Stokely Carmichael and H. Rap Brown. . . .

One place we can spot the erosion of polite protest is in the Freedom Summer of 1964. Among an important group of young SNCC activists there was a certain skepticism about Martin Luther King. For these civil rights workers, nonviolent resistance was understood to be a strategic tactic rather than a principled commitment. And there was a change in style. As sociologist Robert McAdam has noted, there was a feeling among these civil rights activists that they had to free themselves as much as the southern blacks they worked for. And that meant abandoning middle-class norms. Consequently, more rural dress (blue jeans and work shirt) became the mode. . . .

Another sign was the filthy speech movement at Berkeley. In the fall of 1964, the University of California at Berkeley was rocked by the free speech movement, an effort by students to retain their right to distribute political material on campus. Many of the leaders of the free speech movement had worked for SNCC in the South the summer before and a number of Freedom Summer tactics were adopted at Berkeley. Students used mass civil disobedience and sit-ins to pressure campus officials in November and December. They were generally successful. But the next spring, after the campus had quieted, a new twist came. A nonstudent who hung around in New York beat circles drifted to Berkeley to (in his words) "make the scene." On 3 March he stood on Bancroft and Telegraph and held up a sign that just said "FUCK." When asked to clarify his meaning, he added an exclamation point. His arrest threw the campus into another controversy. Other "dirty speech" protests were held, with other students arrested for obscenity.

The counterculture of the 1960s can be traced back to the beats of the 1950s, earlier still to artistic modernism, and even before that to Rousseau's mid-eighteenth-century attack on politeness. But if there is a long subterranean history, a very visible counterculture began to surface in 1964. The first underground newspapers appeared; they were dominated by countercultural themes. By 1966 the counterculture was a mass media phenomenon. Perhaps its height of popularity were the years 1967 and 1968. And while no precise date marks its end, by the early 1970s it was fading fast at least in its most utopian projections.

From Rousseau through the 1960s, advocates of a counterculture valued authenticity over civility. The command to be polite (that is, to *be nice*) does not encourage personal expression. It suppresses impulsive behavior, relying on established social forms to guarantee comity. As Norbert Elias has put it, the civilizing process is about affect control. Counterculture advocates challenged these presumptions, arguing for the liberation of the self. In the name of personal freedom they attacked the restraints and compromises of civil society. In a phrase introduced to American life by sixties freaks, they were dedicated to "doing their own thing."

This translated into an extraordinarily colorful form of life. Shoulder-length hair on men, Victorian dresses on women, day-glo painted bodies, elaborate slang, and more open sexuality—it was all far removed from "straight" (that is, civil) society. Hippies looked different, acted different, were different. At its best, there was a glorious joy in the freedom of hippie life-styles. The "be-ins" of 1967 celebrated the love that would replace the stilted conformity of the established world. . . .

Drugs too were often defended as a liberating experience. (I myself did so in-genuously in the late sixties.) "It's like seeing the world again through a child's eye," one user noted in 1967. Drugs were "a transcendental glory." "When I first turned on," the owner of a San Francisco head shop reported in 1968, "it pulled the rug out from under me. Suddenly I saw all the bullshit in the whole educational and social system. . . . The problem with our schools is that they are turning out robots to keep the social system going." So "turning on, tuning in, and dropping out means to con-duct a revolution against the system." . . .

To those with no respect for the counterculture, the alternative decorum was gross. There was just too much dirt. Hippies did not have the discipline to hold a job. The sex was too loose. The drugs were destructive. Some critics completely missed the claims to liberation and denounced hippies as simply negative. . . .

Yet while the distance from straight culture was deep, the counterculture might best be seen not so much an attack on politeness as an alternative politeness, one not based on the emotional self-restraint of traditional civility but on the expressive individualism of liberated human beings. It is no surprise that "love" was an impor-tant theme running throughout the counterculture. . . .

The counterculture, at its most utopian, tried to invent a new civility. It attacked the social roles of straight society and the implied social order contained within it. But it held firm to the other dimension of civility—that of being nice. But in the end, it could not be yoked together as easily as one thought. To some degree, the roles in-volved in civil etiquette are connected with the avoidance of discord. . . .

By 1965, as the counterculture was coming to national consciousness, there was another debate going on about the civil society. At least some radical activists had moved beyond the talking stage. Violent behavior became a considered option.

This happened first among black activists, later among whites. African Ameri-can radicals like H. Rap Brown and Stokely Carmichael decisively split with the earlier civil rights movement. Carmichael's 1966 call to let the cities burn, the stream of urban riots after 1965, and the growing militancy in general frightened numerous Americans. . . .

Some white student and antiwar activists were making their own transition. The move from dissent to resistance was accompanied by a shift in rhetoric. "We're now in the business of wholesale disruption and widespread resistance and disloca-tion of the American society," Jerry Rubin reported in 1967. To be sure, not all white radicals accepted this, but some did, and the thought of disruption scared Middle America, whose more conservative press responded with almost breathless reports about imminent revolution. The heightened rhetoric, on both sides, contributed to the sense that the center might not hold. A string of burned buildings on university cam-puses as well as a handful of bombings over the next few years contributed as well.

Real violence, against property or person, however, was actually rare. Far more important was the *talk* about violence. The escalation of rhetoric, the easy use of hard words made more centrists very nervous. It reflected, in their eyes, a lack of faith in civil politics.

For these radicals, the hard words were part of their sense that polite society had its priorities backward. There was something grotesquely misguided about a middle-class decorum that masked the profound inequalities of America. The true obscenities, they argued, were the Vietnam War and racial hatred. In fact, some thought, the very idea of obscenity had to be rethought. "The dirtiest word in the English language is not 'fuck' or 'shit' in the mouth of a tragic shaman," one activist wrote, "but the word 'NIGGER' from the sneering lips of a Bull Conner." . . .

By the late sixties, then, countercultural politics might mesh with political radicalism. To be sure, the two movements never fit perfectly together. But there were connections. Even long hair could be a threatening statement laden with political overtones. One participant in the Columbia University uprising in 1968 welcomed the "bad vibrations" his long hair brought: "I say great. I want the cops to sneer and the old ladies [to] swear and the businessmen [to] worry. I want everyone to see me and say: 'There goes an enemy of the state,' because that's where I'm at, as we say in the Revolution game." . . .

The debate in the late sixties was clouded by the polarization of the times. Hippies and violent political radicals were tailor-made for the mass media. But despite the preoccupation with the more extravagant behavior, the nation's manners were changing in more subtle ways. There was a large move toward the informalization of American society.

Informalization is a term invented by sociologists to describe periodic efforts to relax formal etiquette. These periods of informality are then followed by a more conservative "etiquette-prone" reaction. While Americans in the sixties pressed toward more informal social relations, the phenomenon was by no means unique to that period. A significant relaxation of manners took place in Jacksonian America, tied to both egalitarian sentiment and the desire for authenticity. Still another important stage was the 1920s. And as Barbara Ehrenreich has pointed out, sexual mores were becoming less rigid inside mainstream society in the 1950s, a prelude for the next decade.

The counterculture of the mid-1960s was only picking up on debates already under way in mainstream America. Disputes about long hair surfaced not in 1966 with the counterculture but in 1963 when the Beatles first became known in the United States. The *New York Times* first reported on the issue in December 1964, four months after the Beatles began their first full-length tour in the United States. In those early years, the debate over long hair had a very different feel than it would beginning in 1966. The discussion was *not* about basic rottenness of a civilization. Rather, for the boys involved, it was about fun and girls. The look, as it evolved in the United States, was a surfer look. The "mop top," as it was called, was simply a bang swooped over the forehead. The sides were closely and neatly cropped. It was moderate hair by 1966 standards. . . .

Between 1963 and 1965, however, it was controversial. Adults who disliked the bangs claimed they blurred gender lines. Boys looked like girls, something both disquieting and disgusting. Nevertheless, the conservatives on this issue were like the "long hair" kids in not talking about the mop top as a frontal assault on civilization but in the more restricted terms of a threatening relaxation of order. It was only in 1966 that certain forms of male hair became associated with a wholesale attack on what was known as "the American way of life."

Something similar can be said about sexual mores. The urge to liberalize "official" sexual codes was certainly a prominent theme of the counterculture, but it was also a theme of Hugh Heffner's *Playboy,* first published in 1953. And a female variant, Helen Gurley Brown's *Sex and the Single Girl,* was a huge best-seller as early as 1962. By the mid-1960s there were a host of middle-class advocates for a more liberal sexuality, a trend culminating in the early 1970s in books like Alex Comfort's *The Joy of Sex*. The counterculture contributed, but it was neither the beginning nor the end of the change.

The same was true of obscenity. While counterculturalists by 1965 were fighting over "dirty words" at Berkeley, there was a corresponding effort in the mainstream to relax norms. Liberal judges had softened obscenity laws in the 1950s and 1960s. The pornography industry was growing throughout the sixties, with, to take one example, magazines catering to sadists making their appearance early in the decade. . . .

In countless ways you could see the mainstream's mores changing. . . . In August 1971 *Penthouse* magazine first contained pictures of female genitalia. *Playboy* followed five months later. The *New York Times* reported in the fall of 1967 that even doctors and stockbrokers, "traditional squares" the paper called them, were starting to let their hair grow longer. The miniskirt, which first appeared in the mid-1960s, was by no means only worn by girls and women hopelessly alienated from the culture. For its creator, the mini was explicitly tied to sexual liberation. . . .

The changes touched all sorts of mainstream venues. To trace *Cosmopolitan* magazine between 1964 and 1970 is to chart one variation of the move. In 1964 it ran rather staid articles such as "Catholics and Birth Control" and "Young Americans Facing Life with Dignity and Purpose." By 1969, however, *Cosmo* was reporting on "The Ostentatious Orgasm" and "Pleasures of a Temporary Affair." A piece lauding "hippie capitalists" noted how "loose" and "free form" the new entrepreneur was, not tied to confining restraints of Wall Street. "Nobody, *but nobody*," it observed, "calls the boss by anything except his first name." . . .

Parallel changes might be found in other magazines with no commitment to the counterculture, as *Esquire*, with its growing respect for sideburns, or *Ebony*, with its increasing tolerance for moderate Afros. This widespread informalization at the center was often missed during the sixties. It lacked the flair of the counterculture or the drama of the Left. . . .

For writers like Doris Grumbach and Lois Gould, a main point of attack was the older male/female etiquette. If there was one place where the new principle of "nonintervention" was set to the side, it was here. Calling grown women "girls," having men invariably take the lead in dancing, and presuming that men asked women out on dates were mentioned as suspect behavior. These authors introduced to mainstream audiences feminist arguments about the part that male "chivalry" played in female subordination. "If there is to be a new etiquette," Lois Gould wrote in the *New York Times Magazine*, "it ought to be based on honest mutual respect, and responsiveness to each other's real needs." . . .

This shift at the center of American culture did not take place without opposition. There were plaints for the older norms. Nor did the changes take place independent of the law. In fact, they were sanctioned and encouraged through new attitudes toward decorum promulgated by the federal courts, principally the U.S. Supreme Court. A number of decisions, most coming between 1966 and 1973, changed the relationship of the "civilizing process" to the rule of law. This was the legal version of informalization.

In a number of instances, the Court refused to use arguments of bad taste or decorum to uphold a law. In one celebrated case, a young man opposed to the Vietnam

War had been arrested in the corridor of the Los Angeles County Courthouse for wearing a jacket with the words "Fuck the Draft" prominently inscribed on it. The Court overturned the conviction noting that there was no sign of imminent violence at the courthouse and that while the phrase was crude and vulgar to many, the open debate the First Amendment guaranteed necessitated its protection. In a far-reaching departure from earlier decisions, the Court also raised doubts about the possibility of any evaluation of taste: "For, while the particular four-letter word being litigated here is perhaps more distasteful than others of its genre, it is nevertheless true that one man's vulgarity is another's lyric." Since government officials "cannot make principled decisions in this area," it was important to leave "matters of taste and style largely to the individual."

This was a far cry from *Chaplinsky v. New Hampshire* (1942), in which the Court simply asserted that some utterances were of "such slight social value" that the First Amendment did not protect them. In the Chaplinsky case, the defendant was convicted for calling someone a "damned racketeer" and a "damned Fascist." In the next few years, the Court would protect the use of "motherfucker" in public debate. . . .

If the Court moved to open up public space to certain sorts of incivil behavior, there were limits. At no time did it accept the legitimacy of violence. The Supreme Court held fast to the notion that the state had a monopoly on the legitimate use of force. What the Court was doing was rewriting the line between behavior and violence, allowing far more space for aggressive words. Earlier laws had defended civil demeanor precisely because "incivil" behavior was thought to *lead* to discord. Now there was to be a toleration of more insulting behavior although it still had to stop short of violence.

At the same time that this whole string of cases opened up room for more "incivil" action in public, there was a parallel set of cases arguing that decorum had to be maintained. These cases all had to do with the functioning of institutions. In courts, schools, even the workplace, the Court upheld the need for civil decorum and left authorities broad discretion in setting standards.

One case, which had to do with a defendant whose "vile and abusive language" disrupted his criminal trial, prompted the Court to argue that "dignity, order, and decorum" must be "the hallmarks of all court proceedings." The "flagrant disregard of elementary standards of proper conduct . . . cannot be tolerated."

In cases like this, the Court explicitly called attention to the decorum of the protest. As it said in *Grayned v. Rockford* (1971), a case on picketing outside a school: "The crucial question is whether the manner of expression is basically incompatible with the normal activity of a particular place at a particular time."

When protest inside an institution was upheld, it was because it was not disruptive. No doubt the most important case of this kind was *Tinker v. Des Moines,* decided in 1969. A handful of students were suspended from a Des Moines high school in 1965 for wearing black arm bands to protest the escalation of the Vietnam War. Prior to this, the school board had voted to forbid the activity. The Court four years later vindicated the students, but precisely because of the civility of their action. The Court noted how the case did not relate "to regulation of the length of skirts or type of clothing, to hair style or deportment." Nor did it concern "aggressive, disruptive action." There was no evidence "that any of the armbands 'disrupted' the school." The Court, however, added that activity that *did* disrupt a school was *not* protected by the First Amendment.

Debate over institutional decorum also extended to discussion of hair and clothing. In 1975 the Court took up the case of a policeman who had broken the department's dress code by wearing his hair modestly over the collar. While he argued that the code infringed upon his civil rights, the Court's majority disagreed, arguing that the department's need for "discipline, esprit de corps, and uniformity" was sufficient reason for a dress code. Only Justice William O. Douglas dissented, asserting that the policeman should have the right to wear his hair "according to his own taste." . . .

All regimes wind up taking a stand on where decorum can be broken and where it has to be enforced. It is only where there is an abstract commitment to universal equal rights that decorum becomes legally problematic. But, to again repeat, there are different ways that such regimes can handle the issue. In the late 1960s there was a shift in American practice and law. The Supreme Court opened up all sorts of behavior in private life and in public. The Court would do nothing about people yelling "motherfucker" at school board meetings or in street protests. It declared unconstitutionally broad ordinances that outlawed incivil behavior because it "tended" to lead to a breach of the peace. . . . At the same time, however, the Court also carefully maintained the authority of institutions. The running of a school, a courtroom, or a workplace (for example, a police department) all demanded decorum. Here civil behavior, as defined by authorities, could be enforced by law.

Earlier thought had stressed the continuity between everyday life, public drama, and the avoidance of violence. To keep violence from erupting, the first two had to remain "polite." The new thinking cut that relationship. If one thinks about civil behavior as "affect control," the hiding of emotions, some of these new norms were not civil. . . .

. . . As the liberal historian C. Vann Woodward put it in 1975, "freedom of expression is a paramount value, more important than civility or rationality."

By 1990 this would be a controversial position within Left and liberal circles. In the late 1980s the notion of "offensiveness" reentered progressive political thought, at this point connected with arguments about the debilitating effect of rude insults and slurs on historically subjugated peoples. Speech codes adopted by a few campuses explicitly used "offensiveness" as a criterion to forbid some forms of expression. Some law professors indicated qualified respect for *Chaplinsky v. New Hampshire*. For them, it was no longer a matter of principle that the intolerant must be tolerated. The other side on this debate continued to argue that the concern for verbal niceties undermined free speech. In 1989 and 1991, cases reviewing campus codes outlawing offensive speech reached the federal courts. In both, the codes were declared unconstitutional. By the early 1990s, these debates not only divided progressives from conservatives but also split the Left-liberal community itself into those defending the "1970 position" and those adhering to arguments developed in the late 1980s. To some, at least, C. Vann Woodward's attitudes about free speech no longer sounded particularly progressive.

Institutional decorum coupled with a relatively unregulated civic forum is one historic way liberal politics has handled the issue of order and freedom. This was the path chosen by U.S. courts in the late 1960s, a legal version of the informalization going on in American society at large. And for the time being, at least, it has remained the law of the land.

Triumph of the Right: George Wallace, Richard Nixon, and the Critique of Federal Activism

DAN T. CARTER

After his hairbreadth loss to John Kennedy in 1960, Richard Nixon had played the role of the magnanimous loser, congratulating Kennedy and discouraging supporters who wanted to challenge questionable election returns from precincts in Mayor Daley's Chicago. Two years later, faced with another heartbreaking loss to California governor Pat Brown, his mask of control slipped; exhausted, hung over, and trembling with rage, he had stalked into the press room of his campaign headquarters and lashed out at assembled newsmen in rambling remarks so incoherent that reporters—who are not noted for their empathy for wounded politicians—sat in silent embarrassment. For ten minutes (though it seemed like hours to his staff) the former vice president alternated between mawkish self-pity and bitter attacks on the press, which he blamed for his defeat. He closed with the line memorable for its unintended irony: "Well, you won't have Nixon to kick around anymore, because, gentlemen, this is my last press conference. . . ." As stunned aids Herbert Klein and H. R. Haldeman pulled him from the room, the defeated candidate was unrepentant. "I finally told those bastards off, and every Goddamned thing I said was true."

By December 1967, memories of his losses had faded. With the determination that had led his Duke Law School classmates to dub him Richard the Grind, Nixon fought his way back to political center stage. . . .

If there was a turning point in the political recovery of Richard Nixon, it had come in 1964. Faced with the likelihood that his party would nominate conservative standard-bearer Barry Goldwater (and the certainty he would suffer a smashing defeat), the former vice president introduced the Arizona senator at the convention and then dutifully delivered more than one hundred and fifty speeches for Republican candidates in thirty-six states, always emphasizing his support for Goldwater even as he distanced himself from the nominee's more extreme positions. By the time the votes were counted in the Johnson landslide, Nixon had compiled a staggering number of chits from conservative and moderate Republicans. When he embarked on an equally aggressive speaking schedule for party candidates in the 1966 off-year elections, he became the odds-on favorite for the GOP nomination in 1968. And the long-coveted prize—the presidency—appeared within reach as the Democratic Party seemed to implode.

When Lyndon Johnson committed United States airpower and troops to support the tottering South Vietnamese government in 1964 and 1965, only a small minority of intellectuals and students challenged him. As the number of ground troops rose from fifty thousand in 1964 to nearly half a million in January of 1967, as casualties mounted, as the cost of the war doubled, tripled, then quadrupled, members of the antiwar movement, frustrated and impotent, escalated their tactics, from

---

From Dan T. Carter, *The Politics of Rage: George Wallace, the Origins of the New Conservatism, and the Transformation of American Politics* (Baton Rouge: Louisiana State University Press. Revised edition, 2000), pp. 324–334, 337–338, 345, 347–349, 362–367, and 465–468. Reprinted by permission of the author.

teach-ins to rallies to raucous street demonstrations. The war in Vietnam and the explosion of the antiwar movement, coupled with summer after summer of civil disorder, left the incumbent Democratic administration discredited and the nation deeply divided.

. . . Richard Nixon skillfully positioned himself to take advantage of the frustrations of middle-class and working-class Americans by holding out the chimerical promise that he could win the war by relying upon airpower rather than increasing the number of American ground troops.

But first he had to win the Republican nomination. And in that process, the South played a critical role.

To most political reporters, Richard Nixon's "Southern Strategy" was simply a continuation of Barry Goldwater's efforts to woo disgruntled whites in the old Confederacy, but Nixon adamantly rejected the notion that he had picked up where Goldwater left off. . . .

The Arizonan's huge majorities in the Deep South had made possible the election of dozens of Republican officeholders for the first time since the post–Civil War Reconstruction era, but his identification with hard-line segregationists weakened his party's appeal to moderates in the border states and in the North. The GOP, argued Nixon, should reach out to the South's emerging middle-class suburban constituency, more in tune with traditional Republican economic conservatism than with old-style racism.

If Nixon's analysis showed a shrewd grasp of the long-term weaknesses of the 1964 GOP campaign, it was disingenuous to pretend that his own manipulation of the politics of race bore no resemblance to that of Barry Goldwater. The political demands of the hour required him to walk a precarious ideological tightrope—to distance himself from Goldwater's explicit appeal to southern white racism while reaping the benefits of such a strategy. . . .

Nixon realized he couldn't be *too* moderate. Most southern GOP leaders were considerably to the right of the national political mainstream on economic, social, and racial issues. The majority of their mid-level and lower-level cadres had entered the party on the wave of the Goldwater campaign, and—while they were chastened by the Johnson landslide of 1964—they were not about to abandon their conservative and ultra-conservative views. To gain their allegiance required a deft political hand.

In the two years after the 1964 election, Nixon traveled 127,000 miles, visited forty states, and spoke to four hundred groups, nearly half of them in the South. On his southern swings, he was conservative, but not too conservative; a defender of civil rights, but always solicitous of white southerners' "concerns." He often prefaced his remarks with a reminder that he had supported the Supreme Court's decision in 1954 as well as the Civil Rights Acts of 1964 and the Voting Rights Act of 1965. His bona fides established, he would then launch into a stern lecture on the problem of "riots, violence in the streets and mob rule," or he would take a few swings at the "unconscionable boondoggles" in Johnson's poverty program or at the federal courts' excessive concern for the rights of criminals. The real culprits in the nation's racial conflicts were the "extremists of both races," he kept saying. . . .

During one of those southern forays in the spring of 1966, Nixon traveled to Columbia, South Carolina, for a fund-raising dinner for the South Carolina GOP. Senator Strom Thurmond had easily assumed command of the state's fledgling

Republican Party when he officially switched to the GOP during the Goldwater campaign. In the years after his 1948 presidential run, he modulated his rhetoric and shifted the focus of his grim maledictions to the "eternal menace of godless, atheistic Communism." He had even learned (when pressed) to pronounce the word "Negro" without eliciting grimaces from his northern fellow Republicans. But race remained his subtext; he continued to Red-bait every spokesman for civil rights from Whitney Young of the Urban League to Stokely Carmichael of the Black Panthers. For the traditional southern campaign chorus of "Nigger-nigger-nigger," he substituted the Cold War battle cry: "Commie-Commie-Commie." On the eve of Nixon's visit, Thurmond was still attacking the civil rights movement, still accusing the Supreme Court of fostering "crime in the streets" and of promoting "a free rein for communism, riots, agitation, collectivism and the breakdown of moral codes."

The senator assigned Harry Dent to act as the vice president's host. Despite Nixon's reputation as wooden and aloof, he charmed Thurmond's aide by bluntly acknowledging his presidential aspirations and soliciting advice. He had no illusions about the difficulties of getting the nomination and defeating Lyndon Johnson, he told Dent. But the man he feared most was George Wallace.

In his public statements, Nixon always professed to be unconcerned about the Alabama governor. As a third-party candidate, Wallace might hurt the GOP in the South, argued Nixon, but he would draw an equal number of votes from normally Democratic blue-collar voters in the North. "I don't think he'll get four million votes," said Nixon, who pointed to the dismal past experience of third-party candidates. Four million votes would translate into less than six percent of the expected turnout.

He was considerably more frank in his conversation with Dent. . . . If Wallace should "take most of the South," Nixon told Dent, as the Republican candidate he might be "unable to win enough votes in the rest of the country to gain a clear majority." Once the election went to the Democratic-controlled House of Representatives, the game was over.

Dent argued that Thurmond was the key to gaining the support of southern Republicans. Conservatives might privately deride the South Carolina senator as an egotistical fanatic, but his very estrangement from the traditional political process—his refusal to cooperate or compromise with fellow senators—made him the ideological measuring stick for southern GOP leaders baptized in the ideologically pure waters of Goldwater Republicanism.

At an afternoon press conference, Richard Nixon went out of his way to praise the former Dixiecrat. "Strom is no racist," he told reporters; "Strom is a man of courage and integrity." To Thurmond, laboring under the burden of his past as the "Dr. No" of American race relations, it was like being granted absolution from purgatory by the pope of American politics. Almost pathetically grateful, the senator seldom wavered in his support for Nixon in the years that followed.

Nixon's careful cultivation of southern white sensibilities and of power brokers like Thurmond paid off at the 1968 Republican convention. . . .

Flanked by his impassioned sidekick, Strom Thurmond, Nixon summoned the southern delegations to his suite at the Hilton Plaza for a virtuoso performance. (The meeting was captured on tape by an enterprising *Miami Herald* reporter who persuaded a Florida delegate to carry a concealed recorder into Nixon's suite.) Nixon first reaffirmed his commitment to economic conservatism and a foreign policy resting upon equal parts of anticommunism and military jingoism. Still, the issue of race preoccupied the group. Once again, Nixon showed that he was the master of the wink, the nudge, the implied commitment. Without ever explicitly renouncing his own past support for desegregation, he managed to convey to his listeners the sense that, as President, he would do the absolute minimum required to carry out the mandates of the federal courts. In a Nixon administration, there would be no rush to "satisfy some professional civil-rights group, or something like that."

Although some members of his audience believed that George Wallace had the right solution ("take those bearded bureaucrats and throw them in the Potomac") or that the golden-tongued Reagan was the more authentic conservative, the bitter memories of the Goldwater debacle made them pause and listen to Thurmond. "We have no choice, if we want to win, except to vote for Nixon," he insisted. "We must quit using our hearts and start using our heads." Believe me, he said, "I love Reagan, but Nixon's the one."

After the convention, Texas Republican senator John Tower described Nixon's southern brigade as the "thin gray line which never broke." A more appropriate analogy might be found in Margaret Mitchell's *Gone With the Wind.* Like so many Scarlett O'Haras, Nixon's Dixie delegates reluctantly turned their backs on the dashing blockade-runner and resigned themselves to a marriage of convenience with the stodgy dry-goods merchant.

They received their first reward with Nixon's announcement that Spiro Agnew would be his running mate.

A few weeks before the convention, the candidate had accompanied his old law partner, John Mitchell, to an Annapolis restaurant to meet Maryland's governor. Afterward, Nixon told an aide: "That guy Agnew is really an impressive fellow. He's got guts. He's got a good attitude." Although he concealed his decision to the last to gain maximum leverage, it was a done deal. . . .

The former Maryland governor seemed perfectly suited for the job. . . .

. . . He had earned a reputation as a moderate in the Maryland gubernatorial contest when his opponent, a vociferous segregationist, promised to turn the clock back on civil rights. With his typical "on the one hand and on the other hand" rhetoric, Nixon insisted that he chose Agnew because he was a "progressive" border-state Republican who took a "forward-looking stance on civil rights, but . . . had firmly opposed those who had resorted to violence in promoting their cause."

What really sold Nixon, however, was the Maryland governor's performance during the five-day Baltimore race riot that followed Martin Luther King's assassination in April 1968. As the city returned to some degree of normality, Agnew summoned one hundred mainstream black city leaders—respected community organizers, middle-class preachers, lawyers, businessmen, and politicians—to a conference in Annapolis. Instead of holding a joint discussion, the governor lashed out at his audience's failure to condemn the "circuit-riding Hanoi-visiting . . . caterwauling, riot-inciting, burn-American-down type of leader[s]" who, he said, had caused the rioting in the city. Pointing his finger for emphasis, he accused the moderates of "breaking and running" when faced with the taunts of "Uncle Tom" from black radicals like Stokely Carmichael and H. Rap Brown. Three fourths of his audience—many still exhausted from long days and nights on the street trying to calm the rioters—angrily walked out of the meeting. These were the "very people who were trying to end the riots," pointed out the executive director of the city's Community Relations Commission, but Baltimore's television stations reported a flood of telephone calls supporting the governor. . . .

By the end of August, George Wallace held a commanding lead in the Deep South and trailed Nixon narrowly in much of the remainder of the region. In the long run, Nixon believed, Dixie's heartland—Mississippi, Alabama, Louisiana, and Georgia—would come home to the Republican Party because the national Democrats, sensitive to their black constituency, could not appeal to the region's racially conservative white voters. In the meantime, the GOP nominee abandoned his original goal of a southern sweep and adopted a modified Southern Strategy. Thurmond would give him South Carolina; he would work to carry the border South. His main weapon would be Spiro Agnew, who soon began sounding like a rather dignified clone of George Wallace. . . .

A Chattanooga Baptist preacher heralded Wallace's reemergence on the campaign trail with an apocalyptic invocation: "Outside the visible return of Jesus Christ," shouted the Reverend John S. Lanham, "the only salvation of the country is the election of George Wallace." In the city's ramshackle municipal auditorium six thousand Tennessee farmers, factory employees and white-collar workers, small businessmen and retirees gave the Alabamian eleven standing ovations as he laid out his lambasted back-alley muggers, urban rioters, HEW bureaucrats, federal judges, and—most of all—the "out-of-touch politicians" who led the Democratic and Republican parties. "You could put them all in an Alabama cotton picker's sack, shake them up and dump them out; take the first one to slide out and put him right back into power and there would be no change." . . .

More than eighty percent of the nine million dollars raised by the [Wallace] campaign came from small contributions of less than fifty dollars, solicited by the increasingly slick direct-mail fund-raising techniques of televangelists and, more important, by fund-raisers where Wallace was present to press the flesh. Instead of the discreet private "occasions" favored by leading Democratic and Republican candidates, at which donors were asked to contribute from five thousand dollars on up, the Wallace staff emphasized smaller contributions. . . .

Wallace was not the first American political candidate to attract small donors through direct mailings and television appeals, but he broke new ground in the effectiveness of his campaign. In the early spring of 1968, an Alabama-based advertising agency, Luckey and Forney, threw together a half-hour television film, *The Wallace Story*. Little more than a crudely edited summary of the candidate's best applause lines delivered at rallies across America, the narrative was interrupted repeatedly with pleas for viewers to send in their dollars so that George Wallace could "stand up for America." When the agency marketed the film on small television stations in the South and in relatively inexpensive media markets in the Midwest and the Rocky Mountain states, even the Wallace people were stunned at the response. "The money is just coming in by the sackfuls," said an awed Jack House in April 1968. Most of it, he confided, was in small contributions from a dollar to a hundred dollars. "It's a gold mine." . . .

At least a dozen articles that appeared during the 1968 campaign compared Wallace to Louisiana's "Kingfish," Huey Long. Both were authoritarian, but the Kingfish rejected the politics of race. In speech after speech Wallace knit together the strands of racism with those of a deeply rooted xenophobic "plain folk" cultural outlook which equated social change with moral corruption. The creators of public policy—the elite—were out of touch with hardworking taxpayers who footed the bill for their visionary social engineering at home and weak-minded defense of American interests abroad. The apocalyptic rhetoric of anticommunism allowed Wallace to bridge the gap between theocratic and "moral" concerns and the secular issues of government economic policy, civil rights, and foreign policy. . . .

The trick, for candidates who hoped to benefit from the "Wallace factor," was to exploit the grievances he had unleashed while disentangling themselves from the more tawdry trappings of his message. The Republican number-crunchers knew the figures by heart: eighty percent of southern Wallace voters preferred Nixon to [Democratic presidential candidate Hubert] Humphrey; by a much narrower margin, northern Wallace voters preferred Humphrey to Nixon. How could they drive the southern Wallace voters into the GOP without disturbing those in the North? That balancing act was proving more difficult than Nixon had imagined, particularly since he wanted to run a nondivisive campaign.

The counterattack against the Wallace threat to the Southern Strategy was executed by Strom Thurmond's assistant Harry Dent. . . .

Dent repeatedly insisted that neither the Southern Strategy nor Nixon's generally conservative emphasis in 1968 was racist. And, in fact, he (like other members of the Nixon team) scrupulously avoided explicit references to race. The problem with the liberalism of the Democrats, Dent charged, was not that it was too problack, but that it had created an America in which the streets were "filled with radical dissenters, cities were literally burning down, crime seemed uncontrollable," and the vast social programs of the Democrats were creating an army of the permanently dependent even as they bankrupted the middle class. The rising tide of economic and social conservatism clearly complemented opposition to federal activism, north and south.

But the political driving force of Nixon's policies toward the South was *not* an abstract notion about the "preservation of individual freedom"; almost every aspect of the 1968 campaign was tightly interwoven with issues of race. . . .

In much the same way, racial fears were linked to concerns over social disorder in American streets. The threat of crime was real; every index of criminality showed an increase in the number of crimes against property and in crimes of violence. Americans were still more likely to be maimed or killed by their friends and relatives than by strangers, but the growth of random, brutal urban violence—an escalation of black-on-white violence attracted the most attention—made law and order an inevitable issue in the 1960s.

And Wallace simply erased the line between antiwar and civil rights protests, between heckling protesters and street muggers. By the fall, Nixon and even Humphrey were attempting to play catch-up with the crime issue, although both went to great lengths to insist that the issue was nonracial. (As the former vice president pointed out on several occasions, blacks were far more likely to be the victims of crime than whites were.) Occasionally, the façade slipped. Early in the campaign Nixon had taped a television commercial attacking the decline of "law and order" in American cities. As he reviewed it with his staff, he became expansive. That "hits it right on the nose," he said enthusiastically. "It's all about law and order and the damn

Negro–Puerto Rican groups out there." Nixon did not have to make the racial connection any more than would Ronald Reagan when he began one of his famous discourses on welfare queens using food stamps to buy porterhouse steaks. His audience was already primed to make that connection.

For nearly a hundred years after the Civil War, politicians had manipulated the racial phobias of whites below the Mason-Dixon line to maintain a solidly Democratic South. To Nixon it seemed only poetic justice that the tables should be turned. The challenge lay in appealing to the fears of angry whites without appearing to become an extremist and driving away moderates. . . .

. . . Ultimately, an enormous gender gap emerged: women—particularly nonsouthern women—proved far less willing than men to vote for the Alabama politician. In the eleven states of the old Confederacy, half of the men and forty percent of the women were ready to vote for Wallace in late September, at the high-water mark of his campaign. In the North, one-fifth of white males claimed he had their vote, but less than half that number of women supported him.

Cultural and regional differences undoubtedly played a role, but the reason women most often volunteered for opposing Wallace was that he was "dangerous." In his public performances—the speeches and rallies—Wallace often teetered along a razor's edge of violence. Where Nixon and Humphrey hated the hecklers and demonstrators, particularly the antiwar demonstrators, who appeared on the campaign trail, Wallace welcomed them, and had become a master at manipulating them. . . .

. . . And in one rally after another, Wallace's angry rhetoric ignited fist-swinging, chair-throwing confrontations between these hardcore followers and antiwar and civil rights demonstrators, who on occasion pelted the candidate with various objects. Wallace was hit by rocks, eggs, tomatoes, pennies, a peace medallion, Tootsie Rolls, a sandal, and a miniature whiskey bottle. By October, television crews always set up two cameras: one to focus on the stage, the other to capture the mêlées and bloodied demonstrators in the audience.

Wallace's troubles gave Nixon the opening he needed. . . .

During the last two weeks of the campaign, Nixon took to the air himself in advertisements specifically tailored to white southern voters: "There's been a lot of double-talk about the role of the South"—by which he meant the white people of the South—"in the campaign of nineteen sixty-eight, and I think it's time for some straight talk," he told his listeners. Without mentioning Wallace by name, Nixon warned that a "divided vote" would play into the hands of the Humphrey Democrats. "And so I say, don't play their game. Don't divide your vote. Vote for . . . the only team that can provide the new leadership that America needs, the Nixon-Agnew team. And I pledge to you we will restore law and order in this country. . . ." . . .

October 24, 1968, was overcast and drizzly, but unseasonably warm for New York City. More than a thousand police—a hundred of them on horseback—lined up on Seventh Avenue between West Thirty-first and West Thirty-third streets as the crowds began to pour into Madison Square Garden. Twenty thousand of the faithful packed the arena by eight P.M. for the largest political rally held in New York City since Franklin Roosevelt had denounced the forces of "organized money" from the same stage in 1936. At eight-twenty, George Wallace stepped out into the lights and the audience erupted. Although the campaign had another week to run, for Wallace, the evening was the emotional climax of his race for the presidency.

Across the street an astonishing collection of fringe groups gathered: a caravan of Ku Klux Klansmen from Louisiana who had driven all the way to New York; a delegation of followers of the "Minutemen of America," paramilitary ultra-rightists with neatly printed signs and armloads of brochures; a dozen jackbooted members of the American Nazi Party sporting swastika armbands and "I like Eich" buttons worn in memory of Adolf Eichmann, who had been sentenced to death by an Israeli court for his role in supervising the murder of millions of Jews during the Holocaust. New York police maintained an uneasy peace between the far-right contingent and the more than two hundred members of the Trotskyite Workers' World Party and several hundred members of the radical Students for a Democratic Society, bearing the black flag of Anarchy. Altogether, two thousand protesters—most in their early twenties—waved their picket signs and screamed their battle cries. Radical demonstrators mocked: *"Sieg heil! Sieg heil!"* The right wing countered: "Commie faggots! Commie faggots!"

Inside the Garden, while a brass band played a medley of patriotic songs, Wallace strode back and forth across the stage, saluting the crowd, which roared his name again and again in a chant that could be heard by the demonstrators half a block away. Soon he was joined by Curtis LeMay and his wife, Helen.

After more than fifteen minutes, Wallace finally brought his followers to order by having a country singer perform "God Bless America." Apparently overwhelmed by the fervor of the crowd, he began his speech awkwardly. In the southwest balcony of the Garden, a squarely built black man stood and held up a poster proclaiming "Law and Order—Wallace Style." Underneath the slogan was the outline of a Ku Klux Klansman holding a noose. Another demonstrator at his side suddenly turned on a portable bullhorn and began shouting: "Wallace talks about law and order! Ask him what state has the highest murder rate! The most rapes! The most armed robberies." The overwhelmingly pro-Wallace crowd exploded in rage, and police hurried to rescue three suddenly silent black demonstrators who were surrounded by a dozen Wallace followers shouting "Kill 'em, kill 'em, kill 'em."

The heckling seemed to ignite the Alabama governor: "Why do the leaders of the two national parties kowtow to these anarchists?" he demanded, gesturing toward the protesters in the balcony. "One of 'em laid down in front of President Johnson's limousine last year," said Wallace with a snarl. "I tell you when November comes, the first time they lie down in front of my limousine it'll be the last one they'll ever lay down in front of; their day is *over!*"

The crowd was on its feet for the first of more than a dozen standing ovations.

"We don't have a sick society, we have a sick Supreme Court," he continued, as he scornfully described "perverted" decisions that disallowed prayer in the classrooms even as they defended the right to distribute "obscene pornography."

Fifteen minutes into his talk, he shed his jacket as he weaved and bobbed across the stage, his right fist clenched, his left jabbing out and down as if he were in the midst of one of his youthful bantamweight Golden Gloves bouts. "We don't have riots in Alabama," shouted Wallace. "They start a riot down there, first one of 'em to pick up a brick gets a bullet in the brain, that's all. And then you walk over to the next one and say, 'All right, pick up a brick. We just want to see you pick up one of them bricks, now!'" . . .

Richard Nixon always saw the Alabama governor as the key to understanding the reshaping of American politics. Nearly twenty years after the former President left office in disgrace, historian Herbert Parmet interviewed him for a biography, *Richard Nixon and His America.* At the end of his fourth and last question-and-answer session, Parmet methodically outlined the conservative shifts Nixon had made after 1970 to placate the Wallace constituency.

"Your point is that we had to move to the right in order to cut Wallace off at the pass?" asked Nixon.

"Absolutely," replied Parmet.

"Foreign policy was my major concern. You start with that," said Nixon. "To the extent that we thought of it [the Wallace movement] at all—maybe subconsciously—anything that might weaken my base because of domestic policy reasons had to give way to the foreign policy priorities." There was "no question that all these things must have been there. . . . I think," he added, "it's a pretty clear-headed analysis." It was as close as the proud Nixon would ever come to admitting that, when George Wallace had played his fiddle, the President of the United States had danced Jim Crow.

In the decorous landscape of upscale malls, suburban neighborhoods, and prosperous megachurches that has become the heartland of the new conservatism, Ronald Reagan, not George Wallace, is the spiritual godfather of the nineties. During such moments of racial crisis as the spectre of cross-district busing, surburbanites occasionally turned to George Wallace in the 1960s and early 1970s to voice their protest, but he was always too unsettling, too vulgar, too overtly southern. With the exception of a few hard-line right-wingers like Patrick Buchanan, the former Alabama governor has been a prophet without honor, remembered (if at all) for his late-life renunciation of racism. . . .

But two decades after his disappearance from national politics, the Alabama governor seems vindicated by history. If he did not create the conservative groundswell that transformed American politics in the 1980s, he anticipated most of its themes. It was Wallace who sensed and gave voice to a growing national white backlash in the mid-1960s; it was Wallace who warned of the danger to the American soul posed by the "intellectual snobs who don't know the difference between smut and great literature"; it was Wallace who railed against federal bureaucrats who not only wasted the tax dollars of hardworking Americans, but lacked the common sense to "park their bicycles straight." Not surprisingly, his rise to national prominence coincided with a growing loss of faith in the federal government. In 1964, nearly 80 percent of the American people told George Gallup's pollsters that they could trust Washington to "do what is right all or most of the time." Thirty years later, that number had declined to less than 20 percent.

If George Wallace did not create this mode of national skepticism, he anticipated and exploited the political transformation it precipitated. His attacks on the federal government have become the gospel of modern conservatism; his angry rhetoric, the foundation for the new ground rules of political warfare. In 1984, a young Republican Congressman from Georgia explained the facts of life to a group of young conservative activists. "The number one fact about the news media," said Newt

Gingrich, "is they love fights. You have to give them confrontations." And they had to be confrontations in a bipolar political system of good and evil, right and wrong. The greatest hope for political victory was to replace the traditional give-and-take of American politics with a "battleground" between godly Republicans and the "secular anti-religious view of the left" embodied in the Democratic Party.

The notion of politics as a struggle between good and evil is as old as the Republic; that moral critique of American society lay at the very core of populism in the late nineteenth century. But angry reformers of an earlier generation had usually railed against the rich and powerful; Wallace turned the process on its head. He may have singled out "elitist" bureaucrats as symbols of some malevolent abstraction called "Washington," but everyone knew that his real enemies were the constituencies those federal officials represented: the marginal beneficiaries of the welfare state. . . .

Much has changed in southern and American politics in the years since 1958 when George Wallace promised his friends that he would "never be out-niggered again." Middle- and upper-income suburbanites have fled the unruly public spaces of decaying central cities and created (or tried to create) a secure and controlled environment. Isolated from the expensive and frustrating demands of the growing urban underclass, suburbanites could control their own local government; they could buy good schools and safe streets—or at least better schools and safer streets than the inner city. "Big" government—the federal government—they complained, spent *their* hard-earned taxes for programs that were wasteful and inefficient and did nothing to help them. . . .

George Wallace had recognized the political capital to be made in a society shaken by social upheaval and economic uncertainty. As the conservative revolution reached high tide, it was no accident that the groups singled out for relentless abuse and condemnation were welfare mothers and aliens, groups that are both powerless and, by virtue of color and nationality, outsiders. The politics of rage that George Wallace made his own had moved from the fringes of our society to center stage.

He was the most influential loser in twentieth-century American politics.

F U R T H E R   R E A D I N G

David Allyn, *Make Love, Not War: The Sexual Revolution, An Unfettered History* (2000).
John A. Andrew III, *The Other Side of the Sixties: Young Americans and the Rise of Conservative Politics* (1997).
Mary C. Brennan, *Turning Right in the Sixties: The Conservative Capture of the GOP* (1995).
Alice Echols, *Scars of Sweet Paradise: The Life and Times of Janis Joplin* (1999).
Ignacio M. Garcia, *Chicanismo: The Forging of a Militant Ethos Among Mexican Americans* (2000).
Richard N. Goodwin, *Remembering America: A Voice From the Sixties* (1988).
Elizabeth Cobbs Hoffman, *All You Need is Love: The Peace Corps and the Spirit of the 1960s* (2000).
Paul Lyons, *New Left, New Right, and the Legacy of the Sixties* (1996).
Lisa McGirr, *Suburban Warriors: The Origins of the New American Right* (2001).
James Miller, *Democracy is in the Streets: From Port Huron to the Siege of Chicago* (1994).
David Szatmary, *Rockin' in Time: A Social History of Rock-and-Roll* (1997).
Tom Wolfe, *The Electric Kool-Aid Acid Test* (1968).

C H A P T E R
14

Vietnam and the Downfall
of Presidents

The term Cold War *is a misnomer. Although the conflict "froze" borders in Europe, the war burned brightly—indeed raged out of control—for the United States in Vietnam. In Vietnam, the United States experienced what some consider its greatest failure as a nation, as well as the most obvious conflict between its historic "Spirit of 1776" ideal of self-determination and its military practice as a superpower.*

The United States became involved in Vietnam when President Truman decided to back France's attempt to retain its mutinous colony in 1946, following World War II. The American president ignored letters from independence leader Ho Chi Minh, who sought to free his nation from colonialism. Minh asked for U.S. protection, but Truman decided to back his European Cold War ally instead. Retaining the goodwill of France seemed more vital at that time than cultivating the friendship of a fledgling, potentially communist nation in remote Southeast Asia. The French fought the Viet Minh (independence fighters under Ho Chi Minh) for eight bloody years, assisted financially by the United States. By the time France acknowledged defeat in 1954, U.S. leaders had become convinced that it was necessary to divide the small nation permanently to ensure that the popular but communist Ho Chi Minh did not end up ruling the whole country. Flouting the peace treaty signed at Geneva, which temporarily partitioned the country at the 17th parallel in anticipation of elections two years later, the United States opposed a vote that would reunify the nation democratically. What followed was a twenty-year military commitment to the Republic of South Vietnam, a government wracked by civil war, corruption, and the suppression of domestic critics, including the Buddhist clergy. Why the United States decided to pursue the war—despite doubts within the government, the growing objections of our allies, and eventually the opposition of a majority of the American people—remains a subject for debate and national soul-searching.

The war boomeranged on the United States in a number of ways. It fueled a virulent protest movement, weakened the American economy, heightened racial and class conflicts, and brought home a generation of young men who were deeply disillusioned and in many respects damaged by the conflict. More than 58,000 Americans lost their lives. The Vietnamese lost more than one million soldiers in combat, and approximately three million civilians. The war also contributed to the downfall of two American presidents. Lyndon Johnson was the first to be accused of a *"credibility gap" because of his insistence that the United States was not entering into a full-fledged war, even though it was. When it became clear that his Vietnam policy had cost him the confidence of the American people, Johnson announced that he would not run for reelection in 1968. Public mistrust deepened considerably under Richard M. Nixon, who formed a "plumbers' unit" to stop news leaks related to the war and to punish domestic political opponents.*

The Nixon administration eventually brought itself down when it attempted to cover up its "bugging" of the offices of the Democratic National Committee at the Watergate Hotel in Washington. Numerous administration members received jail terms or probation for their crimes, including Vice President Spiro Agnew, Attorney General John Mitchell, Chief of Staff H. R. Haldeman, and White House advisors John Erlichman and John Dean. The bipartisan House Judiciary Committee voted to impeach President Nixon on three counts—obstruction of justice, abuse of power, and contempt of Congress. Before the full House could vote on the motion, Nixon resigned the Oval Office effective August 9, 1974. The president avoided indictment on criminal charges only because his successor Gerald Ford (who had not been elected to either the presidency or the vice presidency) issued him a blanket pardon one month later. The leadership of America was deeply compromised; the nation's people were sorely divided.

Q U E S T I O N S   T O   T H I N K   A B O U T

Was the Vietnam War necessary? Was it a tragic blunder, a noble cause, or a disguised form of anti-democratic imperialism? How did it affect the American people and the American presidency?

D O C U M E N T S

The documents in this chapter reflect different aspects of the Vietnam War. Document 1 sets out the initiating problem for the United States: did it want to support self-determination or colonialism? In this letter to President Harry Truman, Vietnamese independence leader Ho Chi Minh asks for the help of the United States, pointing to Roosevelt's "Four Freedoms" and the recent grant of independence to the Philippines. In Document 2, President Eisenhower articulates the influential "domino" theory: if one country (like Vietnam) falls to communism, so will all the others. In Document 3, a defense analyst assigns percentage weights to U.S. war aims in Vietnam for Secretary of Defense Robert McNamara. The preponderant reason (70 percent) is to "avoid a humiliating U.S. defeat." The least important reason (10 percent) is to help the South Vietnamese enjoy a "freer way of life." Presidential adviser George Ball advises Johnson in Document 4 to compromise with the North Vietnamese. Foreign white troops will not be able to defeat guerrillas who are supported by the local population, Ball asserted in 1965, just before the mass commitment of U.S. troops. The next two documents point to growing concerns about the war amongst Americans, especially the young people called upon to fight. In Document 5, a young marine relates his early idealism and subsequent disillusionment. In Document 6, the Students for a Democratic Society urge Johnson to end U.S. involvement, pointing to the contradiction between the Peace Corps, domestic reform, and the war in Southeast Asia. Document 7 shows the escalating paranoia and vindictiveness of the Nixon administration toward its critics, especially those active in the antiwar opposition. In Document 8, Senator Sam Ervin, head of the Watergate investigation for the Senate, lists the crimes of the corrupt administration. Both the Nixon Administration and the U.S. war in Vietnam, concluded by the Paris Peace Treaty of January 1973, were over.

1. Independence Leader Ho Chi Minh Pleads with Harry Truman for Support, 1946

I avail myself of this opportunity to thank you and the people of United States for the interest shown by your representatives at the United Nations Organization in favour of the dependent peoples.

Our VIETNAM people, as early as 1941, stood by the Allies' side and fought against the Japanese and their associates, the French colonialists.

From 1941 to 1945 we fought bitterly, sustained by the patriotism of our fellow-countrymen and by the promises made by the Allies at YALTA, SAN FRANCISCO AND POTSDAM.

When the Japanese were defeated in August 1945, the whole Vietnam territory was united under a Provisional Republican Government which immediately set out to work. In five months, peace and order were restored, a democratic republic was established on legal bases, and adequate help was given to the Allies in the carrying out of their disarmament mission.

But the French colonialists, who had betrayed in war-time both the Allies and the Vietnamese, have come back and are waging on us a murderous and pitiless war in order to reestablish their domination. Their invasion has extended to South Vietnam and is menacing us in North Vietnam. It would take volumes to give even an abbreviated report of the crimes and assassinations they are committing every day in the fighting area.

This aggression is contrary to all principles of international law and to the pledges made by the Allies during the World War. It is a challenge to the noble attitude shown before, during and after the war by the United States Government and People. . . .

. . . [W]e request of the United States as guardians and champions of World Justice to take a decisive step in support of our independence.

What we ask has been graciously granted to the Philippines. Like the Philippines our goal is full independence and full cooperation with the UNITED STATES.

2. President Dwight Eisenhower Warns of Falling Dominoes, 1954

Q. Robert Richards, Copley Press: Mr. President, would you mind commenting on the strategic importance of Indochina to the free world? I think there has been, across the country, some lack of understanding on just what it means to us.

Ho Chi Minh to Harry Truman, February 16, 1946, reprinted in *Vietnam: The Definitive Documentation of Human Decisions,* ed. Gareth Porter (Stanfordville, N.Y.: Earl M. Corleman Enterprises, 1979), vol. 1, p. 95.

Public Papers of the Presidents of the United States: Dwight D. Eisenhower, 1954 (Washington, D.C.: U.S. Government Printing Office, 1958), 381–390.

The President: You have, of course, both the specific and the general when you talk about such things.

First of all, you have the specific value of a locality in its production of materials that the world needs.

Then you have the possibility that many human beings pass under a dictatorship that is inimical to the free world.

Finally, you have broader considerations that might follow what you would call the "falling domino" principle. You have a row of dominoes set up, you knock over the first one, and what will happen to the last one is the certainty that it will go over very quickly. So you could have a beginning of a disintegration that would have the most profound influences.

Now, with respect to the first one, two of the items from this particular area that the world uses are tin and tungsten. They are very important. There are others, of course, the rubber plantations and so on.

Then with respect to more people passing under this domination, Asia, after all, has already lost some 450 million of its peoples to the Communist dictatorship, and we simply can't afford greater losses.

But when we come to the possible sequence of events, the loss of Indochina, of Burma, of Thailand, of the Peninsula, and Indonesia following, now you begin to talk about areas that not only multiply the disadvantages that you would suffer through loss of materials, sources of materials, but now you are talking about millions and millions and millions of people.

Finally, the geographical position achieved thereby does many things. It turns the so-called island defensive chain of Japan, Formosa, of the Philippines and to the southward; it moves in to threaten Australia and New Zealand.

It takes away, in its economic aspects, that region that Japan must have as a trading area or Japan, in turn, will have only one place in the world to go—that is, toward the Communist areas in order to live.

So, the possible consequences of the loss are just incalculable to the free world.

3. Defense Analyst John McNaughton Advises Robert McNamara on War Aims, 1965

1. U.S. aims:

70%—To avoid a humiliating U.S. defeat (to our reputation as a guarantor).

20%—To keep SVN [South Vietnam] (and the adjacent) territory from Chinese hands.

10%—To permit the people of SVN to enjoy a better, freer way of life.

ALSO—To emerge from crisis without unacceptable taint from methods used.

NOT—to "help a friend," although it would be hard to stay in if asked out.

"Annex—Plan for Action for South Vietnam," memorandum from John T. McNaughton, Assistant Secretary of Defense for International Security Affairs, for Secretary of Defense Robert S. McNamara, March 24, 1965; reprinted in *The Pentagon Papers: As Published by the New York Times* (New York: New York Times Co.,1971), 442.

4. Undersecretary of State George Ball Urges Withdrawal from Vietnam, 1965

Morning Meeting of July 21

The President: Is there anyone here of the opinion we should not do what the [Joint Chiefs of Staff] memorandum says [increase U.S. troops in Vietnam by 100,000]? If so, I want to hear from him now, in detail.

Ball: Mr. President, I can foresee a perilous voyage, very dangerous. I have great and grave apprehensions that we can win under these conditions. But let me be clear. If the decision is to go ahead, I am committed.

The President: But, George, is there another course in the national interest, some course that is better than the one [Defense Secretary] McNamara proposes? We know it is dangerous and perilous, but the big question is, can it be avoided?

Ball: There is no course that will allow us to cut our losses. If we get bogged down, our cost might be substantially greater. The pressures to create a larger war would be inevitable. The qualifications I have are not due to the fact that I think we are in a bad moral position.

The President: Tell me then, what other road can I go?

Ball: Take what precautions we can, Mr. President. Take our losses, let their government fall apart, negotiate, discuss, knowing full well there will be a probable take-over by the Communists. This is disagreeable, I know.

The President: I can take disagreeable decisions. But I want to know can we make a case for your thoughts? Can you discuss it fully?

Ball: We have discussed it. I have had my day in court.

The President: I don't think we can have made any full commitment, George. You have pointed out the danger, but you haven't really proposed an alternative course. We haven't always been right. We have no mortgage on victory. Right now, I am concerned that we have very little alternatives to what we are doing. I want another meeting, more meetings, before we take any definitive action. We must look at all other courses of possibility carefully. Right now I feel it would be more dangerous to lose this now, than endanger a great number of troops. But I want this fully discussed.

Afternoon Meeting of July 21

Ball: We cannot win, Mr. President. The war will be long and protracted. The most we can hope for is a messy conclusion. There remains a great danger of intrusion by the Chinese. But the biggest problem is the problem of the long war. The Korean experience was a galling one. The correlation between Korean casualties and public opinion showed support stabilized at 50 percent. As casualties increase, the pressure to strike at the very jugular of North Vietnam will become very great. I am concerned about world opinion. If we could win in a year's time, and win decisively, world

---

This document can be found in "Cabinet Room, Wednesday, July 21, 1965," Johnson Papers, Meeting Notes File, Box 2, Lyndon B. Johnson Presidential Library, Austin, Texas. Reprinted in Thomas G. Paterson & Dennis Merrill, *Major Problems in American Foreign Relations,* Vol II: Since 1914, Fifth Ed. (Lexington, Mass.: D.C. Heath & Company), 452–454.

opinion would be alright. However, if the war is long and protracted, as I believe it will be, then we will suffer because the world's greatest power cannot defeat guerrillas. Then there is the problem of national politics. Every great captain in history was not afraid to make a tactical withdrawal if conditions were unfavorable to him. The enemy cannot even be seen in Vietnam. He is indigenous to the country. I truly have serious doubts that an army of Westerners can successfully fight Orientals in an Asian jungle.

The President: This is important. Can Westerners, in the absence of accurate intelligence, successfully fight Asians in jungle rice paddies? I want McNamara and General [Earle] Wheeler [chairman of the Joint Chiefs of Staff] to seriously ponder this question.

Ball: I think we all have underestimated the seriousness of this situation. It is like giving cobalt treatment to a terminal cancer case. I think a long, protracted war will disclose our weakness, not our strength. The least harmful way to cut losses in SVN [South Vietnam] is to let the government decide it doesn't want us to stay there. Therefore, we should put proposals to the GVN [government of Vietnam (South)] that they can't accept. Then, it would move to a neutralist position. I have no illusions that after we were asked to leave South Vietnam, that country would soon come under Hanoi control. . . .

The President: But George, wouldn't all these countries say that Uncle Sam was a paper tiger, wouldn't we lose credibility breaking the word of three presidents, if we did as you have proposed? It would seem to be an irresponsible blow. But I gather you don't think so?

Ball: No sir. The worse blow would be that the mightiest power on earth is unable to defeat a handful of guerrillas.

5. A Marine Remembers the Idealism of 1965 (1977)

On March 8, 1965, as a young infantry officer, I landed at Danang with a battalion of the 9th Marine Expeditionary Brigade, the first U.S. combat unit sent to Indochina.

For Americans who did not come of age in the early sixties, it may be hard to grasp what those years were like—the pride and overpowering self-assurance that prevailed. Most of the thirty-five hundred men in our brigade, born during or immediately after World War II, were shaped by that era, the age of Kennedy's Camelot. We went overseas full of illusions, for which the intoxicating atmosphere of those years was as much to blame as our youth.

War is always attractive to young men who know nothing about it, but we had also been seduced into uniform by Kennedy's challenge to "ask what you can do for your country" and by the missionary idealism he had awakened in us. America seemed omnipotent then: the country could still claim it had never lost a war, and we believed we were ordained to play cop to the Communists' robber and spread our own political faith around the world. Like the French soldiers of the late eighteenth century, we saw ourselves as the champions of "a cause that was destined to triumph."

So, when we marched into the rice paddies on that damp March afternoon, we carried, along with our packs and rifles, the implicit convictions that the Viet Cong would be quickly beaten and that we were doing something altogether noble and good. We kept the packs and rifles; the convictions, we lost.

The discovery that the men we had scorned as peasant guerrillas were, in fact, a lethal, determined enemy and the casualty lists that lengthened each week with nothing to show for the blood being spilled broke our early confidence. By autumn, what had begun as an adventurous expedition had turned into an exhausting, indecisive war of attrition in which we fought for no cause other than our own survival.

6. Students for a Democratic Society (SDS) Opposes the War, 1965

Students for a Democratic Society wishes to reiterate emphatically its intention to pursue its opposition to the war in Vietnam, undeterred by the diversionary tactics of the administration.

We feel that the war is immoral at its root, that it is fought alongside a regime with no claim to represent its people, and that *it is foreclosing the hope of making America a decent and truly democratic society.*

The commitment of SDS, and of the whole generation we represent, is clear: we are anxious to build villages; we refuse to burn them. We are anxious to help and to change our country; we refuse to destroy someone else's country. We are anxious to advance the cause of democracy; we do not believe that cause can be advanced by torture and terror.

We are fully prepared to volunteer for service to our country and to democracy. We volunteer to go into Watts to work with the people of Watts to rebuild that neighborhood to be the kind of place that the people of Watts want it to be—and when we say "rebuild," we mean socially as well as physically. We volunteer to help the Peace Corps learn, as we have been learning in the slums and in Mississippi, how to energize the hungry and desperate and defeated of the world to make the big decisions. We volunteer to serve in hospitals and schools in the slums, in the Job Corps and VISTA, in the new Teachers Corps—and to do so in such a way as to strengthen democracy at its grass-roots. And in order to make our volunteering possible, we propose to the President that all those Americans who seek so vigorously to build instead of burn be given their chance to do so. We propose that he test the young people of America: if they had a free choice, would they want to burn and torture in Vietnam or to build a democracy at home and overseas? There is only one way to make the choice real: let us see what happens if service to democracy is made grounds for exemption from the military draft. I predict that almost every member of my generation would choose to build, not to burn; to teach, not to torture; to help, not to kill. And I am sure that the overwhelming majority of our brothers and cousins in the army in Vietnam, would make the same choice if they could—to serve and build, not kill and destroy. . . .

———
Kirkpatrick Sale, *SDS* (New York: Random House, 1973), 242–244.

Until the President agrees to our proposal, we have only one choice: we do in conscience object, utterly and wholeheartedly, to this war; and we will encourage every member of our generation to object, and to file his objection through the Form 150 provided by the law for conscientious objection.

7. White House Counsel John W. Dean III Presents the "Enemies List," 1971

[John W. Dean III to John D. Ehrlichman]   August 16, 1971

CONFIDENTIAL

MEMORANDUM

SUBJECT: *Dealing with our Political Enemies*

This memorandum addresses the matter of how we can maximize the fact of our incumbency in dealing with persons known to be active in their opposition to our Administration. Stated a bit more bluntly—how we can use the available federal machinery to screw our political enemies.

After reviewing this matter with a number of persons possessed of expertise in the field, I have concluded that we *do not* need an elaborate mechanism or game plan, rather we need a good project coordinator and full support for the project. In brief, the system would work as follows:

- Key members of the staff (e.g., [Charles] Colson, Dent Flanigan, [Patrick] Buchanan) should be requested to inform us as to who they feel we should be giving a hard time.
- The project coordinator should then determine what sorts of dealings these individuals have with the federal government and how we can best screw them (e.g., grant availability, federal contracts, litigation, prosecution, etc.).
- The project coordinator then should have access to and the full support of the top officials of the agency or department in proceeding to deal with the individual.

I have learned that there have been many efforts in the past to take such actions, but they have ultimately failed—in most cases—because of lack of support at the top. Of all those I have discussed this matter with, Lyn Nofziger appears the most knowledgeable and most interested. If Lyn had support he would enjoy undertaking this activity as the project coordinator. You are aware of some of Lyn's successes in the field, but he feels that he can only employ limited efforts because there is a lack of support.

As a next step, I would recommend that we develop a small list of names—not more than ten—as our targets for concentration. Request that Lyn "do a job" on them and if he finds he is getting cut off by a department or agency, that he inform us and we evaluate what is necessary to proceed. I feel it is important that we keep our targets

Senate Select Committee on Presidential Campaign Activities, *Hearings* (Washington, D.C.: U.S. Government Printing Office, 1973), vol. 4, pp. 1689–1690.

limited for several reasons: (1) a low visibility of the project is imperative; (2) it will be easier to accomplish something real if we don't over expand our efforts; and (3) we can learn more about how to operate such an activity if we start small and build.

8. Senator Sam J. Ervin Explains the Watergate Crimes, 1974

Watergate was a conglomerate of various illegal and unethical activities in which various officers and employees of the Nixon reelection committees and various White House aides of President Nixon participated in varying ways and degrees to accomplish these successive objectives:

1. To destroy, insofar as the Presidential election of 1972 was concerned, the integrity of the process by which the President of the United States is nominated and elected.
2. To hide from law enforcement officers, prosecutors, grand jurors, courts, the news media, and the American people the identities and wrongdoing of those officers and employees of the Nixon reelection committees, and those White House aides who had undertaken to destroy the integrity of the process by which the President of the United States is nominated and elected.

To accomplish the first of these objectives, the participating officers and employees of the reelection committees and the participating White House aides of President Nixon engaged in one or more of these things:

1. They exacted enormous contributions—usually in cash—from corporate executives by impliedly implanting in their minds the impressions that the making of the contributions was necessary to insure that the corporations would receive governmental favors, or avoid governmental disfavors, while President Nixon remained in the White House. A substantial portion of the contributions were made out of corporate funds in violation of a law enacted by Congress a generation ago.
2. They hid substantial parts of these contributions in cash in safes and secret deposits to conceal their sources and the identities of those who had made them.
3. They disbursed substantial portions of these hidden contributions in a surreptitious manner to finance the bugging and the burglary of the offices of the Democratic National Committee in the Watergate complex in Washington for the purpose of obtaining political intelligence; and to sabotage by dirty tricks, espionage, and scurrilous and false libels and slanders the campaigns and the reputations of honorable men, whose only offenses were that they sought the nomination of the Democratic Party for President and the opportunity to run against President Nixon for that office in the Presidential election of 1972.
4. They deemed the departments and agencies of the Federal Government to be the political playthings of the Nixon administration rather than impartial instruments for serving the people, and undertook to induce them to channel Federal

Senate Select Committee on Presidential Campaign Activities, *Final Report* (Washington, D.C.: U.S. Government Printing Office, 1974), 1098–1101.

contracts, grants, and loans to areas, groups, or individuals so as to promote the reelection of the President rather than to further the welfare of the people.

5. They branded as enemies of the President individuals and members of the news media who dissented from the President's policies and opposed his reelection, and conspired to urge the Department of Justice, the Federal Bureau of Investigation, the Internal Revenue Service, and the Federal Communications Commission to pervert the use of their legal powers to harass them for so doing.

6. They borrowed from the Central Intelligence Agency disguises which E. Howard Hunt used in political espionage operations, and photographic equipment which White House employees known as the "Plumbers" and their hired confederates used in connection with burglarizing the office of a psychiatrist which they believed contained information concerning Daniel Ellsberg which the White House was anxious to secure.

7. They assigned to E. Howard Hunt, who was at the time a White House consultant occupying an office in the Executive Office Building, the gruesome task of falsifying State Department documents which they contemplated using in their altered state to discredit the Democratic Party by defaming the memory of former President John Fitzgerald Kennedy, who as the hapless victim of an assassin's bullet had been sleeping in the tongueless silence of the dreamless dust for 9 years.

8. They used campaign funds to hire saboteurs to forge and disseminate false and scurrilous libels of honorable men running for the Democratic Presidential nomination in Democratic Party primaries. . . .

One shudders to think that the Watergate conspiracies might have been effectively concealed and their most dramatic episode might have been dismissed as a "third-rate" burglary conceived and committed solely by the seven original Watergate defendants had it not been for the courage and penetrating understanding of Judge Sirica, the thoroughness of the investigative reporting of Carl Bernstein, Bob Woodward, and other representatives of a free press, the labors of the Senate Select Committee and its excellent staff, and the dedication and diligence of Special Prosecutors Archibald Cox and Leon Jaworski and their associates.

⬛ E S S A Y S

The Vietnam War remains a political issue in modern America. One of the most contentious problems remains the "necessity" of the conflict. There are at least three different arguments: that the conflict was important to winning the Cold War; that it was an unintentional detour from America's democratic mission in the world; and that it was an expression of covert American imperialism. Concerned about public cynicism toward government following Vietnam and Watergate, former defense secretary McNamara admitted publicly in 1995 that "we were wrong, terribly wrong." In return he received a firestorm of criticism, attesting to the continuing depth of feeling on this subject. After all, many of the military officers, foot soldiers, widows, orphans, and witnesses are still alive. The first essay is from a book by McNamara and historians James Blight of Brown University and Robert Brigham of Vassar College, with the assistance of professors Thomas Biersteker and Herbert Schandler. The book is based partly on transcripts of meetings between 1995 and 1998 that brought together former enemies from Washington and Hanoi. The authors argue that the war resulted from a series of misunderstandings and was a tragedy for both sides. Because the book was written cooperatively, we have indicated in brackets the authors of the different sections. In the second essay, Robert Buzzanco of the University of Houston argues that the war was an expression of liberal imperialism. He asserts that American policymakers were less committed to democracy than they professed to be, both at home and abroad.

Cold War Mindsets and the "Mistake" of Vietnam

ROBERT MCNAMARA, JAMES BLIGHT, AND ROBERT BRIGHAM

[*Blight and Brigham:*] According to an agreement worked out in Hanoi three weeks before the June 1997 conference, the first session would be taken up with presentations on the mindsets of the U.S. and Vietnamese sides.

The initial presentation was by Robert McNamara. It had been circulated in advance and was already familiar to the participants at the table. . . . McNamara admitted that he and his colleagues may well have misjudged Hanoi's motives and intentions due to the obsessive focus in Washington on the fear of falling dominoes. He concluded by inquiring as to whether Hanoi's estimate of Washington's intentions might have been similarly mistaken and thus connected to possible missed opportunities.

Former Foreign Minister Nguyen Co Thach gave the first Vietnamese presentation. He gave no ground whatsoever. The war was caused, he said, by the U.S. desire to become "master of the world." Because the United States backed the brutal and incompetent Diem, he added, it was forced to fight a war against the NLF and Hanoi. Thach agreed with McNamara that the U.S. mindset focused on dominoes as such was wrong. But Hanoi, he concluded, had the correct mindset—that the Americans were the "new imperialists." Nguyen Co Thach delivered this broadside with considerable emotion, and the audience in the large conference hall was utterly silent when he concluded. One wondered: Is it not possible, some four decades after events have transpired, to break into a genuine dialogue about mindsets—about the basic assumptions each side held about the other? The answer: yes—but not quite yet.

The second Vietnamese presentation was by former First Deputy Foreign Minister Tran Quang Co. He began by making a point that was to have considerable impact on the U.S. participants, one that would be made by all the Vietnamese participants: In order to understand the war, one must go back to 1945, not just to January 1961, when Kennedy came to office. He then listed the principal mistakes, as he saw them, in the U.S. mindset toward Vietnam leading to the war. . . .

Following are lengthy excerpts from what participants referred to as the "predialogue" that started off our talks. Robert McNamara begins:

Robert McNamara: My thesis is that we must not permit the twenty-first century to repeat the slaughter of the twentieth; underlying any attempt to reduce the risk of future conflict, will be a better understanding of how past conflicts originated, and what steps might have been taken to avoid them or shorten them.

From Robert S. McNamara, *Argument Without End: In Search of Answers to the Vietnam Tragedy* (Public Affairs, 1999), excerpts from pp. 38–42, 50–51, 62–72, 75–76. Copyright © 1999 by McNamara, Blight, Bingham, Biersteker and Schandler. Reprinted by permission of Public Affairs, a member of Perseus Books, L.L.C.

A retrospective study of the Cuban missile crisis made very clear that the decisions of the Soviet Union, the U.S. and Cuba, before and during the crisis, had been distorted by misinformation, miscalculation, and misjudgment.

Did similar forces shape the decisions of the United States, North Vietnam, and South Vietnam—and hence the course of the Vietnam War—during the 1960s? I now believe so. . . .

Now a major factor, of course, shaping the course of the war was the "mindset" that underlay the decisions of each of the participants. This is the subject of our first session this morning.

Before discussing the U.S. mindset, I want to state, and I want to state it quite frankly, that if I had been a Vietnamese communist in January 1961, when the Kennedy administration came to office, I might well have believed, as I judge they did, that the United States's goal in Southeast Asia was to destroy the Hanoi government and its ally the NLF—that the U.S. was an implacable enemy whose goal, in some fashion, was victory over their country.

Now why might I have believed that? Because the U.S. had:

- Rejected or ignored friendly overtures to President Truman from Ho Chi Minh in the summer and fall of 1945, following the defeat of the Japanese.
- Supported post–World War II French claims to its former colonies in Southeast Asia and had, in addition, throughout the early 1950s financed much of the French war against the Vietminh insurgents, led by Ho Chi Minh.
- Refused to sign the Geneva Accords of 1954, which thus thwarted the planned Vietnamese elections for 1956 that were mandated by the Geneva Agreement.

However, if I had been a Vietnamese communist and had held those views, I would have been totally mistaken. We in the Kennedy administration had no such view; we had no such aims with respect to Vietnam. On the contrary, we believed our interests were being attacked all over the world by a highly organized, unified communist movement, led by Moscow and Beijing, of which we believed, and I now think incorrectly, that the government of Ho Chi Minh was a pawn.

So put very simply, our mindset was indeed one of the fear of "falling dominoes."

Throughout the Kennedy and Johnson administrations, we operated on the premise that the loss of South Vietnam to North Vietnam would result in all of Southeast Asia being overrun by communism and that this would threaten the security of both the United States and the entire noncommunist world. Our thinking about Southeast Asia in 1961 differed little from that of many of the Americans of my generation who, after fighting during World War II to help turn back German and Japanese aggression, had witnessed the Soviet takeover of Eastern Europe following the war and the attempted move into Western Europe. We accepted the idea that had been advanced first by George Kennan in that famous 1947 "X" article anonymously published in *Foreign Affairs:* the view that the West, led by the United States, must guard against communist expansion through a policy of containment. That was the foundation of our decisions about national security and the application of Western military force for the next quarter-century.

Like most Americans, we saw communism as monolithic. We believed that the Soviets and the Chinese were cooperating and trying to extend their hegemony. In hindsight, of course, it's clear that they had no such unified strategy after the late 1950s. . . . At the time, communism still seemed on the march. Don't forget that

Mao Zedong had aligned China to fight with Korea against the West in 1953. In 1961 Nikita Khrushchev had predicted communist victory through "wars of national liberation" in the Third World. Earlier he had told the West: "We will bury you." And that threat had gained credibility when in 1957 the USSR launched Sputnik, demonstrating its lead in space technology. . . .

So it seemed obvious to us that the communist movement in Vietnam was closely related to the guerrilla insurgencies being carried on in the 1950s in Burma, Malaya, and the Philippines. We viewed those conflicts not as nationalistic movements—as I think they were, with hindsight—we viewed them as signs of a unified communist drive for hegemony in Asia. . . .

We also knew that the Eisenhower administration had accepted the Truman administration's view that Indochina's fall to communism would threaten U.S. security. Therefore the Eisenhower administration had sounded the warning of the Chinese threat clearly and often. In 1954, it was President Eisenhower who coined that term "falling dominoes"; he said that if Indochina fell, the rest of Southeast Asia would indeed fall like a "row of dominoes." And he had added that "the possible consequences of that loss are just incalculable to the free world." . . .

Eisenhower wasn't alone in those thoughts. During his years in the Senate, John F. Kennedy had echoed Eisenhower's assessment of Southeast Asia. He had said—and I quote Kennedy's words in a speech he made in 1956: "Vietnam represents the cornerstone of the Free World in southeast Asia. It's our offspring. We can't abandon it, we can't ignore its needs." So we felt beset. We felt at risk. And that fear underlay the Kennedy administration's involvement in Vietnam. . . .

[*Blight and Brigham:*] It is hardly surprising that those who fought a brutal war against each other—whose everyday reality during the war seemed to confirm their assumptions regarding the enemy—that these former officials would only with difficulty, and over time, begin to probe the veracity of their decades-old mindsets.

This especially applies to the Vietnamese. To them, the U.S. was what may be called a "first order" aggressor or enemy. Americans came to their country and killed their people. As they saw it, this was without provocation on their part. As Tran Quang Co said, the Vietnamese did not ask for the war; it was brought to them by the American imperialists. Evidence of U.S. "imperialism," according to this view, is still everywhere to be seen in the unrepaired damage in Vietnamese cities and the countryside.

To the Americans, the Hanoi government was a "second order" aggressor or enemy that had invaded a U.S. ally. It did no direct damage to the United States as such. The damage the war did to the United States was real and is certainly still present, but it is less tangible than that to which the Vietnamese bear witness. Still, even to the participating former U.S. officials, there was a difficulty in facing, for the first time in most cases, in Hanoi, senior representatives of that ostensible "domino" that they had tried unsuccessfully to subdue.

The surprise was that real dialogue began soon after the break following the formal presentations. After some back-and-forth about the fallacy of falling dominoes, and several more attempts by some Vietnamese participants to establish the U.S. imperialist-colonialist "credentials," suddenly the ice was broken.

Chester Cooper, frustrated by the repetition of "imperialist" epithets, turns to the Vietnamese side—to anyone who cared to respond—and asks whether it is possible that they misread the United States. Luu Doan Huynh responds by saying that Hanoi did not want to fight a war with the United States—that they hoped to set up a coalition government in Saigon acceptable to all parties. He does not say Hanoi failed to do so, but that is what he meant, as he later clarified. Robert Brigham then asks the Vietnamese side whether they did not miss an opportunity to explain this to the United States. Nguyen Khac Huynh responds that they tried but that they lacked the sophistication and experience to know how to inform the United States without appearing to be weak.

From that moment, the discussion of missed opportunities, and of mistaken mindsets, became more reciprocal, a joint exploration by colleagues, rather than a latter-day confrontation of wary former enemies.

Luu Doan Huynh: . . . Between the early 1950s and the beginning of the Kennedy administration, the U.S. mindset toward Vietnam was influenced by some sort of irrational apprehension or nightmare. You know, there is something that they call the "blindness of history" that can be applied here. Everything, it seems, was perceived through the lens of Cold War politics. It was because of this that you gentlemen could not understand the rise of nationalist movements throughout the Third World, movements that became powerful in the 1950s and 1960s. These nationalist movements would eventually change the face of international relations. . . .

[*McNamara:*] As our discussions with Vietnamese officials and scholars evolved, I became keenly aware of how ignorant we had been. This first became apparent during our initial visit to Hanoi, in November 1995. At that time I conceived the period to be covered by the project would be the same as *In Retrospect*—that is, it should begin in January 1961, when the Kennedy administration came to office. That was what interested me. My tenure as secretary of defense was a period of escalation of the war. It was this period that I wanted to try to understand, and I went to Vietnam to propose that they join our group in the effort.

On November 8, 1995, I gave a preliminary presentation of our ideas at Hanoi's Institute for International Relations. In attendance was a group of about fifty Vietnamese, including current and former cabinet ministers, high-ranking military officers, and their top scholars of the war. Following my presentation, the floor was given to Nguyen Co Thach, former longtime foreign minister of postwar Vietnam and a key official during the war. He said that he supported the project, except for one flaw, which if not corrected would prevent it from being successful. "The flaw," said Thach, in a refrain we were to hear throughout all our subsequent discussions in Hanoi, "is that the most important missed opportunities happened before January 1961."

In particular, he mentioned two episodes that Vice Pres. Madame Nguyen Thi Binh would also bring up later in our visit: (1) Ho Chi Minh's unanswered appeals for support to Pres. Harry Truman in 1945 and 1946; and especially (2) the failure to implement the Geneva Accords of 1954—specifically, the failure to hold all-Vietnam elections in July 1956, which, he believed, would have permitted the reunification of Vietnam at that point. Thach's remarks were followed by those of Tran Quang Co, then the first deputy foreign minister, who supported Thach and who himself emphasized the singular significance of Geneva. "Without understanding Geneva, and the way we felt about it," Co said, "you will never understand our side of the Vietnam war."

Another member of our U.S. group intervened to say that, with all due respect, the former officials we were proposing to bring to a conference in Vietnam had no relevant experience during the earlier Truman and Eisenhower periods. In any case, he said, most of the relevant participants are dead. At this point Thach, who had been speaking in Vietnamese, intervened in English. Turning to Vietnamese scholar Luu Doan Huynh, seated next to him, Thach said: "Excuse me Huynh, are you dead? You're not dead, are you?" When Huynh reassured Thach on this point, Thach turned to me and said: "You see, he is not dead. And I am not dead either. Many of us on this side of the table are not dead. We would be happy to discuss the significance of the Geneva Conference with anyone you send to Hanoi who is not dead."

Of course, once his remarks were translated, the entire room fell into a fit of laughter, which helped to stimulate discussion following my presentation. But it also made a point that has remained vividly in my mind ever since: The Vietnamese see our conflict within a much longer span of time than we tend to in the United States. Our cabinet-level officials enter and leave government every four or eight years at most. The majority don't last that long. But many of the Vietnamese who would ultimately participate in our project had spent the better part of their long lives engaged in the singular task of fighting for Vietnamese unification and independence: against the French colonialists during the 1930s, the Japanese during the early 1940s, the French again during the 1950s, and later the Americans during the 1960s and 1970s. They thus had long memories and saw connections we needed to know more about if we were to understand their mindset during the 1960s, when the war escalated to an American war. . . .

I recalled the point made by Nguyen Co Thach and Tran Quang Co somewhat later, after we had agreed to include "Geneva, 1954" in our joint agenda. Instinctively, I opened *In Retrospect* to the index and looked up "Geneva," just to see what I had said about it in my memoir. But I discovered that "Geneva" is not an entry in the index. It now seems ironic to me that I had begun the second chapter of that book, "The Early Years," with an epigraph from Montaigne: "We must be clear-sighted in beginnings, for, as in their budding we discern not the danger, so in their full growth we perceive not the remedy." We begin . . . with the same epigraph, to emphasize the necessity of understanding how conflict begins as viewed by both sides. Why both sides? Because I had been equally struck on that first visit to Hanoi by the relative lack of knowledge—and even lack of interest—of the Vietnamese leaders in U.S. thinking during the 1950s and 1960s.

The View from Washington

[*Blight and Brigham:*] World War II ended in August 1945 when Japan surrendered unconditionally following the atomic bombings of Hiroshima and Nagasaki. Almost immediately, the number-one task in U.S. foreign policy became the rebuilding of Western Europe, including Germany, under what became the Marshall Plan. An important part of this effort involved finding ways to bolster the French in Europe and elsewhere, in return for French participation on the side of the West in the emerging confrontation with the Soviet Union, which was proving impossible to dislodge from the Central European countries it occupied after Germany surrendered on May 8, 1945. France, which had capitulated in 1940 and was occupied throughout the war by Germany, was in political turmoil. To policymakers in Washington, including President Truman and the man who would become his secretary of state in 1949, Dean Acheson, even liberated France might be at some risk of a communist takeover, by electoral or other means. Fear of this scenario led the United States to initiate a series of proposals that would, on April 4, 1949, lead to the formation of the North Atlantic Treaty Organization (NATO), with the United States and France among the signatories.

An important French quid pro quo for agreeing to participate in NATO and related collective security arrangements in Europe was U.S. assistance to France in reclaiming colonies in Indochina, including Vietnam. Incrementally, the United States acquiesced, despite its anticolonial past and inclinations. Dean Acheson later recalled:

> The U.S. came to the aid of the French in Indochina not because we approved of what they were doing, but because we needed their support for our policies in regard to NATO and Germany. The French blackmailed us. At every meeting when we asked them for greater effort in Europe they brought up Indochina. . . . They asked for our aid for Indochina but refused to tell me what they hoped to accomplish or how. Perhaps they didn't know.

In this way, with almost no thought given to the fate of Vietnam itself, Truman, Acheson, and their colleagues in Washington struck a Faustian bargain, by which the United States would eventually become the guarantor and underwriter of the unsuccessful French effort to reclaim its prewar colonies in Indochina. This was how U.S. involvement with Vietnam began: absent-mindedly, almost as a kind of "throwaway" in a grand bargain for the heart of Europe, to appease its defeated, temperamental, and proud French ally.

As seen in Washington, the stakes in Vietnam had risen dramatically by 1949. That year, the Soviets successfully tested their first atomic bomb, and the communists under Mao Zedong had simultaneously triumphed in China, raising the specter of a Soviet-Chinese effort to subvert U.S. interests in Asia, as well as Europe. The situation was deemed so dire that Acheson felt compelled to personally resolve a debate then in progress within the U.S. government about the true nature of Ho Chi Minh and his followers. In a May 1949 cable, he declared: "Question whether Ho as much nationalist or commie is irrelevant. All Stalinists in colonial areas are nationalists." Vietnam was about to become a pawn on the great global chessboard of the nascent East-West Cold War.

In mid-January 1950, "Red" China, as it quickly became known, recognized the Vietminh resistance in Vietnam, led by Ho Chi Minh. Ho's government became known as the Democratic Republic of Vietnam (DRV), even though the French still controlled the major Vietnamese cities of Hanoi, Saigon, and Haiphong. A few days after their formal recognition by Beijing, Ho Chi Minh and his colleagues reciprocated, recognizing the communist government in China. This led Acheson to proclaim in response that recognition of the DRV by the Soviet bloc (including Red China) "should remove any illusion as to the nationalist character of Ho Chi Minh's aims and reveals Ho in his true colors as the mortal enemy of native independence in Vietnam." In a countermove on February 7, the United States recognized the government in Saigon of the dissolute and ineffectual former emperor, Bao Dai, brought back by the French from Hong Kong in an attempt to provide a degree of legitimacy for their presence in Vietnam. So rather than recognizing French suzerainty over Vietnam, the United States chose to recognize the French puppet government. . . .

As Dwight Eisenhower, Truman's successor, would soon discover, underwriting the French effort in Indochina was a "dead-end alley." The French capitulation to Vietminh forces at the pivotal battle of Dien Bien Phu in May 1954 left Eisenhower administration officials unsure as to how they should proceed. . . .

The "containment" problem in Southeast Asia would be dealt with first in Geneva, at an international conference cochaired by the British and the Soviets. At first, the United States, Dulles in particular, wanted no part of an international conference cochaired by the Soviets that included communist Chinese participation on an equal footing with the other big powers. When it was clear, however, that the conference would unavoidably be the venue for deciding the Indochina question in the wake of the French defeat, the United States agreed to participate, as an "observer."

Whereas jockeying among the big powers consumed Dulles, the more mundane task of researching the Vietminh fell to Chester Cooper, a young CIA specialist on Southeast Asia. His first task, he later recalled, was to answer this question authoritatively: "Was there really a Ho Chi Minh—or more precisely, was the original Ho Chi Minh still alive?" Such was the level of Washington's knowledge of, and interest in, the Vietminh.

Dulles himself stayed only briefly in Geneva, conducting himself, as one of his biographers put it, like a "puritan in a house of ill repute," around the likes of the old Bolshevik, Vyacheslav Molotov, and "Long March" veteran Zhou Enlai, to say nothing of the representatives of the Vietminh guerrillas who were still at war with the U.S. French ally in Indochina. Dulles was heard to remark that the only way he would ever meet Zhou, who led the Chinese delegation, was if their cars collided. . . .

The Geneva Conference was driven by a deadline: If an agreement satisfactory to the principal participants was not reached by July 20, the new and fragile French government of Pierre Mendes-France would resign. This, it was generally believed, would completely destabilize the situation not only in France but also in Indochina, where the military and political situation was obviously far from resolved. . . .

From Washington's point of view, then, the result of the Geneva Conference was precisely the sort of disaster that had been feared. Among the provisions worked out at the last minute under the pressure of the July 20 deadline, the two most disturbing to the U.S. delegation were these: First, Vietnam would be partitioned at the 17th parallel, north of which the Vietminh would establish a "regroupment area" centered in Hanoi, and south of which France and the United States would organize a "regroupment area" centered in Saigon; and second, all-Vietnam elections would be held two years hence, on July 20, 1956, and based on the results, Vietnam would be reunified and a government established based on the results of the elections. In Washington, this could mean only one thing: A significant part of Vietnam was now "lost" to communism. On July 23, Dulles spoke about "the loss in Northern Vietnam." Walter Bedell Smith, head of the U.S. delegation, refused to sign the Geneva Accords, agreeing only to "take note" of these odious provisions. Smith felt compelled in the aftermath to deny publicly that Geneva was another Munich. But the analogy to the British attempt to appease the Nazis seemed all too apt in Washington.

Washington responded in two ways to this "loss" of part of a Free World "asset" in Indochina. First, the United States would establish the Southeast Asia Treaty

Organization, on the model of NATO, for collective security from communist subversion in the area. But the more important and fateful move was to bring back to Vietnam Ngo Dinh Diem, a Roman Catholic Vietnamese expatriate who had been residing in the United States, to establish a government in Saigon that would provide a "democratic" alternative to the communist DRV. Arriving in early July 1954, Diem, financially underwritten by the United States, moved quickly to consolidate his control of the chaotic situation in South Vietnam—this new entity formally created in Geneva.

With money pouring in from Washington, with the South Vietnamese security forces being advised by the U.S. Military Assistance and Advisory Group in Saigon, and with a tough determination to prevail, Diem at first seemed to be the great foreign policy success Washington had been looking for ever since the Soviet bloc had begun taking assets after World War II. He was hailed as an "Asian liberator" who had succeeded in stopping the spread of communism in Indochina.

However, Diem would prove to be something of a Frankenstein's monster for Washington. The brutality of his regime increased, led by Diem's brother, Ngo Dinh Nhu, who directed internal security in South Vietnam. Predictably, such brutality backfired, and by the late 1950s a communist-led guerilla movement, with close ties to the Hanoi government, was already in control of parts of the South Vietnamese countryside. Moreover, Diem proved to be remarkably impervious to advise and counsel, even if it came from Washington. A mandarin, he believed he ruled with "the mandate of heaven," an attitude that infuriated his American underwriters and estranged his fellow Vietnamese. And so a vicious cycle was created. Diem used ever more brutal and arbitrary means to eliminate suspected communists, which in turn led to increased guerrilla activity. . . .

The View from Hanoi

In March 1945, the Japanese unilaterally ended French rule in Indochina and established a fictitious "independent" Vietnam under the emperor, Bao Dai. Meanwhile, the Vietminh, led by Ho Chi Minh, continued to gain strength, especially in the North and its major city, Hanoi. Following Japan's unconditional surrender on August 15, 1945, the Vietminh moved quickly in the chaos that followed to take the reins of government. During August 18–28, Vietminh-led insurrections occurred throughout Vietnam. Bao Dai abdicated on August 30. With the speed and efficiency of a blitzkrieg, the Vietminh movement had accomplished what would come to be known as the August Revolution. In less than a month, they had triumphed over the French colonialists, the Japanese invaders, and the imperial pretender.

On Sunday, September 2, after consulting with an American official in Hanoi about the wording of some phrases he wished to use from Jefferson's Declaration of Independence, Ho Chi Minh addressed a euphoric crowd of Vietnamese in Hanoi. He began and ended his remarks as follows:

> "All men are created equal. They are endowed by their Creator with certain inalienable rights; among these are Life, Liberty, and the pursuit of Happiness."
>
> This immortal statement was made in the Declaration of Independence of the United States of America in 1776. In a broader sense, this means: All the peoples on the earth are equal from birth, all the peoples have a right to live, to be happy and free. . . .

> We, members of the Provisional Government of the Democratic Republic of Vietnam, solemnly declare to the world that Vietnam has the right to be a free and independent country—and in fact is so already. The entire Vietnamese people are determined to mobilize all their physical and mental strength, to sacrifice their lives and property in order to safeguard their independence and liberty.

This was neither the first nor last time that Ho Chi Minh would reach out to Washington for support in the Vietminh's anticolonial struggle against the French. Ho was encouraged by what he saw as a common cause with the United States—both historically, as former colonies, and during World War II, in their joint fight against the Japanese. But Ho was unmindful of the postwar priorities in Washington, and for this reason his efforts to obtain U.S. support would come to nothing. Ho wrote at least eight poignant cables and letters to President Truman between October 1945 and February 1946, making the case for Vietnamese independence. But to no avail. None of the letters received a reply. At this stage, and for some years to come, Washington regarded France as the principal actor in the unfolding drama in Indochina. The indigenous Vietminh movement was perceived, if at all, as a "native" bit player.

By early 1950, the war against the French had settled into a grinding stalemate, with the Vietminh controlling much of the countryside, the French forces still holding the three major cities of Saigon, Hanoi, and Haiphong. Although the absence of U.S. support for the August Revolution was disappointing, and even though it was known that the United States was providing some support for the French effort in Indochina, Ho Chi Minh and his followers at this point still seem to have regarded the French, and only the French, as their enemy. . . .

The mutual diplomatic recognition in January 1950 (that is, between the government led by Ho Chi Minh and the triumphant forces of Mao Zedong in Beijing) was an interesting and encouraging development. But a millennium of animosity and suspicion between China and Vietnam was scarcely to be overcome by an exchange of letters and diplomats. When criticized for negotiating a five-year term for continued French military presence in Vietnam in March 1946, Ho defended his position by implying that the alternative was to accept Chinese Kuomintang occupation forces of Chiang Kai-chek. He explained: "You fools. . . . The last time the Chinese came they stayed one thousand years. . . . As for me, I prefer to smell French shit for five years, rather than Chinese shit for the rest of my life."

Whatever illusions Ho Chi Minh may have had regarding assistance, or at least benign neglect, from Washington were exploded on May 8, 1950, when U.S. Secretary of State Dean Acheson announced that the United States would hereafter contribute to financing the French in Indochina. . . .

From this point forward—roughly from mid-1950—the Vietminh seem to have regarded Washington as a kind of deus ex machina of the French war effort. There would be no more citations of Jefferson and no more plaintive telegrams to the U.S. president. First, they must deal with the French.

But as Ho Chi Minh would soon discover, the interests of his Vietminh resistance were no safer with his fraternal Soviet and Chinese "allies" than they were with the French "number-one enemy" or the U.S. "interventionists." For in March 1954, when Vietminh forces under Gen. Vo Nguyen Giap were still dug in at the siege of Dien Bien Phu, discussions had already begun—discussions about which the Vietminh leadership knew little or nothing—among the French, British, Soviets, and Chinese regarding the terms under which the war in Indochina might be settled. They had agreed that the venue would be Geneva and had tacitly agreed that the best outcome—best for the big powers, that is—would involve a partition of Vietnam. . . .

Just as the French were surrendering at Dien Bien Phu (May 7, 1954), the Vietminh sent a delegation to Geneva headed by the acting minister of foreign affairs, Pham Van Dong. He was sent, as it were, to claim the spoils of military victory: a unified Vietnam, from which French troops would be withdrawn according to a fixed schedule. . . .

Such proposals were anathema to the Western delegations. The French were being asked to quietly fall on their sword, and their allies were being asked to assist the French in doing so. Of course, to the hardened guerrilla fighters representing the Vietminh in Geneva, the logic of their proposal must have been self-evident. They had won the war and now came to Geneva to take back their country. In theory, if they failed to get their way in Geneva, they could open a final offensive and physically drive the French out. However, the question such a possibility would pose was this: What will Washington do in response?

That question—would the Americans intervene?—may have provided the Soviets and the Chinese with all the leverage they needed with their nascent Vietnamese ally, as they repeatedly pressed Pham Van Dong and his team to agree to compromise after compromise. . . . Zhou and Ho Chi Minh met July 3–5 in Liou-Chow, on the Vietnam-China border, to discuss the Geneva talks, reportedly so Zhou could press Ho personally on the necessity for the Vietminh to accept a temporary partition of Vietnam and thereby avoid a U.S. military intervention.

Finally, they agreed. It must have been a doubly bitter pill to swallow for Ho and his compatriots, since the settlement was virtually identical to the one they had struck with the French in March 1946, with the temporary partition then being at the 16th parallel. Never again, one imagines, would the Vietnamese communists trust their big friends to look out for their interests. In fact, at the Paris Peace Conference, which settled the U.S. war in 1973, there were neither Soviets nor Chinese. They were not invited.

Ho Chi Minh claimed a partial victory on July 15 at a meeting of the Party's Central Committee. He said he understood that the burden of the Geneva settlement would fall hardest on his southern compatriots. He called on them, nevertheless, to "place national interests above local interests and permanent interests above temporary interests" over the following two years, until the elections leading to reunification would be held.

In spite of exuding what must have been forced optimism to buoy his southern comrades, Ho could not avoid expressing his deep concern that the United States was "becoming our main and direct enemy." His fear was prescient. As noted, there would be no elections. The Diem regime would turn out to be more efficient than expected at crippling the resistance movement in the South. As it happened, the situation in the South would become so desperate that Hanoi would be forced to abandon its line of pure political struggle and agree to direct support of an armed revolt south of the 17th parallel.

This shift happened in stages. First, with the passing of the deadline for the elections called for by the Geneva Accords, Le Duan, the Party's chief in the Nam Bo district in southern Vietnam (and destined to be named Party secretary in Hanoi in 1960), in 1956 had published an influential pamphlet called "The Path of Revolution in the South." Although not specifically endorsing armed struggle as the only path in the South, he implied strongly that the conditions there might soon warrant it. . . . Later, returning to Hanoi from a clandestine tour of the South in 1958, Le Duan reported to the Hanoi leadership that many Party organizations had been nearly destroyed by Diem's security forces.

In January 1959, the Party held its Fifteenth Plenum in Hanoi and passed what came to be known as Resolution 15. Declaring "the basic path of development of the revolution in the South is to use violence," Resolution 15 essentially permitted southerners to protect themselves and to fight back when necessary. In May 1959, Group 559 was formed, responsible for establishing the Truong Son Route, or Ho Chi Minh Trail, by which the North would resupply the resistance in the South. The momentum pulling Hanoi into the middle of an increasingly violent situation in the South culminated on December 20, 1960, with the formation of the NLF at a meeting in a secure area of Nam Bo (in the South). The formation and platform of the NLF was announced in an English-language broadcast over Radio Hanoi on January 29, 1961.

Hanoi officials had also apparently learned the lesson of Geneva. Hanoi's official history of the period indicates that in May 1960 the Chinese had exerted pressure on Hanoi to dampen enthusiasm in the South for armed revolt. The entry concludes defiantly: "Masters of their own destiny, the people of Vietnam strongly advanced the revolutionary war in the South." China, however, was only a big bully of an ally. The United States was now the big enemy, as indicated in Article 1 of the NLF Platform: "Overthrow the camouflaged colonial regime of the American imperialists and the dictatorial power of Ngo Dinh Diem, servant of the Americans, and institute a government of national democratic union." . . .

Nguyen Khac Huynh: First, about the Geneva Accords. I would have to say that we on the Vietnamese side regard the failure to implement the Geneva Agreement as the *biggest*—as the greatest and most important—missed opportunity to avoid the war. In retrospect, we can see that the Geneva Accords had wide support. The agreement responded to the hopes of the Vietnamese people and also corresponded, we believe, with the general international trend at that time. All participating countries approved of the agreement. Even the United States did not formally object, although the U.S. did not sign the document.

The implementation of the elections of 1956, as stipulated in the Geneva Accords, would, we believe, have been the best solution of all. Why do we say this? Because: First, the conflict would have been resolved in a free and open manner by all the people of Vietnam; and second, the elections would have been consistent with international law. If this had happened, then the so-called "Vietnam problem" for the U.S. would never have arisen again. Never again. Vietnam would have been unified and free, and thus no conflict among the different sides would have taken place. Mr. McNamara speaks in his book of the "tragedy" of the Vietnam war. The failure to implement the Geneva Accords is, we believe, the origin and main cause of the tragedy. . . .

. . . Historians must begin at the beginning, and the beginning—or at least where we believe it is fruitful to begin—is with the failure to implement the Geneva Accords. To do otherwise, we believe, would be doing an injustice to history.

Anti-Democratic "Containment," No Mistake

ROBERT BUZZANCO

Vietnam and the domestic crises of the 1960s must be understood as unique yet connected consequences of the economic and cultural environment produced in the aftermath of World War II. After 1945, the United States had unrivaled power, but had assumed leadership of a troubled world. The forces of *nationalism*—usually described as Communist by American leaders—were disrupting the US vision of a new world order, especially in the Third World and particularly in Vietnam. Closer to home, blacks, women, workers, students, and others would eventually mobilize to seek greater democracy, often in the streets of major American cities. To face both challenges, foreign and domestic, America's leaders pursued a strategy of *containment,* preventing the political left and forces of nationalism abroad from spreading, while also containing movements for participatory democracy at home. In both cases, the United States tried to limit movements that were based upon the idea that individual citizens—be they Vietnamese peasants, poor African-Americans, or middle-class college students—should have a decisive voice in choosing the nature of their society.

That effort to contain nationalism and democracy in turn motivated many of those whom American leaders opposed—Communists and Vietnamese patriots led by Ho Chi Minh, student protesters on American campuses, African-American activists, champions of women's liberation—to more forcefully, and at times violently, press their agendas. Such tension was already evident by the later 1950s as the United States began to assume greater control over the civil war in Vietnam, while also trying to direct protests over civil rights at home along more manageable and less threatening paths. . . .

While such movements existed in their own right, ultimately all were transformed by the growing commitment in Vietnam, which by the mid-1960s had become a major war and, ultimately, the nation's primary concern, if not obsession. Because of Vietnam, as Martin Luther King charged, other issues were downplayed, ignored, or dismissed. The growing expense of the war meant that less funding was available to address the "War on Poverty" at home. The US attempt to crush Vietnamese nationalism caused millions of Americans—many, but by no means all, young—to question the morality, if not legitimacy, of the government's behavior, and they often took to the streets to express their opinions. Perhaps most importantly, Vietnam exposed the inconsistency in the world-view of the liberal establishment: it was not possible—as Athens had discovered over two millennia earlier—to have a full-fledged democracy at home while extending one's empire abroad. The dreams of a great society indeed were dying on the battlefields of Vietnam. . . .

The war, we shall see, was a product of America's mission to assume world leadership after World War II, was flawed badly from the outset, and was never likely to succeed. It was, most Americans believed, not only a mistake but morally wrong. . . .

Robert Buzzanco, *Vietnam and the Transformation of American Life* (Oxford, England: Blackwell Publishers 1999), 3–5, 7–9, 15, 17–18, 61–62, 72–75, 101, 112–113, 168–169, 176–182, 250–251. Reprinted by permission of Blackwell Publishing.

As we enter a new century, our future is shaped by our past. America's role in the world today, its social system, racial antagonisms, gender relations, and culture can be traced back to an earlier generation when the United States tried to contain a war of national liberation in Vietnam and various democratic movements at home. The triumphs and shortcomings of that era fundamentally transformed the United States and made it what it is today. . . .

World War II created a new global order. Before 1940, Britain, France, and Germany all claimed power to rival the United States, as well as extensive formal empires; the United States was mired in economic depression and was limiting its international political commitments; while the Bolshevik regime was still solidifying internal power in the Soviet Union and hoping to avoid wider European conflict. Faced with the rise of the Nazis in the 1930s, the British and French appeased Adolf Hitler, the Soviet Union agreed to a non-aggression treaty, and the United States basically sat on its hands. Hitler's attacks against Poland, France, Britain, and the Soviet Union, however, finally dragged the major powers into world war (with a huge assist from the Japanese strike at Pearl Harbor, of course) and shattered the existing world order. After World War II, the United States and Soviet Union would emerge as the dominant powers, respectively leading the forces of Capitalism and Communism. . . .

America's containment strategy flowed naturally out of the world liberal system it had established. The term "liberal" today means something much different than it did in the immediate post–World War II period, and that shift in definition was in large measure caused by the Vietnam War. Today, liberals are derided as advocates of big government who want to take away the hard-earned money of working people and redistribute it to the poor and minorities. Culturally, a liberal is often perceived as permissive and lacking traditional values. Liberals, in Richard Nixon's famous phrase from the 1972 campaign, favored "amnesty, acid, and abortion." While the truth of such stereotypes can be questioned, the effectiveness of the post-Vietnam attack on liberalism is quite clear. The war shattered the liberal consensus in the later 1960s and ushered in new world and domestic orders. Since that time, American politicians and pundits such as Nixon, Ronald Reagan, George Will, Rush Limbaugh, Bill Clinton, and countless others have gained power and fame by criticizing the liberalism of an earlier generation.

But liberalism was not always the caricature that Newt Gingrich and others have made it out to be. In the World War II era, liberalism was the organizing principle for the United States to establish hegemony over the globe and unparalleled economic progress and social reform at home. In that period, liberalism was equated with Capitalist expansion, free markets, increases in production at home, good wages, and domestic reform to stabilize the American economic and social systems. Liberals had conducted World War II; established a global economy after the war based on free trade, private investment, and transnational corporations; tried to transport American culture abroad ("Coca-colonization" as critics dubbed it); fostered economic growth at home through a Keynesian system of military spending; and pursued civil rights for African-Americans to end the shame of the southern apartheid system and expand the domestic market as well.

Liberalism, however, also brought with it aggression on a global scale. In their efforts to remake the world along liberal, Capitalist lines after World War II, American leaders such as Secretaries of State Dean Acheson and John Foster Dulles and President John F. Kennedy, among others, essentially held that the United States had the privilege of intervening in the affairs of nations that were not following the US model or were acting too independently. . . . But nowhere did the United States try as hard or for as long to get its way as in Vietnam.

Given the liberal world-view, the effort to make a new world guided by Capitalism, free markets, private investment, and political pluralism may have made conflicts such as Vietnam inevitable anyway, especially given the growth of Nationalist-Socialist-Communist movements in the aftermath of World War II. Vietnam, perhaps, had the bad fortune to become the test case for global liberalism. Even if one does not accept the concept of historical inevitability, it does seem clear that the American war in Vietnam was produced by forces that preceded the 1950s and had significance for all points on the globe, not just Indochina. . . .

In the later 1960s and 1970s the Johnson and Nixon administrations would often justify the American war on Vietnam as an effort to defend an ally, the RVN, from an outside aggressor, the DRVN. The northern Vietnamese, they claimed, had "invaded" the country below the seventeenth parallel, thereby forcing the United States to intervene with advisers, material, and eventually combat troops. But, for several reasons, that justification falls short. Vietnam was historically one nation, albeit "temporarily" divided at Geneva; the RVN was a fictive state, conceived and carried by the United States; and perhaps most importantly, the opposition to Diem arose in the south *despite* Ho's advice to be cautious and patient. Later claims that the north invaded the south notwithstanding, it was in fact southerners who led the struggle against the RVN.

In 1954, as part of the Geneva settlement, Vietnamese on both sides of the partition line were allowed to travel north- or southward. Alarmed by government and church propaganda and afraid of Ho's socialist doctrine, about a million Vietnamese, especially Catholics, moved from the north to the RVN. A smaller yet still significant number of Viet Minh supporters moved to the DRVN. The southern Catholics, American officials hoped, would provide popular support for Diem's state; the Viet Minh in the north hoped to settle down and possibly return to the south after the 1956 reunification. In both cases, they were disappointed. The Diem regime never developed any popular appeal, while many in the north finally did move below the seventeenth parallel, but as soldiers returning to take on the RVN. Thus, when the war began in earnest in 1960–1, the RVN would have little native backing, while Viet Minh forces *in the south,* either those who had remained there or returnees, would fight against the southern military, now known as the Army of the Republic of Vietnam, or *ARVN.* In fact, Ho continued to oppose war in Vietnam. . . .

US military officials were ambivalent about the Americanization of the war in July 1965, in large measure because they remained opposed to war in Vietnam, as they had since the 1950s. Indeed, Ridgway's stand against intervention at Dien Bien Phu was fairly representative of the armed forces approach to Vietnam in the next decade as well. In 1960, a good number of officers, including Generals Maxwell Taylor and James Gavin, had publicly supported JFK's candidacy, and in return the president and McNamara had substantially increased defense budgets once in office. The brass certainly appreciated the money, but did not share Kennedy's enthusiasm for involvement in Vietnam. The heads of the Air Force and Navy, which would fight at a distance and take far fewer casualties, were willing to consider a military role in Indochina, but they were not a majority. More typically, Marine Commandant David Shoup rejected calls for intervention while the Army Chief of Staff, General George Decker, thought that "there was no good place to fight" in Southeast Asia. . . .

General Wallace M. Greene, J, Shoup's replacement as Marine Commandant, was just as candid. "We're up to our knees in the quagmire" already, he said in 1963, and "frankly . . . we do not want to get any more involved in South Vietnam." He then warned fellow Marine officers, "you see what happened to the French? Well, maybe the same thing is going to happen to us." Throughout 1964 and 1965, as the Johnson administration repeatedly escalated the war in Vietnam, the military remained unconvinced of the need for or value of intervention. Indeed, both Generals Taylor and Westmoreland, the ambassador and commander who are remembered as hawks on Vietnam, strongly opposed the introduction of combat troops in the crucial 1964–5 period. To Taylor, it was neither "reasonable or feasible" to expect Caucasian American soldiers to take on the duties of Asian guerrilla warfare. . . .

. . . LBJ was not pessimistic, however, so the military followed the civilian charge into a major war in Vietnam. Perhaps had Taylor made a stand as Ridgway had in 1954, the president would have been more reluctant, but the ambassador and Westmoreland were good soldiers and accepted new and increasing commitments to the RVN. In fact, LBJ was so dedicated to "victory" in Indochina that, in truth, it was doubtful that anyone could have stopped him. As the president himself said in April 1965, "we will not be defeated. We will not grow tired. We will not withdraw . . . We must stay in Southeast Asia." With the Commander-in-Chief thus focused on winning in Vietnam, for reasons of anti-Communism and credibility, the military fell in line. But America's problems were, in a very real sense, just beginning. . . .

Tet ended American hopes for victory in Vietnam. Militarily, the Offensive had exposed the US inability to stop infiltration or destroy the enemy. Worse, politically it showed that the NLF remained popular throughout Vietnam while large numbers of mainstream Americans—those who got their opinions from Walter Cronkite—seemed ready to throw in the towel. American leaders recognized failure too and so began a strategy of "*Vietnamization*"—shifting the burden for warfare to the ARVN while continuing to support Saigon with huge amounts of material and money, but also withdrawing American soldiers to quiet the anti-war movement—in hopes of winding down the war.

But at the same time, new President Richard M. Nixon, who had won office promising to quickly bring "peace with honor," contradictorily intensified the American air campaign and geographically expanded the conflict into Cambodia and Laos. Nixon's strategy, as Dove Senator George McGovern later described it, amounted to maintaining the war while "changing the color of the corpses" from white to yellow. If Tet and the Gold Crisis had signaled a dramatic transformation of American power, then Nixon's policies sent the message that the American empire was still alive and capable of inflicting great damage on its enemies. If Ho and the NLF were to win, it would be at a tremendous cost.

Ironically, however, Nixon's continued withdrawal of American troops—he would pull out 70,000 by 1 May 1972, leaving just 69,000 in Vietnam—took the steam out of the anti-war movement. Although spontaneous protests broke out in numerous areas during the April Linebacker campaign and at the Republican convention in Miami in August, there were no more massive and dramatic demonstrations as there had been in the previous years. But Nixon was unable to understand his success and, in July 1972, burglars authorized by the White House, in an effort to discredit the Democrats' peace candidate, Senator McGovern, and the anti-war movement, broke into Democratic National Committee headquarters at the Watergate complex in Washington—thereby setting into motion a chain of events that would lead to Nixon's resignation in disgrace in August 1974. In the end, the Peace Movement helped drive Nixon out of office, perhaps unwittingly, but, despite its fervent efforts, could not end the war at an earlier date. . . .

Participatory democracy and an interracial movement of the poor could not be achieved in a liberal system that attacked Vietnamese peasants, so stopping the war became the prerequisite for any future New Left political action. As Paul Potter, president of SDS in April 1965, charged at the Washington anti-war rally, "the incredible war in Vietnam has provided the razor, the terrifying sharp cutting edge that has finally served the last vestiges of illusion that morality and democracy are the guiding principles of American foreign policy." Such an analysis was becoming typical, and from that time forward SDS and other groups shifted their priorities from reform at home to anti-war activity, becoming more angry and radical in the process and giving rise to new levels of protest on campus and elsewhere throughout the country. . . .

Clearly, the war had a significantly negative impact on LBJ's plans to help the poor, but even without the US intervention into Vietnam there were a good many structural obstacles to effective reform in the 1960s. The American system of *"corporate liberalism,"* as leftist scholars and activists described it, made it unlikely if not impossible for the government to address the basic problems facing its people. Originally developed and discussed by theorists associated with the journal *Studies on the Left,* the radical scholars Gabriel Kolko and William Appleman Williams, student activists, and especially SDS, the concept of corporate liberalism became the key analytical idea within the New Left and offered a comprehensive explanation for both the Vietnam War and the shortcomings of the Great Society. By 1968 establishment figures like Martin Luther King and Robert Kennedy were addressing this concept as well. To critics on the left, the real barrier to democracy was not the right wing, but in fact the liberals, namely corporate liberals. Wholly supportive of large corporations and defensive of America's unequal class structure, liberals believed in the primacy and importance of big businesses and pursued policies to extend their influence. The goal of liberal reform, therefore, was to create a stable business environment and enable the biggest firms to withstand competition and stave off all but mild labor demands for better wages and conditions. As JFK admitted to an audience of corporate leaders, the government's tax revenues and "thus our success are dependent upon your profits and your success—and . . . far from being natural enemies, Government and business are necessary allies."

Like the president, movement leaders too recognized the convergence of state and corporate interests, but did not share Kennedy's optimism about the arrangement. Dick Flacks, an SDS leader in the early 1960s, explained that "the people who are running society are the corporate liberals. They want to stabilize, not repress. . . . 'Corporate liberalism' meant reforms made by the power elite in the interests of social stability [not] redistribution and social equality." . . .

"We must name that system . . . describe it, analyze it, understand it, and change it," [SDS leader Paul] Potter thundered, in order to stop the war in Vietnam and end oppression and violence at home. Carl Oglesby, SDS president, built upon Potter's critique at the next major anti-war action in Washington in October 1965. Oglesby denounced those officials—LBJ, McNamara, Dean Rusk, the Bundy brothers, Arthur Goldberg, and others—responsible for the war, but also reminded the crowd that "they are not moral monsters. They are all honorable men. They are all liberals." . . .

The New Left, however, ultimately did not offer a popular critique of the liberal order, as SDS and other groups often became more rigid, strident, and violent. But the concept of corporate liberalism remained a highly useful analytical tool for examining the shortcomings of LBJ's programs. The Great Society, as the New Left charged, was inhibited by its own liberalism. While LBJ wanted to offer lower-income Americans "opportunity, not doles," the Great Society tended to be run, as Ted Morgan explained, "from the top down by an elite realm of decision-makers cut off from the world of their subjects, by insiders righteously unaware that their own subjectivity distorted the object of their analysis and policy." . . .

Perhaps the best example of the failure of Great Society liberalism to address the needs of the poor came with the *Community Action Program* (CAP), part of the 1964 Economic Opportunity Act. The CAPs would develop "maximum feasible participation" among the poor. Rather than establish a bureaucracy to make decisions and administer funding, poverty-stricken communities themselves would determine where the money would be spent and organize their own programs to better their lives. Activists and residents in various poor urban areas thus set up community boards to fight their own "wars" against the local political structure. CAP boards thus began to form tenants' unions, conducted rent strikes against slum lords, called for police review boards composed of citizens, lobbied for educational facilities for their youth, registered the poor to vote, and engaged in other political activity that challenged the status quo. In Syracuse, New York, for instance, the famed radical community organizer Saul Alinsky helped establish a CAP which bailed out protesting welfare mothers and became involved in the mayoral election in hopes of defeating the incumbent William Walsh. When the director of the local Housing Authority learned of such CAP actions, he warned that "we are experiencing a class struggle in the traditional Karl Marx style in Syracuse, and I do not like it." . . .

Empowerment and independence were never LBJ's purpose. Vice-President Hubert Humphrey, a liberal icon, told Sargent Shriver, whose agency ran the CAPs, to suppress the citizenry's demands for maximum participation. But Shriver himself bluntly admitted that "we have no intention, of course, of letting . . . the poor themselves . . . 'run the programs.'" Big city Democratic mayors such as John Shelley of San Francisco and Sam Yorty of Los Angeles attacked the CAPs as well, claiming that they were "fostering class struggle" by empowering the poor. . . . When the "kooks and sociologists" in the CAPs, as LBJ called them, tried to redistribute wealth or power, they had exceeded the limits that corporate liberalism had established. . . .

The 1960s, for all its shortcomings, was a decade in which masses of Americans tried to claim, or reclaim, their democratic rights as citizens, end a bloody war, create racial and gender equality, and liberate themselves from often repressive values. Millions of people—crossing class, racial, and gender lines—opposed the war in Vietnam, creating the largest political movement in US history. Others, frustrated by the limited promise and abortive reforms of liberalism, took to the streets and campuses to call for a new kind of politics, one in which people had a voice in the decisions affecting their lives. . . .

. . . The war exposed America's liberal world mission, made clear the contradictions between foreign intervention and domestic reform, energized millions, especially the young, to become involved in the affairs of their country, and led to distinct and often dramatic new social relations and ways of thinking. Because of Vietnam and the 1960s, America is a vastly different place.

F U R T H E R   R E A D I N G

Stephen E. Ambrose, *Nixon* (3 volumes, 1987–1989).
Christian Appy, *Working-Class War: American Combat Soldiers and Vietnam* (1993).
Carl Bernstein and Bob Woodward, *All the President's Men* (1974).
George Herring, *LBJ and Vietnam* (1995).
Mary Hershberger, *Traveling to Vietnam: American Peace Activists and the War* (1998).
David Levy, *The Debate Over Vietnam* (1990).
Michael Lind, *Vietnam: The Necessary War* (1999).
Fredrik Logevall, *Choosing War: The Lost Chance for Peace and the Escalation of War in Vietnam* (1999).
Norman Podhoretz, *Why We Were in Vietnam* (1983).
Jonathan Shay, *Achilles in Vietnam: Combat Trauma and the Undoing of Character* (1994).
Melvin Small, *The Presidency of Richard Nixon* (1999).
Marilyn Young, *The Vietnam Wars, 1945–1990* (1991).

End of the Cold War and New International Challenges: Globalization and Terrorism

In the 1970s, for the first time since the Great Depression, the U.S. economy faltered badly. The Vietnam War, combined with government spending on new social programs, sent the country into a recession. President Nixon devalued the currency, and in 1973 the Organization of Oil Exporting Countries (OPEC) sharply reduced supplies of oil in order to force a steep increase in prices. Cheap gas was history.

Under President Jimmy Carter (1977–1981) conditions worsened. Inflation and interest rates rose to record highs. Then, in 1979, youthful terrorists supported by Islamic spiritual leader Ayatollah Khomeini occupied the U.S. Embassy in Tehran. For fifteen months they held fifty-two people hostage, mostly civilians. Americans suddenly found themselves riveted by ominous events in the faraway Middle East.

President Ronald Reagan (1981–1989) promised that America would "stand tall" again. As president, he brought to Washington the charisma of a former movie star and confidently proclaimed that America was morally entitled to lead the free world. The Republican leader promised to fight the Cold War against the Soviet "evil empire," diminish government interference in the economy, lower taxes, and restore "family values." In office, he presided over a wave of deregulation while increasing military budgets. Because Reagan also cut taxes, the budget deficit soared. By 1985, for the first time since 1914, the United States was a debtor nation.

Of course, many developments were outside the control of any politician. New technologies made possible a level of world integration never before possible. The "dot.com" revolution began during the Reagan years, and the explosion in personal computers, networking, and satellite transmissions exposed Americans to an exhilarating and frightening world of global interdependence. On the geopolitical front, the Cold War unexpectedly came to an end in 1989, when Soviet President Mikhail Gorbachev refused to stop popular movements from overthrowing communist governments in Eastern Europe. President George H. W. Bush (1989–2001) proclaimed the Cold War over.

In 1992 Arkansas Governor Bill Clinton campaigned successfully on a platform of fiscal prudence, economic reinvestment, and post–Cold War reductions in defense. At the same time Clinton supported welfare reform and positioned himself as a New Democrat, neither liberal nor conservative as typically defined. The country entered into another period of economic boom. When Republican President George W. Bush (the son of the first President Bush) took the oath of office in January 2001, the federal government projected an immense budget surplus.

The boom came to an end with the terrorist bombings of the Pentagon and the World Trade Towers on the morning of September 11, 2001. Also at an end was the sense of insulation from international conflict that had nurtured American growth and tranquillity for more than 200 years. On the command of Osama bin Laden, a Saudi Arabian terrorist based in Afghanistan, 2,986 American civilians perished in the space of minutes.

The following years saw an upswing in patriotism, as well as sharp debates over the wisest methods of combating terrorism. Spending on national defense soared once again. On October 7, 2001, the United States and Great Britain initiated war against the Taliban, the theocratic government of Afghanistan, for refusing to give up bin Laden or punish his organization, known as Al Qaeda. Then, on March 20, 2003, the United States began a second war against the dictatorial regime of Saddam Hussein in Iraq, supported by a coalition of forty nations, including the United Kingdom, Italy, Poland, and Spain. But the war sparked intense criticism from domestic opponents, as well as from many post–World War II allies, including France and Germany.

The twenty-first century began with a bang, a terrifying one. Americans showed resiliency in responding to the crises, but they struggled to make sense of where the greatest threats to their future security and prosperity lay: in economic globalization or Islamic terrorism.

◥ Q U E S T I O N S   T O   T H I N K   A B O U T

Is globalization stoppable? What effect have economic and terrorist challenges had on American society? How did social values change in this era?

◥ D O C U M E N T S

The documents in this chapter look at recent decades from a variety of perspectives. In Document 1, President Ronald Reagan praises the American way in his second inaugural address, given on January 21, 1985. In the preceding campaign, Reagan had declared "It's morning again in America." This speech typifies the confidence that Reagan imparted to his fellow citizens. In Document 2, a union organizer gives a contrasting perspective. He sees the export of white-collar jobs with the advent of new technologies as a measure of economic decline. Document 3 reflects the political and economic optimism that initially accompanied the end of the Cold War. In this selection, President George H. W. Bush foresees a more peaceful, prosperous world, free of the arms race with the Soviet Union. Indeed, many expected a "peace dividend" from diminished federal allocations for defense. Document 4 reflects the caution evident after the Cold War when ethnic and religious conflicts broke out in the Balkans and Africa. Problems that might previously have been interpreted as part of the global conflict between capitalism and communism were now seen in humanitarian terms: how to keep people from abusing one another. In this document, Condoleezza Rice, a Stanford University professor who became a George W. Bush campaign adviser and later the secretary of state, warns against humanitarian interventionism. Other great powers, she cautions, might view the United States as exceeding its authority and limiting others' sovereignty. Document 5 describes the inferno inside the World Trade Towers on September 11, 2001, as well as the deep gratitude felt by all Americans toward the common heroes who came to the rescue. In Document 6, journalist David Brooks describes the cultural and economic differences between "Red" and "Blue" America. The response to 9/11 revealed a basic unity amongst Americans, he contends. Document 7 shows the sharp political opposition that President Bush's war in Iraq engendered. Speaking on the floor of Congress, Democratic Senator Robert Byrd of West Virginia excoriated Bush for worsening terrorism and damaging the nation's foreign alliances. In the last selection (Document 8), the president addresses an audience in Riga, Latvia. There he criticizes the United States (and the Roosevelt Administration, by implication) for its caution at the start of the Cold War, when it might conceivably have done more at the Yalta Conference of 1945 to counter the Soviet Union. Bush pledges not to repeat the mistake of "sacrificing freedom in the vain pursuit of stability," and to continue intervening in the Middle East as long as necessary to bring democracy to the troubled region. The Cold War eventually produced just such a result in eastern Europe, but after four decades and at considerable cost. As you read this document, you may want to consider whether Americans were ready in 2005 to make such an extended commitment, once again.

1. President Ronald Reagan Sees a Revitalized America, 1985

There are no words adequate to express my thanks for the great honor that you've bestowed on me. I'll do my utmost to be deserving of your trust.

This is, as Senator Mathias told us, the 50th time we the people have celebrated this historic occasion. When the first President—George Washington—placed his hand upon the Bible, he stood less than a single day's journey by horseback from raw, untamed wilderness. There were 4 million Americans in a union of 13 States. Today, we are 60 times as many in a union of 50 States. We've lighted the world with our inventions, gone to the aid of mankind wherever in the world there was a cry for help, journeyed to the Moon and safely returned.

So much has changed. And yet, we stand together as we did two centuries ago. When I took this oath 4 years ago, I did so in a time of economic stress. Voices were raised saying that we had to look to our past for the greatness and glory. But we, the present-day Americans, are not given to looking backward. In this blessed land, there is always a better tomorrow.

Four years ago, I spoke to you of a new beginning, and we have accomplished that. But in another sense, our new beginning is a continuation of that beginning created two centuries ago, when, for the first time in history, government, the people said, was not our master, it is our servant; its only power that which we the people allow it to have.

Public Papers of the Presidents of the United States: Ronald Reagan, 1985 (Washington, D.C.: U.S. Government Printing Office, 1988), vol. 1, pp. 55–58.

That system has never failed us. But, for a time, we failed the system. We asked things of government that government was not equipped to give. We yielded authority to the national government that properly belonged to States or to local governments or to the people themselves. We allowed taxes and inflation to rob us of our earnings and savings and watched the great industrial machine that had made us the most productive people on Earth slow down and the number of unemployed increase.

By 1980 we knew it was time to renew our faith; to strive with all our strength toward the ultimate in individual freedom, consistent with an orderly society. . . .

At the heart of our efforts is one idea vindicated by 25 straight months of economic growth: Freedom and incentives unleash the drive and entrepreneurial genius that are a core of human progress. We have begun to increase the rewards for work, savings, and investment, reduce the increase in the cost and size of government and its interference in people's lives. . . .

History is a ribbon, always unfurling; history is a journey. And as we continue our journey, we think of those who traveled before us. . . .

A general falls to his knees in the hard snow of Valley Forge; a lonely President paces the darkened halls and ponders his struggle to preserve the union; the men of the Alamo call out encouragement to each other; a settler pushes west and sings a song, and the song echoes out forever and fills the unknowing air.

It is the American sound. It is hopeful, big-hearted, idealistic, daring, decent, and fair. That's our heritage, that's our song. We sing it still. For all our problems, our differences, we are together as of old. We raise our voices to the God who is the Author of this most tender music. And may He continue to hold us close as we fill the world with our sound—in unity, affection, and love. One people under God, dedicated to the dream of freedom that He has placed in the human heart, called upon now to pass that dream on to a waiting and a hopeful world. God bless you, and may God bless America.

2. A Unionist Blasts the Export of Jobs, 1987

For the past 15 years, we have been occupied with the very real problem of jobs leaving this country. In most cases, these are jobs like the making of a wrench, or making apparel, steel, autos. We have tried to deal with this problem through legislation as well as in collective bargaining. However, with the advent of new technology, such as satellite communication and computers, it is easier than ever for employers to move new technology and capital across borders.

One example of this is American Airlines, which historically used keypunch operators earning between $8 and $10 an hour to process the previous day's used tickets and handle the billing and record-keeping. This is now done in Barbados for $2 an hour!

Each day an American Airlines aircraft flies to Barbados and deposits the tickets which are keypunched at one-fourth or one-fifth the U.S. wage level, and then transmitted back to the United States via satellite in finished form.

Speech in possession of Eileen Boris. This document can be found in Eileen Boris and Nelson Lichtenstein, *Major Problems in the History of American Workers* (Boston: Houghton Mifflin, 1991), pp. 646–647.

Trammel Crow Company, the nation's largest real estate company, has established a series of data bases in the People's Republic of China. They train university students in the English language, not in reading and writing, but in the recognition of letters so they can keypunch them into the data base. Then, upon graduation, they are hired at a wage of a dollar a day!

When questioned, Trammel Crow said that it did not go to China for the dollar a day wage, but that the Chinese workers are more efficient because they cannot read and understand the English language, so they don't become engrossed in what they are punching.

Pier 1 Imports became the first American company to store its inventory records in China. Several hospitals followed, and now American hospitals are storing medical records in China.

The scope of this is endless.

Anyone who has a business where record-keeping is a vital part can store data anywhere in the globe through satellite transmission and a relatively simple computer with a printer. And it can retrieve it at will. . . .

What makes all of this technology frightening as well as exciting is that it was supposed to create a new type of service job that was going to somehow supplement, if not totally offset, the blue collar jobs that have been lost.

But the lesson it teaches us is that notwithstanding our particular occupations or job titles, that job, if not now, in the very near future, is going to be totally done in another country where wages are cheaper.

Therefore, it is important that we face these problems today and take charge of our own destiny, because no one else is going to do it.

3. President George H. W. Bush Declares the Cold War Over, 1990

Tonight I come not to speak about the state of the Government, not to detail every new initiative we plan for the coming year nor to describe every line in the budget. I'm here to speak to you and to the American people about the state of the Union, about our world—the changes we've seen, the challenges we face—and what that means for America.

There are singular moments in history, dates that divide all that goes before from all that comes after. And many of us in this Chamber have lived much of our lives in a world whose fundamental features were defined in 1945; and the events of that year decreed the shape of nations, the pace of progress, freedom or oppression for millions of people around the world.

Nineteen forty-five provided the common frame of reference, the compass points of the postwar era we've relied upon to understand ourselves. And that was our world, until now. The events of the year just ended, the Revolution of '89, have been a chain reaction, changes so striking that it marks the beginning of a new era in the world's affairs.

From "Address Before a Joint Session of the Congress on the State of the Union," 31 January 1990, *Public Papers of the Presidents, George Bush 1990* (Washington, D.C.: Government Printing Office, 1991), Book I, pp. 129–134.

Think back—think back just 12 short months ago to the world we knew as 1989 began. . . .

A year ago in Poland, Lech Walesa declared that he was ready to open a dialog with the Communist rulers of that country; and today, with the future of a free Poland in their own hands, members of Solidarity lead the Polish Government.

A year ago, freedom's playwright, Václav Havel, languished as a prisoner in Prague. And today it's Václav Havel, President of Czechoslovakia.

And 1 year ago, Erich Honecker of East Germany claimed history as his guide, and he predicted the Berlin Wall would last another hundred years. And today, less than 1 year later, it's the Wall that's history.

Remarkable events—events that fulfill the long-held hopes of the American people; events that validate the longstanding goals of American policy, a policy based on a single, shining principle: the cause of freedom. . . .

At a workers' rally, in a place called Branik on the outskirts of Prague, the idea called America is alive. A worker, dressed in grimy overalls, rises to speak at the factory gates. He begins his speech to his fellow citizens with these words, words of a distant revolution: "We hold these truths to be self-evident, that all men are created equal, that they are endowed by their Creator with certain unalienable Rights, and that among these are Life, Liberty and the pursuit of Happiness." . . .

For more than 40 years, America and its allies held communism in check and ensured that democracy would continue to exist. And today, with communism crumbling, our aim must be to ensure democracy's advance, to take the lead in forging peace and freedom's best hope: a great and growing commonwealth of free nations. And to the Congress and to all Americans, I say it is time to acclaim a new consensus at home and abroad, a common vision of the peaceful world we want to see.

4. Campaign Adviser Condoleezza Rice Cautions Against Humanitarian Interventions, 2000

Promoting the National Interest

The United States has found it exceedingly difficult to define its "national interest" in the absence of Soviet power. That we do not know how to think about what follows the U.S.-Soviet confrontation is clear from the continued references to the "post–Cold War period." Yet such periods of transition are important, because they offer strategic opportunities. . . .

. . . The next American president should be in a position to intervene when he believes, and can make the case, that the United States is duty-bound to do so. "Humanitarian intervention" cannot be ruled out a priori. But a decision to intervene in the absence of strategic concerns should be understood for what it is. Humanitarian problems are rarely only humanitarian problems; the taking of life or withholding of food is almost always a political act. If the United States is not prepared to address the underlying political conflict and to know whose side it is on, the military may end up separating warring parties for an indefinite period. Sometimes one party

Condoleezza Rice, "Promoting the National Interest," *Foreign Affairs,* January/February 2000, 52–54.

(or both) can come to see the United States as the enemy. Because the military cannot, by definition, do anything decisive in these "humanitarian" crises, the chances of misreading the situation and ending up in very different circumstances are very high. . . .

The president must remember that the military is a special instrument. It is lethal, and it is meant to be. It is not a civilian police force. It is not a political referee. And it is most certainly not designed to build a civilian society. Military force is best used to support clear political goals, whether limited, such as expelling Saddam from Kuwait, or comprehensive, such as demanding the unconditional surrender of Japan and Germany during World War II. It is one thing to have a limited political goal and to fight decisively for it; it is quite another to apply military force incrementally, hoping to find a political solution somewhere along the way. A president entering these situations must ask whether decisive force is possible and is likely to be effective and must know how and when to get out. These are difficult criteria to meet, so U.S. intervention in these "humanitarian" crises should be, at best, exceedingly rare.

This does not mean that the United States must ignore humanitarian and civil conflicts around the world. But the military cannot be involved everywhere. . . . Using the American armed forces as the world's "911" will degrade capabilities, bog soldiers down in peacekeeping roles, and fuel concern among other great powers that the United States has decided to enforce notions of "limited sovereignty" worldwide in the name of humanitarianism. This overly broad definition of America's national interest is bound to backfire as others arrogate the same authority to themselves. Or we will find ourselves looking to the United Nations to sanction the use of American military power in these cases, implying that we will do so even when our vital interests are involved, which would also be a mistake.

5. Two Workers Flee the Inferno in the Twin Towers, 2001

[Mike]

Being blind since birth and having grown up not far from the San Andreas Fault in California, I've had my share of obstacles to deal with in life. But I've also had my triumphs. When the plane struck our tower, I knew the drill. I'd been through the emergency training sessions. We did fire drills every six months. Avoid the elevators. Use the nearest staircase. Don't panic. Follow the fire wardens' instructions. And in my case, keep Roselle at my side. She is a yellow Labrador retriever from Guide Dogs for the Blind. We have a team relationship.

When the building started to vibrate so violently, Roselle got up right away. She'd been napping under my desk. Normally, she wouldn't stir when the wind shook the tower, but this time she was looking around, knowing something needed to happen. I went and stood in a doorway, something you learn to do when you've lived in earthquake country. Roselle was eager for my commands and carefully steered me through the debris in the office and hallway. She remained focused,

David N. Frank and Michael Hingson, "The Gift of Another Life," *September 11: An Oral History,* ed. Dean E. Murphy (New York: Doubleday, 2002) 18–22. Copyright © 2002 by Dean E. Murphy. Used by permission of Doubleday, a division of Random House, Inc.

even with things falling on top of her. I directed her toward the stairs, and with David in front of us, we headed down.

Some people wanted to go faster, so we let them go around us. I was not going to run down the stairs. I stayed to the right and let the dog set the pace. I have had a dog from Guide Dogs for the Blind since I was fourteen. The mantra has always been the same: Follow your dog. So I did. The way down was very organized. Every so often, there were people telling us which way to go. There was an order enforced by all of us in the stairwell. That helped me remain composed and helped Roselle guide better. I never felt a sense of panic. Intellectually, I was looking for that, but it never happened.

I am a physicist by training, so I always intellectualize things. When it got slippery on the stairs, I thought to be careful. I didn't want to become a problem by falling and hurting myself. But instead of getting really worked up about the difficult footwork, I started to think of ways to improve it for next time. When this is over, I thought, I am going to suggest that they install anti-skid strips on the stairs.

[David]

Someone had a radio and turned it on. A plane had hit our building. Then it was two planes. That explained the smell of jet fuel. We certainly had inhaled a lot of it. Around the 40s, we heard voices from above, yelling, "Move right! Burn victims coming down!" I caught my first glimpse of her on the staircase above me. She was in her twenties or early thirties. She turned the corner toward us. Two or three people behind her. She walked like a zombie. Eyes straight ahead, expressionless. Clothes burned off of half her body. Third-degree burns. Skin flapping and falling off her arms, neck and face. Her blond hair caked in gray slime. Fully ambulatory. Totally in shock. I had never seen anything like that. About fifteen minutes later, a second woman followed. It was bizarre. She looked almost the same age, height and weight. She had the same hair color, burns and emotionless expression. She didn't say a thing. I don't think she even touched the hand railing.

As we got into the low 40s, the jet fuel fumes got much more intense to the point where I thought I might pass out. People were clearly suffering and others were beginning to panic. Roselle was not doing well, panting heavily. We all needed water. Some people began passing small Poland Spring water bottles up to us from the floor below. This was a real relief. We gave some to the dog, and she loved it. It cut some of the fuel taste burning our throats and it eased our sense of dehydration and smoke inhalation. . . .

It was somewhere after that, maybe in the high 30s, we ran into our first real hero. A New York City firefighter. He was coming up. Walking from the lobby on his way to the top. He was clothed in a firefighter's hat, a fire-retardant jacket, pants and heavy gloves. He had yellow glow strips around the biceps, thighs and hat. More were behind him. They were carrying an unbelievable array of equipment. Axes, picks, shovels, fire hoses and oxygen tanks. Each guy must have been saddled with 75 pounds, by the time you added in the clothing. They were perspiring profusely and looked exhausted. Some of them were leaning heavily on the railings. And they had to go all the way to the 90s, straight into hell. This was not lost on the crowd. We all broke into applause at one point. It was a wonderful moment. Mike and I patted many of them on the back with a, "God bless you." They were extremely polite and solicitous. "Are you alright?" they'd ask Mike. "I'm fine, thank you," Mike would reply. "Are you with this guy?" they'd ask me. "Yes, I'm with Mike. We are okay, thank you," I'd assure them. We had that conversation with 35 or 40 of them. In a little while, we would be out of the building and they would be inside. And then the building would be gone and they would all be lost. I can't praise their spirit enough.

When we got down to the very last landing in the stairwell, there was water everywhere. It was around 9:35 or 9:40. We proceeded carefully and exited into the lobby. It was a war zone. I know this is an overused phrase, but it really fits. There were pieces of debris—wall material, ceiling tiles, paper and garbage—all in a lake of water that was about ankle deep. Ahead of us, there was a torrential rainfall occurring over the exit turnstiles. I warned Mike that he was about to get soaked but that there was no apparent danger. As we went through the turnstiles, police and security personnel kept yelling and gesturing. "Keep moving!" We went into the underground shopping mall that connects the two towers. More water and lots of noise. We went left and headed north. "Keep moving!" The lights were on. Up some stairs. Down a dark narrow corridor with more light at the end. The sky. We were out. It was about 9:45 or 9:50. . . .

We thought we were clear. As I looked over my shoulder, I saw what I thought was the most monstrous sight of my life. Both towers ringed by fire. Flames sharp and lapping at steel. A huge plume from the North Tower joined up with one from the South Tower, creating a stream of gray and black smoke against a perfectly blue sky. My God, this was no accident. We had to keep moving. . . .

Then we heard a very distinctive and unforgettable sound. The South Tower was coming down. The sound was like a freight train combined with metal poles snapping. The chorus of screams was shrill and terrifying. I was ripped from head to toe with sheer panic, too afraid to even scream. A 300-foot-tall debris cloud came at us at a high speed. We ran for our lives.

6. Journalist David Brooks Sees Basic Unity Between "Red" and "Blue" Americans, 2001

Sixty-five miles from where I am writing this sentence is a place with no Starbucks, no Pottery Barn, no Borders or Barnes & Noble. No blue *New York Times* delivery bags dot the driveways on Sunday mornings. In this place people don't complain that Woody Allen isn't as funny as he used to be, because they never thought he was funny. . . .

The place I'm talking about goes by different names. Some call it America. Others call it Middle America. It has also come to be known as Red America, in reference to the maps that were produced on the night of the 2000 presidential election. People in Blue America, which is my part of America, tend to live around big cities on the coasts. People in Red America tend to live on farms or in small towns or small cities far away from the coasts. Things are different there.

David Brooks, "One Nation, Slightly Divisible," *The Atlantic Monthly,* December 2001, 53–65. Reprinted by permission of David Brooks.

Everything that people in my neighborhood do without motors, the people in Red America do with motors. We sail; they powerboat. We cross-country ski; they snow-mobile. We hike; they drive ATVs. We have vineyard tours; they have tractor pulls. When it comes to yard work, they have rider mowers; we have illegal aliens. . . .

Over the past several months, my interest piqued by those stark blocks of color on the election-night maps. I have every now and then left my home in Montgomery County, Maryland, and driven sixty-five miles northwest to Franklin County, in south-central Pennsylvania. Montgomery County is one of the steaming-hot centers of the great espresso machine that is Blue America. It is just over the border from northwestern Washington, D.C. . . .

Franklin County is Red America. It's a rural county, about twenty-five miles west of Gettysburg, and it includes the towns of Waynesboro, Chambersburg, and Mercersburg. It was originally settled by the Scotch-Irish, and has plenty of Brethren and Mennonites along with a fast-growing population of evangelicals. The joke that Pennsylvanians tell about their state is that it has Philadelphia on one end, Pittsburgh on the other, and Alabama in the middle. Franklin County is in the Alabama part. . . .

There are a couple of long-standing theories about why America is divided. One of the main ones holds that the division is along class lines, between the haves and the have-nots. This theory is popular chiefly on the left, and can be found in the pages of *The American Prospect* and other liberal magazines. . . .

According to this theory, during most of the twentieth century gaps in income between the rich and the poor in America gradually shrank. Then came the infor-mation age. The rich started getting spectacularly richer, the poor started getting poorer, and wages for the middle class stagnated, at best. Over the previous decade, these writers emphasized, remuneration for top-level executives had skyrocketed: now the average CEO made 116 times as much as the average rank-and-file worker. Assembly-line workers found themselves competing for jobs against Third World workers who earned less than a dollar an hour. . . .

Driving from Bethesda to Franklin County, one can see that the theory of a divide between the classes has a certain plausibility. In Montgomery County we have Saks Fifth Avenue, Cartier, Anthropologie, Brooks Brothers. In Franklin County they have Dollar General and Value City, along with a plethora of secondhand stores. It's as if Franklin County has only forty-five coffee tables, which are sold again and again. . . .

And yet when they are asked about the broader theory, whether there is class conflict between the educated affluents and the stagnant middles, they stare blankly as if suddenly the interview were being conducted in Aramaic. . . .

When I rephrased the question in more-general terms, as Do you believe the country is divided between the haves and have-nots?, everyone responded decisively: yes. But as the conversation continued, it became clear that the people saying yes did not consider themselves to be among the have-nots. . . .

Hanging around Franklin County, one begins to understand some of the reasons that people there don't spend much time worrying about economic class lines. The first and most obvious one is that although the incomes in Franklin County are lower than those in Montgomery County, living expenses are also lower—very much so. Driving from Montgomery County to Franklin County is like driving through an invisible deflation machine. Gas is thirty, forty, or even fifty cents a gallon cheaper in Franklin County. I parked at meters that accepted only pennies and nickels. When I got a parking ticket in Chambersburg, the fine was $3.00. . . .

On my journeys to Franklin County, I set a goal: I was going to spend $20 on a restaurant meal. But although I ordered the most expensive thing on the menu— steak au jus, "slippery beef pot pie," or whatever—I always failed. . . .

This leaves us with the second major hypothesis about the nature of the divide between Red and Blue America, which comes mainly from conservatives: America is divided between two moral systems. Red America is traditional, religious, self-disciplined, and patriotic. Blue America is modern, secular, self-expressive, and discomfited by blatant displays of patriotism. . . .

The values-divide school has a fair bit of statistical evidence on its side. Whereas income is a poor predictor of voting patterns, church attendance . . . is a pretty good one. Of those who attend religious services weekly (42 percent of the electorate), 59 percent voted for Bush, 39 percent for Gore. Of those who seldom or never attend religious services (another 42 percent), 56 percent voted for Gore, 39 percent for Bush. . . .

[Yet] almost nobody I spoke with understood, let alone embraced, the concept of a culture war. Few could see themselves as fighting such a war, in part because few have any idea where the boundary between the two sides lies. People in Franklin County may have a clear sense of what constitutes good or evil (many people in Blue America have trouble with the very concept of evil), but they will say that good and evil are in all neighborhoods, as they are in all of us. . . .

The best explanation of the differences between people in Montgomery and Franklin Counties has to do with sensibility, not class or culture. If I had to describe the differences between the two sensibilities in a single phrase, it would be conception of the self. In Red America the self is small. People declare in a million ways, "I am normal. Nobody is better, nobody is worse. I am humble before God." In Blue America the self is more commonly large. People say in a million ways, "I am special. . . ."

These differences in sensibility don't in themselves mean that America has become a fundamentally divided nation. . . .

[T]raveling back and forth between the two counties was not like crossing from one rival camp to another. It was like crossing a high school cafeteria. Remember high school? There were nerds, jocks, punks, bikers, techies, druggies, God Squadders, drama geeks, poets, and Dungeons & Dragons weirdoes. All these cliques were part of the same school: they had different sensibilities; sometimes they knew very little about the people in the other cliques; but the jocks knew there would always be nerds, and the nerds knew there would always be jocks. That's just the way life is. . . .

Never has this been more apparent than in the weeks following the September 11 attacks. Before then Montgomery County people and Franklin County people gave little thought to one another: an attitude of benign neglect toward other parts of the country generally prevailed. But the events of that day generated what one of my lunch mates in Franklin County called a primal response. Our homeland was under attack. . . .

If the September 11 attacks rallied people in both Red and Blue America, they also neutralized the political and cultural leaders who tend to exploit the differences between the two.

7. Senator Robert Byrd Condemns
Post-9/11 Foreign Policy, 2003

To contemplate war is to think about the most horrible of human experiences. On this February day, as this nation stands at the brink of battle [against Saddam Hussein], every American on some level must be contemplating the horrors of war.

Yet, this Chamber is, for the most part, silent—ominously, dreadfully silent. There is no debate, no discussion, no attempt to lay out for the nation the pros and cons of this particular war. There is nothing.

We stand passively mute in the United States Senate, paralyzed by our own uncertainty, seemingly stunned by the sheer turmoil of events. Only on the editorial pages of our newspapers is there much substantive discussion of the prudence or imprudence of engaging in this particular war.

And this is no small conflagration we contemplate. This is no simple attempt to defang a villain. No. This coming battle, if it materializes, represents a turning point in U.S. foreign policy and possibly a turning point in the recent history of the world.

This nation is about to embark upon the first test of a revolutionary doctrine applied in an extraordinary way at an unfortunate time. The doctrine of preemption— the idea that the United States or any other nation can legitimately attack a nation that is not imminently threatening but may be threatening in the future—is a radical new twist on the traditional idea of self defense. It appears to be in contravention of international law and the UN Charter. . . .

This Administration, now in power for a little over two years, must be judged on its record. I believe that that record is dismal. . . .

In foreign policy, this Administration has failed to find Osama bin Laden. In fact, just yesterday we heard from him again marshaling his forces and urging them to kill. This Administration has split traditional alliances, possibly crippling, for all time, International order-keeping entities like the United Nations and NATO. This Administration has called into question the traditional worldwide perception of the United States as well-intentioned, peacekeeper. This Administration has turned the patient art of diplomacy into threats, labeling, and name calling of the sort that reflects quite poorly on the intelligence and sensitivity of our leaders, and which will have consequences for years to come.

Calling heads of state pygmies, labeling whole countries as evil, denigrating powerful European allies as irrelevant—these types of crude insensitivities can do our great nation no good. We may have massive military might, but we cannot fight a global war on terrorism alone. We need the cooperation and friendship of our time-honored allies as well as the newer found friends whom we can attract with our wealth. . . .

The war in Afghanistan has cost us $37 billion so far, yet there is evidence that terrorism may already be starting to regain its hold in that region. We have not found bin Laden, and unless we secure the peace in Afghanistan, the dark dens of terrorism may yet again flourish in that remote and devastated land. . . .

Senator Robert Byrd, "Reckless Administration May Reap Disastrous Consequences," a speech on the Senate floor, Feb. 12, 2003. Obtained at: http://www.commondreams.org/views03/0212-07.htm

One can understand the anger and shock of any President after the savage attacks of September 11. One can appreciate the frustration of having only a shadow to chase and an amorphous, fleeting enemy on which it is nearly impossible to exact retribution.

But to turn one's frustration and anger into the kind of extremely destabilizing and dangerous foreign policy debacle that the world is currently witnessing is inexcusable from any Administration charged with the awesome power and responsibility of guiding the destiny of the greatest superpower on the planet. Frankly many of the pronouncements made by this Administration are outrageous. There is no other word.

8. President George W. Bush Ranks Freedom Above Stability, 2005

This week, nations on both sides of the Atlantic observe the 60th anniversary of Hitler's defeat. The evil that seized power in Germany brought war to all of Europe, and waged war against morality, itself. What began as a movement of thugs became a government without conscience, and then an empire of bottomless cruelty. The Third Reich exalted the strong over the weak, overran and humiliated peaceful countries, undertook a mad quest for racial purity, coldly planned and carried out the murder of millions, and defined evil for the ages. Brave men and women of many countries faced that evil, and fought through dark and desperate years for their families and their homelands. In the end, a dictator who worshiped power was confined to four walls of a bunker, and the fall of his squalid tyranny is a day to remember and to celebrate. . . .

. . . For much of Germany, defeat led to freedom. For much of Eastern and Central Europe, victory brought the iron rule of another empire. V-E Day marked the end of fascism, but it did not end oppression. The agreement at Yalta followed in the unjust tradition of Munich and the Molotov-Ribbentrop Pact. Once again, when powerful governments negotiated, the freedom of small nations was somehow expendable. Yet this attempt to sacrifice freedom for the sake of stability left a continent divided and unstable. The captivity of millions in Central and Eastern Europe will be remembered as one of the greatest wrongs of history.

The end of World War II raised unavoidable questions for my country: Had we fought and sacrificed only to achieve the permanent division of Europe into armed camps? Or did the cause of freedom and the rights of nations require more of us? Eventually, America and our strong allies made a decision: We would not be content with the liberation of half of Europe—and we would not forget our friends behind an Iron Curtain. We defended the freedom of Greece and Turkey, and airlifted supplies to Berlin, and broadcast the message of liberty by radio. We spoke up for dissenters, and challenged an empire to tear down a hated wall. Eventually, communism began to collapse under external pressure, and under the weight of its own contradictions. And we set the vision of a Europe whole, free, and at peace—so dictators could no longer rise up and feed ancient grievances, and conflict would not be repeated again and again. . . .

For all the problems that remain, it is a miracle of history that this young century finds us speaking about the consolidation of freedom throughout Europe. And the

---

"President Discusses Freedom and Democracy in Latvia," Speech at Riga, Latvia, May 2005. Accessed at: http://www.whitehouse.gov/news/releases/2005/05/20050507-8.html.

stunning democratic gains of the last several decades are only the beginning. Freedom is not tired. The ideal of human dignity is not weary. And the next stage of the
world democratic movement is already unfolding in the broader Middle East.

We seek democracy in that region for the same reasons we spent decades working for democracy in Europe—because freedom is the only reliable path to peace. If
the Middle East continues to simmer in anger and resentment and hopelessness,
caught in a cycle of repression and radicalism, it will produce terrorism of even
greater audacity and destructive power. But if the peoples of that region gain the right
of self-government, and find hopes to replace their hatreds, then the security of all
free nations will be strengthened. We will not repeat the mistakes of other generations, appeasing or excusing tyranny, and sacrificing freedom in the vain pursuit of
stability. We have learned our lesson; no one's liberty is expendable. In the long run,
our security and true stability depend on the freedom of others. And so, with confidence and resolve, we will stand for freedom across the broader Middle East.

☛ E S S A Y S

The following essays show two sides to the challenges facing the United States at the
start of the twenty-first century. In the first essay, Bernard Lewis, a professor emeritus
at Princeton University, outlines a profound disjunction between the world-view of
Muslims and "westerners" (which in this case would also include most peoples of the
Far East). Lewis argues that Islamic civilization does not easily embrace the nation-state,
a form of government that is antithetical to its religious teachings. Modernity, secularism, and democracy (all associated with the rise of the nation-state in history) have thus
not proven a good "fit" with the Middle East. This reality has tended to produce dictator-
ships and economic underdevelopment, which in turn spur anger and resentment toward
the West, and especially its most powerful representative, the United States. In the
second essay, Thomas Friedman, a *New York Times* columnist who has written extensively about the Middle East, bypasses cultural explanations for world conflict and
instead calls upon Americans to pay attention to economic globalization. The world has
become "flat," he says, as new technologies and the end of the Cold War have democra-
tized the "global competitive playing field." Economic pressure might produce far more
change in the Middle East than governmental attempts to promote democracy, Friedman
contends. And meanwhile, the United States itself is going to have to struggle to keep
pace with its rivals in a world economy that is changing as rapidly as a computer screen.

Clash of Civilizations

BERNARD LEWIS

President Bush and other Western politicians have taken great pains to make it
clear that the war in which we are engaged is a war against terrorism—not a war
against Arabs, or, more generally, against Muslims, who are urged to join us in this
struggle against our common enemy. Osama bin Laden's message is the opposite.

"The Revolt of Islam" first appeared in *The New Yorker,* November 19, 2001. Later published in Bernard
Lewis, *The Crisis of Islam: Holy War and Unholy Terror,* New York 2003. Reprinted with permission of
the author.

For bin Laden and those who follow him, this is a religious war, a war for Islam and against infidels, and therefore, inevitably, against the United States, the greatest power in the world of the infidels.

In his pronouncements, bin Laden makes frequent references to history. One of the most dramatic was his mention, in the October 7th videotape, of the "humiliation and disgrace" that Islam has suffered for "more than eighty years." Most American— and, no doubt, European—observers of the Middle Eastern scene began an anxious search for something that had happened "more than eighty years" ago, and came up with various answers. We can be fairly sure that bin Laden's Muslim listeners—the people he was addressing—picked up the allusion immediately and appreciated its significance. In 1918, the Ottoman sultanate, the last of the great Muslim empires, was finally defeated—its capital, Constantinople, occupied, its sovereign held captive, and much of its territory partitioned between the victorious British and French Empires. The Turks eventually succeeded in liberating their homeland, but they did so not in the name of Islam but through a secular nationalist movement. One of their first acts, in November, 1922, was to abolish the sultanate. The Ottoman sovereign was not only a sultan, the ruler of a specific state; he was also widely recognized as the caliph, the head of all Sunni Islam, and the last in a line of such rulers that dated back to the death of the Prophet Muhammad, in 632 A.D. After a brief experiment with a separate caliph, the Turks, in March, 1924, abolished the caliphate, too. During its nearly thirteen centuries, the caliphate had gone through many vicissitudes, but it remained a potent symbol of Muslim unity, even identity, and its abolition, under the double assault of foreign imperialists and domestic modernists, was felt throughout the Muslim world.

Historical allusions such as bin Laden's, which may seem abstruse to many Americans, are common among Muslims, and can be properly understood only within the context of Middle eastern perceptions of identity and against the background of Middle Eastern history. . . .

In the early centuries of the Muslim era, the Islamic community was one state under one ruler. Even after that community split up into many states, the ideal of a single Islamic polity persisted. The states were almost all dynastic, with shifting frontiers, and it is surely significant that, in the immensely rich historiography of the Islamic world in Arabic, Persian, and Turkish, there are histories of dynasties, of cities, and, primarily, of the Islamic state and community, but no histories of Arabia, Persia, or Turkey. Both Arabs and Turks produced a vast literature describing their struggles against Christian Europe, from the first Arab incursions in the eighth century to the final Turkish retreat in the twentieth. But until the modern period, when European concepts and categories became dominant, Islamic commentators almost always referred to their opponents not in territorial or ethnic terms but simply as infidels (*kafir*). They never referred to their own side as Arab or Turkish; they identified themselves as Muslims. . . .

In the course of human history, many civilizations have risen and fallen—China, India, Greece, Rome, and, before them, the ancient civilizations of the Middle East. During the centuries that in European history are called medieval, the most advanced civilization in the world was undoubtedly that of Islam. Islam may have been equalled—or even, in some ways, surpassed—by India and China, but both of those civilizations remained essentially limited to one region and to one ethnic group, and their impact on the rest of the world was correspondingly restricted. The civilization of Islam, on the other hand, was ecumenical in its outlook, and explicitly so in its aspirations. One of the basic tasks bequeathed to Muslims by the Prophet was jihad. This word, which literally means "striving," was usually cited in the Koranic phrase "striving in the path of God" and was interpreted to mean armed struggle for the defense or advancement of Muslim power. In principle, the world was divided into two houses: the House of Islam, in which a Muslim government ruled and Muslim law prevailed, and the House of War, the rest of the world, still inhabited and, more important, ruled by infidels. Between the two, there was to be a perpetual state of war until the entire world either embraced Islam or submitted to the rule of the Muslim state. . . .

In practice, of course, the application of jihad wasn't always rigorous or violent. The canonically obligatory state of war could be interrupted by what were legally defined as "truces," but these differed little from the so-called peace treaties the warring European powers signed with one another. Such truces were made by the Prophet with his pagan enemies, and they became the basis of what one might call Islamic international law. In the lands under Muslim rule, Islamic law required that Jews and Christians be allowed to practice their religions and run their own affairs, subject to certain disabilities, the most important being a poll tax that they were required to pay. In modern parlance, Jews and Christians in the classical Islamic state were what we would call second-class citizens, but second-class citizenship, established by law and the Koran and recognized by public opinion, was far better than the total lack of citizenship that was the fate of non-Christians and even of some deviant Christians in the West. The jihad also did not prevent Muslim governments from occasionally seeking Christian allies against Muslim rivals—even during the Crusades, when Christians set up four principalities in the Syro-Palestinian area. The great twelfth-century Muslim leader Saladin, for instance, entered into an agreement with the Crusader king of Jerusalem, to keep the peace for their mutual convenience.

Under the medieval caliphate, and again under the Persian and Turkish dynasties, the empire of Islam was the richest, most powerful, most creative, most enlightened region in the world, and for most of the Middle Ages Christendom was on the defensive. . . .

Then came the great change. The second Turkish siege of Vienna, in 1683, ended in total failure followed by headlong retreat—an entirely new experience for the Ottoman armies. A contemporary Turkish historian, Silihdar Mehmet Aga, described the disaster with commendable frankness: "This was a calamitous defeat, so great that there has been none like it since the first appearance of the Ottoman state." This defeat, suffered by what was then the major military power of the Muslim world, gave rise to a new debate, which in a sense has been going on ever since. . . .

There was good reason for concern. Defeat followed defeat, and Christian European forces, having liberated their own lands, pursued their former invaders whence they had come, the Russians moving into North and Central Asia, the Portuguese into Africa and around Africa to South and Southeast Asia. Even small European powers such as Holland and Portugal were able to build vast empires in the East and to establish a dominant role in trade. . . .

By the early twentieth century—although a precarious independence was retained by Turkey and Iran and by some remoter countries like Afghanistan, which at that time did not seem worth the trouble of invading—almost the entire Muslim world had been incorporated into the four European empires of Britain, France, Russia, and the Netherlands. Middle Eastern governments and factions were forced to learn how to play these mighty rivals off against one another. For a time, they played the game with some success. Since the Western allies—Britain and France and then the United States—effectively dominated the region, Middle Eastern resisters naturally looked to those allies' enemies for support. In the Second World War, they turned to Germany; in the Cold War, to the Soviet Union.

And then came the collapse of the Soviet Union, which left the United States as the sole world superpower. The era of Middle Eastern history that had been inaugurated by Napoleon and Nelson was ended by [Soviet President Mikhail] Gorbachev and the elder George Bush. . . .

These events took place within the context of the Iranian revolution of 1979. On November 4th, the United States Embassy in Teheran [was] seized, and fifty-two Americans were taken hostage; those hostages were then held for four hundred and forty-four days, until their release on January 20, 1981. The motives for this, baffling to many at the time, have become clearer since, thanks to subsequent statements and revelations from the hostage-takers and others. It is now apparent that the hostage crisis occurred not because relations between Iran and the United States were deteriorating but because they were improving. In the fall of 1979, the relatively moderate Iranian Prime Minister, Mehdi Bazargan, had arranged to meet with the American national-security adviser, Zbigniew Brzezinski, under the aegis of the Algerian government. The two men met on November 1st, and were reported to have been photographed shaking hands. There seemed to be a real possibility—in the eyes of the radicals, a real danger—that there might be some accommodation between the two countries. Protesters seized the Embassy and took the American diplomats hostage in order to destroy any hope of further dialogue.

For [Ayatollah] Khomeini, the United States was "the Great Satan," the principal adversary against whom he had to wage his holy war for Islam. America was by then perceived—rightly—as the leader of what we like to call "the free world." Then, as in the past, this world of unbelievers was seen as the only serious force rivalling and preventing the divinely ordained spread and triumph of Islam. But American observers, reluctant to recognize the historical quality of the hostility, sought other reasons for the anti-American sentiment that had been intensifying in the Islamic world for some time. One explanation which was widely accepted, particularly in American foreign-policy circles, was that America's image had been tarnished by its wartime and continuing alliance with the former colonial powers of Europe. . . .

As the Western European empires faded, Middle Eastern anti-Americanism was attributed more and more to another cause: American support for Israel, first in its conflict with the Palestinian Arabs, then in its conflict with the neighboring Arab states and the larger Islamic world. There is certainly support for this hypothesis in Arab statements on the subject. But there are incongruities, too. In the nineteen-thirties, Nazi Germany's policies were the main cause of Jewish migration to Palestine, then a British mandate, and the consequent reinforcement of the Jewish community there. The Nazis not only permitted this migration; they facilitated it until the outbreak of the war, while the British, in the somewhat forlorn hope of winning Arab good will, imposed and enforced restrictions. Nevertheless, the Palestinian leadership of the time, and many other Arab leaders, supported the Germans, who sent the Jews to Palestine, rather than the British, who tried to keep them out.

The same kind of discrepancy can be seen in the events leading to and following the establishment of the State of Israel, in 1948. The Soviet Union played a significant role in procuring the majority by which the General Assembly of the United Nations voted to establish a Jewish state in Palestine, and then gave Israel immediate de-jure recognition. The United States, however, gave only de-facto recognition. More important, the American government maintained a partial arms embargo on Israel, while Czechoslovakia, at Moscow's direction, immediately sent a supply of weaponry, which enabled the new state to survive the attempts to strangle it at birth. As late as the war of 1967, Israel still relied for its arms on European, mainly French, suppliers, not on the United States.

The Soviet Union had been one of Israel's biggest supporters. Yet, when Egypt announced an arms deal with Russia, in September of 1955, there was an overwhelmingly enthusiastic response in the Arab press. The Chambers of Deputies in Syria, Lebanon, and Jordan met immediately and voted resolutions of congratulation to President [Gamal Abdel] Nasser; even Nuri Said, the pro-Western ruler of Iraq, felt obliged to congratulate his Egyptian colleague—this despite the fact that the Arabs had no special love of Russia, nor did Muslims in the Arab world or elsewhere wish to invite either Communist ideology or Soviet power to their lands. What delighted them was that they saw the arms deal—no doubt correctly—as a slap in the face for the West. The slap, and the agitated Western response, reinforced the mood of hatred and spite toward the West and encouraged its exponents. It also encouraged the United States to look more favorably on Israel, now seen as a reliable and potentially useful ally in a largely hostile region. Today, it is often forgotten that the strategic relationship between the United States and Israel was a consequence, not a cause, of Soviet penetration.

The Israeli-Palestinian conflict is only one of many struggles between the Islamic and non-Islamic worlds—on a list that includes Nigeria, Sudan, Bosnia, Kosovo, Macedonia, Chechnya, Sinkiang, Kashmir, and Mindanao—but it has attracted far more attention than any of the others. There are several reasons for this. First, since Israel is a democracy and an open society, it is much easier to report—and misreport—what is going on. Second, Jews are involved, and this can usually secure the attention of those who, for one reason or another, are for or against them. Third, and most important, resentment of Israel is the only grievance that can be freely and safely expressed in those Muslim countries where the media are either wholly owned or strictly overseen by the government. Indeed, Israel serves as a useful stand-in for complaints about the economic privation and political repression under which most Muslim people live, and as a way of deflecting the resulting anger.

This raises another issue. Increasingly in recent decades, Middle Easterners have articulated a new grievance against American policy: not American complicity with imperialism or with Zionism but something nearer home and more immediate— American complicity with the corrupt tyrants who rule over them. For obvious reasons, this particular complaint does not often appear in public discourse. Middle Eastern governments, such as those of Iraq, Syria, and the Palestine Authority, have developed great skill in controlling their own media and manipulating those of Western countries. Nor, for equally obvious reasons, is it raised in diplomatic negotiation. But it is discussed, with increasing anguish and urgency, in private conversations with listeners who can be trusted, and recently even in public. . . .

If America's double standards—and its selfish support for corrupt regimes in the Arab world—have long caused anger among Muslims, why has that anger only recently found its expression in acts of terrorism? In the nineteenth and twentieth centuries, Muslims responded in two ways to the widening imbalance of power and wealth between their societies and those of the West. The reformers or modernizers tried to identify the sources of Western wealth and power and adapt them to their own use, in order to meet the West on equal terms. Muslim governments—first in Turkey, then in Egypt and Iran—made great efforts to modernize, that is, to Westernize, the weaponry and equipment of their armed forces; they even dressed them in Western-style uniforms and marched them to the tune of brass bands. When defeats on the battlefield were matched by others in the marketplace, the reformers tried to discover the secrets of Western economic success and to emulate them by establishing industries of their own. Young Muslim students who were sent to the West to study the arts of war also came back with dangerous and explosive notions about elected assemblies and constitutional governments.

All attempts at reform ended badly. If anything, the modernization of the armed forces accelerated the process of defeat and withdrawal, culminating in the humiliating failure of five Arab states and armies to prevent a half million Jews from building a new state in the debris of the British Mandate in Palestine in 1948. With rare exceptions, the economic reforms, capitalist and socialist alike, fared no better. The Middle Eastern combination of low productivity and high birth rate makes for an unstable mix, and by all indications the Arab countries, in such matters as job creation, education, technology, and productivity, lag ever farther behind the West. Even worse, the Arab nations also lag behind the more recent recruits to Western-style modernity, such as Korea, Taiwan, and Singapore. Out of a hundred and fifty-five countries ranked for economic freedom in 2001, the highest-ranking Muslim states are Bahrain (No. 9), the United Arab Emirates (No. 14), and Kuwait (No. 42). According to the World Bank, in 2000 the average annual income in the Muslim countries from Morocco to Bangladesh was only half the world average, and in the nineties the combined gross national products of Jordan, Syria, and Lebanon—that is, three of Israel's Arab neighbors—were considerably smaller than that of Israel alone. The per-capita figures are worse. According to United Nations statistics, Israel's per-capita G.D.P. was three and a half times that of Lebanon and Syria, twelve times that of Jordan, and thirteen and a half times that of Egypt. The contrast with the West, and now also with the Far East, is even more disconcerting.

Modernization in politics has fared no better—perhaps even worse—than in warfare and economics. Many Islamic countries have experimented with democratic institutions of one kind or another. In some, as in Turkey, Iran, and Tunisia, they were introduced by innovative native reformers; in others, they were installed and then bequeathed by departing imperialists. The record, with the possible exception of Turkey, is one of almost unrelieved failure. Western-style parties and parliaments almost invariably ended in corrupt tyrannies, maintained by repression and indoctrination. . . .

In view of this, it is hardly surprising that many Muslims speak of the failure of modernization. The rejection of modernity in favor of a return to the sacred past has a varied and ramified history in the region and has given rise to a number of movements. The most important of these, Wahhabism, has lasted more than two and a half centuries and exerts a significant influence on Muslim movements in the Middle East today. . . .

From the nineteen-thirties on, the discovery of oil in the eastern provinces or Arabia and its exploitation, chiefly by American companies, brought vast new wealth and bitter new social tensions. In the old society, inequalities of wealth had been limited, and their effects were restrained, on the one hand, by the traditional social bonds and obligations that linked rich and poor and, on the other hand, by the privacy of Muslim home life. Modernization has all too often widened the gap, destroyed those social bonds, and, through the universality of the modern media, made the resulting inequalities painfully visible. All this has created new and receptive audiences for Wahhabi teachings and those of other like-minded groups, among them the Muslim Brothers in Egypt and Syria and the Taliban in Afghanistan. . . .

Osama bin Laden and his Al Qaeda followers may not represent Islam, and their statements and their actions directly contradict basic Islamic principles and teachings, but they do arise from within Muslim civilization, just as Hitler and the Nazis arose from within Christian civilization, so they must be seen in their own cultural, religious, and historical context.

If one looks at the historical record, the Muslim approach to war does not differ greatly from that of Christians, or that of Jews in the very ancient and very modern periods when the option was open to them. While Muslims, perhaps more frequently than Christians, made war against the followers of other faiths to bring them within the scope of Islam, Christians—with the notable exception of the Crusades, which were themselves an imitation of Muslim practice—were more prone to fight internal religious wars against those whom they saw as schismatics or heretics. Islam, no doubt owing to the political and military involvement of its founder, takes what one might call a more pragmatic view than the Gospels of the realities of societal relationships. Because war for the faith has been a religious obligation within Islam from the beginning, it is elaborately regulated. Islamic religious law, or the Sharia, deals in some detail with such matters as the opening, conclusion, and resumption of hostilities, the avoidance of injury to noncombatants, the treatment of prisoners, the division of booty, and even the types of weapons that may be used. Some of these rules have been explained away by modern radical commentators who support the fundamentalists; others are simply disregarded.

What about terrorism? Followers of many faiths have at one time or another invoked religion in the practice of murder, both retail and wholesale. Two words deriving from such movements in Eastern religions have even entered the English language: "thug," from India, and "assassin," from the Middle East, both commemorating fanatical religious sects whose form of worship was to murder those whom they regarded as enemies of the faith. The question of the lawfulness of assassination in Islam first arose in 656 A.D., with the murder of the third caliph, Uthman, by pious Muslim rebels who believed they were carrying out the will of God. . . .

The twentieth century brought a renewal of such actions in the Middle East, though of different types and for different purposes, and terrorism has gone through several phases. During the last years of the British Empire, imperial Britain faced terrorist movements in its Middle Eastern dependencies that represented three different cultures: Greeks in Cyprus, Jews in Palestine, and Arabs in Aden. All three acted from nationalist, rather than religious, motives. Though very different in their backgrounds and political circumstances, the three were substantially alike in their tactics. Their purpose was to persuade the imperial power that staying in the region was not worth the cost in blood. Their method was to attack the military and, to a lesser extent, administrative personnel and installations. All three operated only within their own territory and generally avoided collateral damage. All three succeeded in their endeavors.

Thanks to the rapid development of the media, and especially of television, the more recent forms of terrorism are targeted not at specific and limited enemy objectives but at world opinion. Their primary purpose is not to defeat or even to weaken the enemy militarily but to gain publicity—a psychological victory. The most successful group by far in this exercise has been the Palestine Liberation Organization. The P.L.O. was founded in 1964 but became important in 1967, after the defeat of the combined Arab armies in the Six-Day War. Regular warfare had failed; it was time to try other methods. The targets in this form of armed struggle were not military or other government establishments, which are usually too well guarded, but public places and gatherings of any kind, which are overwhelmingly civilian, and in which the victims do not necessarily have a connection to the declared enemy. Examples of this include, in 1970, the hijacking of three aircraft—one Swiss, one British, and one American—which were all taken to Amman; the 1972 murder of Israeli athletes at the Munich Olympics; the seizure in 1973 of the Saudi Embassy in Khartoum, and the murder there of two Americans and a Belgian diplomat; and the takeover of the Italian cruise ship Achille Lauro, in 1985. Other attacks were directed against schools, shopping malls, discothèques, pizzerias, and even passengers waiting in line at European airports. These and other attacks by the P.L.O. were immediately and remarkably successful in attaining their objectives—the capture of newspaper headlines and television screens. They also drew a great deal of support in sometimes unexpected places, and raised their perpetrators to starring roles in the drama of international relations. Small wonder that others were encouraged to follow their example—in Ireland, in Spain, and elsewhere.

The Arab terrorists of the seventies and eighties made it clear that they were waging a war for an Arab or Palestinian cause, not for Islam. Indeed, a significant proportion of the P.L.O. leaders and activists were Christian. Unlike socialism, which was discredited by its failure, nationalism was discredited by its success. In every Arab land but Palestine, the nationalists achieved their purposes—the defeat and departure of imperialist rulers, and the establishment of national sovereignty under national leaders. For a while, freedom and independence were used as more or less synonymous and interchangeable terms. The early experience of independence, however, revealed that this was a sad error. Independence and freedom are very different, and all too often the attainment of one meant the end of the other.

Both in defeat and in victory, the Arab nationalists of the twentieth century pioneered the methods that were later adopted by religious terrorists, in particular the lack of concern at the slaughter of innocent bystanders. This unconcern reached new proportions in the terror campaign launched by Osama bin Laden in the early nineties. The first major example was the bombing of two American embassies in East Africa in 1998. In order to kill twelve American diplomats, the terrorists were willing to slaughter more than two hundred Africans, many of them Muslims, who happened to be in the vicinity. The same disregard for human life, on a vastly greater scale, underlay the action in New York on September 11th.

There is no doubt that the foundation of Al Qaeda and the consecutive declarations of war by Osama bin Laden marked the beginning of a new and ominous phase in the history of both Islam and terrorism. The triggers for bin Laden's actions, as he himself has explained very clearly, were America's presence in Arabia during the Gulf War—a desecration of the Muslim Holy land—and America's use of Saudi Arabia as a base for an attack on Iraq. If Arabia is the most symbolic location in the world of Islam, Baghdad, seat of the caliphate for half a millennium and the scene of some of the most glorious chapters in Islamic history, is the second.

There was another, perhaps more important, factor driving bin Laden. In the past, Muslims fighting against the West could always turn to the enemies of the West for comfort, encouragement, and material and military help. With the collapse of the Soviet Union for the first time in centuries there was no such useful enemy. There were some nations that had the will, but they lacked the means to play the role of the Third Reich or the Soviet Union. Bin Laden and his cohorts soon realized that, in the new configuration of world power, if they wished to fight America they had to do it themselves. Some eleven years ago, they created Al Qaeda, which included many veterans of the war in Afghanistan. Their task might have seemed daunting to anyone else, but they did not see it that way. In their view, they had already driven the Russians out of Afghanistan, in a defeat so overwhelming that it led directly to the collapse of the Soviet Union itself. Having overcome the superpower that they had always regarded as more formidable, they felt ready to take on the other; in this they were encouraged by the opinion, often expressed by Osama bin Laden, among others, that America was a paper tiger.

Muslim terrorists had been driven by such beliefs before. One of the most surprising revelations in the memoirs of those who held the American Embassy in Teheran from 1979 to 1981 was that their original intention had been to hold the building and the hostages for only a few days. They changed their minds when statements from Washington made it clear that there was no danger of serious action against them. They finally released the hostages, they explained, only because they feared that the new President, Ronald Reagan, might approach the problem "like a cowboy." . . .

Similar inferences are drawn when American spokesmen refuse to implicate—and sometimes even hasten to exculpate—parties that most Middle Easterners believe to be deeply involved in the attacks on America. A good example is the repeated official denial of any Iraqi involvement in the events of September 11th. It may indeed be true that there is no evidence of Iraqi involvement, and that the Administration is unwilling to make false accusations. But it is difficult for Middle Easterners to resist the idea that this refusal to implicate Saddam Hussein is due less to a concern for legality than to a fear of confronting him. He would indeed be a formidable adversary. If he faces the prospect of imminent destruction, as would be inevitable in a real confrontation, there is no knowing what he might do with his already considerable arsenal of unconventional weapons. Certainly, he would not be restrained by any scruples, or by the consideration that the greatest victims of any such attack would be his own people and their immediate neighbors.

For Osama bin Laden, 2001 marks the resumption of the war for the religious dominance of the world that began in the seventh century. For him and his followers, this is a moment of opportunity. Today, America exemplifies the civilization and embodies the leadership of the House of War, and, like Rome and Byzantium, it has become degenerate and demoralized, ready to be overthrown. Khomeini's designation of the United States as "the Great Satan" was telling. In the Koran, Satan is described as "the insidious tempter who whispers in the hearts of men." This is the essential point about Satan: he is neither a conqueror nor an exploiter—he is, first and last, a tempter. And for the members of Al Qaeda it is the seduction of America that represents the greatest threat to the kind of Islam they wish to impose on their fellow-Muslims.

But there are others for whom America offers a different kind of temptation—the promise of human rights, of free institutions, and of a responsible and elected government. There are a growing number of individuals and even some movements that have undertaken the complex task of introducing such institutions in their own countries. It is not easy. Similar attempts, as noted, led to many of today's corrupt regimes. Of the fifty-seven member states of the Organization of the Islamic Conference, only one, the Turkish Republic, has operated democratic institutions over a long period of time and, despite difficult and ongoing problems, has made progress in establishing a liberal economy and a free society and political order. . . .

Meanwhile, there is a more urgent problem. If bin Laden can persuade the world of Islam to accept his views and his leadership, then a long and bitter struggle lies ahead, and not only for America. Sooner or later, Al Qaeda and related groups will clash with the other neighbors of Islam—Russia, China, India—who may prove less squeamish than the Americans in using their power against Muslims and their sanctities. If bin Laden is correct in his calculations and succeeds in his war, then a dark future awaits the world, especially the part of it that embraces Islam.

Clash of Economies

THOMAS L. FRIEDMAN

As an American who has always believed in the merits of free trade, I had an important question to answer after my India trip: Should I still believe in free trade in a flat world? Here was an issue that needed sorting out immediately—not only because it was becoming a hot issue in the presidential campaign of 2004 but also because my whole view of the flat world would depend on my view of free trade. I know that free trade won't necessarily benefit every American, and that our society will have to help those who are harmed by it. But for me the key question was: Will free trade benefit America *as a whole* when the world becomes so flat and so many more people can collaborate, and compete, with my kids? It seems that so many jobs are going to be up for grabs. Wouldn't individual Americans be better off if our government erected some walls and banned some outsourcing and offshoring?

I first wrestled with this issue while filming the Discovery Times documentary in Bangalore. One day we went to the Infosys campus around five p.m.—just when the Infosys call-center workers were flooding into the grounds for the overnight shift on foot, minibus, and motor scooter, while many of the more advanced engineers were leaving at the end of the day shift. The crew and I were standing at the gate observing this river of educated young people flowing in and out, many in animated conversation. They all looked as if they had scored 1,600 on their SATs, and I felt a real mind-eye split overtaking me.

My mind just kept telling me, "Ricardo is right, Ricardo is right, Ricardo is right." David Ricardo (1772–1823) was the English economist who developed the free-trade theory of comparative advantage, which stipulates that if each nation specializes in the production of goods in which it has a comparative cost advantage and then trades with other nations for the goods in which they specialize, there will be an overall gain in trade, and overall income levels should rise in each trading country.

So if all these Indian techies were doing what was their comparative advantage and then turning around and using their income to buy all the products from America that are our comparative advantage—from Corning Glass to Microsoft Windows—both our countries would benefit, even if some individual Indians or Americans might have to shift jobs in the transition. And one can see evidence of this mutual benefit in the sharp increase in exports and imports between the United States and India in recent years.

But my eye kept looking at all these Indian zippies and telling me something else: "Oh, my God, there are so many of them, and they all look so serious, so eager for work. And they just keep coming, wave after wave. How in the world can it possibly be good for my daughters and millions of other young Americans that these Indians can do the same jobs as they can for a fraction of the wages?"

When Ricardo was writing, goods were tradable, but for the most part knowledge work and services were not. There was no undersea fiberoptic cable to make knowledge jobs tradable between America and India back then. Just as I was getting worked up with worry, the Infosys spokeswoman accompanying me casually mentioned that last year Infosys India received "one million applications" from young Indians for nine thousand tech jobs.

Have a nice day.

I struggled over what to make of this scene. I don't want to see any American lose his or her job to foreign competition or to technological innovation. I sure wouldn't want to lose mine. When you lose your job, the unemployment rate is not 5.2 percent; it's 100 percent. No book about the flat world would be honest if it did not acknowledge such concerns, or acknowledge that there is some debate among economists about whether Ricardo is still right.

Having listened to the arguments on both sides, though, I come down where the great majority of economists come down—that Ricardo is still right and that more American individuals will be better off if we don't erect barriers to outsourcing, supply-chaining, and offshoring than if we do. The simple message of this chapter is that even as the world gets flat, America as a whole will benefit more by sticking to the basic principles of free trade, as it always has, than by trying to erect walls.

The main argument of the anti-outsourcing school is that in a flat world, not only are goods tradable, but many services have become tradable as well. Because of this change, America and other developed countries could be headed for an absolute decline, not just a relative one, in their economic power and living standards unless they move to formally protect certain jobs from foreign competition. So many new players cannot enter the global economy—in service and knowledge fields now dominated by Americans, Europeans, and Japanese—without wages settling at a newer, lower equilibrium, this school argues.

The main counterargument from free-trade/outsourcing advocates is that while there may be a transition phase in certain fields, during which wages are dampened, there is no reason to believe that this dip will be permanent or across the board, as long as the global pie keeps growing. To suggest that it will be is to invoke the so-called lump of labor theory—the notion that there is a fixed lump of labor in the world and that once that lump is gobbled up, by either Americans or Indians or Japanese, there won't be any more jobs to go around. If we have the biggest lump of labor now, and then Indians offer to do this same work for less, they will get a bigger piece of the lump, and we will have less, or so this argument goes.

The main reason the lump of labor theory is wrong is that it is based on the assumption that everything that is going to be invented has been invented, and that therefore economic competition is a zero-sum game, a fight over a fixed lump. This assumption misses the fact that although jobs are often lost in bulk—to outsourcing or offshoring—by big individual companies, and this loss tends to make headlines, new jobs are also being created in fives, tens, and twenties by small companies that you can't see. It often takes a leap of faith to believe that it is happening. *But it is happening.* If it were not, America's unemployment rate would be much higher today than 5 percent. The reason it is happening is that as lower-end service and manufacturing jobs move out of Europe, America, and Japan to India, China, and the former Soviet Empire, the global pie not only grows larger—because more people have more income to spend—it also grows more complex, as more new jobs, and new specialties, are created.

Let me illustrate this with a simple example. Imagine that there are only two countries in the world—America and China. And imagine that the American economy has only 100 people. Of those 100 people, 80 are well-educated knowledge workers and 20 are less-educated low-skilled workers. Now imagine that the world goes flat and America enters into a free-trade agreement with China, which has 1,000 people but is a less developed country. So today China too has only 80 well-educated knowledge workers out of that 1,000, and it has 920 low-skilled workers. Before America entered into its free-trade agreement with China, there were only 80 knowledge workers in its world. Now there are 160 in our two-country world. The American knowledge workers feel like they have more competition, and they do. But if you look at the prize they are going after, it is now a much expanded and more complex market. It went from a market of 100 people to a market of 1,100 people, with many more needs and wants. So it should be win-win for both the American and Chinese knowledge workers.

Sure, some of the knowledge workers in America may have to move *horizontally* into new knowledge jobs, because of the competition from China. But with a market that big and complex, you can be sure that new knowledge jobs will open up at decent wages for anyone who keeps up his or her skills. So do not worry about our knowledge workers or the Chinese knowledge workers. They will both do fine with this bigger market.

"What do you mean, don't worry?" you ask. "How do we deal with the fact that those eighty knowledge workers from China will be willing to work for so much less than the eighty knowledge workers from America? How will this difference get resolved?"

It won't happen overnight, so some American knowledge workers may be affected in the transition, but the effects will not be permanent. Here, argues Stanford new economy specialist Paul Romer, is what you need to understand: The wages for the Chinese knowledge workers were so low because, although their skills were marketable globally like those of their American counterparts, they were trapped inside a stifled economy. Imagine how little a North Korean computer expert or brain surgeon is paid inside that huge prison of a nation! But as the Chinese economy opens up to the world and reforms, the wages of Chinese knowledge workers will rise up to American/world levels. Ours will not go down to the level of a stifled, walled-in economy. You can already see this happening in Bangalore, where competition for Indian software writers is rapidly pushing up their wages toward American/European levels—after decades of languishing while the Indian economy was closed. It is why Americans should be doing all they can to promote more and faster economic reform in India and China.

Do worry, though, about the 20 low-skilled Americans, who now have to compete more directly with the 920 low-skilled Chinese. One reason the 20 low-skilled Americans were paid a decent wage before was that, relative to the 80 skilled Americans, there were not that many of them. Every economy needs some low-skilled manual labor. But now that China and America have signed their free-trade pact, there are a total of 940 low-skilled workers and 160 knowledge workers in our two-country world. Those American low-skilled workers doing fungible jobs—jobs that can easily be moved to China—will have a problem. There is no denying this. Their wages are certain to be depressed. In order to maintain or improve their living standards, they will have to move *vertically,* not horizontally. They will have to upgrade their education and upgrade their knowledge skills so that they can occupy one of the new jobs sure to be created in the much expanded United States–China market. . . .

As Romer notes, we know from the history of our own country that an increase in knowledge workers does not necessarily lead to a decrease in their pay the way it does with low-skilled workers. From the 1960s to the 1980s, the supply of college-educated workers grew dramatically, and yet their wages grew even faster. Because as the pie grew in size and complexity, so too did people's wants, and this increased the demand for people able to do complex work and specialized tasks.

Romer explains this in part by the fact that "there is a difference between idea-based goods and physical goods." If you are a knowledge worker making and selling some kind of idea-based product—consulting or financial services or music or software or marketing or design or new drugs—the bigger the market is, the more people there are out there to whom you can sell your product. And the bigger the market, the more new specialties and niches it will create. If you come up with the next Windows or Viagra, you can potentially sell one to everyone in the world. So idea-based workers do well in globalization, and fortunately America as a whole has more idea-driven workers than any country in the world.

But if you are selling manual labor—or a piece of lumber or a slab of steel— the value of what you have to sell does not necessarily increase when the market expands, and it may decrease, argues Romer. There are only so many factories that will buy your manual labor, and there are many more people selling it. What the manual laborer has to sell can be bought by only one factory or one consumer at a time, explains Romer, while what the software writer or drug inventor has to sell— idea-based products—can be sold to everyone in the global market at once.

That is why America, as a whole, will do fine in a flat world with free trade— provided it continues to churn out knowledge workers who are able to produce idea-based goods that can be sold globally and who are able to fill the knowledge jobs that will be created as we not only expand the global economy but connect all the knowledge pools in the world. There may be a limit to the number of good factory jobs in the world, *but there is no limit to the number of idea-generated jobs in the world.*

If we go from a world in which there were fifteen drug companies and fifteen software companies in America (thirty in all) and two drug companies and two software companies in China (four in all) to a world in which there are thirty drug and software companies in America and thirty drug and software companies in China, it is going to mean more innovation, more cures, more new products, more niches to specialize in, and many more people with higher incomes to buy those products.

"The pie keeps growing because things that look like wants today are needs tomorrow," argued Marc Andreessen, the Netscape cofounder, who helped to ignite a whole new industry, e-commerce, that now employs millions of specialists around the world, specialists whose jobs weren't even imagined when Bill Clinton became president. I like going to coffee shops occasionally, but now that Starbucks is here, I *need* my coffee, and that new need has spawned a whole new industry. I always wanted to be able to search for things, but once Google was created, I *must* have my search engine. So a whole new industry has been built up around search, and Google is hiring math Ph.D.'s by the bushel—before Yahoo! or Microsoft hires them. People are always assuming that everything that is going to be invented must have been invented already. *But it hasn't.*

"If you believe human wants and needs are infinite," said Andreeseen, "then there are infinite industries to be created, infinite businesses to be started, and infinite jobs to be done, and the only limiting factor is human imagination. The world is flattening and rising at the same time. And I think the evidence is overwhelmingly clear: If you look over the sweep of history, every time we had more trade, more communications, we had a big upswing in economic activity and standard of living."

America integrated a broken Europe and Japan into the global economy after World War II, with both Europe and Japan every year upgrading their manufacturing, knowledge, and service skills, often importing and sometimes stealing ideas and equipment from the United States, just as America did from Britain in the late 1770s. Yet in the sixty years since World War II, our standard of living has increased every decade, and our unemployment rate—even with all the outcry about outsourcing—stands at only a little above 5 percent, roughly half that of the most developed countries in Western Europe. . . .

As a person who grew up during the Cold War, I'll always remember driving along down the highway and listening to the radio, when suddenly the music would stop and a grim-voiced announcer would come on the air and say, "This is a test of the emergency broadcast system," and then there would be a thirty-second high-pitched siren sound. Fortunately, we never had to live through a moment in the Cold War where the announcer came on and said, "This is not a test." That, however, is exactly what I want to say here: *This is not a test.*

The long-term opportunities and challenges that the flattening of the world puts before the United States are profound. Therefore, our ability to get by doing things the way we've been doing them—which is to say, not always tending to our secret sauce and enriching it—will not suffice anymore. "For a country as wealthy as we are, it is amazing how little we are doing to enhance our natural competitiveness," said Dinakar Singh, the Indian-American hedge fund manager. "We are in a world that has a system that now allows convergence among many billions of people, and we had better step back and figure out what it means. It would be a nice coincidence if all the things that were true before are still true now—but there are quite a few things you actually need to do differently . . . You need to have a much more thoughtful national discussion." The flat world, Singh argued, is now the elephant in the room, and the question is, What is it going to do to us, and what are we going to do to it?

If this moment has any parallel in American history, it is the height of the Cold War, around 1957, when the Soviet Union leaped ahead of America in the space race by putting up the Sputnik satellite. Yes, there are many differences between that age and our own. The main challenge then came from those who wanted to put up walls; the main challenge to America today comes from the fact that all the walls are being taken down, and other countries can now compete with us much more directly. The main challenge in that world was from those practicing extreme communism, namely, Russia, China, and North Korea. The main challenge to America today is from those practicing extreme capitalism, namely, China, India, and South Korea. The main objective in that era was building a strong state; the main objective in this era is building strong individuals.

What this era has in common with the Cold War era, though, is that to meet the challenges of flatism requires as comprehensive, energetic, and focused a response as did meeting the challenge of communism. It requires our own version of the New Frontier and Great Society adapted to the age of flatness. It requires a president who can summon the nation to get smarter and study harder in science, math, and engineering in order to reach the new frontiers of knowledge that the flat world is rapidly opening up and pushing out. And it requires a Great Society that commits our government to building the infrastructure, safety nets, and institutions that will help every American become more employable in an age when no one can be guaranteed lifetime employment. I call my own version of this approach *compassionate flatism.*

Getting Americans to rally around compassionate flatism is much more difficult than getting them to rally around anticommunism. "National peril is a lot easier to convey than individual peril," noted Johns Hopkins University foreign policy expert Michael Mandelbaum. Economics, as noted, is not like war, because economics can always be a win-win game. But sometimes I wish economics were more like war. In the Cold War, we actually got to see the Soviets parade their missiles in Red Square. We all got to be scared together, from one end of the country to the other, and all our politicians had to be focused and serious about marshaling the resources and educational programs to make sure Americans could keep pace with the Soviet Union.

But today, alas, there is no missile threat coming from India. The "hot line," which used to connect the Kremlin with the White House, has been replaced by the "help line," which connects everyone in America to call centers in Bangalore. While the other end of the hotline might have had Leonid Brezhnev threatening nuclear war, the other end of the help line just has a soft voice eager to help you sort out your AOL bill or collaborate with you on a new piece of software. No, that voice has none of the menace of Nikita Khrushchev pounding a shoe on the table at the UN, and it has none of the sinister snarl of the bad guys in *From Russia with Love*. There is no Boris or Natasha saying "We will bury you" in a thick Russian accent. No, that voice on the help line just has a friendly Indian lilt that masks any sense of threat or challenge. It simply says: "Hello, my name is Rajiv. Can I help you?"

No, Rajiv, actually, you can't.

When it comes to responding to the challenges of the flat world, there is no help line we can call. We have to dig into ourselves. We in America have all the tools to do that, as I argued in Chapter 6. But, as I argued in Chapter 7, we have not been tending to those tools as we should. Hence, our quiet crisis. The assumption that because America's economy has dominated the world for more than a century, it will and must always be that way is as dangerous an illusion today as the illusion that America would always dominate in science and technology was back in 1950. But this is not going to be easy. Getting our society up to speed for a flat world is going to be extremely painstaking. We are going to have to start doing a lot of things differently. It is going to take the sort of focus and national will that President John F. Kennedy called for in his famous May 25, 1961, speech to Congress on "urgent national needs." At that time, America was recovering from the twin shocks of Sputnik and the Soviet space launch of a cosmonaut, Yuri Gagarin, less than two months before Kennedy's speech. Kennedy knew that while America had enormous human and institutional assets—far more than the Soviet Union—they were not being fully utilized.

"I believe we possess all the resources and talents necessary," said President Kennedy. "But the facts of the matter are that we have never made the national decisions or marshaled the national resources required for such leadership. We have never specified long-range goals on an urgent time schedule, or managed our resources and our time so as to ensure their fulfillment." After then laying out his whole program for putting a man on the moon within ten years, President Kennedy added, "Let it be clear that I am asking the Congress and the country to accept a firm commitment to a new course of action, a course which will last for many years and carry very heavy costs . . . This decision demands a major national commitment of scientific and technical manpower, materiel and facilities, and the possibility of their diversion from other important activities where they are already thinly spread. It means a degree of dedication, organization and discipline which have not always characterized our research and development efforts."

In that speech, Kennedy made a vow that has amazing resonance today: "I am therefore transmitting to the Congress a new Manpower Development and Training program, to train or retrain several hundred thousand workers, particularly in those areas where we have seen chronic unemployment as a result of technological factors, in new occupational skills over a four-year period—in order to replace those skills made obsolete by automation and industrial change with the new skills which the new processes demand."

Amen. We too have to do things differently. We are going to have to sort out what to keep, what to discard, what to adapt, what to adopt, where to redouble our efforts, and where to intensify our focus. That is what this chapter is about. This is just an intuition, but the flattening of the world is going to be hugely disruptive to both traditional and developed societies. The weak will fall farther behind faster. The traditional will feel the force of modernization much more profoundly. The new will get turned into old quicker. The developed will be challenged by the underdeveloped much more profoundly. I worry, because so much political stability is built on economic stability, and economic stability is not going to be a feature of the flat world. Add it all up and you can see that the disruptions are going to come faster and faster. Think about Microsoft trying to figure out how to deal with a global army of people writing software for free! We are entering an era of creative destruction on steroids. Even if your country has a comprehensive strategy for dealing with flatism, it is going to be a challenge of a whole new dimension. But if you don't have a strategy at all . . . well, you've been warned.

This is not a test.

F U R T H E R   R E A D I N G

Paul Boyer, ed., *Reagan as President: Contemporary Views of the Man, His Politics, and His Policies* (1990).

Douglas Brinkley, *The Unfinished Presidency: Jimmy Carter's Journey Beyond the White House* (1998).

Alison Brysk, *Globalization and Human Rights* (2002).

Beth Fischer, *The Reagan Reversal: Foreign Policy and the End of the Cold War* (1997).

Raymond Garthoff, *The Great Transition: American-Soviet Relations and the End of the Cold War* (1994).

Burton Kaufman, *The United States and the Arab Middle East* (1995).

Joanne Meyerowitz, *History and September 11* (2003).

Joseph Nye, *Bound to Lead: The Changing Nature of American Power* (1990).

Kevin Phillips, *American Dynasty: Aristocracy, Fortune, and the Politics of Deceit in the House of Bush* (2004).

Ronald Powaski, *Return to Armageddon: The United States and the Nuclear Arms Race, 1981–1999* (2003).

Bruce Schulman, *The Seventies: The Great Shift in American Culture, Society, and Politics* (2001).

Gil Troy, *Morning in America: How Ronald Reagan Invented the 1980s* (2005).